DEVELOPI WORLD 97/98

D0478058

Editor

Robert J. Griffiths

University of North Carolina at Greensboro

Robert J. Griffiths is assistant professor of political science at the University of North Carolina at Greensboro. He received his Ph.D. from the University of Connecticut in 1987. His teaching and research interests include comparative and international politics, and he teaches courses in African politics, the politics of development, international law and organization, and U.S. national security policy. His publications include articles on the developing world and global commons negotiations and South African civil-military relations.

Annual Editions

A Library of Information from the Public Press

Dushkin Publishing Group/Brown & Benchmark Publishers
Sluice Dock, Guilford, Connecticut 06437

The Annual Editions Series

ANNUAL EDITIONS is a series of over 65 volumes designed to provide the reader with convenient, low-cost access to a wide range of current, carefully selected articles from some of the most important magazines, newspapers, and journals published today. ANNUAL EDITIONS are updated on an annual basis through a continuous monitoring of over 300 periodical sources. All ANNUAL EDITIONS have a number of features that are designed to make them particularly useful, including topic guides, annotated tables of contents, unit overviews, and indexes. For the teacher using ANNUAL EDITIONS in the classroom, an Instructor's Resource Guide with test questions is available for each volume.

VOLUMES AVAILABLE

Abnormal Psychology
Adolescent Psychology
Africa
Aging
American Foreign Policy
American Government
American History, Pre-Civil War
American History, Post-Civil War
American Public Policy
Anthropology
Archaeology
Biopsychology
Business Ethics
Child Growth and Development
China
Comparative Politics
Computers in Education
Computers in Society
Criminal Justice
Criminology
Developing World
Deviant Behavior
Drugs, Society, and Behavior
Dying, Death, and Bereavement

Early Childhood Education
Economics
Educating Exceptional Children
Education
Educational Psychology
Environment
Geography
Global Issues
Health
Human Development
Human Resources
Human Sexuality
India and South Asia
International Business
Japan and the Pacific Rim
Latin America
Life Management
Macroeconomics
Management
Marketing
Marriage and Family
Mass Media
Microeconomics

Middle East and the
  Islamic World
Multicultural Education
Nutrition
Personal Growth and Behavior
Physical Anthropology
Psychology
Public Administration
Race and Ethnic Relations
Russia, the Eurasian Republics,
  and Central/Eastern Europe
Social Problems
Social Psychology
Sociology
State and Local Government
Urban Society
Western Civilization,
  Pre-Reformation
Western Civilization,
  Post-Reformation
Western Europe
World History, Pre-Modern
World History, Modern
World Politics

Cataloging in Publication Data
Main entry under title: Annual Editions: Developing World. 1997/98.
    1. Underdeveloped areas—Periodicals. I. Griffiths, Robert J., *comp.*
II. Title: Developing World
ISBN 0-697-36333-3   303.4′4   90–660257

Seventh Edition

Printed in the United States of America

Printed on Recycled Paper

Editors/Advisory Board

Staff

To the Reader

In publishing ANNUAL EDITIONS we recognize the enormous role played by the magazines, newspapers, and journals of the *public press* in providing current, first-rate educational information in a broad spectrum of interest areas. Many of these articles are appropriate for students, researchers, and professionals seeking accurate, current material to help bridge the gap between principles and theories and the real world. These articles, however, become more useful for study when those of lasting value are carefully *collected, organized, indexed,* and *reproduced* in a *low-cost format,* which provides easy and permanent access when the material is needed. That is the role played by ANNUAL EDITIONS. Under the direction of each volume's *academic editor,* who is an expert in the subject area, and with the guidance of an *Advisory Board,* each year we seek to provide in each ANNUAL EDITION a current, well-balanced, carefully selected collection of the best of the public press for your study and enjoyment. We think that you will find this volume useful, and we hope that you will take a moment to let us know what you think.

As the post–cold war era progresses, the developing world faces many uncertainties. Although the superpower confrontation no longer distorts our understanding or diverts our attention from the issues and problems that confront the developing countries, there is the danger that many of these countries will become further marginalized. On the other hand, the emerging world order may offer the international community the opportunity to concentrate on seeking solutions to the dilemmas of modernization and development.

The developing world makes up the vast majority of Earth's population. It is incredibly diverse and defies easy generalizations. Increasing differentiation among developing countries further complicates our ability to understand these regions. The problems of developing countries are complex, urgent, and not easily resolved. Peace and security, international trade, the debt crisis, and the environment illustrate growing interdependence and the need for a cooperative approach to addressing these issues. Clearly, however, the developing world's problems are contentious, and points of view differ regarding viable solutions. Moreover, developing world issues compete for attention on an agenda that is often dominated by relations between the industrialized nations, the problems of Eastern Europe and the former USSR, and domestic concerns of individual countries.

This seventh edition of *Annual Editions: Developing World* seeks to give students an understanding of the complexity of the developing world and acquaint them with the challenges that these nations confront. I feel very strongly that there is a need for greater awareness of, and attention to, the developing world. I hope that this volume contributes to these goals.

Over 60 percent of the articles in this edition are new. I have chosen articles that I hope are interesting and informative and that can serve as a basis for further investigation and discussion. The units deal with what I regard as the major issues facing the developing world. In addition to choosing articles that deal with the major issues, I have attempted to suggest the similarities and differences between developing countries and the connections between their problems and those of the industrialized nations.

I would again like to thank Ian Nielsen, publisher of *Annual Editions,* for the opportunity to put together a reader on a subject that is the focus of my teaching and research. As always, his comments and suggestions were valuable. I would also like to thank those who have sent in the response forms with their comments and suggestions. I have tried to take these into account in preparing the current volume.

No book on a topic as broad as the developing world can be comprehensive. There are certainly additional and alternative readings that might be included. As always, suggestions for improvement are welcome. Please use the form at the end of the book for your comments.

Robert J. Griffiths
Editor

Contents

UNIT 1

Understanding the Developing World

Four selections examine how the developing world's problems are interrelated with world order.

UNIT 2

Political Economy and the Developing World

Eight articles discuss the impact that debt has on the developing world's politics and economy.

The concepts in bold italics are developed in the article. For further expansion please refer to the Topic Guide and the Index.

UNIT 3

Conflict and Instability

Eleven articles discuss the current state of ethnic conflicts throughout the developing world.

The concepts in bold italics are developed in the article. For further expansion please refer to the Topic Guide and the Index.

UNIT 4

Weapons Proliferation and Arms Control

Four selections discuss the extent of the global arms trade and the danger of the increasing availability of weapons in the developing world.

UNIT 5

Transitions

Seven selections discuss the problems faced by developing countries as they evolve politically and economically.

UNIT 6

Population, Development, and Environment

Seven articles examine some of
the effects the developing
world's growth has on
Earth's sustainability.

UNIT 7

Women and Development

Six articles discuss the role of women in the developing world.

The concepts in bold italics are developed in the article. For further expansion please refer to the Topic Guide and the Index.

The concepts in bold italics are developed in the article. For further expansion please refer to the Topic Guide and the Index.

Topic Guide

This topic guide suggests how the selections in this book relate to topics of traditional concern to students and professionals involved with the study of the developing world. It is useful for locating articles that relate to each other for reading and research. The guide is arranged alphabetically according to topic. Articles may, of course, treat topics that do not appear in the topic guide. In turn, entries in the topic guide do not necessarily constitute a comprehensive listing of all the contents of each selection.

TOPIC AREA	TREATED IN	TOPIC AREA	TREATED IN
Agriculture	44. Women's Work 45. W = Female + Male	**Economic Growth**	2. Impoverished South 3. Reverse Linkages 4. 'New South' 5. Whither the North-South Gap? 6. Road to Third World Prosperity 7. Immiserating Growth (2)
Arms Control	25. Arming Ethnic Conflict 26. Pelindaba Treaty 27. Levers for Plowshares		
		Economic Reform	6. Road to Third World Prosperity 34. Open for Business
Cold War Legacy	1. Third World and New World Order 13. We Must Hear the Third World	**Education**	42. Burden of Womanhood 43. Female Empowerment
Debt Crisis	1. Third World and New World Order 5. Whither the North-South Gap? 8. Neoliberal Social Policy 9. Credit Where Discredit Is Due 10. Catch-22 of Debt	**Environment**	2. Impoverished South 4. 'New South' 13. We Must Hear the Third World 22. Refugees 35. ICPD Programme of Action 38. Exploding Cities 39. Building a Green Economy 41. Upholding Human Rights and Environmental Justice 44. Women's Work
Democracy	14. Political Islam 15. Middle East on the Brink 16. Gulf between the Rulers and Ruled 19. Nigeria 28. Democracy's Trap 30. Africa Tries Democracy 31. South Africa 32. Mexico 33. Force Is Forever	**Ethnic Conflict**	13. We Must Hear the Third World 18. Awaiting a New Spark 19. Nigeria 22. Refugees 25. Arming Ethnic Conflict 30. Africa Tries Democracy
Development	12. Barefoot Bank with Cheek 27. Levers for Plowshares 35. ICPD Programme of Action 44. Women's Work	**Gender Issues**	42. Burden of Womanhood 43. Female Empowerment 44. Women's Work 45. W = Female + Male 46. Women's Conference 47. Women Redrawing the Map
Economic Assistance	2. Impoverished South 5. Whither the North-South Gap? 6. Road to Third World Prosperity 11. Foreign Direct Investment 12. Barefoot Bank with Cheek 13. We Must Hear the Thrid World	**Globalization of Economy**	3. Reverse Linkages 4. 'New South' 13. We Must Hear the Third World

TOPIC AREA	TREATED IN	TOPIC AREA	TREATED IN
Gulf War	1. Third World and New World Order 13. We Must Hear the Third World 16. Gulf between the Rulers and Ruled	New International Economic Order (NIEO)	1. Third World and New World Order
Human Rights	19. Nigeria 22. Refugees 41. Upholding Human Rights and Environmental Justice 47. Women Redrawing the Map	Nuclear Weapons Population	26. Pelindaba Treaty 13. We Must Hear the Third World 35. ICPD Programme of Action 36. Optimism and Overpopulation 37. Poor Land's Success in Cutting Birth Rate 38. Exploding Cities 43. Female Empowerment
Indigenous Peoples	21. Culture Clash 41. Upholding Human Rights and Evironmental Justice		
Insurgency	21. Culture Clash 25. Arming Ethnic Conflict	Poverty	1. Third World and New World Order 2. Impoverished South 5. Whither the North-South Gap? 7. Immiserating Growth (2)
International Institutions	8. Neoliberal Social Policy 9. Credit Where Discredit Is Due 10. Catch-22 of Debt 23. Mixed Migration 27. Levers for Plowshares	Refugees	22. Refugees 23. Mixed Migration
International Trade	3. Reverse Linkages 4. 'New South'	Structural Adjustment	6. Road to Third World Prosperity 7. Immiserating Growth (2) 8. Neoliberal Social Policy 9. Credit Where Discredit Is Due 10. Catch-22 of Debt
Islam	14. Political Islam 16. Gulf between the Rulers and Ruled 17. Islam		
Middle East	14. Political Islam 15. Middle East on the Brink 16. Gulf between the Rulers and Ruled	Sustainable Development	5. Whither the North-South Gap? 39. Building a Green Economy 40. Voices from the Developing World
Military and Politics	19. Nigeria 33. Force Is Forever	Weapons Proliferation	13. We Must Hear the Third World 24. Third World Militaries 25. Arming Ethnic Conflict

Understanding the Developing World

Understanding the developing world has never been an easy task. The term "developing world" lacks precision and explanatory power. In addition, controversy exists over what actually constitutes development. Lumping together the 100-plus nations that compose this category obscures the wide diversity. Disparities in size, population, resources, forms of government, industrialization, distribution of wealth, ethnic diversity, and a host of other indicators have always characterized the developing world and made understanding this large, diverse group of countries difficult.

Despite this diversity, most nations of the developing world share some characteristics. With very few exceptions, these nations share a colonial past that has affected them politically and economically. Many developing countries have large populations, and almost all are experiencing rapid population growth, with annual growth rates between 2 and 4 percent. Poverty is widespread in both rural and urban areas, with urban areas often containing the poorest of the poor. While the majority of the developing world's inhabitants continue to live in the countryside, there is a massive rural-to-urban migration underway, and cities are growing very rapidly. Wealth is unevenly distributed; education, employment opportunities, and access to health care are luxuries that few enjoy. Corruption and mismanagement are common.

Although there have been some success stories, especially in East Asia, most developing countries continue to lag behind in many indicators of economic and political development. Several of the poorest countries in the developing world finished the 1980s in worse economic shape than they started the decade. The reasons for this poor economic performance are complex. Both internal and external factors play a role in explaining the inability of some developing countries to make economic progress. Among these factors are the colonial legacy, fluctuating prices for exports, increasingly expensive imports, donor fatigue among foreign aid contributors, the debt crisis, and an array of domestic problems these countries face.

As the countries of the developing world continue to struggle to improve living standards, the 1990s offer the prospect of both change and continuity. The end of the cold war eliminated the developing world's role as an ideological battlefield. The emerging world order offers challenges as well as benefits to developing countries, however. While they are no longer the sites of proxy conflicts between the superpowers, some regions of the developing world now face the prospect of becoming even more marginalized as attention and resources are focused on the transition in the former USSR and Eastern Europe. In some countries, the end of the cold war has also allowed subnationalism to surface and threaten further fragmentation. In other cases, weak central governments, no longer able to rely on outside intervention to preserve their power, are under increasing challenges from opposition groups, and order is breaking down. The end of the cold war also offers a great opportunity to direct the world's attention to the plight of the developing world and the need to find solutions to its problems. Whether this will happen remains to be seen. The developing world faces many uncertainties as the post–cold war era progresses. There are reasons to be skeptical about the prospects for many of these countries.

Although the gap between rich and poor nations persists, it is narrowing for some countries, the so-called emerging markets. The developing world's share of output is increasing. If growth continues and stability can be reasonably ensured, the attractiveness of third world investment and markets will also increase. On the other hand, the success of a few countries threatens to further marginalize the majority of developing countries that are not experiencing robust economic growth. This results in further differentiation among developing countries and complicates our understanding of their problems. Moreover, as economic growth takes place, it is important not to focus exclusively on economic factors. Such a focus may obscure important features of the development process such as dignity, empowerment, and other social values.

The post–cold war era represents a crucial period for much of the developing world. While opportunities exist to focus attention on these countries and their problems, the challenges they face threaten to overwhelm their inhabitants. The uncertainty of the future in the developing world emphasizes the importance of a better understanding of the issues and dilemmas that face the majority of Earth's inhabitants.

Looking Ahead: Challenge Questions

What conditions tend to characterize developing world nations?

What potential role does the developing world play in any emerging world order? How might this role differ from its role in the past?

What factors help to account for the disparity between rich and poor nations? Why does this gap persist?

How are the economic circumstances of some developing countries changing? How does this change affect their relationship with industrialized countries?

In what ways might industrialized countries consider growth in developing nations a threat?

What is the "New South"?

What are the reasons for skepticism about the prospects for many developing countries in the post–cold war era?

THE THIRD WORLD AND THE NEW WORLD ORDER IN THE 1990s

Julius O. Ihonvbere

Julius O. Ihonvbere is in the Department of Government, The University of Texas at Austin, 536 Burdine Hall, Austin, TX 78712-1087, USA (Tel: + 1 (512) 471-5121; fax: + 1 (512) 471-1061).

This article examines how well the developing countries fared at the end of the 1980s; identifies contemporary constraints on growth and development in developing formations; and makes projections on the future of Third World economies in view of the developments discussed.

> We can not forget that while the iron curtain has been brought down, the poverty curtain still separates two parts of the world community.
>
> *Javier Perez de Cuellar*[1]

> . . . the decision-making process that govern the international flows of trade, capital and technology are controlled by the major developed countries of the North and by the international institutions they dominate. The countries of the South are unfavourably placed in the world economic system; they are individually powerless to influence these processes and institutions; and hence the global economic environment . . .
>
> The South Commission[2]

> The developing world continued to experience protracted problems of indebtedness, adverse terms of trade, great poverty and deteriorating social conditions. Low-income and least developed countries had been particularly vulnerable.
>
> Commonwealth Heads of Government[3]

The beginning of the 1990s is an appropriate time to assess how well the Third World fared in the 1980s. It is also an opportune moment to make projections into the future based on developments in the global system towards the end of the 1980s. Without doubt, the break down of old ideological orthodoxies, the crumbling of the Berlin Wall, the end of the Cold War, the upsurge of pro-democracy movements the world over and the emergence of the USA as the only superpower in the global system call for a review and analysis of the place of weaker countries in the international division of labour. As well, the unprecedented spate of changes in Southern Africa; the release of Nelson Mandela; the prospects for a United European economy in 1992; negotiations for free trade arrangements in North America; and the triumph of market forces all over the world, except perhaps in Cuba, equally dictate a need to examine how these would affect relations between the developed and developing nations of the world.

In this article, our goals are first to examine how well the developing countries fared at the end of the 1980s; second, to identify contemporary constraints on growth and development in developing formations; and third, to make projections on the future of Third World economies in view of the developments highlighted above.

THE DEVELOPING WORLD AT THE END OF THE 1980s: FROM CRISIS TO CRISIS

It is not possible adequately to study and appreciate the predicaments of developing countries without understanding the historical experiences of the respective social formations. By and large, the contact between these formations and the forces of Western imperialism culminated in the distortion, disarticulation and underdevelopment of these societies. The state structures were severely deformed; the dominant classes were underdeveloped and marginalized in the processes of production and exchange; science and technology policies were relegated to the background; cultural forms were perverted; the local economies were subjected to foreign domination and manipulation and the dominated economies were structurally incorporated into an unequal, exploitative and hostile international division of labour.[4]

At the time these societies won *political* independence, it was obvious that they had not just been relegated to the periphery of global power and production relations but

Reprinted with permission from *Futures*, December 1992, pp. 987-1002. © 1992 by Elsevier Science, Ltd., Oxford, England.

also that they lacked the internal structures to mobilize their peoples, generate capital, promote productivity and participate in international trade on the basis on interdependence. Hence, they were all dependent on the metropolitan countries for technology, foreign aid, military supplies, markets for the sale of their raw materials and other forms of assistance.

The Third World is certainly not a homogenous formation. The contact with the forces of Western imperialism did not have similar effects. The impact and implications of this contact was not uniform. As well, the geostrategic importance of these societies to the metropolitan countries differs significantly, and their resource endowments, populations and vulnerability to external penetration, manipulation, domination and exploitation equally differ. Furthermore, the conditions under which they achieved political independence were not uniform while post-colonial alignment and realignment of class forces within these societies have differed. It is important that we take due cognizance of these critical issues if we are to understand contradictions and coalitions within the ranks of developing countries—why development has been uneven and why they have been unable to take advantage of some concessions in the global system or pressure the developed countries sufficiently to force major concessions. When data on the predicaments of developing countries are provided at the aggregate levels therefore, it is critical that we note the disparities and specificities within and between these societies.

The 1980s were particularly bad for the majority of developing countries. True, a few achievements were made in a handful of African and Latin American countries and perhaps mostly in East Asia in the areas of agriculture and industrialization.[5] However, for the majority of countries, the decade was more or less a disaster. As the World Bank has aptly noted, the 'World economy in the 1980s was dominated first by sharp recession, then by steady and prolonged growth in the industrial countries, high real interest rates, declining real commodity prices, massive movements in exchange rates, and the collapse of voluntary private lending to many developing countries'.[6] Even those countries that had made some concrete economic gains in the 1970s and managed to recover somewhat from the oil shocks were severely affected by massive 'external shocks'. Higher real interest rates, reduced international capital flows, and lower commodity prices[7] contributed to economic dislocation, inflation, unemployment and higher foreign debt profiles.

The 1982 recession caused serious economic dislocations all over the world but affected the developing world the most. The newly industrializing countries (NICs) of East Asia that depended heavily on manufactured exports were badly hit by the recession, although they were to recover by the mid-1980s. Real interest rates in the 1980s 'have been higher than at any time since the great depression'; the price of oil more than doubled and by 1981 it was six times its 1973 price and the majority of

developing countries began to rely on 'external borrowing and too little on domestic sources'.[8] All this encouraged increased protectionism in the developed economies, declining foreign assistance, and resistance to trade concessions to developing countries. The net result was general social, economic and political crisis in the Third World.[9]

In a recent address to the Board of Directors of the World Bank, Barbar Conable, the Bank's President noted that despite the 'impressive advances' in many Third World countries, 'poverty has proven a stubborn foe. For instance, three of the world's most populous nations—India, China and Indonesia—have made great progress toward reducing poverty. Even so, more than 1 billion, half of them in South Asia, still live on less than a dollar a day. During the next ten years, the population of the developing world is likely to increase by at least 850 million people, many of whom will be born into absolute poverty.'[10] Conable further noted that some Third World regions 'have regressed economically' while 'living standards in Latin America have fallen below those of the 1970s'. In the case of sub-Saharan Africa, Conable noted that parts of the region 'have suffered a veritable collapse of living standards, institutions, and infrastructure', and in a rather pessimistic tone the World Bank boss concluded that in view of 'Africa's rapidly rising population, the number of poor people will continue to increase, even if economic growth accelerates. There poverty faces its greatest challenge'.[11] Of course, these problems have now been joined in dangerous proportions by environmental degradation, the rapid spread of the AIDS virus and other natural disasters which underdeveloped countries have been unable to control.

Therese P. Sevigny, the Under-Secretary-General for Public Information at the UN revealed recently that though the organization's second mandate is 'supporting economic and social development in the developing countries', it could not boast of any credible achievement in this area. In fact, according to Sevigny, 'National and international efforts to reduce poverty and narrow the gap between the rich, industrialized North and the poor, developing regions of the South failed abysmally in the last decade'.[12] In terms of actual statistics and data, this 'abysmal failure' can be seen in the fact that of the 84 countries whose economic conditions were examined by the UN Department of International Economic and Social Affairs at the end of the 1980s, 54 of them had 'falling per capita income'. In 14 countries, per capita income fell by over 35%. In 13 years, the debt of Third World countries increased from $170 billion in 1975 to $1200 billion in 1988; and development assistance to the developing countries from the developed countries declined from 0.37% of GNP in 1980 to 0.33% in 1989.

In addition, for at least a billion people in the developing countries, one-fifth of humanity, 'obtaining the most essential elements of social sustenance—food, health care, shelter, jobs, education—continues to be an everyday struggle'.[13] Three million children are still dying every year because they are not immunized; half a million women—99% of them in the developing world—die in childbirth; although the developing world has 80% of the world's population, less than 5% of global spending on health is directed at their health problems and requirements; 900 million adults are illiterate; about 100 million are without shelter, radios, televisions and other basic necessities taken for granted in the developing world; and by the year 2000, 'around 1 billion people in developing countries (will) be living in absolute poverty'.[14] Sevigny summarized the dismal conditions of the developing world at the beginning of the 1990s:

> The statistics of the global divide are striking. Some 70 per cent of world income is produced and consumed by 15 per cent of the world's population. In the 41 least developed countries, average per capita income is well under $300, in sharp contrast to the $14,500 average of developed market economies. In Latin America, living standards are lower today than they were in the 1970s. The situation is even worse in Africa where living standards have fallen to the level of the 1960s. Each year in the developing world, 14 million children die before their fifth birthday, and another 1250 million children under five are malnourished.[15]

The UN now admits that the 'world's poorest, in fact, got poorer in the 1980s' and that there is a direct correlation between poverty and '. . . mounting instability . . . widespread unrest, turmoil and violence which is now afflicting an unprecedented number of countries' in the developing world.[16]

The South Commission, in its 1990 report equally draws attention to conditions of mass poverty, economic dislocation, deindustrialization, declining foreign aid, mass net transfer of resources of about $40 billion a year from the Third World to the developed world, decaying institutions, political tensions and instability and the general inability of poverty-stricken and debt-ridden countries to provide for the basic human needs of the majority. These conditions, coupled with increasing debt-servicing ratios, declining commodity prices, declining investor and donor interest in the Third World; an increasing brain drain, capital flight and deteriorating social conditions led to repressions, riots, coups and counter-coups, political tensions and instability and increasing pressures on the state, its agents and agencies.[17]

Reflecting on the powerlessness of the developing countries, the South Commission wrote that the 'fate of the South is increasingly dictated by the perceptions and policies of governments in the North, of the multilateral institutions which a few of these governments control, and of the network of private institutions that are increasingly prominent. Domination has been reinforced where partnership was needed and hoped for by the South.'[18] Noting that several rounds of multilateral trade negotiations have made little impact towards removing the numerous discriminatory barriers to the exports of the South to the North, the Commission also notes that 'the international financial system has failed to provide the positive flows of capital to the developing countries'

and the result has been 'stagnation and retrogression in most countries of the South'.[19] Thus at the end of the 1980s, the developing countries were hardly better-off than they were at the beginning of the 1960s and the global environment was no more hospitable than it was three decades earlier.[20]

THE THIRD WORLD AND THE NEW WORLD ORDER: ISSUES AND FEARS

Following persistent demands and debates, especially at the level of the UN, the developed countries reluctantly agreed to the need to establish a global basis for a New International Economic Order (NIEO) in 1975. Thus in September 1975, the Seventh Special Session of the General Assembly adopted the Declaration and Programme of Action on the Establishment of a New International Economic Order. This declaration 'formally acknowledged for the first time that economic injustice was as much a threat to world security and peace as were military and political tensions and conflicts'.[21] The broad implications of this Declaration were: (1) that 'the existing system discriminated against the weakest members of the international community through trade barriers, limited access to technology and capital, and inadequate monetary and financial arrangements'; (2) that the developing nations 'deserve at least an equal opportunity to participate in the world economic system without losing control of their natural resources or their freedom to follow their own priorities or policies'; and (3) that the constraints and contradictions in existing political and economic arrangements in the world order can only be resolved through the gradual, rather than violent 'restructuring of international institutions and a reorientation of policies governing relations between the developed and developing countries'.[22]

This Declaration was followed by hundreds of conferences, meetings, negotiations, establishment of institutions and so on, all aimed at restructuring the global flows of resources and capital;[23] the redistribution of power and resources; and the narrowing of the gap between the rich and the poor countries. For instance at UNCTAD IV in Nairobi in 1976, the Integrated Programme for Commodities which made provisions for international intervention to stabilize commodity markets was established. This Programme was to be backed by a Common Fund. As well, the Charter on Economic Rights and Duties of States; the Convention on Multimodal Transport; the Agreement on Restrictive Business Practices and several policies aimed at addressing deteriorating economic and social conditions in the developing world were some of the achievements of the North-South Dialogue which followed the Declaration of the NIEO.

While these and other developments addressed some of the problems facing the poorer countries, in broad terms, they achieved little in terms of democratizing global political institutions, increasing access to the markets of the developed nations for technology, influencing a redistribution of global resources, increasing assistance to developing countries beyond the consideration of ideology and geopolitics and empowering the poorer countries to confront their own economic and social problems.[24] To be sure, many developed countries were plagued with severe economic problems as 'growing unemployment and relatively high rates of inflation which . . . in turn led to serious social and political strains, forcing many governments to plead for inward looking policies in an effort to solve domestic problems in preference for international problems'.[25] These internal pressures provided sufficient excuses for the developed countries to renege on earlier arrangements and agreements on the NIEO.

As the South Commission has argued, most of the gains of the NIEO have had 'little substance beyond declaratory value' because when it came to discussing 'specific aspects of the New International Economic Order . . . the developed countries won the major advantage from the beginning; they ensured that the negotiations would take place in different forums, thus fragmenting them, straining negotiating capabilities of the South, and allowing procrastination in the adoption of agreements capable of being implemented'.[26] Thus, in so 'long as the threat was perceived as possible, the North kept the dialogue going; when it subsided, the North withdrew'.[27] In fact, as soon as the developed countries succeeded in containing the pressures which the OPEC oil price increases had created in the early 1970s, they practically lost interest in any discussions about restructuring the global economy and by June 1977, the expectations for a NIEO 'had disappeared into thin air. The developed countries, having successfully recycled the surpluses of petro-dollars, were no longer interested in a new deal for the Third World. They were in fact, seeking assurance of oil supply and stable oil prices for themselves.'[26]

The final blow to the North-South dialogue came in 1981 at the Cancun Summit of 22 Heads of State and Government. The ideological shifts in the USA—Ronald Reagan; in the UK—Margaret Thatcher; and in West Germany—Helmut Kohl—reflecting an unrepentant belief in market forces and little sympathy for poorer countries resulted in an inability to reach agreement on the need for concessions to the developing world. According to the South Commission, by 1981, the developed countries had become preoccupied with internal problems, and at Cancun they 'gave no priority to agreeing on a new basis for North-South economic relations or to defining the nature, scope, and prospects of interdependence links in the world economy'.[29] In fact at UNCTAD VI in Belgrade in 1983, attempts to revive the North-South dialogue through the efforts of the Group of 77 failed as the developed countries turned down all pleas and arguments taking the position that they, the developed

nations, were already recovering from the global economic crisis; that the benefits of their recovery will ultimately spill over to the developing countries; and that debt-distressed and crisis-ridden Third World nations should approach the IMF and the World Bank to adopt monetarist policies in order to structurally adjust their economies.[30]

By the mid-1980s, several developments in the global system provided some indicators of possibilities for changes in the relations between developed and developing countries. The majority of Third World nations adopted structural adjustment programmes to respond to their deepening economic problems.[31] Policies of deregulation, desubsidization, devaluation, export drive, liberalization and tight fiscal control, in the context of poverty, political instability, corruption, declining foreign assistance and investments, appeared, in the majority of cases, to have deepened the crisis of the developing countries. Beyond this, however, was the diversion of interest, aid and investments away from the developing world to Eastern Europe. Part of the reason for this shift was to prop up the Soviet regime and encourage it on the track of market reforms. Investors argued that the new enthusiasm for the market in Eastern Europe as well as the existence of required infrastructures put it far ahead of most developing regions in terms of investments, political risks and returns. It is true that the West has denied that it was supporting this trend, yet there are sufficient indicators to support the claim.

In any case, the stringent requirements prescribed for further assistance to developing nations have not been extended to the countries of Eastern Europe. When the Soviet Union claimed in late 1990 that it was experiencing problems with moving food from rural to urban centres, the governments in the West rushed to provide it with billions of dollars worth of credit and food aid. For instance, as Edward Greenspan noted, the EC 'agreed to send the equivalent of $1 billion (US) in emergency food aid to the Soviet Union in an undisguised effort to prop up President Mikhail Gorbachev . . . In addition to the Soviet food aid, EC leaders were also discussing a package of emergency food and energy assistance worth the equivalent of about $350 million for Romania and Bulgaria'.[32] A third of this package was to be in the form of a grant while the balance was to be in the form of export subsidies. Canada also opened a $100 million line of credit to the Soviet Union. Other forms of assistance to East European nations included a $970 million assistance to help Czechoslovakia 'make its currency convertible' and a $55 million assistance to Poland in 1989.

Since the collapse of the Soviet Union, aid to the Commonwealth of Independent States has been staggering: Germany gave $34.88 billion; Italy, $5.85 billion; the USA, $4.08 billion; the EC, $3.88 billion; Japan, $2.72 billion; Spain, $1.36 billion; France, $1.22 billion; the UK, $0.07 billion and others, $14.01 billion.[33] The Group of Seven has also promised aid totalling $24 billion to help Russia stabilize its currency and with debt rescheduling.[34] In April 1992, the USA announced a Special Marshall Plan totalling $150 billion to assist the restructuring process in Eastern Europe.

Reflecting on this development in the case of Africa, the Economic Commission for Africa noted in its *1990 Economic Report on Africa* that 'resource flows to Africa will dwindle as and when resources are diverted for the development of depressed areas within the European Economic Community. This prospect is all the more evident with the emerging closer ties between Eastern and Western Europe. These factors . . . can only lead to the further marginalization of Africa in the 1990s and beyond.'[35] Adebayo Adedeji, the Executive-Secretary of the ECA has also noted that the problems of resource mobilization in Africa have been aggravated by the 'declining resource flows to Africa under complaints of aid fatigue, (and) the diverting of such flows to Eastern Europe . . .'.[36] The South Commission, arguing on behalf of the developing countries in general has also noted that with improving relations between Eastern and Western European nations, the East European nations now give 'priority to improving economic relations with the West rather than to negotiations in favour of greater justice for the South'. As well, the Commission argued that 'both attention and technical and financial resources are being diverted from development in the South to economic reconstruction in Eastern Europe'.[37]

To make matters worse, the developing countries lost the Soviet Union as a relatively more reliable ally in the global struggle against exploitation, injustice and foreign domination.[38] In fact, Gorbachev, in trying to reduce the 'over-extension' of the Soviet Union's global responsibilities and generate foreign exchange issued decrees requiring all military and commercial deals with Third World countries to be in hard currencies; and the immediate repayment of all debts owed to the Soviet Union.[39]

Donors have added another conditionality to the stringent conditions for providing further assistance even loans to developing countries—'political conditionality'. To this end, it was demanded that developing countries must show evidence of increasing democratization, political pluralism and respect for human rights before they could be considered for assistance. The World Bank's 1989 report on sub-Saharan Africa was very clear on this conditionality when it made prescriptions on the urgent need to attack corruption, mismanagement, promote the autonomy of the judiciary and create an 'enabling environment' for mobilization, democracy and participatory politics.[40] The UK Foreign Secretary, Douglas Hurd, gave support to this conditionality when he stated recently that 'Aid must go where it can clearly do good' and those who wished to receive UK aid must show evidence of 'pluralism, public accountability, respect for the rule of law, human rights and market principles'.[41]

Of course, it has been argued that the West has adopted this position to complicate the recovery process

in the developing world because, in the first place, it continues to directly and/or indirectly support repressive regimes all over the Third World, and it has resisted all efforts to improve commodity prices and democratize the international system, especially the international financial system.[42] The whole idea of adjustment with a human face which the World Bank started to advocate only in 1989, was an afterthought following the numerous disasters and deteriorations caused by the orthodox adjustment packages imposed on developing countries in the past. The harsh monetarist prescriptions have been politically resisted by the poor. The acts of resistance have been met with increasing repression and political containment. Taken together it remains one major contradiction in the recovery process.[43]

Issues of declining exports and declining foreign exchange earnings in the context of rising costs of imports have added to the rising foreign debt profile of developing countries. As real interest rates continue to increase, the debt-servicing ratios have also gone up averaging between 30% and 135%. This has reduced resources available for developmental purposes and severely constrained the possibilities for recovery. As the South Commission has argued, prospects for recovery and increasing productivity in the South are limited because these debt-distressed countries 'need a substantial reduction of their burden of debt-servicing in order that they may be left with sufficient resources to achieve a level of growth that would enable them to service their debt soundly in the future'.[44] As the regimes are unable to service their debts, credit lines are closed by suppliers and the scarcity of essential goods have led to riots, conflicts, coups and regime turnover.

Sevigny gives the interesting case of Zambia which she describes as 'a simple example of the havoc developing country debt plays with people's lives'.[45] The victory of the Movement for Multi-Party Democracy (MMD) led by Fred Chiluba did nothing to result in increased sympathies for Zambia from the Bank and Fund or from creditors. In the 1960s and until the mid-1970s, Zambia enjoyed an economic boom largely as a result of the high prices of copper, the country's major export. Then copper prices fell precipitously. Zambia, as a result of declining foreign exchange earnings and thinking that the fall in price was only temporary, borrowed heavily from the international community. Unfortunately, the massive decline in the price of copper continued and the country's foreign debts increased from 40% of GDP in 1975 to 400% of GDP in 1986. As Sevigny notes, by 1986, 'Zambia's annual scheduled debt service payment had gone up to $900 million—equivalent to 95 per cent of all its export earnings. That meant that if it paid its obligations, it would have no money at all for its vital imports, which are the basis of much of its economy, and which also includes essentials like food, fertilizer, and medicines.'[46] Like many other developing countries, this situation meant an inability to service foreign debts effectively, keep credit lines open, retain the country's credit worthiness, and provide for the basic needs of the people. Zambia was forced to increase prices of essential items like food, and in line with IMF and World Bank as well as creditor requirements, it embarked on an adjustment programme. The result was political instability, an attempted military coup, several riots and increased repression and human rights abuses.

Debt servicing has now become a new avenue for draining the resources of poorer countries to the developed countries especially by the IMF. Again, the South Commission is clear on the implications of these developments for the survival of developing countries: 'The upshot is that debt has become a form of bondage, and the indebted economies have become indentured economies—a clear manifestation of neo-colonialism. This state of affairs cannot go on. The debt and its service must be reduced to a level that allows growth to proceed at an acceptable pace.'[47] As the maturity dates for loans to developing countries grew shorter by 35% from 6.7 years in 1970 to 4.0 years in 1987, 'interest rates of all creditors increased 172% from 3.7% in 1970 to 10% in 1987'.[48]

These developments have thus encouraged the net flow of resources from the developing to the developed world. With declining investments and declining foreign exchange earnings from exports, most developing economies have become 'collateral for refinancing already existing debt. Refinancing in this way also becomes more a nursing measure to prolong life rather than permit total collapse. Both creditors and debtors find themselves in an almost vicious circle in which the former must give to receive and the latter must receive to give.'[49] But the political implication for poor countries externally is that it mortgages their foreign policies and suffocates their room for manoeuvre in the global system. Internally, it redirects all efforts to satisfying the creditors and leaves very limited resources for meeting the basic needs of the people. The net result is deepening alienation, contradictions and conflicts. Either way, it is the poorer country that loses.

In spite of the apparent changes in the international system, especially in the area of East-West relations, the international economic system was actually moving in the opposite direction. Rather than show evidence of democratization to accommodate the demands of the developing countries, it moved towards the creation of protectionist regional economic blocs. The prospects for a united European market at the end of 1992 set in motion through the 1987 Single European Act, and the December 1987 Canada–US Free Trade Agreement which is now going to include Mexico are not pointers to the democratization of the world economy. The Overseas Development Institute (ODI) made it clear that Europe 1992 is designed in the first instance for the European economy, not for the developing world. As it put it, 'the net effect on ldcs as a whole is likely to be slightly positive. This is not to say that all developing countries will gain. The poorest economies in the least buoyant shape will not

clearly benefit—unless they gain from exporting presently dutiable tropical beverages (commodities which are currently severely depressed).'[50]

What this implies is that only those developing countries that are relevant in supplying required raw materials to the European market will reap some benefits. This will of course increase their dependence on the European market as producers of raw materials. In spite of the Lomé Convention, which through STABEX provides some new arrangements for preferential treatment to African, Caribbean and Pacific states and in spite of Generalized System of Preferences (GSP), the developing countries are certainly going to face increasing marginalization in the emerging international divisions of power and labour. The South Commission has noted that 'the establishment of regional trading blocs raises important issues for the future of the international system' and that the South 'should be alert to the danger that these developments could result in narrowed access to developed country markets for its exports'.[51] The Commission went on to accuse the developed countries of direct and deliberate discrimination against developing countries:

> EC trade policies involve a high level of discrimination against imports from the South . . . the coverage of the GSP and the relief it offers are limited, and furthermore subject to unilateral termination by the EC on grounds of 'graduation' ie the withdrawal of concessional treatment with respect to a developing country that 'graduates' from lower to a higher level of economic development. The Lome Convention, in turn, offers limited concessions on commodities that come within the scope of the EC's Common Agricultural policy . . . In consequence of the recent intensification of protectionism in the developed countries, developing countries' exports have been subjected to discriminatory restrictions precisely in those sectors where they have a clear comparative advantage. . . .[52]

The establishment of a united European market in 1992 will not change the continuing use of tariff and non-tariff barriers, even direct political considerations, to discriminate against the developing countries.

To make matters even worse, the Uruguay Round of multilateral trade negotiation has achieved little. The 13 developing and industrial countries which came together to form the Cairns Group ostensibly to promote common interests as agricultural producers, achieved little as the negotiation broke down over disagreements on the issue of subsidies to farmers. The World Bank had predicted that the 'failure of the Uruguay Round would not only hamper the growth of world trade but also represent a rejection of the development strategy that has been promoted by the international community and multilateral organizations, at the very time the developing countries are coming to accept it'.[53] The developed countries did not go into the negotiations with a view to ensuring its workability given their current interests in regional blocs, hence the irreconcilable conflicts between the USA and the EC. The net losers are the developing nations which had hoped that new agreements would open up new opportunities for their exports to the developed country markets.

It was in the context of the problems above that the Gulf war broke out following the Iraqi invasion of Kuwait in August 1990. The war, which culminated in the US declaration of a new world order on 2 March 1991, revealed in very grim dimensions the marginal role of developing countries in the global system, the real meaning of the new world order as conceived by the USA; the implications of having the USA as the only superpower in the global system and the implications of the disintegration of the Soviet Union.[54] It also revealed clearly how the UN is likely to function under US hegemony and the implications of this for developing countries. We do not go into details on these issues here. We highlight only a few of them as they relate to our overall discussion.

The Gulf war saw in the first place the relegation of the UN to the background by the USA and its manipulation to give global legitimacy to a purely US agenda in the Middle East. That the USA was able to get the support of all the great powers, the Soviet Union and several debt-ridden, dependent and vulnerable developing countries equally provided it with a justification to push for the resolution of the crisis through war. The USA rejected the French and Soviet peace initiatives and proceeded to mount the largest military assault against a debt-ridden Third World country with a largely peasant-based army. The over $55 billion spent on the war is sufficient to eliminate virtually all the economic and social problems plaguing most developing countries if properly managed and invested. In any case, the war did not resolve the crisis in the Middle East and has in fact created new tensions and conflicts in and beyond the Middle East.[55] Since the end of the war, the USA has spent well over $40 million in trying to overthrow the Iraqi regime. What is more, political leaders in the West now openly campaign for the overthrow of legitimate, even if unpopular, governments. The implications of this development go far beyond the character of the Iraqi regime to reflect the open desire to set not just global economic and political programmes but also to determine the internal programmes of certain nations.

Yet, for the developing world, it was a shock to see how powerless the UN became, accepting and supporting through the Security Council all proposals submitted to it by the USA. It was also a shock to see the Soviet Union under Gorbachev, in return for US non-interference in the developments in the Baltic as well as to guarantee continuing US economic assistance in its reform programme, was unable to prevent war between a superpower and its allies and a developing nation. At the Security Council, it either made weak amendments to the US initiatives or simply supported US proposals. The Chinese 'abstained' from supporting US positions, but such abstentions made little difference and could, in the context of US positions, be regarded as support for the USA. The UK was at times even more enthusiastic for war than the USA and France, after initial efforts at the dying minutes to prevent war, did not use its veto power, but gave full support for the war. That France allowed the USA to infest computers ordered by the Iraqi air force for its defence systems before the outbreak of war, reveals the vulnerability of developing nations in a global system dominated and manipulated by the developed nations.

For the Third World, the Middle East crisis showed the preparedness of the West to defend countries that had direct relevance to their geostrategic and economic interests; after all, in spite of the numerous provocative activities of South Africa, the USA never considered a military threat, even less an invasion. Second, it showed that the West was capable of finding the money and resources, and the 'will' to pursue its own interests in spite of the frequent complaint of 'aid fatigue', 'compassion fatigue', and dwindling resources to aid developing countries. Third, the developing countries saw that they had lost the UN, at least for now, as a forum to pursue interests that were not necessarily congruent with the interests of the USA. After all, the USA could get all members of the Security Council to do its bidding even when it was obvious to all that Iraq, with a peasant-based army, stood no chance whatsoever against all the superpowers and great powers. Finally, the developing countries saw the loss of the only real check they had on the USA—the Soviet Union. Long before the war, Al Mazrui had reflected on this issue when he noted that 'We have lost something now that the moral competition is no longer operative. No longer is the Soviet Union acting as the conscience of the US and vice versa. We are also losing other things. There will be diversion of resources from the Third World . . . toward Eastern Europe. There will be diversion of investment, aid and trade. There will be less interest in markets that are regarded as less promising and less likely to maximize returns'.[56]

Since the end of the war, the USA and its allies have been preoccupied with resolving the numerous problems that have become accentuated or were created in the region such as the problems of the Kurds; extinguishing the over 500 burning oil wells in Kuwait; containing political tensions and pressures in many of the countries in the region; trying to redefine power relations especially between Iran, Iraq, Lebanon, Israel and Syria in the region; resolving the Palestinian question without dialogue with Yassar Arafat as the PLO leader; and solving the severe environmental problems caused by the destruction of chemical plants, the pollution of rivers and the impact of heavy weapons employed by the allies against Iraq.

Following the defeat of Iraq, George Bush, declared the dawn of a new world order. The main element of this new order was the USA's absolute and unchallengeable power and dominance of the world system. It involves the ability to get other states to follow its leadership in containing Iraq; the use (even testing) of US weapons in the war and the domination of the UN. The 'American Century' for the USA came from the triumph of the market, the disintegration of the Soviet Union, the heavy reliance of the developing even developed countries on US leadership, and the containment of Iraq (and more recently Libya) as a demonstration of what the USA could do to nations which threatened its interests. As George Bush himself put it, there is 'nothing the American people can't handle . . . The first test of the new world order has been passed'.[57] For Martin Anderson, the new world order means that the 'United States has risen to be the biggest power in the world' and the 'Persian Gulf war has shown, clearly and unequivocally, that we're the number one military power . . . The United States has achieved moral, economic and military supremacy—probably for the first time in history. It is the first time since World War II that the leadership of the United States is undisputed.'[58] What is instructive, however, is that for the USA this 'supremacy' and 'leadership' as well as the 'new world order' which has followed the defeat of Iraq, contains no *economic* programme whatsoever. It is purely a military issue; the economic fall-out from the Gulf war has been to reward some of its allies like Kenya, Turkey, Israel and Egypt.

The new order does not contain any visible programme to redefine the economic relations between the developed and developing nations; calling an international conference on the debt crisis as demanded by the OAU and the South Commission to harmonize responses to the debt crisis; resolving the arms trade as well as the massive net transfer of resources from developing to developed nations; and reorganizing the global flow of resources, aid and investment to favour the developing nations. More important, the new world order contains no programme to deal with growing world poverty which has continued to mediate reform and recovery policies in the developing world as well as generating deep contradictions which culminate in violence, political instability, civil and inter-state conflicts as well as inability to protect the basic rights of people. There is no new approach to the AIDS crisis and the environment. In fact, at the 1992 Earth Summit in Brazil, the USA stood alone in opposition to all other nations on taking decisive steps to protect the environment because of economic considerations. What these show is that the developing nations do not feature seriously in the USA's conception of the new world order.

THE NEW WORLD ORDER AND THE THIRD WORLD: IMPLICATIONS FOR THE 1990S

The UN has projected that 'the lot of the world's poorest, overburdened as it was in the 1980s, is projected . . . to deteriorate even more in the 1990s, just as the already unconscionable gap between the industrialized and developing countries is also projected to widen'.[59] The Economic Commission for Africa, in reviewing the pros-

pects for the region in the 1990s, has also projected that 'given the current world political and economic situation, Africa is becoming further marginalized in world affairs, both geo-politically and economically'[60] and only an alternative set of development policies can generate a basis for recovery. The South Commission in its recent report noted that resource flows to the developing countries have declined; several rounds of multilateral trade negotiations have not removed the discriminatory barriers against exports from the developing world; and in virtually all areas of economic and political relations, the developing countries have been the more vulnerable and exploited. The Commission concluded that 'in the absence of an effective remedial action, stagnation and retrogression in most countries of the South will persist in the 1990s. The "lost decade" may thus be extended'.[61] Pursuing this line a bit further, the Commission argued that 'hundreds of millions of the people living in the South suffer from hunger, malnutrition, and preventable diseases, and are illiterate or lack education and modern skills. The 1990s threaten even more hardship for the people of the South and even greater instability for their countries.'[62] These are not particularly bright projections for the 1990s.

It can be safely argued that not all developing countries are going to slide down the path of economic, social and political decay at the same pace. But, the projections from virtually all international bodies at the end of the 1980s show clearly that the new world order contains few programmes for recovery, growth and development for the Third World. It would seem therefore that a combination of *internal* and *external* policies are urgently required to stem the steady slide towards disaster in the majority of developing nations. In the context of ongoing changes in the world, there is no alternative to empowering popular organizations, rural communities and diverting resources away from flamboyant foreign policies and prestige projects towards rural development, food and cash crop production, industrialization, skills development and the provision of basic needs for the majority. Democratic spaces must be opened up to allow for accountability, respect for human rights, popular participation and a serious check on corruption, waste and mismanagement. Structural adjustment programmes are required in all developing nations, although such programmes must pay serious attention to the survival of vulnerable groups. The new emphasis at the level of policy must be on *productivity* as against mere distribution and consumption. These policies will inevitably lead to a new *national economic order* which is a prerequisite for winning concessions from the global economy.

At the regional level, developing countries must move away from the traditional attitude to regional cooperation. The politicization and proliferation of regional integration schemes as well as the lack of political will, disrespect for protocols and charters, and a general inability to withstand the initial and inevitable costs of harmonization of policies have in the past led to disintegration and decay. Europe 1992, the North American Free Trade Area and developments in the Pacific Rim show very clearly that this is the way to go in the 1990s. A more serious approach than what the OAU is contemplating in the African Economic Community scheduled to come into operation in AD 2025 is required to respond to the rapid creation of trade blocs in the global economy.[63] This would facilitate specialization, the rational utilization of scarce resources, the ability to regulate and perhaps control foreign investments, and reduce unhealthy competition for foreign aid, technology, technical assistance and other supports. Also, regionalism will, if properly organized and taken seriously, have far-reaching implications for resolving political conflicts. The role of the EC in the crisis and conflicts in Eastern Europe is a pointer in this direction.

In spite of the limited concessions currently available in the global system, there is still some room for hope about the future. A new reality will soon dawn on the USA which will compel it to divert attention to its deepening internal crisis, concede the responsibility for maintaining global peace to the UN and to work with other trade blocs on how best to organize the global economy. Before this happens however, the redirection of aid, investment and support for development efforts; the failure of structural adjustment programmes; the addition of 'political conditionality' to the list of conditionalities required by the West to aid developing countries; the implications of US hegemony in the global economy given its poor record of support for development in the past; and the blowing wind of change all over the world, all hold strong possibilities for the required change that will move the Third World out of its present predicaments.

These developments are bound to compel leaders, communities, popular organizations and institutions to ask new questions, plan new models of development, abandon old and discredited orthodoxies and recognize the need to involve the people and their organizations in the new agenda for change and development. The end of the Cold War and the disintegration of the Soviet Union effectively eliminates the tradition of playing the East against the West. It also makes unnecessary the need to support corrupt and repressive regimes in the Third World in the name of containing communism. What becomes possible is a new agenda for mobilizing the people for a struggle for democracy, democratization, empowerment, development and self-reliance. This will undoubtedly be the path for the 1990s. Third World leaders must recognize that the days of political posturing, defensive radicalism, propaganda and rhetoric are over; that new opportunities and markets have opened up in Eastern Europe; and that conditions of political conflicts, instability, deteriorating quality of life, and general uncertainty are bound to scare investors and reduce global compassion and support.

It is instructive to note that all over the Third World dictatorial and repressive regimes are crumbling, popular forces are organizing across ethnic, religious, regional and gender lines for justice, participation, equality, accountability, empowerment and mobilization. The struggle for *democracy* which had been on since the euphoria of political independence evaporated all over the developing world, had received added enthusiasm from the monumental changes in Eastern Europe. As well, issues of the *environment*, gender, popular participation, accountability of the leadership to the people and genuine grassroot democratization have become topical issues for political debates and contests all over the Third World.

It would appear, therefore, that one major hope for recovery and development in the Third World lies in their abandonment of previous structures, institutions and relations of exploitation, repression and mismanagement which have contributed in no small way to the current crisis. This degree of internal restructuring will empower the Third World to wage a new form of struggle for the reform of global power relations on a fairly interdependent basis as against the current grounds of inequality, dependence and marginalization. It is increasingly being recognized that poverty is inimical to peace and that 'deepening poverty is already leading to mounting instability' and that the 'world is currently moving at two wildly divergent speeds that threaten to tear apart the "new world order" that super-powers and regional political agreements are ushering in'.[64] Until the new world order is seriously built around the deepening problems of the developing countries, it is currently unlikely to benefit in any way from the changing conditions in the global system.

NOTES AND REFERENCES

1. Javier Perez de Cuellar, UN Secretary-General, UN Day Message, October 1990.
2. The South Commission, *The Challenge to the South: The Report of the South Commission* (London, Oxford University Press, 1990), page 2.
3. Commonwealth Heads of Government, *The Kuala Lumpur Communique October 1989* (London, Commonwealth Secretariat, 1989), page 27.
4. See the contributions to Toivo Miljan (editor), *The Political Economy of North-South Relations* (Peterborough, Canada, Broadview Press, 1987).
5. See Brandt Commission, *Common Crisis, North-South: Cooperation for World Recovery* (London, Pan Books, 1983); David Goldsbrough, 'Foreign direct investment in developing countries: trends, policy issues and prospects', *Finance and Development*, 22(1), 1986.
6. World Bank, *World Development Report 1989* (New York, Oxford University Press for the World Bank, 1989), page 6.
7. *Ibid.*
8. *Ibid*, page 23.
9. See Thomas M. Magstadt, *Nations and Governments: Comparative Politics in Regional Perspective* (New York, St Martins Press, 1991), Parts IV-VII.
10. Barber B. Conable, *Address to the Board of Governors* (Washington, DC, The World Bank Group, 25 September 1990), page 6.

11. *Ibid*, pages 6–7.

12. Therese P. Sevigny, 'From crisis to consensus: The United Nations and the challenge of development', Keynote Speech at the Inaugural Conference of the Institute for International Cooperation, University of Ottawa, Canada, 14 November 1990, page 2.

13. *Ibid*, page 3.

14. *Ibid*, page 4.

15. *Ibid*, page 4.

16. *Ibid*, pages 3 and 4.

17. See Claude Ake, *Revolutionary Pressures in Africa* (London, Zed Press, 1978); and the South Commission, *op cit*, reference 2.

18. *Ibid*, page 3.

19. *Ibid*, page 19.

20. See Organization of African Unity, *Lagos Plan of Action for the Economic Development of Africa, 1980–2000* (Geneva, Institute for Labour Studies, 1981); Brandt Commission, *North-South: A Programme for Survival. Report of the Independent Commission on International Development Issues* (London, Pan Books, 1980).

21. South Commission, *op cit* reference 2, page 216.

22. Sartaj Aziz, 'The search for a common ground', in Anthony J. Dolman and Jan van Ettinger (editors), *Partners in Tomorrow: Strategies for a New International Order* (New York, E. P. Dutton, 1978), page 14.

23. See Stephen D. Krasner, 'Third World vulnerabilities and global negotiations', *Review of International Studies, 9(4)*, October 1983; P. T. Bauer and B. S. Yamey, 'Against the New International Economic Order', *Commentary (63)*, April 1977; and the contributions to Jagdish N. Bhagwati (editor), *The New International Economic Order: The North-South Debate* (Cambridge, MA, MIT Press, 1977).

24. See Frances Stewart, Brandt II—the mirage of collective action in a self-serving world', *Third World Quarterly, 5(3)*, July 1983; R. Cassen, R. Jolly and R. Wood, *Rich Country Interests and Third World Development* (London, Croom Helm, 1982); and Jimoh Omo-Fadaka, 'The mirage of NIEO: reflections on a Third World dystopia', *Alternatives, 10(2)*, Fall 1984.

25. *Ibid*, page 15.

26. South Commission, *op cit*, reference 2, page 217.

27. *Ibid*, page 216.

28. Aziz, *op cit* reference 22, page 15.

29. South Commission, *op cit*, reference 2, page 217.

30. See *ibid*.

31. See World Bank, *World Development Report 1989* (Washington, DC, The World Bank, 1989); G. K. Helleiner, 'Lessons for sub-Saharan Africa from Latin American experience?', *The African Development Review 1(1)*, 1989; and Albert Fishlow, 'The state of Latin American economies' in *Economic and Social Progress in Latin America, External Debt: Crisis and Adjustment* (Washington, DC, Inter-American Development Bank, 1985).

32. Edward Greenspan, 'Soviets to get $1-billion in EC food aid—European leaders hope to shore up Gorbachev', *The Globe and Mail* (Toronto, Canada), 15 December 1990.

33. *Newsweek*, 30 March 1992, page 9.

34. *Newsweek*, 13 April 1992, page 44.

35. Economic Commission for Africa, *Economic Report on Africa 1990* (Addis Ababa, ECA, 1990), page viii.

36. Adebayo Adedeji, *The African Alternative: Putting the People First* (Addis Ababa, ECA, 1990), page 40.

37. South Commission, *op cit*, reference 2, pages 20–21.

38. This is not to say some aspects of Soviet relations with Third World countries were not exploitative or guided by purely ideological considerations. Yet, on a comparative basis, in the struggle against colonialism, racism, global exploitation and so on, the Soviet Union was a more reliable ally than any Western country. See Noam Chomsky, 'The struggle for democracy in a changed world', and Igor Belikov, 'Perestroika, the Soviet Union and the Third World', *Review of African Political Economy*, (50), March 1991.

39. See Julius O. Ihonvbere, 'The dynamics of change in Eastern Europe and their implications for Africa', *Coexistence— A Journal of East-West Relations, 29(3)*, September 1992; Charles Adade, 'Soviets abandon Africa', *West Africa*, 8 October 1990; and Carol Saivetz, 'New thinking and Soviet Third World policy', *Current History, 88(540)*, October 1989.

40. See World Bank, *op cit*, reference 31, chapters 1-3.

41. 'The prospects for Africa in the 1990s', *West Africa*, 25 June–1 July 1990.

42. See Salim Lone, 'Africa: drifting off the map of the world's concerns', *International Herald Tribune*, 24 August 1990; 'Donors demand political reforms', *Africa Recovery*, July-September 1990; and 'Link national, international democratization', *Africa Recovery*, July-September 1990.

43. See Julius O. Ihonvbere, 'Making structural adjustment programs work in Africa: towards a policy and research agenda', mimeo, University of Texas at Austin, 1991; and 'The crisis of structural adjustment programs in Africa: issues and explanations', *Philosophy and Social Action*, 1992.

44. South Commission *op cit*, reference 2, page 226.

45. Sevigny *op cit*, reference 12, page 6.

46. *Ibid*.

47. The South Commission, *op cit*, reference 2, page 227.

48. Karamo N. M. Sonko, 'Debt in the eye of a storm: the African crisis in a global context', *Africa Today, 37(4)*, 1990, page 21.

49. *Ibid*, page 22.

50. Overseas Development Institute, 'The developing countries and 1992', Briefing Paper, November 1989, page 4.

51. South Commission, *op cit*, reference 2, page 244.

52. *Ibid*, pages 243 and 244.

53. World Bank, *op cit*, reference 31, page 16.

54. See Richard Barnet, Ian Buruma and Owen Harries, 'Defining the new world order, What is it? Whose is it?', *Harper's*, May 1991; Adel Safty, 'Stranglehold on UN no way to a new order', *The Globe and Mail* (Toronto), 5 April 1991; Salim Mansur, 'The United Nations and the Gulf War', *Perspectives* (Canadian Institute of International Affairs), 5(2), March 1991; Kim Richard Nossal, 'The Gulf war and the future of the UN', in *ibid*; and Jeremy Seabrook, 'Gulf war—view from the South', *New Statesman and Society*, 15 February 1991.

55. See David Vick, 'Africa bites the bullet in Gulf war aftermath', *African Business*, May 1991; and Julius O. Ihonvbere, 'The Persian Gulf crisis and Africa: implications for the 1990s', *International Studies*, 1992.

56. Ali A. Mazrui, 'Eastern European revolutions: African origins?', *TransAfrica Forum, 7(2)*, Summer 1990, page 8.

57. Quoted in Linda Diebel, 'US hails 'new world order': but many fear era of intolerance', *The Toronto Star*, 3 March 1991.

58. Martin Anderson quoted in *ibid*.

59. Sevigny, *op cit* reference 12, page 4.

60. Economic Commission for Africa, *African Charter for Popular Participation in Development* (Addis Ababa, ECA, 1990), page 18.

61. South Commission, *op cit*, reference 2, page 19.

62. *Ibid*, page 23.

63. See Julius O. Ihonvbere, 'Towards an African common market in AD 2025?': the African Crisis, regionalism and prospects for recovery', paper presented at the International Workshop on 'Eastern Europe and Africa: parallels and lessons', Queen's University, Kingston, Ontario, Canada, April 1992.

64. Sevigny, *op cit*, reference 12, page 4.

Don't Neglect the Impoverished South

Robin Broad and John Cavanagh

ROBIN BROAD is a professor of international development at the School of International Service, The American University. JOHN CAVANAGH, a fellow at the Institute for Policy Studies and the Transnational Institute, is coauthor, with Richard J. Barnet, of Global Dreams: Imperial Corporations and the New World Order *(Simon & Schuster, 1994). Broad and Cavanagh are co-authors of* Plundering Paradise: The Struggle for the Environment in the Philippines *(University of California Press, 1993).*

For four and a half decades, the Cold War offered Americans a prism through which to view the three-quarters of humanity who live in the impoverished countries of Latin America, Africa, and Asia. The United States fought or funded wars and covert operations in dozens of these countries—including Cuba, the Dominican Republic, Guatemala, Iran, Korea, Nicaragua, and Vietnam—with the stated goal of preventing the spread of Soviet-backed communism. Shaped to meet this goal, U.S. economic and military policies toward the so-called Third World, or South, were relatively simple and straightforward.

Today, a half decade into the confusing post–Cold War era and more than halfway through President Bill Clinton's first term, the Third World still erupts into the forefront of U.S. foreign policy with alarming regularity. The administration and media tend to categorize these episodes into one of three oversimplified images. The first and dominant one can be termed "the Rwanda image," and includes countries where, the media tells us, everything is falling apart, and people kill one another in large numbers. Bosnia in 1995, Haiti in 1994, or Somalia in 1993 fit the bill. A second image, promoted by beleaguered defense contractors and Pentagon hawks, paints certain volatile Third World nations and the former Soviet Union as emerging security threats equal to that posed by Moscow at the height of the Cold War. Here, North Korea and Iraq stand out, each with leaders easily caricatured by the media as Hollywood villains. Finally, there is the much

newer image of a financially tattered Mexico and the fear that other nations may plunge rapidly into similar crises; tens of billions of dollars of short-term speculative capital race around the globe, abandoning yesterday's favorite "emerging market" for promises of quick returns elsewhere.

Content to respond to crises in these three categories, the Clinton administration has yet to forge an overarching policy framework that addresses the deep and changing problems of the South, which comprises approximately 150 countries. In fact, aside from attention to some crisis spots, the administration forfeited its chance to craft a new North-South policy agenda, preferring instead one that places in the foreground only a handful of these countries. And this policy is being managed not by the State or Treasury Department, but by the Commerce Department, which has singled out 10 promising "big emerging markets" for U.S. exports and investments.

When pressed to articulate themes or values that underlie U.S. policy toward these countries and the rest of the South, Clinton administration officials unite around the rhetoric of markets and democracy: Freer markets, through such pacts as the North American Free Trade Agreement (NAFTA), will, they claim, bring both growth and greater democracy. Remarkably, the positions of most Republican leaders in Congress differ only slightly in substance from this agenda. They support the free-trade agenda and the notion that U.S. foreign policy should support U.S. business. A vocal minority who are more protectionist includes the powerful chairman of the Senate Foreign Relations Committee, Jesse Helms (R-NC). Despite his dramatic overstatements and misstatements that seek to distance him from the Democrats, Helms's attack on Clinton's North-South agenda has concentrated on one issue: cutting U.S. aid drastically (much of which, he likes to say, is "going down foreign ratholes").

Thus, Washington is poised to continue neglecting the South, except in response to crisis-based chaos or through free-trade agreements and business promotion aimed at a few Third World countries. This lack of a broader North-South economic agenda, however, may well turn out to be one of the great blunders of the Clinton administration. The danger of neglect lies beneath the facile surface images of the Third World reality: a deteriorating living standard for the poorest 2.5 billion people in the world, widening inequalities in almost every nation on earth, and employment and environmental crises that beg global initiatives.

The Clinton administration and the Republican Congress face three immediate opportunities to address these larger problems—opportunities that should be seized to frame a more comprehensive policy toward the South. First, the administration has begun considering the expansion of NAFTA to include the Caribbean Basin, Chile, and the rest of Latin America. Second, Congress is debating new criteria for giving U.S. aid to poor countries. And finally, the Mexico debacle initiated a propitious international deliberation on fundamental reform of the world's leading multilateral institutions—the World Bank and the International Monetary Fund (IMF)—to meet the new financial crises of the twenty-first century.

What is required to seize these opportunities is a deeper understanding of the new dynamics between North and South and a more comprehensive policy agenda. Unfortunately, Clinton's narrow policies are based on three deeply flawed assumptions (also shared by most Republican leaders) about the nature of the changes in the global economy.

The North-South economic gap is narrowing for about a dozen countries but continues to widen for well over 100 others.

The first incorrect assumption is that free trade and the promotion of U.S. business interests overseas are good for U.S. workers and communities. Commerce Secretary Ron Brown is the clearest articulator of this view, and he supports it with planeloads of corporate CEOs on trips to such "big emerging markets" as Brazil, China, and Indonesia. These trips and the two major free-trade agreements completed under Clinton—NAFTA and a new round of the General Agreement on Tariffs and Trade (GATT)—have offered tens of billions of dollars in new business overseas to the United States's largest firms. As the former deputy director of pol-

icy planning at the State Department, John Stremlau, wrote in the Winter 1994–95 issue of FOREIGN POLICY, the administration's big-emerging-markets program "should create millions of new and better-paying jobs for Americans, spur domestic productivity, ease adjustment to technological change, restrain inflation, [and] reduce trade and fiscal deficits."

The second flawed assumption of U.S. policy is that free trade and increased U.S. engagement in the 10 biggest emerging markets will not only help these economies but will also enhance growth in other Southern countries. Jumping on the big-emerging-markets bandwagon, American CEOs echo administration claims that U.S. policies are leading to the growth of huge middle classes—in such countries as China, India, and Indonesia—that will drive the world economy in the twenty-first century.

A third assumption is that the economic gap between rich and poor countries is now narrowing—a trend that the administration claims is aided by free trade and attention to the 10 Third World countries with big emerging markets. Indeed, there is a widespread perception among U.S. policymakers that the Third World debt crisis that widened the gap during the 1980s has ended, that new capital is flowing into the Third World, and that the gap is beginning to close. These perceptions are reinforced by World Bank projections that over the next decade Third World countries will actually grow faster than richer countries, thus catching up.

A careful analysis of social and economic data from the United Nations, the World Bank, the IMF, and other sources, offers a shockingly different picture of trends in the global economy and the gap between rich and poor countries. There are two ways to measure what is happening economically between North and South. The first is to measure which is growing faster, and therefore whether the gap between them is growing or shrinking. The second is to measure financial resource flows between the two.

On the first issue the picture is clear: The North-South gap widened dramatically in the decade after 1982 as the Third World debt crisis drained financial resources from poor countries to rich banks. Between 1985 and 1992, Southern nations paid some $280 billion more in debt service to Northern creditors than they received in new private loans and government aid. Gross national product (GNP) per capita rose an average of only 1 per cent in the South in the 1980s (in sub-Saharan Africa, it fell 1.2 per cent), while it rose 2.3 per cent in the North.

Situating the "lost decade" of the 1980s within a longer time period reveals no drastic change: In 1960, per capita gross domestic product (GDP) in the South stood at 18 per cent of the average of

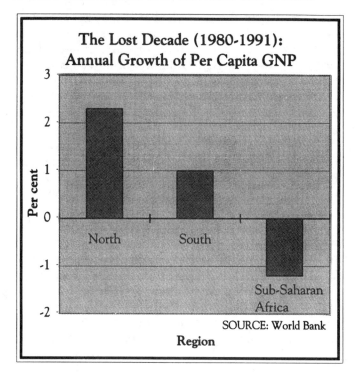

The Lost Decade (1980-1991): Annual Growth of Per Capita GNP

SOURCE: World Bank

Northern nations; by 1990, it had fallen only slightly to 17 per cent. In other words, the North-South gap remained fairly constant.

However, such aggregate figures camouflage a complex reality: For a small group of countries, primarily such Asian big emerging markets as China, Hong Kong, Singapore, South Korea, and Taiwan, the gap with the North has been closing. But—and here is the rub—for most of the rest, the gap has been slowly *widening*. In sub-Saharan Africa the picture is even worse. Not only has the gap expanded significantly, but for many of these countries, per capita GNP has continued to fall.

Likewise, a look at various resource flows between North and South reveals a reality out of sync with prevailing assumptions. Despite the perception of an easing of the debt crisis, the overall Third World debt stock continues to swell by almost $100 billion each year (it reached $1.9 trillion in 1994). Southern debt service still exceeds new lending, and the net outflow remains particularly crushing in Africa. While it is true that a series of debt reschedulings and the accumulation of arrears by many debtors have reduced the net negative financial transfer from South to North over the last few years, the flows remain negative.

Part of the reason some analysts argue that the debt crisis is no longer a problem is that since the early 1990s these outflows of debt repayments have been matched by increased inflows of foreign capital. Here too, however, a deeper look at disaggregated figures reinforces the disconcerting reality. According to World Bank figures, roughly half of the new foreign direct investment by global corpo-

rations in the South in 1992 quickly left those countries as profits. In addition, investment flows primarily to only 10 to 12 Third World countries that are viewed as new profit centers by Northern corporations and investors. More than 70 per cent of investment flows in 1991 and 1992 went to just 10 of the so-called emerging markets: Mexico, followed by China, Malaysia, Argentina, Thailand, Brazil, Indonesia, Venezuela, South Korea, and Turkey.

There is another problem with these capital flows. Several of these countries (Brazil, India, Mexico, South Korea, and Taiwan) have attracted substantial short-term flows by opening their stock markets to foreigners and by issuing billions of dollars in bonds. Between 1991 and 1993 alone, foreign direct investment as a share of all private capital flows into poor countries fell from 65 to 44 per cent as these more speculative flows increased. Recent events in Mexico provide an indication of the fickleness of these new investment flows: During the last week of 1994, an estimated $10 billion in short-term funds fled the country.

In addition, Third World countries have been hurt by the declining buying power of their exports vis-à-vis their imports. Southern nations have long pointed out the general tendency of the prices of their primary product exports to rise more slowly than the prices of manufactured goods imports. This "terms of trade" decline was particularly sharp between 1985 and 1993 when the real prices of primary commodities fell 30 per cent. This translates into billions of dollars: The 3.5 per cent decline in the purchasing power of Africa's 1993 exports, for example, cost the continent some $3 billion.

The inescapable conclusion is that the North-South economic gap is narrowing for about a dozen countries but continues to widen for well over 100 others. Hence, without a major shift in policy, the world of the twenty-first century will be one of economic apartheid. There will be two dozen richer nations, a dozen or so poorer nations that have begun to close the gap with the rich, and approximately 140 poor nations slipping further behind.

GLOBALIZATION OF NORTH AND SOUTH

What about the administration's assumption that policies promoting U.S. business are good for overseas as well as domestic markets—that free markets and globalization raise standards of living across the board in both North and South? Here, too, the Clinton administration has missed a fundamental new reality of the global

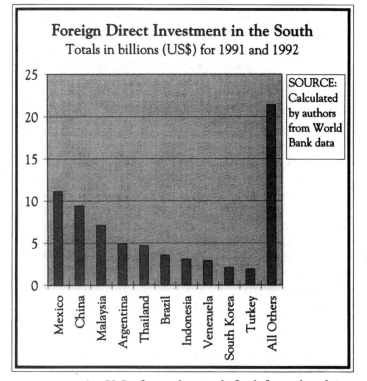

Foreign Direct Investment in the South
Totals in billions (US$) for 1991 and 1992

SOURCE: Calculated by authors from World Bank data

(Bar chart showing: Mexico, China, Malaysia, Argentina, Thailand, Brazil, Indonesia, Venezuela, South Korea, Turkey, All Others)

economy. As U.S. firms have shifted from local to national and now global markets over the past half century, a new division of winners and losers has emerged in all countries. A recent book, *Global Dreams: Imperial Corporations and the New World Order*, written by one of the authors and Institute for Policy Studies co-founder Richard Barnet, chronicles how powerful U.S. firms and their counterparts from England, France, Germany, and Japan are integrating only about one-third of humanity (most of those in the rich countries plus the elite of poor countries) into complex chains of production, shopping, culture, and finance.

While there are enclaves in every country that are linked to these global economic webs, others are left out. Wal-Mart is spreading its superstores throughout the Western Hemisphere; millions in Latin America, though, are too poor to enjoy anything but glimpses of luxury. Citibank customers can access automated-teller machines throughout the world; the vast majority of people nevertheless borrow from the loan shark down the road. Ford Motor Company pieces together its new "global car" in Kansas City from parts made all over the globe, while executives in Detroit worry about who will be able to afford it.

Thus, while on one level the North-South gap is becoming more pronounced for the vast majority of Third World countries, on another level these global chains blur distinctions between geographical North and South. These processes create another North-South divide between the roughly one-third of humanity who comprise a "global North" of beneficiaries in every country and the two-thirds of humanity from the slums of New York to the favelas of Rio who are not hooked into the new global menu of producing, consuming, and borrowing opportunities in the "global South."

In contrast with the Pollyanna-ish assumptions of the Clinton administration, globalization, accelerated by the administration's new free-trade and investment agreements, has deepened three intractable problems that now plague almost every nation on earth including the United States: income inequalities, job losses, and environmental damage.

Income Inequalities

The major adverse consequence of quickening global economic integration has been widening income disparity within almost all nations as the wealthier strata cash in on the opportunities of globalization, while millions of other citizens are hurt, marginalized, or left behind. Years ago, economist Simon Kuznets hypothesized that as economies develop there is initially a growth-equity trade-off, i.e., income inequalities rise as nations enter the early stages of economic growth and fall in more mature economies. Today, however, the inequalities are growing everywhere—to such an extent that in late 1994 the *Economist* acknowledged that "it is no coincidence that the biggest increases in income inequalities have occurred in economies . . . where free-market economic policies have been pursued most zealously" and that "it is a combination of lightly regulated labour markets and global economic forces that has done much more . . . to favour the rich over the poor."

One sees this in the perverse widening of the gap between rich and poor within nations and across the globe. Thirty years ago, the income of the richest fifth of the world's population combined was 30 times greater than that of the poorest fifth. Today, the income gap is more than 60 times greater. Over this period the income of the richest 20 per cent grew from 70 to 85 per cent of the total world income, while the global share of the poorest 20 per cent fell from 2.3 to 1.4 per cent.

The number of billionaires grew dramatically over the past seven years, coinciding with the spread of free-market policies around the world. Between 1987 and 1994, the number more than doubled from 145 to 358. According to our calculations, those 358 billionaires are collectively worth some $762 billion, which is about the combined income of the world's poorest 2.5 billion people. (There are no figures for the combined wealth of the world's poor, but since most have little wealth beyond income, their wealth total would not be much higher than their income total.) At the bottom, 2.5 billion people—approximately 45 per cent of the world's population—eke out an existence using just under 4 per cent of the world's GNP. At the top, 358 individuals own the same per cent.

The impact of free-market policies on this concentration of wealth has been particularly pronounced in Mexico, a country that essentially began its free-market opening in 1986 and that, until the peso debacle of December 1994, was often presented as the model of these policies' success. In 1987, there was just one billionaire in Mexico. By 1994, there were 24 who accounted for $44.1 billion in collective wealth. This exceeded the total income of the poorest 40 per cent of Mexican households. As a result, the 24 wealthiest people are richer than the poorest 33 million people in Mexico.

Job Losses

With the exception of a few East Asian economies, every nation—North and South—is grappling with high or rising unemployment, and many, including the United States, are suffering from deteriorating working conditions for a sizable share of the work-force. Worldwide, more than 800 million people are unemployed or seriously underemployed, with tens of millions more falling into this situation each year. Technology has combined with globalization in a devastating manner to spawn this crisis of work. Unlike previous industrial revolutions, the two most important technological innovations in recent decades—informationl computers and biotechnology—destroy more jobs than they create. At the same time, rapid strides in transportation and communications technologies allow increasing numbers of jobs to be sent to countries other than the United States. Whereas a generation ago, firms shifted only apparel and consumer electronics jobs overseas, today they can move virtually the entire range of manufacturing and agricultural tasks (and a number of service jobs as well) to China, Mexico, or a range of other countries.

As corporations and governments alike strive to compete globally by cutting costs, the move to slash jobs accelerates. *Fortune* 500 firms have cut approximately 400,000 jobs a year for the past 15 years. As many as one-third of U.S. workers are swimming in a global labor pool; their jobs can be moved elsewhere, and this fact confers on their global corporate employers enhanced power to bargain down wages and working conditions.

U.S. car companies, for example, can attain roughly equivalent levels of productivity and quality at their Mexican plants today as in their U.S. plants. The denial of basic worker rights in Mexico,

however, severely hampers Mexican workers' efforts to negotiate improvements in their working conditions, and their wages remain a fraction of those of U.S. autoworkers. The credible threat of moving more production to Mexico gives the U.S. companies bargaining chips against their U.S. workers when wages and benefits are set. Overall Mexican productivity climbed by at least 24 per cent during the boom years from 1987 to 1992, while wages rose only 13 per cent; this gap has increased even more since the peso crisis of late 1994. Likewise, according to the U.S. International Trade Commission, Brazilian workers were 59 per cent as productive in 1986 as U.S. workers but earned 17 per cent of the average U.S. wage. Even in Bangladesh, shirtmakers are about 60 per cent as productive as their American counterparts but earn only 3 to 5 per cent of a U.S. salary.

In the South, roughly 38 million people enter stagnating job markets each year. Markets for Third World products are expanding quite slowly in the rich countries, and biotechnology innovations that create synthetic substitutes for everything from vanilla to cocoa and coffee threaten to eliminate the livelihood of millions of Third World agricultural workers. As in the United States, real wages have fallen in most of Latin America and parts of Asia since the early 1980s—a shock that hits women particularly hard since they earn 30 to 40 per cent less than men doing the same jobs.

As job pressures grow across the South, many people leave for Europe and North America, where job markets are also tight. Violent acts of xenophobia and racism in the North are some of the ugliest manifestations of this current era of inequality and joblessness.

Environmental Damage

Just as jobs and working conditions become bargaining chips for firms in a deregulated global economy, so too do environmental standards. If the Mexican government can attract foreign firms by ignoring violations of environmental laws, it will do so, and, arguably, it must do so or lose investment. The same logic fuels the Republican party's crusade to eliminate a wide range of environmental and other regulations in the United States.

Another pressure on the environment in the South is the constant admonition by the World Bank and the IMF to increase exports. Since most of the world's minerals, timber, fish, and land are in the South, exports tend to be natural-resource intensive. The depletion of these resources hurts yields for millions of small farmers and fishers. The frenzy to ship more goods overseas accelerates environmental degradation and thus diminishes the real, long-term wealth of Southern nations.

On the other hand, as Southern countries have rightly pointed out, most of the world's consumption, greenhouse gas emissions, ozone-depleting chemical emissions, and industrial pollution occur in the North. The heaviest burden for global environmental action rests there. But the creation of a "global North" in the South through the big-emerging-markets strategy also spreads environmental havoc. Following annual economic growth rates averaging 10 per cent since 1978, China's commercial sector consumes more than 1 billion tons of coal annually; thus China produces nearly 11 per cent of the world's carbon dioxide emissions. If this rate of climb continues, the impact on global warming will be catastrophic. In India, increased consumption will exacerbate a situation where scale already exceeds carrying capacity: 16 per cent of the world's population is degrading just 2.3 per cent of the world's land resources and 1.7 per cent of its forest stock. And to compensate for falling oil revenues, Indonesia is tearing down the world's second-largest tropical rainforest, becoming the world's largest exporter of processed wood products.

COMPARATIVE DISADVANTAGE

The North-South reality of the mid-1990s hardly matches the soothing scenario suggested by the Clinton administration. Rather, we find the ominous combination of a growing gap between the majority of the Southern and Northern countries as well as the existence of a privileged minority in a "global North" and a marginalized majority in a "global South." Indeed, our analysis suggests three sets of problems that demand attention:

- Most of the "global South"—some 45 per cent of humanity who reside mainly in the 140 poorest countries of the Third World—is locked in poverty and left behind as the richer strata grow.
- Roughly 20 per cent of the world's population—who are at the upper end of the two-thirds in the "global South," mainly in the big emerging markets—is beginning to enter the global consuming class in a fashion that threatens the environment and exacerbates social tensions.
- An increasing number of workers among the top one-third, or "global North," of the world is experiencing falling incomes and an erosion of worker rights and standards.

Thus far, U.S. policy has largely ignored the bottom 45 per cent, concentrated on the middle 20 per cent in the big emerging markets, and exacerbated the tensions within the top third. The challenge for U.S. policymakers is to focus on this new global picture with a two-tiered set of policies—one aimed at the forsaken 45 per cent primarily in Southern countries and the other focused on the growing inequalities and the job and environmental crises mainly in the big emerging markets and the richer countries of the North. The seeds of what has to change in terms of aid, debt, trade, and investment policies have, in most cases, already been planted. And, as was suggested earlier, the administration has ready venues to change course in the current policy debates on NAFTA expansion, aid reform, and World Bank and IMF restructuring.

The Bottom 45 Per Cent

The main U.S. policy arena addressing the problems of the world's poor is the debate over aid. Helms is achieving deep cuts in aid but wrongly asserts that most poor countries are "foreign ratholes" and are, hence, undeserving of assistance. Virtually all countries in the world now pursue the same basic package of market-opening, privatizing, government-trimming, export-driven policies. While it is true that there is more corruption and inefficiency in some countries than in others, this is as true for favored countries that are at the center of U.S. policy (e.g., Mexico) as for the 140 neglected countries (e.g., Zaire).

At the same time, anyone who has studied development projects and policies on the ground cannot help but acknowledge the truth in some of Helms's criticisms: Much U.S., World Bank, and other aid either fails to ease poverty or is conditioned on the recipient nation adopting policies that deepen social and environmental pain. More of the same aid is not the way to close the gap. The key is to make less aid more effective. The current obsession in Washington with restructuring aid agencies will be misplaced if it does not focus on the quality of aid. Any restructuring must learn from a growing number of aid experiments throughout the world that channel small amounts of funds directly to entities run by local citizen groups with guidelines that stress sustainability, participation, and equity.

While it would be a good step to redirect more aid in this manner, a great deal more needs to be done outside the realm of aid to stop the hemorrhage of resource flows from the bottom 140 countries to the North. The most fruitful avenue is to try to close the gap by taking less money out of the South rather than by getting more money in. Here the focus needs to shift back to debt. The place to begin is with the roughly 17 per cent of Third World debt owed to the World Bank and the IMF—with far higher percentages owed by the poorest African nations. The World Bank and the IMF could readily use their reserves ($17 billion and $40 billion, respectively) to cancel much of the outstanding debt owed to them by the poorest countries. The World Bank could likewise write off loans to other countries for projects and programs that have failed by its own economic criteria and/or have had severe adverse effects on local populations and the environment. (A World Bank study found that in fiscal year 1991 more than one-third of its projects were "unsatisfactory at completion" in meeting a minimum economic rate of return.)

As governments debate World Bank restructuring, it is important to note that there are alternatives to the World Bank's formula of excessive dependence on exports and capital inflows. If the goal is to prevent nations from falling into debt again, then debt reduction can be conditioned on policies that encourage productive investment, provide assistance to small entrepreneurs and farmers, and encourage less indebted economies. One alternative worth considering, proposed by a number of Mexican economists, is the adoption of policies for the World Bank and Mexico that reestablish land rights for the poor, steer access to affordable credit to small farmers and entrepreneurs, and restrict inflows of short-term speculative investment.

Economic reformers in Mexico and elsewhere also push for effective systems of fair taxation, while acknowledging how difficult that goal is since most tax systems are poorly enforced. Most critics of the World Bank model acknowledge the need to maintain smaller export sectors to finance vital imports of capital goods but place greater emphasis on production for the domestic market, as was done in South Korea and Taiwan in their early years of industrialization.

The World Bank and the Agency for International Development should also be restrained from pressing dozens of countries into simultaneous export binges on everything from cut flowers to coffee; the impact of so many countries exporting the same products will inevitably be to depress world prices. And these institutions should nurture the small but growing movement that is stimulating trade in goods produced under conditions that respect worker rights and the environment and recognize the deep discrimination that frequently exists against female producers. "Fair trade" entrepreneurs, who are particularly strong in Europe and are spreading in North America, are now responsible for hundreds of millions of dollars of trade in coffee, textiles, and other products and are devel-

oping new notions of what constitutes socially and environmentally responsible trade.

Not surprisingly, the agenda suggested for the bottom 45 per cent draws from a more traditional set of remedies on how to shrink the North-South gap. However, attacking the trio of problems outlined for the global North and South—the inequities, joblessness, and environmental degradation—demands that these be implemented in conjunction with a newer set of policy instruments.

The Big Emerging Markets and Anxiety at the Top

Rather than quickening the pace to compete in an increasingly deregulated global economy, the United States can lead in calling for new rules to temper economic integration's socially and environmentally destructive effect upon unequal nations. It is important to recall that the United States rose to this same challenge on a national level in the 1930s when large firms were integrating the U.S. national economy and, in the process, playing rich unionized states off poor nonunion states. A strong trade-union movement created the momentum for Franklin Roosevelt's administration to set new national rules for minimum wages, maximum hours of work, and decent health and safety standards.

In the 1990s, this same dynamic now occurs on a global stage, where global corporations play workers and environmental standards against one another to bargain richer countries down to the standards of the poorer ones. Free-trade agreements that accelerate integration without explicitly safeguarding labor and environmental rights and standards are only deepening global job and environmental crises. Therefore, internationally recognized standards on worker rights (including freedom of association, the right to collective bargaining, and a ban on discrimination based on gender or race) and the environment, which have been hammered out by member governments of the International Labor Organization (ILO) and various international environmental treaties, need to be grafted onto new trade agreements so that firms benefiting from lower tariffs would be obligated to respect those rights and standards.

The first steps in this direction have already been taken. Since 1984, U.S. trade law has conditioned the granting of "trade preferences" to a developing country's respect for internationally recognized worker rights. Threats by the U.S. government to withdraw trade preferences have led to important reforms in a number of countries. For instance, in response to looming U.S. sanctions, El Salvador has worked with the ILO to adopt a more comprehensive labor code. The government of Sri Lanka reacted to similar pressure by agreeing to open its garment industry to collective bargaining. Indonesia announced a 29 per cent increase in its minimum wage in 1994 after the United States threatened to remove trade preferences. Building on this U.S. trade law, NAFTA's negotiators crafted side agreements that threaten minor sanctions to encourage enforcement of a small number of labor rights and environmental standards.

In addition to social clauses on trade-agreements, global corporations should be held to codes of conduct that require compliance with these rights and standards. A number of U.S. firms, including Levi Strauss and Sears, have taken a step toward comprehensive corporate codes by agreeing to voluntary codes for the firms with which they subcontract in the Third World.

New corporate codes and socially responsible trade and investment agreements would not solve all the world's job, environmental, and inequality problems, but they could be implemented in the short term and would help reverse the negative dynamic we now face. In the long term, such policies would be more effective if supplemented with strong national policies to address the job and environmental problems jointly.

Even with the best codes of conduct and social clauses on trade agreements, increased trade is likely to continue to be based on the unsustainable exploitation of natural resources. This creates two challenges: first, to raise standards of living in the big emerging markets and other Southern nations without exceeding the Earth's environmental limits and, second, to get Northern societies to acknowledge the costs to the environment of their already high standards of living. Across the board, nations—and individuals—need to acknowledge the environmental costs of economic decisions.

One way to reduce trade in natural resources (such as virgin timber) and the use of resource-intensive products (such as cars) is for governments to adopt accounting systems that factor in the real costs of natural-resource depletion and environmental degradation. In fact, technical work on "environmental accounting" is already quite advanced, as seen in the World Resources Institute's work in Costa Rica, Indonesia, and other developing countries. Even the U.S. Commerce Department has begun recalculations for a "green GDP." In this regard, the World Bank and the IMF should be required to adopt a system of "shadow pricing" that accounts for environmental costs in their projects and programs. This would be an important step in the direction of seeing "green GDPs" become the conceptual framework across the globe.

ENLIGHTENED SELF-INTEREST

For the next year, the Republican Congress will reinforce the Clinton administration's hesitancy to embrace a number of these proposals. Yet, there is an impetus for a shift in policy regarding the poorer majority of the world. In the tough debate over NAFTA, citizens' groups—trade unions, environmental groups, organizations of small farmers, consumer activists, religious groups, women's groups, and others—emerged in Canada, Mexico, and the United States to press for safeguards on labor, the environment, and agriculture. While only small gains were realized in the final agreement, the democratization of the debate over international economic policy continued during the recent GATT deliberation and is likely to characterize the next debates over integration in the Americas and Asia. Similar citizen coalitions throughout the world have likewise gathered momentum for reform of the World Bank and the IMF.

In other words, segments of civil society seem ahead of U.S. policymakers in comprehending that the widening inequalities within nations and between North and South pose crucial challenges that are in our enlightened self-interest to meet. Working conditions in a number of Third World countries have an increasing impact on working conditions in the United States. Growing inequalities in the South are increasing the flow of people, drugs, and environmental problems into the North. The rapid rise of the rich and the emergence of a middle class in the big emerging markets increase instability and tension vis-à-vis the vast numbers of people left behind-witness the growing labor unrest in China, Indonesia, and Mexico, as well as the continuing rebellion in Mexico's Chiapas state.

While the Clinton administration can continue to respond belatedly to crises and fall back on its faulty assumptions about the North-South economic reality, the attendant problems of the post–Cold War global economy will inevitably become clearer as an increasing number of people in the North and South are hurt. There is no way to get around the need for a fundamental rethinking of the North-South agenda. The question is simply whether the United States will take the lead in resolving these problems or will instead wait and be led.

Reverse Linkages:
The Growing Importance of Developing Countries

SWATI R. GHOSH

Swati R. Ghosh, *an Indian national, is an Economist in the International Finance Division of the World Bank's International Economics Department.*

As trade between developing and industrial countries grows and cross-border capital mobility increases, the developing countries will have a greater impact on the global economy. Although public debate has focused on possible adverse effects on the industrial economies, analysis suggests that the latter will benefit from growing integration.

THE DEVELOPING countries' economic prospects have long been heavily dependent on the industrial economies. But the share of world output, trade, and capital flows that can be attributed to developing countries has been increasing over the past two decades. As a result, "reverse linkages"—the impacts of developing countries on industrial countries—are becoming more significant.

Growth of the developing countries' output and trade—and of their share of world output and trade—has accelerated over the past five years (Charts 1 and 2). If this trend continues, over the next 10–15 years, developing countries can be expected to play a much greater role in the world economy—and have a much larger impact on industrial countries. Although the rising importance of developing countries in the international economy has so far been due to a relatively small number of countries, the recent acceleration of growth in the developing world has been broadly based, and this trend is expected to continue.

To date, the debate on reverse linkages has focused almost exclusively on one aspect—the potentially adverse consequences of growing trade between developing and industrial countries on employment and wages in the latter. However, comprehensive analysis of the three factors responsible for the growing impact of developing countries—expanding trade between industrial and developing countries, increasing financial integration, and relatively rapid growth in developing countries—suggests that if the process of integration is properly managed, benefits will outweigh costs to industrial countries.

Trade integration

In 1994, developing countries accounted for 24 percent of world imports; this share could rise to 30 percent by 2010 (Chart 3). Over the same period, their share of world exports of manufactures could increase from 17 to 22 percent. Developing countries currently buy roughly one-fourth of the industrial countries' exports; on present trends, that share could rise to more than one-third by 2010. The main factors driving this increase in trade are the reduction of trade barriers through trade liberalization and other reforms, lower transport and communication costs, and relatively high GDP growth in developing countries.

From *Finance & Development*, March 1996, pp. 38-41. © 1996 by the International Monetary Fund and the International Bank for Reconstruction and Development/THE WORLD BANK. Reprinted by permission.

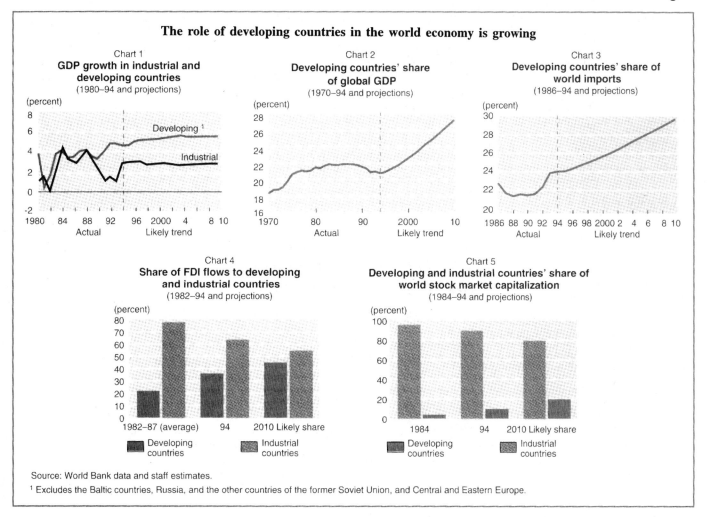

The role of developing countries in the world economy is growing

Chart 1
GDP growth in industrial and developing countries
(1980–94 and projections)

Chart 2
Developing countries' share of global GDP
(1970–94 and projections)

Chart 3
Developing countries' share of world imports
(1986–94 and projections)

Chart 4
Share of FDI flows to developing and industrial countries
(1982–94 and projections)

Chart 5
Developing and industrial countries' share of world stock market capitalization
(1984–94 and projections)

Source: World Bank data and staff estimates.

[1] Excludes the Baltic countries, Russia, and the other countries of the former Soviet Union, and Central and Eastern Europe.

Closer trade links between developing and industrial countries will generate gains for industrial countries at two levels. First, there will be specialization and efficiency gains from the exploitation of the traditional comparative advantages of trading partners, gains from the availability of a greater variety of goods, and, possibly, efficiency gains from economies of scale and increased competition. Second, first-round gains in efficiency and output will provide a second-round boost to output over the medium term. Increased efficiency in the first round will raise the return to capital, thereby leading to increased investment. Savings will also rise, either because of higher returns to savings or because part of the initial increase in output is saved—or both. A study by Levine and Renelt (see references) provides empirical evidence of increased openness leading to higher levels of investment. The second-round effect could take the form of a permanent increase in the growth rate of output if there are sufficient spillovers or economies of scale.

In theory, such "endogenous growth" could happen in several ways. For example, trade integration could allow firms to spread the costs of research and development over a larger market, thus reducing unit costs and encouraging greater innovation and technical progress. This can, in turn, generate positive spillovers as successful innovations are applied more broadly. Innovation could also be spurred by increased competition. Furthermore, innovation, by adding to the stock of public knowledge, can stimulate further innovation. Integration can also boost productivity growth by allowing increased specialization.

How large are the potential gains from trade integration likely to be? Price differences between countries for similar products provide a broad indication—the larger the differences, the greater the gains from specialization. Data compiled under the UN International Comparison Program indicate that these differences tend to be much larger between the industrial and the developing countries than between industrial countries.

Estimating the actual gains from growing trade integration is very difficult, however, because increased trade integration occurs in different ways with a variety of different effects. The gains from the one-off multilateral trade liberalization under the Uruguay Round agreement provide one measure of possible gains. It is estimated that the Uruguay Round will lead to gains for industrial countries ranging from 0.3 percent of industrial country GDP under constant returns to scale to 0.4 percent under monopolistic competition and internal increasing returns to scale (when a doubling of inputs more than doubles output), and 0.75 percent under increasing external or industry-wide returns to scale, which can come into play as trade increases market size. Although these estimates may be seen as overstating benefits from trade integration with developing countries because they are, to a large extent, based on the liberalization of markets in industrial countries, they may actually understate gains because they do not include the effects of the substantial liberalization that developing countries had already undertaken as well as the efficiency gains from increased competition, foreign direct investment (FDI) flows that reinforce these gains, or potential benefits from trade in services.

The magnitude of the second-round boost to output will depend on the share of accumulable capital in production and on the externalities or spillovers associated with this capital.

If both physical and human capital can be accumulated and are stimulated by the increased returns to their accumulation, the induced second-round effect could amount to 0.8 percent of GDP (following an initial increase of 0.4 percent). If, however, there are also sufficient positive externalities associated with this capital that prevent the returns to it from diminishing over time, the second-round effect could take the form of an increase in the growth rate, as opposed to just an increase in the level of output. Although empirical testing of the significance of endogenous growth is at an early stage, there appears to be some preliminary support for this outcome. Studies have found a positive correlation between trade openness and total factor productivity (Wolff 1995), which could stem from some of the potential spillovers or externalities mentioned above. A study by Backus and others (1991) provides some sectoral evidence of one of the potential externalities: the dynamic economies of scale associated with learning-by-doing and specialization.

Positive spillovers would lead to substantial benefits for industrial countries. To illustrate, if the externalities associated with physical and human capital were large enough to prevent the returns to capital from diminishing—that is, to ensure endogenous growth—the initial increase in output and income resulting from the Uruguay Round trade liberalization would lead to an increase of 0.1 percentage point in the growth rate of industrial countries in the second round. Expressed as discounted income, this could amount to a second-round increase in output of about 3.2 percent of industrial country GDP. The gains from overall growth in trade integration with developing countries—not just those resulting from a one-off round of trade liberalization—would be much higher.

Financial integration

In 1992–94, developing countries received about 40 percent of global FDI inflows, compared with 23 percent in the mid-1980s, and the share of FDI flows going to the developing world is likely to keep going up as more developing countries open their markets and improve their growth prospects (Chart 4). In addition to the gains from FDI associated with trade and the globalization of production, investors enjoy high rates of return. Over the past three years, according to the US Department of Commerce's *Survey of Current Business*, the rate of return on FDI flows from the United States to the other Group of Seven nations averaged about 8 percent annually;

returns on FDI flows to the eight largest recipients among developing countries averaged about 21 percent annually. To some extent, of course, the higher returns reflect the greater risk in developing countries but, even adjusted for risk, rates of return are likely to be substantially higher in developing countries.

Investors from industrial countries also can diversify risk by investing in stock markets in developing countries because of the relatively low correlation between returns in emerging markets and those in industrial

". . . fears of decapitalization and the hollowing-out of industries do not appear well founded."

countries. The typical pension fund in the United States invests only 1–2 percent of its portfolio in emerging markets. Yet calculations for 1989–94 (Ghosh 1995) suggest that, if this share were increased to about 20 percent, the annual return on the entire portfolio would rise by almost 2 percentage points without increased risk. Although it may be difficult for developing countries to absorb such large magnitudes of investment at present, increases in market capitalization (Chart 5) will increase opportunities for portfolio diversification.

Rapid growth

The faster growth of the GDP of developing countries can lead to greater trade integration, generating first- and second-round gains for industrial countries. Indeed, over time, growth could be more important than trade liberalization as a source of gains from trade integration. Besides generating gains from trade integration, the rapid outward-oriented growth of developing countries will benefit industrial countries in other ways.

First, it stimulates demand for industrial country output. Growth in investment in developing countries boosts demand for imports of capital goods and services. The growing shift to the private sector and the prospective expansion of infrastructure investment in developing economies offer new opportunities for exports from industrial countries. In addition, income growth in developing countries will increase demand for more, increasingly sophisticated consumer goods, boosting imports from industrial countries. By 2010, there could be more than one billion consumers in developing countries (more than the current total population of all the industrial

countries) with per capita incomes exceeding those of Spain or Greece today. If developing countries continue to run current account deficits over the medium term, and if there is unemployed capacity in industrial countries, developing countries' increased demand for imports will lead to higher output in industrial countries. Based on current structure, a 1 percentage point increase in GDP growth in the developing countries could lead to an increase of 0.2 percentage points of GDP growth in industrial countries.

Second, the relatively faster growth of developing countries could improve the industrial countries' terms of trade. Terms of trade gains will depend on the relative growth of exportables and importables in the two groups of countries and income and price elasticities. Since developing countries tend to grow faster than industrial countries, supply of their exportables will tend to grow faster, other things being equal, than supply of industrial countries' exportables. The demand for exportables from industrial countries will also tend to rise more than the demand for exportables from developing countries because industrial countries tend to produce goods with greater income elasticity.

Third, to the extent that developing countries grow more rapidly than in the past, they will offer investors even higher rates of return, both on FDI and portfolio flows.

Adjustment costs

In the public debate about the benefits and costs to industrial countries of increased trade and financial integration with developing countries, the benefits generally fail to be recognized, in part because they are diffuse, often indirect, and accrue over time. The costs are likely to receive much more attention because they are concentrated in specific sectors and tend to be much more immediate in their impact; moreover, the surge in developing countries' trade with industrial countries over the past few years has coincided with adverse labor market conditions in the latter. The debate has focused on a number of issues: the effect of exports from developing countries on manufacturing output and employment in the industrial countries; the relationship between trade with developing countries and deindustrialization in some industrial countries; the effect of trade on widening wage inequality between skilled and low-skill workers in industrial countries, and on unemployment, especially of low-skill labor; and "decapitalization"—the possible decline in industries and jobs as a result of the increased flow of capital to developing countries.

Imports by countries belonging to the Organization for Economic Cooperation and Development (OECD) of manufactured goods from developing countries increased, as a share of the value of OECD manufacturing output, from 3 percent in 1970 to 12 percent in 1992. Over the same period, manufacturing in the industrial countries, as a share of GDP and source of jobs, suffered a decline. Empirical analysis suggests, however, that, while trade with developing countries has certainly affected the structure of manufacturing in the industrial economies—the contraction of some activities and the expansion of others are the very means by which gains from trade are realized—it is not the principal cause of the manufacturing sector's decline, which can be attributed to higher productivity growth, compared with the expanding services sector.

The surge in trade with developing countries has also coincided with a widening wage gap between skilled and low-skill workers, especially in the United Kingdom and the United States, and with increasing unemployment in Europe, especially of low-skill labor. However, evidence from the United States suggests that the effects of trade on the labor market have not been significant. More important has been the impact of labor-saving technological change. Europe's relatively high unemployment rates seem to be due mainly to rigidities in labor and product markets. Finally, fears of decapitalization and the hollowing-out of industries do not appear well founded. Over the past 25 years, cumulative net flows to developing countries have accounted for only 2 percent of the industrial countries' capital stock.

In the future, as trade between the developing and the industrial countries continues to increase, some industries will shrink while others expand, and the structure of the world economy will change. Labor-intensive and low-skill industries in the industrial economies will no doubt be affected. At the same time, those industries and services in which industrial countries retain a comparative advantage will expand. It is also important to note that the increases in output and incomes in industrial countries from trade and financial integration with developing countries will increase demand for services that have high income elasticities in the industrial countries. Part of this increase will be for low-skill intensive services. For industrial countries, the challenge is to minimize the social costs of adjustment while reallocating resources to industries that will benefit from integration. Flexibility in labor markets is crucial. To keep unemployment down, these markets need to function smoothly.

This article is based on a World Bank report, Global Economic Prospects and the Developing Countries 1995 *(Washington).*

References:

D. Backus, P. Kehoe, and T. Kehoe, 1991, "In Search of Scale Effects in Trade and Growth," Research Department Working Paper, Federal Reserve Bank of Minneapolis.

W. H. Buiter and S.R. Ghosh, 1995, "Economic Integration, Scale Effects, Market Structure and Growth" (unpublished, World Bank, International Economics Department).

S.R. Ghosh, 1995, "Reverse Linkages—The Effects of Developing Countries on Industrial Countries: A Conceptual Framework" (unpublished, World Bank, International Economics Department).

R. Levine and D. Renelt, 1992, "A Sensitivity Analysis of Cross-Country Growth Regressions," American Economic Review, *Vol. 82 (September), pp. 942–63.*

E. Wolff, 1995, "Productivity Growth Among OECD Countries: Historical Record and Future Prospects" (unpublished, World Bank, International Economics Department).

The 'new South'[*]

Maurice Strong

Maurice Strong was a moving force behind the Earth Summit in Rio de Janeiro in 1992. He has been an Under-Secretary General of the United Nations several times, and is now Chairman and Chief Executive of Ontario Hydro, the largest utility company in North America.

As we move into the twenty-first century, human ingenuity and the miracles wrought by our mastery of science and technology have produced a civilisation beyond the wildest dreams of earlier generations, and given us the tools with which to shape an even more exciting and promising future. But these same forces have also given rise to some serious and deepening imbalances which must be seen as ominous threats to our common future.

These threats stem primarily from the concentration during this century of economic growth, and its benefits, in the industrialised countries, and population growth, with its attendant costs and pressures, in the developing countries. This is accentuating the differences between rich and poor both within and among nations. It is also compounding the problems of managing co-operatively the risks to our common future arising from the growing pressures on the earth's resource and life-support systems.

The prospects for a secure and sustainable future for the human community will largely be determined by the nature and direction of the major changes which are transforming the developing world into what I call the 'new South', and the ways in which we in the traditional industrialised countries contribute and respond to these changes.

[*]This article is an edited and slightly extended version of a talk given at Chatham House on 8 September 1995.

Today's 'world order' is quite different from that which prevailed at the time of the 1972 Stockholm Conference on Human Environment. The line between the traditional have and have-not nations is blurring as the result of the economic progress being made by some developing countries. There has also been a movement towards democratising the political process in some key countries of Latin America and Asia, and the emergence of a multi-social democracy in South Africa. The more rapidly developing countries of Asia and Latin America are leading the revitalisation of the global economy, challenging its domination by the traditional industrialised countries and reshaping the geopolitical landscape.

A recent World Bank report points out that even in the two decades from 1974 to 1993, developing countries as a whole grew at a rate slightly higher (3 per cent) than the rich industrialised countries (2.9 per cent) and are expected to grow by almost 5 per cent per year in the next decade, compared with 2.7 per cent in the traditional industrialised countries.

On this basis, as *The Economist* noted in a survey of the global economy, China will replace the United States as the world's largest economy by 2020, and 9 of the top 15 economies of the world will be today's developing countries. India will replace Germany as the fourth largest economy. The same survey projects that developing countries' share of world output will grow to 62 per cent by 2020, while that of the rich industrialised countries will decline to 37 per cent.

It is always dangerous to put too much weight on surveys based largely on the extrapolation of current trends. There seems little doubt that the direction pointed up by *The Economist* is valid. As the recent crisis in Mexico demonstrates, the rapidly developing countries are vulnerable to severe setbacks. But through a combi-

From *The World Today*, November 1995, pp. 215-219. © 1995 by The Royal Institute of International Affairs. Reprinted by permission.

nation of radical and enlightened policy changes and the support of the international community, the setback to Mexico seems to have been temporary and its economy is now on the move again.

The basic character of the economies of the developing countries is also undergoing a major transformation. Although the majority of the poorest and least developed countries have been largely by-passed by this movement, many others have moved beyond their traditional role as exporters of raw materials and commodities. Manufactured goods now constitute some 60 per cent of developing countries' exports, compared to only 5 per cent in 1955. And their share of world manufacturing exports rose from 5 per cent in 1970 to 22 per cent in 1993.

Fortress North?

In the light of these forecasts, the G-7 group of industrialised nations, which today does not include a single developing country, is clearly becoming an anachronism. The current 'world order' continues to be rooted in the past, particularly our notions regarding North–South relationships. We in the West have not yet really begun to appreciate and come to terms with the immense geopolitical implications of this shift of economic power to the South. Despite the movement towards a global economy and a more open trading system, I see signs of a 'fortress North' mentality developing in the wealthy industrialised countries which would not bode well for future relations with the developing world.

The major movement of economic growth to the South is evoking mixed feelings, and responses, from the traditional industrialised countries – the member states of the Organisation for Economic Cooperation and Development (OECD). On the one hand, their export industries have welcomed – and been quick to exploit – the opportunities that have opened up in the rapidly growing economies of the developing world. A recent OECD report postulates that if China, India and Indonesia continue to grow at current rates, without changing current patterns of income distribution, some 700m people in these three countries alone – more than the combined populations of America, the European Union and Japan – will, by the year 2010, have an average income equivalent to that of Spain. This compares with only 100m today.

On the other hand, OECD countries increasingly look on developing countries as competitors. Low labour costs and rising productivity are making their manufactured products highly competitive in northern markets, helping to keep consumer prices down but evoking strong and growing resistance from those in the industrialised countries who see their investments and jobs at risk.

There is a chorus of powerful voices, including that of the British financier and European Parliamentarian, Sir James Goldsmith, predicting that freer trade with developing countries will lead to a massive movement of industry to the third world and large-scale unemployment in OECD countries as well as in developing countries. Similar concerns are beginning to surface in Japan.

While the borders have been opening to trade in goods and services and flows of capital, the movement has been in the opposite direction in respect of the flows of people. No sooner had the Berlin Wall come down, symbolising the removal of the boundaries that had separated East and West in Europe, than new walls were being erected against those who are uprooted, dispossessed and persecuted. This comes at a time when political turbulence, conflict and economic hardship in the developing world, as well as in parts of Eastern Europe and the former Soviet Union, are creating increased pressures for emigration. In a very real sense, these barriers are creating a new Iron Curtain separating rich and poor. For the same countries that are tightening their borders against the poor and dispossessed welcome and even woo those with capital and marketable skills. Thus far we have only seen the tip of the iceberg of human trafficking on a global basis.

Environment South

The new South continues to be home to most of the world's poverty and much of its conflict, at the same time as it is generating the lion's share of economic growth. But the developing world has never been homogeneous and the new South is much less so. The rapid changes occurring there are deepening the processes of differentiation, particularly between those who are growing and who continue in the grip of economic stagnation and poverty. These changes have immense implications for all of us. In environmental terms alone, they could be decisive for the human future.

Whether or not developing countries follow the same growth path as that taken by the more mature industrialised countries, their impacts will undoubtedly move us beyond the thresholds of safety and sustainability. Our environmental future will be largely determined by what happens in the developing world. Yet we who have created most of these risks, and have benefitted most from the processes of industrialisation that have given rise to them, can scarcely deny the right of developing countries to grow. Nor would it be fair or practical to seek to impose unilaterally constraints on their growth in the name of environment.

Some of the most environmentally devastated areas of the world are in the former Soviet Union and Eastern Europe. We have a compelling interest in helping to ensure that they rebuild their economies on an environmentally sound and sustainable basis.

The new South is contributing more and more to the larger global risks, such as climate change, ozone depletion, degradation of biological resources, and loss or deterioration of arable lands. China has already become the second largest source of CO_2 emissions, and will almost certainly succeed the United States to the dubious honour of becoming number one. Meanwhile, in our countries, as these issues have somewhat receded from our own immediate experience, it has become more difficult to maintain the levels of public interest and commitment required to deal with them. This year's hot summer in Europe and America, whatever its real causes, brought the issue close to home for many. But we cannot wish for the heat and climatic turbulence to continue just to make the point. It is sobering to remind ourselves that all of the environmental deterioration and risks that have arisen to date have occurred at levels of population and economic activity that are much less than they will be in the period ahead.

A series of paradoxes is developing which will soon confront both industrialised and developing countries with some very painful tensions and challenges. While efficient and competitive economies produce more gnp, the benefits accrue disproportionately to the minority which has capital and knowledge. This class is highly mobile and those in it can move their assets and activities across national borders.

Meanwhile, the continued existence of extreme poverty, with its attendant deprivation and suffering, affecting some 1.3bn of the world's people, is an affront to the moral basis of our civilisation – all the more so because the means to eradicate it clearly exists. What is needed is the assertion of a new political and moral will which would, in turn, produce the social and economic innovation required to devise the means to deal effectively with it. The gaps between rich and poor, privileged and underprivileged, are deepening, both within and amongst societies. This process, if it is not reversed, will inevitably lead to greater social tensions and potential for conflict.

In the early stages of a major new cycle of economic growth, these pressures may be relieved as some of the benefits trickle down to the poorest sectors of society. This happened in the United States between 1929 and 1969, and there is evidence that it is now occurring to some extent in countries like India. But the fact that modern, competitive, industrial societies require proportionately less labour and more capital will ultimately widen, and entrench, the rich–poor gap, as the current experience of the United States and Britain demonstrates.

Democratic market capitalism must find ways of dealing with these emerging dilemmas or risk becoming the victim of its own success. It must become just as effective at meeting society's environmental needs as it is in generating economic growth. A recent article in *The Economist* – hardly a radical publication – stated that 'if the Marxist prediction of a proletariat plunged into abject misery under capitalism has so far been unfulfilled, the widening gap between haves and have-nots is causing some to think that Marx might yet be proved right on this point after all'.

The globalisation of capitalism

The globalisation of capitalism is producing a new and universalising culture symbolised by CNN, brand-name consumer products like Coca-Cola, McDonald's and Levis, pop music, shopping malls, international airports, hotel chains and conferences. For the privileged minority who participate fully in this culture, it provides an exciting and expanding range of new opportunities and experiences. But for the majority, particularly in the non-Western world who live on its margins, and feed on its crumbs, it is often seen as alien and intimidating. Caught up in the dynamics of modernisation of which they are more victims than beneficiaries, it is no wonder that many react with anxiety and rejection, seeking refuge and identity in their own traditional values and cultures. The clash between modernism and fundamentalism has deeply rooted secular as well as religious dimensions and is producing a new generation of conflict and turbulence.

The Canadian ecologist, Professor Thomas Homer-Dixon, cites the growing potential for eco-conflicts, as a result of competition for land and other resources that become locally scarce, and competition for shared resources like river systems and common areas like the oceans. The recent confrontation between Canada and the European Union over depleting fish stocks is a portent of this.

Meanwhile, medical scientists warn of the growing risks from the emergence of new forms of disease, and the resurgence of new strains of traditional communicable diseases, like tuberculosis and malaria. While these problems will arise primarily in developing countries, there is no way in which we can be isolated from them or their consequences.

Changing course?

What, then, is the answer to this bewildering complex of forces that are shaping our future? The Earth Summit held in Rio de Janeiro in 1992, and the subsequent conferences on Human Rights in Vienna, Population in Cairo, the Social Summit in Copenhagen, and now the Women's Conference in Beijing have pointed up the need for more concerted, cooperative and integrated action by the world community to deal with these issues. The Earth Summit produced two landmark conventions, on Climate Change and on Biological Diversity, and initiated the Convention on Desertification, which has now been agreed in addition to the Declaration of Rio, and a programme of action to give effect to it: Agenda 21.

With all their shortcomings, the Rio Agreements represent the most extensive and comprehensive programme of action for the future of our planet ever agreed by governments. And the fact that they were agreed – word by word – by virtually all of the nations of the world, most of them represented at the highest levels, provide them with a unique degree of political authority. But, as I made clear in my final statement at Rio, this does not guarantee that these agreements will be implemented.

Three years after the Earth Summit, it is still too early to pronounce final judgment as to its results. Despite progress in a number of areas, it has to be said that there is all too little evidence of the fundamental change of course it called for. Although the first meeting of the parties to the Climate Change Convention in Berlin, earlier this year, did manage to patch together an agreement that will keep the process of implementation and further negotiation alive, it highlighted the continuing differences that exist, particularly between industrialised and developing countries, and the degree to which political will has receded since Rio.

Even the progress that has been made in dealing with many of the most visible and acute environmental problems of the United States and other industrialised countries is fostering a growing sense of apathy and complacency. The environmental journalist, Gregg Easterbrook, in his recent book *A Moment on the Earth* strikes a responsive cord in many when he says that environmentalists have been too pessimistic. But he also concedes that the progress that has been made in the industrialised countries has come about largely as a result of government regulations and incentives and confirms the importance of these rather than supporting the arguments for their rescision or relaxation.

A new generation of enlightened leaders in both business and government is realising that sound economic policies and practices must integrate environmental and social considerations. This was the basic message of the book *Changing Course* by the leading Swiss industrialist, Stephan Schmidheiny, and some 60 other Chief Executive Officers of major corporations, in their report to the Earth Summit. It called for fundamental changes in economic practices and behaviour based on a commitment to 'eco-efficiency' – efficiency in the use of energy and resources and in the prevention, disposal and recycling of wastes. Eco-efficiency is good for business as well as for the environment.

The old maxim that 'knowledge is power' is now being accompanied by the realisation that 'knowledge is money', and therefore a primary economic resource. The growing drive to convert knowledge into proprietary intellectual property could tend to reduce the total stock of knowledge, and restrict access to the products of research and development for those who do not have the means to purchase it. This could especially disadvantage those, particularly in developing countries, whose needs are greatest. Yet it is in our common interest to ensure that they have access to the best state-of-the-art technologies and techniques so that in the course of their own development they do not add unnecessarily to the pressures on the earth's environment and resources.

We must leave 'space' for developing countries to grow, and set them an example that enables them to avoid the abuses and the costs of our own growth experience. For they will be much more influenced by our example, and by evidence that sustainable development is in their own interest, than by our exhortations. It is clearly in our own interest to ensure that the new South has both the incentives and the means to make the transition to sustainability. This means facilitating their access to the latest technologies and to the additional capital they will need to employ them. It would be unrealistic to expect that this would come through increases in foreign aid in traditional terms. But governments everywhere continue to spend hundreds of billions of dollars on direct and indirect subsidies for activities which run counter to sustainable development – as, for example, to chemically-intensive agriculture and to fossil fuels. These impose costly burdens on people as taxpayers and consumers, as well as encouraging environmentally unsound and unsustainable practices. A reorientation and redeployment of these resources would provide all the resources required to effect the transition to sustainable development, at home and abroad, while improving economic efficiency.

Developing countries would also attract major new funds for investment in sustainable development if industrialised countries were willing to accord to the indispensable services they provide to the world community (for example, as custodians of most of its precious and irreplaceable biological resources and life-supporting ecosystems) the real value of these services, and reflect this in the terms of trade and the prices they pay for the relevant products of the developing countries. This will require radical changes in the current policies and priorities of governments and a substantial revamping of the system of incentives and penalties by which governments motivate the economic behaviour of individuals and corporations.

Energy for growth

Energy is at the centre of the environment development nexus. Already consumption of commercial energy by the developing countries of Asia is growing at a faster rate than in OECD countries. The 1993 report of the World Energy Council's task force on 'Energy for Tomorrow's World' estimated that by 2020 developing countries will need some $30 trillion of new investment in energy facilities if they are to meet their growing needs on the basis of current patterns of use and efficiency. This is nearly 50 per cent greater than the entire world gnp – clearly an impossible prospect.

A massive commitment to energy efficiency is the only answer. It is as essential in economics as in environmental terms – the most cost-effective and sensible investment in the energy future of developing as well as more developed countries. My own company, Ontario Hydro, is carrying out a massive programme of energy efficiency and recently joined other electric utilities and policy institutes to form a Global Energy Efficiency Collaborative to foster the movement towards energy efficiency throughout the world.

Foreign aid is in decline and private investment now accounts for the principal flows of financial resources to the rapidly developing countries. Accordingly, we must develop the incentives and innovative financial mechanisms to ensure that private capital will support development that is sustainable. Such new financial mechanisms as tradeable emission permits can utilise markets to channel funds available for environmental improvement to the places where they can be employed on the most cost-effective basis. Only by the 'greening' of private capital can we make the transition to sustainability provided for in Rio's Agenda 21.

Agents for change

A wide variety of new non-governmental actors is emerging which are becoming primary agents of change. In a thoughtful article in the summer 1994 issue of *Foreign Affairs*, Lester M. Salmon compared the growth in the numbers and influence of voluntary, non-governmental organisations in the last half of this century with the emergence of the nation-state system in the eighteenth century.

In the field of environment and sustainable development, the most exciting and promising post-Rio developments are occurring outside of governments, where there has been a virtual explosion of activities and initiatives on the part of grassroots organisations, citizen groups and other key sectors of society, including the private sector. One of the most promising vehicles for this is the establishment of National Councils for Sustainable Development in almost 100 countries, bringing together representatives of governments with those of civil society to develop their own national and local 'Agendas 21'. I am pleased to note that the British government has established its own National Council for Sustainable Development (NCSD), under the Chairmanship of Sir Crispin Tickel, one of Britain's most consistently enlightened and effective environmental leaders.

The Earth Council, headquartered in San José, Costa Rica, is a unique product of the Earth Summit. It is a new kind of global, non-governmental organisation, designed to act as a catalyst to facilitate and support implementation and follow-up of the results of Rio. In doing so, it consults a network of some 20,000 organisations, most of them of a grassroots nature, and also including a broad cross-section of development, environmental, social and public policy leaders and experts throughout the world. Its principal mission is to help to support and empower people and provide them with information and tools with which to develop

Agendas 21 and to help to link people at the community and grassroots level with the broad policy- and decision-making processes which affect them, and to amplify their voices in these processes – voices that are too seldom heard or heeded.

Not all non-governmental actors are, of course, of the benevolent kind. Organised crime built on the profits of drug trafficking and other illicit activities has been growing to an alarming degree, increasingly pre-empting the attention of government.

Developing countries which once saw pollution as a problem of the rich are now experiencing these problems in even more acute form than we did. The cities of the developing world are growing at rates beyond anything experienced in the industrialised countries – outstripping their capacity to provide even the most basic housing, infrastructure, health, education and social services to their exploding populations. Cities like Cairo, Manila, Bangkok, Calcutta and Mexico City are amongst the most polluted on earth. Many are faced with the prospect of environmental and social breakdown which would make them festering cauldrons of conflict, suffering and disease. The United Nations Conference on Habitat, the last in the series of great UN conferences of this decade, to be held next June in Istanbul, Turkey, will focus world attention on these issues.

The need for a cooperative alliance with the new South and the nations of the former Eastern bloc is particularly compelling when it comes to management of the 'commons' beyond the jurisdiction of individual nations – the oceans and Antarctica, comprising some two-thirds of the area of the earth, the atmosphere and outer space. Perhaps the most important 'commons' of all is the global system of interacting cause-and-effect relationships on which the survival and well-being of all life on earth ultimately depends. The care and management of this system requires a degree of cooperative stewardship beyond anything we have yet realised. The multilateral institutions, particularly those established since the Second World War, provide the institutional framework for the system of governance required to exercise such stewardship. But they are the newest, least developed, least appreciated and least supported of all the levels in our hierarchy of governance.

At the global level, the United Nations and its specialised agencies and organisations, including the World Bank and the International Monetary Fund, constitute the principal elements of this international system. On the occasion of the fiftieth anniversary of their establishment following the Second World War, there has been a plethora of studies and proposals for reforming and strengthening them. Particularly noteworthy among these is the report 'Our Global Neighbourhood', by the Commission on Global Governance headed by the Swedish Prime Minister, Ingvar Carlsson, and the former Commonwealth Secretary-General, Sir Shridath Ramphal. This study and others have produced some valuable ideas for fundamental changes in the United Nations and the Bretton Woods Organisations.

But the reality is that, if we went back to the drawing-board to renegotiate the terms of the United Nations Charter and the agreements establishing the constitutions of the other agencies and organisations of the system, it is unlikely under current conditions that agreement could be achieved on the kind of fundamental changes in their structures and mandates that these

studies call for. The shortage is not of ideas, but of will. I believe at this point the most important priority is to improve the management and performance of these institutions, which would go a long way towards restoring confidence in them and building the political will required for fundamental change.

A decisive century

I am convinced that the twenty-first century will be decisive for the human species. For all the evidences of environmental degradation, social tension and inter-communal conflict have occurred at levels of population and human activity that are a great deal less than they will be in the next century. Theoretically, one can make a case that these problems will be manageable. But in practice, it will require that we extend to the global level the kind of social discipline and cooperative management that some of the more successful modern societies, including Canada, have developed. Prospects for this are not promising. Some of the poorer and least developed nation-states of Africa, particularly those which had artificial boundaries imposed upon them, are already proving to be virtually ungovernable. And the political and institutional structure of even the most rapidly growing developing countries is often fragile and vulnerable.

The risks we face in common from the mounting dangers to the environment, resource base and life-support systems on which all life on earth depends, are far greater as we move into the twenty-first century than the risks we face or have faced in our conflicts with each other. All people and nations have in the past been willing to accord highest priority to the measures required for their own security. We must give the same kind of priority to environmental security. This will take a major shift in the current political mind-set. Necessity will compel such a shift eventually; the question is: can we really afford the costs and risks of waiting?

A global alliance for environmental security would not require world government or the homogenisation of cultures and behaviour. Rather, it would require agreement on the fundamental boundary conditions which all nations and people must respect to ensure that our collective behaviour does not transgress the thresholds of safety required to ensure our common survival and well-being. It would require a major strengthening of the programmes through which the scientific community seeks to identify and probe such thresholds, understand and monitor the human activities that impinge on them, give early warning of pending risks and opportunities, and evaluate the evidence resulting from the continuing process of change which affects these boundary conditions. The foundations for such a system already exist in such organisations as the Global Environmental Monitoring System (GEMS) of the United Nations Environment Programme, the various research programmes sponsored by the International Council of Scientific Unions (ICSCU), and those set up under treaties, such as the Intergovernmental Panel on Climate Change (IPCC).

In the final analysis, the behaviour of people as well as the priorities of society respond to the deepest moral, ethical and spiritual values of people. I am convinced that the radical changes now occurring in our society are producing a historic convergence between our traditional perceptions of relationships, between the practical aspects of human life and its moral and spiritual dimensions. It has too often been assumed in the past that there is an essential dichotomy between the 'real world' of practical affairs and the more ethereal, ideal world of morals and spirit.

Concepts of mutual respect, caring for, sharing with and cooperating with our brothers and sisters both at home and internationally can no longer be seen as mere pious ideals divorced from reality, but as indispensable prerequisites for our common survival and well-being. The profound changes taking place in the new South, I submit, provide both new imperatives and new opportunities to forge a new set of cooperative global relationships which move beyond outmoded, traditional notions of North and South. They must take into account the shift in economic growth and political weight towards the new South as well as the continuing entrenchment of dire and debilitating poverty. Both extremes, and the growing dichotomy between them, pose major risks to the security and sustainability of the human community which must move to the centre of our agenda for the twenty-first century.

The primary task of this new global alliance will be to produce a comprehensive security regime which will ensure at least certain basic minimum standards of security for nations and peoples as well as the integrity of the environment, natural resources and life-support systems of the planet as a whole. This may seem somewhat idealistic, even unrealistic, given today's conditions. But we cannot – must not – settle for less, if we are to avoid the risks and realise the opportunities that confront us in the new millennium.

Political Economy and the Developing World

Economic issues are among the most pressing concerns that face the developing world. Progress on the variety of problems that developing countries confront requires economic growth and stabilization. A combination of internal and external factors complicates the quest for these goals.

The position of the developing world in the international trading system contributes to the difficulty of achieving consistent economic growth. From the incorporation of these countries into the international economic system during colonialism to the present, their role has been primarily as suppliers of raw materials and agricultural products. Dependence on commodity exports has meant that developing countries have had to deal with fluctuating, and frequently declining, prices for their exports. At the same time, prices for imports have remained constant or have increased. At best, this has made development planning difficult; at worst, it has led to economic stagnation and decline.

Most developing nations have had limited success in breaking out of this dilemma by diversifying their economies. Efforts at industrialization and export of light manufactures have led to competition with less efficient industries in the industrialized world. The response of industrialized countries has often been protectionism and demands for trade reciprocity, which can overwhelm markets in developing countries. Efforts to avoid the consequences of protectionism and increase international trade will be a primary focus of the newly created World Trade Organization (WTO). Preliminary indications are that some of the same differences between the developing countries and the industrialized world that existed under the General Agreement on Tariffs and Trade (GATT) will persist in the WTO. Some critics continue to charge that international trade favors the industrialized countries, while others contend that the developing world benefits as well.

The economic situation in the developing world is not entirely attributable to colonial legacy and protectionism on the part of industrialized countries. Trade and industrialization schemes involving heavy government direction were often ill-conceived or resulted in corruption and mismanagement. Industrialized countries frequently point to these inefficiencies in calling for market-oriented reforms. But market solutions can only be effective in conjunction with reductions in trade barriers, which allow the developing world greater export opportunities.

In the past, developing countries received substantial amounts of foreign aid. This effort was a disappointment for both donors and recipients. The need for development aid exceeds the ability or willingness of donors to provide it and aid levels have been declining. Critics from developing countries complain not only about the amount of aid available, but also about tying aid to political objectives and equity in distribution. Donors are dismayed at the lack of development progress, corruption and mismanagement, and a thankless attitude on the part of some recipients. Donor fatigue has been exacerbated by domestic problems within industrialized countries that make aid even less politically popular. Clearly, foreign aid is less than satisfying or productive from the standpoint of both donors and recipients.

Foreign direct investment in some developing countries has been increasing. The bulk of this investment, however, goes to those countries that are already growing. The poorest countries are less attractive to investors. Consequently, they are falling further behind.

The debt crisis has further compounded economic problems in the developing world. During the 1970s, developing country economic performance and the availability of petro-dollars encouraged extensive commercial lending. Developing countries sought these loans to fill the gap between revenues from export earnings and foreign aid and expenditures for increasing development. The second oil price hike in the late 1970s, declining export earnings, and worldwide recession in the early 1980s left many developing countries unable to meet their debt obligations. By the mid-1980s, this debt crisis threatened commercial banks that had extended loans to developing countries. The debt plans formulated by U.S. Treasury secretaries James Baker and Nicholas Brady advocated debt rescheduling and continued lending in return for growth-oriented economic reforms. Access to World Bank and International Monetary Fund financing became conditional on the adoption of structural adjustment programs that involved steps such as reduced public expenditures, devaluation of currencies, and export promotion, all geared to debt reduction. The consequences of these programs have been painful for developing countries. Fewer public services, higher prices, and greater exploitation of resources have resulted from these programs, causing some countries to abandon the plans, jeopardizing their creditworthiness and continued access to additional funds. The commercial banks have weathered the crisis, with some

actually profiting. Some middle-income developing countries have made progress in getting their economies back on track. The poorest countries, however, continue to struggle with their debt burdens. Debt servicing requirements in a number of these countries have resulted in debt repayments exceeding new foreign aid and investment. In other words, poor countries are paying Western donors more than they are receiving in new aid.

Despite the generally bleak economic picture in much of the developing world, there have been some success stories. The success of the newly industrializing countries in East Asia and the emerging markets of countries such as China, Argentina, Thailand, and Brazil have led analysts to question why these countries have prospered while others have lagged behind. Reasons advanced for this discrepancy include lack of resources, poor economic management, the colonial legacy, and corruption. Whatever the reasons, the discrepancies further underscore the diversity of the developing world as well as its continuing economic differentiation.

Looking Ahead: Challenge Questions

Why are some observers skeptical of the World Bank's assertion that the gap between rich and poor nations is narrowing? What do they contend is actually happening?

What steps contribute to economic growth in developing countries?

Why might economic growth be a mixed blessing?

What was the origin of the debt crisis? How has this crisis affected developing countries?

What are structural adjustment programs? How do social policies under structural adjustment differ from a traditional Keynesian approach?

What are the differing views regarding the effectiveness of the World Bank's structural adjustment programs?

What are the arguments against reducing the debts of the most seriously affected countries?

Where does the bulk of foreign direct investment go?

How does the Grameen Bank differ from other commercial lenders?

Whither the North–South Gap?

Robin Broad & Christina Melhorn Landi

Robin Broad is at the School of International Service, The American University, 4400 Massachusetts Avenue, NW Washington, DC, 20016-8071, USA

> ... the economies of the developing world ... are, in aggregate, growing faster than those of the major industrial countries. World Bank, *Global Economic Prospects and the Developing Countries,* 1994, p. 5.

During much of the Cold War, the central dilemma of development economics was how to reverse the growing economic gap between the rich and poor countries of the world. In recent years, the World Bank has declared a victory on that front. The Bank asserts that not only is the gap no longer growing, but indeed that it has begun to narrow. Moreover, the Bank claims, the free market policies it has spearheaded are at the core of the developing country turnabout that is closing the North–South gap.

This article challenges the World Bank assertion of a narrowing North–South gap. Rather, we argue, economic data from the World Bank and other United Nations agencies suggest that the North–South gap continues to widen in all but roughly a dozen Third World countries, and there remains a net flow of resources from most Southern nations to the North.

The Bank bases it claim of a closing gap on two primary assertions: that the economies of the developing countries are growing faster than industrial countries' economies, and that large net capital flows are now flowing into developing countries.

Based on an examination of World Bank and United Nations data, this article refutes both of these assertions. We first compare the growth rates of Northern versus Southern countries. Then we survey the nature and levels of the financial flows between North and South.

As we discover, a major problem with the Bank's gap closing projections is that they are based on aggregate data and often on the strength of only one to three years of data from the early 1990s. Disaggregating the data paints a vastly different picture of the dynamics and consequences of these economic flows and trends for the majority of developing countries. A closer and longer look at North–South data reveals that, while the gap may be closing between a few developing countries—particularly the 10 'big emerging markets' (BEMs) pinpointed by the US Department of Commerce[1]—and the industrial countries, the vast majority of Third World countries are slipping further behind the North.

We focus on the World Bank not only because it is the major donor to the Third World. In recent years, its influence has outstripped its lending and it has become the preeminent source of policy advice and development research and writings. Its annual texts—*The World Development Report, The World Debt Tables, Global Economic Prospects* and others—and its numerous publications in effect define the conventional paradigm of development. They are read in college courses, quoted by the media, and relied upon by policy makers. But they are far too seldom subject to careful review. And the fact that we can reach opposite conclusions based partially on the Bank's own data lends support to those who argue that World Bank development advice is based too much on inflexible ideological positions rather than rigorous analysis.[2]

To be fair, many who criticize the World Bank's analysis of the state of the Third World base their own predictions of a widening North–South gap on the reality of the 1980s' 'lost decade'. But this simplistic 'one-gap' analysis too is lacking, as the current article will show.

The gap

The World Bank's assertion that Southern countries are growing faster than Northern ones can be dissected in a number of ways. First, one must consider the time frame in which such an analysis is made. Whether one finds that the aggregate gap between North and South is growing, remaining constant or shrinking is determined, in part, by what time period one chooses to examine. Consider the period 1960–1990; in 1960 developing countries' gross domestic product (GDP) per capita was 18% of the industrial nations; in 1990, at 17%, the gap was almost unchanged.[3] On the other hand, during the disastrous decade of the 1980s (1980–91), gross national product (GNP) per capita increased only by an average of 1% in the South (and in sub-Saharan Africa, it declined by 1.2%), while it increased 2.3% in the North—suggesting a widening gap.[4]

Recent higher aggregate growth rates for the South in the 1990s—highlighted by the Bank in, for example, its *World Atlas 1995* and its *Global Economic Prospects 1994*—may help ameliorate some of the damage these countries suffered in the 1980s, but they do not reverse it. In sub-Saharan Africa, for example, as the Bank's 1994 *Global Economic Prospects* points out: 'Although growth . . . is expected to accelerate, per capita incomes until the year 2000 will be well below the level reached in 1980.'[5]

Thus, key to assessing the relative positions of rich and poor countries is not only the time period but also the phrase 'in aggregate'. The engine of economic growth of the developing countries taken as a whole is not evenly distributed among the roughly 150 countries that now make up the South. (This 150 ballpark number includes the countries of the former Second World.) More precisely, it is only a small number of leading Southern countries that are driving such economic performance: the BEMs of East Asia (especially China) and Latin America. Even the World Bank points out that 'about one half of the acceleration of developing-country growth since 1990 is due to East Asia, primarily China, where growth has averaged about 10% a year in the past four years' (although it conveniently ignores this crucial caveat in its conclusions.)[6]

If the data behind the highly touted economic trends of the early 1990s are disaggregated between the BEMs and the rest of the South, then the gap is indeed closing between the BEM developing countries and the industrial countries. As former US Commerce official Jeffrey Garten noted in a speech outlining a US policy towards the BEMs, 'of all the world trade growth in the next two decades, almost three-fourths is expected to come from the LDCs. But a small core of those LDCs, the biggest of them, just ten countries, is likely to account for more than half of that growth.'[7] The bottom line is that about a dozen countries have been doing well for the past few years, while the vast majority of the South is either slipping backwards, stagnating, or growing slower than the North.

Once these big emerging markets are excluded from the picture, the scenario for closing the gap via economic growth appears more troublesome for the majority of countries in the South. Consider the World Bank's projections for growth in Latin America and Africa. (Note, however, that a decade ago, one of us examined the World Bank's projections for economic and trade growth and found them egregiously over-inflated.[8]) In the World Bank's 1994 *Global Economic Prospects,* Africa is projected to grow annually at 3.9% (with a low projection of 0.8 percent).[9] Let us give the World Bank the benefit of the doubt and assume that Africa does reach the higher projected growth rate of 3.9% a year. Compare this, however, to University of Sussex professor Hans Singer's calculation that sub-Saharan Africa would actually have to grow by 8.8% a year for 'very much more than a decade'—or more than twice the rate of the World Bank's high end projection—to return its average income levels to where they would have been had its growth rates from 1965–1980 continued to the present. Latin America and the Caribbean, Singer calculates, would need to grow annually by 10.5% in order to return to their 1965–1980 trajectory. As Singer concludes: 'In other words, the task is impossible (except perhaps for the upper-middle-income countries).'[10]

Net private financial flows

During the 'lost decade' of the 1980s, not only did the South grow more slowly than the North, but a dangerous trend emerged of a net financial flow of resources from South to North as debtor nations were pressed to service growing debts. From 1985 to 1992, the net negative flow from South to North on debt service alone totaled $280 billion.[11] This net negative transfer became a focal point for those arguing that the North–South gap was widening precipitously in the 1980s' 'debt crisis', creating a polarized world of Northern winners and Southern losers. The World Bank now asserts, however, that this negative flow has stopped and, indeed, has started to be reversed. The reason: an explosion of new private capital flows into the South. The World Bank points to record new levels of foreign investment and bond and portfolio investment flowing into developing countries since the early 1990s. Indeed, these flows are the basis for many of its projections about higher economic growth in the South.

While commercial banks, the centerpiece of the debt surge of the 1970s and 1980s, have largely lost interest in the South, a variety of other sources of private capital has emerged. Between 1991 and 1993, the movement of portfolio equity flows into the South surged from $7.6 billion to $46.9 billion as a number of debtor countries followed Bank advice (often in order to satisfy loan conditionality) and opened their stock markets to foreign investors.[12] Over this same period, foreign direct investment flows into the South rose from $36.8 billion to $66.6 billion; private sector bond flows jumped from $5.3 billion to $27.6 billion.[13]

We now turn to an analysis of these short-term capital flows, followed by an assessment of the status of the debt crisis. In a subsequent section, we examine other sources of continued South-to-North drain, namely the declining terms of trade suffered by the South, as well as human and natural resource flows. Finally, we assess the sustainability of the factors that fuel the World Bank's optimism about the North–South gap.

With the new short-term private capital flows, the devil is once again in the details of disaggregation. First, as we saw in looking at economic growth rates, here too Africa is a distressing exception to the Bank's rosy financial flows scenario. Africa barely figures in these flows; the continent is simply not on the radar screen of most financial institutions and investors at the core of the new flows. While the World Bank in its 1994–95 *World Debt Tables* estimates that 'aggregate private to private flows . . . accounted for about 70% of the net long term flows to developing countries in 1993, up from 45% in 1990,[14] that same publication buries in a footnote the fact that 'in 1993 about 90% of [these] net flows to the low-income countries *excluding China and India* . . . came from *official* sources'.[15] Thus, the large majority of poor countries remain outside these new types of capital flows and any projected economic growth they might bring.

Let us further disaggregate these figures by looking at the major forms of new capital flows one at a time.

2. POLITICAL ECONOMY AND THE DEVELOPING WORLD

Foreign direct investment (FDI) is considered a valued source of capital by the World Bank and others because, unlike debt, it adds no recurring interest based on variable international rates. In addition, FDI is seen as a stamp of approval by global corporations in an international arena of competition and change; one firm's interest often piques others'. The World Bank also supports FDI as a source of capital because it is considered the least volatile and 'should allow for the transfer of technology in production and management practices'.[16] And FDI does have a growing, significant role in North–South flows: in the 1990s, over 40% of private capital flows to the South have been in the form of FDI.[17] In addition, the percentage of global FDI that went to developing countries reached 37% of the world total in 1993, up from 29% in 1992.[18]

However, once again, disaggregation reveals that these unprecedented FDI flows did not spread equally into all developing countries. During 1989–92, 72% of private capital flows went to only 10 countries: China, Mexico, Malaysia, Argentina, Thailand, Indonesia, Brazil, Nigeria, Venezuela and South Korea.[19] (Note that, of these, six are on the US Commerce Department's BEM list.) On the other hand, the approximately four-dozen least developed countries (a majority of which are in sub-Saharan Africa) received only 2%.[20] In addition, global FDI is highly concentrated by region. Sub-Saharan Africa received just 6% of the FDI that flowed to the South in the late 1980s. In 1993, East Asia and the Pacific received 55% of all FDI flowing to the South, Latin America and the Caribbean received 24%, and Europe and Central Asia obtained 14%, while the Middle East and North Africa received 3%, Sub-Saharan Africa received 3% and South Asia just 1%.[21] China, by far the largest recipient of these flows,[22] completely skews the FDI tables: the annual average growth rate of FDI flows to the World Bank's low income Southern countries (defined by the World Bank as countries with a 1993 GNP per capita less than or equal to $695) in 1990–1993 was a staggering 70%. But once China is removed, the average was 6%.[23]

There is one other component of foreign direct investment that affects the North–South gap to the South's detriment. According to the World Bank, around half of the new foreign direct investment into the South in 1992 left those countries as profits.[24] Still more dollars leave the South as royalty and licensing payments, a stream of cash that will probably increase with the new trade-related intellectuals property rights (TRIPS) rules of the Uruguay Round of GATT.

Other forms of capital flows to the developing countries that have burgeoned in the last few years are portfolio equity and bond issuance. Once again, however, these are highly skewed in terms of who received the flows. Specifically, Latin America and East Asia—the main regions in which the BEMs are located—'together accounted for more than 90 percent of the gross portfolio equity flows to developing countries between 1989 and 1993'.[25] To be more precise, only 10 countries issued nearly 90% of all developing country bonds in 1993:[26] Mexico, Brazil, Argentina, Hungary, South Korea, Greece, Turkey, China, Venezuela and Thailand (listed in descending order of the dollar value of bonds issued).[27] (Note again how the disaggregated lists of 'winners' overlap; six of these are on

the Commerce Department's BEM list.) Of these, the top five accounted for 58% of all bonds issued that year by developing countries.[28]

In addition, in recent years, foreign purchases of bonds have grown to encompass a significant proportion of these emerging bond markets. In Mexico, for example, foreigners held more than $23 billion in Mexican government securities (a third of the market) as of May 1994, up from $1.8 billion in 1990—roughly a 1200% increase.[29]

The extreme concentration of portfolio flows is only one element of the highly problematic nature of these flows. Since a major source of the stock market booms in several Southern nations has been the privatisation of state enterprises[30] (a practice promoted by the World Bank), this source has a finite life given that there is a fixed amount of capital for divestment. In other words, at least some of this privatisation represents a one-time, non-replicable increase in portfolio flows.

Overall, these new private capital sources reinforce the conclusion we reached on GNP growth figures: perhaps a dozen countries are the prime beneficiaries and are not currently suffering a South-to-North resource drain; the rest of the Southern countries have not benefitted to any significant extent.

The debt crisis

For the majority of Southern nations left out of the new private flows, do debt obligations still translate into a net negative drain? The evidence suggests that they do.

While the World Bank has proclaimed the 'twilight of the commercial debt crisis',[31] a look at the debt situation in developing countries reveals the existence of still burdensome debt stocks. There are three main dimensions to the current debt situation: the debt burden (as measured by the ration of debt servicing to export earnings and of debt to GNP), international interest rates and the changed nature of new debt.

First, a look at the overall debt burden. Let us begin with the relatively good news. Debt-to-GNP and debt-to-export ratios did peak for almost all countries in the late 1980s and are decreasing—except for Africa, where debt as a percentage of GNP is growing, reaching 75.5% of GNP in 1990. However, even those decreasing amounts remain taxing. According to the United Nations Conference on Trade and Development (UNCTAD), the ratio of debt to GNP peaked in 1987 for all developing countries at 42.4% of GNP. By 1990, it was still 32.3% of GNP for all developing countries; in Latin America it was 46%.[32]

The difference between the aggregate and regional figures is accounted for partially by East Asia, which has for the least few decades maintained a relatively low and stable debt burden because of high investment, increased productivity and GDP, and export growth. Thus, the region brings down the aggregate debt ratios for developing countries.

Also, as some of the above statistics reveal, while it is true that across time debt burdens are relatively lower compared to the onerous levels of the 1980s, this does not negate the still high absolute levels of debt obligations. The overall stock of

Third World debt continues to rise by around $100 billion a year and reached $1945 billion in 1994.[33] As the 1994 World Bank *World Debt Tables* noted, even assuming full application of the additional bilateral debt relief offered by the enhanced Toronto terms and Paris Club reschedulings of official development assistance, 29 of the 32 severely indebted low income countries would still have debt-to-export ratios exceeding 200%.[34] Commercial banks may no longer totter at the edge of collapse; the debt burden of developing countries, however, continues to exert a cost on their national plans and possibilities as well as on their citizens.

Second, let us look at interest rates. The World Bank emphasizes that international interest rates have stabilized at levels that are adequate for developing countries to service their debts: the Bank predicts that if international interest rates are sustained for five years at the Banks' forecasted low levels, this will add half a percentage point to the annual GNP growth of developing countries.[35] However, this 1994 assessment of stabilization failed to foresee events that were then already on the horizon: the 1994 fall of the dollar in international markets, the peso plummet and the bailout of Mexico by the USA. While an appreciation of the US dollar decreases dollar-denominated debt stocks (for example in 1991, by an estimated $24 billion), in 1990 the fall in the US dollar increased dollar-denominated debt stocks by $51.5 billion—a trend that continued with the dollar devaluations of 1993 and 1994.[36] Overall, the World Bank's rosy predictions of stabilization on this front deny the fragility of financial markets. With instantaneous market response and computerized investment and speculation, projecting stabilization over the medium to long term seems disingenuous. Debt is not a problem that is going away quickly or smoothly.

In addition, debt is changing in nature, and this portends some new potential problems and challenges for developing countries, as partially discussed above. A new form of debt is becoming prominent in overall debt stocks of developing countries: the insurance of bonds. In 1993, this accounted for 92% of net private debt flows.[37] On one hand, this may be a positive change to the extent that it represents diminished exposure to the vagaries of commercial banks. But, on the other hand, considering the withdrawal of investment from Mexico after the December 1994 peso plunge, switching the vagaries of the commercial banks for those of private investors may not be much of an improvement.

Overall, the ease with which a positive inflow can switch to a net outflow, and the high level of foreign ownership, raise crucial questions of vulnerability—questions that go unasked and unanswered in many of the Bank's hopeful projections about capital flows.

Terms of trade

There is another source of South-to-North financial leakage that seldom enters the Bank's calculations of the status of the North–South gap: the diminishing purchasing power of Southern commodities in international trade or the so-called declining 'terms of trade'.

Inasmuch as primary commodities continue to be central to the foreign exchange earnings of most non-BEM Southern nations, the prices derived from commodity exports remain the most important terms of trade indicator. In 1992, the overall real price of commodities, with 1985 as the base of 100, was only 71.[38] Different regions have been affected to differing degrees. In 1991, with 1987 as the base year of 100, sub-Saharan Africa's terms of trade was 85 and South Asia's terms of trade was 94.[39] These movements can translate into billions of dollars: the 3.5% decline in Africa's terms of trade from 1992–93, for example, meant that the purchasing power of the continent's exports fell by some $3 billion. And this was not an isolated 'bad' year for Africa: from 1991–92, its terms of trade had fallen by 3.4% and from 1990–91, by 7.9%.[40]

Expanding the focus from Africa, if one looks specifically at exporters of non-oil primary products, the terms of trade record remains dismal. From 1974–80, the terms of trade deteriorated by 5.7% a year; from 1981–86, terms of trade for these non-fuel primary product exporters declined by 3% a year; from 1987–93, the decrease was 1.8% a year.[41] Yet, in its 1994 *Global Economic Prospects,* the World Bank advocated primary commodities as a foundation for economic development—using studies of the USA and Australia to bolster such assertions.[42]

Non-financial flows

In addition to flows of investment and trade, there are two other flows of resources between North and South exercising a drain on the South in recent decades that merit mention, if only briefly: human resources and natural resources. These 'social and environmental' flows have only recently begun to be included in some quantitative assessments of resource flows between the North and South, and they add significantly to the conclusions of such analyses. Notable is the recent work by Keith Griffin and Terry McKinley for the United Nations Development Programme.[43]

In terms of human resource flows from South to North, Southern nations invest billions of dollars each year in the education of skilled workers who often leave the country for greener pastures in the North. The United Nations estimated that between 1961 and 1972, Northern nations received around $51 billion of 'human capital' through the migration of Southern professionals.[44] The movement has grown substantially since then. Today, for example, there are more Filipino doctors and nurses overseas than there are in the Philippines. Some 60,000 middle and high-level managers left the African continent between 1985 and 1990. From four Asian nations alone—the Philippines, India, China and South Korea—nearly 150,000 scientifically trained workers came to the United States between 1972 and 1985.[45]

One final component of the South-to-North resource flow that is difficult to measure, but that will be a crucial determinant of future development problems and possibilities, is the export of non-renewable Southern national resources to the North in the form of forest products, minerals and marine resources. At the economic core of most colonial relationships was the exploitation of silver, gold, timber, fish and other raw products for Northern use, and many of these patterns continue to the present.

Analysis by the World Resources Institute indicates that South-to-North natural resource flows are greatest in petroleum and minerals, but the South is also sending more resources to the North than vice versa in industrial raw materials such as cotton and rubber, and food and agricultural raw materials.[46] In addition, one of the least studied South-North flows occurs offshore and hence off camera: the fishing fleets of the North, having depleted fisheries off Newfoundland, New England, the North Sea and elsewhere, have increasingly moved into the rich fishing banks of the South.[47] While Southern governments receive foreign exchange for their exports of natural resources, the depletion of these resources hurts millions of small farmers and fisherfolk who face falling yields as a result of deforestation and over-fishing. The real wealth of Southern nations is being depleted in the process.

Sustainability

In the World Bank's 1994–95 *World Debt Tables,* it put forward the argument that the short-term flows that are the basis of so much of the Bank's optimism concerning the future of the South are 'sustainable', meaning that one could count on them to help fuel growth in years to come. Part of the Bank's argument around sustainability is that changes in the world economy that are beneficial to developing countries are 'structural rather than temporary'.[48] The Bank pinpoints 'factors underlying the much higher private capital flows [that] are unlikely to be reversed in the aggregate—the sea change in developing countries' policies that makes them more creditworthy and more attractive to international investors, the integration of global financial markets, and the fall in international interest rates from their highs in the 1980s . . .'[49] And, the Bank continues in its lengthy exposition of its sustainability thesis, 'the upward FDI trend is being driven by structural and secular (as opposed to cyclical) developments such as the global integration of production'.[50]

Our analysis of these flows suggests that the Bank's 'sustainability' conclusion is premature. Rather, we would agree with the United Nations' 1993 *World Economic Survey's* blunt warning: 'developing countries are hosting large stocks of volatile funds'.[51] One cannot help but question the Bank's definition of structural.

Much of our discussion thus far already suggests this point. Case in point is the volatility of the dollar which has a huge effect on debt stocks held by developing countries. The recent fluctuations in the dollar, where the dollar's value has been falling against the yen in international markets, do not augur well for stable and sustainable debt reduction in the near and medium term for developing countries.

Consider the case of Mexico, a model BEM. The collapse of the Mexican peso in December 1994 led to the flight of around $10 billion in short term US funds from that country in just the last week of 1994. Within days of the onset of the Mexican crisis, stock markets and currencies from Brazil and Argentina to Thailand and India plunged in value. These events reveal how increasingly deregulated international financial markets, with a growing array of financial instruments, are interconnected and volatile in ways that are only beginning to be apparent.[52]

Another basis for the World Bank's hypothesis of sustainability is its assertion that developing countries are becoming *less* dependent on the performance of industrial countries.[53] Hence, the Bank's argument goes, slower growth in industrial countries should not have much of a negative impact on the South. Yet, elsewhere, the Bank seems to contradict itself by arguing that 'if growth in industrial countries were much higher than expected, this would fuel inflationary expectations—pushing up interest rates and slowing growth in these countries. This, in turn, could hurt developing-country growth and erode developing-country creditworthiness—dampening private capital flows.'[54] In other words, an industrial country-developing country performance link still exists and the South remains vulnerable to growth trends in the North.

Conclusion

The World Bank has long argued that it has the solution to Southern problems. For some 15 years, it has implemented its solution through the vehicle of structural adjustment loans (SALs) in dozens of countries; it has been one of the leading—and most effective—advocates of privatisation, freer trade and increased emphasis on exports.[55] Its publications of recent years have declared success. Not only is the South growing, it argues, but the North–South gap is now narrowing.

Travelling through the data on the past, current and projected economic prospects of industrial and developing countries reveals a more complex and problematic situation than the World Bank suggests in its conclusions. It is not enough to simply look at aggregate growth rates of developing and industrial countries. Equally important are the disaggregated statistics which offer a strikingly different picture of the dynamics between North and South.

The representation of the South as a monolith was flawed back in the 1960s, but, in light of the discussion above, it is increasingly misleading today. Over the next generation, if current trends continue, some 10–12 Southern nations are likely to join the ranks of the North or at least move much closer to Northern levels of economic performance. The remaining 140-odd Southern nations, however, are likely to slip further behind. Yet, since the 10–12 rapidly growing Southern nations include some of the largest economies in the world, including those of China and India, aggregated figures of the South's performance will increasingly mask a complex pattern of a few winners and a much larger group of losing nations.

It is ironic that we reach the conclusions we do—conclusions very different from those of the Bank—in large part based upon closer examination of World Bank data. The World Bank provides many of the elements for uncovering the volatility, vulnerability and variability of the increasing complex South, but neglects to connect the dots that would illuminate the shifting landscape of rich and poor in the global economy.

Notes

1. Jeffrey Garten, then US UnderSecretary of Commerce for International Trade, in January 1994 identified the 10 BEMs as: China, Indonesia, India, South Korea, Mexico, Argentina, Brazil, South Africa, Poland and Turkey. Jeffrey Garten, 'The big emerging markets: changing American interests in the global economy', remarks before the Foreign Policy Association, New York, 20 January 1994, pp 2, 8.
2. See, for instance, Susan George & Fabrizio Sabelli, *Faith and Credit: The World Bank's Secular Empire,* London: Penguin, 1994; and Bruce Rich, *Mortgaging the Earth: The World Bank, Environmental Impoverishment, and the Crisis of Development,* Boston, MA: Beacon Books, 1994.
3. United Nations Development Programme, *Human Development Report 1994,* New York: Oxford University Press, 1994, p 143.
4. World Bank, *World Development Report 1993: Investing In Health,* New York: Oxford University Press, 1993, p 239.
5. World Bank, *Global Economic Prospects and the Developing Countries 1994,* Washington, DC: World Bank, 1994, p 5.
6. Ibid., p 9.
7. Garten, 'The big emerging markets', p 8.
8. Robin Broad & John Cavanagh, 'No more NICs', *Foreign Policy,* 72, Fall 1988, pp 93–94; and Robin Broad & John Cavanagh, 'Flawed World Bank report could cause wrong policies for Third World', *Third World Network Features,* 176, 1987, pp 1–5.
9. World Bank, *Global Economic Prospects 1994,* p 20, table 1.4.
10. H W Singer, 'Beyond the debt crisis', *Development: Journal of the Society for International Development,* 1, 1992, p 35.
11. Calculated from World Bank, *World Debt Tables 1992–93: External Finance for Developing Countries,* Vol 1: *Analysis and Summary Tables,* Washington, DC: World Bank, December 1992, p 160.
12. World Bank, *World Debt Tables, 1994–95: External Finance for Developing Countries,* Vol 1: *Analysis and Summary Tables,* Washington, DC: World Bank, 1994, p 11.
13. World Bank, *World Debt Tables 1994–95,* p 11.
14. Ibid, p 10.
15. Ibid, p 24, note 1 (emphasis added).
16. Ibid, p 16.
17. Ibid, p 18.
18. Ibid, pp 3–4.
19. UNDP, *Human Development Report 1994,* p 62, New York, Oxford University Press.
20. Ibid.
21. World Bank, *World Debt Tables 1994–95,* p 4, figure 2.
22. Ibid, p 3.
23. Ibid, p 160, table A 5.2. The definition of 'low income' is on p 186.
24. Some $19 billion of the $38.3 billion in new direct investment left the countries. World Bank, *World Debt Tables, 1992–93,* pp 16, 17.
25. World Bank, *World Debt Tables 1994–95,* p 14.
26. Ibid, p 12.
27. Ibid, p 12, table 1.3.
28. Calculated from World Bank, *World Debt Tables 1994–95,* p 12, table 1.3.
29. Ibid, p 13.
30. Ibid, p 15.
31. Ibid, p 4.
32. United Nations Conference on Trade and Development, *Handbook of International Trade and Development Statistics 1992,* New York: United Nations, 1993, p 420, table 5.14.
33. World Bank, *World Debt Tables, 1994–95,* p 25.
34. Ibid, p 43.
35. World Bank, *Global Economic Prospects 1994,* p 1.
36. World Bank, *World Debt Tables 1991–92: External Debt of Developing Countries,* Vol 1: *Analysis and Summary Tables,* Washington, DC: World Bank, 1991, p 13.
37. World Bank, *World Debt Tables 1994–95,* calculated from p 7, table 1.1.
38. United Nations, Department of Economic and Social Information and Policy Analysis, *World Economic Survey 1993: Current Trends and Policies in the World Economy,* New York: United Nations, 1993, p 227, table A.21.
39. UNDP, *Human Development Report 1994,* pp 168–169, table 20.
40. United Nations, Department of Economic and Social Information and Policy Analysis, *World Economic and Social Survey 1994: Current Trends and Policies in the World Economy,* New York: United Nations, 1994, p. 96 and p. 277, table A.20.
41. World Bank, *Global Economic Perspectives 1994,* p 15, figure 1.5.
42. Ibid, p 34. Note, however, that in its 1995 *Global Economic Prospects,* the Bank problematised such a plan, pointing out that ' . . . the long-term outlook for commodity prices remains unfavorable' (p 7).
43. See, for example, Keith Griffin & Terry McKinley, 'A new framework for development cooperation', paper presented to the UNDP Roundtable on Change: Social Conflict or Harmony?, Stockholm, 22–24 July 1994.
44. From a 1982 UNCTAD study cited in Martin Khor, 'South-North resource flows and their implications for sustainable development', *Third World Resurgence,* 46, 1994, p 25. See this whole issue of *Third World Resurgence* entitled 'The Drain from the South'.
45. UNDP, *Human Development Report 1994,* p 65.
46. World Resources Institute in collaboration with United Nations Environment Programme and United Nations Development Programme, *World Resources 1994–95: A Guide to the Global Environment,* New York: Oxford University Press, 1994, ch 1 and p 263.
47. 'Overfishing: causes and consequences', *The Ecologist,* 25 (2) (3), 1995.
48. World Bank, *World Debt Tables 1994–95,* p 18.
49. Ibid, p 4.
50. Ibid, p 8.
51. United Nations, *World Economic Survey 1993,* p 104.
52. See Richard J Barnet & John Cavanagh, *Global Dreams: Imperial Corporations and the New World Order,* New York: Simon and Schuster, 1994, part IV.
53. See, for instance, World Bank, *Global Economic Prospects 1994,* p 8.
54. World Bank, *World Debt Tables 1994–95,* p 18.
55. See Robin Broad, *Unequal Alliance: The World Bank, the International Monetary Fund, and the Philippines,* Berkeley, CA: University of California Press, 1988; George & Sabelli, *Faith and Credit;* and Rich, *Mortgaging the Earth.*

The Road to Third World Prosperity

William C. Freund

Many Third World countries, hoping to lift their people out of dismal poverty, had their hopes dashed when the roof fell in on Mexico's economy, one of the world's promising candidates for rapid development.

Foreign capital, which provided the lubrication for Mexico's economic development, turned tail, seeking greater safety and opportunity elsewhere. Foreign capital also reversed course in other Latin American countries for fear that Mexico's disease might be contagious.

Despite these events, there is cause for optimism about longer-term growth prospects in the less-developed countries. Indeed, opportunities for raising living standards in these countries are

better than they have ever been in the history of the world. The reason: the ongoing internationalization of productivity growth through technology transfers. Let us examine this proposition.

PRODUCTIVITY CONVERGENCE

Professor William Baumol of New York University has developed important new insights into what he calls "productivity convergence" among the already industrialized countries of the world. As is customary, he defines productivity growth as the annual increase in output per person-hour. Productivity growth is the stuff of which economic progress and rising living standards are made. Indeed, it is the only means of lifting countries out of

poverty and raising the per capita living standards.

The average gross domestic product (GDP) per worker has narrowed considerably since World War I and especially since World War II. By 1990, the productivity gap among the world's five leading economies (the United States, Japan, Germany, Great Britain, and France) had narrowed to only 20 percent. Today, that gap is on the verge of disappearing altogether.

Baumol offers good reasons not only for the convergence of productivity growth but for convergence to occur at ever faster rates. With modern communications, countries with lagging productivity can copy or transfer technological innovations more rapidly than ever before.

As Baumol puts it: "Better communications permit innovative techniques to move from one country to another far more quickly than in the past. Better and more widespread education permits countries to learn technical details from one another and to train their labor forces rapidly to make use of them."

Moreover, Baumol believes, the transfer of technology is continuing to accelerate. When the steam engine was invented in England at the beginning of the eighteenth century, it took 50

Projected Growth of Real GDP*	1994-2003
East Asia	7.6%
South Asia	5.3%
Sub-Sahara Africa	3.9%
Middle East and North Africa	3.8%
Latin America and Caribbean	3.4%
All Other Countries**	5.2%
OECD (Projected by Freund)	2.7%
U.S. (Projected by Freund)	2.7%

*Percent per annum   **Except Europe & Central Asia

SOURCE: *GLOBAL ECONOMIC PROSPECTS*, WORLD BANK, 1994

years for it to spread to western Europe and America. In contrast, innovations in transistor and semiconductor technology since World War II have, on average, taken only about 2 years to spread among countries.

One further factor has vastly increased countries' ability to transfer technology at an unprecedented pace. New technology has become miniaturized to a significant degree, making it unnecessary to transfer mammoth machinery and equipment as in the past.

The new age of electronics and telecommunications has led to a significant downsizing in the technology of both the manufacturing and services industries. Modern microchips are doubling their capacity every few years, while the costs of encoding millions of bits of information are dropping. The result of this miniaturization and cost reduction has been to make the new technology more rapidly available, at lower cost, especially to countries on the cusp of economic development.

LABOR PRODUCTIVITY, 1870-1989

Legend (Real GDP per Work Hour ($) vs. Year):
- United States
- France
- Germany
- Great Britain
- Japan

SOURCE: Angus Maddison, *Dynamic Forces in Capitalist Development*, (Oxford University Press, 1991.)

NEW HOPE FOR EMERGING COUNTRIES

Emerging countries, which in the past would not have enjoyed substantial economic progress, now have new opportunities to achieve higher levels of per capita income through the transfer of modern technology. But countries can capitalize on their new opportunities only if they are prepared to embrace private initiative and provide the basic education needed to absorb the new technology. Fortunately, recognition of unprecedented opportunities for real economic growth is spreading among emerging countries.

In a recent report, *Global Economic Prospects and the Developing Countries*, the World Bank projects GDP growth rates to the year 2003 for major regions of the world.

The fastest-growing area is expected to include Cambodia, China, Indonesia, Laos, and Vietnam in eastern Asia. If the growth rate of this region in fact equals the projected 7.6 percent per annum, these countries will work their way into the tier of middle-and upper-income countries.

It will take time for the new trend of productivity convergence to become apparent. But, if these projections are at all in the ballpark, the striking result will be that many countries we now call Third World will achieve second-and first-rank status.

We do not yet know all of the countries that will succeed in making this leap, but the list will exclude some now viewed favorably and include others not yet recognized. Candidates for success include Thailand, Korea, and the Philippines, as well as Bhutan, India, Pakistan, and Sri Lanka.

I would also include some

countries in the Americas—perhaps Argentina, Bolivia, Chile, Mexico, Peru, and Venezuela. Even among the most successful countries, there will be considerable differences in actual growth rates achieved.

What is particularly striking about many of these countries is the size of their populations. The four "Asian tigers"—Hong Kong, Singapore, South Korea, and Taiwan—well known for their past strides in economic growth, are home to some 75 million people. But the countries in Asia and Latin America with the greatest opportunity for economic progress number upward of three billion people, quite a different order of magnitude.

The dramatic possibility now exists that the living standards of billions of poor people will reach unimagined levels of achievement within a historically short period.

It should be recognized that to achieve rising levels of per capita income will require more rapid growth in the emerging countries than in already industrialized countries. The reason is that populations are rising much faster in developing countries.

In Mexico, for example, the annual population gain is about 3 percent. That means that even if Mexico enjoys as much as a 3 percent per annum growth rate, there can be no improvement in per capita income. Only if incomes rise at twice that rate, say 6 percent per annum or more, will living standards show any clear improvement.

Fortunately, these opportunities for rapid growth of real GDP now exist in many countries around the world. Whether these opportunities will be realized will depend heavily on the adoption of policies conducive to economic growth. To succeed, emerging economies must embrace policies that encourage the flow of domestic and foreign savings.

Achieving Economic 'Tigerhood'

To be prosperous, Third World countries today must:

Rapidly transfer Western technology to their own economies, taking advantage of modern communications and miniaturization.

Use foreign capital for productive purposes, not consumption.

Encourage domestic savings and investment.

Avoid deficit spending.

Adopt other sound fiscal and monetary policies.

Provide a dependable political framework, a corruption-free judiciary, and a legal system that respects human rights and property.

Improve primary and secondary schooling.

POLICIES TO ENCOURAGE GROWTH

The road to economic prosperity is lined with both opportunities and pitfalls. To realize the new opportunities, countries must be able to attract foreign capital. But there are two additional caveats: The foreign capital must be used for productive purposes rather than consumption, and countries must not rely exclusively on foreign capital.

Mexico offers a striking illustration of the dangers of both an overreliance on foreign capital and the excessive use of foreign savings to finance consumption instead of investment. The result was a large balance-of-payments deficit that might have worked out all right if it had been used to finance basic investment in production facilities. But the use of foreign savings for domestic consumption ultimately led to a collapse in confidence in the value of the peso. In turn, these events triggered a collapse in domestic financial markets.

Mexico also illustrates the importance of maintaining a good balance between foreign investments and domestic savings. In the longer term, governments cannot rely solely on foreign capital. They must encourage domestic saving and investment through a variety of policies, including a limit on government deficit spending.

Indeed, economic history shows the interdependence of policies affecting domestic and foreign capital. If a country is unable to produce the conditions favorable to mobilizing domestic capital, it is unlikely that foreign capital will enter for any prolonged period of time. Short-term portfolio investments require a high degree of confidence and are vulnerable to any shocks in expectations.

It is worth noting that in the high-growth economies of eastern Asia, domestic savings rates have run twice as high as in Mexico.

Emerging countries can never forget that they are competing for foreign capital in a world where demands are enormous, where competition is increasingly intense, and where capital flows are extremely mobile. Signs of a faltering resolve to adhere to sound domestic policies or to treat foreign capital fairly will trigger a quick exodus.

In fact, the world's financial markets have become the watchdogs over domestic economic, political, social, and legal policies. They are judge and jury. Instead of governments dictating to markets, international markets oversee governmental policies.

International investors require confidence in the continued existence of societies that have sound fiscal and monetary policies and provide a dependable framework of political and legal stability. Countries will not stay ahead in the competitive race for international capital unless confidence and stability prevail.

International capital can be divided into two parts: *portfolio capital*, which invests in stocks and bonds, and *direct capital*, which invests in plants, equipment, stores, offices, and the like. Emerging countries need to recognize that portfolio capital is often short-term and nervous, seizing new opportunities as soon as doubts appear about any one country's economic prospects.

THE TRUST FACTOR

Portfolio capital turns tail whenever uncertainty or turbulence appears, as it did in Mexico. Foreign portfolio investors can halt further inflows as well as liquidate existing holdings and exit a country on short notice. Developing countries should favor the attraction of direct investments in longer-term physical assets. But here, too, building investor confidence is essential.

Market opportunities in populous China are apparent to international investors everywhere, from suppliers of consumer products to distributors of capital equipment, to builders of roads and telephone systems. But foreign direct capital takes a dim view of officially sanctioned activities considered illegal in free-market economies. Any piracy of private property, whether it be copyrights, computer software, CDs, or movies—such as still occurs in China—poses a strong deterrent to private capital. Where the sanctity of private contracts is in doubt—as has also been the case in China—foreign direct capital will always be hesitant.

The *Economist* magazine noted recently that, because venture capital is scarce, entrepreneurship must be prodded by an efficient banking system and a stock market capable of mobilizing domestic and foreign savings. But above all, the magazine said,

the best long-term way to improve the lot of the poorest is better primary schooling. An understand-

able obsession with quantity must give way to an emphasis on improving quality. That does not mean elitism. . . . It means tackling entrenched bureaucracies and public-sector trade unions, to extract more value from limited funds.

Capital of any stripe favors countries with political stability, a respect for human rights and property, and a judiciary free of corruption and contempt for law.

A number of international lending institutions have had a hand in stimulating Third World economic growth. And perhaps none has been more involved than the World Bank. But over the years, many observers believe, this organization has become encrusted with layers of bureaucracy at its Washington headquarters.

Now, however, there is a new broom ready to sweep in. James Wolfensohn, an investment banker, philanthropist, musician, and public servant, has become the World Bank's new president. He traveled to at least 18 countries in his first few months in office to find out what the bank is doing in the field. Rumor has it that he wants to create a more outward-looking organization with less power in the hands of the Washington staffers and more decision making devolving to local staffs. As one observer put it, he wants more money to go into education and preserving the wilderness, and less into clearing forests and pouring concrete.

There has already been a 10 percent staff reduction, and more job cuts seem to lie ahead. Wolfensohn wants to broaden the bank's perspective, respond to local needs, deemphasize massive projects such as dams and power plants, and favor smaller projects and local partnerships. It won't be easy, however, to create a new

philosophy and a new culture at the bank.

A NEW GLOBAL PROSPERITY

It took over a hundred years for a middle class to develop in Great Britain. Given the right policies, even poor countries can now achieve that goal within decades. That is the modern-day promise of productivity convergence.

But the competition for world capital will be keen, and the prize will go to those countries that implement private markets, free competition, and an environment of stability. The world has discovered the awesome power of private entrepreneurship and risk taking. Experience has also shown that countries must promote domestic savings rather than rely primarily on foreign capital for economic development.

Emerging countries able to grasp the new opportunities provided by productivity convergence and technology transfers will have an unprecedented chance of improving the living standards of billions of people. That is the exciting prospect for the next two decades.

Achieving a growth of 6–7 percent per annum depends on the right combination of domestic policies, domestic savings, and stable longer-term foreign direct investments. But these levels of growth also promise a revolution in living standards within one or two generations for many of the world's emerging countries and for billions of people who, so far, have known only poverty.

William C. Freund is New York Stock Exchange Professor of Economics at the Lubin School of Business at Pace University in New York City and director of the Center for the Study of Equity Markets. He was chief economist of the New York Stock Exchange for 18 years.

Immiserating Growth (2): The Third World

Kuznets Law built on sketchy data

E d w a r d   S .   H e r m a n

In the early Cold War years the dominant aims of establishment intellectuals analyzing Third World issues were, first, to counter leftist ideas of exploitation, dependency, immiseration, and the necessity of radical change; and, second, to rationalize the planned and ongoing reshaping of the globe for U.S. imperial advantage. The best publicized analysis along these lines was Walt Rostow's *The Stages of Economic Growth* (1960), subtitled "A Non-Communist Manifesto," which described a sequence of development whereby Third World countries, with judicious foreign aid and investment, would gradually modernize their institutions and value systems, increase their rates of investment and per capita incomes, and take off into sustained growth. In the end they would become like us, the obvious final product of human development (and history). The possibility that the great powers might obstruct or skew the Third World development process in accord with their own interests was recognized by Rostow, but dismissed. As a model Cold Warrior, Rostow naturally found the Soviet leadership to be "expansionist" and convinced that the rest of the world "must ultimately be conquered," whereas the West only sought "partnership" and encouraged Third World change that would "keep open the possibility of progressive, democratic development."

Another influential and less blatantly ideological strand of establishment thought arose out of the empirical work of the distinguished economist Simon Kuznets, who found a tendency for income distribution to become less equal during five to seven decades of rapid growth, but then to become more equal. Such a pattern, which could be graphed as an inverted U curve, seemed to fit a number of cases of western economic development. Although Kuznets offered the relationship tentatively and with qualifications, it soon became "Kuznets law." The law was simple and politically convenient: it could explain, and implicitly justify, deteriorating income distributions in Third World development under First World tutelage. The masses might be miserable now, but in place of the old exhortation that they wait for their reward in heaven, they could take solace in the prospect that their grandchildren might benefit from a delayed trickle-down.

At the very same time as establishment thought was giving these benign views of presumably freely-chosen development processes in the Third World, the U.S.—following closely World War II and early postwar plans for "Grand Areas" under U.S. control, with the Third World serving the needs of the Western great powers—was actively intervening to make sure that oligarchic structures of control were preserved and social democratic reforms would pose no threat to foreign investment. Kuznets classic article appeared in 1956; Rostow's *Stages of Economic Growth* was published in 1960. Meanwhile, the U.S. had put the Shah on the throne in Iran by covert subversion in 1953, and had organized the overthrow of an elected government in

Guatemala in 1954, installing in its place a regime of permanent state terror. The important and pace-setting Brazilian coup in 1964, which also displaced a democratic government with a military dictatorship, was enthusiastically supported by the liberal Democrats in power in Washington (the coup was "the single most decisive victory for freedom in the mid-twentieth century" according to U.S. Ambassador Lincoln Gordon, later president of Johns Hopkins University). Trujillo in the Dominican Republic, Duvalier in Haiti, and the Somoza family in Nicaragua had taken power following extended U.S. occupation and tutelage. The World Bank and IMF were already in place, serving to guide Third World countries in proper directions. In the mainstream, however, these were all defensive, stabilizing, and apolitical efforts, in accord with accepted ideological premises.

Kuznets Law: An Aberration

Kuznets law was built on sketchy data drawn from western experience. It doesn't apply to Third World development, as was apparent even before the final victories of the National Security State and the full global triumph of the transnational corporation (TNC) and neoliberal ideology. Furthermore, the curve of inequality has been moving upward again in the West itself, suggesting that the earlier decline may have been transitory, eventually to be reversed with the full maturation of a global capitalism.

Irma Adelman and Cynthia Taft Morris carried out a major test of Kuznets law in application to the Third World in their *Economic Growth and Social Equity in Developing Countries* (1973). They examined the relationship between 31 different economic, political, and cultural variables, and income concentration, for 44 Third World countries. Their results were "consistent with the view of economic backwardness under colonialism held by such political economists as Paul A. Baran, according to which very uneven income distribution is a typical outcome of a narrowly based growth process where natural resources are exploited for the primary benefit of a small class of wealthy, usually expatriate, businessmen....An even more disturbing implication of our findings is that development is accompanied by an absolute as well as a relative decline in the average income of the very poor. Indeed, an initial spurt of dualistic growth [where technological improvement and income growth are confined to one sector, while another frequently traditional sector remains small-scale, poor, and politically powerless] may cause such a decline for as much as 60 percent of the population. The absolute position of the poorest 40 percent apparently continues to worsen as countries

move toward less dualistic growth patterns unless major efforts are made to improve and expand human resources. Thus our findings strongly suggest that there is no automatic, or even likely, trickling down of the benefits of economic growth to the poorest segments of the population in low-income countries."

Economist David Felix also studied Kuznets law with particular application to Mexico for the period 1885-1975 ("Income Distribution Trends in Mexico and the Kuznets Curves," in S. Hewlett and R. Weinert, *Brazil and Mexico: Patterns in Late Development, 1982*). Felix found that Mexico's high level of income concentration failed to decline, as had those of Great Britain, the U.S., and Germany, despite a higher growth rate over a longer period than it took the others to produce a turnabout. (His finding for the years 1885-1975 was reinforced by the substantial further increase in Mexican income inequality after 1975.) Felix argued that Mexico is hardly a special case; that its leveling revolution and reformist institutional changes of the post World War I era provided conditions more favorable to "extensive trickling down" than in a majority of Third World states.

Durable Immiseration Factors

Why did inequality not fall in Mexico or Brazil after many decades of growth? One reason is that the ruling oligarchies rarely projected a national vision of independent development; they were satisfied to prosper via export bonanzas in indigenous raw materials and produce, and they were fearful of depleting the supply of cheap agricultural and mining labor. Their lack of national-cultural vision and identity was also manifested in their long aping of the styles and other cultural innovations of Europe and the U.S. This made them object lessons in the workings of the "international demonstration effect," whereby national surpluses of relative poor countries were frittered away in elite purchases of fashionable foreign consumer goods rather than being used to stimulate domestic industry or provide investment funds for indigenous development.

In Britain, the U.S., and Japan, industrialization was closely tied in with the development of artisan industry, which filled niches not adequately supplied by factories and provided a technological base important to future industrial development. Its growth, along with that of factory industry, helped absorb labor surpluses coming out of a shrinking or industrializing agriculture. In Brazil and Mexico, by contrast, artisan industry declined with economic growth, as the elites, who captured virtually all the national surplus, preferred foreign made and modern goods; artisan industry was left to supply the poor. Its decline, and the heavy reliance on foreign produced goods, made for technological backwardness and technological dependency.

This form of development also helped consolidate dualism and economic-social polarization. In Brazil, some 30-35 million of the 150 million population, or between a fifth and a quarter of the total, live in circumstances comparable to those of the middle classes and rich in the United States or France. They consume the great bulk of fashionable new goods supplied by the modern sector and TNCs. Studies of Mexican consumption patterns show that "the demand of the lowest 60 percent was concentrated on products whose national sales were stagnating [i.e., traditional and artisan supplied goods], while the top 20-40 percent made up the market for successive new goods in the dynamic growth phases of their product cycles" (Felix). When puffers of Latin American "reform" refer to surging new markets and sales in Mexico (or Chile, or Brazil) they are speaking of only 20-25 percent of the population—the people who count for the puffers.

The remaining 75-80 percent—the other pole of Brazil's dual society—live in wretched conditions in huge shantytowns around Rio de Janiero and Sao Paulo, or in numerous poor agricultural communities, and consume a minute fraction of the hot new consumer goods. Many work small land holdings or as part-time agricultural laborers in the countryside; those in the shantytowns provide a reserve army available to the affluent for household service or to the "modern" sector in factories or as employees of subcontractors in the "informal market." A large fraction of this Brazilian majority are without potable water or sewage facilities, have grossly inadequate medical care, and their educational resources are reflected in a 35 percent illiteracy rate—the percentage of children finishing grade school in this fairly wealthy country approximates that in Haiti and Guinea-Bissau. It is estimated that some 8 million Brazilian children under 14 are homeless and live as beggars, thieves, and prostitutes. Several thousand of them are murdered each year by police death squads, some hired by local businesses to improve the climate for tourism.

The benefits of growth in Brazil and Mexico, both in the past and today, have flowed almost entirely to the affluent 20-25 percent of the population, plus, importantly, foreign TNCs and banks. The residual majority is seen by the leadership (and by IMF and World Bank officials) largely as a means to elite ends, and concern for its well-being almost invariably reflects worry that it might cease to be apathetic and upset "stability." The condition of the majority therefore constitutes a "management problem," and considerable thought is given to token allocations of resources, strategically placed, that will placate, divide and immobilize them.

There have been brief interludes in which the welfare of the majority received attention in Mexico. Felix

notes that the two Mexican presidents who tried to tilt toward equity, Adolfo Lopez Mateos (1958-74) and Luis Echeverria (1970-76), suffered in consequence from strongly adverse reactions by Mexican and foreign business interests, including reductions in private investment, and they were unable to fulfill their promises. Echeverria "left office in a major foreign exchange crisis and amidst rumors of a military coup, a novel and portentous phenomenon in postwar Mexico." Peter Evans and Gary Gereffi point out, in reference to Echeverria's experience, that "Mexico, one of the richest and best-behaved nations in the Third World, had only to stray slightly from the path of sound business practice to end up . . . [suffering a shift] of TNC capital and profit flows from a positive $179 million in the 1960 to 1969 period to a negative $349 million in the period from 1970 to 1976. Since one can hardly accuse Echeverria of being a radical, it would appear that the band of acceptable policy is exceedingly narrow and that the penalties for straying outside it are strict and swift" (Hewlett and Weinert, p. 151).

The experiences of Allende (Chile, 1973), Goulart (Brazil, 1964), Bosch (Dominican Republic, 1963 and 1965), Arbenz (Guatemala, 1954), and the Sandinistas (Nicaragua, 1979-90) show that military intervention, sponsored or supported by the U.S., is a very real possibility where there is too much "straying" beyond the boundaries of service to local and expatriate elites. "Security" expenditures remain enormous in Latin America; in Argentina, the military budget is three times that for education, and more than the aggregate for education, health, culture and justice combined. In Chile, also, "the military budget in 1989 outstripped by $432 million the housing, health and education budgets combined" (Joseph Collins and John Lear, *Chile's Free-Market Miracle: A Second Look*, p. 9). The Chilean military budget is exempt from neoliberal "shrinking" of government, and is the only governmental activity where salaries are linked to the cost of living. This priority system is understandable: the armed forces preserve the right to immiserate the majority.

The spendthrift habits of Latin elites has also been a long-standing factor in periodic balance of payment crises: spurts of income growth and inflows of foreign capital have led to large increases in consumer imports, leaving little margin for adverse changes (declines in export prices, sudden fears on the part of foreign investors!), which have produced balance of payments deficits, panic outflows of capital, and consequent deflationary policies and further increases in external debt. These developments have enhanced the power of foreign lenders and the international financial institutions like the IMF, which have forced upon the debtor countries policies that worsen all the indigenous trends toward inequality. That is, they enforce a primary focus on paying the foreign debt, privatization (benefiting foreign and local elites), export orientation (further concentrating land ownership and accelerating the expropriation and marginalization of peasants), cutbacks in public expenditures (except export subsidies and those for "security"), and deflationary macro policies (increasing unemployment, but helping creditors).

Law of Increasing Immiseration

Immiseration rests on the implementation of class power in the economy and political arena. A surge of immiseration is usually associated with changes in technology and markets that create opportunities for the dominant class and interest groups. Taking advantage of these requires the dispossession of peasants, the mobilization of a pliable and cheap labor force, intensified exploitation, and the aggressive application of state power to further serve business profitability.

Over extended periods of capitalist development in the technologically advanced countries of the West, real wages rose markedly and welfare states were put in place, although large pools of misery persisted even in good times. This came about as a consequence of periods of relative labor scarcity, the gradual emergence of labor unions, and painfully slow but real gains wrested from a capitalist-dominated but not entirely closed political system. To this important degree democracy in the West has worked; the propertied classes, often not completely unified, were induced to allow concessions rather than suffer more severe class conflict or take a chance on authoritarian rule at home.

In the 1970s and thereafter, however, international competition intensified, and the burdens of high wages and a welfare state began to seem intolerable to the U.S. business community. New communications technology helped make restructuring and foreign outsourcing more practicable. The labor movement was in retreat, and the power of business was further enhanced by the fluidity of money capital, the further centralization of the media, and the increased importance of money in politics. Any populist tendencies in politics could be snuffed out by sustained media assaults, money market discipline, and the funding (and defunding) of political campaigns. So business could hog-tie and discredit Carter and put in place their own servant (Reagan, formerly a hired propaganda gun of General Electric Company) to help it implement an accelerated program of "reform" cum "immiseration."

The key factor in this renewed phase of immiserating growth, which is taking place on a global basis, is the enhanced mobility of capital, which has allowed an increasingly active global process of wage-tax-regulation arbitrage (i.e., shifting between markets to take advantage of price and other differences) and bargaining down. The TNCs have been able to tap the vast pools of impoverished and underemployed labor in the Third World, which provide what economists call an "elastic" supply of cheap labor—i.e., wages do not go up as the supply is tapped, helped along by regressive political regimes, as in Mexico, Indonesia, or China, where strikes must be approved by the state and the dominant unions are government-controlled. In Indonesia an estimated 30 percent of the 83 million workforce is underemployed, and another 2 million-plus enter the work force each year, "eagerly competing for the $1.75-a-day jobs being created in the cities" (Merrill Goozner, "Asian labor: Wages of shame," *Chicago Tribune,* Nov. 6, 1994).

Since 1979, China's "market socialism" leaders have allowed some 177,000 foreign-organized joint ventures or independent firms to set up shop in special economic zones, tapping some 60-100 million peasants, millions of them young women, lured by the promise of factory jobs. These workers have been subjected to "working conditions that have not been seen since the dawn of industrial capitalism in the early 19th century," a "killing field" of workers (206 factory fires resulting in 10 or more deaths, 19,000 work fatalities in the first 8 months of 1994 by official estimate), with the enforcement of law and worker protection non-existent. Attempts to create independent labor organizations to correct the severe abuses have been met with "fierce repression" in both China and Indonesia, and Tribune reporters put the two countries in the same class: "The one-party regimes of nominally communist China and right-wing authoritarian Indonesia have reacted to the labor unrest in a similar fashion for similar reasons"—they worry about challenges to authoritarian rule and the demands of foreign investors (Uli Schmetzer and Merrill Goozner, "Growing workplace fatalities dim glow of Chinese economy," *Chicago Tribune*, Nov. 8, 1994).

These supply conditions disconnect wages and productivity, so that economic growth "is not lifting all boats" in China and Indonesia, the world's first and fourth most populous nations, and "a wave of labor unrest has swept over both countries in the last year as the promise of a better life from working in industry proved false for millions of uprooted agricultural workers." The delinkage can go far, with real wages sometimes declining while productivity soars; thus, real wages in Mexico in the years 1980-1992 fell 32 percent while manufacturing productivity increased by 41 percent.

Arbitrage, along with Third World labor supply conditions, necessarily affects wages and working conditions in the high income countries, by putting steady downward pressure on the higher wage levels. This has weakened the relationship between productivity and wage rates in the high wage countries as well, where real wage growth is now consistently below the rate of productivity increase. In the U.S., between 1973 and 1992 average hourly real wages fell 1 percent, while productivity rose by more than 15 percent. The other side of the coin, of course, was the sharp increase in executive pay (19 percent, 1979-89) and, more important, the enormous increase in capital income (up 65 percent, realized capital gains up 205 percent, 1979-89), all reflected in the substantial increase in income inequality.

These numbers show that at this juncture a very large fraction of any global productivity advances are being captured by a small elite of local compradors and political and military leaders, and foreign banks and TNCs. This elite is even able, brazenly, to impose further absolute reductions in the living standards of the already impoverished majority to sustain elite incomes in times of difficulty—thus Zedillo's adjustment package to meet Mexico's current crisis centers on forcing real wages down, and IMF imposed austerity plans consistently involve budget cuts, deflationary macro policies, and wage restraints that put the burden of adjustment on the impoverished. The poor majority, who do not share in the gains of productivity growth, still must provide the fallback resources to assure payment to those who do benefit from growth.

In sum, the technological, economic, political, and ideological environment of the New World Order has strengthened the traditional forces making for inequality and immiseration. TNC mobility and power in economic life, the media, and politics, has entrenched the belief that there is no other policy option than creating a favorable climate for investment; it has put opposition groups into disarray and in weakened positions, and with no obvious strategies for defense or means of regaining initiatives; it has unleashed the forces of irrationality (immigrant threat, racism) to help smooth the way to dismantling the welfare state; and it has led us into a new era of renewed aggressive class warfare and unconstrained search for global advantage. A revised "law" of the trend in inequality seems plausible: that, given the increasing imbalance in the global power of capital and labor, we may expect inequality and immiseration to increase until either a new and potent resistance force emerges from the oppressed or the now unconstrained forces of capital produce a Big Bang (with unknown fallout effects thereafter).

Neoliberal Social Policy

Managing Poverty (Somehow)

Neoliberalism considers the
growth of poverty to be a
pathology, not a consequence of
the economic system. By isolating
poverty from the process of
economic development, it
reduces the solution to designing
temporary social policies.

CARLOS M. VILAS

Carlos M. Vilas is a sociologist and historian at the Center for Interdisciplinary Research at the National Autonomous University of Mexico (UNAM), and a member of NACLA's editorial board. His most recent book is Between Earthquakes and Volcanoes: Market, State, and the Revolutions in Central America *(Monthly Review Press, 1995).*
Translated from the Spanish by NACLA.

The debt crisis of the early 1980s and the macroeconomic adjustment and neoliberal reforms that the region's governments implemented to deal with it resulted in a dramatic increase in the number of people living in poverty. In 1980, 118 million Latin Americans—about a third of the region's total population—were poor. By 1990, that number had increased to 196 million, or nearly half the total population. Eighty percent of these 78 million "new poor" live in cities, which helps explain the congestion and deterioration of many Latin American capitals.[1] This 42% growth rate of the "new poor" between 1980 and 1990 was almost double the 22% population growth rate in the region during the same period.

This veritable process of poverty production contrasts sharply with socioeconomic trends of the preceding decades. The proportion of poor people within the overall population in Latin America fell from 51% in 1960 to 33% in 1980. During this 20-year period, the number of poor people increased by 9 million, or 8%, while the total population grew by 145 million, or 67%. This drop in the percentage of poor people was obtained *without programs designed to "combat poverty."* It was, rather, the result of the overall functioning of the economy, which integrated large segments of the population by creating new jobs, and helped to progressively distribute income through business-labor negotiations regulated by the state.

Latin America's economy began to rebound from the economic recession in the mid-1980s. Gross domestic product (GDP) grew 9.5% between 1986 and 1990, and another 15% between 1991 and 1995.[2] As poverty levels remained constant or increased despite economic growth, it became clear that structural adjustment does not by itself reduce poverty and macroeconomic recovery does not translate into significant social improvement. This provoked alarm among Latin American govern-

From *NACLA Report on the Americas*, May/June 1996, pp. 16-25. © 1996 by the North American Congress on Latin America, Inc. Reprinted by permission.

ments and the multilateral lending institutions like the World Bank and the Inter-American Development Bank (IDB) that were advising them on how to implement the adjustment measures. This burgeoning poverty was seen as a source of political instability, and as fertile terrain for demagogues and populists that might threaten the neoliberal restructuring process. As a result, these multilateral agencies began to emphasize the need to create programs to combat poverty.

In this way, social policy entered into the neoliberal reform agenda as a question of poverty and, in fact, was reduced to that. Neoliberalism considers the growth of poverty to be a pathology, not a consequence of the economic system. Hence it isolates poverty from the process of capital accumulation and economic development, and reduces the solution to designing specific social policies.

Any social policy performs two essential functions. First, it supports the process of capital accumulation through the social reproduction of the labor force. Second, it legitimizes the overall political order by offering social services that help create consensus among the population that benefits from them. The way in which these two functions are performed depends on the political and social dynamics of each country. Social policy is an arena of social and political conflict among social groups, whose outcome is expressed in government decisions.

Over the past decade, the passage from a Keynesian-Fordist model of economic development to a neoliberal one has had significant repercussions on the nature of social policy in Latin America. In the Keynesian-Fordist model, the state regulated economic activity and intervened in specific sectors, including the establishment of state-owned enterprises. Increases in economic productivity led to salary increases and expanded employment, which benefited the population as a whole.

Social policy in this model reinforced the process of capital accumulation to the degree that it created externalities for private enterprises.[3] For example, public investment in education, health care, worker training, and low-income housing represented a savings for the private sector, which would otherwise have had to invest in these areas. Meanwhile, employment, wage and pricing policies improved the purchasing power of individual workers and the domestic market as a whole. Social policy was seen as an element of investment, not an expense. But economic and social policies in the Keynesian-Fordist model facilitated the incorporation of broad sectors of the poor, especially the urban poor, into the political and economic system.

Latin America during this period was characterized by widespread social mobility, stimulated—within certain limits—by the state. Together these varied elements helped constitute what was known as the "national-popular state," or the "national-developmentalist state"—the Latin American proxy of the western European "welfare state." Social policies contributed to capitalist development, were reformist by nature, and fed social mobility. As a result, they gave broad legitimacy to the political system. Citizen rights were thus imbued with socioeconomic rights. Citizen rights were also expanded into the political realm, as women and indigenous people were granted the right to vote. The implicit paradigm of social policy—and of state policies in general—was integration.[4]

With variations from country to country, the Keynesian-Fordist model peaked between the 1930s and 1970s. It entered into crisis because of changes in the international system since the 1950s, increasing divergence between business interests and labor demands, and recurring fiscal crises. Military dictatorships, authoritarianism, and later, the debt crisis that detonated in 1982, led to the exhaustion of this model of development and its corresponding social policies.

Recognizing the limitations and inefficiencies of the Keynesian-Fordist model should not lead us to minimize its successes. The integrating dynamic of this model reduced poverty by moving labor from low-productivity activities to modern ones, improving employment levels and the quality of jobs, and increasing disposable income through wage hikes and price subsidies for urban workers as well as redistributive state social policies.

The crisis of the 1980s created the conditions for the application of the neoliberal model. This model is characterized by the deregulation of the economy, trade liberalization, the dismantling of the public sector, and the predominance of the financial sector of the economy over production and commerce. The state has abandoned its role as an agent of social development and integration. Instead, it helps define winners and losers in the marketplace by setting the exchange rate, interest rates and tax policy, all of which pump income toward the financial sector.

Social policy is reduced to a limited series of measures intended to compensate the initial negative effects of structural adjustment among certain sectors of the population. These negative effects, neoliberal policy makers purport, are rooted in the irrationality of the previous system's distribution of resources. Social policy is considered transitory: after an initial painful phase, structural adjustment will reestablish basic macroeconomic equilibrium and promote economic growth without inflation. New jobs will be created within the modern sector of the economy—the "trickle-down" effect—which will raise incomes and leave only a small proportion of the population in need of public attention.

As a matter of principle, neoliberal economics does not concern itself with social policy. A strong economy, it is argued, will make permanent social policies unnecessary. Social issues are considered a government expense, not an investment; the concept of social development gives way to that of social compensation. With the drastic cuts in social spending, however, only minimal compensatory mechanisms can be sustained. As a result, social policy has contracted, and its two traditional functions—accumulation and legitimization—have experienced severe adaptations.

Neoliberal social policy helps promote capital accumulation through financial maneuvers. For example, the privatization of the retirement and pension systems in many Latin American countries has handed over huge financial resources to the private capital market. For their part, social-investment funds promote capital accumulation by supporting small-business activities like repair shops and industrial homework enterprises.

For the rest, neoliberal social policy operates like a charity, directing aid toward the extremely poor. Rather than improving the working and living conditions of low-income groups, social policy tries to assist the many victims of structural adjustment, and to prevent further deterioration in the living standards of the population already below the poverty line. Neoliberal social policy doesn't help these people get out of the hole of poverty; it simply tries to prevent them from sinking further into it.

These characteristics of neoliberal social policy severely limit its capacity to fulfill a legitimizing function for the political system. In fact, social policy is essentially reduced to putting out fires so that situations of extreme social tension do not become larger political problems. Neoliberals fear that such problems would create a climate of instability that might negatively affect the inflows of foreign capital, putting the whole economic model at risk. In this sense, social policy becomes closely linked to the politics of the moment. On the eve of the 1994 presidential elections in Mexico, for example, the government of Carlos Salinas poured huge sums of money into "Procampo," a new program to provide temporary relief to the rural poor. The implicit objective of the Mexican social-investment fund Pronasol was to reduce the level of political conflict in those parts of the country where the opposition might gain ground.[5]

Neoliberal social policy doesn't help people get out of the hole of poverty; it simply tries to prevent them from sinking further into it.

Central America's health-sector reform dramatically illustrates the internal tensions and contradictions of neoliberal social policies in poverty-stricken countries. Although Central American governments began discussing the need to reform the health sector in the late 1980s, the recent health-care reform was prompted by loans offered by the World Bank and the IDB. These loans were granted only on the condition that governments implement broader public-sector reforms. The development banks' concern with health reform reflects their wider interest in macroeconomic adjustment and state deregulation. The scope and content of reform in the health sector are tailored to the overall goals of neoliberalism.

Since macroeconomic reform usually involves sharp cuts in already meager public spending on infrastructure and social services, the impact of health reform has been ambivalent and even contradictory. In Nicaragua, for example, public spending on health dropped from 5% of GDP in 1990 to 4.4% in 1994. Today the government spends an average of $19 per person a year on health services, or $1.50 per person per month. The figures for Guatemala are even worse. Public health expenditures dropped from 1.5% of GDP in 1980 to 0.9% in 1990, climbing to just over 1.3% in 1993. Costa Rica, on the other hand, spent 7.5% of its GDP on public health in 1993, an average of $60 per person.[6] Efficiency, cost-cutting, and better managerial skills—all of which are urgently needed in Central America—are emphasized. Yet, efficiency is undermined by budget cuts that reduce the impact of policies and actions. Cost-cutting is urged upon countries that already devote meager resources to health and other social services. The emphasis on management skills and techniques is abstract, and frequently bears little relation to the specific character and needs of the health sector.

Most health ministries in Central America face increasing shortages in infrastructure, equipment and personnel—shortages that cannot be offset by the "self-management" of civil society in countries in which the overwhelming majority of the population is poor. In recent years, greater emphasis has been placed on improved training for health-care specialists, but low salaries and poor working conditions jeopardize efforts to recruit and retain skilled personnel. Since health is not—despite the rhetoric—a priority for most Central American governments, high turnover of personnel in top-level positions in health ministries reinforces the lack of continuity and the loose commitment to health-care reform.

Within this general framework, differences exist among countries. In Costa Rica, decision-making regarding health-care reform is more independent from the multilateral lending agencies. Even as reform takes the shape that these agencies favor, the notion of health as a social service has been preserved. By contrast, in the health-reform program designed by the IDB in Guatemala, the Ministry of Health must get explicit IDB approval for 43 out of 63 components of the program in order to move to the next step and have funds disbursed.[7]

Neoliberal social policy has three basic characteristics, which are tightly interwoven: privatization, targeting, and decentralization. Privatizing social services is considered a way to alleviate the fiscal crisis, to make service delivery more efficient, and the avoid the micro- and macroeconomic distortions that arise from free public services. Users' fees have been imposed or increased, and new operating principles based on the criteria of business and commercial profit have been introduced. These have had significant repercussions on the quality and breadth of coverage. Users' fees, it is argued, are a way of reducing the financial burden assumed by lending agencies. They are also supposedly a way of ensuring that public services will be used only by those who really need them, avoiding the waste of resources.

Privatization implies the abandonment of the notion of public service, and its replacement with that of a business out to make a profit. Access to social services is no longer considered one's right as a citizen, but is based on one's ability to pay. The privatization of social services generates new social inequalities because only

---

> **With privatization, health and education have become pieces of merchandise to be bought and sold in the marketplace.**

---

wealthier groups can now afford them. This explains the resistance to privatization from broad sectors of the lower and middle classes who believe that they have a right to health care and education. In Argentina, for example, low-income salaried workers lost access to medical attention when the social-security system was privatized. As a result, these workers are forced to rely on the public health system, which is already overwhelmed. In a domino effect, the poorest of the poor have ended up excluded from public hospitals. Making matters worse, after problems in his economic program became apparent last year, President Carlos Menem and his minister of economics, Domingo Cavallo, ordered further cuts in social spending. As a result, several public hospitals in Buenos Aires have been forced to close, leaving thousands of people completely without access to basic medical care.

Privatization also entails the loss or reduction of state financing for projects once run by the government as a function of its role as representative of the public interest. In El Salvador, for example, the government delegated to the Business Foundation for Educational Development (FEPADE), a business-oriented think tank, several important worker-training programs for ex-combatants from the Farabundo Martí National Liberation Front (FMLN) and demobilized members of the armed forces. The program was designed by FEPADE, and financed with foreign funds.

The efficiency of the privatization process usually depends on the state's regulatory capacity. In Latin America today, however, the state has abdicated this

function, paving the way for the formation or consolidation of oligopolies in the health, education, and social-security markets. As a result, social policy becomes shaped in ways amenable to particular groups and special interests that can exert the most pressure. In the case of the health sector, for example, medical laboratories, large private clinics, and professional organizations have gained significant influence. In housing policy, construction companies and banks have become major players.

With privatization, health and education are no longer rights. They are luxuries or, at least, pieces of merchandise to be bought and sold in the marketplace. If you cannot afford the merchandise, don't buy it. In other words, if you can't afford medical care, die. If you can't pay for education, stay illiterate and sell chewing gum on the street corner. The privatization of pensions

Making the World Bank Mo[re]

The World Bank and the Inter-America[n] Development Bank (IDB) extol the importanc[e] of involving civil society in the projects that the[y] fund. From the Amazon rainforest to souther[n] megacities like São Paulo, local communities an[d] non-governmental organizations (NGOs) in Braz[il] understand how things really work: despite th[e] rhetoric, the Brazilian government and the multi[-] lateral lending institutions lack the political will t[o] create institutional mechanisms to facilitate democratic dialogue with the populations affecte[d] by the projects.

To give one example, the World Bank investe[d] more than US$500 million over the course of th[e] 1980s to support the Brazilian government['s] Polonoroeste project in Rondônia, which has bee[n] called the greatest ecological disaster ever funde[d] by the Bank. This megaproject was supposed t[o] rationalize the colonization process, provide loca[l] infrastructure, and protect indigenous areas in th[e] Amazon. Hundreds of indigenous peoples, rura[l] workers and rubber-tappers were expelled fro[m] their lands after a road to the interior was pave[d] yet they had no say in the project's design at all.

Acknowledging its part in that debacle, the Ban[k] is now investing US$167 million in a new projec[t] called Planafloro, which is supposed to refle[ct] a more sustainable approach to development i[n] the area affected by the previous project[.] Although good in intention, Planafloro was no[t] designed with the involvement of local communi[-] ties either. The Bank only initiated a process of con[-] sultation after being pressured by Northern envi[-] ronmental groups. Local organizations are no[w] petitioning the World Bank's Inspection Panel t[o] investigate Planafloro. Neither the Brazilian gov[-] ernment nor the Bank seems to be interested i[n] pursuing this investigation even though local orga[-] nizations have presented compelling evidence o[f]

Fátima Vianna Mello is a member of the Federation of Educational and Social Assistance Organizations (FASE), one of the founding organizations of the Brazil Network on Multilateral Financial Institutions.

in Bolivia illustrates this logic with particular cruelty: the government set the age to begin to "enjoy" retirement benefits almost ten years higher than the life expectancy of the average Bolivian.

The second principal tenet of neoliberal social policy is targeting. Given the contraction of funds assigned to social policy, targeting is promoted as a way to guarantee that resources effectively reach those to whom they are directed. The arguments in favor of targeting echo the criticisms of the Keynesian-Fordist model. That model was based on the principle of universal, free social services. Neoliberals argue that the model benefited workers in the urban wage-labor force and the middle classes, but did not reach the poorest of the poor—the rural poor and the informal sector.

Targeted social programs, specifically designed to reach the neediest, impose new management practices and efficiency criteria on state social policy. Clearly, however, targeting responds less to the supposed inefficiencies of the Keynesian-Fordist social-security model, than to the need to respond to mounting social problems with scarce resources.

In theory, targeting aims to fulfill a basic requirement of any public policy: reaching the intended constituency, and optimizing the use of resources. The first obstacle is defining the beneficiary group given the magnitude of needs. This process normally involves much more than a technical breakdown of the population according to particular statistical indicators. Who benefits from these special programs is the outcome of a complex interplay of pressures and competition among

---

ccountable: Activism in the South

BY FÁTIMA VIANNA MELLO

ignificant problems with the way the project is being implemented.[1]

Brazil is among the five biggest World Bank borrowers, along with China, Mexico, Indonesia and Russia. In 1994, Brazil had the most projects funded by the World Bank, and was third in total amount of loans.[2] Brazilian activists have become fed up with the lack of transparency and accountability that has resulted in socially and environmentally unsustainable projects like the Polonoroeste and Planafloro.

For many years, Brazilian organizations turned to their international allies—mainly U.S. NGOs—to stop or give a more sustainable direction to development-bank projects. Brazilian groups found it difficult to coordinate their local organizing efforts and municipal and federal governments were not open to a dialogue, leading to a reliance on Northern allies. These international alliances are still crucial. Besides putting Brazilian struggles in international context, their Northern allies feed Brazilian activists information and advocate on their behalf in Washington, D.C.

Brazilian NGOs, however, felt that Brazil lacked a domestic forum that could highlight and link up the many localized struggles taking place across the country. Various Brazilian organizations were already monitoring the development banks, and working with local populations affected by their projects. But to be effective in an immense and complex country like Brazil, activists began to realize the importance of fortifying their struggles at the national level. With a national organization, the Brazilian government and the multilateral lending institutions would be pressured on two fronts: from domestic forces in Brazil as well as from their international allies.

n March, 1995, 35 groups came together to form the Brazil Network on Multilateral Financial Institutions. So far, the Network includes development, environmental, labor, research, educational, urban, religious, cultural, and rural workers' organizations. ts main goal is to increase civil society's participation n the design, planning and implementation of development-bank projects. The organization also hopes to influence public policy by promoting a dialogue between civil society and the Brazilian government. To that end, the Network is lobbying the federal government and the National Congress to create a permanent institution that would give civil society more input into the allocation of development-bank funds.

Another central goal of the Network is to publicize and support local organizing experiences. The national media rarely cover grassroots social movements, even when they successfully derail environmentally and socially destructive projects and propose innovative alternatives. The Network intends to publish information about these local struggles and to widen public awareness more generally about the presence of multilateral lending institutions in the country. The Network also maintains an electronic conference where it posts information about its activities as well as urgent-action appeals.

At the international level, the Network has built excellent working links with the Latin American and Caribbean Network on Multilateral Banks, with focal points in Montevideo (at the Third World Network) and in Washington, D.C. (at the Bank Information Center). The Network also supports initiatives such as the 50 Years is Enough campaign in the United States, and disseminates information about these campaigns in Brazil.

The creation of the Brazil Network will hopefully contribute to the struggle to democratize multilateral lending institutions. In concert with other such movements across the globe, the Network is pushing institutions like the World Bank and the IDB to promote development strategies that work for people, not against them.■

---

1. Stephan Schwartzman, "A Sociedade Civil e os Bancos Multilaterais no Brasil: Diagnóstico e Propostas Para Discussão," Environmental Defense Fund and Instituto Socioambiental, August, 1995.

2. Henrique Barros and Michael Bailey, "Para Comprender e Dialogar com Organismos Multilaterais: Um Guia Sobre o Banco Mundial no Brasil e no Mundo," OXFAM Brazil/INESC, September, 1995.

potential beneficiary groups. In this sense, targeting is highly sensitive to struggles over income redistribution, which grow more acute as the economic crisis deepens and resources become scarcer. These programs are also used as patronage tools to create and maintain clientelistic relationships. In the same way, targeting is open to bureaucratic or political manipulation for electoral purposes.

Experience shows that it is extremely difficult to redirect resources that used to go to the middle class toward the poorest. In general, the poor exert little pressure, either because of their lack of experience or their sheer vulnerability. Moreover, it is usually middle-class professionals, not the poor, who design the projects. In Bolivia, for example, the Social Emergency Fund (FSE) did not reach the poorest Bolivians. The majority of the projects were carried out in the wealthier or relatively less-impoverished areas, since there was little demand for funding from groups in the poorest regions of the country. Targeting may in fact aggra-

Making the World Bank More Accountable: Activism in the North

In early October last year, over a thousand marchers left Dupont Circle and proceeded up Connecticut Avenue to the Washington Sheraton, site of the annual meetings of the World Bank and the International Monetary Fund (IMF), which are held in Washington, D.C. every two out of three years. While Bank/IMF meetings in Europe have often been marked by big street demonstrations, this was the first large-scale action in the United States focusing on those two multilateral lending institutions.

The march came at the end of a two-day conference on the Bank and IMF, and preceded a week of vigils, street theater, and other actions to protest the destructive impact of IMF and World Bank policies. The conference, which offered workshops and panels on issues ranging from "The Cold Reality of Hot Money" to "Struggling for Health in Unhealthy Economies," brought together over 300 U.S. solidarity and grassroots activists as well as nearly 100 activists from abroad. The conference was organized by members of the grassroots working group of the 50 Years is Enough (50YIE) campaign, while the demonstration was organized jointly with the National Commission for Democracy in Mexico.

The 1995 events were a high watermark for the 50YIE campaign. The campaign emerged in early 1994 out of discussions among six organizations with extensive experience monitoring and lobbying the Bank and the IMF: Oxfam-America, the Development GAP, Global Exchange, International Rivers Network, Friends of the Earth, and the Environmental Defense Fund. These groups wanted to take advantage of the educational, media and advocacy opportunities opened up by the fiftieth-anniversary celebrations of the founding of the World Bank and IMF.

The campaign rapidly grew to include over 140 U.S. groups, including faith-based justice and peace organizations, environmental groups, solidarity groups, and development organizations. It forged alliances with over 170 partner organizations worldwide, including more than 40 in Latin America and the Caribbean. The 50YIE campaign is the U.S. version of a broader international movement that also uses the slogan "50 Years is Enough."

Campaign members united around a set of proposals based on a five-point program: openness and full public accountability of the Bank and IMF, an participation of affected women and men in a aspects of their projects and policies; the reorienta tion of Bank and IMF economic-policy reforms t promote more equitable development; an end t environmentally destructive lending and support fo self-reliant, resource-conserving development reduction of the size and power of the two organi zations, and rechanneling of resources into othe more participatory and accountable developmen initiatives; and multilateral debt reduction.

Based upon this platform, issue-oriented workin groups drafted comprehensive background an briefing papers on different aspects of Bank and IM operations. Functional working groups then focuse on getting this information and analysis out to th media and policy makers as well as to different grass roots communities. A group of women formed gender caucus both as a response to the absence i the campaign of a clear gender-based critique o Bank and IMF policies and practices, and to ca attention to the lack of women in leadership pos tions within the organization.

Juliette Majot, a steering committee member fror the International Rivers Network, points out that key element of 50YIE's success was that it built upo the foundation of an already well-established mult lateral development-bank campaign largely com prised of Third World activists and their Washingtor based allies. A broad range of organizations—includ ing groups that view themselves as "abolitionists" a well as those that see themselves as "reformists"– united behind the campaign's radical reform ager da. This unity was based on the reputation of th founding member organizations in the broader env ronment and development community as well as o the profound restructuring envisioned in the pla form which, in effect, erased the distinction betwee radical reform and abolition. The major differenc between 50YIE and other efforts was the campaign public willingness to attack U.S. appropriations fo the Bank and IMF, a stance other advocacy group had been unwilling to take as a means of exertin pressure.

During its first year, the campaign focused on ger erating media publicity, which peaked with th 1994 Bank-IMF annual meetings held in Madrid. was able to get widespread coverage in the U.S. an foreign press of its criticisms of Bank and IMF pol

John Gershman is a research associate at the Institute for Development Research and the Institute for Health and Social Justice.

vate inequality, since targeted programs can improve the situation of one particular community while others languish in poverty. In the end, the desire to keep people who are not poor from receiving benefits often results in the exclusion of many of the poor.

Targeting frequently puts a heavy burden on women. In particular, community-based programs such as food supplements rely on the direct involvement of women. Women can gain important organizing experience by participating in these programs, which have the poten-

tial to become the basis for a truly participatory social policy. At the same time, however, they make women's workload heavier. As unpaid female labor grows, gender inequality is reinforced.[8]

But above all, the neoliberal approach to fighting poverty has proven incapable of answering a fundamental question: What does the notion of target groups mean when 60 to 80% of the population lives below the poverty line, either because of the impact of structural reform or for pre-existing or other reasons?

BY JOHN GERSHMAN

A 50 Years is Enough protest in San Francisco in October, 1995.

cies. After the Madrid meeting, media interest shifted away from the Bank and the IMF, with brief blips around the December, 1994 peso crisis in Mexico, and the appointment of investment banker James Wolfensohn as president of the World Bank in June, 1995. The campaign shifted its emphasis to grassroots education, mobilization and advocacy.

The campaign's outreach coordinator worked with local coalitions in half a dozen cities nationwide, including San Francisco, Chicago, and Burlington, Vermont. These local coalitions organized teach-ins, conferences and guerrilla theater, and developed popular-education materials and a poster series. A bimonthly letter-writing campaign on issues advanced by campaign members gave Washington lobbying efforts a grassroots base. The combination of principled unity with decentralization has, says steering committee member Juliet Majot, allowed the campaign to "shift its strategic priorities from lobbying, to media, to mobilization, depending on the situation." The October, 1995 gathering marked a convergence of the principal streams of activity: the conference reflected the campaign's outreach and education efforts; the demonstration, its grassroots mobilization; and the 24 meetings between campaign members and Bank and IMF directors, its lobbying and advocacy component.

The campaign's media visibility and policy leverage were principally due to two factors: the fiftieth anniversary, and support from a handful of Congress members including Barney Frank of Massachusetts. In the absence of the fiftieth-anniversary news hook, 50YIE has become much less successful at using the media to advance its agenda. Partly in response to the bad press generated by 50YIE, Wolfensohn has developed a much more sophisticated Bank public-relations campaign. He canceled the economically and environmentally catastrophic Arun Dam project in Nepal shortly after assuming office, and has proposed decentralizing the Bank's operations and increasing the involvement of non-governmental

organizations (NGOs) and civil society in Bank activities. As a result, the Bank has become a more complex target, to which the campaign has yet to develop a compelling response.

Historically, the U.S. Congress and the Treasury Department have been the two main channels to influence Bank and IMF policy. When the Republicans assumed the majority in Congress in October, 1994, the campaign concentrated its lobbying efforts primarily on the Treasury Department and the U.S. executive directors of the two agencies. "The capacity to convert grassroots pressure into changes at the Bank and Fund without Congress is one of the largest challenges that the campaign faces," says John Ruthrauff of the Center for Democratic Education.

The campaign is currently in the midst of a major transformation. A name change is on the agenda. 50 Years is Enough, while having gained some press recognition, has built-in obsolescence as a name. The organization also has had to grapple with its own weaknesses and limitations. Most of the campaign's efforts to date have focused on the issues most familiar to its members: the environmental damage caused by large infrastructure projects, the social and economic impacts of structural-adjustment programs, and information-transparency issues. The campaign is working to develop greater expertise about the kinds of lending increasingly favored by the Bank, such as social-sector lending and direct support to the private sector. In order to strengthen its ties with other U.S. grassroots activists, the campaign has also formed a Making the Links caucus, whose task is to develop clear analytical and activist connections between economic restructuring in the United States and abroad.

Despite the need for retooling, the campaign has had an important impact on a number of fronts. The demands of Southern groups—such as conditioning Bank and IMF appropriations on greater transparency—are now more forcefully heard in Washington, D.C. The campaign has also carved out space in the mainstream media for critical analysis of the impact of Bank and IMF operations. The fact that the World Bank felt compelled to build a more sophisticated public-relations campaign, including a ten-page response to the 50YIE platform, demonstrates that it takes the campaign seriously. And as a result of 50YIE's work, the Bank and the IMF are now firmly on the agenda of solidarity and other grassroots groups in the United States. ∎

The final basic tenet of neoliberal social policy is decentralization. Neoliberals criticize the Keynesian-Fordist model for being too centralized. They argue that decisions concerning social policy should be assumed by lower echelons of government such as provinces or municipalities, and eventually by the local organizations of the affected population and other NGOs.

Decentralization can give people a sense of the importance of working together to directly confront their problems. It encourages the development of local leadership and gives poor people training in management practices. The Orçamento Participativo—the participatory budget—under the municipal administrations controlled by the Workers' Party in Brazil is an example of a genuine decentralization of social policy. Citizens participate directly in the decision-making process both in terms of defining government policies and determining how money is spent. This experience, however, belongs to a specific political project that is completely at odds with neoliberalism.

Up to now, decentralization in the neoliberal context has focused on program implementation, not program design. This amounts to functional decentralization—also referred to as "deconcentration"—but not political decentralization. This lack of political decentralization lends credence to the hypothesis that the objective of decentralization is not the democratization of social programs and policies, but rather achieving greater efficiency from scarce resources.

Making the transition from a highly centralized system to a decentralized one is complex and takes time. This is particularly true when the centralized structures have been around for more than a century and have become part of the mindset of the actors. One of the problems facing the decentralization process—including the operative kind—is the inability of actors at the local level to assume the tasks delegated to them. Virtually overnight, for example, municipalities have found themselves responsible for providing a gamut of social services without the necessary financial, human, administrative, and material resources. This often translates into inefficiency—at least initially—in service delivery, deterioration in the quality of services, and the emergence of multiple entities that perform functions that used to be the responsibility of a single institution.

While it is true that grassroots participation in social-policy implementation is greater in local structures than in the centralized entities that were usually far away and bureaucratic, not all sectors of society get involved. Participation is the result of an array of factors that are normally absent, or exist to a lesser degree, in the neediest social groups: organizing capacity, a sense of efficacy, and basic education. Without the presence of a central state with the political will to correct inequalities, decentralization ends up leaving out the weakest social groups.

Criticism of the inefficiencies of the Keynesian-Fordist social policy points to its limitations and uneven reach, but doesn't improve the results of neoliberal social policy. Even if we evaluate neoliberal social policy only in the limited sense of combating poverty, the results after a decade of neoliberalism are meager. The majority of the poverty-alleviation programs represent a new form of relating with the poor, but this hasn't translated into a significant reduction in overall poverty.

Until now, neoliberal social programs have demonstrated their capacity only to reduce the number of people living in *extreme* poverty. Emergency employment programs, food subsidies and the like can effectively attend to extreme needs. Rising out of poverty, however, is a much more complicated process that depends on a diverse set of economic, financial, political and institutional factors that go far beyond social policies.

Simply put, neoliberalism marginalizes and expels people at a greater rate than poverty-alleviation programs can compensate.

All models of capital accumulation assume a given portion of "surplus population"—in others words, people who look for work, but don't find it.[9] Since neoliberalism privileges the financial sector of the economy over the productive one, it presumes a much larger portion of surplus population than the Keynesian-Fordist model of the past. In this context, one can expect little of neoliberal social policy, regardless of its technical merits.

Simply put, neoliberalism marginalizes and expels people at a greater rate than these programs can compensate. The case of Mexico is especially illustrative of the tension between the technical efficiency of a particular sectoral policy and the logic driving the overall economic model. While Pronasol, Salinas' poverty-alleviation program, succeeded in reducing the number of extremely poor Mexicans by 1.3 million between 1989 and 1992, the very same number of people lost jobs in the industrial sector of the economy between 1988 and 1992.[10]

This kind of juxtaposition highlights the inability of targeting to have any significant impact given the profound social inequalities that the economic system generates. In Chile in 1970, for example, only 17% of households were poor; in 1989, after almost two decades of neoliberalism and dictatorship, poor households represented 38.1%.[11] In 1995, the richest 20% of Chilean households earned 18 times the income of the poorest 20%. Chile, praised as a neoliberal success story, now has the fifth worst income distribution in the region.[12]

Overall neoliberal economic restructuring defines the possibilities and limitations of the new social policy much more than the technical limitations of the programs themselves or the "errors of the past." For example, this year Mexico will have to make more than $32 billion in payments on its debt to foreign creditors, which equals 35-40% of the total value of its exports. In such circumstances, there isn't much money left over to fight poverty or to promote social development.

The neoliberal hypothesis that economic growth ultimately generates increased employment and lessens poverty doesn't hold up against the facts. The passage from economic crisis to economic recovery in much of Latin America has not produced substantial social improvements. The increase in productivity and economic output have not generated corresponding increases in employment levels and better working conditions. Employment, when it expands, does not keep pace with population growth. Real wages remain depressed as well. The biggest surge in employment is taking place in the informal sector, which offers work that is precarious and low-paying. Of the 15.7 million jobs created in all of Latin America over the last five years, 13.6 million of those came from the informal sector.[13]

Faced with the rigidities of the free market and the bias of government policies, there is little that neoliberal social policy can accomplish with respect to legitimation of the social order either. Job insecurity, violence, urban congestion, rising common crime, and growing social inequality are products of the crisis of the 1980s and the social and economic policies adopted to confront that crisis. The economic recovery that followed the initial period of structural adjustment has left a trail of victims among small and medium-sized business owners and employees, urban wage earners, women, rural communities, and children.

Costa Rica represents an example of the positive results that can be obtained in a public welfare system when equity is genuinely valued. Direct public subsidies through health programs, education, housing, food, social security, and water and sewage infrastructure have reduced total poverty by two-thirds over the course of the 1980s.[14] Thanks to its heterodox, balanced and creative approach, Costa Rica is one of the two countries in Latin America which in that traumatic decade succeeded in reducing poverty levels, even in the countryside. The other country is Cuba.

1. Economic Commission for Latin America and the Caribbean (CEPAL), "El Perfíl de la probreza en América Latina a comienzos de los años 90," Santiago de Chile, November, 1992.
2. CEPAL, "Balance preliminar de la economía de América Latina y el Caribe," Santiago de Chile, December, 1995.
3. Externalities are the effects that the economic activity of an actor (a person, a business, government, etc.) provokes in other economic actors.
4. Carlos M. Vilas, ed., *La democratización fundamental: El populismo en América Latina* (Mexico: Consejo Nacional para la Cultura, 1995).
5. Sara Gordon, "La política social y el Programa Nacional de Solidaridad," *Revista Mexicana de Sociología*, Vol. 54, No. 2 (April, 1993), pp. 352–366.
6. Social Cabinet, Government of Nicaragua, "Estudio sobre el gasto social, 1990–1994," Managua, November, 1994; "Lineamientos de política de salud 1994–1995," Guatemalan Ministry of Public Health and Social Assistance, 1993; Organization for Health/World Health Organization, "Representación de Costa Rica, Costa Rica: Información básica," May, 1995, mimeo.
7. Government of Guatemala, "Programa Sectorial de Salud," Guatemala City, May, 1995, Annex III-I.
8. See Diane Elson, ed., Male Bias in the Development Process (Manchester: Manchester University Press, 1990); Lourdes Benería and Shelley Feldman, eds., *Unequal Burden: Economic Crises, Persistent Poverty, and Women's Work* (Boulder, CO; Westview Press, 1992).
9. This is also true of Soviet-style economies, where surplus population is usually hidden as unproductive or redundant employment.
10. Figures for the reduction of poverty are from CEPAL/INEGI, "Informe sobre la magnitud y evolución de la probreza en México, 1984–1992," Mexico City, October, 1993. Figures for the decrease in workers in the industrial sector are from *El Financiero* (Mexico City), December 13, 1995, p. 26.
11. CEPAL, *Focalización y pobreza* (Santiago de Chile: CEPAL, 1995), p. 81.
12. World Bank, *World Development Report 1995* (New York: Oxford University Press, 1995). Chile follows Brazil, Panama, Guatemala and Honduras in terms of social inequality.
13. Carlos M. Vilas, "Economic Restructuring, Neoliberal Reforms, and the Working Class in Latin America," in Sandor Habelsky and Richard Harris, eds., *Capital, Power and Inequality in Latin America* (Boulder, CO: Westview Press, 1995), pp. 137–163.
14. Marvin Taylor-Dormand, "El estado y la pobreza en Costa Rica," in *Revista de la CEPAL*, No. 43 (April, 1991), pp. 133–150.

A CRITIC'S VIEW:
CREDIT WHERE DISCREDIT IS DUE

Structural adjustment has failed in most low-income countries. And where it has succeeded, it may have been in spite of World Bank policy packages.

John Weeks

John Weeks is a professor of development economics at the Centre for Development Studies of the School of Oriental and African Studies, in London, England.

When Mexico announced in 1982 that it could no longer service its debt, it shocked the financial world. At a stroke, what had previously been viewed simply as "difficulty"—created by the pressure of Third World debt, low primary product prices and a reluctance of commercial banks to make further loans—was suddenly converted into an international crisis.

The alarm generated by the subsequent fear that major commercial banks could collapse prompted a dramatic change in the priorities of international lending agencies, from their previous emphasis on poverty reduction and equity to a fixation on debtservice. Debtservice required immediate current account surpluses, which would be achieved through import reduction and export expansion.

The method by which the current accounts of developing countries would be brought into surplus quickly became a subject of intense controversy—and still is 10 years later, as the world continues to struggle with the pros, cons and very real pains of structural adjustment.

To understand this ongoing struggle, and decide whether it is worth the suffering, a brief review of post–Second World War financial history is needed.

A FAVORABLE ENVIRONMENT

While the terms of trade for many of the non-industrialized countries declined during the first 25 years after the war, flows of private and official capital tended to offset this. The great majority of financial inflow went to non-agricultural projects, mining, manufacturing, and infrastructure. However, agriculture performed reasonably well, and the proportion of developing country population suffering from malnutrition actually declined significantly (see the FAO *Fifth World Food Survey*). Throughout the 1950s and '60s, the non-industrialized countries experienced moderate to strong growth, attributable to a great extent to the relatively favorable world economic environment. Overall, they benefited from a fairly stable world trading system of fixed exchange rates overseen by the International Monetary Fund (IMF), preferential trading agreements, and an increasing number of operative commodity agreements between producing and consuming countries.

So sustained was the growth of developing countries that, by the end of the 1960s, distribution of the gains from growth was being emphasized, even to the point of making equity considerations integral to the very definition of "economic development." Where earlier development theory tended to stress the likely positive relation between income inequality and growth (usually through the saving rate, based on the influential work of Nobel laureate W. Arthur Lewis), by the early '70s precisely the opposite view gained respectability. Inspired by innovative theoretical and empirical work, especially from the World Bank, a "basic needs" approach emerged which placed alleviation of poverty at the centre of economic policy in developing countries.

Then, just as a consensus was forming about the central importance of distribution to the development process, several shocks to the international system occurred—and dramatically altered the world economic environment. As the 1970s began, the international trading system was first shaken by the decision of the United States to suspend the fixed-price convertibility of the dollar for gold. This ushered in a new set of international rules for trade and finance based on managed, but variable currency exchange rates in the member countries of the Organization for Economic Cooperation and Development (OECD). The new rate regime proved especially problematic for developing countries, due to their economies' vulnerability to world market fluctuations, as well as their comparative lack of skilled people to take on the increased burden of economic management.

Next came the epic oil price hikes of 1973–74, which generated large trade deficits for developing countries that were dependent on oil imports.

In the wake of these initial shocks—and long before "structural adjustment" became a household term—a period of substantial policy change occurred in developing countries. One means of adjustment was the accumulation of foreign debt (both private bank and official) to finance balance-of-payments deficits. The overwhelming consensus in the '70s was that growing indebtedness posed no long-term danger; on the contrary, without indebtedness the hard currency surpluses of the oil-exporting countries wouldn't have been "recycled" into the international spending stream. Further, world inflation in the '70s resulted in buoyant primary product prices, generating optimism about the ability of the non-industrialized countries to service their debts.

The early 1980s, however, brought still further unexpected shocks for developing countries. Most serious was the severe recession in OECD member countries, which provoked a rapid drop in the world inflation rate. Somewhat differently from previous postwar downturns, the recession partly reflected the conscious policy of some industrialized countries of making control of inflation their policy priority, even at the cost of high unemployment. For the developing countries, the recession generated high real interest rates and falling primary product prices. At this point, many developing nations, especially the heavily indebted ones, found they could not service their debts and turned to crisis borrowing on terms starkly unfavorable, compared to the previous decade.

MULTILATERAL AGENCIES' ROLE

Then came Mexico's momentous 1982 announcement that it could no longer service its debt at all—and the subsequent push for current account surpluses.

Due partly to political changes in the major market economies, however, balance-of-payments adjustment became equated with policies of trade liberalization, market deregulation, fiscal austerity and privatization. These contentious policy packages unfortunately sparked debate over abstract and generalized issues of economic philosophy, rather than pragmatic discussion of policy options appropriate to each country's circumstances. Arguments focused on justifying normative judgments, rather than on the actual behavior of economies in the developing world. From the viewpoint of developing countries, the debate over adjustment appeared all the more frustrating because of the asymmetry in pressures for policy change. While governments of developing countries came under heavy external pressure to liberalize trade, the OECD countries exhibited increasingly protectionist tendencies with respect to both agricultural products and labor-intensive manufactures from the Third World.

The lead role in protecting "free market" structural adjustment packages was assumed by the IMF and World Bank. These packages involved governments agreeing to major policy changes stipulated in loan agreements, and were described by the generic term "policy-based lending." Formally, there was a strict division of labor between the IMF and the bank. IMF lending aimed at "stabilization," short-run reduction in inflation and balance-of-payments correction, while it fell to the bank to fund "structural adjustment," medium- and long-term supply-side (namely, monetarist or based on money supply) "reforms" to shift resources from domestic production to production of internationally competitive goods and services (from "non-tradeables" to "tradeables"). IMF and bank lending tended to go together, so the formal division of tasks proved difficult to distinguish in practice. By the early 1990s, almost 80 developing countries had accepted World Bank adjustment programs and many others had introduced essentially similar policy frameworks in anticipation of such funding.

While the World Bank had previously made loans with policy conditions attached to them, the scope and scale of structural adjustment lending represented a qualitative change in the institution's role (and this was even more the case for the Inter-American Development Bank which began policy-based lending somewhat later).

. . . the pros, cons and very real pains of structural adjustment

---

The rapid expansion of conditional lending by the World Bank provoked controversy on several grounds. First, critics pointed out that structural adjustment loans, unlike the bank's traditional project lending, created no assets. Countries, almost invariably already deeply in debt, incurred still further debt—but debt that was not directed at creating any productive capacity which could generate a flow of foreign exchange for debt service. As a result, a tremendous burden fell upon the policy packages: if they proved unsuccessful in increasing export capacity via indirect means (namely, market incentives), the borrowing government would find itself worse off than before it borrowed.

Second, the predicted success of the packages in stimulating exports was based on the conclusion that deregulation of markets would increase the efficiency with which resources, goods and services were allocated in the countries in question. Most economists agreed that, under carefully specified assumptions, market deregulation would have such an effect because the free market is generally seen as an efficient arbiter. However, the market does not correctly value so-called "public goods" (including social needs)—and there was no agreement that the operation of markets in each developing country actually conformed to the economists' assumptions.

Third, and more important economic theory provides little support for the view that greater allocative efficiency fosters faster growth, either of exports or national income. Indeed, critics noted a number of cases where export growth has been spectacularly successful under governments allegedly violating the rules of static allocative efficiency—the Republic of Korea being a frequently cited example. They maintained it was an empirical question as to whether increased allocative efficiency would call forth dynamic growth, and insisted that generalizations were impossible.

Fourth, some evidence suggested that policymakers should not presume that export growth would translate into rising national incomes. Latin America's experience seemed to support this criticism: according to data from the Inter-American Development Bank, its 26 Latin American and Caribbean members enjoyed export growth in current prices of five per cent per year during the 1980s, but national incomes increased barely one per cent per year in real terms over the same period (well below the population growth rate).

LOST IN CONTROVERSY

Stepping back from the heat of debate over whether the World Bank's policy packages brought improvement, the most important lesson from the '80s seems to be the great diversity of developing country experience. However, this diversity tended to be lost in the controversy over whether bank-funded programs could be judged a success.

Most attempts to evaluate the situation have tended to start by dividing all observations of the impacts of policy-based lending into categories of bank-assisted or non-bank-assisted countries. On the surface, this may seem an obvious and sensible division, but in practice it isn't.

The central issue is really whether it is the *policy packages* fostered by the World Bank—as opposed to its financing *per se*—that promote medium- and long-term recovery and growth in developing countries. The position taken by the World Bank in all its official documents is precisely to credit these policy packages. Indeed, one of the strongest critical objections has been that the bank claims too much for its policy prescriptions—crediting them with rapid, positive results and marketing them with undue optimism.

Yet many critics claim that, when structural adjustment policies are successful, it isn't due to the packages, but because bank-funded countries enjoy an inflow of capital and debt-rescheduling benefits not available to other countries. They insist that there are many sets of policies—not just those of the bank—that would not only succeed, but prove *more* effective than the bank's, if enhanced by such lending.

If one tests for the effectiveness of policies by dividing countries between those receiving bank funds and those that don't, an implicit assumption is made, namely, that the bank-funded set of countries must have implemented broadly similar policy packages. Thus, taken together, they can be treated as operating under a roughly common policy regime significantly different from those implemented by non-bank-funded countries. Yet numerous studies have shown that this is *not* the case. There is in fact considerable variation in policy regimes among bank-funded countries, and even greater variation among non-bank-funded countries. In the technical language of statistics, *the variance within groups is greater than the variance between groups*. Further, bank-supported countries differ greatly in the amount of lending they receive, the number of loans, the number and importance of conditions, and the degree to which conditions are executed as policy. The methodological problems can be summarized by saying that the population of countries receiving bank support can't be treated as synonymous with the population of countries implementing liberalization policies; the former group excludes many countries in the latter, while including many whose degree of liberalization was limited.

This fundamental methodological problem hasn't prevented studies—several by the bank itself (1988, '90 and '92)—that compare bank-supported and non-bank-supported countries across a range of economic indicators. These empirical studies have produced broadly similar results: "bank countries" tend on average to show greater export growth than "non-bank countries" and, therefore, greater improvement on the current account of their balance of payments. Trade balance improvement could be interpreted as derivative from gains in static allocative efficiency, though the benefits to the current account as a whole may result largely from debt rescheduling facilitated by the bank's seal of approval. As for increases in national income (the translation of allocative efficiency into dynamic growth), the performance of the two groups of countries proves not significantly different—which is what theory would suggest. The disappointing empirical results cast even more doubt on the effectiveness of World Bank lending if one is convinced by the argument of the critics that the bank's studies incorporate systematic biases that tend to make adjustment programs seem more successful than they actually are.

The strongest empirical result, by both bank and non-bank studies, is that investment tends to fall in countries implementing structural adjustment programs; and there is some evidence that the decline is strongest in countries that adhere most closely to bank conditions. In World Bank documents, the negative impact on investment is conceded and explained away as the result of an increased efficiency of investment. That is, increased allocative efficiency is seen as allowing less investment to generate the same or greater increases in national income. But critics dismiss this claim as unsubstantiated. They argue instead that what growth occurs is a result in reduction of idle capacity, which implies that the recovery of bank-supported countries is fuelled by temporary capital inflows and is unsustainable due to declining investment.

GENERAL LACK OF SUCCESS

A second finding common to all of the empirical studies is the general lack of success of bank programs in low-income countries, especially in sub-Saharan Africa. In terms of growth and other domestic indicators, sub-Saharan countries implementing bank programs performed worse on average than non-bank countries. So strong is the negative evidence (augmented by numerous cases in which the bank unilaterally cancelled programs in process) that in 1992 the bank's own Country Economics Department issued a study which conceded that adjustment policy had not been successful in the region.

Criticism of structural adjustment programs has not been limited to academics and such developing country organizations as the Economic Commission for Africa. In 1991, a Japanese aid agency, the Overseas Economic Cooperation Fund (OECF), issued a position paper in which it took issue with the market liberalization philosophy of the bank programs. The OECF document argued that the experience of several Asian countries, especially the Republic of Korea and Japan itself, suggested market interventions play an essential role in fostering an export-led development strategy. This is a particularly impor-

tant commentary, since Japan will probably be the single largest financial contributor to the World Bank in the 1990s.

In the mid-1980s, World Bank documents frequently referred to a "Washington Consensus" on structural adjustment, the essence of which was the market liberalization philosophy of structural adjustment programs. While it is probably too early to pass definitive judgment on the effectiveness of such programs, one can conclude that the putative consensus, if it ever prevailed, no longer does.

A positive development in the empirical assessment of adjustment programs is that recent work has tended to abandon the unsatisfactory approach of comparing bank-supported to non-bank-supported countries. Analytical work now seeks to investigate the impact of specific policy instruments independent of the funding a country may or may not receive. Hopefully, the lessons that come out of this work will help in designing more effective, appropriate policy advice for developing countries.

The catch-22 of debt

Since 1987 the IMF has received $4 billion more in debt repayments for Africa than it has provided in new finance. **Kevin Watkins** reports on the failure of will among multinational creditors to find a solution to the third world's debt problems.

When Moses relayed the word of God to the people of Israel, there was a blunt message for creditors recorded in Leviticus. "When your brother-Israelite is reduced to poverty and cannot support himself, you should assist him as you would an alien or a stranger. . . . You shall not charge him interest on a loan, either by deducting it in advance from the capital sum, or by adding it on repayment."

By contrast, the great official creditors of our age—northern governments, the World Bank and the International Monetary Fund (IMF)—have been subjecting the world's poorest countries to a debt strategy moulded solely around the interests of creditors. The result has been destroying the lives of vulnerable communities on a scale that dwarfs the casualty figures from civil wars and natural calamities.

Today, international efforts to end this destruction have reached a watershed. Last year, the Halifax summit of the Group of Seven countries called for a comprehensive solution to the debt problems of these countries, and a World Bank task force report acknowledged, for the first time, the need for multinational creditors to reduce their claims. Since then, normal service has resumed. The IMF has ruled out participation in a debt-reduction initiative, the World Bank is suffering from a schism, with senior figures uncritically endorsing the Fund's stand, western governments are gripped by a familiar combination of inertia and indifference, and Africa's governments are characteristically silent. Hopes for a breakthrough in advance of the spring meeting of the IMF and World Bank are fading fast.

The social and economic costs of failure will be inestimable. There are 32 states classified by the World Bank as severely indebted low-income countries (or SILICs), 25 of them in Africa. Collectively, these countries owe their external creditors $210 billion, or some four times more than they did in 1980. Viewed globally, the SILIC debt is the small change of the world total, representing less than 10 percent of all developing country debt. Measured in terms of ability to pay, however, it represents a massive burden. The average ratio of debt to national income in the SILICs is in excess of 110 per cent, which is higher than in Latin America at the height of the debt crisis in that region. In countries such as Uganda and Nicaragua, every man, woman and child owes the equivalent of more than six times their entire annual income.

Efforts to meet the demands of external creditors are imposing a huge strain on the world's most fragile economies. Contrary to the impression of sub-Saharan Africa as a bottomless pit for western generosity, governments in the region have been transferring in excess of $12 billion annually to western creditors. The sum represents around one-quarter of their export earnings. But even this is only part of the story, since actual repayments represent less than half of scheduled payments, so the arrears have quadrupled since 1989 to $56 billion.

Even stated in cold financial terms, the dimensions of the debt crisis facing the world's poorest countries retain the power to shock. But the human costs of that crisis defy description. Five years ago the United Nation's Children's Fund (Unicef) estimated the costs of meeting the targets for human welfare improvements agreed by governments at the 1990 World Summit for Children. These targets included reducing, by 2000, infant mortality rates by a third, lowering maternal mortality rates by a half, and providing universal primary education. For sub-Sahara Africa, it was estimated that governments would need to mobilize $9 billion to meet these targets.

Between 1990 and 1993, Zambia spent $1.3 billion in debt repayments, or 35 times what was spent on primary education.

The urgent need for such investment in Africa ought to be beyond serious dispute. By the end of the decade, more than half the region's population—300 million people—will be living in poverty. One in five African children does not live to see its fifth birthday, and, of those that do, one in two will not complete its primary education.

An international debt-reduction strategy could help to change this picture. Take the case of Uganda, with one of the world's highest maternal and infant mortality rates. According to the World Bank, it would cost around $12 per capita to provide the country with a health service capable of eradicating preventable diseases such as malaria, measles and respiratory infections, the main killers. For a country in which the government spends only $3 per person on health, that appears a huge investment. But it is considerably less than the $15

From *New Statesman & Society*, March 1, 1996, pp. 30-31. © 1996 by New Statesman & Society. Reprinted by permission.

that every Ugandan pays to the country's external creditors.

It is a similar story in Zambia, which spent over $1.3 billion in debt repayments between 1990 and 1993, or 35 times what was spent on primary education. Repayments to the IMF alone amounted to more than the combined spending of the government on primary health and primary education. This is in a country where child mortality has risen by 20 percent in the past decade.

Of course, debt relief would not translate automatically into human welfare improvements. Most governments in Africa would be more likely to invest the resulting benefits in military hardware, expensive teaching hospitals, universities or even Swiss bank accounts. But an international compact in which debt reduction was linked to increased spending on basic human needs could provide opportunities that will otherwise be lost. Debt reduction would also improve the prospects for an investment-led recovery and a reduction in aid dependence.

So, why has the SILIC debt crisis been allowed to drag on for so long? Partly because successive debt-reduction initiatives by northern governments have done little more than slow the rate at which arrears are building up; and partly because of the increasing weight of multilateral debt, owed mainly to the IMF and the World Bank. Repayments to multilateral creditors now account for about one-half of total SILIC debt repayments or some $3.3 billion in 1994. Maintaining these payments is beyond the fiscal and export capacity of the SILICs, yet in contrast to governments and commercial banks, the IMF and the World Bank have refused to contemplate debt reduction, claiming that this would jeopardise their financial integrity. The upshot is that to-

day more than 25 countries face chronic problems with multinational creditors.

Efforts to protect the "preferred creditor" status of the Bretton Woods agencies have created an increasingly bizarre financial circus, in which creditors devise ever more elaborate ways of repaying one another. In 1994, aid donors pledged $550 million for Zambia's development efforts, out of which $350 million went to repay external creditors. Prominent among these was the IMF, which since 1987 has received $4 billion more in debt repayments for Africa than it has provided in new finance. These repayments are sustained partly through the World Bank's International Development Association (IDA), in effect by transferring cheques across 19th Street in Washington. Some cheques make an even shorter circuit. Out of every $3 in IDA grants ostensibly directed toward poverty-reduction, $2 comes straight back to the World Bank as repayments on past debt.

The case against multilateral debt relief is built upon three arguments. The first, especially popular in some quarters of the World Bank, asserts that there is "no free lunch" in debt relief, since any debt-reduction initiative will have to be paid for by diverting aid. In fact, aid is already being diverted away from long-term development to multilateral creditors on a massive scale, with some $2 billion annually—or 10 per cent of total aid flows—being used for this purpose. As aid budgets decline, debt refinancing will absorb a growing share of a diminishing cake.

The second strand in this case against multilateral debt reduction is that it would erode the standing of the World Bank in the international bond markets where it raises finance, forcing it to raise interest rates and raise the cost of borrowing. Such arguments were heard *ad nauseam* from commercial banks in the 1980s, until they were forced to reduce

debt and markets responded positively. In the case of the World Bank, it is unlikely in the extreme that, even without the implicit guarantee provided by northern governments, markets would react unfavourably to an ordered reduction in its outstanding SILIC debt, which amounts to less than 3 per cent of its authorised capital. It is equally unlikely that financial markets are sufficiently myopic to imagine this debt is payable.

In fact, as an Oxfam paper published this month sought to show, it would be possible to raise new and additional debt-relief resources from within the IMF and the World Bank without any adverse implications for their financial stability. Cautious use of the World Bank's reserves and provisions against loss, the sale of IMF gold stocks and a new issue of Special Drawing Rights, the Fund's currency reserve, could mobilize $13 billion for a debt-reduction operation which, as most commercial bankers acknowledge, would barely register on international bond markets.

The third argument against multilateral debt reduction is that it will lead to what bankers euphemistically describe as "moral hazard"—a situation in which debtors fail to behave responsibly in managing their debt. That many of the governments—from Idi Amin's Uganda to Kenneth Kaunda's Zambia and Arap Moi's Kenya—that accumulated today's debt behaved irresponsibly is beyond dispute. So too is the complicity of western creditors and of multilateral institutions in pouring funds into wasteful projects and corrupt regimes. The real question, surely, is who would pay for the mistakes of the past. Morality and enlightened self-interest both demand that it should not be the poor.

Kevin Watkins is senior policy adviser, Oxfam.

Foreign Direct Investment in Developing Countries: Progress and Problems

JOEL BERGSMAN AND XIAOFANG SHEN

Joel Bergsman, *a US national, is a Manager in the Foreign Investment Advisory Service.*

Xiaofang Shen, *a Chinese national, is an Investment Policy Officer in the Foreign Investment Advisory Service.*

ANY developing countries have made notable efforts to attract foreign direct investment in the past decade. Although total flows to the developing world have exploded, they are unevenly distributed. Countries that have aggressively reformed policies have been far more successful than countries whose reforms have been half-hearted.

Foreign direct investment (FDI) is playing a growing role in economic development. FDI flows to the developing world quadrupled from an annual average of $12.6 billion in 1980–85 to $51.8 billion in 1992–93, and rose to $70 billion in 1994. Developing countries received 32 percent of total world FDI during 1992–94, up from 20 percent in the first half of the 1980s. The share of FDI in the gross capital formation of developing countries more than doubled between 1986 and 1992, surpassing 6 percent in 1993.

While FDI is surging, other forms of capital flows to developing countries are diminishing (see table). Aid has continuously declined as a share of capital inflows since the 1960s, when it was the most important source of external finance for developing countries; it now accounts for only one fourth of their capital inflows. Commercial loans, a major source of capital flows in the 1970s, have virtually disappeared since the debt crisis of the 1980s. Portfolio investment, which boomed when stock markets in developing countries caught the attention of investors in the 1980s, is important but is also volatile and risky—as demonstrated by outflows from Mexico in December 1994.

Unlike other forms of capital inflows, FDI almost always brings additional resources—technology, management know-how, and access to export markets—that are desperately needed in developing countries. Investors are exacting, however, when it comes to deciding which countries are the most desirable sites for investment, and the lion's share of FDI has been going to a handful of countries, mostly in East Asia and Latin America

(see chart). In 1994, 11 countries accounted for about 76 percent of total FDI flows to the developing world. Nevertheless, some small countries (including many island countries) have received amounts of FDI that are large in proportion to the size of their economies. But FDI flows to many other countries, particularly in sub-Saharan Africa, have stagnated.

Why East Asia and Latin America?

More and more developing countries have reduced barriers to FDI and improved their business climates. At the same time, multinational corporations are responding to increased competition by considering a broader range of locations for their facilities. These mutually reinforcing trends have combined with technological changes in communication, transportation, and production to make "the global marketplace" a reality for investment decisions. The days of producing shoddy, high-cost products for sale in local markets are passing; most foreign investors are interested only in sites where they can produce to international standards of quality and price.

This globalization means that the old distinction between export-oriented production and production destined for the local market is weakening and even disappearing. Countries that want to develop must offer good business conditions both for exporters and for production for local markets. The emphasis may differ, depending mainly on the size of the local market, but providing the combination is increasingly important. Countries in East Asia and Latin America have received the most FDI because they have adjusted their strategies to keep up with globalization.

Some of these countries initially based their development on exporting labor-intensive manufactured goods to the industrial countries. Recently, many have recognized that technological advances and intensified competition have increased the capital and skill intensity of production in many industries. This means that countries can no longer count on low labor costs alone but also need high-quality, productive labor to sustain their comparative advantages. Those that have succeeded in attracting FDI have focused on improving general education, industrial skill training, and labor and managerial discipline. Facilitating companies' efforts to upgrade technology has also been crucial in maintaining their competitive edge.

The development of other successful countries was initially based on import-substituting industrialization. This strategy produced valuable skills, institutions, and physical infrastructure, but was inherently limited because of small domestic markets and the inefficiencies caused by continuing protection. These countries were either forced by economic crises or inspired by countries that succeeded through more outward-looking policies to reduce protection, privatize state enterprises, and make their productive apparatus competitive internationally.

Whatever route they took, the rapid, sustained economic growth of the successful countries of East Asia and Latin America has earned them the name "emerging markets." They are even beginning to rival the industrial countries as export markets because of strong, consistent increases in the demand for consumer goods and services. All this has made them extremely attractive to international investors.

Companies interested in establishing facilities in emerging markets need access to quality supplies of parts, components, and supporting services. For manufacturing industries, especially, a major force driving success is a "flexible" system of intercorporate relations under which companies specialize in different stages of production, either

upstream or downstream in a production chain, and cooperate closely with each other through networking and long-term buyer-supplier relationships. This type of system helps integrate foreign investment into host economies and allows the latter to derive more benefit from FDI through induced economic activities, the transfer of technology and management skills, and better access to export markets. But companies need great flexibility and highly developed skills to ensure "just-in-time" delivery of quality intermediate goods and services, without defects. Countries that have the conditions that facilitate these kinds of operations have become much more competitive in the eyes of foreign investors.

None of the countries that have attracted significant FDI inflows could have done so without sustained trade reform enabling them to keep up with the pressure of international competition. All have carried out substantial domestic economic reforms to encourage private sector development. Many have essentially succeeded in stabilizing the macroeconomic environment, reducing price distortions, deregulating investment procedures, and increasing general economic efficiency—getting the "fundamentals" right for *all* private investment, domestic and foreign.

What about other countries?

Many other developing countries have also embarked on reforms, addressing the same issues—fiscal and monetary imbalances, price distortions, bloated public enterprises, and unnecessary regulations, among others. Many have made significant progress, winning deserved praise from economists, banks, and international institutions, including the World Bank and the IMF. But FDI has either not appeared or, if it has, still falls short of the amount desired. What is wrong?

One basic problem is that some countries possess few attractions for foreign investors. One traditional attraction of developing countries—cheap labor—is becoming less important in investment decisions. Economies at an early stage of industrialization do not offer the sophisticated providers of inputs—both goods and business services—that most foreign investors need to be competitive. Another factor that deters investment is poor economic performance—FDI tends to follow growth, not to lead it.

A closer look at the less successful countries, however, reveals that many that are potentially attractive to FDI simply have not carried their reforms far enough. Foreign investors do not come just because *some* progress has been made; to attract FDI, countries must have made enough progress to meet worldwide best-practice standards.

Obstacles to entry. Many countries have liberalized entry policies over the past few years. They have relaxed restrictions on foreign ownership and entry in certain sectors, and they have also introduced "negative lists"

Selected capital flows to developing countries
(million 1993 dollars)

	1960s	1970s	1980s	1991	1992	1993
Net foreign direct investment	304	3,024	12,988	34,475	44,868	63,999
Portfolio investment	13	423	3,353	17,505	24,250	86,569
Net commercial bank lending	384	9,839	11,791	1,892	14,541	5,482
Grants and official debt flows	1,466	9,854	34,366	59,301	47,383	52,336
Total	**2,167**	**23,140**	**62,498**	**113,173**	**131,042**	**208,386**

Sources: IMF, *Balance of Payments Statistics Yearbook*, various years; and World Bank, *World Debt Tables*, various years.
Note: Figures for the 1960s, 1970s, and 1980s represent the annual averages for those decades.

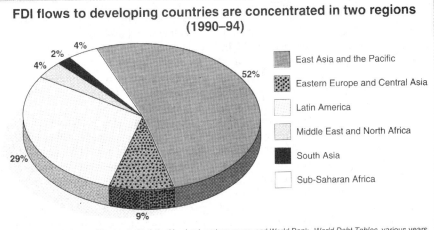

FDI flows to developing countries are concentrated in two regions
(1990–94)

- East Asia and the Pacific — 52%
- Eastern Europe and Central Asia
- Latin America — 29%
- Middle East and North Africa — 4%
- South Asia — 9%
- Sub-Saharan Africa — 2%, 4%

Sources: IMF, *Balance of Payments Statistics Yearbook*, various years; and World Bank, *World Debt Tables*, various years.

to limit the types of investments that require screening and approval. In many countries, however, entry is still needlessly restricted and/or arbitrarily regulated—often because of pressure from domestic interest groups or from regulatory authorities with vested interests in screening.

Inadequate legal protection. Most governments have recognized the need for investment protection, and many have guaranteed equal treatment for foreign and national investments. An increasing number of countries have enacted laws forbidding expropriation or guaranteeing prompt and adequate compensation in the event of expropriation. In more and more countries, foreign investors have recourse to international arbitration for settling investment disputes.

Legal reforms are still far from adequate in most countries, however. In many cases, laws still implicitly allow expropriation of investors' property for arbitrary reasons. The very poor functioning of judicial systems in many countries calls into question the "prompt and adequate compensation" promised by law. Finally, investors are often required to exhaust domestic means for settling disputes before resorting to international arbitration. In the context of a weak domestic court system, this dramatically weakens investors' confidence.

Overvaluation and restricted access to hard currencies. Since the late 1980s, a growing number of developing countries have taken steps to liberalize their foreign exchange systems. Many have devalued their currencies, and some have allowed market determination of the exchange rate. In spite of considerable adjustments, however, many currencies are still overvalued, and extensive controls on exchange transactions are still seen as necessary. Moreover, foreign exchange liberalization in many countries has been accomplished by decree but not followed up by appropriate legislative steps, creating an atmosphere of uncertainty for investors.

Trade barriers. In the past, many developing countries that had adopted an import-substitution strategy attracted FDI by offering investors a protected domestic market. Recognizing the importance of competing in global markets, most have now reduced protection and taken steps to promote exports. In too many instances, however, trade reforms have still not gone far enough. Some countries have reduced protection significantly, but still have too much to foster real competition at home or to provide an exchange rate that is conducive to exports. There is also a widespread problem in the developing world with customs services. Better trade policies may be negated by bureaucratic customs pro-

cedures and the obstructionist attitude of customs agents. Thus, imported capital equipment and other inputs do not arrive at production sites on time; drawback payments due to exporters are delayed for months or even years; and going through the multilayered clearance process is very costly.

Tax distortions. To attract foreign investment, some countries use special investment incentives, including tax holidays, tax credits and exemptions, and reduction of duties. However, experience shows that such strategies have had little, if any, impact on most long-term investors. Tax holidays create distortions of tax regimes; they favor new investors and discriminate against existing ones—in some countries, they discriminate against domestic investors. The expiration of tax holidays causes sudden increases in tax burdens on companies. Moreover, these incentives are often granted through complex and bureaucratic administrative procedures that encourage corruption. A stable, automatic tax system with reasonable rates and without discretionary incentives is better both for investors and for the host country. Many countries have a long way to go to reach that goal.

Getting the word out. Investment promotion—persuading investors to come—has become widespread in recent years. More countries, however, need to have a carefully planned program of making the improvements achieved at home known to the world—not so much through expensive advertising supplements but rather through sophisticated, long-term public relations campaigns. Providing effective assistance to interested investors and businesslike follow-up, and helping existing investors to solve administrative problems are important parts of promotion that are too often neglected.

Role of governments

For many countries that have not achieved the expected results, the problem is that reforms have been inadequate. Governments need to persevere with reforms already under way. Intensified global competition has put companies under greater pressure, and they are responding by investing only in the most favorable places. Countries should take this as a challenge rather than a threat if they want to win the battle for FDI.

Furthermore, policy liberalization alone may not increase competitiveness sufficiently. Economic opening is the necessary "stick" to force competition and shift resources to their most productive uses. Experience in many countries suggests that "carrots"—public support of efforts to make firms more efficient—are also urgently needed. For example, now that international investors have

begun to be more interested in high productivity than in low labor costs, government assistance is needed to upgrade technology and labor skills. Access to information and technical services, general education, and specialized industrial and managerial training are more important than ever.

"Public support" does not mean, however, that governments should do, or even pay, for it all. To the contrary, many of the support services required by industries are best delivered by private institutions. Foreign investors themselves can provide assistance, motivated by their own business interests. Private companies not only benefit from such a supporting system but also can play a crucial role in the design and operation of it, and they must bear at least part of the cost.

The role of governments is thus becoming more complex. Governments can no longer act simply as monopolies providing certain services or goods, or even simply as regulators; their functions must include those of organizer, coordinator, assistant, and partner. To succeed, governments will need to change their orientation and acquire new skills. Commitment, creativity, and willingness to learn from mistakes are crucial assets that can lead to success.

The Foreign Investment Advisory Service

This article is based, in part, on the experience of the Foreign Investment Advisory Service (FIAS). Created ten years ago by the International Finance Corporation (IFC), FIAS is now jointly operated by IFC and the World Bank. Its mission is to help governments of developing countries to attract foreign direct investment through improved policies, sensible deregulation, and more effective institutions.

Governments that request FIAS's help get frank and confidential analysis of the problems that concern them. FIAS's advice reflects the experience of other countries but also takes into account the political and administrative realities of the client. FIAS works informally and closely with client countries to build relationships of trust and understanding with them. By now, FIAS's clients number about 90, including developing countries all over the world, as well as transition countries in Eastern Europe and the former Soviet Union.

Clients pay part of the costs of FIAS's advisory work. The rest of FIAS's expenses are underwritten by IFC and the World Bank, and by donations from the United Nations Development Program and individual industrial countries.

The Barefoot Bank With Cheek

*The Grameen Bank, in Bangladesh, which
makes small loans to some of the poorest people on
earth, has become a model for economic
developers all over the world*

David Bornstein

*David Bornstein, a journalist, spent three
years doing research on the Grameen
Bank for his book* The Price of a Dream:
The Story of the Grameen Bank, *published by Simon & Schuster (1996).*

BUSES and trucks barrel down
Mirpur Road, in Dhaka, Bangladesh, blasting their horns and
leaving trails of black smoke to settle on
rickshaws and oxcarts. By the side of
the road a high brick wall encircles four
buildings in a compound, one of which is
dominated by a tropical garden that opens
to the sky. On many afternoons rain falls
into the garden, and at their desks accountants can pause to listen to the sound
of water slapping leaves. This is the
head office of a bank that does its work
in the countryside.

Thousands of visitors have traveled to
Bangladesh to learn from this bank, and
many arrive carrying tape recorders and
note pads. When they enter the office,
they find no receptionist, no carpets, no
elevators, and few telephones. The rooms
are equipped with ceiling fans, manual
typewriters, paperweights, and stacks of
ledgers. Only the computer room, on the
fifth floor, is air-conditioned. Here programmers monitor operations and prepare reports, which they love to fill with

wild-looking graphs depicting their organization's growth.

The graphs all look basically the
same: like ski hills, rising slowly at first,
and then shooting up at impossibly steep
angles toward the sky.

For two decades the Grameen ("Village") Bank has been extending small
loans for self-employment purposes to
some of the poorest people on earth—
landless women in Bangladesh—and its
financial performance has never been
stronger. The bank's founder, the Bangladeshi economist Muhammad Yunus,
continues to win international honors—
the 1992 King Baudouin Development
Prize, the 1993 CARE Humanitarian
Award for Development, the 1994 World
Food Prize—but his bank is hardly a one-
man show. Grameen's loans are administered by more than 10,000 university and
high school graduates scattered throughout Bangladesh—no small organizational
feat in a country notorious for corruption
and mismanagement, a country that since
its birth, in 1971, has absorbed more than
$25 billion in foreign aid and seen the
majority of its citizens grow poorer.

The Grameen Bank, once dubbed the
"barefoot bahk," can no longer be described in quaint terms. With more than
1,050 branch offices that serve 35,000
villages and two million customers, 94
percent of them women, Grameen is the
largest rural lender in Bangladesh, and
the proportion of its loans that are repaid,
97 percent, is comparable to the repay-

ment rate at Chase Manhattan Bank. Last
year, after eighteen years of making small
loans, Grameen had disbursed more than
$1 billion; at the present rate the bank
will cross the $2 billion mark sometime
next year. "It's like McDonald's," Yunus
says. "People know the quality of our
service. Our job at head office is to make
sure it doesn't deteriorate in any corner
of the country."

Given that Grameen's banking system
is based on trust and mutual accountability, that is quite a task. To qualify for a
loan, a villager must demonstrate that her
family assets fall *below* the bank's threshold. She will not be required to put up
collateral; instead she must join a five-
member group and a forty-member center and attend a meeting every week, and
she must assume responsibility for the
loans of her group's members. This is
crucial, because it is the group—not the
bank—that initially evaluates loan proposals. Defaulters spoil things for everybody else, so group members choose
their partners wisely. If all five repay their
loans promptly, each is guaranteed access
to credit for the rest of her life—or as
long as she elects to remain a customer.
In this fashion Grameen is faithful to the
Latin from which "credit" derives: *credere*
—"to believe."

"The myth that credit is the privilege
of a few fortunate people needs to be exploded," Yunus explains. "You look at
the tiniest village, and the tiniest person
in that village: a very capable person, a

From *The Atlantic Monthly,* December 1995, pp. 40-47. © 1995 by David Bornstein. Reprinted by permission of Mildred
Marmur Associates, Ltd.

very intelligent person. You have only to create the proper environment to support these people so that they can change their own lives."

Pure idealism? Well, yes. Nonetheless, these words come from a man who has designed a bank that forces its borrowers to save money for emergencies, provides them with benefits in the event of death, and is in the process of instituting a village-based health-care and insurance program, which will be self-financing. Today, against the backdrop of two and a half decades of often-wasted international aid, Grameen's entrepreneurial approach stands out as singularly effective and sustainable. Up to 1994 the bank had revolved its loan capital more than five times. Along the way it helped millions of villagers to move from one or two meals a day to three, from one or two sets of clothing to three or four. Grameen members have borrowed money to pay for their children's education, to buy medicine, to build houses, to accumulate assets for old age, and—like the peddler Oirashibala Dhor—to pay for their daughters' weddings.

INSIDE, the mud walls were smooth to the touch. Above a table hung a framed birth certificate and a political-campaign poster featuring the party's logo—a riverboat. Another wall was decorated with yellowed pages from *USA Today*.

Oirashibala Dhor set her basket on the ground beside my translator. She appeared to be constructed entirely of angles—knees and elbows jutting sharply from beneath her plain white sari. Her hair was silver, her brow deeply creased, and she had only half her teeth. She was born, as she put it, "before the British-Japanese war of 1943."

Whispers could be heard from behind a bamboo screen. Two young sisters and an older woman emerged, and were joined by several neighbors and their children. Oirashi, as everyone calls her, took up a red capsule from her basket. "Lip gloss," she announced. "You put this over lipstick, your lips shine."

"How much is the lip gloss?" a young girl asked. "Give it to me for six takas."

Another girl, browsing through Oirashi's basket, inquired, "How much is this hair clip?"

"Don't be so extravagant," her mother said.

The girl dropped the hair clip and picked up a jar of Fair and Lovely beauty cream, which promised "noticeably fairer" skin in six to eight weeks.

"That's for older people," Oirashi said. She selected a glass bangle, polished it with her sari, and asked the girl if she liked the color. The girl nodded. Oirashi requested soap and water. She wet the girl's tiny wrist and then squeezed and twisted until the bangle slid on. The girl extended her arm to show her mother. Children at the door pressed forward to see.

"Stop blocking the door," an older woman yelled. "Let the breeze in."

"Nowadays children are so disrespectful."

"Please give me the lip gloss for three takas less," the first girl said, her final plea.

"Don't kill me," Oirashi replied.

Oirashi has been supporting herself and her two daughters since the death of her husband, twenty-five years ago. "He died of frozen Satan's gout," she told me on my recent visit to her village. "Nowadays the doctors call it pneumonia." Every morning except Sunday, when her Grameen Bank meeting is scheduled, she gets up with the sun, offers a prayer, places her basket on her head, and sets out to sell her wares. She walks for miles. Though she sells sandals, she never wears them. I asked her why.

"I'm just a simple peddler," she replied. "How can I be seen wearing sandals?"

As Oirashi walked along the narrow partitions separating rice plots, she drummed on her thighs. I asked about the basket balanced on her head. "It's not heavy," she replied. We approached a cluster of huts situated atop a mud plateau that rose four feet above the bristling green field. "Those are all Grameen Bank house loans," she explained. "All the old houses were washed away in the [1991] cyclone."

Several women waved. "These women have become a lot braver because of the Grameen Bank," Oirashi said. "Previously, if any strange man came, they would go into their houses and sit behind the purdah" (literally, "veil"; figuratively, the Muslim code of conduct that confines women to their homesteads). "Now they come out and they talk."

The bank's repayment rate, 97 percent, is comparable to that of Chase Manhattan Bank.

Oirashi passed by one woman who called her over. "I'll only come if you cook me a hen," Oirashi joked. She had no time to waste with nonbuyers, she said. "People take a lot of time picking and choosing from my basket. If I could go to more places, I'd be rich."

Oirashi's overriding concern is finding a husband for her second daughter, who is in her mid-twenties and still unmarried. In Bangladesh daughters usually move in with the families of their husbands after marriage. Oirashi's first daughter lives ten miles away. But Oirashi doesn't want to be left alone in her old age. This time she is looking for a *ghor jamai*: a son-in-law who agrees to live in his mother-in-law's house. Finding one is not easy; most men look down on the idea. Oirashi knows that if her plan has a hope, she must sweeten the pot. She will have to come up with a sizable dowry and expand her house.

"When I have all the jewelry and money," she explained, "then I will tell my elder daughter and her husband to find a boy. After they have found one, I will go and see for myself. If I like him, then the wedding will take place."

"Will you ask your daughter's consent?" I asked.

"Of course," Oirashi said. "Is this my marriage?"

The wedding (dowry included) will cost more than 15,000 takas (about $375). For many villagers such a sum represents two or three years' income. Oirashi has been working to save it for the better part of a decade. Fortunately, in the past few years her peddling sales have increased. Oirashi often sells on credit, but when she buys merchandise in the bazaars, she does better to pay cash. Cash flow had always been her major business constraint. To overcome it, Oirashi joined the Grameen Bank. In six years her annual borrowing increased from about $60.00 to about

$260. Each loan was for one year, payable in fifty equal weekly installments, with annual interest of 20 percent (calculated on a declining principal) due in the last two weeks. After her house was destroyed in the cyclone, Oirashi also assumed a $375 long-term mortgage, at eight percent interest, to rebuild it.

Like all retailers, with cash in hand she found herself in a stronger position. She could haggle with vendors over price, stock higher-quality merchandise, and take advantage of volume discounts. Before the Grameen Bank came along, Oirashi borrowed from moneylenders, whose interest rates ranged from 10 to 20 percent a month. "Now I always buy with cash," Oirashi explained. "Look—I do my business for profit."

FOR the thousands of men and women who staff the Grameen Bank, the story of their organization's birth has the resonance of myth. One afternoon in 1976 Muhammad Yunus was taking a walk in a village a mile from Chittagong University, where he was the head of the Department of Economics, when he encountered a woman weaving bamboo stools.

Yunus had returned to Bangladesh in 1972, after the country had become independent. Prior to that he had spent seven years in Nashville, Tennessee, completing a Ph.D. at Vanderbilt University. Yunus had been influenced by the student activism of the late 1960s, especially the civil-rights movement, and the message he carried home was that it was possible for young people to change society. As a professor of economics in Bangladesh, he asked his students if, for all their knowledge of equations and formulas, they really knew how 90 percent of the people in their country lived. He challenged them to close their textbooks and get involved with local villagers, and for four years he spent his afternoons with them in villages, studying the informal economy, organizing immunization programs, and helping local farmers to grow more food.

Yunus had never met Sufiya Khatun on his many walks through her village. Sufiya, a widow, was trying to support herself by constructing and selling bamboo stools. She earned two cents a day. When Yunus asked why her profit was so low, she explained that the only person

who would lend her money to buy bamboo was the trader who bought her final product—and the price he set barely covered her costs.

Yunus's instinct was to dig into his pocket. But first he wanted to see if there were other villagers in similar circumstances. He and a few students canvassed the village and compiled a list of forty-two people whose capital requirements, in order to buy materials and work freely, added up to about $26.00.

Through the years he would recount that story hundreds of times. A decade later, testifying before the U.S. Congress Select Committee on Hunger in a hearing devoted to micro-enterprise credit, he recalled what had gone through his mind: "I felt extremely ashamed of myself being part of a society that could not provide twenty-six dollars to forty-two able, skilled human beings who were trying to make a living."

He gave his graduate students the money and instructed them to distribute it to the villagers. He arranged for the loans to be repaid in small installments at a local tea stall. A short time later he felt dissatisfied. "They couldn't come to me every time they needed money," he said. Where should villagers be able to go when they needed a loan?

Yunus paid a visit to the manager of a local bank. "He gave me a big laugh," he recalls. "He said the amounts were not worth the paperwork." Most of the villagers were illiterate, the manager explained, and they had nothing to offer as collateral. No bank lent money to people without collateral.

Two years later, with his graduate students, Yunus established the first branch of the Grameen Bank. Conscious of the dismal performance of credit cooperatives in Bangladesh, he resolved to be different on three counts: First, the loans were to be repaid, and on time. Second, only the poorest villagers—the landless—were eligible. Third, he would make an effort to lend money primarily to women, who were socially, as well as economically, impoverished.

With support from the Bangladesh Bank, the Ford Foundation, and the International Fund for Agricultural Development (IFAD), an aid organization created by the United Nations, Grameen was

Once it was popular enough to surmount religious opposition, the bank made loans almost entirely to women.

by 1983 an independent bank operating eighty-six branches and serving 58,000 clients. As it grew popular enough to surmount religious opposition, the bank began providing loans almost exclusively to women. "When a woman brings in income," Yunus explains, "the immediate beneficiaries are her children."

The following year, after years of development washouts, foreign donors began taking Yunus very seriously. In 1984–1985 IFAD, Ford, and the governments of Norway and Sweden stepped in with $38 million in low-cost loans. By 1988 Grameen had 501 branches and 490,000 borrowers. In 1989 Canada and Germany joined the team of donors, and the bank received an additional $87 million. In 1992 Grameen opened its thousandth branch office. It also raised credit ceilings and introduced various new kinds of loans intended to boost revenues. In the past three years disbursements have soared to $40 million a *month,* with only a marginal increase in staff. Grameen has moved, as one manager puts it, "from Mach one to Mach two."

TYPICALLY, Americans are reluctant to look to other countries for help with their social problems. Think of health care. However, as the current political debate rages over how big government should be, Grameen's experiences are more relevant to the United States than ever before. The Grameen Bank has received praise from U.S. commentators and policymakers on both the left and the right. Being Bangladeshi, it has the advantage of being seen as a perennial underdog. And, no doubt, the bank speaks to something at the core of the American ideal: what Ralph Waldo Emerson called "the heroism and grandeur which belong to acts of self-reliance."

Grameen is a political chameleon: it has the ability to affirm beliefs that both conservatives and liberals hold dear. From the right Grameen can be seen as an entrepreneurial institution that makes the case for less government; from the left it appears to be an enlightened social-welfare program that argues for the value of government involvement. Some see Grameen as an example of reinvented government. Muhammad Yunus disagrees. He sees his bank as an example of reinvented capitalism. In fact, he calls it a "socially conscious capitalist enterprise."

Consider: the Grameen Bank charges interest four points above the commercial rate. It never forgives loans, not even after a flood or a cyclone, although it restructures them when necessary. It provides no free services to its borrowers, charging fees even when it distributes such essential items as water-purification crystals, vegetable seeds, and iodized salt. Although the bank has received tens of millions of dollars in grants and low-cost loans from foreign governments, it remains a private enterprise, with 90 percent of its shares controlled by its two million borrowers. For all its efforts to contain costs, Grameen remains committed to a clientele that is inherently expensive to serve—a clientele that in the absence of an ethical imperative would probably never have been discovered by the free market.

Today Grameen's annual report lists more than 400 different kinds of businesses initiated by borrowers, who husk rice or make ice-cream sticks, trade in brass or repair radios, process mustard oil or cultivate jackfruit. For each activity the bank lists the number and amounts of loans disbursed. It would be a commercial banker's nightmare.

As a rule, the statistics on which Grameen prides itself most—volume of customers and disbursements—do not excite bankers. Two million small, short-term loans are much more expensive to manage than a few big, long-term loans. Bankers care about the costs and revenues associated with a loan portfolio. But in this area Grameen is also fast gathering strength. The bank's operating income jumped from $19 million in 1992 to almost $50 million in 1994, and is expected to exceed $60 million this year. In five of the past seven years Grameen has reported small profits, which are reinvested in its revolving loan fund; however, analysts are quick to point out that those profits are

not "real," because the bank has received its funding at concessionary rates.

But recently Grameen has taken a number of decisions to demonstrate that it is serious about being seen as a capitalist enterprise: It has declined donor funds in favor of $150 million in loans at the bank rate from the Bangladesh Bank, and in the past two years has raised $125 million through bond issues. Despite much higher interest expenses, Grameen continues to report profits. The bank has begun providing an early-retirement option for older employees, to cut salaries; and, to reduce overhead further, it is testing computers in branches with access to electricity. As borrowers mature, they become more stable and their demand for credit increases. Down the road, if Grameen can shift from weekly to, say, bi-weekly installments and still maintain its rate of loan repayment, administrative costs will drop by a third without affecting revenues.

Laissez-faire or interventionist? Either way, Grameen is a performer—which is why, this past July, the World Bank broke with its tradition of financing primarily large-scale infrastructure-development projects by launching a drive to raise more than $200 million for Grameen-style lending, and why, over the past few years, many Americans have attempted to tackle poverty in the United States in similar ways. Part of a movement some call the "first Third World technology transfer," the Association for Enterprise Opportunity, a network of micro-enterprise development organizations established in 1991, lists 400 members across the country. Yunus is excited by the spread of these programs. "If the United States becomes convinced that poverty can be eliminated," he told me, "then it can be done."

But given the canyon of cultural and economic differences separating the two countries, the technology transfer poses difficulties. To begin with, Bangladesh has a long tradition of self-employment. By comparison, very few Americans—not even one in ten—work for themselves, and low-income Americans who wish to be self-employed typically require training, technical assistance, and, perhaps most important, access to business networks along with credit.

One of the veteran micro-enterprise programs in the United States, begun in 1986, is the Women's Self-Employment Project, in Chicago. WSEP has extended close to $1 million in loans to more than 300 businesses and has offered business-counseling services to 5,000 women. Its repayment rate is 93 percent. Mary Houghton, the president of Shorebank Corporation, which oversees the project, believes that WSEP has demonstrated that there is "a big market in Chicago for self-employment among single women who are either very low-income or on welfare." Micro-bankers have yet to develop a systematic, self-sustaining methodology for turning low-income Americans into successful businesspeople, she told me recently, "but they've discovered a fair number of ways by which people can add to their incomes by two or five or ten thousand dollars a year."

Because of the high cost of training and the low disbursements, to date no micro-enterprise lender in the United States has come close to breaking even, and only a handful have more than a few hundred borrowers. The people running these programs prefer to avoid comparisons with the Grameen Bank; many have abandoned the hope of achieving financial self-sufficiency. Instead they defend their program costs by framing the issue in terms of social justice, arguing that every American, rich or poor, should be entitled to a limited quantity of resources on loan, at the commercial rate or higher, provided that he or she demonstrates commitment, a desire to work, and what appears to be a viable business plan.

An attractive idea—but is it politically feasible? One of those who think not is Jeffrey Ashe, the director of Working Capital, based in Cambridge, Massachusetts. Ashe worked in micro-enterprise in South America, Africa, and Asia for more than a decade before he founded Working Capital, in late 1990, to provide group-based support, credit, training, and technical assistance to low-income people throughout New England. Unlike the Grameen Bank and other micro-enterprise programs, Working Capital does not target the poorest of the poor. Its market, best described as "the entrepreneurial poor," is made up of people already involved in income-generating activities who lack access to financial resources and other support services. However, like Yunus, Ashe does not attempt to turn poor people into entrepreneurs; he supports people who are already entrepreneurs, or at least show promising signs of soon becoming entrepreneurs. In this sense he is, in his approach, closer to Yunus's pragmatic spirit than are micro-lenders who target poorer clients. Writing in the July, 1994, issue of *The Atlantic Monthly,* Amitai Etzioni argued that it is "wise policy" for social programs to seek early success by starting with a "realistic notion of human transformation"—in this case, not expecting poor people just to go out and start viable businesses. Ashe agrees. In five years Working Capital has extended $1.5 million in loans, of amounts ranging from $500 to $5,000, to more than 1,100 businesses; its repayment rate is 98 percent.

Ashe is unique among his colleagues in his determination to demonstrate that it is possible to be a banker for poor Americans and still cover costs. "Almost everybody has rejected this out of hand," he told me recently. "But the truth is, for these programs to reach any appreciable scale, we have to show that they can be self-sustaining. And if we can prove that, we can blow this whole movement to another level."

"I figure that micro-enterprise in this country has a window of opportunity for the next four or five years," he added. "Right now there's interest among funders, but already major questions about cost-effectiveness are being raised."

Ashe has plans to franchise his operation, to support as many as 4,000 businesses by the end of 1997, and has started franchises in Delaware and South Miami. His cost per borrower continues to drop; it is somewhere between 10 and 20 percent of the cost in other programs; and he is looking for new ways to increase revenues, including raising the loan ceiling to $10,000 and charging membership fees to groups. He projects that with an investment today of $5 million over five years, Working Capital could generate $60 million in new jobs by the end of the sixth year and could break even in the seventh year.

"People latch on to the concept of micro-enterprise pretty fast," Ashe said, "but the trick is actually designing a structure that will produce sustainable results. More and more, as I slog through this on a day-to-day basis, I appreciate what Yunus has accomplished."

Conflict and Instability

Conflict and instability have frequently characterized the developing world. During the cold war, many observers traced this conflict and instability to the ideological struggle between East and West. Despite the end of the cold war, however, these twin problems persist throughout the developing world. Their persistence drives home a point that those who viewed international politics from a purely ideological perspective often overlooked: the sources of conflict and instability were deeper, more varied, and much more complicated than simply a struggle between communism and capitalism. Whatever the causes, conflict and instability in developing countries remain a major threat to global peace and security.

Conflict and instability stem from a combination of sources. Among these are ethnic and religious diversity, nationalism, the struggle for state control, and the cold war legacy. In many cases, boundaries that date from the colonial era encompass diverse groups. Their diversity can increase tension among groups competing for scarce resources and opportunities. Where some groups benefit or are perceived as enjoying privileges at the expense of others, ethnicity can offer a convenient vehicle around which to organize and mobilize. Moreover, ethnic politics lends itself to manipulation both by regimes seeking to protect privileges, maintain order, or retain power and by those challenging existing governments. The situations in Nigeria, Rwanda, and Burundi demonstrate the desire to wield power and the influence of ethnicity. In such a politically and ethnically charged atmosphere, conflict and instability often result, as groups vie to gain control of a state apparatus that can extract resources and allocate benefits. Even ethnic homogeneity is no guarantee against disorder, however, as Somalia illustrates. The fighting there that led to the breakdown of civic order and to international intervention was based on rival clan affiliations among ethnically homogenous Somalis.

Early literature on modernization and development speculated that as developing societies progressed from traditional to modern, primary attachments such as ethnicity and religious affiliation would fade and be replaced by new forms of organization. Clearly, however, ethnicity remains a potent force, as does religion. Ethnic politics and the resurgence of religious fundamentalism demonstrate that such attachments have survived the drive toward modernization.

Islamists are active throughout the Middle East, Africa, and Asia. Rejecting secularism and vehemently anti-Western, these fundamentalists seek to install governments based on Islamic law. Inspired and encouraged by the theocratic regime in Iran, Islamists are challenging a number of governments, particularly in the Middle East. For many in the West, this resurgence of Islam, perceived as anti-Western and intolerant, looms as possible successor to the communist threat. The 1993 World Trade Center bombing and the plot to bomb other targets in New York by Islamic radicals elevated the threat from regional to international. While this Islamic movement certainly represents a serious challenge to some governments, it is far from unified. Instead, there are different strands of Islamic thought lumped under the fundamentalist category. Moreover, while these movements may reflect a disillusionment with Western cultural influences, they often represent the only way to challenge authoritarian regimes. On the positive side, Islam may contribute to the restoration of order in countries like Somalia.

India has recently experienced a resurgence of Hindu nationalism. Violence erupted between Hindus and Muslims after a Hindu mob destroyed a mosque in Ayodhya in December 1992. Separatist movements in Punjab and Kashmir have contributed to this resurgent Hindu nationalism and have increased tensions between India and Pakistan. India's internal politics have been further complicated by the rise of the Hindu nationalist Bharatiya Janata Party (BJP) and by efforts of lower castes to gain more political power.

In the Middle East, many factors contributing to conflict and instability come together, resulting in a complex and tense situation. In 1993, Israel and the Palestine Liberation Organization (PLO) signed an agreement to grant limited autonomy to Palestinians in the Gaza Strip and the West Bank town of Jericho. The opposition of hard-line elements within the PLO complicates the implementation of the agreement. The influence of hard-liners in Israel who reject a land-for-peace deal was strengthened by the recent election of Benjamin Netanyahu as prime minister. Regional instability resulting from Islamic fundamentalism and intra-Arab struggles also remains a distinct possibility. For instance, a gap between rich and poor Arabs emerged during the Persian Gulf War, as haves and have-nots lined up on different sides of the war. With progress on the Palestinian issue, other potential conflicts such as the gap between rich and poor or the struggle for water rights may become more prominent. Indeed, there seem to be more areas of disagreement than agreement throughout the region.

Conflicts may also stem from the domination of indigenous peoples by outsiders. Indonesia's treatment of the inhabitants of Irian Jaya and its exploitation of the region's resources have sharpened tensions there.

The end of the cold war has eliminated a simplistic approach to the problems of conflict and instability in the developing world. The current, less ideological climate has forced the international community to recognize that though these threats are far more complicated, they are no less dangerous.

Looking Ahead: Challenge Questions

What are the sources of conflict in the developing world? What factors contribute to the intensity of these conflicts?

What could account for Islamic militancy?

Why does Islamic fundamentalism pose a threat to governments, particularly in the Middle East?

Why is it inaccurate to equate Islam with fanaticism?

Why is there potential for political instability in the Persian Gulf monarchies?

How might Islam contribute to the restoration of order in Somalia?

What factors could account for the violence in Rwanda and Burundi?

Why has Nigeria failed to make the transition to civilian rule?

What are the sources of conflict between India and Pakistan? Why is this potentially dangerous?

What are the sources of tension between Indonesia and the people of Irian Jaya?

What factors account for the increasing numbers of refugees and economic migrants worldwide? How might this problem be managed?

We must hear the Third World

MICHAEL T. KLARE

Michael T. Klare is Five College Associate Professor of Peace and World Security Studies at Hampshire College in Amherst, Massachusetts.

The end of the Cold War has produced or revealed global changes that have enormous significance for the U.S. peace movement. It is vitally important that the peace movement attempt to analyze these changes and reconstruct its strategy accordingly. While the threats associated with the Cold War have largely disappeared, the world still faces many threats to peace and security. Some of these threats arise from the legacy of the Cold War, a legacy that will imperil the world for generations to come. This legacy includes the large stockpiles of nuclear warheads that we must somehow locate, monitor, safeguard, and destroy. This may not prove an easy task, given the disintegration of the Soviet Union and the unrest in Eastern Europe. Indeed, controlling and eliminating all of these weapons—and preventing their accidental use—may prove the most important and difficult task facing the world community in the months and years ahead.

There are also large stockpiles of chemical weapons that we must safely dispose of, and large quantities of conventional weapons that we must destroy or place in safe storage, lest they flow into the international arms market. The poisonous nuclear wastes produced by forty-five years of bomb production must be disposed of in a safe manner. And we must convert the immense military-industrial infrastructures of the Cold War to productive use without causing great social and economic hardship.

That is the legacy of the Cold War. But a host of other threats to international peace and stability command our attention. Most of these threats arise from social, political, and economic stresses and strains in the Third World, and in parts of what used to be called the Second World—that is, the Sino-Soviet bloc.

As the divide grows between North and South, rich and poor, haves and have-nots, frustrations and resentments among the less fortunate tend to increase and often find expression through the reassertion of traditional ethnic, national, religious, and tribal identities. This reassertion intensifies the hostility toward those of differing identities. Such a clash is occurring on a global basis, and it represents the greatest source of conflict in the current, post-Cold War environment.

Most of the stresses we now see in the Third World and Eastern Europe have been developing over a long period—going back in many cases to the onset of the colonial era. But they appear to have gained increased urgency and vigor with the end of the Cold War. I say "appear" because in some cases we simply didn't *see* these stresses before because of our preoccupation with East-West security concerns. Had we been watching more closely over the past decade or so, we would have been able to detect these developments.

The end of the Cold war and the erosion of central Soviet power (and central Yugoslav power) allowed the ethnic antagonisms that have simmered beneath the surface to erupt with extra vigor. It is a mistake, however, to view these explosions as a result of the Cold War's end; rather, they should be seen as a consequence of the central authorities' failure to address existing ethnic and national aspirations in an honest and constructive way.

The turbulence in the Third World and in Eastern Europe affects world peace and security at three levels. It is increasing tension between North and South; it is fueling interstate rivalries in the Third World; and it is exacerbating ethnic, tribal, religious, and caste antagonisms within Third World countries.

Many of the existing conflicts operate at all three levels. The "Arab-Israeli dispute," for instance, entails ethnic conflict between Jews and Palestinians, regional conflict between Israel and its Arab neighbors, and a welter of stressful relations between these countries and the major Northern powers. The same was true of the Persian Gulf conflict, which entailed ethnic fighting within Iraq, regional conflict between Iraq and its neighbors (especially Kuwait, Saudi Arabia, and Israel), and North-South conflict between Iraq and those Northern powers that feared its growing military potential. This interplay of internal, regional, and global hostilities is likely to be more and more common in the conflicts of the future.

Among the major threats to global peace and security in the post-Cold War era are these:

1. Efforts by nations of the South to enhance their military power vis-à-vis the North (through the acquisition of nuclear, chemical, and conventional weapons).

2. Efforts by nations of the North, especially the United States, to assert dominance throughout the Third World by direct military action, as in Operation Desert Storm.

3. Arms races and hostilities between competing regional powers of the South, as in the Iran-Iraq war, the Arab-Israeli conflicts, the India-Pakistan conflict, and the conflict between the Koreas. An especially dangerous aspect of such rivalries is the tendency of nations on one side of

such disputes to foment or support internal ethnic or tribal disorders within the territory of their rivals.

4. Conflicts over borders or territorial dispositions originally constructed by the colonial powers and now considered illegitimate by the current leaders of the countries involved (e.g., Ethiopia/Somalia, Iraq/Kuwait, and the conflict over the Falklands/Malvinas).

5. Efforts by ethno-nationalist groups within multi-ethnic states to secede and establish their own nation-states, along with efforts by central government authorities to suppress such drives (as, for instance, in Croatia, Eritrea, Kashmir, Iraqi Kurdistan, the southern Sudan, and the Tamil-populated parts of Sri Lanka).

6. The channeling of socio-economic antagonisms into armed violence, as in Lebanon, Burundi, Guatemala, and the Punjab region of India. Similarly, the intensification of conflict between settler (ex-colonial) societies and indigenous peoples, as in South Africa, Israel and the West Bank, and much of the Western Hemisphere.

7. Violent struggles between authoritarian governments and popular forces seeking social and political change, as in Algeria, Burma, El Salvador, and Haiti.

8. The persistence of revolutionary movements employing a guerrilla strategy, as in Colombia, Peru, and the Philippines.

Three developments are intensifying these long-simmering conflicts: the globalization of the economy, environmental degradation and population growth, and the growing availability of modern arms.

With capital moving rapidly from one location to another around the world, some states and peoples find it easier to integrate themselves into the global economy; others do not. And within states, new pockets of wealth appear alongside stretches of desperate poverty.

The legacy of colonialism often has a hand in this uneven pattern, since those Third World peoples who were given at least minimal educational and employment opportunities are now better positioned to adapt to the needs of the world economy, while those excluded from educational opportunities often find themselves at a distinct disadvantage.

As some peoples prosper while others stagnate, there is a natural tendency for the less fortunate to emphasize the ethnic, religious, and tribal identities that separate themselves from the more fortunate, and to express these differences in violent forms.

There is also a natural tendency for some groups within a multi-ethnic system to break out of their existing state structure and seek economic alliances with more affluent centers. Hence, the desire of the Bal-

tic republics and Slovenia and Croatia to remove themselves from the economically depressed Soviet Union and Yugoslavia and to forge links with the European Community.

Uneven economic development brings additional destabilizing pressures—particularly the migration of huge numbers of people. Two migratory patterns can be discerned:

First, there is a growing migration of impoverished peoples to the megalopolises of the South—Mexico City, São Paulo, Lima, Cairo, Bombay, Bangkok, Manila. This intensifies ethnic and class warfare and results in growing unemployment, criminality, and the deterioration of the urban infrastructure.

Second, there is a growing migration of Southern (and Eastern) peoples into the affluent areas of the North (and West), sparking anti-immigrant sentiment in the Northern countries, along with increased ethnic and racial conflict within the immigrant communities of the North. This tension has recently flared up, for instance, in ethnically based gang warfare in Los Angeles and rioting in Brooklyn and Washington, D.C.

As global industrialization proceeds and the pace of economic activity accelerates, more and more stress is being placed on the global ecosphere. This process of environmental decay tends to affect some peoples more than others, and it usually exacerbates the existing conflicts and tensions.

The uneven impact of environmental degradation is most evident in the so-called marginal lands—the highlands, jungles, swamps, and deserts where indigenous peoples have scratched out a sustainable existence. But as a result of environmental and climatic changes, they are losing their capacity to do so. As a result, many of these peoples have been forced to join the vast migratory streams described above.

What's more, the untapped resources of lands once considered too remote or too inhospitable for successful economic exploitation—such as the Amazonian rain forest, the forests of Borneo and New Guinea, the oil-rich areas of Alaska's North Slope, and the rivers of northern Quebec—are now falling prey to resource companies seeking new areas for exploitation. These intrusions inevitably threaten indigenous peoples, in some cases resulting in the virtual extermination of tribes and cultures.

Adding to environmental stress is uncontrolled population growth, which increases demands on limited water, forest, and land resources and heightens frictions along ethnic and tribal lines. In areas where one major river system empties through several countries and is the source of drinking and irrigation water for many

If the Third World continues to be shut out of political and economic decisions that affect it, a paralyzing new Cold War could break out.

peoples (e.g., the Nile, the Jordan, or the Euphrates), there is a growing risk of conflict and violence.

Finally, the growing availability of modern arms—including nuclear, chemical, and high-tech conventional weapons—raises the stakes in all of the conflict types described above. As we move into the 1990s, more and more countries will acquire the skills and technology to produce modern weapons on their own. Even more widespread is the ability to manufacture conventional weapons, especially the sort that are employed in local, internal, and insurgent conflicts.

As these capabilities grow, it becomes easier for belligerents (whether states, guerrillas, terrorists, or sectarian militias) to conduct wars of great violence and duration. This became particularly evident in the Iran-Iraq war, which lasted eight bloody years and took the lives of one million people, and in such long-lasting guerrilla and sectarian conflicts as those in Afghanistan, Angola, El Salvador, Ethiopia, Lebanon, and the Sudan.

Even as some of these conflicts are brought to a conclusion, the weapons employed in them have found new use in emerging conflicts. For instance, a shipment of weapons no longer needed by Lebanon's warring factions was reportedly sent to the newly constituted armed forces of Croatia.

How should the peace movement repond to these daunting challenges? It is obviously difficult to spell out a blueprint for successful peace action in all of these areas, but it is nevertheless essential that we begin to develop an agenda to deal with the problems that loom ahead of us.

Here, then, is my list of major peace-movement priorities for the 1990s:

First, we must confront and overcome the legacies of the Cold War. This means continuing our campaigns for nuclear and chemical disarmament, the dissolution of the nuclear-weapons production complex, the dissolution of NATO, and the con-

3. CONFLICT AND INSTABILITY

version of military industries into productive civilian enterprises.

Second, we must oppose the tendency of the U.S. Government to act as the world's policeman. For the Pentagon, Iraq was prologue. American military officials fully expect that Operation Desert Storm will be succeeded by a continuing series of armed confrontations between the emerging military powers of the Third World. "The Gulf War presaged very much the type of conflict we are likely to confront again in this era," Secretary of Defense Dick Cheney told Congress last spring. The Pentagon insists that U.S. forces maintain a substantial capacity for military intervention abroad, and the peace movement needs to recognize this and resist it.

Third, we need to campaign for the adoption of rigorous multilateral controls on the export of nuclear, chemical, and conventional weapons. To encourage Third World states to cooperate in nonproliferation efforts, we should insist that increased economic and technical assistance be provided to countries which agree to reduce their military spending. At the same time, we must oppose the use of military action as a substitute for effective nonproliferation.

Fourth, we need to redesign the major international institutions so as to give real power and authority to Third World countries. Two institutions in particular demand a more democratic structure: the Security Council of the United Nations and the International Monetary Fund. If the Third World continues to be shut out of the major political and economic decisions that affect it, a paralyzing new Cold War could break out between North and South.

Fifth, we need to place more emphasis on international peacekeeping, mediation, and conflict resolution. We need to work through the United Nations and regional peacekeeping efforts, such as the Arias plan for Central America, the Treaty of Tlatelolco, and the South Pacific Nuclear Free Zone.

Sixth, we need to support increased economic assistance to the poorest Third World countries, with this aid provided in such a fashion as to benefit needy communities directly. Likewise, we should support U.S. assistance (whether through governmental or nongovernmental channels) for environmentally sound self-help development projects in poor Third World countries.

And lastly, we need to encourage dialogue and cultural understanding across ethnic, religious, tribal, racial, and national boundaries—the front lines of the post-Cold War period. This is by no means a complete or comprehensive list, but I offer it as a starting point for thinking about the peace movement's strategy in the crucial years to come.

> "To equate Islam and Islamic fundamentalism uncritically with extremism is to judge Islam only by those who wreak havoc—a standard not applied to Judaism and Christianity... There are lessons to be learned from a past in which fear of a monolithic Soviet threat often blinded the United States to the Soviet bloc's diversity, led to uncritical support for (anti-Communist) dictatorships, and enabled the 'free world' to tolerate the suppression of legitimate dissent and massive human rights violations by governments that labeled the opposition 'Communist' or 'socialist.'"

Political Islam: Beyond the Green Menace

JOHN L. ESPOSITO

JOHN L. ESPOSITO *is a professor of religion and international affairs and director of the Center for Muslim-Christian Understanding at Georgetown University's School of Foreign Service. Among his books are* The Islamic Threat: Myth or Reality? *(New York: Oxford University Press, 1992),* Islam: The Straight Path, *(New York: Oxford University Press, 1991), and* Islam and Politics *(Syracuse, N.Y.: Syracuse University Press, 1991).*

It is the mightiest power in the Levant and North Africa. Governments tremble before it. Arabs everywhere turn to it for salvation from their various miseries. This power is not Egypt, Iraq, or indeed any nation, but the humble mosque.[1]

From Ayatollah Khomeini to Sheik Omar Abdel Rahman, from Iran to the World Trade Center, government leaders and opinion makers in the West and in the Middle East have warned of the dangers of militant Islam. If the 1980s were dominated by images of embassies under siege, American hostages, and hijackings, the 1990s bring prophecies of insurgent movements wielding nuclear weapons and employing urban terrorism. Headlines announce the possibility of a worldwide Islamic uprising and a clash of civilizations in which Islam may overwhelm the West. Television viewers see the bodies of Coptic Christians and tourists killed by Egyptian extremists and take in reports of Algerian militants' pitched battles with police. All fuel alarmist concerns reflected in publications and conferences with titles like "Roots of Muslim Rage," "Islam: Deadly Duel with Zealots," and "Awaiting God's Wrath: Islamic Fundamentalism and the West."

For more than four decades governments formulated policy in the midst of a superpower rivalry that defined the globe and the future in terms of the visible ideological and military threat posed by the Soviet Union. In the aftermath of the cold war, the fall of the Soviet Union and the discrediting of communism have created a "threat vacuum" that has given rise to a search for new enemies. For some Americans the enemy is the economic challenge the Japanese or the European Community represent. For others it is an Islamic world whose 1 billion Muslims form a majority in more than 48 countries and a rapidly growing minority in Europe and America. Some view Islam as the only ideological alternative to the West that can cut across national boundaries, and perceiving it as politically and culturally at odds with Western society, fear it; others consider it a more basic demographic threat.[2]

The 1990s, however, reveal the diversity and complexity of political Islam and point to a twenty-first century that will shake the assumptions of many. While some Islamic organizations engage in terrorism, seeking to topple governments, others spread their message through preaching and social services and demand the right to gain legitimate power with ballots rather than bullets. But what of militant Islam? Is there an international Islamic threat? Will humanity witness the rise of a "new Comintern" led by "religious Stalinists" poised to challenge the free world and impose Iranian-style Islamic republics through violence, or through an electoral process that enables Islamic movements to "hijack democracy"?

FAITH, FUNDAMENTALISM, AND FACT

Muslims vary as much in their interpretations of Islam as followers of other faiths with theirs. For the vast majority of believers, Islam, like other world religions, is a faith of peace and social justice, moving its adherents to worship God, obey His laws, and be socially responsible.

Indiscriminate use of the term "Islamic fundamentalism" and its identification with governments and

---

[1] "The Islamic Threat," *The Economist*, March 13, 1993, p. 25.

[2] See John L. Esposito, *The Islamic Threat: Myth or Reality?* (New York: Oxford University Press, 1992), which I have drawn on for this study.

movements have contributed to the sense of a monolithic menace when in actuality political Islam is far more diverse. Saudi Arabia, Libya, Pakistan, and Iran have been called fundamentalist states, but this tells us nothing about their nature: Saudi Arabia is a conservative monarchy, Libya a populist socialist state headed by a military dictator. Moreover, the label says nothing about the state's Islamic character or orientation. Pakistan under General Muhammad Zia ul-Haq embodied a conservative Islam, and Saudi Arabia still does; Islam in Libya is radical and revisionist; clerics dominate in Iran. Finally, although fundamentalism is popularly equated with anti-Americanism and extremism, and Libya and Iran have indeed often denounced America, Saudi Arabia and Pakistan have been close allies of the United States and the mujahideen that resisted the Soviet occupation of Afghanistan received support from Washington for years.

The Iranian revolution of 1978–1979 called attention to a reassertion of Islam in Muslim personal and public life that subsequently came to be referred to by many names: Islamic resurgence, Islamic revivalism, political Islam, and more commonly, Islamic fundamentalism. The totally unexpected ousting of the shah of Iran by an Islamic revolution led by the charismatic Ayatollah Ruhollah Khomeini and the creation of an Islamic republic under the mullahs stunned the world. Fear that Iran would export Islamic revolution to other countries of the Middle East became the lens through which events in the Muslim world were viewed. When Khomeini spoke, the world listened—supporters with admiration, detractors with disdain and disgust or, often, anxiety.

The 1979 takeover of the United States embassy in Teheran and Khomeini's expansionist designs, Libyan leader Muammar Qaddafi's posturing and promotion of a third world revolution, and Egyptian President Anwar Sadat's 1981 assassination by Muslim extremists supported the projection of a militant Islamic fundamentalism. Hostage-taking, hijackings, and attacks on foreign and government installations by groups such as the Islamic Liberation Organization, Jihad, and Takfir wal Hijra (Excommunication and Flight) in Egypt and by the Iranian-funded Hezbollah and Islamic Jihad in Lebanon received enormous publicity. In the late 1970s and throughout the 1980s the prevailing picture of the Islamic world in the West was of militants bent on undermining countries' stability, overthrowing governments, and imposing their version of an Islamic state. The result was the facile equation: Islam = fundamentalism = terrorism and extremism.

THE ROOTS OF RESURGENCE

The reality is that Islamic revivalism was not the product of the Iranian revolution but of a global reassertion of Islam that had already been under way and that extended from Libya to Malaysia.

The causes of the resurgence are many and differ from country to country, but common catalysts and concerns are identifiable. Secular nationalism (whether in the form of liberal nationalism, Arab nationalism, or socialism) has not provided a sense of national identity or produced strong and prosperous societies. The governments in Muslim countries—mostly non-elected, authoritarian, and dependent on security forces—have been unable to establish their political legitimacy. They have been blamed for the failure to achieve economic self-sufficiency, to stem the widening gap between rich and poor, to halt widespread corruption, to liberate Palestine, to resist Western political and cultural hegemony. Both the political and the religious establishments have come under criticism, the former as a westernized, secular elite overly concerned with power and privilege, and the latter (in Sunni Muslim nations) as leaders of the faithful who have been co-opted by governments that often control mosques and religious universities and other institutions.

The disastrous defeat of Arab forces by Israel in the 1967 war discredited Arab nationalism and triggered soul-searching in the Arab world. In South Asia, the 1971 civil war in Pakistan leading to the creation of Bangladesh undermined the idea that Islam and Muslim nationalism could act as the glue to hold together an ethnically and linguistically diverse Muslim population. One finds similar catalytic events or conditions in Lebanon, Iran, Malaysia (the riots of 1969), and many other countries.

Islamic revivalism is in many ways the successor to failed nationalist programs. The founders of many Islamic movements were formerly participants in nationalist movements: Hasan al-Banna of the Muslim Brotherhood in Egypt, Rashid Ghannoushi of Tunisia's Renaissance party, and Abbasi Madani of the Islamic Salvation Front in Algeria. Islamic movements have offered an Islamic alternative or solution, a third way distinct from capitalism and communism. Islamists argue that secularism, a modern bias toward the West, and dependence on Western models of development have proved politically inadequate and socially corrosive, undermining the identity and moral fabric of Muslim societies. Asserting that Islam is not just a collection of beliefs and ritual actions but a comprehensive ideology embracing public as well as personal life, they call for the implementation of Sharia, or Islamic law, as a social blueprint. While the majority within the Muslim world seek to work within the system, a small but significant minority believes that the rulers in their countries are anti-Islamic and that they have a divine mandate to unseat them and impose their vision.

In general, the movements are urban-based, drawing heavily from the lower middle and middle classes.

They have gained particular support among recent university graduates and young professionals, male and female. The movements recruit from the mosques and on campuses where, contrary to popular assumptions, their strength is not so much in the religious faculties and the humanities as in science, engineering, education, law, and medicine. Organizations such as the Muslim Brotherhood of Egypt, Jordan, and Sudan as well as South Asia's Jamaat-i-Islami consist in great part of university graduates and professionals. The Islamic Salvation Front's Abbasi Madani, for example, earned his doctorate in education from a British university, while his younger colleague Abdelqader Hachani is a petrochemical engineer and a doctoral candidate at a French university. Seventy-six percent of the Front's candidates in municipal and parliamentary elections in 1990 and 1991 held postgraduate degrees, and a significant portion of the leadership and membership can be described as middle-class professionals.

In many Muslim countries an alternative elite exists, its members with modern educations but self-consciously oriented toward Islam and committed to social and political activism as a means of bringing about a more Islamic society or system of government. This phenomenon is reflected in the presence—and often dominance—of Islamists in professional associations of lawyers, engineers, professors, and physicians. Where permitted to participate in society, Islamists are found in all sectors, including government and even the military.

FROM PERIPHERY TO CENTER

Demonization of Islam proceeded throughout the 1980s, but by late in the decade a more nuanced, broad-based, diverse Islamic world was increasingly evident. Beneath the radical façade, apart from the small, marginalized extremist groups, a quiet revolution had taken place. While a rejectionist minority had sought to impose change from above through holy wars, many others reaffirmed their faith and pursued a bottom-up approach, seeking a gradual Islamization of society through words, preaching, and social and political activity. In many Muslim countries Islamic organizations had become energetic in social reform, establishing much-needed schools, hospitals, clinics, legal societies, family assistance programs, Islamic banks and insurance companies, and publishing houses. These Islamically oriented groups offered social welfare services cheaply and constituted an implicit critique of the failure of the regimes in the countries to provide adequate services.

Along with social activism went increased political participation. In the late 1980s economic failures led to mass demonstrations and food riots in Egypt, Tunisia, Algeria, and Jordan. Moreover, the demand for democratization that accompanied the fall of the Soviet Union and the liberation of Eastern Europe touched the Middle East as well. Throughout the decade many governments in the Muslim world charged that the Islamic activists were merely violent revolutionaries whose lack of popular support would be evident if elections were held, but few governments showed themselves willing to put this claim to the test. When political systems were opened up and Islamic organizations were able to participate in elections, the results stunned many in the Muslim world and in the West. Although Islamists were not allowed to organize separate official political parties, in Egypt and Tunisia they emerged as the leading opposition. In the November 1989 elections in Jordan they captured 32 of 80 seats in the lower house of parliament and held five cabinet-level positions and the office of speaker of the lower house. Algeria, however, was the turning point.

Algeria had been dominated for decades by a one-party dictatorship under the National Liberation Front (FLN). Because the FLN was socialist and had a strong secular elite and feminist movement, few took the Islamic movement seriously; moreover, the movement had been among the least well known of the country's groups outside its borders, even among Islamists. The stunning victory of the Islamic Salvation Front (FIS), an umbrella group, in 1990 municipal elections sent a shock wave around the globe.

Despite the arrest of front leaders Abbasi Madani and Ali Belhadj; the cutoff of state funds to municipalities, often crippling FIS officials' ability to provide services; and gerrymandering to create districts more favorable to itself, the ruling party failed to prevent an even more stunning sweep by the FIS in parliamentary elections held in December 1991. As Islamists at home and across the Muslim world celebrated, the military intervened, forcing the resignation of Algeria's president, arresting FIS leaders, imprisoning more than 10,000 people in desert camps, and outlawing the front, and seizing its assets.

In the face of the repression much of the world stood silent. The conventional wisdom had been blind-sided. While most feared and were on their guard against "other Irans," the Islamic Salvation Front's victory in Algeria raised the specter of an Islamic movement coming to power through democratic elections and ballots worried many world leaders even more than bullets. The justification for accepting the Algerian military's seizure of power was the charge that the FIS really only believed in "One man, one vote, one time." The perceived threat from revolutionary Islam was intensified by the fear that it would capture power from within the political system by democratic means.

THE TRIPLE THREAT

In contrast to other parts of the world, calls for greater political participation and democratization in the Middle East have been met by empty rhetoric and repression at home and by ambivalence or silence in the West. Middle Eastern governments have used the danger posed by Islamic fundamentalism as the excuse for increasing authoritarianism and violations of human rights and the indiscriminate suppression of Islamic opposition, as well as for the West's silence about these actions.

Fear of fundamentalism, like fear of communism, has made strange bedfellows. Tunisia, Algeria, and Egypt join Israel in warning of a regional and international Islamic threat in their bids to win Western aid and justify their repression of Islamists. "Israel, which for years won American and European backing as a bulwark against the spread of communism through the Middle East, is now projecting itself as the West's defense against militant Islam, a movement it is portraying as an even greater danger."[3] Israeli Prime Minister Yitzhak Rabin justified the expulsion of 415 Palestinians in December 1992 by saying that "Our struggle against murderous Islamic terror is also meant to awaken the world, which is lying in slumber. . . We call on all nations, all peoples to devote their attention to the greater danger inherent in Islamic fundamentalism[, which] threatens world peace in future years. . . [W]e stand on the line of fire against the danger of fundamentalist Islam."

Israel and its Arab neighbors have warned that a resurgent Iran is exporting revolution throughout much of the Muslim world, including Sudan, the West Bank and Gaza Strip, Algeria, and Central Asia, as well as to Europe and America; indeed, Egyptian President Hosni Mubarak has urged the formation of a "global alliance" against this menace.

Islam is often portrayed as a triple threat: political, civilizational, and demographic. The fear in the 1980s that Iran would export its revolution has been superseded by the larger fear of an international pan-Islamic movement with Iran and Sudan at its heart. In this decade, despite Iran's relative failure in fomenting revolution abroad, visions of a global Islamic threat have proliferated, combining fear of violent revolution and of Algerian-style electoral victories. French writer Raymond Aron's warning of an Islamic revolutionary wave generated by the fanaticism of the Prophet and Secretary of State Cyrus Vance's concern over the possibility of an Islamic-Western war have been succeeded by columnist Charles Krauthammer's assertion of a global Islamic threat of "fundamentalist Koran-waving Khomeniism" led by Iran.

The Ayatollah Khomeini's condemning of novelist Salman Rushdie to death for blasphemy for his *Satanic Verses*, combined with Iraqi President Saddam Hussein's call for a holy war against the West during the 1991 Persian Gulf War, reinforce fears of a political and cultural confrontation. This is magnified by some who, like Krauthammer, reduce contemporary realities to the playing out of ancient rivalries: "It should now be clear that we are facing a mood and a movement far transcending the level of issues and policies and the governments that pursue them. This is no less than a clash of civilizations—a perhaps irrational but surely historic reaction of an ancient rival against our Judaeo-Christian heritage, our secular present, and the worldwide expansion of both."[4]

Muslim-Western relations are placed in the context of a confrontation in which Islam is again pitted against the West—"our Judaeo-Christian and secular West"—rather than specific political and socioeconomic grievances. Thus the assault on the West is seen as "irrational," mounted by peoples peculiarly driven by their passions and hatred; how can Western countries really respond to this?

The politics of the Middle East refutes theories of a monolithic threat. Despite a common "Islamic" orientation, the governments of the region reveal little unity of purpose in interstate or international relations because of conflicting national interests and priorities. Qaddafi was a bitter enemy of Anwar Sadat and Sudanese leader Gaafar Nimeiry at the very time that all were projecting their "Islamic images." Khomeini's Islamic republic consistently called for the overthrow of Saudi Arabia's Islamic state on Islamic grounds. Islamically identified governments also differ in their stance toward the West. Libya's and Iran's relationships with the West, and the United States in particular, were often confrontational; at the same time, the United States has had strong allies in Saudi Arabia, Egypt, Kuwait, Pakistan, and Bahrain. National interest and regional politics rather than ideology or religion remain the major determinants in the formulation of foreign policy.

The World Trade Center bombing last year gave impetus to a third current, the portrayal of Islam as a demographic threat. The growth of Muslim populations in Europe and the United States has made Islam the second-largest religion in Germany and France and the third-largest in Britain and America. Disputes over Muslim minority rights, demonstrations and clashes during the Salman Rushdie affair, and the Trade Center bombing have been exploited by strident voices of the right—politicians such as France's Jean-Marie LePen, neo-Nazi youth in Germany, and right-wing political commentators in the United States.

NO DEMOCRACY WITHOUT RISKS

For Western leaders, democracy in the Middle East raises the prospect of old and reliable friends or client states transformed into more independent and less predictable nations, which generates worries that West-

---

[3]Emad El Din Shahid, "The Limits of Democracy," *Middle East Insight,*, vol. 8, no. 6 (1992), p. 12.

[4]Charles Krauthammer, "The New Crescent of Crisis: Global Intifada," *Washington Post,* January 1, 1993.

ern access to oil could become less secure. Thus stability in the Middle East has often been defined in terms of preserving the status quo.

Lack of enthusiasm for political liberalization in the region has been rationalized by the assertion that Arab culture and Islam are antidemocratic (an issue never raised to a comparable degree with regard to the former Soviet Union, Eastern Europe, or Africa). The proof offered is the lack of a democratic tradition, and more specifically, the glaring absence of democracies in the Muslim world.

The history of that world has not been conducive to the development of democratic traditions and institutions. European colonial rule and postindependence governments headed by military officers, ex-military men, and monarchs have contributed to a legacy in which political participation and the building of strong democratic institutions are of little concern. National unity and stability as well as the political legitimacy of governments have been undermined by the artificial nature of modern states whose national boundaries were often determined by colonial powers and whose rulers were either put in place by Europe or simply seized power. Weak economies, illiteracy, and high unemployment, especially among the younger generation, aggravate the situation, undermining confidence in governments and increasing the appeal of "Islamic fundamentalism."

Experts and policymakers who question whether Islamic movements will use electoral politics to "hijack democracy" often do not appear equally disturbed that few rulers in the region have been democratically elected and that many who speak of democracy believe only in the risk-free variety: political liberalization so long as there is no danger of a strong opposition (secular or religious) and loss of power. Failure to appreciate that the issue of hijacking democracy is a two-way street was reflected in the West's responses to the Algerian military's intervention and cancellation of the election results.

Perception of a global Islamic threat can contribute to support for repressive governments in the Muslim world, and thus to the creation of a self-fulfilling prophecy. Thwarting participatory politics by canceling elections or repressing populist Islamic movements fosters radicalization. Many of the Islamists harassed, imprisoned, or tortured by the regime, will conclude that seeking democracy is a dead end and become convinced that force is their only recourse. Official silence or economic and political backing for regimes by the United States and other Western powers is read as complicity and a sign that there is a double standard for the implementation of democracy. This can create the conditions that lead to political violence that seemingly validates contentions that Islamic movements are inherently violent, antidemocratic, and a threat to national and regional stability.

More constructive and democratic strategies are possible. The strength of Islamic organizations and parties is also due to the fact that they constitute the only viable voice and vehicle for opposition in relatively closed political systems. The strength at the polls of Tunisia's Renaissance party, the Islamic Salvation Front, and Jordan's Muslim Brotherhood derived not only from a hard core of dedicated followers who backed the groups' Islamic agendas but from the many who wished simply to cast their vote against the government. Opening up the political system could foster competing opposition groups and thus weaken the monopoly Islamic parties have on opposition voters. (It must be remembered that the membership of Islamic organizations does not generally constitute a majority of the population.) Finally, the realities of a more open political marketplace—having to compete for votes, and once gaining power having to govern amid diverse interests—could force Islamic groups to adapt or broaden their ideology and programs.

The United States should not in principle object to the involvement of Islamic activists in government if they have been duly elected. Islamically oriented politicians and groups should be evaluated by the same criteria as any other potential leaders or opposition parties. While some are rejectionists, most will be critical and selective in their relations with the United States, generally operating on the basis of national interests and showing a flexibility that reflects understanding of the globally interdependent world. The United States should demonstrate by word and action its belief that the right to self-determination and representative government extends to an Islamically oriented state and society, if these reflect the popular will and do not directly threaten United States interests. American policy should accept the ideological differences between the West and Islam to the greatest extent possible, or at least tolerate them.

All should bear in mind that democratization in the Muslim world proceeds by experimentation, and necessarily involves both success and failure. The transformation of Western feudal monarchies to democratic nation states took time, and trial and error, and was accompanied by political as well as intellectual revolutions that rocked state and church. It was a long, drawn-out *process* among contending factions with competing interests and visions.

Today we are witnessing a historic transformation in the Muslim world. Risks exist, for there can be no risk-free democracy. Those who fear the unknown, wondering how specific Islamic movements will act once in power, have legitimate reasons to do so. However, if one worries that these movements might suppress opposition, lack tolerance, deny pluralism, and violate human rights, the same concern must apply equally to the plight of those Islamists who have shown a willingness to participate in the political process in Tunisia, Egypt, and Algeria.

Governments in the Muslim world that espouse political liberalization and democracy are challenged to promote the development of civil society—the institutions, values, and culture that are the foundation of true participatory government. Islamic movements, for their part, are challenged to move beyond slogans to programs. They must become more self-critical, and speak out not only against local government abuses but against those of Islamic regimes in Iran and Sudan, for example, as well as acts of terrorism by extremists. They are urged to present an Islamic rationale and policy that extend to their opposition and to minorities the principles of pluralism and political participation they demand for themselves. The extent to which the growth of Islamic revivalism has been accompanied in some countries by attempts to restrict women's rights and public roles; the record of discrimination against the Bahai in Iran, the Ahmadi in Pakistan, and Christians in Sudan; and sectarian conflict between Muslims and Christians in Egypt, Sudan, and Nigeria pose serious questions about religious pluralism, respect for human rights, and tolerance in general.

Islamic revivalism has run counter to many of the presuppositions of Western liberal secularism and development theory, among them the belief that modernization means the inexorable or progressive secularization and Westernization of society. Too often analysis and policymaking have been shaped by a liberal secularism that fails to recognize it too represents a world view, not the paradigm for modern society, and can easily degenerate into a "secularist fundamentalism" that treats alternative views as irrational, extremist, and deviant.

A focus on "Islamic fundamentalism" as a global threat has reinforced the tendency to equate violence with Islam, to fail to distinguish between illegitimate use of religion by individuals and the faith and practice of the majority of the world's Muslims who, like adherents of other religious traditions, wish to live in peace. To equate Islam and Islamic fundamentalism uncritically with extremism is to judge Islam only by those who wreak havoc—a standard not applied to Judaism and Christianity. The danger is that heinous actions may be attributed to Islam rather than to a twisted or distorted interpretation of Islam. Thus despite the track record of Christianity and Western countries when it comes to making war, developing weapons of mass destruction, and imposing their imperialist designs, Islam and Muslim culture are portrayed as somehow peculiarly and inherently expansionist and prone to violence and warfare.

There are lessons to be learned from a past in which fear of a monolithic Soviet threat often blinded the United States to the Soviet bloc's diversity, led to uncritical support for (anti-Communist) dictatorships, and enabled the "free world" to tolerate the suppression of legitimate dissent and massive human rights violations by governments that labeled the opposition "Communist" or "socialist." The risk today is that exaggerated fears will lead to a double standard in the promotion of democracy and human rights in the Muslim world as can be witnessed by the Western concern about and action to support democracy in the former Soviet Union and Eastern Europe but the muted or ineffective response to the promotion of democracy in the Middle East and the defense of Muslims in Bosnia and Herzegovina. Support for democracy and human rights is more effective if it is consistent around the world. Treating Islamic experiences as exceptional is an invitation to long-term conflict.

THE MIDDLE EAST ON THE BRINK: PROSPECTS FOR CHANGE IN THE 21ST CENTURY

In the past fifty years, the various leaders of the Middle East have tried to make the newly independent states work. On the whole, they have not done very well in forging viable economies or in providing a modicum of social justice for their populations. To do better as the 21st century approaches, they will need to improve the governance of their societies, which will entail some measure of democratization and accountability.

William B. Quandt

William B. Quandt holds the Byrd Chair in Government and Foreign Affairs at the University of Virginia. This article is adapted from his keynote address at the Middle East Institute's 49th annual conference in Washington, DC, 29–30 September 1995.

As the century draws to a close, one should reflect on what a remarkable era the Middle East has been passing through. Just a century ago, the Ottoman empire was still intact and was struggling to find a constitutional formula to keep its increasingly assertive national groups together. That effort failed, in part because of World War I. Then, the imperial powers of the day, primarily Britain and France, intensified their domination over most of the area. Inevitably, foreign domination gave rise to nationalist movements, and within a few decades newly independent countries, including Israel, were taking their place in the United Nations.

All of that happened, more or less, in the first fifty years of the current century; and the past fifty have been spent by various leaders and regimes trying to make the resulting national states work. On occasion, those leaders have resorted to force, and other times to diplomacy, to settle a wide variety of interstate disputes. On the domestic front, they have faced the need to create viable economies and provide a modicum of social justice for populations long denied the most elemental of rights. Everywhere, populations new to independence have struggled with the clash between modernity and various forms of tradition. Many wrenching changes took place in a relatively short period. Small wonder, given all of these challenges, that the Middle East in recent years has seemed like a troubled, confused, unstable, and sometimes violent region—a region of uncertainties.

One should not focus only on what has gone wrong, or poorly, in the Middle East in recent years. There have been some real achievements. Colonial rule was ended almost everywhere with comparatively little resort to violence (Algeria being the noteworthy exception). Despite the artificiality of borders, especially in the Arab world, most inter-Arab disputes did not lead to war (Iraqi president Saddam Husayn's 1990 invasion of Kuwait stands as the most glaring counter-example). The Arab-Israeli conflict, which so dominated the life of the region until recently, has been partially resolved, and the near-term prospects for war have been reduced. And here and there in the region, genuine development has taken place; great works of literature and art have been produced; and life expectancy and basic literacy have improved dramatically. All of these achievements deserve recognition.

On balance, however, one must conclude that the twentieth century has not been kind to most peoples of the Middle East. Far too many have died in wars; far too many have lived in poverty and ill health; far too many have been deprived of basic human rights; some, notably Palestinians and Kurds, are still denied secure national existence; far too many may still die in future wars in which weapons of mass destruction may very well be used; and far too many still live under repressive, unaccountable political regimes. For a region rich in human and natural resources, this is not a record of which to be proud.

3. CONFLICT AND INSTABILITY

A CRISIS OF GOVERNANCE

The worst part of this story is that none of it was inevitable. Of course, one can always find excuses—colonialism and imperialism were particularly harsh in the Middle East; foreign powers did continue to intervene even after most countries had achieved independence; loyalty to the new states was often weak in the face of both local primordial attachments and broader ideological claims; the Arab-Israeli conflict was devastating in its impact. And the list can be extended.

But when all the excuses are made, all the extenuating circumstances accounted for, one point remains to be emphasized: many of the problems of the Middle East today are the result of decisions made by leaders who could have acted otherwise. Choices were available, and bad decisions were made time after time. Many of those responsible for disastrous developments are still in power. This suggests that the source of the region's unhappiness lies, to a very large degree, in the political realm. It does not lie with its culture, with the structure of its society, or with its economic potential, but with its politicians. In short, those who have acquired power often have used it poorly on behalf of their peoples. If the next century is to be different in fundamental ways from the present one, this core political deficit will have to be overcome.

The biggest challenge facing the Middle East in the years to come is the development of better systems of governance. This means governments that are accountable, in some acceptable manner, to their people. Without some means of accountability, mistakes, which all governments make, cannot readily be corrected; the art of compromise, necessary in any healthy polity, will not flourish; and individual rights will be ignored.

Some will say that this view assumes that a Western model of government can be exported to the Middle East. But accountable, responsible government can take root anywhere and in several different forms. And such governments will be no more foreign to the region than the police states that now exist (with their uncanny resemblance to the repressive, bureaucratic regimes of the former Soviet empire). They will be no more foreign than the Gulf Cooperation Council (GCC) monarchies, which, in their modern guise, have little to do with long-established tradition and much to do with consumerism, patronage, and corruption—all ingredients found in other places where sudden wealth coincides with unbridled power. One must look hard today to find what is authentic about regimes of the Middle East and what is simply a local variant of the game of politics and privilege. Leaders, of course, claim that they are ruling in the best interests of their people, who are not ready for Western-style democracy. Until "their" people have been given a chance to express themselves, one ought to be very skeptical of all such self-serving claims. (Ironically, these "Oriental despots" are espousing a kind of Orientalism, arguing that they and their people are different, exceptional, immune to the rules that govern the lives and feelings of ordinary people elsewhere. Such theories of Middle East "exceptionalism" should not be given any serious consideration.)

Excuses for the status quo also come from cynics who argue that people get the governments they deserve. It is not at all clear how this is supposed to work in dictatorial systems. Does it mean that "bad people" deserve "bad governments"? Such a view is remarkably simplistic. After all, many people today enjoy democracy who just a decade or so ago were ruled by dictators. It would be hard to make the case that the "people" somehow changed in such a short time. What does seem to be true is that dictatorships, once they take root, are difficult to dislodge, and most people are not prepared to go to the barricades to fight for political freedom. It takes extraordinary circumstances for people to revolt.

It is certainly understandable if Middle Easterners are skeptical about importing some Western models of government. After all, the colonial powers that ruled them professed to be democratic and respectful of human rights. Disillusioned by the hypocrisy of the West, Middle Easterners seek indigenous traditions upon which to build more responsive, humane, and stable political systems. Such traditions do exist: in the late Ottoman period, for example, government interfered relatively little in people's everyday lives. Distinctive communities often lived side-by-side in harmony, the entrepreneurial spirit was given wide scope to express itself, people crossed administrative borders easily, intellectual exchange within the region and the outside world was normal, and concepts of individual and communal rights were seriously debated by intellectuals. There were many unpleasant sides to life in the previous century as well, but some of the principles of limited government, of tolerance for those of other nationalities, of open borders and economic exchange are not just Western inventions. They have roots in the region.

Unfortunately, the combined effect of colonial domination and fierce struggles to establish independent states has been to weaken traditions of tolerance, civility, and pluralism. We have witnessed, in this century, a messianic era of intense nationalism (which has sometimes degenerated further to ethnic particularism). This disease struck Europe in the interwar period and is flaring up again in the Balkans. It has also been a feature of today's Middle East, although one can detect the emergence of a more pragmatic style of politics in many countries of the region. Perhaps ordinary people in the Middle East have concluded that they will be better off without modern zealots who believe they are God's chosen people, whether Jewish, Muslim, or Christian.

Each major national group in the Middle East has been guilty in this century of this type of exclusivist zeal. There is no shortage of examples—from the modern Turks who argued that they were the race from which all others had descended; to Zionists claiming Biblical sanction for their expropriation of land; to Arab Ba'thists who proposed a mystic bond that would erase the very real differences among Arab peoples, and who showed little tolerance for minorities in their midst; to the arrogance of Iran's Shah Muhammad Reza Pahlavi, who saw in his Aryan people a racially superior breed, even while treating ordinary Iranians with contempt; to the pretenses of current religious zealots who claim that God is on their side. Who needs such visions today? Are Israelis, Turks, Arabs, and Persians—Muslims, Christians, and Jews—so insecure in their national and religious identities that they must be told by their leaders that they alone of the peoples of the Middle East deserve pride of place? I doubt it. These claims are simply the tactics of power-hungry demagogues in the region. By this point in the twentieth century we should have little trouble spotting the seeds of fascism in claims of religious or racial superiority.

Based on the evidence to date, when politics and religion are closely mixed in the Middle East, religiosity suffers and extremism wins out. But religion does not necessarily breed intolerance. Indeed, popular religious traditions are often much more tolerant than the official, politicized versions. Sufism may be looked upon with condescension by religious scholars, but as a popular form of Islam it has promoted a spirit of acceptance and personal piety. Religious leaders in all communities have strong traditions to draw on that respect the rights of individuals, that resist oppression, and that uphold a moral code for society.

POLITICAL DECISIONMAKING: LACK OF ACCOUNTABILITY

One of the manifestations of the crisis of governance in the Middle East, of the lack of accountable leadership and dictatorial methods, is the frequency of reckless decisions that have led to disasters.

We can start our list of unfortunate decisions with Egypt's President Jamal 'Abd al-Nasir's ordering of his troops into the Sinai in mid-1967. Nasir's defenders will say that he was provoked, that he fell into a trap, that the Soviets supplied false information, and that Israel was the first to fire in the June 1967 War. All of that may be true, but in those crucial days of May it was Nasir who took the initiative to turn a relatively quiescent front of the Arab-Israeli conflict into a battlefield. Leaders must bear the responsibility for their decisions, and Nasir, whatever his earlier achievements, was responsible for taking his people, along with other Arabs, into a war with Israel for which they were not prepared. How different the Middle East might have been if there had been no war in 1967. Of course, it might have happened later. But not necessarily, or not necessarily in the same way.

Wars, because of their appalling human and economic costs to societies, reveal most clearly the disastrous quality of leadership in the region. Saddam Husayn deserves the prize for the worst leader in this regard. He not only took his country to war with Iran in 1980—ignoring the very sound principle of never attacking a revolution—but he also then added to his people's misery by invading Kuwait in 1990 in a war that, once the West decided to intervene, he could not possibly win. Along the way, he was guilty of launching the Anfal campaign against his own Kurdish people. This man alone is responsible for hundreds of thousands of deaths, untold suffering, and a setback to his country's economic prospects that will take decades to repair. And none of it had to happen.

Although Iraq was the aggressor in 1980, Ayatollah Ruhollah Khomeini, the Iranian leader, bears the responsibility for deciding to fight on after recovering Iranian territory in 1982.

Rather than accept a truce and turn to the task of rebuilding Iranian society on the model he had propounded, Khomeini sought to punish Saddam Husayn for his impertinence. And how many more Iraqis and Iranians died because of this old man's intransigence? Again, the numbers must be in the hundreds of thousands. In the end, when Khomeini decided to accept a cease-fire in 1988, he had nothing to show for the added years of war. His troops were just where they had been in 1982, plus or minus a few kilometers, and the economy was in ruins. Yet the war did help Khomeini to consolidate power and to eliminate all opposition to his regime.

Israel, despite its democratic form of government, also had autocratic leaders who made decisions in secret that were disastrous for its people and for its neighbors. A case in point is Defense Minister Ariel Sharon's war for Lebanon in 1982. Although the Israeli cabinet went along, as, perhaps, did the US government, few had any idea how grandiose Sharon's plan really was. And ultimately the plan failed, but only after tens of thousands were dead, much of Beirut was in ruins, and the delicate balances of Lebanon's political fabric were ripped almost beyond repair. At least democracies offer remedies, however imperfect. Alone of my list of leaders who have taken their countries into foolish wars, Sharon was temporarily removed from office because of public outrage at his conduct. Democracies do not prevent bad decisions, but they have much more resilient, self-correcting mechanisms than dictatorships.

ECONOMIC CHOICES: REGIONAL IMPACT

The horror of war magnifies the impact of bad decisions. But other, less dramatic decisions may be equally catastrophic in the long run. We really do not yet know the consequences of some economic choices, but we can easily imagine the day when some angry Middle East citizens will ask who made the decision to drain the fresh water aquifers under the Libyan and Saudi deserts, or under the West Bank? Will it be faceless bureaucrats who are blamed, or international consulting companies, or greedy politicians? Whatever the outcome, we can already say that these decisions, which may affect millions of people, have been made in secret, with no accountability, and possibly with large payoffs and kickbacks involved. Until political systems open up to public scrutiny, this is how decisions will continue to be made.

The Middle East has not only suffered from a "democracy deficit." There also has been a related "development deficit." Simply put, a small proportion of the population of the Middle East—perhaps ten percent of the total—lives very well, while the rest lives in very modest conditions or on the borderline of poverty. This in a region that produced well over 150 billion dollars in oil revenue in 1980 alone. The development problem becomes most evident when we look at what regimes have produced for their people with the resources they have at hand. And here international comparisons are telling. The best source is the United Nations' (UN) annual *Human Development Report,* which assesses each country in the world in terms of a variety of measures of human development—literacy, economic well-being, life expectancy—and gives a composite score to each country. One can quibble about the indicators, but they seem to be applied without any apparent bias.

Most Middle East countries have a higher rank with respect to per capita income than they have on human development. If these rankings are reasonably accurate, this means that regimes are doing a poor job of translating wealth into improvements in the everyday lives of their citizens. Countries elsewhere, at the same level of per capita income, are doing more for their populations in terms of health and education. This could be due to the fact that wealth in the Middle East is going primarily to the elite, or is going into foreign bank accounts, or is being spent on the military sector at the expense of the civilian sector. We do know that defense spending consumes much more of national wealth in the Middle East than elsewhere in the world, and some of that is due to conflicts in the region. But defense spending alone is unlikely to account entirely for the development deficit. Poorly designed economic and social policies bear part of the blame as well. Here again, governance is at the heart of the problem. Leaders are making bad choices in economic and social policies, and their people are suffering as a result.

ROLE OF WESTERN POWERS

What, if anything, can the West, and the United States, in particular, do to help facilitate the transition toward better governance and more equitable development in the Middle East? Not too much—that is, the United States and other developed democracies cannot simply impose their preferred economic and political models on the Middle East. But there are ways in which the West can be helpful, if only at the margins. First, there is a continuing role for the United States, in particular, to help contain and resolve regional conflicts. If successful, those efforts might free up considerable amounts of capital for development instead of arms acquisitions. Second, the rich countries should make their markets available to exports from the Middle East. It is hypocritical for the United States to preach free markets to the Egyptians, for example, and then to limit their access to the US textile market. Third, the rich countries can decide to forgive or to reschedule the debts of poor countries. (For example, Iraq, after Saddam Husayn's demise, will be desperate to have the sanctions ended, debt repayments waived, and demands for reparations dropped. How these issues are handled will have an enormous impact on Iraqi society).

Are the prospects good for Arab-Israeli peace, as some are eager to have us believe? Or should we conclude from the Israeli-PLO (Palestine Liberation Organization) agreement of September 1995 that we are still far from a comprehensive peace? And how will the assassination of Israeli Prime Minister Yitzhak Rabin affect the chances for peace? At each stage of Arab-Israeli peacemaking, it has taken some time to gain perspective on current events, and the same will be true following the dramatic events of the fall of 1995. My early assessment, however, makes me worried about the next stage of negotiations. It is not so much a matter of figuring out whether the proverbial glass is half empty or half full. It is more the growing conviction that this may well be the last negotiated agreement between Israelis and Palestinians for many years to come, especially now that Rabin is no longer on the scene to reassure a skeptical Israeli public that peace is worth the price of ceding territory. Instead of building momentum for peace, inspiring mutual trust and confidence, recent events could portend a long, dry—and possibly quite violent—period ahead.

There are several reasons for my concern. By now, we can see what the pattern of negotiations is likely to be. Israelis determine how far they are prepared to go; the Palestinians protest and threaten to walk out; the United States urges both sides to be reasonable; and after many delays and much shouting, the Israelis get most of what they initially proposed. This is not surprising, given the disparities between the parties concerned and the lack of any real leverage on the Palestinian side, but it does suggest that the final-status negotiations, due to begin in May 1996, will be extraordinarily difficult. There, the parties will be dealing with settlements, borders, Jerusalem, and refugee claims. Based on how difficult recent talks have proved to be, it is hard to imagine that Israel and the Palestinians will reach mutually acceptable positions. And if the peace process stalls, instead of Israel living in peace alongside a viable democratic Palestinian state, Israel will remain in control of much of the West Bank and Gaza, but at one step removed.

Perhaps this initial assessment will prove wrong. After Rabin's death, Israelis may throw their support behind his program of negotiating, while shunning the radical right. Any real progress toward ending the Israeli occupation over much of the West Bank should certainly be welcomed and the release of political prisoners applauded. The political courage that it takes to keep returning to the negotiating table in the face of fierce domestic opposition is admirable; and the Palestinian elections for a self-governing authority may well produce a responsible, accountable government. If Oslo II[1] is just an interim step on the way to a final agreement, then its equivocal and complex terms, per se, are not of great importance. But if the final agreement remains elusive, this "interim" deal could well turn out to be the "final" agreement. In that case, Palestinians will feel cheated, Israeli settlers will have proved their political clout, and political extremists in both camps will have gained strength. The "settlement" may fail the crucial test of legitimacy in the eyes of one or both constituencies. Without some sense that security and justice have been achieved, no agreement stands much of a chance of lasting, a lesson that should have been learned from the ill-fated 17 May 1983 agreement between Israel and Lebanon.

While it is hard to judge the merits of any interim step without knowing where it will lead, it is not difficult to describe the outlines of a workable Arab-Israeli peace: the territorial concessions the Israelis will have to make, the

---

1. Oslo II, the agreement expanding Palestinian self-rule in the West Bank, was signed by former Israli Prime Minister Yitzhak Rabin and PLO Chairman Yasir Arafat on 28 September 1995, in Washington, DC.

commitments to peace that will be required of the Arabs, the security arrangements that will accompany any agreement, the payoffs, the formalities—all of this is well understood. But whether the political will exists in Israel, in Syria, and among the Palestinians to make the remaining hard decisions is unclear, although we do see some hopeful signs on the Israeli-Syrian front.

What is clear, alas, is that Washington is not very interested in providing leadership, or acting as a catalyst, or pressuring the parties to do what they must for the sake of peace. This is not to say that the current administration of President Bill Clinton is indifferent. It would like to see peace, it would like to host more grand events at the White House—but it does not want to exert itself, it does not want to spend much capital, political or otherwise, and it seems to have few creative ideas of its own. And Congress is even worse. Few in either house have much interest in, or knowledge of, the Middle East to buttress their opinions. They mechanically vote each year for billions in aid to the region, but largely because they know that this stance is politically sanctioned by the pro-Israeli lobby. But can they bring themselves to provide needed help to the emerging Palestinian entity, or to send a token peace-keeping force to the Golan? The signs of serious thinking on Capitol Hill on Middle East affairs are few indeed.

Without US leadership to help, the burden of peacemaking lies primarily on the shoulders of Israel's prime minister, Syria's President Hafiz al-Asad, and PLO Chairman Yasir Arafat. Each will have to show strong leadership if peace is to be secured. Israeli prime minister Shimon Peres, or his successor, will have to deal with Israeli extremists and settlers who oppose any further territorial concessions; Arafat will have to mobilize the large majority of Palestinians who favor peace in the face of the determined opposition of the minority that feels the Palestinians have nothing to gain from the peace process; and Asad will have to transcend his narrow, parochial view of Syria's interests to lead his country into a new set of relations with its neighbors. Each needs to be able to point to the gains that will justify the risks, and this is where the United States could conceivably help. But this administration does not seem prepared to lead the peace process. Once the hard work has been done by others, it may tell us that it really orchestrated the whole thing from behind the scenes—or by telephone. And if it fails? Will it also take credit for that?

As the pall of re-election-year politics begins to descend over Washington—and soon over Jerusalem as well—it seems unlikely that US politicos will do much to help the forces of peace. Instead, pointless calls will be made to move the US

embassy to Jerusalem, to cut off funding to the PLO because it has not yet crushed HAMAS (Islamic Resistance Movement), and no one will think to criticize the continuing building of settlements and expropriation of land in the West Bank and Jerusalem. Small wonder that Likud leaders can try to convince their followers that Israel does not have to make a choice between settlements and support from the United States. It can have both.

If the peace effort fails, the consequences will be terrible for the region. It will mean more suffering for Palestinians and Israelis, a strengthening of extremist sentiment at the expense of moderation and pragmatism, and the possible return to power of Likud. It could also weaken the underpinnings of the Egyptian-Israeli peace. None of this need happen, however; an alternative is on the horizon. Without being pollyannish, one can imagine the emergence of a zone of peace in the Eastern Mediterranean in the coming decade that would allow for a flourishing of democratic politics and economic growth in Israel, Palestine, Jordan, and Lebanon, with beneficial spillover in Syria and Egypt as well.

If this corner of the Middle East, possibly along with North Africa and Turkey, enters the next century in conditions of improved governance, greater economic prosperity, and peace, a genuine revolution will have taken place. The region could become one in which real national independence might be achieved, cultural life would recover from the dead hand of bureaucratic control, diversity might be seen as a source of strength, individual rights would not be considered a threat to collective identities, and wasteful spending on arms might be reduced.

Needless to say, this vision is far from becoming a reality; but it is not a vision that is foreign to the aspirations of the people in the region, who, after all, are not so different from people elsewhere. They, like others, hope for lives of security, identity, economic well-being, peace, and justice. For too long they have been deprived of these elemental rights, either by foreign powers who saw the Middle East as little more than a chess board on which to play out their rivalries, or by indigenous regimes that valued power and gestures over tangible accomplishments for their people.

Of course, it is difficult to predict the future in the Middle East. Uncertainties abound on all fronts. In confronting those uncertainties, leaders and citizens of the Middle East will need to be guided by a vision of the future, a future that need not resemble the recent past. Central to that vision should be accountable governance, equitable development, and peace.

The Gulf between the rulers and the ruled

The Gulf war ended two years ago. . . . Yet still, says Dilip Hiro, the reigning oligarchies, in particular the Saudis, refuse to countenance promised reforms

The two major problems facing the Middle East are: self-determination for the Palestinians, and the grossly unequal ownership of petroleum among Arab countries. While continued denial of national rights to Palestinians is widely recognised as a major barrier to stability in the region, there is scant awareness of the destabilising effect of the perilously wide gap between the oil haves and have-nots in the Arab world.

Facts are stark enough. While six Gulf monarchies, with a mere million inhabitants, possess 46 per cent of the proven global petroleum reserves, the remaining 15 members of the Arab League, with an aggregate population of 170 million, have only a third of the Gulf states' share. With world reserves at 1,012 billion barrels, the per capita figure in the Gulf monarchies is 25,700 barrels as opposed to 870 elsewhere in the Arab League. That is, the disproportion in oil wealth is 30:1.

The wealth accruing from the extraction of petroleum in the oil sheikhdoms, accomplished by tens of thousands of local and expatriate workers, ends up as the private property of the ruling oligarchies. Since the aggregate oil reserves of Bahrain, Kuwait, Oman, Qatar, Saudi Arabia and the United Arab Emirates (more specifically, three of its seven principalities) amount to 462.6 billion barrels, and since all these countries are run as feudal autocracies, eight ruling families now possess oil reserves which, priced at $20 a barrel, are worth $9,252 billion.

Such outrageously skewed ownership of property in the world's most heavily armed region, with a long history of volatility and violence, is an ongoing recipe for destabilisation and violent upheavals.

After the quadrupling of the petroleum price in 1973–74 had inflated their riches to unimagined heights, the oil sheikhs became the target of Ayatollah Ruhollah Khomeini, the leader of the 1979 Islamic revolution in Iran. He attacked them for perpetuating hereditary power which, he argued, was not sanctioned by Islam. He condemned them for refusing to share power with their subjects as enjoined by the Koran; being morally and materially corrupt; selling oil cheaply to the west, particularly America, the Great Satan; and having failed to liberate Palestine, including Jerusalem—which contains Islam's third holiest shrine—from the Zionists.

Khomeini's condemnation was a source of great worry to the oil sheikhs, who claimed to derive their political legitimacy from Islam and Islamic precepts. So acute was their fear that the Saudi rulers, the single most important group in the Arabian peninsula, encouraged the Iraqi president, Saddam Hussein, to attack Iran in September 1980.

Saddam Hussein accomplished what he set out to do even though it took him eight years: he contained the tide of revolutionary Islam, and made the future of the Gulf monarchies safe. But two years after the end of the Iran-Iraq war in August 1988, he adopted, consciously or subconsciously, the two-point programme for the Gulf that Khomeini had conceived but failed to implement: raising oil prices and overthrowing the Gulf monarchs.

In his speech on 10 August 1990, Saddam Hussein articulated his viewpoint. "Through its partitioning of the [Arab] lands, western imperialism founded weak mini-states and installed the families who rendered it services that facilitated its [exploitative] mission," he said. "Thus it prevented the majority of the sons of the people and the [Arab] nation from benefiting from their own wealth. As a result of the new wealth passing into the hands of the minority of the [Arab] nation to be exploited for the benefit of the foreigner and the few new rulers, financial and social corruption spread in these mini-states . . . [and from there to] many quarters of the majority of the Arab countries." It is a viewpoint shared by an increasing number of Arab intellectuals and religious leaders.

The onus is thus on the Gulf sheikhs to redress the situation by following just external and domestic policies. Following Islamic edicts, they should show concern for those Arabs who live in countries with large populations but little or no oil wealth, and share their wealth with them. The best way to do so would be through a multilateral aid agency funded by them on the basis of an equitable formula. This would end the use of oil money on a bilateral basis as a tool to impose the will of the donor on the receiver, a strategy used most blatantly by the Saudi royals.

External security is best achieved through regional pact(s), and not by relying on western powers, however friendly and willing. Having backed the Damascus Declaration in early March 1991 on the posting of a joint Arab peacekeeping force, consisting of 35,000 Egyptian and 20,000 Syrian troops, in the region, Kuwait reneged.

From *New Statesman & Society,* February 26, 1993, pp. 18-20. © 1993 by New Statesman & Society. Reprinted by permission.

Six months later, it signed a 10-year defence cooperation agreement with America, allowing it to stockpile military supplies, conduct training exercises, and have access to Kuwaiti ports and airfields. It thus upset such Arab stalwarts as Egypt and Syria, and provided ammunition to those Arab nationalists who depict the Gulf sheikhs as avaricious ogres more ready to buy western protection through monetary inducements of arms purchases, and a sustained strategy of keeping oil prices low to subsidise western economies, than serving the interests of fellow Arabs.

Kuwait has a problem in motivating even its own nationals to fight for its territorial integrity. The rate at which Kuwait's 20,000-strong armed forces melted in the face of the Iraqi invasion on 2 August 1990 was scandalous. A similar situation prevails in other Gulf monarchies, whose armed forces rely to a very substantial degree on foreign nationals—or mercenaries, to put it bluntly.

The primary reason for the lack of loyalty among the subjects of the Gulf monarchies is that they have no stake in the social system, which is best secured through representative government, public accountability, and civil and human rights for all.

Such a scenario is nowhere in sight, given the vehement resistance to electoral politics, based on adult franchise, in the Gulf monarchies, especially in Saudi Arabia. "The democratic system prevailing in the world does not suit us in the region," King Fahd declared on 29 March 1992. "Islam is our social and political law. It is a complete constitution of social and economic laws and a system of government and justice."

King Fahd seemed oblivious of the fact that, just across the Gulf, the Iranian regime, also claiming legitimacy from Islam, had held four parliamentary and four presidential elections since the revolution in 1979. Iran's electoral system, based on universal suffrage, rests on the Koranic verses that read: "Consult them on affairs" (3:159), and "Their affairs are by consultation among them" (42:38). The Iranians interpret "them" to mean citizens of a realm, not hand-picked advisers, as the Saudi monarch would have it.

The Iranian elections are conducted within the context of a written constitution—something Saudi Arabia, founded 61 years ago, still lacks. When a draft constitution, prepared under his order,

was presented to King Saud in 1960 for approval, he rejected it, saying: "The Koran is the oldest and the most efficient of the world's constitutions."

After the seizure of the Grand Mosque in Mecca on 20 November 1979 by 300 militant Islamists in protest at the autocracy and corruption of the Saudi royal family, and the subsequent bloodshed, King Khalid (1975–82) appointed a committee to draft a constitution, followed by an announcement by Crown Prince Fahd that a Consultative Council of 60 to 70 nominated members would be established "in the near future".

Nothing happened for 13 years.

Then, on 1 March 1992, a year after the cataclysmic Gulf war, King Fahd referred to "the momentous events in the recent past" as the (implied) reason for the political reform he announced. His decrees promised a Consultative Council of 60 commoners to be nominated by him within six months, adherence to the rule of law, and an enlarged body of princes to select a new monarch.

Actually, the demand for a Consultative Council to "debate and decide on all domestic and foreign affairs" was the first of ten demands made by more than 100 leading religious scholars, judges and academics, and submitted to King Fahd by Sheikh Abdul Aziz ibn Baz, the head of the country's 17-member Supreme Religious Council (SRC) in May 1991. Since Saudi Arabia was created by Abdul Aziz, the present king's father, in 1932 by an alliance between his family and the leader of the puritanical Wahhabi sect in central Arabia, the SRC is one of the two main pillars on which the kingdom rests.

Other demands of the SRC included reforming the military and arms suppliers with a view to creating "modern, strong and independent Islamic armed forces" backed by a sophisticated arms industry; preserving the interests, purity and unity of the country by "keeping it out of non-Islamic pacts and treaties"; comprehensive social justice based on "equality for all citizens" within the framework of Islamic laws; and, equally important, punishment of all who enriched themselves by illegal means "whoever they are, wherever they are, without any exception of rank".

As before, there was no follow-up on the establishment of the promised Consultative Council. But, in August, about 100 Islamic luminaries submitted to King Fahd a 45-page memorandum, widening

and deepening the scope of the ten-point petition of May 1991.

The monarch was not amused. Nor was the head of the SRC. In September, the SRC issued a denunication of the latest memorandum. This statement was signed by only ten of the 17 SRC members, giving rise to rumours that the remaining seven (implicitly) backed the document—a disturbing development for the Saudi monarch. Early in October, he had another piece of bad news. Elections to the revived parliament of Kuwait (which had been dissolved in June 1986 by the emir of Kuwait, under Saudi pressure) were held as promised, and—horror of horrors—the opposition had triumphed.

Only 15 of the 50 elected parliamentary seats went to the pro-government candidates. Of the 35 seats won by the opposition, 16 went to those who belonged to one of the three Islamist parties or had Islamist endorsement. This despite the fact that voting was limited to only 81,400 men out of a total of 410,000 adult citizens who would be eligible to vote under the universal suffrage that exists in such Muslim countries as Iran and Pakistan. And the Kuwaiti government had spent $10 billion to bribe the voters by raising salaries by 25 per cent, writing off the personal debts of all Kuwaiti citizens, and paying seven months' salary to those who had stayed on during the Iraqi occupation.

Due to the traumatic experience of foreign occupation and war, the Kuwaiti voters had become politically more conscious. Instead of enquiring about public services during the election campaign, as they did before, they focused on Kuwait's investments abroad, and the country's security and defence.

Not surprisingly, the new parliament has busied itself with these issues. It passed a law that authorised it to scrutinise all state investments. Its select committees have decided to investigate *inter alia* the depletion of the Reserve Fund for Future Generations by about $55 billion; the government decision in October to buy up all of Kuwaiti banks' debts; and the virtual disappearance of $5 billion of public money invested in a Spanish chemical company, the scandal involving two important members of the ruling al Sabah family.

Established in 1976, the Reserve Fund for Future Generations was built up by injecting 10 per cent of oil revenues into it each year. This brought the total to $85 billion in 1989, seven-eighths of it invested abroad, and managed mostly by the Kuwait Investment Authority, a department of the finance ministry. It is now believed to be worth only $30 billion. Allowing for the $23 billion that Kuwait contributed towards the Gulf war fund, $32 billion remain to be accounted for.

As for the government wiping out Kuwaiti banks' debts, 9,300 debtors are involved. About one-sixth of these are reportedly responsible for 90 per cent of the total debt of $22 billion. They include some of the richest merchants and members of the ruling family. To protect their foreign assets, they have refused to declare them to their creditors' banks.

Financial scandals in Kuwait are nothing new. When the informal stock exchange, Suq al Manakh, collapsed in September 1982, the government stepped in to save the situation, and found itself lumbered with $97 billion in paper debt. When the parliament of the day attempted to discover which al Sabahs owed money and how much, it was dissolved.

As then, so now, the real target of the parliamentary investigators is believed to be Sheikh Ali Khalifa al Sabah, former oil and finance minister, and a powerful member of the ruling family. The opposition see him as arrogant and authoritarian. Though the parliamentary committees lack judicial powers, MPs maintain that if they uncover any wrongdoing, they reserve the right to prosecute.

The moral for the Gulf's ruling dynasties is plain. Representative government can put in jeopardy the future of even the most powerful oligarchs. Thanks to the limited parliamentary democracy in Kuwait, it has been possible to pinpoint instances of major scandals of corruption and mismanagement of public funds. But in the absence of any representative chamber in Saudi Arabia, rumours and innuendos abound.

Since a free press does not exist in the Saudi kingdom, the task of circulating the stories of corruption and other misdemeanours by the ruling elite has fallen on clandestine audio-tapes carrying the sermons of several prominent dissident clerics. Among many such tapes, the one nicknamed "The Supergun" is particularly noteworthy. It denounces royal princes, ministers, high-ranking officials and army officers for corruption, drug-taking, alcoholism and other deviations from the path of Islam. It accuses the royal family of embezzlement and squandering the country's oil wealth which, it claims, ends up in the pockets of the leading princes. The speaker is Abu al Bara al Najidi, *nom de plume* of a former Islamic judge in Saudi Arabia, now reportedly based in Pakistan/Afghanistan.

The government's response has been to offer large rewards for identifying the author(s) of such tapes and banning 40 clerics from delivering sermons in mosques. In mid-December, King Fahd warned Islamic preachers against using the mosque for political purposes, and replaced those SRC members who three months earlier had failed to sign the condemnation of the demand for comprehensive reform along Islamic lines.

But, unlike in the past, the signatories were not cowed by this. In late December, following the shooting down of an Iraqi warplane by the US aircraft in southern Iraq's no-fly zone, they warned the Saudi government against siding with "the infidels" in their battle with "our Muslim brethren in Iraq". That explained why, following the western air strikes against Iraqi targets in mid-January, Riyadh maintained official silence about the use of Saudi airbases by US warplanes.

Undoubtedly, the House of Saud faces rising opposition—primarily from the traditional religious leaders who see Islam undermined by the waywardness of the ruling family at home and western pressures abroad, and secondarily from foreign-educated intellectuals who desire democratic liberties.

For both groups, the reform package offered by the monarch last March was too little too late. Eleven months later, all they had was the name of the chairman of the promised consultative council: Sheikh Abdullah ibn Jubair, a member of the SRC.

A striking feature of this phenomenon has been America's total silence. Washington knows well that the rigorous censorship that blocked news of Iraq's invasion of Kuwait for three days is very much in place. It knows too that there are at least 100 political prisoners, that torture of detainees is routine, that detention without trial can last years and that there is no appeal against wrongful arrest.

America, the foremost upholder of civil and human rights and democracy, has so far refrained from cajoling the Saudi royals towards political pluralism. Why? First, it is much simpler to manipulate a few ruling families—to secure fat orders for arms and ensure that oil price remains low—than a wide variety of personalities and policies bound to be thrown up by a democratic system. Second, elected governments in the Arabian peninsula would reflect the ideologies of Arab nationalism and Islamic fundamentalism prevalent among large sections of the population, and veer away from the west, stressing self-reliance and Islamic fellowship.

The free and fair poll in Jordan in November 1988 resulted in the election of 32 Islamic fundamentalists or their sympathisers in a house of 80, and about half as many Arab nationalists. The distance that the Jordanian government and King Hussein put between themselves and the west during the Gulf crisis of 1990–91 reflected this reality.

More seriously, if the status quo continues undisturbed, it is only a matter of time before another Saddam or Khomeini moves against the avaricious oil sheiks. And next time, the "infidel" west would not find it so easy to intervene militarily, albeit under the umbrella of the United Nations, as it did in 1991.

The current western policy of over-arming these monarchies with sophisticated weapons without any pressure for political liberalisation is a rerun of what was done in the case of Iran under the Shah in the mid- and late-seventies. The consequences of that disastrous policy—manifested in the emergence of a revolutionary Islamic Iran—are still with us. Will the west ever learn from the past?

Islam: promise or peril?

Asteris C. Huliaras

A new chapter in the history of the Horn of Africa[1] began to unfold in 1991: Eritrea won its independence after Africa's longest war; the regime of Mengistu Haile Mariam collapsed in Ethiopia; and Siyad Barre's overthrow in Somalia was followed by extremely violent inter-clan conflict. During the Cold War, the Horn owed its strategic significance to its proximity to the oil-rich Middle East. 1991 also marked the decline of the strategic value of the region to the major powers.[2] The US intervention in Somalia was nothing more than an interlude: it actually reduced the importance to the West of sub-Saharan Africa—including the Horn—even further. Will Islam now replace communism on the agendas of the Western powers?

In general, the 'threat of Islamic fundamentalism' is over-estimated by many journalists and politicians in the West. Samuel Huntington's thesis about an emerging conflict between the West and other civilisations[3]—a view held widely among US foreign policy and military strategies—has been sharply criticised by many academics. As John Esposito correctly observed: 'The defeat of communism has crated a "threat vacuum" that has given rise to a search for new enemies'.[4]

The American military intervention in Somalia was partly caused by the creation of a Somalia Islamic organisation called *al-Itahad* which, in June 1992, occupied (not for long, as it turned out) many towns in the country, including the important port of Bosaso. American foreign policy-makers were particularly concerned about the possible spread of Islamic influence to neighbouring Ethiopia and Kenya.

The same considerations continue to dominate US foreign policy vis-à-vis the Horn of Africa: Washington fears that Sudan, backed by Iran, might become a 'new Lebanon', using terrorist groups to export the Islamic revolution across Africa. Thus, the Clinton Administration is reported to have braced itself to provide help to Ethiopia and Eritrea to counter Sudanese military attempts to expand Islam.[5] However, it is quite clear that the United States is unwilling to interfere in the region's affairs to the extent that some local governments would wish, or to the extent it did in the recent past.

Islam on the march

In 1993, a group called Jihad-Eritrea launched an attack against Eritrean government soldiers in an area close to the Sudanese-Eritrean border. On 22 February 1995, at least 11 people were killed and more than 150 wounded when Muslim factions opened fire on each other outside Addis Ababa's Grand Anwar Mosque. At the beginning of 1995, Islamic law was enforced in northern Mogadishu, nominally controlled by the Somali warlord Ali Mahdi Mohammed. In Djibouti, 'more and more women are wearing the veil'.[6] Is Islamic fundamentalism spreading in the Horn of Africa?

The recent incidents can be attributed to both internal and external factors. Unlike elsewhere, the increasing influence of Islamic militancy in the Horn of Africa is not primarily due to a religious renaissance in reaction to processes of Westernisation. Islamic activism in the region is only secondarily the response of traditional societies to the forces of modernisation and Western materialism. In Ethiopia and Eritrea—as in many countries in eastern Europe—the Islamic resurgence is not so much a consequence of the confusion and anxiety produced by modernity, as a reaction to religious repression by a totalitarian regime.

Marxism-Leninism in Ethiopia under Mengistu moved against both Christianity and Islam. In 1977, the head of the Ethiopian Orthodox church was removed from office and arrested. Later other religious leaders, both Orthodox Copts and Sunni Muslims, were arrested or assassinated. Since the collapse of the Ethiopian communist state, and after decades of anti-religious propaganda, churches and mosques in Ethiopia and Eritrea are full of people practising their religion. From this perspective, what is happening in the Horn of Africa is not so much an Islamic 'resurgence' as an Islamic 'reassertion'.

An ideological vacuum

As in the Maghreb region, the collapse of socialism in the Horn of Africa has created an ideological vacuum. Young people, in particular, are looking for answers in an era of economic decline and political disillusionment and find in the Koran, or in the Bible, an intellectual and sentimental refuge. In Ethiopia, the collapse of the unitary state, the independence of Eritrea, and the introduction into its constitution of a clause that allows secession, have created confusion and a sense of insecurity, leading people to an idealisation of a supposedly 'glorious past'. Ethiopian Christians and Muslims, feeling lost in a period of rapid and radical change, look for answers in religion. For Eritrea, Ethiopia is no longer a unifying external threat. For Muslims, Eritrea is a part of the Muslim and Arab world.

In an era characterised by political apathy, political forces tend to look for new sources of ideological legitimacy. Muslims in all four countries of the Horn form significant constituencies. Almost all of Djibouti's and Somalia's inhabitants, the absolute majority of Eritreans (probably 55 per cent) and about 45 per cent of Ethiopians are Muslims.[7] The Eritrean Liberation Front (ELF), an organisation of Muslim lowlanders, has recently reemerged, and some of its leading members attended the conferences of *Rabita Islamia* (the Muslim League). In Ethiopia, the leaders of three Muslim Oromo opposition groups (the Islamic Front for the Liberation of Oromiya, the Oromo Liberation Front and the United Oromo Peoples Liberation Front) met in Saudi Arabia and agreed to coordinate their struggle against the government.

As in other parts of the world—especially Algeria—the religious resurgence reflects the economic situation. In sharp contrast to Libya and Iran, where fundamentalism is a product of material wealth, Islamic militancy in the Horn is partly the product of hardship. Desperate people seek a sense of direction in the strict Muslim morality, 'as if the physical barrenness of the soil has given rise to spiritual fertility'.[8] But sometimes the causes are far less spiritual than one might suppose. Many people in Ethiopia, Eritrea and Somalia, hit by price increases, unemployment and poor social services, find refuge in religious institutions which distribute food, provide shelter and offer basic health care. This explains to a large extent the success of many Western evangelical churches in the Horn and is, in part, responsible for the emergence of radical Muslim groups.

Rivalry over the control of foreign funds, mainly from Saudi and Sudanese Islamic organisations, appears to be the main reason for the fighting in Addis Ababa's largest mosque.[9] According to Western diplomats in the Ethiopian capital, the creation of the Islamic Front for the Liberation of Oromiya reflects clearly the ambitions of Muslim elites to attract Saudi money. Economic strength can easily ensure public support in 'subsistence' economies like those of Ethiopia, Eritrea or Djibouti.

Although the internal factors should not be underestimated, external powers are particularly important in the recent emergence of Islamic militancy in the countries of the Horn. In the past, Djibouti, Somalia and Sudan, as members of the Arab League, were favoured by Arab institutions. The received financial aid from the Arab Aid Fund for Africa and its successor, the Arab Bank for Economic Development in Africa, from the Islamic Development Bank and from the Islamic Solidarity Fund. However, as pan-African ideological considerations receded and superpower involvement in the region intensified, the Arab states' ambition to transform the Red Sea into an 'Arab lake' gradually declined. Economic aid declined as well. Although Eritrea has recently become a member of the Arab League, hoping to attract investment from the countries of the Middle East, prospects are not very promising: the 'Arab factor' in black Africa is far less dominant than it used to be.

Sudan as a threat

At the beginning of the 1990s, the collapse of power structures in Somalia, the crucial transitional period in Ethiopia, and questions regarding Eritrea's viability, contributed to the emergence of Sudan as a key power in the Horn of Africa and the Red Sea littoral. In December 1991, the Iranian President, Ali Akbar Hashemi-Rafsanjani, visited Khartoum, and a number of commercial, economic and military agreements were signed.[10]

As expected, the strengthening of the relationship between the two countries aroused the interest of US diplomats who feared the creation of a triangular Islamic alliance (Iran, Sudan and the Algerian opposition). In 1993, the new transitional Eritrean government accused Khartoum of organising and arming Eritrean refugees in southern Sudan (in mid-1994 there were about 500,000 Eritreans in Sudan). In December 1994, and after a number of military actions by Muslim guerillas on Eritrean soil, Asmara severed diplomatic relations with Khartoum. Some analysts contended that Eritrea's move reflected a wider regional effort involving Egypt, Uganda and Ethiopia, and was aimed at isolating Sudan.[11] Kampala, supporting this view, severed diplomatic relations with Khartoum a few months later.

Although, at the beginning, the government of Umar Hasan Ahmad al-Bashir dismissed Eritrea's allegations, a conference of Arab and Islamic nations in Khartoum in 1995 decided on the need to 'support in all ways the oppressed Eritrean Muslims', while Eritrea-Jihad continued its attacks in a number of Eritrean provinces. It seems that Eritrea-Jihad is linked to the Muslim Eritrean Liberation Front, which in the 1960s had begun the Eritrean insurgency against Ethiopia. Eritrean Muslims and Christians have a history of conflict since the beginning of the 1970s, when their respective guerrilla movements fought for dominance of the secessionist movement. Thus, Eritrea seems particularly vulnerable to Sudanese destabilisation in its first steps as an independent entity.

As far as Ethiopia is concerned, it was reported in May 1995 that leaders of the Oromo Liberation Front (OLF), which had taken part in the insurgency against Mengistu but later withdrawn from the transitional government, had discussed ways of military training, material assistance and strategic bases in a meeting with officials of the al-Bashir government.[12]

Thus, Sudan emerges as a strategic threat in the Horn, spreading Islamic militancy and trying to undermine the legitimacy of the governments of Ethiopia and Eritrea.

Africanising Islam

In the Horn of Africa, Islamic practices were mixed with pre-Islamic African religions, enabling the creation of a tradition of political adaptability, flexibility and tolerance.[13] This tolerance allows the peoples of the region to have, for example, both Muslim and Christian members in the same families. Particularly in Ethiopia, Islam is characterised by a rich and revealing syncretism: the Afar and the Oromo Muslims still believe in a god called *Waq*, who is the sky and whose blessing is the rain. Many Muslims of the Horn 'simply adopt the external trappings of Islam but are [not] coverted in mind, heart and soul, and essentially remain embedded in traditional religion'.[14] This characteristic of Islam in north-eastern Africa makes it difficult for fundamentalism to grow.

Islam in the traditional sense is dominant only on the Eritrean coast among Arab or Arabised population s as well as in Hararge and a few other big Ethiopian cities. Among Somali nomads there is no strict observance of even the most important practices of the Islamic faith, such as regular payer and fasting during the Ramadan period. The Somali pastoralists and some Eritrean clans do not follow the basic Islamic principle of division of property among their heirs. Historically, as Trimingham has observed in his important study, while Christian expansion in the Horn took place essentially by conquest, Islam spread mainly by peaceful means.[15] Thus, there is no tradition of an aggressive Islam in the region, and consequently, Islamic fundamentalism cannot spread easily.

Boosting strategic values

Another very important reason for the recent talk of an 'Islamic peril' is the policies of governments. Apart from the officials in Western capitals searching for new enemies, after the end of the Cold War, the governments of Ethiopia and Eritrea—as those of Turkey, Saudi Arabia and Pakistan, among others—tend to overemphasise the Islamic threat, hoping to stop the erosion of public support and, more important, to increase their countries' weakened strategic value after the collapse of the bipolar system.

The leaderships of the countries in the Horn are, of course, no exception to this rather common and widespread tactic: the political stance of both Meles Zenawi of Ethiopia and of Isayas Afeworki of Eritrea against Sudan is a reflection of their efforts to increase their countries' leverage in Western capitals. Zenawi has confirmed Sudanese support for Muslim fundamentalists in Ethiopia, and Eritrea has served diplomatic relations with Khartoum. Both governments, according to Western diplomatic sources in Addis Ababa, has asked the United States to help them halt Sudanese efforts to expand Islam. Particularly in the case of Ethiopia, the Ethiopian Peoples Revolutionary Democratic Front (EPFRD) government emphasises the 'Islamic danger', not only in the hope of receiving Western economic and military assistance, but also to decrease inter-Christian ethnic rivalries between Tigre and Amhara. At the same time, inter-ethnic religious cleavages can be accentuated, especially in the case of the Oromo, where the OLF, the EPRDF's strongest rival, is influential.

There is another factor which reduce the possibility of an Islamic fundamentalist movement in the Horn: ethnic and religious identities do not coincide. In sharp contrast to the Middle East, ethnic identity has always been much more important than religion in the Horn of Africa. It continues to be so today. Mainly Christian Tigreans have fought the Christian Amharas for years. Muslim Somali factions battled with each other before and after the collapse of the Siyad Barre regime. In Djibouti, Muslim Afars started an insurgency against a government dominated by Muslim Issas.

The most numerous people in Ethiopia, the Oromo (about 40 per cent of a population of 53 million) offer a very clear picture of the religious diversity within ethnic groups in the Horn. The eastern Oromo of Harar and the Muslim urban population of towns like Hararge and Dire Dawa have traditional links with the Arab world, and their local leaders have a strong Islamic identity. In sharp contrast, the Western Oromos share the Christian culture of the Amharas. In an era of intense ethnic consolidation in Ethiopia, Muslim identity cannot unify the various ethnic groups since it frequently does not coincide with ethnicity.

In Eritrea, Muslims belong to a variety of ethnic groups and they speak Tigre, Arabic, Saho, Afar and other languages. And, of course, clan and sub-clans divide an almost entirely Muslim population in Somalia. As Mazrui has emphasized, when religious differences coincide with ethnic and linguistic divisions, the natural ecumenism of indigenous Africa is overwhelmed by the competitiveness of Christianity and Islam.[16] Divisions and the interests in the Horn are basically ethnic-, class- (mainly agricultural/pastoral) and clan-oriented, and are only secondarily of a religious character.

We have seen that outside forces, and especially Sudan, have played an important role in the recent developments in the countries of the Horn. At the same time, however, external factors contribute to the gradual decline of this influence. With economic problems mounting, including a debt of $15 billion (about 150 per cent of its gross national product), Sudan is in no position to offer serious economic or military aid to Islamic groups. Furthermore, Khartoum's support for Baghdad in the Gulf war worsened its relations with Saudi Arabia, Kuwait and other Arab states, and does not appear to have improved its relations with Iran. The recent assassination attempt against President Mubarak of Egypt, and the ensuing crisis in Egyptian-Sudanese relations, undoubtedly increased the security concerns of al-Bashir's government: Khartoum will probably hesitate to open new fronts on the country's southern borders.

3. CONFLICT AND INSTABILITY

Although there is a strong religious component in Iran's foreign policy, it pragmatic leadership is now more concerned with promoting the country's interests than with spreading Islamic fundamentalism in sub-Saharan Africa. Finally, Saudi Arabia seems to face internal economic problems that impose serious constraints on its willingness to offer financial support to Muslim movement abroad.

An antidote to anarchy?

Robert Kaplan, in his now notorious article "The Coming Anarchy',[17] reflected on the predicament of a number of West African states and predicted a Hobbesian vision for most of the globe. 'West Africa', he wrote, 'is becoming the symbol of worldwide demographic, environmental, and societal stress, in which criminal anarchy emerges as the real "strategic" danger'. In an interview with a West African Minister, Kaplan is told that 'in the poor quarters of Arab North Africa there is much less crime, because Islam provides a social anchor of education and indoctrination', but that 'in West Africa we have a lot of superficial Islam and superficial Christianity'. The same is true, as far as Muslims are concerned, in the Horn of Africa where, as we saw, Islam is also lightly worn.

Can Islamic fundamentalism act as an antidote to the collapse of states and societies in the Horn? This is a question which has been largely ignored in academic discussions of the so-called 'Islamic peril'. If Islam can become a stabilising factor in an increasingly volatile region characterised by chaotic criminality, why should the West regard it as a danger? In northern Mogadishu, the enforcement of the *Sharia* law, some lashings and amputations were enough to eliminate crime and to establish a sense of order.[18]

In February 1995, Islamic tribunals started to operate in southern Mogadishu, where General Aideed is in control, while reports from the north-eastern part of the country suggest that the Islamic law will soon be implemented by the Democratic Front for the Salvation of Somalia.[19] Why should these be regarded as 'negative' developments?

A clear distinction appears. In societies where Islam is the absolutely dominant religion (Somalia, Djibouti, the Ethiopian Ogaden) and where the social order has collapsed (recent Somali experience), Islamic fundamentalism could act as a stabilising factor. In societies where the population is multi-religious (Eritrea and most of Ethiopia's provinces), fundamentalism is divisive and acts as a destabilising factor. So although Islamic fundamentalism can be regarded as a threat to stability in multi-religious societies, in Muslim societies and in situations of extreme chaos, it can also offer a viable law-and-order alternative to state institutions. Consequently,

it should not always be considered as a 'peril'. Thus, if 'the magic word for Western interests in the Horn is "stability"', as one European diplomat in Addis Ababa put it, then the introduction of the *Sharia* law in Somalia could be regarded as a positive development because it is a law that prevents crime and establishes internal order, despite the fact that it does not respect Western humanitarian anxieties.

Although it would be wrong to underestimate Islam's increasing influence on the political agendas of the countries of the Horn, fundamentalism is only a secondary factor in the current alignment of political forces in the region. Ethnic rivalries are far more important, and since they do not coincide with religious differences, they do not permit the emergence of a religious conflict. Furthermore, the ability and willingness of outside powers to influence political developments in the region is undoubtedly in decline. The Horn of African does not represent any serious Islamic 'danger'. And even when Islam does emerge in chaotic situations, as in post–Siyad Barre's Somalia, it promotes rather than threatens stability.

Notes

1. Here, 'the Horn of Africa' is defined as consisting of Djibouti, Eritrea, Ethiopia and Somalia.
2. For an excellent introduction to the security problems in the Horn and its strategic significance, see Samuel M. Makinda, *Security in the Horn of Africa*, Adelphi paper No. 269 (London: The International Institute for Strategic Studies, 1992).
3. Samuel P. Huntington, 'The clash of civilisations?', *Foreign Affairs*, Vol. 72(3), 1993, pp. 22–49.
4. John L. Esposito, 'Political Islam: Beyond the green menace', *Current History*, Vol. 93(579), 1994, p. 19.
5. *Ethiopia: Seven Days Update*, Vol. 2(59), 24 April 1995, p. 8; The Economist Intelligence Unit, *Country Report: Ethiopia, Eritrea, Somalia, Djibouti*, 2nd Quarter 1995, p. 21.
6. Jean-Pierre Tuquoi, 'Djibouti survives on French handouts', *The Guardian Weekly*, 20 August 1995, p. 16.
7. Estimates of Western diplomats in Addis Ababa and Asmara.
8. Ali Mazrui, 'African Islam and competitive religion: between revivalism and expansion', *Third World Quarterly*, April 1988, p. 515.
9. The Economist Intelligence Unit, *op. cit*, 1st Quarter 1995, pp. 9–10.
10. Abdal Salam Sid Ahmed, 'Tehran—Khartoum: a new axis or a warning spot?', *Middle East International*, 2 February 1992, p. 18.
11. *Africa Confidential*, 16 December 1994, p. 8.
12. *Ethiopia: Seven Days Update*, Vol. 2(57), 10 April 1995, pp. 4–5.
13. Ali Mazrui, *The African Condition. A Political Diagnosis* (Cambridge: Cambridge University Press, 1980, p. 54; A. Mazrui, 'African Islam', *op. cit.*, pp. 499–501.
14. Mario Azevedo and Gwendolyn S. Prater, 'The Minority Status of Islam in East Africa: A Historico-Sociological Perspective', *Journal of the Institute of Muslim Minority Affairs*, July 1991, p. 488.
15. John Spencer Trimingham, *Islam in Ethiopia* (London: Cass, 1965).
16. A. Mazrui, 'African Islam', *op.cit.*, p. 503.
17. Robert D. Kaplan, 'The Coming Anarchy', *The Atlantic Monthly*, February 1994, p. 46.
18. 'Somalia after the peacekeepers go', *The Economist*, 18 February 1995, p. 52.
19. The Economist Intelligence Unit, *op.cit.*, 2nd Quarter 1995, p. 34.

Awaiting a new spark

Genocide and civil war stalk bloodied Burundi and Rwanda — again

Bujumbura, the capital of Burundi, strains for an aura of normalcy. Streets are quiet and neat. Locals sip sundowners at the yacht club as they watch hippos snorting in Lake Tanganyika's muddy waters. Diplomats and government officials trade handshakes and polite cocktail chatter beside glowing hotel pools.

But amid the perfume of Bujumbura's lush gardens there is a whiff of Saigon, circa 1965. The city's calm comes courtesy of an 8-mile *cordon sanitaire* hacked into the hills by the Tutsi-dominated Army, which has evacuated entire villages to strip antigovernment Hutu militias of cover. Receptions end early, as guests rush home to beat a strict 9 p.m. curfew. And out in the countryside of the Massachusetts-size Central African nation, Western officials estimate that as many as 100 Burundians are dying every week in an intensifying cycle of Hutu insurgent attacks and Army reprisals.

Despite millions in aid and determined diplomatic efforts, Central Africa remains on the brink of chaos. While Burundi slides into a civil war that could sow the seeds of genocide, neighboring Rwanda is recovering from a genocide that appears to have planted the seeds of civil war. The desperate plight of both countries highlights yet again the world's continuing inability, short of massive intervention, to stop the ethnic conflicts that are becoming the hallmark of the post-cold-war world. "We still do a much better job managing the consequences of disaster than we do preventing disaster," says J. Brian Atwood, administrator of the U.S. Agency for International Development, who visited the region last week as part of a joint U.S.-European mission to assess its troubled future.

In 1988 the developed world spent $500 million on humanitarian relief worldwide. In 1993 the annual tab had exploded to $3.5 billion. Benaco refugee camp in Tanzania is a testament to the skill and efficiency with which the world has learned to respond to the crises that it does not prevent. It is an orderly city of 158,000, with regular food deliveries and health, education and sanitation services.

But the accelerating cost of humanitarian relief is creating a vicious dilemma. Refugee camps in Central Africa (see map) cost about $2 million a day; amid tightening aid budgets, that is money not being spent on long-term development projects that might prevent future Rwandas and Burundis elsewhere.

Burundi's worries are more immediate. As in Rwanda before the 1994 genocide, which killed as many as 800,000 Tutsis and Hutu moderates, Hutus in Burundi make up a largely disenfranchised 85 percent majority that is dominated by a small Tutsi elite. An estimated 100,000 have died in fighting since 1993, and now three

STEPHEN ROUNTREE—*USN&WR*

ZAIRE · **UGANDA** · Goma · Lake Kivu · **RWANDA** · ★ Kigali · Ngara · Bukavu · Cibitoke · **TANZANIA** · Ngozi · Bujumbura · Ruyigi · Area of detail · **BURUNDI** · △ Refugee camps · ✂ Recent clashes · Bururi · Lake Tanganyika · 0   50 · **MILES**

USN&WR—Basic data: United Nations High Commissioner for Refugees; Search for Common Ground; U.S. Committee for Refugees

Hutu insurgencies are trying to topple the country's weak coalition government. Still, most local observers doubt that the violence will escalate to genocidal proportions, in part because there is a rough military balance between the Tutsi-controlled Army and the Hutu forces.

Nevertheless, the situation is dangerous enough that the United States and Europe have suspended about $100 million in development assistance over security concerns. And last month, the U.N. Security Council voted to begin contingency planning for a possible multilateral intervention force. The Clinton administration and its European allies are hoping that war weariness and political dialogue will instead defuse the crisis. But that appears increasingly doubtful: The Tutsi elite, which is also fighting to protect its domination of the economy, has been hardening its line in the face of widening Hutu militia attacks. "There's no room for dialogue with proponents of genocide," says Burundian Prime Minister Antoine Nduwayo.

Threats from without. Rwanda is comparatively stable—for now. A new government includes Hutus and Tutsis and is making steady progress toward restoring order and infrastructure. Streets in the capital of Kigali are bustling and, according to the International Monetary Fund, the war-devastated economy grew about 40 percent last year.

Rwanda's problems lie just outside the country's borders. Nearly 1.7 million Rwandan refugees, mainly Hutu, remain in teeming camps in Zaire, Tanzania and Burundi. Some, mostly women and children, are innocent of genocide but are afraid to return to Rwanda for fear of revenge killings. But among them are thousands of murderers and members of the former Rwandan Army, which orchestrated much of the genocide. These Hutu leaders intimidate the other refugees—violently, if necessary—to discourage them from going home. Worse,

3. CONFLICT AND INSTABILITY

they are using the camps, the surrounding countryside and a steady flow of covert arms from Zaire and elsewhere in the region to organize and train insurgents to regain power in Rwanda. These militia leaders seem to have learned that genocide is no longer an acceptable goal: Their propaganda pamphlets, captured by the Rwandan Army, refer instead to the coming "insecticide" campaign.

Relief officials, lacking support from the international community and the Zairian and Tanzanian governments, can do little to control these extremists. "I cannot kick them out. I do not have an army," says a frustrated Joel Boutroue, who directs the operations of the United Nations High Commissioner for Refugees in Goma, Zaire.

Meanwhile, the ethnic antagonisms continue to fester in Bujumbura's squalid camps for displaced persons. Credos, a 45-year-old Hutu, fled to one last summer after the Army cleansed his village as part of its fight against Hutu militias. His uncle, brother, sister and three children were killed by the Tutsi soldiers, who he says bayoneted the women and children who were too slow to outrun them. Nikodeme, a 40-year-old Tutsi, lives in another of the capital's camps. He arrived there in 1993, shortly after paratroopers from the Tutsi-dominated Army assassinated Burundi's Hutu president. In re-venge, Hutus in Nikodeme's village started slaughtering their Tutsi neighbors. His 15-year-old daughter was murdered.

Each man insists he wants peace and ethnic harmony in Burundi. But at the same time, each refuses to concede any wrongdoing by his faction or acknowledge any right on the other side. They can agree on only one point, which Nikodeme puts this way: "If we do not resolve this problem immediately, Burundi will be worse than Rwanda."

TIM ZIMMERMANN IN BURUNDI, RWANDA AND TANZANIA

Nigeria: Inside the Dismal Tunnel

"Nigeria first entered. . .'the dismal tunnel' on January 15, 1966, when the military overthrew all the institutions of a democratically elected government. . . If there is light at the end of [this] tunnel, it is imperceptible to anyone not paid to see it."

RICHARD JOSEPH

RICHARD JOSEPH, *a visiting professor of political science at the Massachusetts Institute of Technology, has written extensively on Nigerian politics. His books include* Democracy and Prebendal Politics in Nigeria: The Rise and Fall of the Second Republic *(Cambridge: Cambridge University Press, 1987). This article is based on a paper presented at a conference on the "Dilemmas of Democracy in Nigeria" at the University of Wisconsin at Madison, November 10-12, 1995.*

The November 10, 1995, execution of Ken Saro-Wiwa and eight other activists from the Movement for the Survival of the Ogoni People by the military government of General Sani Abacha quickly earned worldwide condemnation. It also led to greater international awareness of the regime's repressive policies and highlighted the fact that, although Nigerians have been governed longer by soldiers than by elected politicians since independence in October 1960, the legitimacy and efficacy of military rule have always been vigorously contested.

One month after the regime of General Yakubu Gowon was overthrown in a palace coup in July 1975, Obafemi Awolowo published a set of recommendations to the new rulers. Awolowo had been a civilian member of the Gowon government, but left once the Biafran war ended. Although it promised to return power to civilians in a measured manner, the Gowon government had begun implementing a vast number of far-reaching policies—a pattern that would be followed by all its military successors. Awolowo's admonitions are as relevant today as they were two decades ago: the military administration should serve as "an essentially corrective regime, and not a reconstructing administration with ready and lasting answers to all our political and economic ills. . . It would be too much of a task for it to attempt the massive and neverending task of rebuilding or reconstructing the body politic."

This advice has never been heeded by Nigeria's military rulers. Although General Ibrahim Babangida spent eight futile years between 1985 and 1993 directing a large number of structural reforms, including a complicated transition to civilian rule, the Sani Abacha regime has unveiled a similar set of initiatives to justify remaining in power. Awolowo had his own motives in counseling the armed forces to limit its political agenda. However, in this and other matters, his comments went to the heart of the Nigerian dilemma.

Nigeria first entered what Awolowo labeled "the dismal tunnel" on January 15, 1966, when the military overthrew all the institutions of a democratically elected government. That date echoed in the decision of the constitutional conference, established by Abacha after he seized power on November 17, 1993, to set January 1996 as the date his regime would return power to elected civilians. It took considerable effort and persistence to obtain such a declaration from a conference packed with Abacha appointees and subject to all forms of inducements, co-optation, and coercion. But in April 1995 the conference reversed itself and left the termination date open. On October 1, 1995, Abacha demonstrated his dominance over all internal political forces and his disregard for international opinion by declaring that he would remain in power until 1998. The execution of the

Ogoni activists a month later was a clear signal that only extraordinary measures will loosen the military's grip on power.

Although Nigeria has seen the arrival of an entirely new generation of political, military, and civilian elites and has undergone several regime changes, purges, dismissals, and detentions of members of the political class, the criticisms of Major Kaduna Nzeogwu, who led the seizure of power in northern Nigeria in the January 1966 coup, are as pertinent today as they were 30 years ago. Nzeogwu identified Nigeria's main "enemies" as "the political profiteers, the swindlers, the men in high and low places. . .those who seek to keep the country divided permanently so that they can remain in office as ministers or VIPs at least; the tribalists, the nepotists, those who make the country look big for nothing before international circles, those who have corrupted our society and put the Nigerian political calendar back by their words and deeds."

There is little dispute about what Nigeria has become. The economy is in shambles, kept afloat only by the continued production and export of petroleum. All major public institutions are in a state of advanced decay; social services have deteriorated steadily for over a decade. Once described as kleptocratic, the conduct of public officials merits a stronger designation as the society has become increasingly criminalized. Nigeria is now a major transit point in international drug trafficking and in the laundering of illicit fortunes. Although it has been a major oil producer for over two decades, Nigeria is now included among the debt-distressed nations. Moreover, it lacks the governing capacity even to manage the effective servicing of its estimated international debt of $37 billion.

Even more troubling, Nigeria has become a rogue state, and as such refuses to abide by prevailing international ethical and legal norms in the conduct of public affairs. There are many indications of this new status: suspension of Nigeria's membership by the Commonwealth of States; universal criticism of the continued detention of president-elect Moshood Abiola along with scores of journalists, lawyers, human rights monitors, and political activists; condemnation of the June 1995 secret trials and subsequent sentences imposed on accused coup plotters, including the former president, General Olusegun Obasanjo, and his former deputy, General Shehu Yar'Adua; decertification by the United States government because of drug trafficking (which excludes Nigeria from most forms of assistance); designation, together with Burma, as one of the worst human rights abusers in the United States State Department March 1996 annual report; cancellation of sporting events, including an international soccer tournament scheduled to take place in Nigeria in 1995; tight restrictions on the issuance of visas to Nigerian public officials and their families seeking visas to visit Western nations; and suspension of new loans and investments by multilateral agencies.

Although Nigeria's status has fallen internationally, it is still being given every chance to "return to the fold" before more drastic measures are imposed, such as a ban on arms sales and purchases of Nigerian crude oil. Even the Commonwealth chose to suspend Nigeria for two years rather than expel it after the November 1995 executions.

How did this state of affairs come to pass? Why has Nigeria, which has conducted perhaps the most extensive attempts of any developing nation to construct a constitutional democracy, failed so abysmally? Why has the Nigerian military, after governing the country during much of the post-civil war decade in a manner that permitted a wide degree of openness and autonomy in civil society, produced one of the few regimes on the continent still characterized today as "authoritarian"? How did a country that had a deserved reputation as a principled leader of the continent on international matters, especially the struggle against the racist regimes of Rhodesia and South Africa, come to be described by a British foreign minister as a place of "growing cruelty"?

THE PREBENDAL REPUBLIC

The current crisis in Nigeria can be seen as the outcome of a number of forces whose interactions have pushed the nation down a particular path. One of the elements that should not be overlooked is the repeated failure of civilian politics. As General T. Danjuma, the chief of the army staff under Obasanjo, pointed out with some exasperation in the 1970s, "It is now fashionable in Nigeria to talk about a military regime being an aberration, and that a return to civilian rule means a return to democracy. This is a fallacy because we never had a democracy in Nigeria."

A critical moment came in 1979, following a careful attempt to lay the basis for a stable democracy, that masked a deep flaw that would undermine the new system. That flaw was the relationship between the administration of public office and the acquisition and distribution of material benefits. These practices had also become central to the processes of party building and the making of political alliances. The party that won power in the elections did so for a number of reasons, including its willingness to capitalize on this logic. These well-established practices in Nigerian sociopolitical life can yield short-term gains but also contribute to the sapping of the authority, legitimacy, capacity, and finances of the state.

According to the theory of prebendalism, state offices are regarded as prebends that can be appropriated by officeholders, who use them to generate material benefits for themselves and their constituents and kin groups. In Nigeria, the statutory purposes of such offices became a matter of secondary concern. With the National Party of Nigeria (NPN)—which regarded itself as Nigeria's natural party of government—leading the way in entrenching these practices at the federal level, and all other parties doing likewise in the state and local governments they controlled, Nigeria during the Second Republic between 1979 and 1983, evolved into a full-fledged "prebendal republic."[1] The state was a national cake to be divided and subdivided among officeholders. Politics degenerated, as the scholar Claude Ake has pointed out, into an unrelenting war to acquire, defend, or gain access to state offices.

The state was a national cake to be divided and subdivided among officeholders.

Although civilians had fashioned this system while Nigeria was under colonial rule, the Nigerian military contributed to its extension. There was little difference between the final years of the Gowon administration and those of the Second Republic in this regard. In fact, the members of every Nigerian government, from the regional administrations under colonial rule in the 1950s to the Abacha regime, have demonstrated an increasing propensity to divert public funds for their personal use. Justice Akinola Aguda stated it quite simply when he remarked in the late 1970s that the one achievement of every Nigerian government is that it has created more millionaires than its predecessor. Today, with the emergence of "pharaonic" in place of the milder "prebendal" corruption, that comment should be amended to "multimillionaires."

[1]The first independent civilian government, between 1960 and 1966, is often referred to as the First Republic. The Third Republic, constructed under Babangida, was stillborn.

BABANGIDA'S BOGUS TRANSITION

Despite these failings, Nigeria has usually remained a place of hope. It was, and still is, the greatest agglomeration of African peoples within the boundaries of a single nation-state, and it still possesses considerable natural resources. Nevertheless, in 1989 there came a moment when it became evident that the country was lost in the "dismal tunnel." General Babangida, having already postponed the promised date for the handover of power to civilians from 1990 to 1992, allowed political associations being formed to seek registration as political parties. However, the requirements were grossly unreasonable. The number of offices that associations had to open, the lists and photographs of supporters that had to be provided, and the timetable imposed on them—everything had to be done in a matter of only a few months. The regime set the rules and it could impose any criteria it wished.

After the mountains of materials were delivered to the Electoral Commission in Lagos, the verdict soon followed: none of the associations had met the test and the government would create its own political parties, name them, write their manifestos, and oversee their development. The military regime had embarked on what Awolowo and others had long cautioned against as "the massive and neverending task of rebuilding or reconstructing the body politic"; it was assuming full responsibility for establishing the instruments by which Nigerian civil society would be allowed to pursue its political and social objectives. Little wonder that Nigerian critics dismissed the new parties as parastatals (state-financed enterprises).

As was revealed to participants in an August 1990 conference, the two-party system imposed by the Babangida regime after it dismissed all political associations in 1989 was a preconceived plan. All the political aspirants and entrepreneurs who took part in these exercises have been dupes to one extent or another, since the regime had no intention of ceding power. The transition to democracy became a game in which the rules were changed as soon as the civilian politicians felt they had mastered them. In the hope of inheriting power, or some parcel of it, many Nigerians—soldiers, trade unionists, established politicians, traditional rulers, intellectuals, businesspersons—had been led by Babangida further into the dismal tunnel.

In the election of June 12, 1993, Babangida

finally allowed two affluent businessmen—who considered themselves his cronies—to contest the presidency. They were only the last of the many individuals who had been led to believe that Babangida supported their candidacies only to find themselves dismissed as they reached for the brass ring. On the very eve of his June 23 annulment of the elections, some of Babangida's advisers left a meeting with him reassured that the next day he would announce the winner and next president of the nation.

After 1989 it seemed that there was little new to be said about Nigerian politics. The prebendal character of the state and political life generally had been repeatedly confirmed. Rather than changing what had become fundamental to Nigerian political life, the major developments under the Babangida regime—the considerable growth of the powers of the presidency, Babangida's domination over all aspects of political and social life, the colossal sums privately appropriated (especially by senior members of the regime), the minute stage managing of an elusive transition process—only deepened the contradictions that had been identified by many analysts.

Throughout this period, concerned Nigerians were unable to arouse awareness of the direction Babangida was leading Nigeria as long as the regime repeated its promise to transfer power to an elected government. Following a byzantine series of developments, Babangida was induced by the military hierarchy to leave office on August 26, 1993, clearing the way for Sani Abacha to brush aside Ernest Shonekan's "Interim Civilian Government" less than three months later. Abacha, a man Obasanjo has described as Babangida's "eminent disciple, faithful supporter, and beneficiary," proceeded to take the nation deeper into the dismal tunnel after seizing power on November 17, 1993.

THE MILITARY-CIVILIAN REVOLVING DOOR

Although Awolowo claimed that military rule was an abnormality in Nigeria, it is also the case that civilian rule has not left a commendable record. The violence and mayhem, especially in western Nigeria at the time of the 1983 elections, were reminiscent of the carnage and confusion during the final years of the First Republic. The corrupt behavior of public officials and the gross mismanagement and increasing repressiveness of the federal and state governments during the Shehu Shagari era raised fears that Nigeria would experience a severe crisis if it continued to be inef-

ficiently and corruptly governed while becoming increasingly impoverished. When the armed forces stepped in on December 31, 1983, the ease of their takeover reflected the extent to which the civilian government had lost legitimacy in the eyes of the demoralized and anxious population. Even the embryonic Third Republic, in the form of elected governments at the local, state, and federal levels under Babangida, showed signs of continuing this pattern. As Obasanjo has noted, "In very few states were cases of corruption and obscene malpractice and abuse of office not the order of the day. At the national level, the scale of corruption was monumental."

But Nigeria has also known peace, some economic progress, and a sense of hopefulness during certain periods of military rule. This was the case during the first years following the Biafran war, for much of the Murtala Muhammed-Obasanjo regime, between 1975 and 1979, and for the early years of the Babangida administration. During each of these episodes a distinctly Nigerian military system of governance was in evidence. This system, beginning with Gowon, was refined by each subsequent military administration. In both federal and state governments, a relatively small group of military officers were assisted by civilian appointees, who included well-known politicians as well as private citizens from the professions and the business world. The effective sharing of power took place between the higher military and civil bureaucracies.

This system allowed considerable freedom and autonomy within civil society. Indeed, Nigeria had a freer press during these episodes and a more active, autonomous, and effective array of interest and professional groups than most African countries. Moreover, the balancing of representation of Nigeria's major ethnic groups in the government and in the major public institutions was also handled reasonably well by this system.

Each military government, however, was subject to decay because the military was an unaccountable body that could not restrain the inevitable abuses of office and, except for the Obasanjo regime, was unable to arrange a smooth succession. It thereby increasingly invited countercoups. When Sani Abacha seized power in November 1993, even he temporarily aroused hopes that this known system of governance would be reinstalled. Although Abacha dismissed all the elective political institutions, he managed to draw into his government an impressive group of national politicians, including the long-time human rights lawyer Olu Onagoruwa, who became his minister of justice. By this time, however, such gestures no longer had any substantive meaning; they were merely rituals aimed at obtaining compliance with continued military rule.

When Babangida came to power in August 1985, it seemed that Nigeria was returning to the familiar conciliar system of governance. As Babangida stated in criticizing his predecessors, "A diverse polity like Nigeria required recognition and the appreciation of differences in both cultural and individual perceptions." In fact, the first year of Babangida's rule, characterized by his wide degree of consultation and an open style, kept at bay criticisms of his self-described "military democracy."

By the end of his eight years in power, what the country had experienced, in the words of one of its erstwhile agents, was "organized confusion." Babangida's government claimed to be laying the basis for a "stable liberal democracy" and in its early years pushed through reforms intended to create the foundation for a more market-oriented economy. The Political Bureau appointed by Babangida shortly after he came to power recommended the construction of a socialist republic, a goal the regime rejected while accepting the need for extensive social and ethical mobilization of the population and the creation of a costly bureaucracy to fulfill that role. It initially adopted the conciliar mode of interest accommodation, but gradually supplanted it with a corporatist propensity to charter new institutions and make formerly autonomous bodies dependent on presidential largesse. And after promoting a vigorous human rights policy, it moved to harassing and imprisoning the country's leading human rights lawyers and activists, detaining journalists and banning publications.

ANOTHER REPLAY?

At the end of the 1980s the Campaign for Democracy and its affiliates had called for a national conference to lay the basis for a genuine transition process in place of Babangida's manipulations. In the neighboring francophone countries of Benin, Congo, and Niger, this approach had brought an end to military regimes, but it had been stoutly resisted or derailed in others, such as Cameroon and Zaire. Nigeria needed a new basis for civilian politics that would emerge from an "ingathering" of all political and social forces rather than a renewed top-down crafting by a military regime.

In addition to the need for a transitional process that would mobilize the broad forces of Nigerian society, another issue needed to be addressed: that these transitions were largely phases in the circulation of powerful elites. Since civilians have held government posts under military as well as civilian regimes, they have tended to become involved in promoting changes within military systems, or even military coups (as in 1983 and 1993), that benefit their own material interests.

The idea of a period of nonpartisan civilian government as a kind of "probationary" exercise has regularly surfaced in Nigerian political discourse. One flaw in the transition to the Second Republic was the absence of such an experience at the national level. Indeed, three of the regime's four years in power were devoted to the making of the constitution and only one year to legalized party building, campaigning, and elections.

What was required was a bridge between the system of governance established by the military and the reestablishment of a fully open system of competitive party politics. Such a "bridge" was also advocated in 1975 by Awolowo, who suggested that Nigeria should not move directly to a winner-take-all system. He therefore revived a recommendation put forward earlier by Aminu Kano, a populist opposition leader, that any "political probationary period" should last five years, during which a sharing of all government positions would be proportional to the votes won by parties in the elections—a proposal remarkably similar to the transitional arrangements put into effect in South Africa two decades later. Such an idea, if adopted in Nigeria, should not be introduced as another superficial exercise in political engineering but should be anchored to a broader institutional process, such as a national conference or its equivalent.

The Abacha regime has unveiled a new draft constitution whose most striking feature is the introduction of a rotational presidency in which the position of head of state will revolve among the country's major ethnolinguistic groups. And on October 1, 1995, Abacha announced a new three-year "transition program." Already, Nigerian polit-

> [T]he military was an unaccountable body that could not restrain the inevitable abuses of office.

ical aspirants have begun creating political associations, anticipating the starting pistol for the formation of political parties and renewed competition for electoral office. But as long as a Nigerian military regime maintains effective control of the security forces, it can dictate any "transition" program it wants with the knowledge that politically ambitious Nigerians will dance to the new tune. Despite the country's economic shambles, oil production continues and there will always be major fortunes to be made by holding state office.

What, therefore, are Nigeria's options three years after the Babangida regime was forced out? The most likely is another replay of the Babangida scenario: a supposedly democratizing regime that uses its leverage to keep revising the "transition program," thereby prolonging its stay in power until it is forced out. A second option is a different transition program based on a national conference or power-sharing framework, as suggested earlier. This option would depend on the termination of Sani Abacha's rule and its replacement by a military regime committed to a genuine transition. A third option was taking shape within the Babangida "transition" and was blocked by a preemptive military coup by Babangida himself against an incipient "citizens' republic" when he canceled the elections of June 12, 1993.

A fourth option has always been rumored within the country but has never been carried out—a radical military coup comparable to the second seizure of power by Jerry Rawlings in Ghana in 1981, with the intention of establishing a revolutionary government and sidelining the established military and civilian political class. Although junior officers have often played a significant role in coups in Nigeria, once successful, they have usually ceded place to more senior officers. The threat of the dire actions the "Young Turks" would unleash once in power has often been used to justify a preemptive move by more conservative senior officers. The bloodbath at the time of the attempted overthrow of the Babangida regime in April 1990 is an indication of the carnage that would ensue if a military faction tried to seize power without having firm control of core units of the army.

DEMOCRACY DEFERRED

Pini Jason, a Nigerian journalist, contends that "General Babangida annulled Nigeria's best chance

to enter the 21st century as a modern democracy." Something unusual did take place in Nigeria on June 12, 1993, and the report by Peter Lewis, who was present for the occasion, is instructive. He notes that the party-building process up to the presidential elections had replicated the misconduct normally associated with civilian politics in Nigeria; "aspiring political factions employed fraud, financial inducement, and violence in the bid for advantage."[2] It seemed that hardly a week went by when one party official or another was not suspending a colleague, or defecting to the opposition. In 1992 the regime had canceled the presidential primaries on the basis of alleged irregularities and substituted an even more complicated system. When the day of the presidential elections arrived in 1993, however, Nigerians performed a collective and national act that made these elections one of the most peaceful to take place in Africa during the current wave of democratic transitions.

Lewis's report confirms one issued by the Nigerian Center for Democratic Studies, which had organized its own election-monitoring exercise. The election campaign was conducted with "unprecedented decorum; [it] was marked by little of the political violence and electoral manipulation of the past; there was limited evidence of fraud and vote-rigging; polling was generally conducted in a peaceful and orderly manner" and the results were promptly collated by the [National Electoral Commission]."

Any observer of previous Nigerian elections—even the Babangida "transition"—is likely to blink on reading these words. Something very remarkable had happened in Nigeria. The unannounced results of the election, which would have shown a 58 percent majority for Moshood Abiola, were also noteworthy both for the size of his plurality and for the fact that he drew significant support from all areas of the country, including several major northern precincts.

The deliberately contrived judicial pronouncements canceling the elections, then blocking the announcement of the returns, and the bizarre exertions of Arthur Nzeribe's Association for Better Nigeria to get the government to scuttle the entire process, reflect the panic within government circles and among some of its constituencies that, despite all the roadblocks and "organized confusion," the Nigerian people were going to elect a president who could not be relied on, once in office, to do the bidding of the outgoing regime.

---

[2]"Endgame in Nigeria: The Politics of a Failed Democratic Transition," *African Affairs*, vol. 93 (1994), p. 324.

Moshood Abiola is no paragon of democratic accountability; he has become fabulously wealthy by mastering the strategies for acquiring power and wealth in Nigerian society. However, only someone with his wide networks of political and business associates could have reached the end-point in Babangida's "transition." But the Nigerian electorate was voting for much more than a man. After all the delays, it had been granted one final chance to get the military out of power and restart the Nigerian "political calendar"—and it made the most of it. As Lewis points out, "the combined influences of apathy, apprehension and confusion kept many away from the polls." The resulting 35 percent turnout was subsequently used by the regime's supporters in its campaign to weaken Abiola's claims. In view of all that Nigerians had experienced since the "transition" began eight years earlier, it is remarkable that so many were still prepared to go to the polls.

June 12, 1993, should not be seen in isolation. The argument can be made that it represents one of several elements of a citizens' republic whose emergence has been stymied by the misconduct of civilian politicians as well as the deliberate interference of a politicized military. Thus, during the First Republic a political system with two broad political groupings evolved. A similar process was in evidence during the Second Republic. Both trends were halted by the irresponsible behavior of the political class and the military's arrogation of the absolute right to rule. Rather than the military rushing in to "save" the Nigerian nation, it is Nigerian civilian politicians who will have to experience, and surmount, the deepest challenges to the nation, whether they take the form of economic difficulties, internal discord, or external threats to the nation's security.

Chief Adisa Akinloye, a leading politician in the National Party of Nigeria during the Second Republic, made the observation that "there are really two parties in Nigeria: the military and the civilians." Only the latter can still give rise to a sustainable democracy in Nigeria. When Babangida rounded up a number of politicians and detained them for violating the ban on political activities in 1991, another remarkable event occurred that presaged what took place in June 1993. Although these politicians came from different parts of the country and belonged to different political formations, they discovered that they shared much common ground. When they were released they put forward a set of common positions on the political process, much to the chagrin of the Babangida administration. This is an indication of the kind of experience that a national conference or its equivalent could force Nigeria's senior politicians to undergo, similar to the transition proceedings in South Africa. It could also lead to the fashioning of a common political program, together with a commitment to overcome the country's regional, ethnic, and religious divisions and make possible the national concord that could sustain an extended period of civilian rule.

BEYOND THE ROGUE STATE

It is in the behavior of the ruthless security services, which proliferated under the Babangida regime, that the embryonic rogue state may be discerned. When the dynamic journalist and publisher Dele Giwa was blown apart in October 1986 by a parcel bomb while he was investigating the connections between the criminal and military networks, a signal was sent of what could be in store for other Nigerians who threatened the consolidation of mafia-style governance. With each reshuffling of Nigerian military rulers, the risk of an unbridled tyranny grew. As a private citizen commented with chilling prescience just before Babangida stepped down: "Unless we say never again, we will wake up one day and a psychopath in uniform will usurp authority, use and abuse power to plunder the nation, and dare us speak."

With each reshuffling of Nigerian military rulers, the risk of an unbridled tyranny grew.

Less than a year after he had handed power to civilians, General Obasanjo took part in a debate with a law lecturer on the campus of the University of Ibadan. That confrontation can now be seen as having taken place across the fault line in the construction of the Nigerian polity. Rejecting the argument that the Nigerian military undermined the rule of law, Obasanjo contended that the military invoked an alternate and equally authoritative legal system whenever it dismissed civilians and suspended the constitution. As a consequence, he argued, the "ability, competence, and authority" of the Nigerian military "to make law that is valid and binding on all citizens should not be in doubt or questioned once they are effectively in political power." He also extended such authority to include the right to disregard not just constitutional procedures but such fundamental principles as the inadmissibility of retroactive laws; "when occasions do call for such laws to save the nation from political or economic destruction, the governing majority must be able to act in defense of the nation."

Fifteen years later Obasanjo has been arrested, tried, and imprisoned on the basis of the very alternate "legal system" he once defended. A spokesperson for the Abacha regime brushed off criticisms of the 1995 secret trials by arguing that "this is not the first time we have had this type of trial" in Nigeria, and wondered why "past secret coup trials in Nigeria did not attract this kind of attention." In the kafkaesque world that Nigeria has become since the Babangida era, Emeka Ojukwu, who led an armed struggle against the Nigerian nation between 1967 and 1970, can rebuke Olusegun Obasanjo, who defended the nation in that civil war: "If there is any punishment that comes, should he be found guilty of whatever it is, it will be prescribed by no other person than himself."

As any passing knowledge of the speeches and writings of Obasanjo would indicate, the former military ruler has come a long way from his defense of the military's right to disregard fundamental rules of jurisprudence in "the defense of the nation." When the Abacha regime declared in 1994 that it was suspending habeas corpus, and when it detains lawyers who try to defend their clients, what exists is no longer a "militarized Leviathan" that seeks to preserve organized society but a rogue state whose motivations cannot be predicted, and whose boundaries for irrational behavior are unknown.

In exiting this tunnel, Nigeria cannot just go back to the "good old days" of the prebendal republic, whether in its military or civilian form. It must go further back to a citizens' republic. This republic can only be brought into being incrementally and through an extended period of accommodation and power-sharing among civilian groups in an open and accountable national unity government.

The June 1993 elections demonstrated that the Nigerian people may be ready for such an exercise. In 1975 they believed that Murtala Muhammad would create such an opportunity; in 1985 and 1986, Ibrahim Babangida sparked similar hopes. In the various regions of Nigeria other civilian politicians have also emerged from time to time to rekindle that vision. But the solemn fact is that, by the end of this century, Nigerians will have experienced nearly 50 years of political experimentation, beginning with the formation of the first major political parties around 1950, followed by elected regional administrations. These experiments, many inspired by the finest democratic ideals, have resulted in a ravaged economy, a poorly functioning state, and recurrent social upheavals.

The Abacha regime has shown little sign of veering from its determination to undertake its own reconstruction of the body politic. Commissions have been established to supervise a new "transition," to oversee elections from the local to the national level, and to review the number and composition of states and local governments. In the meantime, sporadic bombings and attacks on individuals continue, as well as arrests and harassment of political opponents.

The United States government is calling for increasing international sanctions on Nigeria, but the discovery of new oil deposits and major foreign investments in natural gas production are enhancing the leverage of the regime. Despite an aggressive public relations campaign, the transition program lacks international legitimacy. Nevertheless, a new set of Nigerian politicians, and some old ones, will be induced to take part as long as there is hope of reaching the political trough that the state now exclusively represents. If there is light at the end of the dismal tunnel, it is imperceptible to anyone not paid to see it.

No War, No Peace

Fears of war between India and Pakistan are overblown, but the dispute over Kashmir and warnings of a nuclear race on the Subcontinent contribute to a dangerously edgy stalemate.

V. G. Kulkarni

Islamabad, Lahore and New Delhi

The welcome arches on the broad boulevards of Lahore were drenched by the spring drizzle of Punjab. The city was returning to normal in late March after the excitement generated by the finals of the World Cup cricket tournament. Pointing to the fading cardboard cut-outs of cricket heroes next to Pakistan People's Party posters showing Prime Minister Benazir Bhutto, a burly Punjabi driver remarked: "Thank God India lost the World Cup semifinals in Calcutta; had they come to Lahore and won the finals there would have been a battle on the streets here." Shaking his head in despair, he added: "You know how crazy people can be."

From playing fields to battlefields, there is almost no neutral ground in the rivalry between India and Pakistan. Yet many in both countries, as the Pakistani taxi driver's last comment indicates, recognize that it's a rivalry that too often threatens to go out of control. The battle for the World Cup—in which India beat Pakistan in the quarter-finals—came after troops from the two sides traded fire across the border. Those shots were echoed in skirmishes between Indian security forces and Muslim separatist guerrillas in the disputed territory of Kashmir. With Washington, meanwhile, warning of an India-Pakistan nuclear race, outsiders could be forgiven for thinking the Subcontinent was in imminent danger of implosion.

The reality is less grim. Officials in Washington may say their words of caution are well meant for an "accident-prone" region; the two neighbours have, after all, fought three wars in the past five decades and are now considered nuclear-threshold states. But in separate interviews with the REVIEW neither Bhutto nor Indian Prime Minister P. V. Narasimha Rao anticipates full-blown hostilities between their countries any time soon. That view is shared by the United States' ambassador to Islamabad, Thomas Simmons. "It doesn't seem to us," he says, "that either side is spoiling for a war."

Still, with the relationship already as tense as a bowstring, it wouldn't take much to make it snap. The nervousness born of deep-rooted mutual suspicions could easily lead to hasty moves, warn independent observers. Even Ambassador Simmons injects a cautionary note to his belief that neither side wants war, warning that "mistakes could occur; it's a deadly embrace in a very nervous region." Civil disturbances within each country and border skirmishes tend to feed the tension, leading to belligerent exchanges between Delhi and Islamabad that sound like the verbal equivalent of war.

Some recent incidents that have fuelled the fire:

- In the middle of last year, India began erecting an electrified barbed-wire fence along the de facto border of Kashmir to prevent armed Islamic militants from crossing over from the Pakistani side. Islamabad objected, and artillery bombardments ensued, with the inevitable loss of life on both sides.
- On January 26, India's Republic Day, a mosque close to the border on the Pakistani side of Kashmir burned down, resulting in the deaths of 20 people. Islamabad promptly blamed Indian bombardment and publicized the issue internationally, despite Indian denials, but did not provide conclusive proof of Indian malfeasance. The incident remains unexplained.
- In late March, armed separatists took over the Hazratbal Mosque in Srinagar, the holiest Muslim shrine in the state. Indian forces laid temporary siege to the mosque to flush out the militants, who were allowed to leave the building after a couple of days of protest. Back in Islamabad, there were violent demonstrations against the Hazratbal incident. By month's end, 24 people from the same militant group and their leader, Shabir Siddique, were killed in a fire-fight with Indian forces in Srinagar. Pakistan's Parliament passed a resolution condemning the killing and called on the government to take up the matter internationally.
- In December, American intelligence sources leaked a story that India was probably preparing for a nuclear test at Pokhran in the Rajasthan desert. Pakistan immediately acted as if the story was true, though the Indians denied it and the U.S. did not come up with any follow-up evidence. In March came Pakistan's turn, when U.S. intelligence leaked news that it had satellite evidence of nuclear-related activity in Pakistan's Baluchistan area. Islamabad blamed it on American "misinterpretation of intelligence." Meanwhile, Pakistani officials and politicians continued to allege an Indian blast was imminent—al-

From *Far Eastern Economic Review*, April 11, 1996, pp. 18-20. © 1996 by Review Publishing Company Limited. Reprinted by permission.

though in private most of them thought it unlikely.

But New Delhi and Islamabad agree on one thing: both view the U.S. intelligence reports as less-than-discreet pressure on them to sign the Comprehensive Test Ban Treaty, and both decry the alarms that senior officials in Washington have sounded repeatedly.

Most of the Indian and Pakistani policymakers that the REVIEW spoke to reject the American fears of a nuclear exchange. Even retired Lt.-Gen. Hameed Gul, the former head of Pakistan's Interservices Intelligence and an avowed nuclear hawk, says mutual deterrence has worked quite well on the Subcontinent. But the policymakers do concede that it would be difficult to resolve the Kashmir issue to Pakistan's satisfaction.

According to Prime Minister Bhutto, "India is trying to inherit the mantle of the British raj" and the Kashmir dispute "is the root cause" of all bilateral problems. Independent observers maintain that the insurgency in the valley is a product of both Kashmiri grievances and Islamabad's help to the militants, who have included Pakistanis, Afghans and even some Arabs.

K. Subrahmanyam, a leading Indian defence expert, says that Kashmir has become Pakistan's main obsession because of domestic political problems. To Bhutto's frequent remarks on human-rights violations in the Kashmir Valley, Indian Premier Rao retorts: "Has Pakistan become the custodian of all Muslims? There are as many Muslims in India as in Pakistan. Pakistanis should worry about human rights of their own citizens first."

Rao says India has dealt with its diverse, secular milieu by making adjustments and concessions through the democratic political process, and is addressing the Kashmir question in the same spirit. The dialogue with several militant groups in Kashmir and the coming parliamentary elections in the state are part of that process, he says. Indian officials also point to the growing human-rights movement in the country and official mechanisms to deal with such issues.

Diplomats say a series of visits to Kashmir by foreign ambassadors in India have helped allay fears of human-rights violations in the state. But Islamabad has declared the planned elections and New Delhi's talks with the Kashmiri militants—who it says do not represent the people of the territory—unacceptable. Still, independent observers believe that even a marginally credible election could put Kashmir on the back burner of international concern. And that could lead to a "no war, no peace" situation resembling the Middle East of the mid-1970s, says a European envoy in New Delhi.

As Indians and Pakistanis continue to engage in their primordial conflict, however, they risk being left behind in the worldwide race to economic prosperity. Though both countries have launched free-market reforms and made some economic progress, old mindsets continue to handicap attempts to tap into Subcontinental synergies.

K. D. Kurtkoti, an eminent Indian cultural and literary scholar, depicts the Subcontinental divide in historical terms: "The pan-Indian civilization has for millennia faced outside invaders but slowly absorbed them. Our enmities always lie within. Our epics are full of our own brothers turning into our enemies from time to time. Sadly, the Indo-Pak problems will have to run their course before another era of harmony comes in."

Policymakers, of course, can't wait for historical cycles to play themselves out. To push a dialogue, New Delhi says that it is amenable to discussions on a broad range of bilateral issues, but that Pakistan is bent on resolving the Kashmir question to its own satisfaction—meaning wrenching it away from India. Efforts to agree on international mediation—including by the U.S.—have come to nought. As Ambassador Simmons says: "Probably Pakistan would like us to deliver Kashmir to them," something he describes as an impossibility.

Besides, both sides have their grievances against the U.S. Islamabad considers itself a moderating factor in a militant Islamic region teeming with anti-Western forces. But with the end of the Cold War, it believes, America sees no further use for its faithful anti-communist ally.

The Indians, for their part, believe they have always received a raw deal from the U.S. Washington, they say, has looked at the Subcontinent only through the prism of its security concerns. Even with the end of the Cold War and the opening up of the huge Indian market to Western investment, there has been no appreciable change in the American view of the Subcontinent, says A.P. Venkateshwaran, a former Indian foreign secretary.

Indian opinion-makers, hawks and doves alike, charge that Washington is still not prepared to take into account the concerns voiced even by East and Southeast Asia about the emergent power of China, a concern at the forefront of Indian planners' minds.

Yet even as the two Subcontinental establishments squabble with each other, liberal and reformist groups of Indians and Pakistanis have exchanged visits in recent years and found a lot in common. Mubashir Hasan, a leading liberal and former Pakistani cabinet minister, says there is a lot of goodwill among ordinary people and businessmen on both sides which needs to be nurtured. This, in turn, could gradually influence their political masters.

But the reformist dialogue has a long way to go before it can bring real change. Hasan recalls an occasion at his Lahore home a few years ago. Well-meaning Indians and Pakistanis argued the evening away—agreeing on most issues, differing on some. Amid the garrulous confusion of unending debate, one of the guests, a visiting American professor, asked: "You gentlemen have impeccable credentials and seem to agree on a lot of things. Why don't you go and do something about it?" The host explained: "In the Subcontinent, we talk a lot; most of the time we agree on a lot; sometimes we differ and score debating points; then we think the job is done. There is no follow-up action. Even our governments occasionally behave like that." According to the host, the American visitor must have concluded: No war, no peace, any time soon.

CULTURE CLASH

*Why anger and resentment in Indonesia's eastern frontier
province are rising to dangerous levels*

Keith Loveard

JAYAPURA

A first sighting of Irian Jaya reveals a land of immense natural wealth. To fly over Indonesia's eastern frontier is to witness one of the world's last untouched tropical rain forests, rising to snow-covered peaks rich in copper, gold and other minerals. But an on-the-ground look soon makes it clear that all is not well in paradise. Jakarta's efforts to integrate the province into its vast confederation have made the Irianese an underclass of strangers in their own land.

In the central market of the capital Jayapura, a few Irianese traders sit on the ground with their vegetables and fruit. Behind them, businessmen from Java and Sulawesi occupy the stalls, selling food, clothing and shoes. The minivans that serve as public transport are painted with names redolent of Java, Sulawesi and North Sumatra. It is Javanese not Irianese who ply the streets at night, selling chicken satay from carts lit by hurricane lamps. Government and private offices are full of outsiders and formal commerce is dominated by immigrants for Sulawesi.

Jakarta has tried to help ease the western half of New Guinea into the 20th Century. But the bald fact, say the Irianese, is that the effort has largely been a failure. A mixture of prejudice, discrimination and government neglect has put the Irianese at risk of becoming paupers in their rich province. With hopes of a fair deal from Indonesia consistently dashed, the people are increasingly translating their anger and resentment into violence. The recent kidnapping of foreign and Indonesian researchers by members of the Free Papua Organization (OPM) shot the tensions into international headlines. Indonesians were shocked when two captives were hacked to death with axes only minutes from rescue.

The incident was hardly isolated. Riots on both sides of the main island in March raised alarm bells in the faraway national capital. But rather than sit down and talk, Jakarta, long wary of moves for greater autonomy for the regions, seems set on facing the problems with force. For the people of Irian, the outcome will inevitably be disastrous. Foreign diplomats say privately they fear the province could eventually make Indonesia's security problems in volatile East Timor look like child's play.

What is going wrong? I got my first hint before my plane even landed in Sentani near the capital. "We have to realize that the native Irianese aren't capable of doing many jobs," one Balinese tells me matter-of-factly. "They are no good as drivers. Just making iced drinks they get it wrong. And if you were to be offered a meal made by one of them, you wouldn't want to eat it." Like most others on the plane, the man is a civil servant returning from a break in his native island. "It will take time—two or three generations—before they can be capable of working properly," he says. "In the meantime, people from the other islands are needed to do the jobs."

The reality on the ground is a more complicated story. In Irianese-run offices, indigenous people are fully integrated into modern society. But in the marketplace, where attitudes such as the Balinese offical's are common, finding a decent job is tough, if not impossible, for local residents. One Irianese hotel worker blames his own people. "I started here as a room boy 14 years ago and worked my way up," he says. "But most people believe they should sit in the boss's chair and only show up at the office for four hours, then go home again." A Christian foundation worker, also an Irianese, agrees. "The people who build our roads are immigrants. If an Irianese works, he'll last five meters, then want to sit down and smoke or drink tea."

Those attitudes were ingrained when times were good, says Augustinus Rumansara, executive secretary of the Foundation for Entrepreneurship Development, a private non-governmental organization (NGO). "Before other people came here, there were enough fish, fruit, vegetables for everybody," he says, sitting in his tidy office near the capital. "Living didn't require too much energy. But the way people live in Java, where there is so much competition, means that newcomers are prepared to do any job. Irianese have to learn to accept that as today's reality."

Attitudes toward the ownership of land create another divide between Irianese and outsiders. The modern view of land, says anthropologist Benny Giay, the first PhD from the Irian highlands, "is only as an economic asset. We don't recognize that. The land means everything to us, it is something we can look at to connect with the past. A newcomer can use it for as long as he wants, but then we will take it back."

Among those who cannot accept that they have no rights to their traditional land are the Amungme people who live near the PT Freeport Indonesia copper and gold mine in the south. Tribal leader Tom Beanal has hit the U.S.–based company with a $6 billion law suit. He accuses Freeport of destroying the local environment and "cultural genocide." The on-off suit, withdrawn once by Beanal and then presented again, is seen as symptomatic of the confusion among the Amungme leadership. "We are just stupid people up against these smart people from Freeport," Beanal says sarcastically.

One church source says Freeport has to accept some blame for failing to encourage real communication with the local people. "The Amungme people are not jealous of the money that Freeport is making. What they do not like is the lack of dialogue and the apparent refusal to acknowledge their rights," the source says. "The people still believe that this is their land." The arrival of Freeport and its multi-million-dollar development program in 1967 suddenly threw the people out of the Stone Age, adds Brother Theo van den Broek, a Catholic priest and a resident in Irian for 21 years. "It is completely unimaginable for local people. They don't understand what is going on."

In private, senior Freeport officials admit their record is imperfect. As a mining company, they say there is bound to be environmental impact. But Jakarta, which takes an average $250 million a year from Freeport in tax and royalties, has to bear some of the responsibility, an executive says. When it comes to employment practices, the company has few options. "We hire people from outside Irian," he says. "The people from Irian simply do not have the skills we require, and that's going to take a long time to address."

Another Freeport spokesman, public-affairs chief Edward Pressman, puts it this way: "We've tried to understand the people. There are very distinct clashes between the two cultures." He insists that the company has the interests of the locals at heart. Last year, it contributed $22.7 million to social-development projects in the area and plans to spend $34.3 million this year. That means schools, health centers, agribusiness pilot projects and other schemes. The lack of employment opportunities for local people nonetheless continues to lead to tension. In March, tribesmen in Freeport for a traditional feast ran through the area smashing windows and vehicles.

That riot was followed by another in Abepura, the university town 10 km from Jayapura. About 4,000 Irianese attacked and set fire to a market and nearby shops mostly owned by Sulawesi immigrants. The mob then marched toward the capital, smashing windows and destroying government vehicles. Some scrawled OPM slogans on walls. The Irianese were protesting official refusal to allow a traditional burial for Thomas Wainggai. The former university lecturer's body had just been returned from Jakarta, where he had died serving a 20-year jail sentence. Wainggai had sinned against Indonesia by raising the Free Papua flag at the Jayapura sports ground in 1988.

By mid-May, the Abepura market was being rebuilt. Long timber frames were in place, and the debris from the fire that destroyed the original market was slowly being carried away. Helping the Sulawesi settlers was Nicholaas Elly, a descendant of the original tribe of this magnificent Jayapura valley. He and his friends say they lived peacefully with the newcomers for years before the rioting. "We would visit each other in our houses, and when they came to ask my help in the rebuilding, I could not refuse." Despite sympathy for his neighbors, the drop-out from a university in west Java sees himself as another victim of development. "We are being marginalized," Elly says. "We have sold our land. We live by looking for timber in the forests. But the woods are getting thinner as time goes on. I have tried to look for work but there is little hope."

Complicating the picture in Irian Jaya is the role of the Military. Legal aid worker Paul Prout is willing to discuss the issue while others in his office near the Abepura market are not; they are aware that a visit from a foreign journalist is bound to be noted by intelligence operatives. "It's clear from the national perspective that the army is needed here, to guard the border with Papua New Guinea, for instance," Prout says. "But what happens is that they create a climate of fear."

Indeed, negative reports about the army's presence are rampant. "We are constantly hounded by the military," says one Irianese academic. "If you say one word out of place we can be grabbed and questioned. There is an accumulation of fear." Such is the mounting distrust of the military that theories are circulating that the two Indonesians who died in the recent hostage incident were in fact killed by Irianese in the pay of the army, hoping to discredit the OPM. "Even if the OPM did kill those two hostages," insists a rebel sympathizer, "we have to say, 'Wait, who started this?' "

The military, however, says its forces are the ones who are on the receiving end of the violence. The deaths of two soldiers in the highlands in early May justifies at least part of that claim. The soldiers were hacked into pieces by presumed OPM guerrillas or sympathizers. At military headquarters in Jayapura, information officer Capt. Sulistiadi says the military does what it can to help people. He cites as an example soldiers standing in for teachers who have failed to turn up for work. Still, he says his men live in fear. "We feel naked here," Sulistiadi says. "We can never know who is our friend and who is our enemy."

The Catholic Church was a critical element in bringing the first allegations of the military's human-rights violations. That led to the sentencing of four soldiers found to have exceeded authority in the shooting and killing of 16 demonstrators in Timika. The church is widely seen as one of the few real challenges to the rule of power in Irian. "These people have a right to participate fully in what is going on," Brother Van den Broek says. "But the Irianese don't have status. They don't have the ability to compete with others. These people are told they are stupid and over time they begin to believe it themselves. You have to question the process of development."

That is not something many Indonesian businessmen bother to do. The province, after all, represents rich pickings. Forestry and fisheries have been divided up among a variety of interests. The Irian Jaya Rural Development Foundation, another private NGO, says that more than 10 million hectares of land have been handed to national forestry interests. The companies see the province as the next target for their operations, though some have reportedly been scared away by the recent violence.

Research and Technology Minister B. J. Habibie has few such misgivings. His research body is working on an ambitious plan to dam the Mamberamo river and create industrial areas and rice fields in an enormous swath of swampland to the west of Jayapura. A group of hydroelectric power plants would produce a massive 15,000 megawatts of electricity, making it feasible to produce liquid hydrogen cheap enough to transfer elsewhere in the country. Similar schemes, though on a far smaller scale, are being sketched out for the Arso region, southeast of the capital near the PNG border. Many Javanese transmigrants have been introduced here to provide a buffer to rebel elements who seek refuge across the border.

Many question the scale of Habibie's huge Maberamo plan, not least the Irianese who fear thousands of outsiders will be brought in to build the project. Meanwhile, there is quiet talk of more protests, even revolution. A receptive white ear attracts whispered accounts of plans for revolt, of clandestine groups. One older Irianese recalls that he told his children nothing of the province's past, in which the Netherlands was preparing it for independence. But he says they discovered the history themselves. The flag that Wainggai raised in 1988 was the same one that would have been the symbol of an independent West Papua. Those plans came to naught when Indonesia pushed its right to all former Dutch territories in the East Indies, winning control of the territory in 1963. That was later cemented by the United Nations-supervised Act of Free Choice in 1969.

The government has made efforts to help Irian. In the wake of the Rioting at Freeport and Abepura, President Suharto announced that the year's intake of 17,000 civil servants would include a special placement of 2,000 jobs for Irianese. And Jakarta continues to remind the people of Irian of their place in the brotherhood of Indonesian communities. But most Irianese say they want much more: better schools, jobs and, above all, respect. Virtually every Irianese I spoke to had the same complaint. "We want to be treated as real citizens of this country, not like children," one NGO official says. Sporting the bushy beard that marks him as a highlander, he adds: "As things stand it is hard for us to accept we are part of Indonesia. We don't want to have to go as far as to fight for a free Papua, but we do want to be treated as equals."

For now, anthropologist Giay and others predict that local anger will continue to rise. "I could see that in the recent riots," Giay says. "People expressed their frustrations. They shouted 'We are free.' This sort of thing happens when people can no longer tolerate their position." He shakes his head. "I think this type of riot will continue. More people will be shot and killed." There is a "second possibility," Giay says. The government can get together with churches or NGOs to set up "programs to help the people, to get more understanding." So far though, that doesn't seem too likely. And Jakarta, apparently unwilling to sit down and discuss what its Irianese citizens want, will have to face the costs of that refusal.

REFUGEES
THE RISING FLOOD

SPREADING VIOLENCE IS DRIVING GROWING
NUMBERS OF PEOPLE FROM THEIR HOMELANDS,
AND THE COUNTRIES OF ASYLUM ARE FINDING IT
HARDER TO ACCOMMODATE THEM.

Kathleen Newland

Kathleen Newland is a senior associate at the Carnegie Endowment for International Peace, and principal author of the United Nations High Commissioner for Refugees' State of the World's Refugees 1993 *(Penguin Books, New York and London), from which much of this article is adapted. Formerly a senior researcher at the Worldwatch Institute, she is author of* Worldwatch Paper 43, Refugees: The New International Politics of Displacement.

Virtually every political upheaval in today's increasingly crowded and dangerous world uproots people from their homes and sends them fleeing from violence and persecution. Those who manage to cross an international border to seek protection are called refuges. Their numbers now approach 19 million worldwide. In addition, 2.7 million Palestinian refugees and their descendants live in Jordan, Syria, Lebanon, and the occupied territories. There are at least another 25 million people who have fled from violence and persecution but have not crossed an international border: the internally displaced. All told, roughly one of every 123 people on earth is among the dispossessed.

The number of refugees has been climbing for the past 30 years or more. The reasons are complex: an amalgam of political violence, conflict over economic resources, environmental degradation, ethnic or religious persecution, and abuses of human rights. Increasingly often, such turmoil takes place against a background of disintegrating governments—the very institutions that should be expected to mediate conflict, or at least shelter people from its worst effects. In many cases, the government itself is the agent of persecution.

The inability to count on the protection of their own governments is what sets refugees apart from other migrants, however desperate, and other people in need of humanitarian assistance. Refugees know that they cannot expect, at home, the protection of the police, access to a fair trial, redress of grievances through the courts, prosecution of those who violate their rights, or public assistance in the face of disaster. In a world made up of sovereign states, people who do not have access to the legal and social protection that a properly functioning government normally extends to its citizens, as best it can, must look to the international community for protection.

Refugee laws, laid down in international treaties and adopted into national legal codes, acknowledge and spell out legal obligations toward people whose own governments are unwilling or unable to protect them. These laws define a refugee as any person who, "owing to a well-founded fear of being persecuted for reasons of race, religion, nationality, membership of a

From *World Watch*, May/June 1994, pp. 10-20.

particular social group, or political opinion, is outside the country of his nationality and is unable—or, owing to such fear, unwilling—to avail himself of the protection of that country. . . ." The most fundamental obligation to refugees is to ensure that they are not sent back to a place where they would face persecution.

The international system of refugee protection was consolidated in the aftermath of World War II and during the tense early stages of the Cold War. To negotiators looking back to the Nazi persecutions and Stalinist repression, the causes of the refugee problems did not seem excessively complicated. A political consensus among Western democracies that the people of Eastern Europe were persecuted by their governments meant that the limited numbers who managed to flee were automatically granted asylum. As conflicts over decolonization in the late 1950s and 1960s—such as those in Algeria, Angola, and Zaire—generated large numbers of refugees, the causes again seemed self-evident.

But refugees' numbers escalated sharply in the 1970s, and set off a vigorous debate about the root causes of their movement. Although individually targeted persecution was still rampant, more and more people were fleeing from general violence, severe disruptions of public order, and the inability to feed themselves in the midst of armed conflict. Moreover, many refugees were intermingled with people who moved not out of fear for their lives and freedom, but in search of better economic opportunities. As the numbers continued to rise throughout the 1980s and into the 1990s, policymakers began to focus more sharply on how they could prevent conditions from deteriorating to the point at which people feel compelled to flee.

POLITICAL ROOTS

The main instrument of international refugee law, the 1951 Convention Relating to the Status of Refugees, identified what is still a major reason that people are forced out of their native countries: persecution based on who the refugee is (race, nationality, membership in a particular social group) or what he or she believes (religion or political opinion). Persecution usually takes place when there are fundamental political disputes over who controls the government, how society organizes itself, and who commands the power, privileges, patronage, and perks that go with political control. These disputes are at their most heated during periods of intense change—in the aftermath of a revolutionary struggle (successful or failed), at the moment of a far-reaching change of regime, or at the emergence of a new state.

Virtually all of the conflicts that caused people to flee their homes during 1993 and early 1994

were civil conflicts. Weak states, such as Liberia or Haiti, are especially prone to internal violence, since credible mechanisms for resolving conflicts peacefully or seeking redress for violations of rights in such states have usually eroded or ceased to function altogether. The lack of representative political institutions, an independent judiciary, impartial law enforcement, or free elections may lead people to conclude that armed resistance is the only way to bring about change. In many cases, no party or faction is able to establish control, and political conflict degenerates into anarchy, with no one able to provide security to the people. Somalia, with its tens of thousands of dead, hundreds of thousands of refugees, and millions of internally displaced, is today's example of this kind of nightmare—but elements of the pattern have also been visible in Afghanistan, Haiti, and Liberia.

As the superpower rivalry of the Cold War all too clearly demonstrated, external political support for one side or the other prolongs internal conflict and raises the level of violence. The largest refugee movements of the last three decades—from Afghanistan, Vietnam, Cambodia, the Horn of Africa, Angola, and Mozambique—were exacerbated by superpower involvement. External intervention in local disputes often disrupts local traditions of bargaining and compromise by giving one party, clan, or faction a definitive upper hand. An outside patron may prop up leaders who have little if any domestic legitimacy, and give them the firepower to enforce their will. An infusion of military aid increases the destructiveness of confrontation, while economic aid raises the stakes in the contest for control of domestic institutions.

ECONOMIC ROOTS

Economic tensions are among the major underlying causes of refugee movements, but the relationship is not as straightforward as it may seem. It is too simple to say that poverty begets refugees. In relatively static situations, extreme deprivation is as likely to breed resignation as resistance.

More combustible situations are produced by a deterioration of economic standing. Bitter disputes among national groups (such as the Serbs and the Croats in former Yugoslavia) arise from efforts to preserve or advance the standing of one group at the relative expense of others. Disputes over the distribution of resources during general economic decline are the most politically explosive. Leaders, trying to avoid the blame for deteriorating economic conditions, frequently turn to scapegoating, and minority groups often provide the most convenient targets.

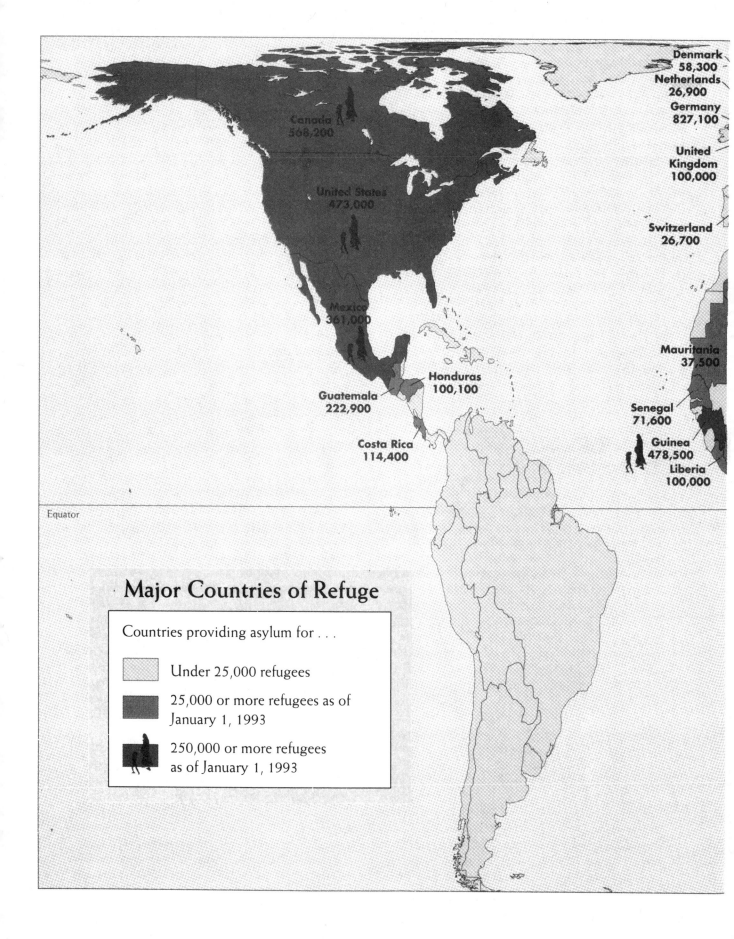

Denmark
58,300

Netherlands
26,900

Germany
827,100

United
Kingdom
100,000

Switzerland
26,700

Mauritania
37,500

Senegal
71,600

Guinea
478,500

Liberia
100,000

Canada
568,200

United States
473,000

Mexico
361,000

Guatemala
222,900

Honduras
100,100

Costa Rica
114,400

Equator

Major Countries of Refuge

Countries providing asylum for . . .

Under 25,000 refugees

25,000 or more refugees as of
January 1, 1993

250,000 or more refugees
as of January 1, 1993

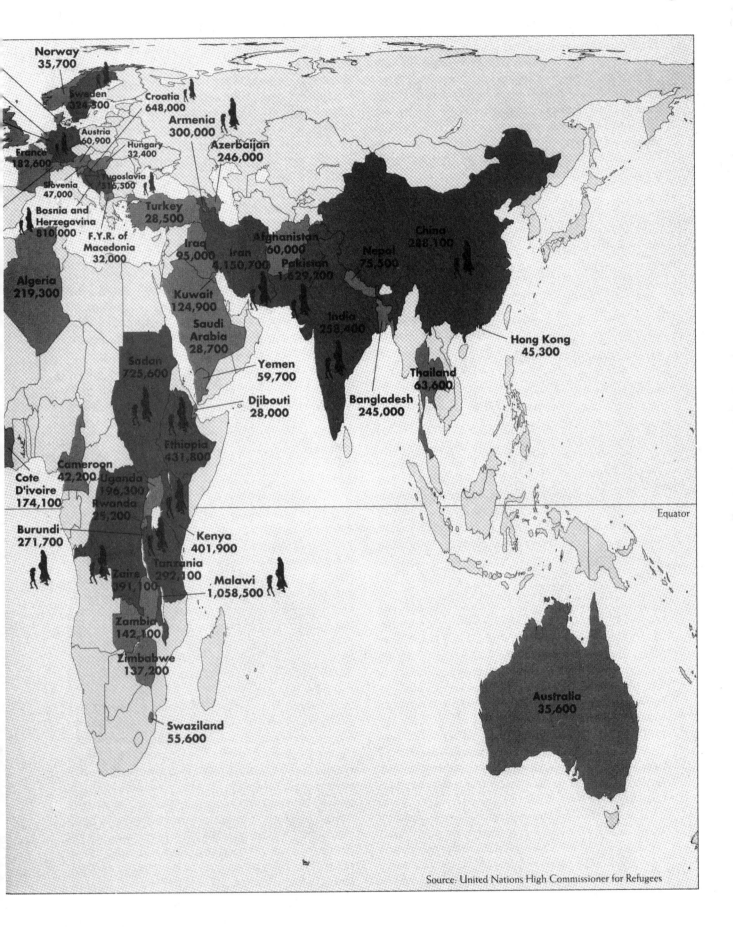

Norway
35,700

Sweden
324,500

Croatia
648,000

Armenia
300,000

Azerbaijan
246,000

Austria
60,900

Hungary
32,400

France
182,600

Yugoslavia
516,500

Slovenia
47,000

Turkey
28,500

China
288,100

Afghanistan
60,000

Iran
4,150,700

Nepal
75,500

Bosnia and
Herzegovina
810,000

F.Y.R. of
Macedonia
32,000

Iraq
95,000

Pakistan
1,629,200

Algeria
219,300

Kuwait
124,900

Saudi
Arabia
28,700

India
258,400

Hong Kong
45,300

Sudan
725,600

Yemen
59,700

Djibouti
28,000

Bangladesh
245,000

Thailand
63,600

Ethiopia
431,800

Cameroon
42,200

Uganda
196,300

Rwanda
25,200

Cote
D'ivoire
174,100

Burundi
271,700

Kenya
401,900

Tanzania
292,100

Malawi
1,058,500

Zaire
391,100

Zambia
142,100

Zimbabwe
137,200

Swaziland
55,600

Australia
35,600

Equator

Source: United Nations High Commissioner for Refugees

3. CONFLICT AND INSTABILITY

Impoverishment undoubtedly exacerbates ethnic and communal tensions. To know that the number of rural poor has doubled since 1950, that per capita incomes have fallen steadily in a number of regions, and that malnutrition has risen, is to know that the stage is set for continuing floods of refugees—but this is only one part of the dynamic of people being forced out of their homes. Worldwide, nearly one billion people live in absolute poverty. Only a small proportion of them will become refugees. In fact, the total number of refugees amounts to less than 3 percent of the destitute. Economic deprivation interacts with other circumstances to heighten instability and aggravate conflicts, but is itself rarely a direct cause of refugee flows.

In near-subsistence economies, violent conflict disrupts food production and distribution even as it displaces people. When the conditions of daily life, precarious to begin with, are disrupted by war, the ensuing famine and disease often become greater threats to the population than the fighting itself. In Sudan's civil war, for example, 600,000 people are thought to have died so far, the vast majority of whom have starved or succumbed to diseases that they would probably have been able to resist had the situation been more stable.

It seems obvious that stagnation and decline aggravate conflict—but it is also true that rapid growth can have the same effect. Every process of change has winners and losers. The dislocations of development result in imbalances, with some classes, regions, or ethnic groups benefiting disproportionately. The ethnic Chinese led the boom in trade and manufacturing in many Southeast Asian countries. South Asians dominated trade in a number of African countries—Uganda being one example, until the entire ethnic group was expelled by Idi Amin. Such groups may become the targets of resentment, or may themselves assert a claim for self-determination in order to be free of what they see as the drag of less dynamic elements of society. The secession of Slovenia from Yugoslavia, and of Eritrea from Ethiopia, are examples of the latter. Either reaction may provoke violent confrontation.

ENVIRONMENTAL ROOTS

Millions of people have been forced to leave home because their land has become uninhabitable or is no longer able to support them. In some cases the cause is a natural disaster; in others, the catastrophe is caused by people. It may be sudden, as at Chernobyl or Mount Pinatubo, or as gradual as the spread of a desert or the retreat of a forest.

The terminology for describing this kind of migration is controversial. For many observers, "migration" does not convey the fact that the people affected are *forcibly* uprooted. And to call them refugees makes it clear that they left their homes involuntarily, for reasons not of their own making. Accurate use of the term "refugee," however, implies a need for international protection. Most people whose homes have become uninhabitable turn first to their governments and communities for recourse. Although they undoubtedly need assistance, they don't necessarily require the kind of international protection implied by the term "refugee."

Nevertheless, there are clear links between environmental degradation and refugees. Deterioration of natural resources, coupled with demographic pressure and chronic poverty, can *lead* to conflicts that force people to flee. Africa, for example, accounts for 10 percent of the world's population and hosts more than 25 percent of its refugees. It is no coincidence that those parts of the continent that are most affected by soil erosion, drought, and other environmental disasters are also the main theaters of armed conflicts, recurrent famine, and consequent refugee movements.

In the Sahel and the Horn of Africa, the combination of rapidly expanding populations, drought, and competition between nomads and settled agriculturalists has erupted into violence along a number of fronts. Fighting arising from disputes over irrigable land in the Senegal River basin has pushed thousands of Senegalese and Mauritanian refugees across their common border in both directions. In southern Ethiopia, incursions by certain clans into the traditional grazing lands of other clans have led to fierce and bloody clashes, and to a large, though temporary, flow of refugees into northern Kenya. Further south, in Mozambique, civilians already under severe pressure from the effects of civil war were pushed to the very edge of survival—and in many cases beyond it—by the effects of drought in 1992. More than 100,000 of them took refuge in neighboring Malawi in that year alone.

Occasionally, habitat destruction takes on the character of persecution—for example, if it occurs as a result of deliberate governmental action or gross negligence and no effort is made to compensate or assist the people affected. Indigenous people are particularly vulnerable to this kind of assault, as their way of life is often closely connected to a particular terrain. In extreme cases, for example in the southern marshes of Iraq, destruction of habitat may be used as a deliberate weapon of war. People who are uprooted because of willfully negligent or intentional destruction of the environment may indeed need international protection.

Long-term prevention should address the potential role of environmental damage in refugee flight. There is no comfort in the realization that today only a minority of environmentally displaced people need international protection. The international community has every interest in responding to the need for assistance to preserve and rehabilitate the environment before degradation begets violence and persecution and produces a mass of homeless people who easily *do* meet the conventional definition of refugees.

ETHNIC TENSIONS

Conflicts between ethnic groups have proliferated in recent years. Armenia and Azerbaijan, Burma, Burundi, Ethiopia, Georgia, Iraq, Sri Lanka, Sudan, and, of course, the former Yugoslavia are among a long list of countries where ethnic tensions have flared into civil war. Ethnic diversity is part of human geography almost everywhere: the 180 or so independent nations currently in existence are home to at least 5,000 ethnic groups. As a result, the notion of an ethnically pure nation-state is far-fetched—it could only be realized at an unacceptably high human cost.

Ethnic tensions can be seen as a root cause of refugee flows for two reasons. First, they are highly susceptible to political exploitation. Factions seeking to mobilize support commonly seek to fan ethnic antagonisms for their own ends. Ethnic conflict is a likely outcome when control of the state is captured by a single ethnic group that uses its power to further its own interests at the expense of others.

Second, despite the fact that most states contain a variety of ethnic groups, the ethnic identity of a single group is all too often made into a defining characteristic of nationality. Some minority groups may be seen as an obstacle to nation-building, incapable of fitting into a homogeneous national identity. Ethnic Albanians and Bosnian Muslims, for example, have no place in extreme nationalist visions of an Orthodox Christian "Greater Serbia." The ideology of *apartheid* in South Africa defined the non-white population out of citizenship. Members of groups other than the dominant one may be exposed first of all to discrimination, then to forced assimilation, persecution, expulsion, or even genocide. In many refugee crises, ethnicity is the criterion by which people are denied the protection of their national governments.

Recurrent conflict among ethnic or communal groups within a state calls for mediation by the central government. If the government is unwilling or too weak to perform this role effectively, "ethnic cleansing" or other forms of forcible segregation of populations may be the result, leading to a mass exodus—as in Palestine and the Punjab in 1948, and in Bosnia-Herzegovina today.

Ethnic tensions are also vulnerable to manipulation by external forces. Irredentism—the attempt to unite all territories occupied by a single ethnic group into one political entity—is the most obvious form of manipulation, and has played a large part in refugee-producing conflicts in the Horn of Africa and the former Yugoslavia, for example. Somalia's ambition to incorporate Somali-inhabited areas of the Ethiopian Ogaden led to a war in 1977, and the population of much of the region remains unsettled to this day, owing to a combination of political instability, ethnic tension, economic collapse, and recurring drought.

Throughout the Cold War period, superpower rivalry was a source of patronage for ethnic factions in many conflicts. Like European colonialism before it, the Cold War fostered or even created ethnic tensions. The recruitment of local factions into strategic alliances with East or West disrupted historical balances between groups, and artificially strengthened the position of client groups by arming them, arranging sanctuaries in neighboring countries, and providing diplomatic support for them. The Nicaraguan *contras* were given all three kinds of assistance from the United States.

Leaders trying to avoid the blame for failing economies frequently turn to scapegoating, and minority groups often provide convenient targets.

Members of certain ethnic groups were systematically co-opted to act as preferred proxies, intermediaries, or fighters—for example, the Hmong in Laos or the Miskitos in Nicaragua—thereby exposing the whole group to retribution. Local impulses toward accommodation or reconciliation were sometimes submerged by a powerful patron's interest in continuing the conflict. Refugees themselves became pawns in disputes that had little to do with their own immediate concerns.

If the Cold War era was dominated by ideological conflict, the fear is widespread that the 1990s mark the beginning of a new era of ethnic violence that will uproot additional millions of people from their homes. Already, refugees from dozens of ethnic conflicts look to the international community for material assistance and protection. Supposedly ancient hatreds, to which many people attribute the savagery of ethnic conflicts, can be invented, revived or kept from dying a natural death by opportunists who see in them a vehicle for personal or political profit. The Serbian strongman Slobodan Milosevic and other Serbian nationalists of the extreme right have made much of the entrenched enmity between Serbs and Croats, going back to (and indeed beyond) World War II, when the Croat allies of the Nazi regime in Germany inflicted great suffering on Serb communities. Yet in the post-war period, more than 20 percent of the adults of these two groups in the former Yugoslavia married someone from their "enemy" ethnic group—a testament to the mutability of supposedly immutable ethnic hatreds.

The challenge for modern nations is to alleviate ethnic tensions through mediation and prevent them from turning into violent conflict. This preventive role is set within a more positive responsibility: to manage ethnic diversity in a way that promotes tolerance within and beyond national borders.

HUMAN RIGHTS VIOLATIONS

Forcing people to flee is a violation of the human right to remain peacefully in one's home. The direct denial of other basic rights, including the rights of civilians not to be targeted in military actions, often provides the immediate impetus for flight. Indirectly, protest about or resistance to human rights violations may provoke violent retaliation, or take a violent form itself. An accumulation of abuses accompanied by violence, which leads to further abuses and a general climate of fear, is a sequence that frequently sparks mass exodus. In Iraq, Bosnia-Herzegovina, Myanmar, Guatemala, and elsewhere, human rights violations have been at the core of major humanitarian emergencies.

The types of refugee floods that have occurred over the past decade cannot be handled solely by providing protection in countries of asylum.

A number of countries remain unwilling to acknowledge the growing international consensus on human rights standards, much less to subject themselves to international scrutiny. China, for example, rejects any attempt at international oversight of its policies in Tibet, or criticism of its treatment of Chinese dissidents. Premier Li Peng told the U.N. Security Council summit in 1992 that "the issue of human rights falls within the sovereignty of each country. . . . China is opposed to using human rights as an excuse for interference in the internal affairs of other countries."

But as refugee problems increase and come to be seen by many receiving states as a threat to international peace and security, the responsibility of governments toward their citizens is coming under closer scrutiny. Both humanitarian and security concerns have focused attention more sharply on the causes of mass exodus, bringing human rights out from behind the shield of national sovereignty. Responsibility toward one's own citizens is being extended to encompass a responsibility to the international community for the way those citizens are treated. Protection against the most threatening forms of abuse, such as arbitrary killings, detention, torture, and disappearance, can have a profound impact on the cycle of violence and fear that impels so many people to flee.

Human rights violations do not occur in a vacuum. Like other causes of refugee flows, they exist in a complex environment of economic strain, political instability, a tradition of violence, ecological deterioration, and ethnic tensions. One factor or another may dominate a particular situation while interacting with others. By the time serious and massive abuse of fundamental rights occurs, the chances of averting refugee flows are slim indeed.

PREVENTION

Prevention, where possible, is the most effective form of protection for people in danger of becoming refugees. As recent events have shown all too clearly, the international community needs to take earlier and more effective action if it is to prevent potential refugee-generating situations from degenerating to the point where people feel that flight is their only option. The crises in the Horn of Africa, the former Yugoslavia, the Caucasus, and elsewhere have followed a broadly similar pattern of evolution, albeit under very different circumstances: in each case, tensions arising from unresolved political, ethnic, religious, or nationality disputes led to human rights abuses that became increasingly violent. Left unchecked, this process has often developed into armed conflicts that force people to flee their homes, and often their countries, in search of safety. By then, it has proved too late to avert widespread suffering, and far more difficult to assist and protect people or to achieve lasting solutions.

The types of refugee floods that have occurred over the past decade or so cannot be handled solely by providing protection in countries of asylum. Of the three conventional solutions for refugees—local integration in the country of first asylum, resettlement in another country, or voluntary repatriation—the first two are under severe pressure because of the sheer magnitude of the exodus. The

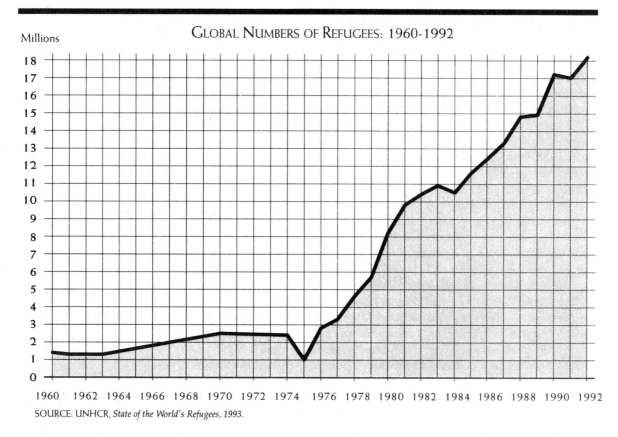

GLOBAL NUMBERS OF REFUGEES: 1960-1992

Millions

1960 1962 1964 1966 1968 1970 1972 1974 1976 1978 1980 1982 1984 1986 1988 1990 1992

SOURCE: UNHCR, *State of the World's Refugees, 1993*.

developing countries that provide sanctuary for the vast majority of the world's refugees face economic, environmental, and political problems that make it increasingly difficult for them to shelter masses of people for long periods. Small and densely populated Malawi, for example, has hosted one million refugees from war-torn Mozambique—a number equivalent to 10 percent of its own population. Their presence has put a tremendous burden on the local economy and infrastructure—on eveything from schools to water supplies. The refugee settlements are located in some of the most ecologically vulnerable areas of the country, and their needs for fuel and building materials have exacerbated deforestation and land degradation; Malawi is losing about 3.5 percent of its forest cover each year. The peace plan that allowed the repatriation of Mozambican refugees to begin in 1993 came not a moment too soon for hard-pressed Malawi.

Wealthier countries also have faced pressures to adopt more restrictive policies toward asylum-seekers as their numbers have grown. In 1983, some 100,000 people requested asylum in Europe, North America, Australia, and Japan. By 1992, the number of applications passed 800,000. Germany was most seriously affected by the sharp increase, with asylum applications rising from 121,000 in 1989 to 438,000 in 1992. The surge, coinciding with the strains of German reunification, led to a drastic

tightening of Germany's asylum law. Lawmakers in many other countries, including Austria, Switzerland, Canada, the United States, Britain, and Spain, have introduced similar legislation. Many of the countries that traditionally welcomed foreigners who wanted to settle there are showing greater reluctance. In some, there is an indiscriminate social backlash against all forms of immigration.

While very few people would argue with the truism that prevention is better than cure, in practice prevention is often controversial. The concept itself is open to misinterpretation, and even to misuse. Preventive action can take a positive or negative form. It can be aimed at protecting potential victims, promoting solutions to their problems before they are forced to flee. Alternatively, prevention can simply mean that a government throws up barriers to try to stop victims of persecution and violence from entering the country. Positive prevention aims to reduce or remove the conditions that cause people to flee, while the negative version—which should more properly be called obstruction—makes escape from persecution and danger more difficult, or impossible.

Unfortunately, obstruction is not uncommon. It ranges from forcibly turning back refugees at frontiers to intercepting them on the high seas and sending them back immediately, or to demanding that refugees show documentation in advance of entry. Pakistan has closed its border to further entries from Afghanistan, and the United States continues a policy of intercepting would-be refugees from Haiti on the high seas and returning them to Haiti without even a hearing on their claims to asylum. The United Kingdom requires Bosnians to hold a visa for direct entry to Britain, but does not have a consulate in Bosnia where they could obtain one—and will claim that those who go to a third country to apply should seek asylum in that country rather than Britain. Milder forms of obstructive prevention go under the name of "deterrence," a tactic that erects barriers to all immigrants and imposes harsh conditions upon reception, on the questionable assumption that economically motivated migrants will be discouraged while refugees will not. In reality, practices that raise barriers for one group raise them for all.

Prevention of refugee situations can be initiated long before, immediately before, or at various stages during the development of a crisis. At the most general level, prevention is—or should be—aimed at root causes, and goes far beyond the scope of humanitarian concerns alone. Displacement is the symptom of a host of the ailments of human society. Preventing the accumulation of social and economic strains that produce refugee-generating conflict and persecution is a many-faceted undertaking. It involves promotion of human rights, economic development, conflict resolution, the establishment of accountable political institutions, and environmental protection. It encompasses, in other words, virtually the whole agenda for constructing a sustainable society, with particular emphasis on the responsibilities of governments to care for all their people without discrimination.

In some countries there has been indiscriminate social back-lash against all forms of immigration.

Truly massive, far-sighted prevention has rarely been attempted, and generally only on a remedial basis in order to prevent the recurrence of major disaster. Perhaps the most spectacular examples are the post-World-War-II reconstruction of West Germany and Japan, designed to avoid repeating the mistakes made in the aftermath of World War I, and the Marshall Plan for western European recovery. Of a lesser magnitude, but still important, are current programs to consolidate the peacemaking processes in Cambodia and Central America. These involve a very broad program of reconstruction and

reconciliation, addressing issues as diverse as disarmament, land tenure, and human rights safeguards.

Rather than addressing root causes well before people are obliged to flee, most preventive efforts focus on immediate causes, when flight is imminent or has already started. Typically, they involve attempts to repair relations between people and their government before it is too late, and to provide supplementary or substitute protection until this can be accomplished. Efforts to stabilize internal population movements and provide protection and humanitarian relief to civilians within their home country involve, in many instances, the same measures that make possible the voluntary return of

Extreme deprivation is as likely to lead to resignation, as to flight. It is abrupt *deterioration* of status that causes refugee flows.

those who have already left. Finally, prevention involves helping states set up effective institutions, laws and procedures that enshrine the principles of national protection and guarantee the rights of minorities. The cost of failing to take preventive action can be very high, as illustrated by the situation of the Kurds and Shiites in Iraq, and of the Muslims in Bosnia and Herzegovina.

RESPONSES

The once hospitable climate for refugees has cooled in many asylum countries. Economic difficulties, domestic political instability, the resurgence of ethnic tensions, and the rolling up of the West's ideological welcome mat for refugees from communist countries are among the explanations. There is also an increasing sense of weariness at the apparent intractability of refugee problems. In virtually all regions, the persistent growth in numbers of actual and potential refugees has prompted a more conservative approach. The authorities in many industrialized countries are increasingly inclined to interpret their obligations to refugees according to a narrow "persecution standard" and to apply a restrictive definition of what constitutes persecution. Fewer asylum countries remain willing to accept what they see as an unlimited obligation to people fleeing violence.

Maintaining a humane refugee policy in the current political and economic climate requires firm responses. To begin with, the refugee problem, large and growing though it is, must be kept in perspective. Worldwide, less than 20 percent of international migrants are refugees. In many countries, refugees make up a still smaller proportion of immigrants. For example, in the United States in the fiscal year that ended in September 1992, legal immigration amounted to 973,977 people. The much harder to measure number of illegal immigrants was assumed to be about 300,000. Of this total of perhaps 1.3 million, refugees and asylum-seekers whose claims have been accepted accounted for only 132,173. The often-invoked image of a country overrun with refugees hardly conforms to the facts.

The manageability of the refugee problem depends on four elements of policy, the first of which must be an insistence that treaty obligations be met. That means, first and foremost, that refugees should not be returned to the countries where they face persecution and should be allowed to seek asylum in safe countries.

Second must be the provision of tough, fair, and fast determination procedures for asylum seekers, so that the system meant to protect refugees is not clogged with people trying to use it as a back channel for voluntary migration.

Third is generous international support for refugee assistance programs, so that those states that live up to their obligations but are unlucky enough to be located next door to a refugee-pro-ducing country do not bear unfair burdens of a kind that might tempt them to slam the door on refugees.

Finally, a more activist foreign policy to prevent the causes of refugee flows from developing to the crisis stage, and to bring about conditions in which refugees may safely return to their homes, is the only framework in which the manageability of the global refugee problem can be maintained.

Achieving an international consensus on these points will not be easy, and no country can pursue them successfully in isolation. But there are few subjects on which the commonality of interests of people and countries across the entire economic and political spectrum is so apparent. Long-term solutions for refugees involve a basic rebuilding of societies' capacities to manage change—the same capacities that will be needed to solve the other major issues on the human agenda. The rapid growth in the global refugee population is symptomatic of the inadequacy of our efforts to date. Refugees are the human fallout of the explosive tensions that have been allowed to accumulate around economic maldistribution, environmental degradation, militarization, and a host of other ills. They are not the only people who have a stake in addressing the causes of their plight.

Mixed Migration

Strategy for Refugees and Economic Migrants

TODAY, MORE THAN EVER, the tumultuous movements of people occurring throughout the world are pushing the problems of migration and forced displacement to the top of the international agenda. A complex mix of economic, demographic, social, religious, ethnic and political processes occurring simultaneously at the local, national and international levels are forcing people to move away from their homes and countries. This article focuses on one aspect of the larger migration debate: refugee movements—particularly where these refugee movements are mingled with economic migration.

SADAKO OGATA

Sadako Ogata is the United Nations High Commissioner for Refugees.

The security concerns of affected states are dominated by the violent causes of forced displacement, but the problem of migration has many different facets. Poverty, economic decline, environmental degradation and demographic pressures lead people to move to new areas in search of a better livelihood. These factors also exacerbate the inequities arising out of religious, ethnic or political divisions that may lead to violence and further refugee flow. Thus, the same or similar situations may produce both refugees and economic migrants. Given the ease of international travel, both groups may move to the same countries or areas. This mixed character of today's movements necessitates a comprehensive strategy that meets the diverse needs of refugees and economic migrants and simultaneously addresses the causes and solutions of their problems.

Any comprehensive response to population movement must be based on a clear understanding of the international refugee system and the fundamental difference between refugee flows and migratory movements.

Responses to Forced Migration

Today, there are over 20 million refugees and persons of concern to the United Nations High Commissioner for Refugees (UNHCR) who have been forced to flee their country in fear of persecution, war and violence. The majority of refugees and other persons of concern to UNHCR are in Africa (7.5 million) and Europe (6 million), followed by Asia (5.7 million) and the Americas (1.4 million). The number of migrants worldwide is estimated to be over 100 million.

Their need for international protection sets refugees apart from economic migrants. Refugees flee because their governments are unwilling or unable to protect them from persecution for reasons of race, nationality, political opinion or religious belief. More commonly, refugees flee from the brutal effects of internal conflict and violence. Economic migrants, on the other hand, move in search of improved employment opportunities or for other personal reasons. Though their reasons for moving may be compelling, they are not of the same life-threatening quality as in the case of refugees.

Perhaps because of this difference, the issue of interstate migration has remained within the sovereign prerogative of states, whereas the granting of international protection to refugees has come within the purview of international law. UNHCR and the 1951 Convention relating to the Status of Refugees form the basis upon which the post World War II refugee system was established. UNHCR was mandated by the UN General Assembly to provide international protection to refugees and to find solutions to their problems, such as voluntary repatriation or integration in a new community. The 1951 Convention relating to the Status of Refugees binds party states to internationally agreed standards for the admission, protection and treatment of refugees. One of the most important

From *Harvard International Review*, Spring 1995, pp. 30-33. © 1995 by the Harvard International Relations Council. Reprinted by permission.

principles of refugee protection, contained in the 1951 Convention, prohibits contracting states from returning a refugee to a territory where his life or liberty could be threatened. 123 States are party to the 1951 convention, among them the Russian Federation and several of the newly independent Republics of the former Soviet Union.

The international refugee system has been shaped by the political context in which it developed. In the 1950s, the ideological and strategic interests of Western states coincided with the granting of asylum to those fleeing from communist repression in Eastern Europe. Refugees were either integrated in the country of asylum or resettled elsewhere in the West. As a result, neither prevention of refugee movements nor voluntary repatriation were considered feasible policy options.

Decolonization in Africa and Asia during the 1960s and 1970s, however, led to a different type of flight, characterized by large-scale displacement of people seeking protection from general violence rather than individual persecution. Although neighboring countries generously provided protection to these refugees, neither the refugees nor the receiving states desired local integration. Instead, temporary asylum and voluntary repatriation were emphasized as solutions. The different nature of the refugee problem faced by Africa was acknowledged by the 1969 OAU Convention Governing the Specific Aspects of Refugee Problems in Africa. This Convention broadened the definition of refugees to include those fleeing war, violence and serious public disorder and promoted the principle of voluntary repatriation of refugees. In succeeding years, however, the extension of the Cold War rivalry to and the political and socio-economic inequities in these newly independent states led to prolonged civil wars that exacerbated the refugee crises to an unprecedented scale in countries such as Mozambique, Ethiopia, Sudan, Angola, and Afghanistan.

The end of the Cold War has provided valuable opportunities to resolve some of these long-standing conflicts and has also facilitated the return of refugees. For example, 375,000 Cambodians, 600,000 Ethiopians and 1.5 million Mozambicans have returned to their homes in recent years. At the same time, however, the end of the Cold War has unleashed and intensified internal conflicts—particularly ethnic ones—on a scale rarely seen before. Since 1991, the international community has been confronted by at least four major emergencies in Iraq, Somalia, the former Yugoslavia and Rwanda, each of which has produced more than 1 million refugees.

The failure of the international community to address the issues of poverty, famine, environmental degradation, high population growth and urbanization in the Third World underlies these recurrent humanitarian crises. Development efforts have brought little improvement in income, life expectancy or the provision of basic needs for the vast majority of the population of this planet. Yet, they have heightened expectations while the gap between rich and poor nations has increased. Television exposure to the lifestyle of the West and the ease of air travel has led a growing number of people, both refugees and economic migrants, to seek new lives beyond their region of origin.

Europe has been the recipient of many of these refugees and economic migrants. Since the late 1970s, however, immigration to Western Europe has been virtually stopped, leaving the asylum channel as the only gateway. Abuse of the asylum procedures and growing xenophobia have led governments to adopt restrictive measures affecting both illegal immigrants and genuine asylum seekers. In the United States, which in the past admitted many refugees, particularly from Central America and Southeast Asia, there is growing pressure to limit immigration.

Particularly in countries ravaged by conflict and war, democratic institution-building and rehabilitation and development programs are essential. Otherwise, circumstances may force returnees to move again.

Against this background of deepening refugee crisis, growing migratory pressures and waning hospitality in receiving countries lies the challenge of promoting a policy that distinguishes refugees and economic migrants and meets their differing needs. For refugees, ensuring their protection and removing the causes of flight are the most obvious needs. To be fully effective, however, a refugee strategy must be complemented by immigration and economic development policies.

A Comprehensive Strategy for Mixed Migration

In its broadest sense, a comprehensive strategy consists of the variety of concerted measures that aim to break the vicious cycle of exile, return and internal displacement which typifies the many refugee crises in the Third World. The strategy must seek to enhance the overall stability of the affected country by promoting respect for fundamental human rights, economic and social development and the maintenance of peace and security. To achieve these goals, a wide range of governmental, intergovernmental and non-governmental actors must cooperate and coordinate their activities.

Prevention, protection and solutions are the key elements of a comprehensive strategy. The *prevention* element tackles the causes that compel people to move. A wide variety of activities, such as the promotion of human and minority rights, ethnic and religious tolerance, economic development, conflict resolution and the adoption of an accountable political system, fall into this category. Such measures aim at both avoiding refugee movements and at reducing uncontrolled and irregular migratory movements. Mass information campaigns in countries of origin, such as those organized by UNHCR and the International Organization for Migration in Albania, Vietnam and Romania, may reduce irregular migration by making potential migrants better aware of the consequences of their decision to leave or stay.

As a minimum standard, international *protection* for refugees should include temporary admission, no forcible return to danger and repatriation when the conditions in the country of origin permit it. Protection of internally displaced persons might also prevent people who are in a refugee-like situation from moving abroad.

In most instances, voluntary repatriation of refugees and the return of migrants is the most appropriate solution. This approach can only be successful, however, if conditions for the successful economic and political reintegration of the returnees exist. Particularly in countries ravaged by conflict and war, democratic institution-building and rehabilitation and development programs are essential. Otherwise, circumstances may force returnees to move again.

Such comprehensive approaches to address mixed migration have rarely been attempted. One example of a limited effort is the Comprehensive Plan of Action (CPA) for Indo-Chinese

Emergency relief is only part of the solution.

Refugees adopted in June 1989. Vietnamese boat people had, since 1979, been granted temporary asylum by countries in the region before being resettled as refugees in Western countries. By 1987, however, it had become apparent that economic conditions, rather than persecution, were the predominant motives for departure from Vietnam. At the same time, resettlement places were dwindling as countries tightened their admission policies for refugees.

UNHCR initiated a process of consultations with governments, including the Vietnamese government, which led to the 1989 International Conference on Indo-Chinese Refugees during which the CPA was adopted. The CPA has allowed for temporary refuge for all those arriving in first asylum countries. For the first time, however, it has

introduced screening procedures to differentiate between refugees and migrants. Refugees are resettled in third countries while non-refugees are encouraged to return to Vietnam in an orderly and humane manner. CPA has had three objectives: to protect "genuine" refugees, to stop the flow of boat people out of Vietnam and to adopt a "humane" solution for non-refugees. The CPA has sought to reduce the clandestine departures of economic migrants and accelerate orderly departures. It has done this by promoting an emigration program and initiating an information campaign so that those wishing to leave are better aware of the consequences of their decision.

The CPA's relative success has been largely due to the inter-locking and mutually reinforcing obligations placed on the main actors involved—Vietnam, countries of asylum, countries of re-settlement and donors. An important element of the CPA's success has been Vietnam's recognition of its responsibility to its citizens in accepting their return and in scrupulously observing the "guarantees" of their safety. Apart from the limited assistance for the economic reintegration of the returnees into their host communities, however, the root causes of departure have not been touched, limiting the scope of the CPA.

Although each situation of mixed migration is different, the experiences gained in Southeast Asia provide useful lessons on how to respond to recent mixed outflows from Haiti and Cuba. Though both Caribbean states have had regular mixed outflows in the past, the response to the outflows of each of the countries has been markedly different. Despite the serious human rights situation in Haiti, the United States has viewed the outflow of Haitians as primarily economically motivated. This perspective led the US Government, in 1991, to adopt a policy of interdiction on the high seas and the return of nearly all Haitians to Haiti following a preliminary screening on Coast Guard vessels. Under the 1966 Cuban Adjustment Act, however, Cubans have been allowed to enter and reside in the United States—regardless of the reasons for their departure. The policy amendments with respect to both groups during the summer of 1994 reflect efforts to differentiate more effectively between those who need protection and migrants.

Following the 1991 military coup in Haiti and the ouster of President Aristide, the international community responded by imposing an economic embargo. These events, combined with the deteriorating human rights situation in the country caused nearly 30,000 Haitians to leave their country by boat. International and domestic pressure led the US Government to announce in May 1994 that Haitian boat people would no longer be interdicted at the high seas and returned, but would instead pass through a screening process. Boat people recognized as refugees would be transferred to the United States and rejected persons would be returned to Haiti. The prospect of resettlement in the United States, however, caused the number of new arrivals to rise dramatically.

The US subsequently adjusted its policy: pending a more durable solution, all new arrivals from Haiti were granted safe haven outside the US—mainly at the US military base at Guantanemo—resulting in a steep decline in the number of departures from Haiti. Meanwhile, pressure on the Haitian regime to abide by the election results of 1991 culminated in Security Council resolution 940 of July 1994 authorizing the formation of a multinational force under Chapter VII of the Charter and the use of "all necessary means" to implement the Governors Island Agreement. Following the military intervention and the return of President Aristide, the majority of Haitians in the temporary safe havens opted to return home. The problem remains, however, of building a democratic society and improving Haiti's economic situation. Without a long-term international commitment to such measures, the people of Haiti will continue to find the shores of the US, the world's richest country, extremely attractive.

While Haitians were refused asylum, Cubans were welcomed by the United States. When 36,000 Cubans departed for the US during the summer of 1994, the issue was not whether to grant asylum but how to restrict it. To deter further arrivals, the United States provided assistance to Cubans at Guantanemo but did not permit them to enter the US. Instead, bilateral negotiations were opened with the Cuban government, and a Migration Accord was signed on September 8, 1994, to "ensure that migration between the two countries is safe, legal and orderly." Similar to the Orderly Departure Programme for Vietnamese within the context of the CPA, the Accord provides several measures to facilitate emigration to the United States, while Cuba agrees to take effective measures "... to prevent unsafe departures using mainly persuasive methods." However, as long as the socio-economic causes that force Cubans to leave are not addressed, the threat of disorderly movement will continue.

The long-term prospect for solving the refugee and migration problem in Vietnam, Haiti and Cuba depends on two factors: the continuing commitment of these countries to address this issue in a responsible and humane manner and the adoption of economic development projects that absorb returning refugees and migrants and share equally the benefits of growth among the population. In turn, the international community can assist these countries in reaching these objectives through targeted trade, investment and aid programs.

The continent of Europe presents a mixed scene. In Western Europe, a highly developed asylum system is under pressure from a mixed group of refugees and economic migrants, as well as those fleeing war in the Balkans who need temporary protection. In Central Europe, countries are facing refugees and migrants from Eastern Europe, Africa and Asia seeking to enter Western Europe. Within the fifteen Republics formerly constituting the Soviet Union simmering ethnic and political conflicts are producing refugees and internally displaced persons on a large scale, whether in Georgia, the Caucasus or central Asia. This picture is further complicated by the movement of people, such as Crimean Tartars or Meshketian Turks, who had been deported from their countries in the past and who now seek to reclaim their land and rights. Political and economic restructuring has also led a significant number of the 25 million Russians living outside the Russian Federation to move "homewards." Changing nationality laws increase the risk of statelessness and add to the complexity of the refugee and migration question.

As refugees become part of a larger movement of people, responses must be fashioned to include measures to address both refugees and economic migrants.

Facing these difficulties, Europe could be a new context for comprehensive approaches. In the case of the Republics of the former Soviet Union, after consultations with interested governments, UNHCR is organizing a regional conference. This process should contribute to the development of a comprehensive strategy—of prevention, protection and solutions—to address population movements in the region. A regional strategy can only succeed, however, if all parties in the region are politically committed to a sustained effort and are aided by the international community.

Beyond any doubt, the issue of mixed migration is of major concern to the international community. As refugees become part of a larger movement of people, responses must be fashioned to include measures to address both refugees and economic migrants. In such situations, traditional responses which focus primarily on the conditions in the receiving country fall short. Instead, the situation in the country of origin should be the focus of efforts to implement the most appropriate solution to the crisis and to adopt measures that may prevent or minimize disorderly or coerced movements. As the causes of and solutions to population movements are often primarily of a political and socio-economic nature, closer cooperation is required between refugee and migration agencies, political actors and development and financial institutions.

Weapons Proliferation and Arms Control

Weapons proliferation in the developing world constitutes a threat to regional, as well as international, peace and security. The potential for conflict and instability in the developing world has generated a strong demand for weapons and has resulted in a large market for international arms traders. Arms sales to the developing world during the 1980s totaled over $300 billion, providing many developing countries formidable arsenals of conventional weapons for use against both internal and external security threats. The largest portion of these arms sales went to the Middle East and the Indian subcontinent, two regions where tensions have always been high. Arms expenditures worldwide have slowed, but the availability of increasingly sophisticated weapons provides consumers with the incentive to upgrade their arsenals, especially if their adversaries do so. The demonstrated capability of sophisticated weapons in the Falklands/Malvinas and Persian Gulf wars increased both the demand and cost of such weapons technology.

Arms producers have their own incentive to increase their market shares in order to improve economies of scale, contribute favorably to their balance of payments, and perhaps increase their influence in the developing world. Although cold war rivalry is no longer a contributing factor to arms sales, regional conflict continues to provide markets for conventional weaponry.

Another contributing factor to the international arms trade is the entry of developing world arms producers into the market. A number of developing countries have gained the capacity to produce arms and are actively seeking to promote exports. While these weapons may not rival the technical sophistication of those produced by industrialized countries, their cost makes them an attractive alternative. This arms production increases the availability of weapons, stiffens competition within the market, and offers diversity of supply. These factors complicate efforts to control conventional weapons transfers.

Even more disturbing than the availability of sophisticated conventional weapons is the potential for proliferation of nuclear weapons. The Nuclear Nonproliferation Treaty (NPT) came into force in 1970 and requires signatories that possess nuclear weapons to refrain from transferring this technology to nonnuclear weapons states. The treaty also obliges nonweapons states that have signed not to attempt to acquire nuclear weapons. Over 150 nations are party to the agreement, including all five countries that have declared their possession of nuclear weapons. India, Pakistan, and Israel, all assumed to either have the weapons or the ability to manufacture them, remain outside the treaty. Argentina and Brazil also remain outside the treaty but are cooperating with other Latin American countries to establish a nuclear-free zone in the region. South Africa disclosed that it had built six nuclear weapons, but subsequently dismantled them. Pretoria joined the Nonproliferation Treaty as a nonweapons state in 1991, but questions have arisen regarding its compliance with International Atomic Energy Agency (IAEA) inspections. A number of NPT signatories appear to be working toward developing nuclear weapons. These countries include North Korea, which never fully complied with the treaty's inspection terms and has been locked in a dispute with the United States and the IAEA regarding inspection of its nuclear facilities, and Iran, Libya, and Iraq. However, the indefinite extension of the Nuclear Nonproliferation Treaty, the conclusion of the Pelindaba Treaty, and the efforts to conclude a Comprehensive Test Ban Treaty help to strengthen the nonproliferation regime. Some developing countries are also engaged in an effort to eliminate nuclear weapons.

Many consider the spread of nuclear weapons to be a major threat to international peace and security, generating regional arms races and increasing the likelihood that such weapons will be used. Others regard the proliferation of nuclear weapons with less alarm, claiming that deterrence will work at the regional level in much the same fashion as it worked between the superpowers during the cold war. Whatever the perspective, the proliferation of nuclear weapons remains a controversial issue.

Ballistic missile technology to deliver nuclear weapons is increasingly available, too. Perhaps even more dangerous, however, ballistic missiles can be adapted to deliver chemical and biological weapons, the so-called poor man's nuclear weapons, which are easier to obtain and produce. Concerns about chemical weapons capability were evident during the Persian Gulf War, when the coalition forces feared that their troops might face Iraqi chemical weapons on the battlefield. Iraq's SCUD missile attacks against Israel also raised fears that these inaccurate and unpredictable missiles might be equipped with chemical weapons. Although these fears never materialized, the attacks raised awareness regarding this combination of threats.

While most of the attention has been focused on sophisticated conventional weapons, chemical and biological weapons, and nuclear weapons, it is small arms and mines that represent perhaps the biggest threat to civilian populations. The mindless killing in Liberia and the casualties caused by mines in places like Cambodia, Angola, and Afghanistan illustrate these problems.

Weapons proliferation and militarization in the developing world not only increase the potential for conflict and instability, but also drain resources away from development efforts. The more money that is spent on the military, the less is available for education, health care, family planning, and other social needs. How to encour-age a reduction in military spending and the channeling of resources toward more productive purposes remains a dilemma.

Looking Ahead: Challenge Questions

What are the implications of increasing the developing world arms production?

What are the sources of arms for ethnic conflicts? What are the obstacles to controling this arms trade?

What is a nuclear-weapon-free zone?

What is the significance of the Pelindaba Treaty?

Why is control of nuclear weapons so complicated?

Third World Militaries: New Suppliers, Deadlier Weapons

Amit Gupta

Amit Gupta, a junior fellow at the Center for the Study of Developing Societies, Delhi, is currently with the Program in South and West Asian Studies at the University of Illinois, Urbana-Champaign.

Until the 1980s, the global arms bazaar was dominated by the Western states and the Soviet Union, who were thus able to use arms transfers to further their political goals vis-à-vis a recipient country. In the 1980s, Third World countries such as Brazil, Israel, and the two Koreas emerged as major arms exporters. This rise of Third World arms producers has changed the arms bazaar from a sellers' market to a buyers' market, and recipient countries are now able to procure arms on commercially better terms and with less political dependency on their suppliers.

Yet these commercial and political changes are not what worry policy makers in Washington. Instead, concern is being voiced because of the range and lethality of weapons produced in the Third World. This weapons production capability, it is feared, will give Third World countries the ability to prosecute their ambitions more freely and aggressively. It will also make Western intervention more difficult as Third World states continue to acquire weapons of mass destruction and the means to deliver them. At the very least, it is believed, profit-hungry arms industries in the Third World will go in for the unrestricted transfer of weapons to other states, thereby increasing the level of regional conflict the world over.

THE ARMS MARKS IN THE 1980S

One reason Third World arms industries found a niche in the arms bazaar of the 1980s was their attractive sales packages—a combination of low prices, good customer service, and guaranteed availability. The net result of such policies was especially beneficial for two Third World countries: Israel and Brazil. Brazil was the tenth largest exporter of armaments in the world between 1986 and 1990, with sales of $1.189 billion. Israel was the twelfth largest with sales of $1.094 billion.[1]

A second reason lay in a set of opportunities that arose in the 1980s that allowed Third World countries to achieve substantial military exports. Specifically, the complexity of new Western weapons systems created a demand for simple rugged weaponry, and this demand was met by countries like Brazil. The Brazian arms industry specialized in producing weapons systems that were based on easily available components and low technology. Since most Third World countries did not expect to fight a technologically advanced opponent, they saw such low- and medium-tech systems as better satisfying their needs.

But this second reason also set limits for the Third World arms industries. Sales were primarily to other Third World countries rather than in the lucrative Western market. The only major South-North arms deal was the Brazilian sale of the Tucano turboprop trainer to the Royal Air Force in the late 1980s. Perhaps as a result, the prevailing hierarchy of arms producers and arms suppliers did not change despite the rising sales of Third World producers. During the period that the Brazilians and the Israelis sold a billion dollars each worth of armaments, the superpowers sold approximately $64 billion worth of weaponry.[2] Too, one must note that the Iran-Iraq war accounted for the bulk of arms sales by Third World countries. Indeed, one could make the case that if the Iran-Iraq war were set aside Third World arms sales would be miniscule.

Nevertheless, Third World arms producers hoped that the weapons programs they had embarked on in the 1980s would, in the 1990s, allow them the opportunity to compete with the Northern states for the advanced weapons market. Is this possible, in light of recent trends?

THE ARMS MARKET IN THE 1990S

Many analysts initially drew on the Gulf War experience to forecast the arms market of the 1990s. They saw that war as demonstrating the superiority of advanced-technology weapons; as showing the utility of anti-missile defenses; and as proving that crude ballistic missiles needed more lethal—nuclear, chemical, biological—warheads to be effective weapons. Given these assumptions, they believed the arms market would be marked by large sales of high-technology weapons systems and particularly by ballistic missiles with a capacity for mass destruction.

But a number of factors run counter to such a scenario. The high cost of weapons systems has created major problems for arms producers in the developed world. Individual countries, barring the United States and now Japan, are finding it increasingly difficult and expensive to design and produce weapons systems by themselves. Sweden and France are the only two West European countries left with national programs for producing supersonic combat aircraft. The ability of such states to off-set domestic costs with exports is diminishing, as competition among arms producers is increasing while the global market for weapons shrinks.

The market is further complicated by changes in the former Soviet Union. As the Russians reduce their armed forces, they will have a large surplus of weapons to sell. With changes in the global environment, markets hitherto closed to the Russians may open up and Moscow should be able to offer its large surplus of arms at bargain basement rates. Witness the attempt to sell the MiG-29 to Switzerland or the sale of the Su-27 to China. More recently, Ukraine has offered to sell China an aircraft carrier and has reportedly put nineteen Tu-16O strategic bombers on the market as well.[3]

Lastly, consider the Third World arms industries themselves. During the 1980s, there was a general upgrade in the quality of weapons produced by Third World countries—especially in countries that had extensive military-scientific bases, such as Brazil, Israel, and India. Thus twenty-six countries had on-going missile programs and at least four were developing combat aircraft (Israel, India, Taiwan, and South Africa). Other systems put into production included ships, tanks, and guided missiles (India, Israel, and Brazil). Brazil and India also initiated programs for the construction of nuclear-powered submarines. Coupled with the development of such systems was the growing capability of Third World countries to produce weapons of mass destruction. Libya and Iraq produced chemical weapons; North Korea and Pakistan embarked on nuclear programs.

But most of these countries will be hurt by their industries, heavy dependence on exports. Brazil, for example, has a very small internal market for its weapons systems and consequently its arms industry depends on exports for its survival. This is further complicated by a dependence on only a few countries for export orders. Brazilian firms have been particularly hurt by the inability of Iraq to pay for the systems that it purchased in the 1980s. Embraer, Brazil's leading aeronautics manufacturer, has been forced to declare bankruptcy and is being sold off to private firms. ENGESA and Bernadini Brothers

invested heavily in developing the Osorio tank for Saudi Arabia, but Riyadh decided against purchasing it. Chile, another country dependent on arms exports to sustain its arms industry, was also hurt by the closure of the Iraqi market.[4] Thus the international arms market will witness an even more intense rivalry in the 1990s than it did in the 1980s.

Coupled with these trends is the entry of new producers. Iran, for example, has started showing its indigenously produced armaments in international exhibitions. Taiwan and Indonesia are also trying to enter the arms market as exporters. Significantly, all these countries provide the same sort of low-technology equipment; none has bridged the gap to provide high-technology weaponry such as supersonic fighters. Until they do, the goal of all Third World countries will be to seek the low-technology end of the market.

MISSILE PROLIFERATION

The threat posed by the proliferation of nuclear and chemical weapons would seem to have risen substantially by the increased availability of capable delivery systems. Ballistic missiles in the Third World, it is thought, may provide these states the capability to launch nuclear and chemical strikes against traditional rivals and to fend off Western interventionist forces. Thus, the West has placed an emphasis on pressuring Third World producer states to restrict the sales of such systems. Equally important has been the Missile Technology Control Regime (MTCR) of 1987, which prohibits exports of missiles or missile components by the cooperating countries. These countries were originally the Western powers but now include Russia, with China agreeing to follow similar constraints. In this context, recent U.S. insistence that Israel become an ICR signatory is a significant breakthrough.

One restraint on missile sales may come from the potential for mutual vulnerability. India, for example, is seen as a potential salesman of ballistic missiles, but its most likely market is the Middle East, and it would not be in India's interest to sell such weapons there because in every India-Pakistan war the Middle Eastern states, in the interests of Islamic solidarity, have supplied weapons to Pakistan. Israel, another state that has the technology and needs the money from such sales, faces a similar situation in the Middle East and an equally constraining situation outside its region. Israel has supplied technological assistance to the South African missile program in the past, but the continuation of such assistance may be in doubt given the changes in the South African political scene. And it would be difficult for Israel to sell weapons elsewhere within the international system, except to states facing a similar security dilemma, like Taiwan.

THE ROLE OF TECHNOLOGY

By the start of the 1990s, the attempt by Third World countries to advance a technological level had met with mixed success. On the production side, most were able to expand their range of systems and to upgrade the quality of these systems. Thus the Israelis and the Brazilians produced tanks, the Chileans and South Africans produced aircraft, and India began to build a new range of naval vessels. Further, in specific areas of weapons technology, particularly the development of a series of missiles, the research efforts of countries like India, Israel, and Iraq bore fruit. Certain Third World states were also able to make advances in the production of electronic subsystems—Israel and Singapore being the most prominent examples.

But when it came to developing state-of-the-art conventional weapons, the track record was far less successful. A number of programs were either terminated or pushed to the point of becoming uneconomical because of high development costs, technology restrictions, and external pressures. The most complete program to develop a supersonic fighter was Israel's Lavi fighter, but this was scrapped in 1987 owing to escalating costs and pressure from American aerospace firms, which saw the plane cutting into their market. India's Light Combat Aircraft program has been plagued by developmental delays and by a restricted production quota (400) that may lead to an astronomical price tag for the entire program.[5]

In sum, the rise in technological level that was expected to emerge from the weapons programs of the 1980s did not take place. Third World states will therefore tend to compete for the low-tech end of the global market as far as major weapons systems are concerned, the one notable exception being perhaps missile technology. Given these facts where are the Third World arms industries headed?

TRENDS: PREDOMINANCE OF LOW-TECH

First, the Gulf War will not spell the doom of low- and middle-tech systems. Most Third World countries do not have the resources to invest in expensive high-tech systems, and they do not face technologically advanced opponents in their immediate environment.

The conventional military build-ups of most Third World countries in the 1980s were due to the availability of subsidized weaponry from a superpower. Thus Afghanistan, India, Syria, and Vietnam were the largest recipients of Soviet military aid, while Israel, Egypt, and Pakistan benefitted from ties with the United States. India became the second largest importer of armaments in the 1980s (Iraq was the largest), primarily because the Soviet Union provided its most modern weapons systems on highly favorable terms.

With the cold war gone, such subsidies are going to be increasingly hard to come by and the potential of most Third World countries to buy such large amounts of weapons is going to decline. Consider that one estimate puts the cost of a Pakistani military satellite capability against India in the range of $4.2 billion.[6] Yet the total

annual Pakistani defense budget is $3.19 billion.[7] No wonder current U.S. arms sales efforts are centered on the Middle East: it is the one region where states can afford to pay for such systems. The bulk of the Third World can acquire such systems only with Western loans or subsidies.

Also telling against the dominance of high-tech arms is the fact that Third World states do not expect to face a superpower as an adversary. They expect to fight their traditional rivals, who are at a similar technological level. Saddam Hussein's preparations, for instance, were aimed at combatting Israel. Similarly, India's principal military concerns, despite the growth of its naval power and the development of an intermediate-range ballistic missile, remain its South Asian neighbors and the still disputed Sino-Indian border. Third World countries will likely make token purchases of advanced weapons systems to be the showcase of their inventory, but this will not lead to a substantial increase in their capabilities.

Thus though high-tech arms sales will be dominated by Western companies, this domination will not lead to the complete exclusion of Third World arms industries. A major export market for less capable systems remains and will remain. It is instructive in this regard to remember that the overwhelming majority of orders placed with U.S. companies in 1990 were from Saudi Arabia.

TRENDS: SUB-NATIONALISM

A second area of opportunity for Third World arms industries lies in the rising tide of sub-nationalism and ethnic conflict that is sweeping the world. From Quebec to Tibet, ethnic groups are once again seeking to break away from the states in which they are presently located. Sub-nationalism creates opportunity for arms sales to insurgent groups or newly emerged states, and this may be an important market for Third World producers. The weapons such groups require are not high-tech systems; indeed, most groups would lack the military training to use such systems. Instead, these groups require the rugged middle- to low-tech weaponry that the Third World produces. Such armaments could include fixed and rotary wing aircraft for close support, but the bulk of such sales will be of weapons that can be supplied covertly to insurgent groups and are useful for waging guerrilla warfare. Assault rifles, anti-tank weapons, surface-to-air missiles, and anti-personnel weapons are likely to be in demand. Israel, for example, sold the Tamil Tigers Eagle pistols, Galil rifles, Uzi submachine guns, light machine guns, and shoulder carried field missiles.[8] Similarly, the Croatian national guard has received arms from Hungary, Romania, South Africa, and Singapore.[9] In fact, Singapore has sold the Croatian national guard a weapons package of SAR-80 assault rifles, Ultimax 100 Mk III light machine guns, and Crossbow light anti-tank weapons. The Croatians have also obtained 7.62mm rifles from Argentina and grenade launchers from South Africa's ARMSCOR.[10]

Ethnic conflicts also create a demand for counterinsurgency weapons from the beleaguered state. Third World arms industries that specialize in light arms (Israel), anti-personnel munitions (Chile, which makes cluster bombs), and counterinsurgency aircraft (Brazil) could take advantage of the situation. Sri Lanka, for example, raised its military expenditures from $25 million in 1982 to $583 million in 1988, in order to combat the Tamil secessionists. (By 1991, the military budget had slimmed down to $450 million.[11])

The opportunity to make sales in such situations will be dependent on the extent to which the supplier state is itself vulnerable to similar pressures. An India or an Iraq, which itself faces secessionist pressures, would increase its own vulnerability by making such arms sales. A hostile state could respond by providing weapons to insurgent groups in the supplier country. Mutual vulnerability, therefore, will condition such arms sales.

TRENDS: NORTH-SOUTH COLLABORATION

The third major trend will be increased collaboration between the arms industries of the North and the South. Western arms producers started transferring technology to Third World industries in the 1980s in order to penetrate these markets. Countries in the Asia-Pacific region, for example, demanded some form of technology transfer and co-production in the deals they cut with Western aerospace companies. Indonesia's IPIN aircraft company received significant technology transfers under the NBO 105 helicopter program and through its partnership with the Bell Helicopters. More recently, the Franco-German consortium, Eurocopter, had to agree to the joint development of the P120L helicopter with China and Singapore.

Further North-South collaboration is likely to take place in the development and production of new weapons systems. Examples include programs like the joint development of the Super Sabre by Grumman and the Chinese aircraft industry, and the co-development of the AMX fighter by Brazil and Italy. The Russians are also going in for joint development with both Western and Third World countries. The Yakovlev design bureau, for instance, is targeting both India and China for co-development and co-production of the Short Take Off and Vertical Landing Yak-141. Such collaboration is also likely to be seen in the research and development (R&D) of weapons systems. One means by which Western companies could hold down spiralling production costs is by transferring part of the R&D process for new weapons systems to the Third World industries. Both France and Sweden sought to interest India in tying its Light Combat Aircraft project to their own.

A number of Third World industries also have top-flight skilled labor that can be hired for a fraction of the cost of comparable labor in the West. Such skilled labor can be used for establishing computer-aided-design and computer-aided-manufacture programs. The German aeronautical company, VFW, for instance, has taken the first step in this direction by asking India's Aeronautical Development Agency to do a preliminary study for co-development of a 100-seater commuter aircraft that can be sold in both civilian and military markets.[12]

But the demand for North-South collaboration is not restricted to a top-down process, where the technologically advanced Northern states are seeking partners to decrease costs and gain access to markets. In a growing trend, Southern states seek Northern partners to gain entry to the markets of developed states. For example, Israel has sought to create joint companies with American firms so as to get a slice of the U.S. defense budget. Singapore is also seeking joint ventures so as to gain greater access to Northern markets.

Systems being phased out of production may also get a new lease on life by transferring assembly lines to Third World countries. In the mid-1980s, Northrop offered India the production line of the Northrop F-5 fighter/trainer, with the suggestion that Hindustan Aeronautics Limited might later be provided with the blueprints of the more modern F-20 Tigershark fighter. The French, similarly, want to transfer the Alpha Jet production line, which is being shut down, to South East Asia or India. The French Air Force would buy aircraft from this line to make up for attrition.[13]

Controversy over weapons might be muted by North-South collaboration. A forerunner of that trend could be the funding of the Israeli Arrow anti-missile program—72 percent of total program costs—by the American SDI program.[14]

North-South transfers need not go through government channels. One critical example may be the transfer of scientific personnel. The media have given attention to the possibility that Third World countries seeking to manufacture nuclear weapons could use the services of former Soviet scientists who are available on the international market. But the former Soviet Union is just one of a growing number of sources for Third World and East European countries seeking scientific personnel who might give them a nuclear capability. South African, Israeli, Brazilian, Pakistani, Indian, and possibly Korean scientists could also be asked to do the job. Moreover, as Western defense industries continue to face harder times, even Western scientists have come on the market. Argentina's Condor missile program, for instance, was to be developed by a team of freelance German scientists. Trying to control the spread of the relevant knowledge will thus be next to impossible, and alternative measures will have to be sought.

TRENDS: SOUTH-SOUTH COLLABORATION

Another feature of the arms trade in the 1990s will be increased South-South collaboration in the field of weapons production. In the 1980s, attempts at South-South collaboration were proposed to lessen development costs, to avoid restrictions on technology transfers, and to allow countries to develop weapons of mass destruction and the means to deliver them. Thus South Africa hired Israeli scientists who had worked on the Lavi—which incorporated a large amount of American technology—to work on its own fighter aircraft program. Israeli assistance was also sought by the South Africans for the development of ballistic missiles. Collaboration on both ballistic missile and nuclear development emerged between the Brazilians and Iraqis. Iran built up its domestic arms industry with the help of Argentina, Brazil, Taiwan, and Pakistan. And Iranian advances in missile technology came from Chinese and North Korean assistance, yielding the Iranian variant of the Chinese M-11 missile.[15]

Such collaboration is likely to increase in the 1990s, for the transfer of complete systems will be difficult to achieve given the current international mood. Rising non-proliferation concerns in the West and attempts to give teeth to regimes like the MTCR will make it tougher for countries such as North Korea and China to export such systems—especially if future trade, economic, and technology agreements are linked to the observance of non-proliferation regimes. For countries desiring ballistic and guided missiles, therefore, the easiest route to acquisition will be through technology and personnel transfers from other Southern states.

In addition, Third World arms industries are now facing the same problem which arms industries in the West face—the skyrocketing costs of development require the co-development of systems in order to reduce costs and enlarge markets. The ASEAN countries, therefore, are considering how to coordinate production from each member country's facilities and how to go in for joint procurement. Collaboration should also grow in the area of conventional weapons production, as exemplified by the Pakistani-Chinese co-development of the K-8 trainer aircraft.

There will also be a market for spare parts, as a result of the break-up of the Soviet Union, which has created a major shortage in the South of spare parts for Soviet weapons systems. This has led India to go in for the rapid indigenization of spare-part production, and exporting spare parts throughout the South could provide a means for retaining aging Soviet weapons systems in the armed forces of many countries.

OUTCOMES

Given these constraints and opportunities what impact are the Third World countries going to have on the international arms market? First, the stratification of the market that took place in the 1980s—with the North selling high-tech systems and the South providing low-

and medium-tech ones—is likely to continue. Most of the Third World's advanced weapons programs have run into major developmental delays or have been scrapped outright. Southern producers' capacity to emerge as challengers to Northern producers has been severely hampered.

The results of this stratification can be seen in the small percentage of arms sold by the Third World in the latter half of the 1980s. According to the Stockholm International Peace Research Institute, the top 15 arms exporters to the Third World in the period 1986–1990 sold a total of $101 billion worth of weapons. Third World suppliers accounted for approximately $11 billion. Thus controlling the spread of weapons around the world still lies in the hands of the Western powers—a group to which Russia now belongs.

Despite restrictions on technology, Third World arms industries have increased their products' level of lethality.

Secondly, the move towards North-South collaboration, which began in other areas of high technology such as the development of software, is now being replicated in the global arms industry. Escalating development costs are pushing towards such collaborative efforts and this will have a major impact on the restriction of technology. As Third World countries get involved in such R&D processes, Western efforts to restrict technology transfers will be negated.

Thirdly, market forces will weed out the more vulnerable arms industries. As more and more countries enter the arms market, drawn by the success stories of the 1980s, a larger number of Third World states will be providing similar types of weaponry. To take just the example of field artillery, Israel, South Africa, Yugoslavia, Chile, Argentina, and Brazil are vying in this market. In this situation, countries with a large domestic clientele (such as China, India, and Israel) will be best able to deal with the difficult export market.

Fourthly, South-South military cooperation will have interesting implications for inter-state relations. Cooperation within regions, as in ASEAN, could work to increase regional integration as the integration of defense industries breaks down barriers imposed by national security concerns. Cooperation across regions on the other hand could lead to de facto alliances between states, thereby complicating the security environment. Now that India and Israel have established diplomatic relations, for example, defense cooperation between the two states could lead to a reshaping of threat perceptions in both South Asia and the Middle East.

Lastly, despite restrictions on technology and the delay or failure of advanced weapons programs, Third World arms industries have increased their products' level of lethality. Over twenty countries have ongoing ballistic missile programs, increasing the range, the magnitude, and the level of the destruction they can inflict on their enemies. Similarly, while these industries may not be able to produce state-of-the-art systems, they do have the capability to produce an entire range of weapons—ships, tanks, aircraft, and missiles. This increases the level of destruction at the regional level and potentially leads to the bridging of what were otherwise discrete regions. Thus the Indian acquisition of ballistic missiles has implications not only for South Asia but also for South West Asia and South East Asia. Similarly, the Saudi acquisition of the CSS-2 intermediate-range ballistic missile from China has implications for South Asian security.

POLICY IMPLICATIONS

What policy implications are suggested by the future capabilities of Third World arms industries?

One must recognize first that Third World arms industries are not going to change current patterns in the conventional arms trade. The Western countries still monopolize the sale of advanced weapons systems and the Third World lacks the capability to alter this state of affairs in the near future. The Third World can supply weapons to ethnic groups around the world, but this does not shift the arms transfer pattern or create significant instability within the international system. Such brush-fire wars have occurred frequently since the end of the Second World War and they have had international implications only when large-scale external support (not just arms sales) led to the broadening of the conflicts.

The real issue is the transfer of weapons of mass destruction and the means to deliver them. These weapons are not a threat because "crazy Third World dictators" have plans to hold California to nuclear ransom. Nor are they a threat because Third World countries are targeting downtown New York, Moscow, or Paris. Third World states have very small nuclear inventories or for that matter ballistic missile forces. For them to try such offensive actions would be suicidal. Would even Iraq, with 25–50 nuclear weapons, have been a threat to the continental United States?

One real threat is that, if Third World countries possess weapons of mass destruction, then invading them, or intervening in their regional conflicts, becomes an increasingly costly process. If countries like Israel, Iraq, Pakistan, India, North Korea, and Taiwan have the power to send large numbers of invading troops back in body bags—which weapons of mass destruction do give them—then it could serve as a deterrent against invasion. On the other hand, if these countries cannot produce such weapons, intervening in their affairs becomes much easier. Thus the real threat is not that Third World military industrialization is going to hurt the West's defensive capability, but it will blunt the offensive capability of the

West. The Pentagon in fact, in its recently leaked report on threats in the post-cold war era, expects to face such threats in future regional conflicts.[16]

The answer to such threats does not lie, however, in trying to check Third World arms production capabilities. Technical solutions to what is essentially a political problem are not going to suffice. Political solutions on the other hand reduce or contain conflicts which give rise to the pressures for Western intervention. One move that needs to be pursued is creating regional arms control arrangements, which would lead to confidence building and a reduction in regional force levels. Most Third World states face a significant military burden and such moves could help redeploy it for economic development purposes.

It is also important to remember that some of these Third World countries are regional powers and that they should be included in plans for global security arrangements. Regional powers can be used for peacekeeping and could also form a more acceptable basis for intervention than Western armed forces. While such a role may still be difficult in the Middle East, it can be carried out in the Indian Ocean as well as in South East Asia. In fact, there is large-scale coordination between the different ASEAN states and, increasingly, Australia. Such regional security arrangements would obviate the need for a Western interventionist capability and provide Third World states with the security guarantees they desire.

Another useful step would be to broaden existing international regimes to incorporate Third World countries in them. One step in this direction may be to expand the Nuclear Non-Proliferation Treaty to include a new category—nuclear states. These would be states that have acquired the capability to produce nuclear weapons but do not have a visible nuclear force. Such states could be asked to help restrict technology transfers and the transfer of personnel.

In conclusion, therefore, the growth of Third World arms industries is not going to alter fundamentally the balance of military power or significantly alter trade patterns in the international arms market. What it will do is increase the lethality of regional conflicts and make external intervention in regional affairs an increasingly costly process. It has to be recognized that the military capability accorded by these industries cannot be taken back without expensive future conflicts, so the best solution is to work to create a new international system in which these states can be accommodated rather than contained.

NOTES

1. Stockholm International Peace Research Institute, *SIPRI Yearbook 1991: World Armaments and Disarmament* (Oxford: Oxford University Press, 1991), p. 198.

2. Ibid., p. 198.

3. Christopher K. Hummel, "Ukrainian Arms Makers Are Left On Their Own," *RFE/RL Research Report,* August 14, 1992, p. 36.

4. Adrian English, "Industry After Eldorado," *Jane's Defence Weekly,* June 15, 1991, p. 1037.

5. For a discussion of India's Light Combat Aircraft program, see Amit Gupta, "The Indian Arms Industry: A Lumbering Giant?" *Asian Survey,* September 1990, pp. 851–53.

6. Cited in Vipin Gupta, "Sensing the Threat—Remote Monitoring Technologies," in Stephen P. Cohen, ed., *Nuclear Proliferation in South Asia: The Prospects of Arms Control* (Boulder, Colo.: Westview, 1991), p. 260.

7. *The Military Balance,* 1991–92 (London: IISS, 1991).

8. Thalif Deen, "Sri Lanka Mauls Tamil Tigers in 'Mother of All Battles,' " *Jane's Defence Weekly,* August 17, 1991, p. 272.

9. Paul Beaver, "Croatia's Arms Revealed," *Jane's Defence Weekly,* October 5, 1991, p. 599; and "Armour to Small Arms," *Janes Defence Weekly,* February 22, 1992, p. 292.

10. Paul Beaver, "Croatian Armed Forces Open New Front," *Jane's Defence Weekly,* June 27, 1992, p. 1133.

11. *Jane's Defence Weekly,* August 17, 1991, p. 272.

12. Author's interview with Dr. Kota Harinarayana, Director, Aeronautical Development Agency, Bangalore, India, July 15, 1991.

13. "Asians Could Build Alpha Jet," *Jane's Defence Weekly,* March 7, 1992, p. 385.

14. "Defence Still Top Priority," *Jane's Defence Weekly,* February 15, 1992, p. 234.

15. Tony Banks and James Bruce, "Iran Builds Its Strength," *Jane's Defence Weekly,* February 1, 1992, p. 158–59.

16. *The New York Times,* February 17, 1992.

Arming Ethnic Conflict

Aaron Karp

Aaron Karp is a research associate with the Department of Political Science and Geography at Old Dominion University in Norfolk, Virginia. He is currently preparing a book on this subject for the United Nations University in Tokyo.

O ne of the more interesting side effects of the end of the Cold War has been the increased international awareness of the dangers posed by the continuing flood of conventional weapons worldwide. Until recently, debates over the arms trade were merely a sideshow; most attention was focused on international security and arms control. Yet even as the international community begins to take a closer and more serious look at the arms trade, one of its most deadly and anarchic aspects—the transfer of weapons to sub-state groups—is being overlooked.

Discussions tend to focus on major conventional weapons such as combat aircraft, naval vessels, armored vehicles and long-range missiles—weapons that symbolize international warfare. Greater control over the trade in major conventional armaments is essential to building regional peace and security. But these controls will have little effect on the weapons most likely to be used in war.

Least Glamorous, Most Deadly

Unlike the major weapons systems that dominate arms trade discussions, the weapons used by breakaway groups consist mostly of small and light arms: machine guns, automatic rifles, mortars, grenades, landmines and raw explosives. Such weapons have none of the exotic appeal or engineering elegance of big-budget equipment, and their cost is almost trivial by comparison. They are disarmingly ordinary and familiar, and compared to the major weapons systems their potential destructiveness is easily overlooked. Most are based on technologies 40 to 100 years old. Even the most sophisticated light arms, like shoulder-fired anti-aircraft and anti-tank mis-

> *"Ultimately, the goal should be to begin dealing with the stark realities of the carnage caused worldwide by these most-used but least controlled weapons by establishing procedures that ensure any transfer reflects a broad international consensus."*

siles, are not counted in the new UN Conventional Arms Register.

Yet while such weapons rarely have much political significance in peacetime, they are the likely weapons of choice for insurgent groups of every stripe and the cause of the vast majority of military and civilian casualties. Of the 30 major conflicts currently in progress according to the 1993 *Sipri Yearbook*, all but four are being fought almost entirely with small and light armaments, mostly the cheapest and least advanced kinds. And while there is more to resolving regional conflict than simply controlling small arms sales and deliveries to sub-state groups, the availability of these weapons directly affects the pace and direction of ethnic conflict. Any serious efforts to control such conflicts will need to focus considerable attention on these less glamorous but more lethal and destabilizing weapons if long-term stability is to be assured.

Major arms deals gain much of their significance from their diplomatic and symbolic implications; weapons procured

by ethnic and other insurgent groups serve more basic roles—above all, as instruments of survival. Often arranged at great political and personal risk, these deals are the product of extreme ambition and perceptions of dire necessity. Mostly covert and rarely acknowledged, the scale of such transfers is almost impossible to estimate accurately; it is even difficult to determine basic trends or discern whether the trade is increasing or decreasing at any particular moment. What is beyond question is that its significance for the international community is increasing tremendously.

New, Different Threat to Stability

The end of the Cold War has made it possible for most governments to relax their military preparations, but it has created new pressures in which the invisible and seemingly insignificant arms of sub-state actors are increasingly threatening. As ethnic, national and regional conflict has risen to the top of the international agenda, transfers to sub-state groups became the most dynamic aspect of the weapons trade. These actors, be they nationalist insurgents, ethnic rebels, political extremists, terrorists, drug cartels or other groups, are rapidly emerging as the most destabilizing arms buyers of the post-Cold War world.

Insofar as policy-makers and analysts have dealt with the problem of small arms transfers, it has been treated as a miniature version of the traditional state-to-state transfers of major weaponry, focusing on arming police and gendarmerie. This approach misses many of the most distinctive aspects of the arms trade to sub-state groups, which involves very different motives, processes and equipment. Nor do these arms transfers respond to many of the policy instruments currently under consideration to control the conventional arms trade.

To understand the problems in dealing with arms transfers to ethnic and sub-state groups, it is important to first develop a better appreciation of the nature and seri-

4. WEAPONS PROLIFERATION AND ARMS CONTROL

ousness of this threat. While the arms control community has become increasingly sensitive to the problem by working to control landmines and explosives like Semtex, these are just two elements of a broad phenomenon.[1]

Scope of the Problem

A comprehensive understanding of the trade in arms to sub-state groups will be a long time in coming; nonetheless, the problems can better be understood by examining a few fundamental propositions.

The most revealing general indicator of the scope of the covert arms trade also is the most elusive. Arms transfer statistics are of little use. The most comprehensive data source—the Arms Control and Disarmament Agency's annual *World Military Expenditures and Arms Transfers*—excludes transfers to non-state actors, as does its sister publication, the annual *Conventional Arms Transfers to the Third World* published by the Congressional Research Service. Both include transfers to sub-state groups under national categories but this is not systematic, nor does either source distinguish such transfers from state-to-state transfers. The data published by the Stockholm International Peace Research Institute (Sipri) includes such transfers when possible, but covers only major weapon systems, not the small and light weapons that comprise most of the arms inventories of sub-state forces.

Typically, the dollar amounts of small arms sales will be much lower, involving arms worth no more than a few million dollars. But these kinds of arms can have implications far greater than many massive major weapons deals. At the height of the "Reagan Doctrine" in the mid-1980s, American military support for insurgencies reached unprecedented heights, with annual figures of $670 million for arms aid to the Afghan Mujahedeen alone. In many years the armed factions of the Palestine Liberation Organization (PLO) received comparable levels of support from their Arab and East European sponsors. Even much smaller levels of support have had dramatic effect: the $70 million Washington allocated annually

for the Nicaraguan Contras and the $30 million to the Union for the Independence of Angola (UNITA) in the 1980s transformed the nature and scale of conflict in those regions.

As a general rule, the total cost of maintaining a well-equipped militia involved in periodic firefights amounts to roughly $75 million annually per 10,000 troops. Of this, some $40 million will be for arms, billeting and supplies like food and clothing; the rest is for salaries. Procurement of major weapons systems like armored vehicles, artillery or anti-tank missiles usually requires much greater outlays. Few groups appear actually to spend this much money, tending instead to rely on direct transfers from sponsors and other sources.

Insurgent's Supplies

If accurate figures were available, they would most likely reveal enormous volatility in the value of this trade, often rising or falling by over 50 percent every year. This depends in part on the vicissitudes of battlefield operations and the ability of groups to find and keep support. Groups that do not control territory or enjoy the support of

a generous sponsor rarely can sustain the levels mentioned above.

An extreme example was the PLO's forces in Lebanon. With near-sovereign control of much of the country, loyal supporters elsewhere and strong state sponsors, it had all the advantages. Income from taxes plus contributions from a sympathetic population and donations from several Arab and East European states gave the PLO an annual income of several billion dollars. In the late 1970s much of this went to weapons and training. The PLO developed a ground force that was better equipped than those of any country in Latin America or Sub-Saharan Africa. When Israel invaded Lebanon in 1982, it captured a large share of the PLO's heavy equipment. This did not include the fighter and transport aircraft of PLO air units based in Yemen and Libya.

As the PLO case, and in contrast, the plight of the Philippine New People's Army (PNPA) illustrate, control of territory is especially important for weapons acquisition. It provides a reliable source of income through taxation or extortion of local civilians. It also makes large transfers of arms physically manageable. Without territory, a group can neither acquire nor keep

Washington's decision in the mid-1980s to supply the Afghan Mujahedeen with U.S.-made Stinger ground-to-air missiles (above) is widely credited with dramatically shifting the balance of power in their struggle against occupying Soviet armed forces.

large weapons inventories. At its height in the 1980s, the PNPA could draw upon perhaps 25,000 fighters. But lacking control of territory or other major sources of supply or income, the willing followers could not be transformed into an effective major force. No more than a few thousand could be armed at a time and few were well trained. While the PNPA threat has not disappeared, it has failed to develop into a major challenge to the Manila government.

Captured Weapons

For a typical sub-state group, with its lack of modern military industries, strong finances or steady outside military support, the most reliable way to acquire weapons is to take them. The military history of most insurgencies begins with carefully planned raids on government units and bases to capture arms and other equipment.

A well-documented case in point is the Viet Cong after 1958. Lacking the complete commitment of the Hanoi government, Viet Cong forces in South Vietnam depended on the same source of supply as the South Vietnamese Army: the United States. The Viet Cong collected U.S.-supplied rifles and ammunition on the battlefield or extorted them from the government-sponsored militia. Not until their first major military success at Ap Bac on January 2, 1963, did the Viet Cong begin to receive

steady assistance from the North. Hanoi supplied larger weapons like 12.7 millimeter machine guns, mortars, 57 millimeter recoilless rifles and radios.[2]

Small arms continued to come indirectly from the United States as escalating American involvement accelerated the process. In the first six months of 1964, some 200,000 rifles were captured from South Vietnamese forces. According to reporter and author Neil Sheehan, the Viet Cong refined theft into a science. Many southern militia garrisons were left unmolested in the fall 1963 offenses to serve as quartermasters for fresh ammunition. Sheehan says a standard price for a month's survival was 10,000 rounds. Not until the fall of 1967, when Hanoi committed its own army to the war in the South, did the Viet Cong generally cease to use the last of their American weapons.

Groups go to elaborate lengths to capture weapons. Terrorist groups routinely replenish their stocks by breaking into military and police facilities (and, in the case of the Irish Republican Army (IRA) and others, by robbing banks to finance bribes and purchases). Most armed forces suffer from some degree of pilferage and theft. U.S. armed forces lost an average of 2,000 weapons this way every year before instituting rigorous security programs in the mid-1970s.[3]

Where all this equipment goes is a matter of speculation. Some stolen American

military equipment has fallen into the hands of separatist insurgent groups like the IRA. European armed services have similar problems. In 1989 two dozen anti-tank missiles and other weapons were stolen from the Danish army, while the Norwegian army lost 40 anti-tank missiles in a single incident that year. In November of the following year, terrorists in Greece stole at least 60 anti-tank rockets from a military base at Sikouri.

The hemorrhage of small arms from Western armed forces is a relatively minor compared to the problem in the former Soviet Union. The Red Army's immense inventories are a major source of weapons for ethnic minorities. In some cases, even artillery and armored vehicles have been pilfered, although this may have been arranged with the connivance of sympathetic base commanders. Armenian, Azerbaijani and other nationalists have raided Russian territory in search of weapons. In an exceptional case, Armenian nationalists captured a group of Russian army officers in March 1992 as hostages in exchange for weapons.

Historically, the only reliable means to obtain small arms, ammunition and supplies for guerrilla groups was to capture them, and because they usually lacked the resources and training to use more advanced equipment when they came across it, they would usually destroy any major, advanced weapons that fell into their

The huge arms inventories of the former Soviet armed forces have been a major source of weapons for combatants in many of the conflicts now raging throughout the former Soviet Union. The ongoing fighting between Armenians and Azerbaijanis over the disputed territories of Nagorno-Karabakh and Nakhichevan has involved large quantities of former Soviet arms. Above, a member of the Armenian self-defense force prepares to fire a bazooka during a clash last year near the Azerbaijani village of Sardarak.

4. WEAPONS PROLIFERATION AND ARMS CONTROL

hands. This now appears to be changing, especially for ethnic separatist groups whose numbers often include men with formal military training. This was true in the latter stages of the war in Afghanistan, and in the former Yugoslav republics captured tanks and artillery play a prominent role in the fighting. Croatian units were especially successful in capturing Yugoslav bases and supply trains in 1991-92 and took about 160 tanks, several hundred howitzers and anti-tank rockets, dozens of anti-aircraft missiles and patrol boats. The nucleus of Croatia's air force was created with MiG-21 fighters brought by defecting pilots.

in Pakistan, although probably not as much as some Indian sources assert.

Ideological support for sub-state groups is no less common, but elicits weaker support in the quest for armaments. In practice, surprisingly few individual supporters are willing to take the personal

there is a risk that the client cannot or will not pay, or which could invite prosecution from their own government.

Thus, the principal barrier to wider use by insurgent groups of most private arms dealers is the caution and resistance of these dealers. Private dealers long ago ceased to

> *"Of the 30 major conflicts currently in progress . . . all but four are being fought almost entirely with small and light armaments, mostly the cheapest and least advanced kinds."*

Disguising Secret Transfers

In many cases, however, weapons are presented to the public as captured booty to disguise their actual origins. When the weapons supply is sensitive, coming from foreign powers or the black market, it is in the interest of those concerned to claim that the equipment was captured, if only to protect the real supplier. This may well be the case with some of the equipment allegedly captured by Slovenian and Croatian forces, but which may in fact have been purchased from other Central European governments. It almost certainly is the case in Cambodia, where the Khmer Rouge claim to be using captured tanks and artillery that more probably were purchased from China, plus rockets from other suppliers across the Thai border.

Private Assistance

Appeals to altruism have been effective for some groups in need of arms supplies. The emotional involvement of foreigners and outsiders often creates opportunities for private contributions of arms. Although supporters rarely can furnish arms directly, their financial support can be instrumental, especially for smaller groups.

Ethnic ties are most readily manipulated for support. For years, the IRA found generous financial support in the Irish community in North America, much of it used to buy weapons in the long conflict against Protestants and the British army. Tamil separatists in Sri Lanka rely even more heavily on the assistance of India's Tamil community on the nearby mainland. The extent of such ties as a source of arms can be obscured by political claims. An example is Kashmir, whose Muslim separatists receive arms and training from sympathizers

risks of providing food and shelter, or funds. When they do, the effects can be dramatic. This is a tradition that goes back at least as far a the 19th century anarchists. More recently it has been a source of success for the German Red Army Faction. In directing its Latin American policy, the Reagan administration had to contend with the unwanted interference of private groups supplying financial and sometimes military aid to the Contras.

The scale of private assistance usually is too small to be of much use to an army. Usually it is more appropriate to the needs of a terrorist group. Even terrorists, however, use sympathizers mostly for practical help; but for arms they rely more on stolen and captured arms, revenue-generating crimes or state sponsorship.

The Relevance of Private Dealers

Some private arms dealers have supply capabilities that theoretically could be of great use to sub-state groups. One of the most outspoken private arms dealers, who lives in the Washington, D.C. area, is fond of claiming he can instantly equip two entire divisions of troops. With an annual turnover of over $100 million, he also has the financial resources.

What most private dealers lack is not the means but the interest in supplying clients that their governments turn away. Made visible by the very publicity they generate to help their businesses, and carefully observed by customs authorities, established private dealers must be especially scrupulous. The appeal of short-term profit through questionable transaction is negated by the promise of steady legal business. They tend to avoid transactions where

be romantic, swashbuckling crusaders. Nor are they maniacal profiteers. Rather, most successful private arms dealers are careful businessmen who generally avoid unnecessary risks. Their trade requires government licensing and certification. For most of them to stay in business they must respect the export restrictions of their governments. With rare exception, this makes them, in effect, agents of official policy.

The biggest exception is a private dealer operating in a loosely regulated environment. At present this is an apt description of the situation in the former Soviet Union, where entrepreneurs have tried to spirit tanks and other large weapons out of the country. Huge and mysterious consignments of Russian armaments—in one case 40,000 rifles—have been discovered in Western ports without any indication of their final destination. Russian officials are trying to cope with the problem of illegal and unlicensed arms exports, but for some years to come, it seems unavoidable that former Soviet republics and other East European countries will remain important sources of unlicensed exports.

Another supply source that deserves closer attention is the transfer of demilitarized weapons for private customers. Second-hand armored vehicles and military aircraft, stripped of key military components and destined for private collectors constitute a growing inventory of fully serviceable weapons platforms which can easily be converted back. For decades this trade was limited to obsolescent piston engine aircraft and jet trainers. More recently buyers have been able to acquire high performance jet fighters like the Northrop F-5 and the Swedish Draken. China, Russia and several East European countries will sell second-hand jet fighters directly out of their air forces to private buyers, and the 1992 Conventional Armed Forces in Europe (CFE) Treaty let loose onto civilian markets an unprecedented wave of armored vehicles. The danger is that these demilitarized platforms will find their way back to other military clients. An aging Chinese MiG-21 may be entertainment for a retired pilot in Cleveland, but refitted by technicians in the mythical kingdom of Freedonia it is a weapon once again.

The Black Market Myth

Contrary to popular belief, the black market is surprisingly marginal to the success of insurgencies. A marriage between black marketeers and an insurgent group is unlikely to be an arrangement of convenience or conviction. Both black marketers and insurgents would prefer not to deal with each other. Black market exporters need immediate payments and prefer that their clients make shipping arrangements, which also is difficult for all but the best organized sub-state groups.

Nor is there much of substance that the black market can offer that holds great interest to sub-state actors. Insurgents typically require large quantities of prosaic items, while the black market is better suited to small transfers of high-value items. The exorbitant price of illegally transferred equipment—often three to 10 times market value—is another serious obstacle. Most groups can afford such purchases only intermittently, and only the best financed groups can afford such prices regularly. But these same groups usually have the advantages of state-sponsorship and little need for the black market.

Another major problem is the inability of illegal dealers to include the many services needed to complete an arms transfer in ways that integrate equipment into operational service. An illegal trading network must complete its transactions as rapidly as possible to avoid detection. The sale of illegal arms is a serious business with risks ranging from prosecution to assassination, so no black market conspiracy can accept the risk of maintaining an open pipeline that furnishes training, operating assistance, spare parts, maintenance and overhaul services as part of the "sales package."

One of the most serious disadvantages is the lack of help with financing. Black marketers have no interest in extending credit. They tend to be cash-on-the-barrel operators. Recipient are expected to complete all financial arrangements themselves. But financing can be especially troublesome for a stateless, impoverished insurgent group. Even a financial institution as corrupt as BCCI, which routinely helped countries like Iran and Pakistan with loans and letters of credit for *sub rosa* purchases of military technology, apparently balked rather than provide the same facilities to insurgents. Only if such groups had unambiguous support from a government, which in effect co-signed the arrangement, would BCCI get involved.[4]

The black market is of greatest utility to isolated *states* trying to circumvent international restrictions on their armed forces or military industries. While not suited to shipping large quantities of major weapons, the black market is ideal for transferring weapons components and manufacturing technology, which are less likely to attract the attention of customs authorities. By concentrating on these areas and using the black market, South Africa was able to develop its arms industries and overcome the UN embargo, and Iraq was able to build up its nuclear weapons and ballistic missile capabilities.[5]

Among sub-state actors, the black market probably is of greatest importance to drug cartels. They have the financial and organizational resources to acquire large-scale capabilities through numerous small transactions. Latin American narcotics traffickers have acquired much of their firepower from unlicensed purchases on the U.S. private gun market where, with over 200 million firearms in private hands, there is unlimited potential for illegal diversions.

But even drug dealers prefer to buy through licensed exporters when possible. Through legal deals they receive better quality equipment at a lower price, and they eliminate the risk of prosecution. One of the biggest examples was a 1989 consignment of 500 Israeli rifles plus ammunition transferred through Antiqua to Colombian cocaine barons. Lack of Israeli concern and the cooperation of Antiquan officials allowed the entire transaction to be completed on the books. When that is possible, the black market is irrelevant.

State Sponsorship: the Ideal

While captured weapons can sustain a sub-state group, they usually are not sufficient for victory. This is partly because dependence on captured weapons sacrifices the military initiative; to prevent arms from being taken the government merely has to cease fighting and retreat into its bastions. It also reflects the limitations of low-intensity, guerrilla operations. Small-unit actions with light weapons may be enough to bring an adversary to crisis, but victory usually is won through combat against large units and major weapon systems.

While captured weapons are the means of survival, major weapons are more likely to lead to victory. As the only reliable source of major weapons and advanced equipment, state sponsors play a decisive role in the distribution of armaments to sub-state actors.[6] The Vietnamese experience is again illustrative. With captured weapons the Viet Cong could do little more than stay even with the South Vietnamese. Heavy armaments from Hanoi helped shift the balance of power in 1963-65, precipitating a series of crises that left the United States with the choice of defeat or direct intervention. Once the United States entered the ground war and began building up the South Vietnamese Army, however, the Viet Cong no longer could find victory on the battlefield and the initiative gradually passed to North Vietnamese regular forces. It was the latter, fighting with tanks and heavy artillery, who won the war in 1975, some two years after the withdrawal of U.S. ground forces and the drawdown in financial and other U.S. support to the Saigon government.

It was state sponsorship from the Soviet bloc that made it possible for the PLO to accumulate the enormous inventories of major weaponry uncovered in 1982.[7] It was Libyan state sponsorship that provided the IRA with its most sophisticated training and equipment, including SA-7 surface-to-air missiles and Semtex, an especially versatile explosive made in Czechoslovakia. In South Africa the apparently spontaneous emergence of the Zulu raiders in the early 1990s was made possible by extensive support from the South African military and police. And it was U.S. state sponsorship, most notably a decision to supply Stinger ground-to-air missiles and other more advanced weaponry, that revived the fortunes of the sagging Afghan resistance in the mid-1980s.

Without state sponsorship, some insurgencies must struggle for survival, while others simply give up. The Nicaraguan Contras showed no serious interest in continuing their struggle after U.S. aid evaporated. Deprived of Soviet sponsored assistance, the El Salvadoran rebels quickly accepted negotiated terms. The East Timor resistance groups have seen their capabilities against the Indonesian central government decline steadily over the years; although their cause has widespread moral support, no state has been willing to support it materially.

Conclusion: The Riddle of Control

In at least one critical respect, arms transfers to sub-state actors are no different from orthodox state-to-state trade: there is no single panacea for greater control over this or any other aspect of arms transfers. Some types of transfers to sub-state groups will always be difficult to control. The immense flow of captured weapons, for example, seems especially intractable. In the long run, arms transfers of all kinds can be brought under control and sharply reduced only through a combination of diplomatic, political and economic instruments, culminating in regional conflict resolution. Nothing will undercut all aspects of the arms trade so effectively as wider acceptance of the political status quo.

But numerous approaches can be pursued to reduce the dangers of arms transfers to sub-state actors in the near term. Controlling the black market is probably the easiest, depending largely upon better law enforcement. Current efforts to improve export control in former Soviet republics, Eastern Europe and the Third World should be re-directed to emphasize small and light arms more than is the case at present. But controlling the black market will not have much effect on the most important ethnic conflicts, which rely on other sources of supply.

So far, the greatest successes in dealing with state-sponsored small and light arms have focused on particular weapons and war materials, such as landmines and Semtex. There will be a continuing need to create ever more export control regimes to deal with specific weapons. But this approach will be limited mostly to sophisticated and scarce light armament like anti-aircraft missiles.

To deal with the most important aspect of the trade in arms to sub-state actors the international community must focus on state sponsorship. This issue will be difficult, forcing governments to acknowledge policies they traditionally regarded as highly sensitive. But there is room for optimism in this regard: there appears to be less interest in supporting insurgencies and terrorist factions now that the Cold War is over. Washington has abandoned the Reagan doctrine, and with it, support for many rebel groups. Those that formerly relied on Soviet-sponsored assistance are in serious trouble today and moderate Arabs have reassessed their support for the PLO and more

radical groups. Even Libya appears to have dropped its support for the IRA.

This positive trend easily could be reversed; it has not yet affected sponsors like Iran, Syria and North Korea. To strengthen this positive but serendipitous trend and minimize backsliding requires formal, codified restrictions based on international consensus. The trend would be greatly reenforced if small and light arms were added to the agenda of international arms transfer regimes and registers. In particular, the "Permanent-5" process should examine this aspect of the arms trade as it regains momentum. Aggressive action also is necessary to make the UN Arms Register more meaningful by widening its categories and lowering its thresholds to include at least the largest transfers to sub-state groups.

Certainly there will be circumstances when the international community wants to encourage arms transfers, especially to ethnic nationalists whose situation is dire and whose demands are legitimate. The recent debate over the wisdom of arming the Bosnian Muslims illustrates the difficulties of such cases. Ironically, a credible policy to stifle the flow of small and light arms may have to be balanced with consultative mechanisms to permit such transfers in desperate cases.

At a minimum, the international community can establish standards determining when such arms transfers are permissible and when they must be

stopped at all costs. Ultimately, the goal should be to begin dealing with the stark realities of the carnage caused worldwide by these most-used but least controlled weapons by establishing procedures that ensure any transfer reflects a broad international consensus.   ACT

NOTES

1. Senator Patrick Leahy, "Landmine Moratorium: A Strategy for Stronger International Limits," *Arms Control Today*, January/February 1993; Stephen Goose and Steve Asklin, "Global Production and Trade in Antipersonnel Landmines." Paper prepared for the 43rd Pugwash Conference, Hesseludden, Sweden, 9-15 June 1993.

2. Neil Sheehan, *A Bright Shining Lie: John Paul Vann and America in Vietnam* (New York: Random House, 1988) pp. 312-314.

3. Hearings on Theft and Losses of Military Weapons, Ammunition and Explosives, U.S. House, Committee on Armed Services, Subcommittee on Investigations (Washington, D.C.: U.S. Government Pringting Office, 1976.

4. The BCCI Affair: A Report to the Senate Committee on Foreign Relations, U.S. Senate, Subcommittee on Terrorism, Narcotics and International Operations (Washington, D.C.: U.S. Government Printing Office, 1992.

5. Michael Klare, "The Thriving Black Market for Weapons," *Bulletin of the Atomic Scientists*, April 1988.

6. A Similar Conclusion Is Reached by William E. Odom, *On Internal War: American and Soviet Approaches to Third World Clients and Insurgents* (Durham: Duke University Press, 1992).

7. Raphael Israeli, ed., *PLO in Lebanon: Selected Documents* (London: Weidenfeld and Nicolson, 1983) pp. 78-101, 177-181, 206-210, 270.

While Serbian forces in the former Yugoslavia have had the most access to the arms of the well-equipped former Yugoslav national army, both Bosnian and Croatian fighters have gained additional arms by capturing weapons, including tanks and howitzers, from Serbian nationalist forces. A Croatian soldier, above, keeps watch during a lull in the fighting in Bosnia-Herzegovina.

The Pelindaba Treaty:
Africa Joins the Nuclear-Free World

David Fischer

If "Pelindaba" has meant anything at all to students of arms control, it has been in connection to the nuclear research center near Pretoria where, during the 1970s, South Africa conducted much of its secret research and development work on the country's now-dismantled nuclear weapon capability. Today, however, Pelindaba has taken on a distinctly peaceful connotation: The "Pelindaba Treaty" is the informal name of the soon-to-be-signed pact that will establish Africa as the world's fourth nuclear-weapon-free zone (NWFZ). When the treaty enters into force—perhaps as early as next year— it will, along with the 1959 Antarctic Treaty, the 1967 Tlatelolco Treaty (for Latin American and Caribbean states) and the 1986 Rarotonga Treaty (covering the South Pacific), transform most of the Southern Hemisphere into a zone free of nuclear weapons.

The negotiation of the Pelindaba Treaty has been a long and arduous task. It has taken more than 35 years to complete the treaty since African states first voiced interest in an NWFZ in 1960. In February of that year France conducted its first nuclear test—above ground—in Algeria, during the U.S.-British-Soviet testing moratorium that began in 1958. (France conducted three additional atmospheric tests in Algeria before it moved its testing program there underground in 1961.)

In swift reaction, a group of eight African countries proposed a resolution at the UN General Assembly calling on all states to respect Africa as a nuclear-weapon-free zone and to refrain from testing, storing or transporting nuclear weapons in Africa. While the 1960 resolution was never put to a vote, the General Assembly approved a

David Fischer, a distinguished scholar in residence at the Monterey Institute of International Studies, was assistant director general for external relations at the International Atomic Energy Agency.

"[T]he Pelindaba Treaty will encourage the creation of other nuclear-weapon-free zones, particularly in Southeast Asia and the Middle East, and set new patterns and precedents for such regional endeavors."

similar resolution the following year. In 1964, African countries intensified their efforts by adopting a "Declaration on the Denuclearization of Africa" at the first summit conference of the Organization of African Unity (OAU)—a move that the General Assembly endorsed in 1965 and every year thereafter until 1990.

When France stopped testing in Algeria in 1966 after 13 underground tests, the immediate incentive to ban nuclear weapons from the African continent receded. But in 1970, the government of South Africa announced that it had developed a new technology for enriching uranium, and suspicions soon mounted that Pretoria was intent on acquiring nuclear weapons. While the uncertainty surrounding South Africa's nuclear intentions was heightened mostly by a series of deliberately ambiguous policy statements emanating from Pretoria, much more ominous signals were on the horizon. In August 1977, Soviet and U.S. satellites detected what appeared to be preparations by South Africa for an underground nuclear test in the Kalahari Desert. Strong diplomatic demarches by the United

States, Britain and France compelled Pretoria not to test any nuclear explosive device at the site. Suspicions over South Africa's weapons program were further heightened in September 1979, however, when a U.S. VELA satellite registered what could have been a flash from a nuclear test over the South Atlantic, prompting speculation that South Africa had tested an explosive device.[1]

As long as South Africa was believed to have a nuclear arsenal, it was impossible for other African countries to conclude a nuclear-weapon-free-zone treaty. Their first objective was to rid the continent of existing weapons; only then could meaningful negotiations begin on a treaty. But throughout the late 1970s and early 1980s, South Africa remained politically and economically isolated and seemingly intent on building up its suspected arsenal.

However, with the election of Frederik W. de Klerk as president of South Africa in September 1989 and the promise of political reform, the 1990s offered African countries a new window of opportunity and they acted on it immediately. In December 1990, the General Assembly approved a new Africa-sponsored resolution that, in part, called on the UN secretary-general to assist the OAU in convening "a meeting of experts" in 1991 to discuss the drafting and implementation of a denuclearization accord. Two "groups of experts," one designated by the United Nations in cooperation with the OAU and the other an OAU intergovernmental panel, began their joint efforts. The groups were joined by experts from the International Atomic Energy Agency (IAEA) and the treaties of Rarotonga and Tlatelolco.

At their first meeting in May 1991 in Addis Ababa, Ethiopia, the participants recommended that, in view of the changing situation in Southern Africa and the world, the time was right to begin working on a treaty for the denuclearization of Africa. They also emphasized that South Africa's participation in the treaty would be essential.

On July 10, only weeks after the Addis Ababa meeting, South Africa acceded to the nuclear Non-Proliferation Treaty (NPT) as a non-nuclear-weapon state, and, in September, concluded a comprehensive safeguards agreement with the IAEA. In April 1992, the groups convened their second meeting in Lome, Togo, and recommended that the draft process begin. The formal drafting of the African NWFZ treaty began at the third meeting in April 1993 in Harare, Zimbabwe, where South Africa participated for the first time.

At the fourth meeting in Windhoek, Namibia, in March 1994, representatives of the five nuclear-weapons states (the United States, Russia, China, Britain and France) offered their views of the treaty's proposed protocols, and by the time of the fifth meeting that May in Addis Ababa, the participants were able to adopt the first complete draft treaty. The final treaty text, which was completed at a joint meeting of experts in Johannesburg and Pelindaba in May and June 1995, was approved by African heads of state on June 23. In the fall of 1995, the General Assembly approved a resolution that welcomed the adoption of the treaty by African leaders, called on African states to sign and ratify the accord, and urged relevant non-African states to subscribe to its protocols.[2]

Although the Pelindaba Treaty contains a number of new, innovative measures for a regional nuclear-weapon-free zone, it benefitted from experience gained in drafting and implementing the Tlatelolco Treaty. Most of the African accord's 22 articles correspond closely to those of the Rarotonga Treaty (with 16 articles), which in many cases served as the treaty model for the Pelindaba pact. The following analysis highlights the main points of each of the treaty's articles and any significant differences, or similarities, between them and corresponding articles in the NPT and the other regional treaties.

Definitions and Terms

Article 1 defines the African nuclear-weapon-free zone as the continent of Africa, island states that are members of the OAU and all islands considered by the OAU to be part of Africa. (Fifty-four countries will be eligible to sign the treaty.) The zone includes territorial seas and archipelagic waters as well as the airspace above them and the sea bed beneath. A map of the zone, appended as Annex I to the treaty (see p. 143), shows the states and territories to which the treaty applies.

The Pelindaba Treaty uses essentially the same definitions as the Rarotonga Treaty for two important terms: "nuclear explosive device" and "stationing." Unlike the Tlatelolco Treaty, which defines a nuclear explosive device as having "a group of characteristics that are appropriate for use for warlike purposes," the Pelindaba definition includes any device "capable of releasing nuclear energy" irrespective of how it is used. It also includes devices that are unassembled or only partly assembled. The Pelindaba Treaty defines stationing to include the implantation, emplacement, transport, stockpiling, storage, installation and deployment of nuclear devices.

While the Rarotonga Treaty does not define the terms "nuclear installation" and "nuclear material," the Pelindaba text specifies installations as including research and power reactors; conversion, fabrication, reprocessing and isotope separation plants; and "any other installation or location in or at which fresh or irradiated nuclear material or significant quantities of radioactive materials are present." The treaty's definition of nuclear material incorporates by reference that used in Article XX of the Statute of the IAEA. Although IAEA document INFCIRC/153 excludes uranium ore and ore residue from the agency's definition, and contains the qualification that extension of safeguards to additional materials included in the definition by the Board of Governors will be subject to acceptance by the concerned states, the Pelindaba definition omits both the exclusion and the qualification.

Treaty Application

Article 2 of the treaty, which is closely modelled on the corresponding article in the Rarotonga Treaty, defines the zone of application as that illustrated by the map in Annex I, and includes a disclaimer stating that nothing in the treaty will affect in any way the rights of states with regard to the freedom of the seas. There is no such disclaimer in the Tlatelolco Treaty.

Unlike the Tlatelolco and Rarotonga treaties, the Pelindaba Treaty does not cover adjacent oceans. In the case of the first two treaties and the Antarctic Treaty, oceanic coverage is extended to make the zones they cover contiguous.

One territorial issue within the African nuclear-weapon-free zone, with possible implications for U.S. nuclear weapons policy, involves the ongoing dispute between Britain and the African island-nation of Mauritius, both of which claim sovereignty of the Chagos Archipelago in the Indian Ocean. Britain currently exercises sovereignty over the archipelago, which includes the island of Diego Garcia. Located some 3,600 kilometers east of the African continent, the United States has leased portions of the island from Britain for military purposes, including as a staging base for nuclear-capable P-3 naval aircraft; as a "support" facility for carrier battle groups operating in the Indian Ocean; as a home-port facility for Navy Maritime Prepositioning Ships; and for a range of communications, satellite tracking and monitoring activities. In the past, the United States has authorized the wartime deployment to the island of nuclear depth bombs for P-3 operations.

Because the sovereignty issue remains in dispute, the map contained in Annex 1 of the Pelindaba Treaty shows that the archipelago lies within the zone of application, but indicates that it appears "without prejudice to the question of sovereignty." If British sovereignty had been acknowledged by the treaty, Britain would have been invited to sign Protocol 3 (as France and Spain are), which commits the extra-regional states to apply the treaty's relevant provisions to the territories in the zone for which they are internationally responsible.

While U.S. access to Diego Garcia may be affected by a future determination of sovereignty over the Chagos Archipelago, the Arms Control and Disarmament Agency has stated that the notation on the annex map adequately protects U.S. interests because any resolution of the issue will have to occur outside the framework of the treaty.

Renunciation of Explosive Devices

The Pelindaba Treaty prohibits parties from developing, manufacturing, stockpiling, possessing or otherwise acquiring any kind of nuclear explosive device, but the treaty's Article 3 goes further than those accords by banning research on nuclear explosive devices.[3] It also bans parties either from seeking or receiving assistance in pursuit of any of the above-mentioned activities, or from assisting in or encouraging such activities. This stricture would presumably have the effect of prohibiting any research on subjects such as implosion technology, hydronuclear testing or computer simulation of nuclear tests. While the IAEA is not explicitly called upon to verify compliance with this provision, the agency would have difficulty doing so under existing safeguards arrangements, which largely confine the IAEA to monitoring nuclear material and this constraint is incorporated in Annex II (Paragraph 3) of the Pelindaba Treaty. However, the IAEA's current review of the safeguards regime may enable the agency to monitor nuclear research that does not involve nuclear material.

Prevention of Stationing

As in the Rarotonga Treaty, but unlike the NPT, each party to the Pelindaba Treaty "undertakes to prohibit" the stationing of any nuclear explosive device in its territory. However, like the corresponding article in the Rarotonga Treaty, which has been interpreted as permitting the "home-porting" of U.S. warships in the territorial waters of states-parties and visits by warships that may carry nuclear weapons, the Pelindaba text allows each party to decide whether to allow its ports, air fields and air space to be used by foreign ships and aircraft "in a manner not covered by the rights of innocent passage," that is, in addition to the right of innocent passage on the high seas that is enjoyed by ships of all navies whether or not they are in an area covered by a nuclear-weapon-free zone. Article 4 therefore seemingly allows parties to permit foreign warships or aircraft that may be carrying nuclear weapons to enter their harbors, overfly their territories and land on their airfields.

Prohibition of Testing

Article 5 of the treaty, which commits each party to "prohibit" the testing of any nuclear device in its territory, goes further than the corresponding article in the Rarotonga Treaty by including an explicit undertaking by each party "not to test any nuclear explosive device." The Pelindaba Treaty would be, in effect, a regional test ban treaty.

Destruction and Conversion

Article 6 in the Pelindaba text is a novel clause not found in any other treaty. It requires each party

to declare any capabilities it may have for the manufacture of a nuclear explosive device, to dismantle and destroy any such device in its possession and to destroy or convert to civilian use facilities for making such devices.

The article also provides for verification by the IAEA of all such activities. This provision presumably stems from the fact that one potential party, South Africa, at one time possessed a nuclear weapons capability. The treaty, however, does not address the problem of ensuring that international verification of the dismantlement process does not disseminate information about the design and manufacture of nuclear weapons.

Article 6 may set a useful precedent for potential nuclear-weapon-free-zone treaties in the Middle East and South Asia, where the suspected weapons programs of the so-called "threshold" nuclear-weapon states (India, Israel and Pakistan) will greatly complicate the negotiation of such treaties.

Dumping of Radioactive Wastes

While the Rarotonga Treaty commits each party not to dump radioactive wastes and other matter *at sea* anywhere within the zone, Article 7 of the Pelindaba Treaty extends this prohibition to the whole of the African zone. Presumably, this would not prevent controlled surface storage or underground storage or disposal of nuclear waste that countries operating nuclear reactors would eventually have to undertake, and for which South Africa already has a program.

Peaceful Nuclear Activities

Under Article 8, each party to the Pelindaba Treaty undertakes to promote the peaceful uses of nuclear science and technology and to establish and strengthen mechanisms for nuclear cooperation. Parties are also encouraged to make use of IAEA technical assistance and to

The African Nuclear-Weapon-Free Zone

Appears without prejudice to the question of sovereignty.

strengthen cooperation under the African Regional Cooperation Agreement for Research, Training and Development Related to Nuclear Science and Technology (AFRA) established by the IAEA. Neither the Rarotonga or Tlatelolco treaties explicitly seeks to promote nuclear energy.

Verification of Peaceful Uses

Like the Rarotonga and Tlatelolco treaties, Article 9 of the Pelindaba Treaty requires each party to conclude a comprehensive safeguards agreement with the IAEA. The Pelindaba Treaty also follows the Rarotonga accord's obligation of requiring full-scope IAEA safeguards on all nuclear exports to any non-nuclear-weapon state. It does not, however, contain the Rarotonga Treaty's requirement for item-related safeguards (safeguards on the exported item and its products) on nuclear exports to nuclear-weapon states.

With the closure of South Africa's two enrichment facilities, there will be no reprocessing or enrichment activities in the African zone. It might have been possible to include a legal proscription of such proliferation-sensitive activities (along the lines of the still unimplemented agreement between South Korea and North Korea that bans reprocessing of spent fuel and enrichment of uranium) and thus set a precedent for other regions such as the Middle East, but the opportunity was not taken.

Protection of Materials and Facilities

Article 10 of the treaty commits each party to "maintain the highest standards of security and effective physical protection of nuclear materials, facilities and equipment to prevent theft or unauthorized use and handling." The measures must be equivalent to those prescribed by the Vienna Convention on Physical Protection of Nuclear Material and in the guidelines developed by the IAEA. This article offers an innovative and useful precedent for other nuclear-weapon-free treaties.

Prohibition of Armed Attack

In an obligation not found in other regional treaties, Article 11 of the Pelindaba Treaty commits each party "not to take, or assist, or encourage any action aimed at an armed attack by conventional or other means" on any nuclear installation in the zone. The inclusion of this commitment in other potential nuclear-weapon-free zone treaties would provide an important confidence-building measure, particularly in the Middle East, for example, where such attacks have already occurred.

Mechanism for Compliance

Article 12 of the Pelindaba Treaty establishes the African Commission on Nuclear Energy (AFCONE) to supervise implementation of the treaty and ensure compliance. The 12-member commission will be responsible for collating reports submitted by parties, arranging consultations between parties and convening conferences on any matter arising from treaty implementation. AFCONE will also review the application of IAEA safeguards, activate the complaints procedure and encourage cooperation on the peaceful uses of nuclear energy. Slated to meet in ordinary session once a year, the commission will hold extraordinary sessions as necessary to hear complaints and settle disputes.

Reports and Information Exchanges

Article 13 requires each party to report annually to AFCONE on its nuclear activities and to notify the commission of any significant event affecting treaty implementation. The commission is also directed to seek an annual report from the IAEA on the activities of AFRA.

Conference of the Parties

According to Article 14 of the treaty, the secretary-general of the OAU (the sole depositary of the treaty) will convene a conference of the parties as soon as possible after the treaty's entry into force, which, among other duties, will elect the members to AFCONE, determine its headquarters (which South Africa has offered to host) and adopt its budget. Thereafter, conferences will be held as necessary but "at least every two years."

Other Treaty Matters

The treaty's final eight articles deal primarily with implementation and operational issues. The treaty, which will not be subject to reservations (Article 16), is of unlimited duration and shall remain in force indefinitely (Article 17). According to Article 18, the treaty will enter into force when the 28th instrument of ratification is deposited, and for any state that joins after that date, the treaty will enter into force on the date it deposits its instrument.

Once the treaty enters into force, it will, in accordance with Article 2, apply to all of Africa, but the obligations that the pact imposes upon parties can only be legally binding on those states that have ratified the treaty. However, for those signatories that have not yet ratified the treaty but are parties to the Vienna Convention on the Law of Treaties, they are bound by that convention to refrain from any act contrary to the purposes of the Pelindaba Treaty.

Under Article 19, any party may propose an amendment to the treaty, which must be approved by two-thirds of the parties and will enter into force for all parties after a majority of states deposit their instruments of ratification.

The Pelindaba Treaty contains essentially the same withdrawal clauses as the NPT. According to Article 20, withdrawal is permissible if a party decides that extraordinary events related to the subject matter of the treaty have jeopardized its supreme interests. However, the treaty requires 12-months' notice before the withdrawal takes effect instead of the three months stipulated by the NPT.

Treaty Annexes

If a party to the Pelindaba Treaty does not already have a standard NPT-mandated safeguards agreement with the IAEA (based on IAEA document INFCIRC/153), under Annex II of the treaty, it must conclude an equivalent agreement so that it is in force within 18 months of the treaty's entry into force for that country. An innovation in the treaty is that each party must include in its annual report to AFCONE "a copy of the overall conclusions of the most recent report" by the IAEA on its inspection activities in the territory of the party.

The only potential parties that now operate nuclear plants that would be inspected by the IAEA are Algeria, Egypt, Ghana, Libya, Zaire (all of which operate research reactors) and South Africa.

Annex III of the treaty outlines briefly the composition, structure, tasks and voting procedures of AFCONE, which should be elected "bearing in mind the need . . . to include Members with advanced nuclear programmes."

On the model of the Rarotonga Treaty, Annex IV of the Pelindaba Treaty prescribes a fairly elaborate procedure for the investigation of complaints and the settlement of disputes. If circumstances so warrant, AF-CONE is empowered to ask the IAEA to make an unrestricted access inspection (which apparently would not constitute a "special inspection" under Paragraphs 73 and 77 of the standard IAEA safeguards agreement based on INFCIRC/153). In the event of a breach of the treaty, the commission may make recommendations on appropriate action to the OAU which may, in turn, refer the matter to the UN Security Council.

Treaty Protocols

Like the Rarotonga Treaty, the Pelindaba Treaty is amplified by three protocols. Protocol I, which will be open to signature by the five nuclear-weapon states, will commit each country to give assurances that they will not use, or threaten to use, nuclear explosive devices against any party to the treaty, or against any territory within the zone for which an extra-regional state is internationally responsible. These are so-called "negative security assurances." Reportedly, the U.S. Department of Defense is concerned about the implications of the obligations that will be imposed on the United States should Washington sign Protocol I. For example, should Libya sign and ratify the Pelindaba Treaty and in the future use or threaten to use chemical or biological weapons, the negative security assurances called for under the protocol would apply to Libya, thereby eliminating the threat of nuclear weapons use as a U.S. deterrent option.

Protocol II, which will also be open to signature by the nuclear-weapon states, will commit each adherent not to test or assist or encourage the testing of any nuclear explosive device anywhere in the zone. This protocol will also commit each adherent not to contribute to any act that violates the treaty.

Protocol III, which will be open to signature by France and Spain, will apply the relevant provisions of the Pelindaba Treaty to the territories within the zone for which they are internationally responsible.

All of the treaty's protocols are to be formally ratified by the eligible states and are of indefinite duration. The withdrawal clauses contained in the protocols mirror those contained in the treaty's main text.

Support for the Treaty

All delegations that referred to the Pelindaba Treaty during the NPT Review and

Extension Conference, including the United States, Russia and the European Union (EU), affirmed their warm support for the treaty and these affirmations were repeated last fall at the General Assembly. It thus seems likely that the three protocols will be ratified more swiftly by the nuclear-weapon states and Spain than was the case for the protocols to the Tlatelolco and Rarotonga treaties.[4] There could, however, be lengthy delays if the reported reservations of the U.S. Defense Department about giving negative security assurances to all treaty parties in the region determined official U.S. policy toward the treaty.

It would be desirable for the United States, Russia, China, Japan and the EU countries to reaffirm their support for the Pelindaba Treaty when it is opened for signature in Cairo—probably at the end of February 1996—and to encourage all eligible states to ratify it and its protocols as early as possible.

It would also be desirable if they would help the IAEA and South Africa make AFCONE an effective body for promoting peaceful nuclear applications of nuclear technology (for example, in African agricultural research, medical research and treatment, hydrology and other areas) by making available a reasonable flow of resources. Western European countries, with their historical connections to Africa, can ensure that the EU plays a key role in this regard.

The world's major nuclear exporters and other NPT states may be able to use AFCONE meetings as a forum for explaining and gaining support for policies that are often misunderstood, such as restrictions on the transfer of sensitive nuclear technologies and the work of the Nuclear Suppliers Group (NSG). South Africa has recently joined the NSG, and other African countries that export uranium (namely Gabon, Namibia and Niger) should be encouraged to join.

The Role of the Arab States

Eight of the nine Arab League states in North Africa (Algeria, Egypt, Libya, Mauritania, Morocco, Somalia, Sudan and Tunisia) are already non-nuclear-weapon states parties to the NPT (Djibouti is not). Yet, despite this edge, there remains a question as to whether some or all of these countries may be reluctant to ratify the treaty.

> "It would be desirable for the United States, Russia, China, Japan and the EU countries to reaffirm their support for the Pelindaba Treaty when it is opened for signature in Cairo—probably at the end of February 1996—and to encourage all eligible states to ratify it and its protocols as early as possible."

The fact that the treaty will be opened for signature in Cairo appears to confirm Egypt's commitment to the accord, and for many years Egypt has also been the leading proponent of a Middle Eastern nuclear-weapon-free zone. Egypt's fellow African Arab League countries are all potential members of a Middle Eastern accord.

Before NPT parties decided at the 1995 review and extension conference to indefinitely extend the treaty, some of the African Arab League states might have perceived a negotiating advantage in delaying formal membership in an African treaty of unlimited duration as long as Israel retained its nuclear arsenal. According to this rationale, by signing and ratifying the Pelindaba Treaty, these states would permanently renounce nuclear weapons without any comparable commitment from Israel. However, the NPT's indefinite extension eliminates this "advantage." For the African Arab states party to the NPT, their renunciation of nuclear weapons has become permanent.

Nonetheless, there have been informal indications that while all the eligible Arab states may sign the Pelindaba Treaty, all of them, including Egypt, may withhold formal ratification until Israel renounces nuclear weapons.

Entry Into Force

Since more than 50 states are eligible to join the Pelindaba Treaty, at first sight it appears that it would not be difficult to attain the 28 ratifications needed to bring the treaty into force. But if the reports about the intentions of the African Arab League states are correct, the number of potential ratifiers drops significantly, possibly complicating prospects for early entry into force.

In addition, experience with other multilateral arms control treaties does not encourage hopes for an early entry into force of the Pelindaba pact. It took nearly two years to collect the 40 ratifications needed to bring the NPT into force despite the determined efforts of the treaty's three depositary governments (the United States, Britain and the former Soviet Union) and the fact that the treaty's potential membership included a far larger and diverse group of states. Although more than 180 countries are eligible to join the Chemical Weapons Convention, which was opened for signature and ratification on January 13, 1993, only 47 states have so far deposited their instruments of ratification, still shy of the 65 ratifications now needed to bring the treaty into force.

Moreover, for many African states, there are other matters more pressing than ratification of the Pelindaba Treaty. Unless a determined effort is made by the OAU, South Africa, Nigeria, Zimbabwe and other strong supporters of the treaty, it will be surprising if the pact enters into force before the first meeting of the preparatory committee for the next NPT review conference in 1997. With their historical ties to Africa, France, Britain, the EU and the Commonwealth secretariat could all help speed the ratification process. Timely ratification of the protocols by the nuclear-weapon states would undoubtedly generate substantial support for the treaty among African countries.

Significance of the Treaty

Before NPT parties decided in May 1995 to indefinitely extend the treaty, the regional treaties, each of which is of unlimited duration, provided a permanent barrier to nuclear proliferation in the various regions even if the NPT were allowed to lapse. Now that the NPT is permanent, it is important to remember that there are several non-proliferation benefits that the Pelindaba Treaty, and other similar regional accords, can bring to the participants.

First, unlike the NPT, the Pelindaba Treaty will explicitly ban nuclear explosive devices from the area of application. There can be no development, acquisition, manufacture, deployment, stockpiling or testing of any device. Furthermore, the treaty prohibits the dumping of radioactive wastes and other matters anywhere in the zone.

Second, through their participation in negotiating the treaty and in the future meetings of parties, the states of the region become directly involved in the task of preventing the spread of nuclear weapons. This should help them to appreciate more fully the risks inherent in nuclear proliferation. It should also strengthen the constituencies at the United Nations, the IAEA and within the NPT regime that seek to reinforce the barriers to proliferation and to maintain pressure on the nuclear-weapon states to shrink their nuclear arsenals.

Third, the Pelindaba Treaty will encourage the creation of other nuclear-weapon-free zones, particularly in Southeast Asia and the Middle East, and set new patterns and precedents for such regional endeavors. As previously noted, the Pelindaba Treaty goes further than the NPT by explicitly requiring full-scope IAEA safeguards as a condition for nuclear supply, and it extends *treaty-based* negative security assurances to an additional region of the world. One of the frequently heard complaints made by non-aligned states at NPT meetings is that the generalized security assurances given so far by the nuclear-weapon states are not incorporated in a binding treaty and are thus revocable. The Pelindaba Treaty also goes further than the NPT and other regional treaties by requiring effective physical protection of nuclear operations and prohibiting armed attacks on nuclear facilities. It also sets an important precedent by banning research on nuclear weapons.

When considering what lessons the Pelindaba Treaty may hold for other regions, one fact stands out. The treaty became possible only when South Africa abandoned the nuclear weapons option, and it did so only when those factors that it perceived as being threats to its security had disappeared. What is unique in the South African case is that this change in threat perception hinged not only on external factors (such as the settlement in Namibia and the withdrawal of Cuban troops from Angola), but on internal factors as well. Without a fundamental transformation of its domestic policies—the elimination of apartheid and transition to full democracy—Pretoria would be unable to escape either the political, economic and military isolation imposed by the international community or the threats to its security, real or perceived, resulting from its internal politics.

Now that South Africa has dismantled its nuclear weapons program and acceded to the NPT—joining the other five African countries whose nuclear programs are under international safeguards (Algeria, Egypt, Ghana, Libya and Zaire)—should one regard the Pelindaba Treaty as a symbolic political statement rather than a purposeful non-proliferation measure? Much of the answer has already been given. The Pelindaba Treaty sets many useful non-proliferation precedents, and will eventually impose an additional barrier to clandestine nuclear programs and to any backsliding from the international non-proliferation regime.

The move toward complete nuclear disarmament is a process that began with the Antarctic Treaty in 1959, and has progressed northward step-by-step with the conclusion of the Tlatelolco Treaty, the Rarotonga Treaty and now the Pelindaba Treaty. It remains for the Northern Hemisphere to follow the good example set by the southern half of the world.

NOTES

1. President Jimmy Carter set up a "blue ribbon" panel under the chairmanship of Jack Ruina, a Massachusetts Institute of Technology professor, to investigate the matter. The panel concluded that the event picked up by the satellite was probably not a nuclear explosion. Other U.S. scientists and intelligence officials contest this conclusion. The assessment today is that if there was a nuclear test, it was more likely to have been carried out by Israel, helped by South Africa, but in the author's view this is doubtful. As parties to the Limited Test Ban Treaty, Israel and South Africa, had they wished to collaborate in a nuclear test, could have used the South African underground test site in the Kalahari Desert, which would not have breached the LTBT. For a South African account of the incident, see Waldo Stumpf, "South Africa's Nuclear Weapons Program: From Deterrence to Dismantlement," *Arms Control Today*, December 1995/January 1996, pp. 3-8.

2. UN document A/C.1/50/L.23 of November 6, 1995. The resolution was proposed by South Africa on behalf of the UN members that are also members of the African Group of States.

3. The original ambiguity in the Tlatelolco Treaty, which was interpreted by Argentina and Brazil, but not by other parties, as permitting them to manufacture and use nuclear explosives for peaceful purposes, was eliminated when Argentina and Brazil renounced all nuclear explosions for any purposes, established the Argentine-Brazilian Accounting and Control Committee (ABACC), accepted full-scope IAEA safeguards and when the text of the Tlatelolco Treaty was subsequently amended.

4. France's signature and ratification of the Treaty of Rarotonga's protocols will become possible only after the completion of the country's current nuclear test program in the South Pacific.

Levers for Plowshares:
Using Aid to Encourage Military Reform

Nicole Ball

Nicole Ball, a visiting fellow at the Overseas Development Council (ODC), is the author of Pressing for Peace: Can Aid Induce Reform? *(ODC Policy Essay no. 6, 1992), from which this article is drawn.*

In a December 1991 *Washington Post* article, former World Bank President Barber Conable noted that "where military expenditures rise above, say, 5 percent of GNP (or, as in the case in some developing countries, more than expenditures on health and education combined), it is hard to see the good sense of lending to such nations and in doing so reduce the capital available to other borrowers."[1]

Was this just another case of a senior official now safely out of office prescribing policy in an area he had ignored during his tenure? On the contrary. Along with International Monetary Fund (IMF) Managing Director Michel Camdessus, Conable began speaking out on the imbalances between military spending and the resources available for economic and social development in 1989—months before the Berlin Wall crumbled, well before the demise of the Soviet Union and the end of the Cold War, and long before the Gulf War revealed that the major powers' arms transfer and nonproliferation policies were an emperor with no clothes.

The need for reductions in military spending in the developing world—as well as continued reductions in the developed world—is clear. During the Cold War, the developing world spent over five percent of its gross national product on the military, depriving economies of desperately needed resources. While millions of people were struggling in poverty, developing countries spent $167.7 billion on their military forces in 1989—the last year for which official figures are available—according to the U.S. Arms Control and Disarmament Agency (ACDA). Nearly a fifth of the world's developing countries spend more on their militaries than on education and health

> *"Among the major international lenders, consensus on the importance of considering military spending in aid decisions is slowly building—stemming in significant part from the World Bank and International Monetary Fund efforts."*

programs combined—sometimes by a significant margin. Nor is the issue only misallocation of economic resources. Iraq, which used external loans to free up funds for military purposes, provides a clear example of the threats to international security posed by large military budgets and an unrestrained arms trade. By the time the Cold War ended in 1990, some 40 million people had died as a result of wars in the developing world—wars which often blocked or rolled back any economic development in the area where they took place.

In short, as a 1991 report of the U.N. Development Programme put it:

> "If a government chooses to spend more on its army than on its people, it cannot be regarded as committed to human development, and this bias should certainly count against it in aid negotiations. High military expenditure should be a legitimate area of policy dialogue in all forums of development cooperation."[2]

The Game So Far

Among the major international lenders, consensus on the importance of considering military spending in aid decisions is slowly building—stemming in significant part from the World Bank and IMF efforts. This is key, as the greater the consensus and coordination among the lenders, the more effective they will be in influencing government policies among the borrowers.

At first glance, the World Bank and the IMF might seem unlikely leaders of an effort to introduce security-related considerations into the development dialogue. Their mandates are economic, prohibiting them from tying lending decisions to political criteria. Many developing countries point to this fact in strenuously opposing any link between these institutions' lending policies and the size of borrowers' military budgets. Yet where military spending poses a substantial drag on a country's economy and its ability to develop, it is a legitimate subject to place on the table. Already, the World Bank and the IMF routinely insist on economic steps that have important political implications, from cutting budget deficits to valuing currencies. And few institutions are as well equipped to examine the developmental impact of government priorities skewed in favor of the military sector as the World Bank and the IMF, with their capacities to delve deeply into the economies of member states. Moreover, these institutions wield enormous influence, both through the billions of dollars in annual financing each provides directly to borrowers and through the impact their policies have on individual lending countries.

With the end of the Cold War, Camdessus, Conable, and Conable's successor, Lewis Preston, have argued forcefully that changing international conditions create opportunities for transferring resources from the military to economic and social development in all countries. The World

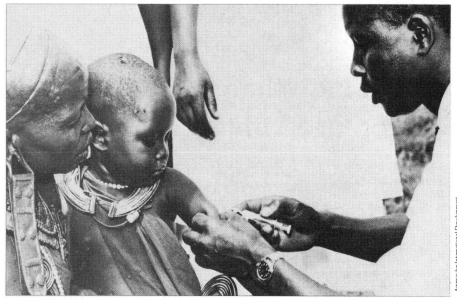

A Masai child in Kenya being immunized in a program sponsored by the U.S. Agency for International Development. Unlike Germany and Japan, the United States has so far failed to develop any policies for using its aid as a lever to discourage excessive military spending.

Agency for International Development

Bank-IMF activity began in earnest in 1989, with public statements questioning excessive military spending and justifying the idea that such issues should be considered in aid discussions. Both institutions, however, have made clear that they will not force countries to meet specific military-related conditions to qualify for funds. These statements were complemented by numerous in-house seminars, training sessions, and the like. The discussions reached a new pitch of intensity in 1991. In April, military spending was one of the "cutting edge" issues addressed at the World Bank's annual Conference on Development Economics, when former bank President Robert McNamara gave a major address calling for drastic military budget cutbacks worldwide, to be encouraged, in part, by links to aid. That fall, after the joint World Bank-IMF meeting in Bangkok, Preston said publicly that while "it is the sovereign right of nations to decide" how much to spend on their military, "if we found a situation where defense expenditure was 35 percent to 40 percent of the [government] budget, we might wonder if it was an appropriate use for [World Bank] funds." While Camdessus was more circumspect, he too made clear that the IMF would be putting military spending on the table in lending discussions.[3]

Both institutions have also raised military expenditure issues privately with a growing number of governments. In South Asia, for example, press reports indicate that both the World Bank and the IMF have pressed for cuts in military spending. In 1991, the last part of a World Bank aid

package for Pakistan was reportedly held up, in part, because Islamabad was initially unwilling to discuss reductions in military spending as part of efforts to cut its deficit, and the IMF, by one report, called for a nine percent cut in military spending. Germany and Japan have exerted similar pressure on Pakistan, and while Islamabad has yet to announce any reductions in the absolute level of military spending, it has spoken of a freeze, while budgets for health, housing, education, and rural development have increased. India has also reportedly been subject to World Bank-IMF pressures for military cutbacks. By some reports, New Delhi is now reducing military spending in real terms, and in September 1991, the IMF approved nearly $3 billion in new loans to India. Another example is Uganda, where the military budget has consumed about a third of the national budget in recent years. Aid institutions urging lower military spending have received a sympathetic hearing from the Ugandan government, and in June 1992, Kampala announced a plan for deep cuts in the military.

The World Bank has also begun to respond to requests for demilitarization assistance, such as helping demobilized soldiers and their families find housing, training, and employment, and converting **defense industries to civilian production. In 1991, for example, Argentina and the World Bank began negotiating a loan that would support the privatization of firms in the defense industry that produce primarily civilian goods.**

While lenders have made it clear that they believe military spending in a siz-

able number of member countries is excessive, they are less certain as to how much is "too much." Conable has raised the five-percent-of-GNP standard and Preston the possibility of a 35-to-40-percent-of-state-spending guideline, while Camdessus has repeatedly pointed out how much certain nations could save if they reduced their military spending to the world average of roughly 4.5 percent of GNP. But officials in both institutions recognize that a broader analysis is needed. In a December 6, 1991 memorandum, senior management at the World Bank indicated that it would be appropriate to raise the issue of resource allocation to the military with countries where development-related outlays are "seriously inadequate" and military budgets are high—vague but potentially flexible guidelines.[4]

Equally important, the willingness of the multilateral lending institutions to address military spending has encouraged individual national donors to formulate their own policies. Germany and Japan are the donors that have gone furthest in formulating and implementing policies linking economic assistance with military factors. Neither country absolutely conditions aid on meeting any particular military criterion, and each uses more complex analyses than a flat percentage of GNP or of government expenditure.

Germany begins by examining a borrower's military spending as a share of GNP and of central government spending, arms imports as a share of total imports, arms production as a share of industrial output, military spending as a share of domestic savings, and soldiers as a share of total population. Any recipient of German aid that exceeds the regional average in any one of these areas is subject to a more in-depth study focusing on qualitative factors. These factors include possession of or efforts to obtain weapons of mass destruction, long-range delivery systems (both missiles and aircraft), and other technologically sophisticated weapons (fighter aircraft, electronic warfare equipment, and precision-guided munitions); the nature of the domestic arms industry; the role of the military in politics and domestic conflicts; and the domestic use of repression. The recipient's attitude toward international arms control negotiations and treaties and the effect of military spending on the economy are also factors in this assessment.

While the German Ministry of Foreign Affairs has accepted this approach (developed by the Ministry of Economic Cooperation), there have been some disagreements between the two over its implementation. After Syria's participation in the Gulf War, for example, the Foreign Ministry ensured that questions about Syria under these criteria would not hold up aid. Similarly, in the case of India, the Ministry of Economic Cooperation agreed with the World Bank and the IMF that military spending was too high (as were the budget deficit and restraints on free markets), and proposed cutting German aid to New Delhi by 25 percent. But after discussions in which Indian leaders pointed out the progress they were making in these areas, the Foreign Ministry convinced the Ministry of Economic Cooperation to reconsider.

In April 1991, Japan announced that three military-related criteria would be taken into account when determining aid allocations to developing countries: military spending, the development and production of weapons of mass destruction and ballistic missiles, and participation in the arms trade (as both importers and as exporters). These criteria were codified in Japan's Official Development Assistance Charter of June 30, 1992. Concrete examples of Japan's policy include Tokyo's October 30, 1991 announcement that it will not provide recognition or aid to North Korea unless it dismantles the plutonium reprocessing plant at Yongbyon, and its October 1992 threat to cut aid to China if Beijing proceeds with plans to purchase an aircraft carrier from Ukraine, a sale which seems to have fallen through for a variety of reasons.

In April 1992, the Japanese government urged its partners in the Development Assistance Committee of the Organization for Economic Cooperation and Development (OECD)—a group of Western developed nations—to "take into account the trend of military expenditures and arms trade of recipients in their provision of assistance, and request recipients to cut 'excessive military expenditures.'"[5] To identify countries whose military budgets are "excessive," the Japanese government proposed examining trends in military spending, both in absolute terms and as a share of GNP. Resources allocated to the military would then be compared with those available for development purposes, particularly social expenditure. Finally, the Japanese government suggested that these factors be weighed against determinants of military spending—such as external threats, internal security requirements, geographic loca-

tion, length of borders, and collective security arrangements.

Unfortunately, the United States, with its billions of dollars in annual foreign aid, has so far been conspicuously absent in this dialogue. The U.S. president is required, under section 620(s) of the Foreign Assistance Act of 1961, to take into account the share of each recipient's national budget that goes to the military, and the amount of foreign exchange used for arms procurement. But no country has ever been denied aid on the basis of such a review. Indeed, for much of the Cold War, the United States,

like the former Soviet Union, explicitly provided aid to friendly countries to allow them to spend *more* on their militaries. Virtually every country in the developing world has received some portion of the billions of dollars of military hardware, training, technology, and aid that the United States, the Soviet Union, their allies, and a few wealthy oil-producing countries provided on concessional terms during the Cold War. Even today, the United States continues to spend a substantial part of its foreign aid budget on military assistance, and is by far the world's largest arms

H. Arvidsson/United Nations

Iraq's "supergun" (above), and the Iraqi buildup it was part of, are archetypal examples of the dangers of unrestrained military spending. During the Cold War, nearly 40 million people died in dozens of wars in the developing world.

exporter. And like other arms exporters, the United States continues to subsidize many of its sales—a policy IMF head Camdessus has explicitly criticized. The links between development, military issues, aid, and arms exports cry out for attention from the new Clinton administration—particularly as the president-elect has indicated that he supports efforts to restrain the international arms trade.

The German and Japanese methodologies require the collection and evaluation of a considerable amount of information—though they rely on published tabulations from the Stockholm International Peace Research Institute, the International Institute for Strategic Studies, and ACDA for quantitative information. Some analysts have suggested that such information-intensive methodologies are too cumbersome to be of real use in the policy process, and have suggested relying on simple approaches, such as cutting aid to all countries spending more than a certain percent of their GNP on the military. To arrive at well-informed decisions about the complex relationship between a developing country's military sector and its economic situation, however, a relatively detailed analysis is required. The alternative of applying simple formulas across-the-board fails to take into account regional and local differences or special circumstances, and relies too heavily on quantifiable data that may be of very low quality.

What The Lenders Can Do

There are major differences between what multilateral lenders such as the World Bank and the IMF can do and what individual lending countries can do. The mandate of the World Bank and the IMF is to strengthen the economies of member governments, therefore the objective of enhancing security will always be secondary, at the very best. In contrast, individual countries providing aid can address overtly political issues, if they choose to do so, by using economic tools to alter government policies on weapons procurement and conflict resolution as well as on the level of military budgets. They may also have the capability (although not in their aid agencies) to evaluate the security needs of other governments, help restructure security forces, and provide them with professional training.

Thus, Japan can insist that North Korea dismantle the Yongbyon plutonium facility before providing aid, and the United States can tie the resumption of aid to Pakistan to specific nuclear nonproliferation steps from Islamabad. The World Bank, however, is likely to rely more on persuasion, support for reform-minded governments, and pressure to spend more in economic and social sectors—designed to squeeze the military budget indirectly.

All of the lenders, however, have a fairly broad menu of possible strategies open to them for bringing military issues into the development dialogue, from simple persuasion at one end of the spectrum to sanctions on the other. This is in sharp contrast to the public debate on the subject that has focused heavily on only one of these tools, known as "conditionality," which provides particular amounts of aid only if the recipient agrees to take certain actions (such as cutting the defense budget to a specific level) or not to take others (such as acquiring nuclear weapons). While conditionality may be effective in some cases, many of the other approaches are less confrontational and more flexible, and therefore may have a better chance of producing the desired results. The following are a few of the different, but often complementary, strategies lenders are developing.

Persuasion

Persuasion—designed to convince borrowing governments that changes in military policy are in their own best interests—has played a central role in recent efforts to bring military budgets and policies into the development dialogue.

Public expressions of concern by lenders about the competition between military spending and development have served to warn the recipients of international financing that the rules of the game are changing. Henceforth, military spending will be viewed as an economic as well as a strategic or political issue. Giving such notice, both publicly and privately, should be a precondition for applying more direct pressure for change.

Some governments would like to change their spending priorities, but face substantial obstacles in doing so because of the political power of the military, which often controls the defense budget process. External support, beginning with policy dialogue, can help such governments raise the issue with their armed forces. As Conable has commented, "Weak or uncertain civilian governments may publicly protest, as invasion of their sovereignty, admonitions that arms expenditures be reduced. I speak from experience when I say that such pressure may be privately welcomed by the

new democracies."[6] Indeed, in some cases it may be desirable to reward countries that make steady progress in reducing military budgets, even if expenditure remains relatively high at the outset.

Policy dialogue is also important because the more borrowers feel that the reform programs are theirs and not imposed from outside, the more likely these programs are to succeed. Lenders should give high priority to identifying ways to avoid appearing to force one specific course of action on borrowers. Even governments that are already seeking external support for locally initiated reform programs can be sensitive on this point.

In the same vein, lenders should also accord high priority to working through multilateral forums in which military expenditure and other related issues can be raised in a nonconfrontational fashion. The Global Coalition for Africa—whose members include African governments, bilateral donors, and multilateral organizations—is addressing the possibility of reducing military expenditure as one element of improved governance. In Central America, consultations between regional governments and industrial countries under the San Jose accords (which involve the European Community and its members) or under the Partnership for Democracy and Development (which includes all OECD governments) could be broadened to include opportunities for lowering military spending.

Support

External support in various forms can facilitate borrower governments' efforts to implement military changes.

Financial support can help governments absorb extra costs associated with reform, such as compensating soldiers released from the armed forces or workers laid off from defense jobs. The World Bank negotiations with Argentina to help with privatization of defense firms producing civilian goods is a good example. Similarly, several major lenders to Nicaragua and Uganda are working with those governments to underwrite programs designed to integrate demobilized soldiers into the civilian economy. In a November 11, 1992 op-ed in *The New York Times*, Oscar Arias, former president of Costa Rica, pointed out that a Panamanian referendum on a package of constitutional amendments, which included banning military forces entirely, "might have stood a better chance" of passing if

Panamanians had been assured "that a positive vote would have met with a favorable response from creditor governments, lending institutions and investors."

Technical support can provide skilled manpower or equipment to carry out specific demilitarization tasks, from weapons destruction to monitoring to conversion. The Organization of American States, for example, provided demobilized Nicaraguan resistance fighters with construction materials and farm implements to assist their transition to civilian life, while bilateral donors have provided training to enhance their skills.

Pressure Without Conditions

As mentioned, the World Bank and the IMF have clearly stated that they will not apply specific military-related conditions to their lending. If policy dialogue is to be a credible tool for these two institutions, however, they must have some means of motivating borrowers to reexamine their military budgets.

One tool the World Bank has developed is to use structural adjustment lending to squeeze military budgets. The bank sets expenditure targets in economic and social sectors that cannot be met without a significant reallocation of resources, leaving governments little choice but to shift funds from other sectors the bank sees as unproductive, including the military. A similar strategy is available to the IMF when it sets targets for cutting fiscal deficits. For these institutions, this approach, combined with policy dialogue and targeted support for reforms, is among the most promising, as it directly addresses the link between wasteful military spending and domestic development without straying beyond these institutions' economic mandates.

Conditionality

Conditionality can take several forms and be applied with varying degrees of stringency. Most lenders are reluctant to identify specific military expenditure targets that borrowers *must* meet to obtain financing. Aid suspension and other forms of sanctions have been applied, however, particularly by the United States, in response to specific activities such as military *coups d'etat*, efforts to obtain nuclear weapons, and failure to negotiate in good faith. Thus, Washington sought to encourage the Israeli government to enter into

Nearly one-fifth of the world's developing countries spend more on their militaries than on education and health combined, diverting desperately needed resources. Above, schoolchildren in Bangladesh.

significant negotiations with the Palestinians and several of its Arab neighbors by threatening to place conditions on the $10 billion in housing loan guarantees requested by Israel in 1991.

Although bilateral donors may link aid to particular actions to promote nonproliferation, conflict resolution, and regional arms control, few are likely to tie their aid absolutely to a specific level of military spending. As described above, while the lenders generally agree that lower military budgets are preferable, there is no agreement on how much is too much. Lenders are therefore more likely to press for sustained progress in cutting military spending than to insist that borrowers meet a particular target level.

Nevertheless, some military expenditure "threshold"—perhaps along the lines of Preston's reference to countries devoting more than 35–40 percent of their budgets to military spending—might eventually be established. If pre-

ceded and combined with intensive policy dialogue, support for desired changes, and diplomatic efforts to reduce security threats in particular regions, such an approach could ultimately be effective.

Explicit conditionality raises hackles in many countries in the developing world, as it suggests a loss of sovereignty over providing for their own defense (a function guaranteed to them by the U.N. Charter), and often involves little, if any, consultation with the borrower or flexibility on the part of the lender. Many borrower countries have argued that demanding reductions in military spending without reference to security needs is a dangerous exercise. In their view, only the country concerned has the capacity to define those needs and the resources needed to meet them. After the October 1991 joint World Bank–IMF meeting, for example, the "Group of 24" developing countries circulated a communique warning "against the involvement of the fund and the bank in issues beyond their strict economic and financial mandate."

Nevertheless, while there is clearly a need for lenders to work collaboratively with borrowers, lenders should not allow their desire to "persuade" rather than "force" to serve as an excuse for allowing the military *status quo* to go unchanged. The human, financial, and material losses that wars, excessive arms procurement, and high military budgets have inflicted in the developing world over the last four decades render the sovereignty argument increasingly invalid. It may at times be necessary to place conditions on economic cooperation to force a government to reconsider a policy that a majority of the international community—and perhaps of its own people—views as unacceptable.

"Carrots" Instead of "Sticks"

Lenders may choose not to impose specific conditions on their aid, but to give preference to governments whose performance is favorable. The Japanese government is particularly interested in rewarding good behavior, reserving denial of aid for rare occasions when governments fail to pursue certain policies. A reward-based strategy is grounded upon the premise that positive reinforcement is more likely to produce change than punishment.

While such an assessment may be valid for governments with a fairly firm commitment to reform, it is unclear how much leverage this sort of strategy provides over less committed countries. Furthermore, desirable as it may be to offer the carrot rather than the stick, reward strategies virtually always require official lenders to *shift* resources from one country to another. Japan, whose aid budget has been expanding more rapidly than most other countries, may find it easier to reallocate resources. A number of other OECD countries are facing cuts in aid budgets, as recessions push up fiscal deficits. And in the United States, congressional earmarking of substantial portions of aid resources imposes significant limits on the U.S. capacity to offer rewards substantial enough to make a difference.

Next Steps

The international lending community is making progress in bringing military issues into the development dialogue, but specific policies are still embryonic. The following are four suggestions for next steps.

1. Actively seek to support and promote military reform—including cutbacks in military spending—in the developing world.

All lenders should adopt policies that actively promote reform, rather than simply punishing bad behavior or passively rewarding good behavior. Specific conditionality may at times prove necessary, but the core of lenders' policies should be policy dialogue and financial and technical support designed to assist governments in restraining and reforming their military sectors. The objectives should include establishing greater transparency and accountability in the military sector; encouraging civilian control over the armed forces, paramilitary groups, and the police; supporting reductions in the size of military forces and domestic arms industries; and promoting new security arrangements that will enable governments to provide enhanced security at lower levels of expenditure.

One of the most important contributions that lenders can make is simply helping governments to integrate the military sector into normal development practices, such as assisting in strengthening government management and in increasing the efficiency of the money that is spent.

2. Build cooperation among national and multilateral lenders, borrowers, and relevant political institutions to create the conditions needed for enhanced security at lower levels of military spending.

For the purposes of devising strategies in this area, developing countries can be divided into two broad groups. The first group—which includes countries such as Egypt, Paraguay, and Uganda—spends demonstrably more on the military than is warranted by existing internal and external security threats, compared to development needs. These are the countries with which lenders feel most comfortable discussing military reform—particularly those among them that have already decided to undertake military cutbacks. Even in these cases, the international community may need to provide assistance in reaching arms control agreements or creating regional security mechanisms that will reduce the likelihood of renewed emphasis on the military in the future. Lenders should explore opportunities for using their lending to encourage such activities.

In the second group of countries, the security picture, either external or internal, will have to be changed before the economic burden of the military sector can be significantly reduced. In South Asia and the Koreas, for example, some reductions in military spending are possible now, but fundamental changes would require resolving outstanding political and armament issues. Here, political institutions must take the lead in pursuing the kinds of negotiated settlements, arms control pacts, and regional security arrangements that would make enhanced security at lower levels of military spending possible. Again, lenders should actively cooperate with these efforts, using their financial and technical resources to encourage the necessary changes in policies.

Although the bilateral donors and organizations such as the United Nations may be best suited to link official financing with arms control and conflict resolution, the World Bank and the IMF can clearly participate in certain activities, such as helping to devise and implement job creation and retraining programs for demobilized soldiers.

In addition, it would be worth exploring whether the multilateral development banks (the World Bank and the African, Asian, and inter-American regional development banks) could, under certain circumstances, link development assistance to the cessation of hostilities and the inauguration of serious negotiations between disputing parties. If it were agreed that a high level of military spending in a particular area or an ongoing conflict constituted a serious obstacle to development, and that only negotiations to resolve underlying security imbalances could free up resources urgently needed by economic and social sectors, multilateral development bank action might be justifiable on economic grounds.

3. Build agreement among the bilateral donors and U.N. agencies that countries receiving their financial support will generally conform to certain internationally agreed-upon security standards.

These standards should generally be norms of behavior that are already internationally accepted, such as international treaties and conventions. As a first step, they might include:

• adherence to international arms control treaties such as the nuclear Nonproliferation Treaty, the Biological Weapons Convention, the Environmental Modification Convention, and the just-completed Chemical Weapons Convention, or to internationally recognized alternative arrangements;

• respect for the territorial integrity of other countries, including support for the principles of nonaggression and nonintervention;

• participation in dialogues designed to increase regional security and stability, where these exist;

• a willingness to negotiate in good faith as necessary to end longstanding conflicts, both internal and external;

• participation in the United Nations' standardized military expenditure reporting exercise and the U.N. arms register; and

• a willingness to subject the military sector to the same scrutiny and discipline as other public sector expenditure.

4. Match the donors' policies to those expected of developing countries, wherever possible.

To build credibility and avoid charges of discrimination and unwarranted interference in borrowers' affairs, lenders and developed nations in general should be willing to accept the same norms for themselves that they are applying to developing countries. The military cutbacks already underway in the industrial countries have given greater authority to calls from the international lending community for military reform in the developing world, but there is more that the developing countries should do. It will be difficult for the lenders of the developed world to demand that developing countries spend less than five percent of their GNP on the military, for example, if the lenders are spending substantially more than that themselves.

Military cutbacks should continue in many countries, as military spending in most of the developed world remains substantially higher than is justified, given the benign security environment most developed countries now face. To the extent possible, future international arms control agreements and supplier groups should be universal in membership and nondiscriminatory in scope, treating all states alike. When military intervention in the developing world is necessary, it should be multilateral, not unilateral, in nature, and given legitimacy in some broadly accepted way; for example by the United Nations or a regional organization.

One of the areas of greatest disparity between the objectives industrial countries are pursuing in the developing world and their own behavior is the arms trade, in which virtually all developed countries take part. The United States, Russia, France, and Britain export a substantial amount of arms to the developing world and are currently seeking to expand their share of the market in the face of declining domestic orders, sometimes using unrealistically low prices and subsidized financing. Clearly, countries that aggressively promote arms sales—including the United States—seriously undermine their ability to promote military reform. Eliminating arms sale subsidies, as IMF Managing Director Camdessus has urged, would offer concrete proof that the industrial countries do not expect all concessions to be made by the borrowing countries. More broadly, the largest arms exporters have a special responsibility to work toward genuine international limits on the arms trade.

Conclusion

The end of the Cold War has brought many positive changes in international relations, creating new opportunities for military reform in both the developed and developing worlds. But continuing problems from Yugoslavia to Cambodia make clear that conflicts have by no means been eradicated. The challenge of the 1990s is to ensure that emerging trends toward international cooperation in security and other fields, reduced military spending, and domestic political participation are maintained and strengthened.

The international lending community clearly has a role to play in this process. Lenders can help to change norms of behavior—from military secrecy to appropriate means of settling disputes within and among states. Where the objective is primarily to free resources for development, lenders, including the World Bank and the International Monetary Fund, can legitimately act on their own initiative. Where the objective is primarily to alter the security environment, as in constructing a regional

security and arms control regime, political institutions will take the lead, but lenders will continue to have an important role to play in nurturing and supporting the process.

While far-reaching military reform in developing countries will occur only if governments in those countries accept the need for change, lenders have a role to play in building that acceptance. It is past time for the developing nations to take a hard look at their priorities and devise policies that will promote reduced tensions and increased development. For their part, the industrial countries can underline their commitment to the emerging norms they promote by applying them to their own behavior as well, and by using all the strategies outlined above to encourage beneficial changes. But it is ultimately the people and the governments of developing countries who must seize the current opportunities to create a more equitable and prosperous future for themselves.

NOTES

1. Barber B. Conable, Jr., "Growth—Not Guns," *The Washington Post*, December 24, 1991.

2. U.N. Development Programme, *Human Development Report 1991*, New York: Oxford University Press, 1991, p. 83.

3. Paul Blustein, "World Bank, IMF to Press Defense Cuts: Institutions Hint at Withholding Loans," *The Washington Post*, October 18, 1991.

4. Jonathan E. Sanford, *Multilateral Development Banks: Issues for Congress*, IB87218, Washington, DC: Congressional Research Service, March 13, 1992, p. 13.

5. Japan International Cooperation Agency, *Annual Report 1991*, Tokyo, 1992, p. 19; and statement by Nobuyuki Sugimoto, director of Multilateral Cooperation Division, Economic Cooperation Bureau, Ministry of Foreign Affairs of Japan, at the Informal Meeting on Participatory Development and Good Governance, Organization of Economic Cooperation and Development, April 9, 1992, p. 2. See also, "Japan's ODA Policies for a Peace Initiative," address by Takao Kawakami, director-general, Economics Cooperation Bureau, Ministry of Foreign Affairs, to the Tokyo Conference on Arms Reductions and Economic Development in the Post-Cold War Era, November 5, 1992.

6. Conable, "Growth—Not Guns," op. cit.

Transitions

The trend toward democratization in the developing world has been fueled by a legitimacy crisis, demands for greater political participation, and the collapse of the Soviet Union, which effectively reduced the socialist alternative of development. The developing countries' experience with democratization has varied, and its success is by no means guaranteed. Nevertheless, democratic reform efforts offer fascinating and complex issues and problems for those interested in political development.

Few developing countries have a democratic past. The colonial powers often failed to adequately prepare their colonies for democracy at independence. Even where there was an attempt to foster parliamentary government, the experiment frequently failed, due to such factors as a lack of democratic tradition or factionalism. Leaders frequently resorted to centralization of power and authoritarianism, either to pursue ambitious development programs or simply to retain their own power. In some cases, leaders experimented with socialist development schemes that emphasized ideology and the role of party elites. The promise of rapid, equitable development proved elusive, and the collapse of the Soviet Union discredited this strategy. Other countries had the misfortune to come under the rule of tyrannical leaders who were concerned with enriching themselves and who brutally repressed anyone with the temerity to challenge their rule. Although there are a few notable exceptions, the developing world's experiences with democracy have been very limited.

During the 1980s, much of Latin America underwent redemocratization after a period of authoritarian rule. This trend toward democracy spread to some Asian countries, such as the Philippines and South Korea, and by 1990 it also began to be felt in sub-Saharan Africa and the Middle East.

Democracy's "third wave" has been a sporadic and uneven process in the developing world and is likely to

continue in this fashion. In Latin America, Mexico's democracy is undergoing a stiff test, while Venezuela, Peru, Guatemala, and Nicaragua have all had to contend with challenges to their democracies. Chile's democracy must deal with threats of military intervention. These circumstances highlight the tenuous hold that democracy has in some parts of that region.

Beginning in 1990, a wave of democratization swept over Africa. Many leaders, some of whom had held power since independence, were seriously challenged or ousted. Kenneth Kaunda of Zambia and Hastings Kamuzu Banda of Malawi, both of whom had ruled their countries since independence, were ousted in multiparty elections. International pressure forced President Daniel arap Moi of Kenya to agree to multiparty elections in December 1992. Although Moi survived these elections, and the political process has opened up for opposition groups, ethnic violence has increased since the elections. President Marshal Mobutu of Zaire is besieged by challenges to his rule, but he continues to cling precariously to power. In the meantime, Zaire appears to be edging toward collapse. In a number of other countries throughout Africa, during a populist wave in the early 1990s, constituent assemblies stripped leaders of power and forced elections. In South Africa, the last vestiges of formal apartheid were swept away in April 1994 when blacks finally participated in democratic elections for the first time and elected a government dominated by the Africa National Congress party (ANC). South Africa's experience illustrates the complexity of the democratic transition process. Democratic reform has been complicated by deep factionalism, political violence, and controversy over future constitutional arrangements, especially regarding federalism and civil-military relations. Economic issues also contribute to the complexity of South Africa's political situation. The prospects for successful democratic consolidation appear good, but the enormous problems the government faces in overcoming the legacy of apartheid could still complicate democratization.

There have also been movements toward democratic reform in the Middle East, although, as in other regions, the results have been varied. In Algeria, the military annulled the 1991 elections when the Islamic Salvation Front was on the brink of winning, bringing an end to Algeria's democratic experiment and ushering in a deadly conflict between Islamic militants and the military government. This situation serves as a reminder of the potential for political intervention by the armed forces, who are frequently major political players in developing countries. The promise of democratic reforms in Kuwait in the aftermath of the Persian Gulf War remain unfulfilled. Egypt faces a serious challenge by Islamists, resulting in govern-

ment suppression of this opposition. The Israeli-PLO agreement has increased the chances of regional peace, but the Palestinian leadership's commitment to democracy in the autonomous areas is untested. Overall, the pace and scope of reform in the Middle East have not been as sweeping as they have been elsewhere.

In 1993, internationally supervised elections in Cambodia produced a 90 percent turnout and were judged free and fair. Cambodia's fragile democracy continues to face numerous challenges to consolidation, including a resurgent Khmer Rouge.

While democratic transitions have begun throughout the world, there is no guarantee that these efforts will succeed. Indeed, challenges loom large as fledgling democracies seek to consolidate. The lack of a democratic tradition, factionalism, resistance by powerful interests, and military intervention are among the obstacles to democratic transition and consolidation in the developing world.

Looking Ahead: Challenge Questions

What are the dangers of quick attempts at democratic transition?

What challenges does the Middle East peace process face in the aftermath of Israel's 1996 election of Benjamin Natanyahu?

What are the obstacles to successful democratic consolidation in South Africa?

What accounts for Africa's mixed results with democratization?

What are the major challenges facing Mexico?

What changes are under way in Cuba?

How do the Chilean armed forces represent a potential threat to the country's democracy?

Democracy's Trap

Robert D. Kaplan

Robert D. Kaplan, a contributing editor of The Atlantic Monthly, is the author of "The Ends of the Earth: A Journey at the Dawn of the 21st Century" (1996).

WASHINGTON

America needs to curb its missionary zeal to establish multiparty systems in every third world country as fast as it can. Our rote prescription for underdeveloped and newly "liberated" nations—elections within one year, followed by stability—is more likely to lead to chaos than democracy.

This is not to deny democracy's successes, especially in some Eastern European states. But we must acknowledge its limitations, at least as a quick fix, in a world torn by exploding populations, diminishing natural resources, struggling governments and ethnic rivalries. We should shift our foreign development strategy from one of instant gratification to one of mature patience, encouraging a slower, but more realistic, route to democracy.

We seem to assume that our victory in the cold war has paved the way for worldwide democracy. But the demise of the Soviet Union does not necessarily justify creating political parties in, say, Rwanda, where the establishment of a multiparty system and a coalition Government in 1992 hardened ethnic divisions that erupted into civil war and genocide in 1994.

Or in Cambodia, where the United Nations spent several billion dollars on a high-profile election in 1993 that has given us an increasingly dictatorial, corrupt and brutal Government that cannot even control its army.

Or in Haiti, where we can only hope that Jean-Bertrand Aristide, whom we did not allow to run for a second presidential term, can keep the country together from behind the scenes.

States are not formed by elections. They are formed by geography, war, settlement patterns and the rise of literate bourgeoisies. Nor are countries necessarily strengthened by elections. Indeed, democracy initially weakens many states because it demands ineffectual compromises. Totalitarianism is anathema to us, but remember that Bosnian Muslims, Croats and Serbs lived together peacefully and intermarried under Tito's jackboot.

Yet even the Balkan countries—with their high literacy rates, low birthrates and some tradition of a middle class—are better candidates for democracy than much of the third world. When elections are introduced suddenly into societies where the poor predominate, random crime and gangsterism often fill the void vacated by tyranny.

Witness South Africa, where in the past year violent crime has increased by as much as 75 percent in some areas. Of course, this is preferable to apartheid, and political violence there has greatly subsided. But if the Government cannot eventually stabilize crime rates, a new form of tyranny, or chaos, could evolve.

From Cambodia to Haiti, quick-fix elections invite disaster.

Democratic elections often intensify ethnic and regional divisions rather than heal them. In the Caucasus, the collapse of the Soviet Union brought nationalist-democrats to power in Armenia and Azerbaijan. Each leader furthered his country's slide into a brutal war against the other. Only after the freely elected President of Azerbaijan, Abulfez Elcibey, had been toppled in a coup that brought a former Communist leader to power did a modicum of stability return. Some months later, the two countries agreed to a cease-fire.

Because democracy neither forms states nor strengthens them initially, a multiparty system is best suited to nations that already have an established bureaucracy and a middle class which pays income tax and where the main issues of property and power-sharing have been resolved, leaving politicians to argue about budgets. Two perfect examples are Taiwan and Greece, both middle-class, ethnically homogeneous societies that have moved fitfully but successfully toward democracy for decades. Likewise, Chile's impressive economic growth and the withering away of its military dictatorship have made it a suitable candidate for real democracy.

Sometimes an authoritarian regime becomes so odious that out of concern for its citizens (or out of worry that it will destabilize its region) we feel compelled to get involved. Thus Nigeria may be the next battleground of democracy—and we need to be cautious there.

Nigeria has a volatile mixture of ethnic and regional divisions, and it has a long history of money laundering, drug smuggling and forgery scams. Its increasingly urbanized population is doubling every 22 years and its natural resources are rapidly being depleted. If the West were to force the reintroduction of democracy before attending to other changes, like a reorganization of the military, and leave the day after a "successful" election, Nigeria could slowly unravel.

The example of Nigeria also illustrates how hypocritical Americans can be about exporting democracy. Nigeria is far less developed than, say, Egypt, according to the U.N. Yet, with an eye on geopolitical priorities, the United States doesn't even dare to consider where a real democracy might lead Egypt.

What can we do? We should shift our emphasis in the third world from holding elections to promoting family planning, environmental renewal, road building and other stabilizing projects. We need to sponsor more bread-and-butter literacy and agricultural programs (especially those that focus on women, who in many societies are the keys to cultural transformation). Yes, some dictators may take advantage of such programs, but this approach is better than throwing up our hands and more practical than elections.

History and cultures can rarely be forced by expensive stunts like the United Nations elections in Cambodia. And each failure only provides more ammunition for American isolationists.

This is why even in the Balkans, where there has been a level of social development not enjoyed in Haiti or Cambodia, arming the Bosnia Muslims to create a regional balance of terror is a safer bet than risking NATO's reputation on elections within a year, followed by peace.

On Course for ... What?

Netanyahu has been clearer about what he *won't* do than what he will. And the empowered far right will have its own agenda. By Tom Masland

"PEACE WITH SECURITY." THAT'S A slogan to win an election with, but what does it really mean? The liberals who last week piled fresh flowers and notes on the spot where former prime minister Yitzhak Rabin was assassinated thought they could read through Bibi Netanyahu's artfully ambiguous message. "Rabin was killed on Nov. 4—Peace was killed on May 29," one sign said. Settlers on the West Bank had another view. "We feel like this is salvation," said Aryeh Saraf, a security guard in a settlement called Beit El. "Bibi will keep us here," said Moshe Ben Ami, 19, who lives outside Ramallah. "This is Israel, where we are fighting the Arabs." Both sides' fervor was understandable. But oddly, Israel's course under Netanyahu, at least in the short term, is likely to be little different from what it would have been under his opponent.

Israel's formal commitments are a fact—something both the White House and nervous Arab leaders were quick to point out. Netanyahu is first of all a pragmatist. And any attempt to reverse course on dealings with the Palestinians would immediately put him up against the powerful forces both within Israel and abroad that have driven the peace process as far as it is. There is a new Mideast reality, and that includes a place at the table for Yasir Arafat and the Palestinian majority he represents. But Arafat is said to be deeply anguished by Shimon Peres's loss, and with reason. Even if Netanyahu wanted to push the peace process ahead, he would have to bow to the new power of splinter parties in Israeli politics. Israel's Orthodox were the big winners. "People forget that this is a Jewish country," said Shlomo Aminov, one of the swing voters who gave Netanyahu the nar-

row win. The emergent right wing could bedevil his decisions on such hot-button issues as settlements, terrorism and the Palestinians' place in Jerusalem.

Whatever Netanyahu really intends, Israel's new voting system has sapped the government's power. Designed by a group of Tel Aviv university professors to strengthen both major parties, it instead spread authority to narrow interests. For the first time Israelis voted separately for the prime minister and for the Knesset. The result was that Likud enters government with just over a quarter of the Knesset's seats. Nearly half of the seats went to small parties, including the new, pro-immigrant Yisrael B'Aliya movement of former Soviet dissident Natan Sharansky (graphic). Conservative religious parties hold an unprecedented 20 percent of the seats.

On the peace issue, it won't be easy for Netanyahu to please this powerful camp while not alienating the entire Middle East—and Israel's protector, Washington. "Our minimum expectation is that agreements made will be honored," said one White House aide. As soon as the result became official, Netanyahu and his aides went into what one White House source called "reassurance mode." The new prime minister is "deeply committed to continuing the peace process with the Palestinians and all of Israel's neighbors," he said through a spokesman. That seemed aimed partly at quieting markets fearful that a new, hard-line policy could end an economic boom brought about by the apparent end of Israel's isolation. And Clinton, who had all but campaigned openly for Peres, hurried to reciprocate. As soon as the result was official, he invited the new prime minister to the White House—while teasingly congratulating him on his

"Israeli landslide"—less than 30,000 votes out of 3 million.

Soon, though, Netanyahu must begin to show his hand. He is unlikely to break much new ground in his first official declarations, but his cabinet choices will send a signal of moderation; hard-liners won't get the defense or foreign-affairs portfolios. As a professed peacemaker, Netanyahu so far has mainly said what he will not do. He won't give up the Golan Heights to win a peace treaty with Syria. That disappoints a White House that has invested heavily in the Syria talks—and would love to stage a ceremony on the South Lawn before Election Day. But the Syria talks were bogged down anyway. "Assad is hopeless," said Peter Rodman, a former National Security Council adviser to President Ronald Reagan. "He had a chance with Labor and he wasn't willing to pay the price." Netanyahu also rules out considering a Palestinian state and negotiating over the status of Jerusalem—and says he would prefer not to meet with Arafat at all. That doesn't leave much hope for progress on a final agreement with the Palestinians.

The settlement issue puts the newly empowered religious right squarely in conflict with U.S. policy. To authorize new settlements would put the government right back where Likud was during the Bush administration, when the White House threatened to withhold loan guarantees. Likud was bruised in that debate—especially when Secretary of State James Baker declared that Israelis must abandon the claim of a greater Israel. Baker actually barred Netanyahu, then a deputy foreign minister, from entering the State Department after Netanyahu accused the U.S. government of "building its policy on a foundation of distortions and lies." Netanyahu doesn't want a replay. But a moderate increase in support for settle-

A New Day for Hard–Liners and the Orthodox

Although the margin of victory in the race for prime minister was paper thin, new electoral rules led to dramatic parliamentary gains for religious and single-issue parties.

Upheaval in the Knesset

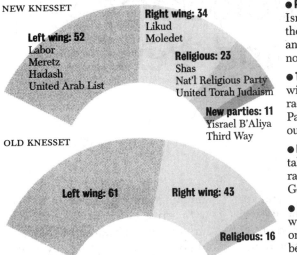

NEW KNESSET

Right wing: 34
Likud
Moledet

Left wing: 52
Labor
Meretz
Hadash
United Arab List

Religious: 23
Shas
Nat'l Religious Party
United Torah Judaism

New parties: 11
Yisrael B'Aliya
Third Way

OLD KNESSET

Left wing: 61

Right wing: 43

Religious: 16

Netanyahu's Platform

● **Palestinian state:** Ruled out. Israel will never cede authority over foreign affairs and security ; Jerusalem is nonnegotiable.

● **The West Bank:** Settlements will be permitted to expand. Israeli troops will be sent into Palestinian-run towns to root out guerrillas.

● **Relations with Syria:** In theory talks could go forward, but Israel won't discuss returning the Golan Heights.

● **Relations with Jordan:** Ties would be strengthened to build on a "strategic convergence" between the two nations.

in order to stall it. "This is the same agenda," said Sheik Sayed Abu Mesameh, a spiritual leader of the Islamic Resistance Movement (Hamas), which rejoiced in the election result. Natanyahu likely will acknowledge Palestinian frustration with a short-term fix: relaxing the border controls, put in place this year to protect against terrorism, which have impoverished the West Bank and Gaza.

The West Bank's hottest flash point, Hebron, poses the same kind of threat. The Oslo deal calls for the withdrawal of all Israeli forces, but that has been delayed since March because of security concerns. If Netanyahu moves forward with the withdrawal, Orthodox settlers who revere the city as Abraham's burial place will revolt. Another trigger could be Orient House, Arafat's headquarters in East Jerusalem. Netanyahu's supporters want it closed.

Even those who know Netanyahu well can't completely explain his philosophy or predict what course he'll take. Most expect a moderate path—a continuation of the peace process but at a slower, more complicated pace. "The goal should be to preserve what has been achieved," said Richard Haass, Mideast adviser to George Bush. That may not sound like much, but only recently an interim solution to the Palestinian question seemed like the best hope for taming the conflict. And Netanyahu seems far too nimble a politician to be trapped into fighting reality.

With Joseph Contreras in Jerusalem, Christopher Dickey and Mark Dennis in Gaza and Tara Sonenshine in Washington

ments won't necessarily court that kind of censure. Quietly, some West Bank settlements have continued to grow slightly under the outgoing Labor government.

That why many Palestinians were cynical about the election results. For Arafat, the challenge now will be to contain the frustration of Palestinians who expected him to widen the agreement that gave the Palestinian Authority the right to govern Gaza and Palestinian towns on the West Bank. Netanyahu rejects any effort to limit Israel's right to seek out its enemies wherever they might hide, raising the specter of a return to the days when Israeli soldiers with tear gas and rubber bullets confronted groups of stone-throwing Palestinian kids. Israel's foes were quick to point out that the last Likud prime minister, Yitzhak Shamir, admitted after leaving office that he signed on to the peace process mainly

Africa Tries Democracy, Finding Hope and Peril

John Darnton

Special to The New York Times

NAIROBI, Kenya—Despite economic collapse, countries are proclaiming democracy throughout Africa. With a raft of elections and sometimes a multitude of parties, their governments are beginning to tolerate a once forbidden sound—that of the political opponent.

Already the drive for political rights has consigned the archetypal autocrat—the "president for life" who rules with a fly whisk and a squadron of secret police—to the same graveyard as apartheid, African socialism and the ships that brought the first European colonizers 500 years ago.

But what lies ahead is uncertain. The trend toward reform is not uniform and certainly not universal.

Most ominously, there are signs that in some countries political liberalization may be widening ethnic cleavages. These rivalries could grow to touch off movements for secession or even lead to the kind of horrific tribal massacres convulsing Rwanda.

A more open political process can lay bare ethnic tensions that have long simmered under the suppression of a dictator's boot. Having several political parties may mean that they will take on ethnic identities. And underneath all the rallies and hoopla of a campaign, there is the danger that groups may jostle for control or that a ruling minority will sense the risk of being turned out of power and resort to subversion and violence.

A rise in ethnic tension, while part of the worldwide explosion of claims of sovereignty and self-determination in the post–cold-war era, is particularly dangerous in Africa, where the boundaries inherited from colonialism do not correspond to the areas inhabited by ethnic groups.

The political ferment has unquestionably led to new freedoms. More than half of the 48 countries south of the Sahara have held or promised multiparty elections. Fifteen years ago, only two—Nigeria and Kenya—could be said to have had influential and independent newspapers. Now most have them. Groups to monitor human rights have sprung up everywhere, even in repressive countries like Zaire.

Africans welcome these changes. They are glad to wave good-bye to the old world of one-man rule. It ended symbolically several weeks ago when Hastings Kamuzu Banda, the last surviving independence leader, shuffled off Malawai's stage, turned out by voters after running the country like a private preserve for 30 years.

But conversations with scores of Africans in the course of a six-week visit to nine countries suggest that these changes are only a first step. Genuine democracy, they say, has yet to arrive in most countries.

In some it has been stymied by the old power elite or hijacked by a new one. In others, the opposition is so fragmented—sometimes into a plethora of parties following ethnic divisions—that it is too ineffectual for the system to function. De facto single-party rule returns by default.

"They say the newspapers are free, but a minister can still put a journalist in jail," said Halidou Ouedraogo, president of the Burkina Faso Movement for the Rights of Man. "They say the courts are independent, but there are always pressures from behind the scenes. We still don't have real participation of the people at a grass-roots level.

"Take Rwanda and Burundi. Both signed the International Convention for Protection and Defense of Human Rights. But look at the massacres. The gap between a piece of paper and what is reality can be frightening, truly frightening."

Significantly, the continent's political reform is proceeding under a giant question mark because it coincides with a downward economic plunge. Throughout the 1980's and into the 1990's the vast majority of the countries—with a few exceptions like diamond-producing Botswana—experienced negative per capita growth.

This means that these nations are experimenting with bold new political ideas and structures at a time when living standards are dropping, health and education are declining and the people are consequently most prone to strikes, demonstrations and the appeals of demagogues.

It is not lost on the experts that the country that has made the most economic progress, according to the World Bank, is Ghana and that it did so during the decade when it was under the tight military rule of Jerry J. Rawlings, who has since won election as President. Authoritarian rule makes it more possible to impose the stringent measures that the international financial institutions demand.

And what is sound economically may clash with what is politically sensible. At the stroke of a pen in January, the value of the French-backed currency called the C.F.A. franc was cut in half. It was a move that most financial experts felt was long overdue, but overnight it destabilized 14 countries in West and Central Africa.

The Alternatives
Hope and Horror In Two Nations

The imaginations of Africans everywhere, it is clear, have been seized by two seismic events in recent months. One is the election of President Nelson Mandela in South Africa. It was not just that Mr. Mandela triumphed in the last redoubt of white minority rule. It was that he welcomed his former foes, F. W. de Klerk and Chief Mangosuthu G. Buthelezi, into his administration with open arms, providing an object lesson in the value of tolerating the opposition as a form of good, stable, even shrewd government.

The other is Rwanda. To the outside world, the tribal massacres there were an inexplicable horror, an atavistic replaying of ancient hatreds. But to many Africans, there is another troubling aspect.

The slaughter of Tutsi by Hutu represents what can happen when there is a dangerous brew and the lid is lifted off too quickly, they say. It is

a parable of reform-minded change under the prodding of Western countries gone horribly wrong.

Some assert that the West shares the blame by pushing for a democratic form of government that would inevitably mean power-sharing between the Tutsi, who had a privileged position during colonial days, and the more numerous Hutu, who were beginning to control the army.

From the point of view of Western diplomats, talks involving regional governments held over the course of two years at Arusha, Tanzania, were aimed at smoothing out the differences between the two hostile groups by providing for such things as integration of the armed forces. But this is not the way some Africans perceive it.

"The outside powers, Belgium, France, the U.S., they all exerted a lot of pressure on Rwanda," said Alberto Bento Ribeiro, the Angolan Ambassador to Zimbabwe. "They wanted to get the Hutu into the power structure, to move them up in the army. All that upset the established order, which had Tutsi at the top.

"Democracies can work in our countries only if the internal forces are allowed to work without outside manipulation," he concluded.

Jonathan Moyo, a political scientist now working for the Ford Foundation in Nairobi, drew a parallel between Rwanda and white-ruled South Africa. "The cruelty of the system of oppression is the same. When you set one group above another and close all channels of political expression, you sow the seeds of eruption further down the line.

"The difference is, South Africa underwent a process of managed change. It started in 1986. If they had suddenly lifted the lid off back then, people would have been slaughtering each other too. That's what happened in Rwanda—it was too much too quickly for a system that had been totally closed.

"Today the one-party structure is ending all over Africa and people demand elections within 21 days," Mr. Moyo said. "The South Africa

experience teaches us it should be done gradually by people of vision, allowing the structures to evolve and preaching values of tolerance the whole way."

The Danger
Ethnic Tensions Erupt Into Strife

Everywhere, the point is the same: Africa cannot just transplant foreign models, like the parliamentary system, and hope it will take root in native soil.

"It's a mistake to copy Western democracies because it's artificial," observed Cyril Goungounga, an engineer and national assembly deputy in Burkina Faso. "Look at the U.S. You elect a President. He's in office for four years, eight years. Then he's out. That's what the Constitution says."

"We have a constitution too," he said. "But it doesn't work. It's just a piece of paper. Because we have two civilizations here. The Western one on top where everything is fine and differences are submerged in talk of national unity. And a parallel one underneath, an African one where ethnic groups are a reality."

The "reality" is readily apparent when it reaches the point of armed conflict. For decades, the conventional wisdom was that Africa was the scene of so many wars because the superpowers were fighting each other through their client states. But now that the superpowers have withdrawn their sponsorship, many of the conflicts are continuing. The reason, experts say, is that they have a strong ethnic component.

In some countries, like Liberia and Somalia, ethnic turmoil came in the wake of victories by insurgents. In others, like Angola and the southern Sudan, ideological differences have largely dropped away and the contending factions are becoming more sharply defined by ethnicity or religion.

What's more, new outbreaks of tribal violence and "ethnic cleansing" are erupting in backwaters where

161

Africa, Politically

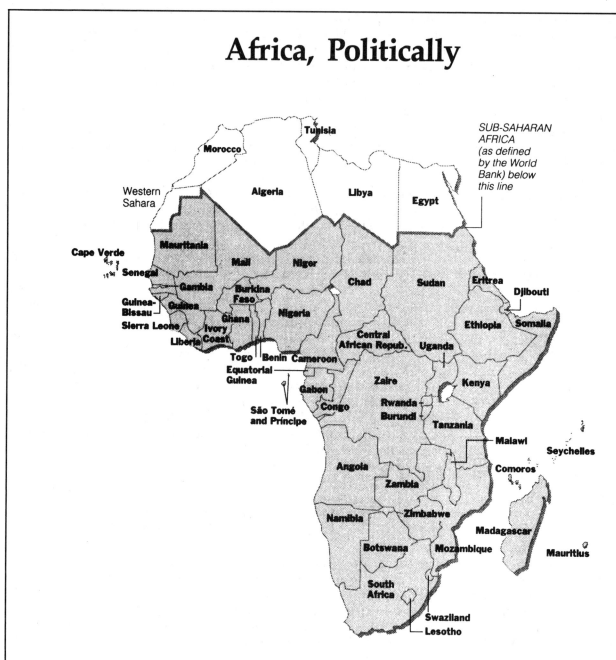

SUB-SAHARAN AFRICA (as defined by the World Bank) below this line

ANGOLA
Rich in resources but racked by civil war, now in its 19th year. Peace talks muddling along in Lusaka, Zambia. José Eduardo dos Santos is the current leader.

BENIN
First French-speaking country to successfully navigate the shoals from dictatorship to multiparty state.

BOTSWANA
Long an island of relative prosperity and democracy in a once-troubled region of black-white, East-West conflicts.

BURKINA FASO
Desperately poor, drifting since the 1987 coup that killed the radical, charismatic military leader, Thomas Sankara. Blaise Compaoré is the current leader.

BURUNDI
Scene of recurring tribal massacres, lost its chance for reconciliation with last year's coup that killed first Hutu president.

CAMEROON
Split between French- and English-speakers, fighting with Nigeria and the World Bank, ruled by a corrupt, ethnically based and repressive elite.

CAPE VERDE
A nation of volcanic Atlantic islands that abandoned Marxist economics but needs aid to survive; chronically drought-stricken.

CENTRAL AFRICAN REPUBLIC
Undergoing a difficult but so far successful passage to democracy. Former Emperor Jean-Bédel Bokassa, now out of jail, wanders in white robes, crazy.

CHAD
Long in the shadow of Libya's territorial claims, rife with jockeying among clans; President Idriss Déby's guards commit human rights violations.

COMOROS
Had been run for years by a French mercenary who helped South Africa evade sanctions; still the scene of intrigue that undercuts elections.

CONGO
Held elections to replace longtime Marxist dictator, unsettled by fighting between ethnic militias; Israelis in charge of presidential security.

DJIBOUTI
Elections inspired by Paris uncovered deep divisions between two main groups, Afars and Issas; French maintain large military presence.

EQUATORIAL GUINEA
One of Africa's true horrors, now ruled by the nephew of Macias Nguema Biyoko, who once mowed down opponents in soccer stadium as rock music was played.

ERITREA
The only country to change colonial-era boundaries, after a 30-year independence war with Ethiopia; self-reliant and tough.

ETHIOPIA
Threw out its brutal Soviet-backed dictator in 1991; the old empire is breaking into ethnic groupings to prepare for more elections.

GABON
Swimming in oil and also swimming in discontent and debt; the longtime leader Omar Bongo's claim to have won December election widely disbelieved.

GAMBIA
The English-speaking sliver in French-speaking Senegal has long practiced multiparty politics.

GHANA
Africa's first in everything in the postwar wave of decolonization—in revolving-door coups, in hitting bottom and in climbing back through I.M.F. program. Jerry J. Rawlings is the current leader.

GUINEA
Saw a hotly contested election; still unable to shake off legacy of Ahmed Sékou Touré's African socialism, which bankrupted a once-rich land.

GUINEA-BISSAU
The Government has allowed a multiparty system to descend slowly, almost reluctantly, on a backwater former Portuguese colony.

IVORY COAST
Former economic "miracle" now down on its luck; the new President, Henri Konan Bedié, jails journalists for writing insulting articles.

KENYA
Heading downhill fast under Jomo Kenyatta's successor, Daniel arap Moi, who plays tribal politics, crushes dissidents and permits widespread corruption.

LESOTHO
The tiny kingdom surrounded by South Africa has byzantine politics and a restive, underpaid army that killed the Deputy Prime Minister in April.

LIBERIA
Civil war has claimed more than 150,000 lives, brought in an all-African intervention force; peace talks reduce fighting but it continues.

MADAGASCAR
Had successful elections, lengthy but free; the new President, Albert Zafy, faces huge economic decline after 20 years of one-man rule.

MALAWI
With the old tyrant in a homburg hat, Hastings Kamuzu Banda, struck down at the polls, his successor, Bakili Muluzi, promises reforms.

MALI
The revolution that dumped the dictator Moussa Traoré has given way to elected Government, but it faces poverty and uprisings by Tuaregs in the north.

MAURITANIA
Opposition boycott of elections has kept old powers in control, the Maurs still dominate the blacks, and the desert encroaches.

MAURITIUS
Its economic growth rates, stability and assiduous regard for multiparty democracy have long made it an island in more ways than one.

MOZAMBIQUE
At long last the civil war is winding down and a peace agreement is holding; everything depends on demobilization of armies and elections.

NAMIBIA
Under its new Swapo leadership, it is practicing democratic Government and market economics; future is closely tied to South Africa next door.

NIGER
A multiparty system voted into place in 1992; Government is fighting on all fronts—rebel Tuaregs, falling uranium prices, growing Islamic militance.

NIGERIA
The swaggering giant of West Africa reneged on elections after they were held; still ruled by confused and rapacious military Government. Gen. Ibrahim Babangida is the current leader.

RWANDA
Africa's hell, pure and simple, with prospects ahead of more grisly killings by either Hutus or Tutsis, barring outside intervention.

SAO TOMÉ AND PRINCIPE
A smooth democratic transition, helped by much aid from France and Portugal, has a decade of mismanagement to overcome.

SENEGAL
Long a multiparty democracy, has been unsettled by February riots over devaluation; two principal opposition leaders held in jail without trial.

SEYCHELLES
Its strongman, France Albert René, won 1991 election; the biggest problem for the island paradise is a decline in tourism caused by European recession.

SIERRA LEONE
Besieged in the east by Liberian-supported rebels, lacking in popular support, a corrupt military Government has promised civilian rule.

SOMALIA
The case study in the failure of international intervention; Gen. Mohammed Farah Aidid is still a power, the clans are still at each other's throats.

SOUTH AFRICA
The recent election serves as a model throughout Africa; leaders admire President Nelson Mandela's courage in embracing the opposition.

SUDAN
Africa's largest country is devastated by Africa's longest war, the Islamic Government in the north against the Christian-animist rebels in south.

SWAZILAND
King Mswati II is still following a conservative course of maintaining traditional practices but with a slight opening to democratic principles.

TANZANIA
Facing a long uphill climb to economic recovery; former President Julius K. Nyerere's high-minded but disastrous rule is receding; elections scheduled.

TOGO
A popular push for democracy was thwarted by sleight of hand from the longtime dictator, Gnassingbé Éyadéma; turmoil and ethnic tensions result.

UGANDA
Trying to overcome a two-decade curse of dictatorship and ethnic warfare, President Yoweri Museveni is experimenting with single-"movement" politics.

ZAIRE
The gold standard in corruption and mismanagement, the personality cult rule of Mobutu Sese Seko is gradually fading away amid anarchy and poverty.

ZAMBIA
Kenneth D. Kaunda surprisingly lost elections and surprisingly turned over power; new President, Frederick J. T. Chiluba, beset by burden of economic catastrophes.

ZIMBABWE
An economic and political success under President Robert Mugabe, though still fraught with tensions involving whites, parties and land.

foreigners rarely venture to tell the outside world about it—places like eastern Zaire, northern Ghana, and the north of Mali and Niger.

Togo is a prime example of a country where the step toward democracy proved inflammatory. For years President Gnassingbé Éyadéma based his dictatorial rule upon his own group, the Kabye from the north. Through clever manipulation, he has managed to cling to power through two elections by splintering and outfoxing the opposition, based largely upon southern tribes like the Ewe. Now his dictatorship still reigns, and ethnic strife is so high that several hundred thousands have fled to neighboring countries.

Scholars point out that the ethnic divide has been there all along but sometimes was hidden.

"Many military coups of the 1960's and 70's had an ethnically based component," said Donald L. Horowitz, author of Ethnic Groups in Conflict (University of California Press, 1985). "After the coup things settled down in a quieter pattern. It didn't mean ethnicity had been suppressed. It meant competition had been suppressed. So in the early 80's it felt as if a lot of these conflicts had gone away while in fact they were simply driven underground."

Two countries are in fact experimenting with new political systems to try to overcome the legacy of ethnicity.

One is Uganda, where President Yoweri Mouseveni, who came to power as head of a rebel military group in 1986, is deeply conscious of the country's agony of the last 23 years. The despotic regimes of both Idi Amin and Milton Obote were thinly disguised masks for tit-for-tat ethnic subjugation and slaughter.

The 50-year-old President argues that multiparty systems were created by industrial societies and fit them because they tend to divide along fluid lines of class. But in pre-industrial Africa, countries split vertically, along rigid tribal lines, and so competing parties can lead to group warfare.

His broadly based National Resistance Movement suspended party politics and instead is trying to promulgate a system for grass roots participation through "national resistance councils." It claims to be a sort of grand coalition, though critics charge it is a one-party state by another name. Voting was held in March to elect a constituent assembly. The delegates are largely N.R.M. supporters and may well decide to try the new system for five years and then hold a referendum.

The opposite approach is unfolding in Ethiopia, where the Marxist dictator, Mengistu Haile Mariam, was overthrown in 1991. Ethiopia has long been an uneasy assemblage of regions dominated by distinct groups and under the sway of the Amhara in the center. In the north the Eritreans successfully prosecuted a 30-year war and became the only secessionist movement to achieve an independent state in Africa.

The example has not been lost on other groups, such as the Tigreans and the Oromo. Now temporarily under the fractious Ethiopian People's Revolutionary Democratic Front, Ethiopia appears to be headed toward a federal system with strong regional governments. By their very nature they would become avowedly ethnic—another first for the continent.

The Legacy
Closing the Book On
One-Man Rule

The rush toward new democratic forms of rule has been called by Colin Legum, a British scholar and writer on Africa, a "second independence." The era of one-man rule that began when hastily constructed parliamentary regimes collapsed in the 1960's was widely conceded to be disastrous.

Though these dictators managed to hold their countries together, often by draconian means, that was about all they did. They were often corrupt, like Mobutu Sese Seko of Zaire, or monomaniacally doctrin-

aire, like Ahmed Sékou Touré of Guinea, or mad like Jean-Bédel Bokassa of the Central African Empire.

Even when they were relatively benign and paternalistic, like Félix Houphouët-Boigny of the Ivory Coast, they favored their own groups, in his case the Baoule. With no check on their power they often pursued ruinous economic policies. By the time Houphouët-Boigny died in December, after squandering millions on grandiose monuments, the Ivory Coast, once hailed as the "economic miracle" of West Africa, was $16 billion in Debt.

For over a decade there were only four multiparty states on the continent—Mauritius, Gambia, Senegal and Botswana. When the political map began to change in 1990, it did so with a vengeance, prompted in part by the dramatic spectacle of Communist regimes falling like bowling pins throughout Eastern Europe.

The causes were both internal and external. Growing economic discontent gave rise to opposition movements and emboldened them, especially among hundreds of thousands of young graduates who could find no work and saw little reason to respect doddering leaders. In February 1990 France told its client states that it would no longer prop up single-party governments. Then in June Britain told its former colonies that henceforth aid would be tied to political pluralism and good government.

The unraveling began with Benin, a sliver of a West African country that had been under military-type Marxist rule for 17 years. Under pressure, the Beninese strongman, President Mathieu Kérékou, convened a "national conference" of eminent citizens to recommend reforms. The conference promptly declared itself sovereign and set off on a course that led to elections and Mr. Kérékou's defeat.

By 1993, nine countries—all of them French-speaking—had held such conferences. Six of them resulted in a change in regime, most notably in Congo, Mali and Niger. In Zambia, the longtime "African humanist" leader, Kenneth D. Kaunda, was forced to hold an election and when he lost he gracefully stepped down.

The process has been a failure elsewhere. In Nigeria, the military government, which had been laying plans for six years to return to civilian rule, abruptly reneged on the promise after presidential elections in June. In Ghana and Burkina Faso, military leaders who came to power in coups were able to sail through elections and gain an imprimatur of legitimacy.

Cameroon and Gabon have made no strides toward democracy. And in Zaire, President Mobutu has successfully confounded the opposition during four years of maneuvering that has seen two competing prime ministers, two Cabinets and two constitutions—a development aptly labeled "le doublement d'institutions."

The Holdout
Kenya's Leader Defies the Trend

Perhaps nowhere has the failure been as flagrant as in Kenya. President Daniel arap Moi, a 69-year-old given to seeing plots in the air, has been an implacable opponent of democracy, warning that it would breed ethnic strife. Meanwhile, he has flagrantly played the tribal card himself, ousting the once-powerful Kikuyu from all positions of influence and replacing them with members of his own Kalenjin and related groups.

Forced by a cutoff of foreign aid to call elections in December 1992, President Moi split the opposition, which divided on ethnic lines, and won what most diplomats view as rigged balloting. Opponents, whom the President once called "rats," have been harassed, jailed and even killed. Thirty-six members of the opposition were arrested last year and 14 so far this year.

Even more unsettling has been a series of armed attacks beginning in 1991 by Kalenjin raiders against Kikuyu, Luo and Luhya communities in the lush farmland of the Rift Valley. About 1,000 people have been killed and some 250,000 run off their land. Diplomats and many Kenyans are convinced the Government is behind the raids and indeed Government figures declare publicly that what was once the "white highlands" belongs to their ethnic group.

"Kenya is sitting on a volcano," a Kikuyu said. "I don't know what would happen tomorrow if Moi chokes on a chicken bone."

All this has proved disillusioning to Africans in everyday life. "Look at Rwanda, Burundi, Zaire," said Dr. Aliou Boly, a young Ph.D. in business management in Ouagadougou.

"If that's democratization, I'm not for it. Look at Togo—worse off than before. Benin, Mali, Zambia. They've all had elections but it didn't change anything. There's a new elite but it behaves the same as the old one."

The political liberalization means that many countries where dissent once meant courting imprisonment or execution, now have a free and at times boisterous press. There is an increasingly independent judiciary and even functioning human rights groups that are not afraid to post their names on their doors.

But there are still obstacles on the road to full democracy. Sometimes there are too many opposition parties—Zaire has 200 of them—for the system to function. Sometimes the levers of power and state-controlled television and radio are temptations too strong for an incumbent to resist. And many politicians have learned how to win an election, but not how to lose one.

"No country in Africa since the winds of change started blowing four years ago has really achieved democracy," Mr. Moyo said. "The triggering of change has led to political liberalization but not to democracy.

"Democracy is much more far-reaching. It requires changes in institutions. They have to become strong and competing and they have to recognize each other's legitimacy. That's far down the line. Who knows how far it really is?"

South Africa: Putting Democracy to Work

"South Africa's accomplishments have so far surpassed most expectations, including those of the masses still waiting for tangible evidence that majority rule will deliver the benefits for which they struggled all those years."

KENNETH W. GRUNDY

KENNETH W. GRUNDY *is the Marcus A. Hanna Professor of Political Science at Case Western Reserve University. His most recent book is* South Africa: Domestic Crisis and Global Challenge *(Boulder, Colo.: Westview, 1991).*

An open, competitive general election is as good a place as any to begin—for launching a democracy and for analyzing the partisan political winds in contemporary South Africa. For the record, from April 26 through 28 (the 29th in some areas), nearly 20 million voters participated in South Africa's first nonracial national election. Nineteen parties offered candidates for the National Assembly (a legislature that also sits jointly with the Senate as a constituent assembly to draft a new constitution). Nine provincial legislatures were also elected.

The election was a gigantic educational exercise. Because only white voters and a limited number of Indian and "Coloured" (mixed race) citizens had any direct experience with national elections, people needed instruction in the mechanics and the meaning of the process, and reassurance about how the secret ballot worked. The electoral machinery—the ballots, 80,000 voting booths at 9,000 voting stations, 5,000 election observers (2,000 from abroad), and 190,000 election workers—had to be coordinated by a newly formed Independent Electoral Commission, which had been given just three months to prepare for the polling. The logistics became even more complicated with the Inkatha Freedom Party's last-minute decision to participate. There were glitches, but the election went off smoothly and without rancor. The world watched, impressed by the patience and tolerance voters showed, and the nation savored a well-earned sense of accomplishment.

The campaign, too, went well, though it was not perfect. The radical right and the militant left did not take part. Inkatha, at first critical if not hostile, did not join the process until one week before the balloting. Al worked to undermine the election and to disparage the results. In some neighborhoods, townships, and regions, workers from certain parties could not safely speak out. Even among the participating parties, a few local leaders sought to keep the "enemy" off their turf.

When the results were in, the African National Congress under Nelson Mandela had captured some 63 percent of the vote, winning 252 of 400 seats in the National Assembly; the Afrikaner-dominated National Party of President F. W. de Klerk was a distant second; and Inkatha had placed third. The ANC also emerged as the majority party in seven provinces, while Inkatha prevailed in Natal and the National Party in the Western Cape.

From afar this looks like a workable multiparty system. In reality, however, power is parceled out locally, and the picture at the local level sometimes resembles a checkerboard of one-party enclaves with little pretense of diversity. Nevertheless, internal monitors and foreign observers endorsed the election and declared it essentially free and fair. This, then, is the foundation on which South Africa's democracy will be built. In compliance with several multiparty agreements leading up to the election, including an interim constitution adopted in late 1993, South African leaders began the task of hammering together a viable system of government.

The first order of business was to create a national unity government that would guide the new South Africa through its first five years. Mandela was elected president by the National Assembly without opposition. Parties that had won 80 or more assembly seats were entitled to designate a deputy president. The ANC named Thabo Mbeki first deputy president, and the National Party chose de Klerk.

The new government is composed of 27 ministers. Six are from the National Party and 3 from Inkatha, including its leader, Mangosuthu Gatsha Buthelezi, who heads the home affairs ministry; the rest are ANC members. (According to the interim constitution, each party that received 5 percent or more of the vote was entitled to join the cabinet.) This lineup is very much the product of hard-nosed negotiations, as much within the ANC as between the eligible parties.

The provisions for minority party representation are a significant departure from the winner-take-all system normally associated with parliamentary government. The president is obliged to consult with the deputy presidents on a wide range of matters, but they cannot veto his decisions; similarly, he does not have to obtain the cabinet's consensus to carry out his central executive functions. However, the "consensus-seeking spirit underlying the concept of a government of national unity," as a pre-election agreement put it, reflects a commitment to reconciliation and cooperation on the part of the parties.

The task of governing in the new South Africa has proved complex and vexing. Removing the legal superstructure of apartheid has been relatively simple, but apartheid's social and economic substructure and the ensuing tensions and inequities defy quick remedies. Delays in resolving long-standing grievances have provided ammunition for the government's critics and will contribute to further dissatisfaction and unrest.

UNITY AT A PRICE

South Africa's transformation has created popular expectations that would be difficult for even the most popular, practiced, and gifted government to satisfy.

SOUTH AFRICA

Capital:
Pretoria, administrative
Cape Town, legislative
Bloemfontein, judicial

*Pretoria-Witwatersrand-Vereeniging

0   100   200   300 Miles

model of parliamentary democracy, coalitions are normally fashioned when no party has a majority of seats in the legislature or when parties are so close in their goals and policy preferences they decide to cooperate to strengthen the government. In South Africa's case, the ANC has a solid majority, with 252 of 400 seats, but had agreed before the election to form a government of national unity for five years. And since constitution writing requires a two-thirds majority, the ANC must persuade additional legislators to support its proposals.

The National Party and Inkatha joined the government because they feared that if they stayed out they might be weakened and further marginalized, and because neither wanted the ANC to have unfettered control of the state machinery. Yet they are not sure what their roles in government are to be. How critical can they be? How can they avoid being used by the ANC as a rubber stamp to legitimize the dominant party's policies?

Their early experience in the government confirmed their apprehension. The National Party and Inkatha charge that their cabinet members had their responsibilities reduced, and that ANC deputy ministers were appointed to "spy" on them. In some cases their objections to ANC policies were overridden rather than used to temper policy. And the principle of proportional representation that applied to cabinet seats was not extended, they contend, to parliamentary committees or government agencies. Critics believe the ANC has taken sole credit for the reconstruction and development program on which government policy is based. In short, the role and powers of the cooperating parties are being worked out on the run, and the minority partners are not satisfied with them. (In December Inkatha and National Party hard-liners separately be-

The idea of a government of national unity was adopted to buy time for the country's new leaders and to co-opt centers of opposition to the ANC. The ANC, realizing its governing policies would require sacrifices from the prosperous white community and knowing it needed the National Party to help implement these demands, agreed to bring the Nationalists into government; the personal chemistry between Mandela and de Klerk also contributed to the spirit of consensus. The National Party saw the new government as enabling its senior people to continue to play an important part in the power structure. Strictly speaking, the national unity government is not a coalition government. In the Westminster

gan to press their party leaders to withdraw from the government and go into open opposition.)

All the parties are feeling their way through this transitional scheme. They do not want to jeopardize the current arrangements or the climate of national consensus, but they also do not want to be taken advantage of or to weaken their hand in any emerging constitutional order. As several commentators have said, it is not so much the results of the first election that matter, but what happens in the second election, which is set for 1999. All are deeply aware that how they perform during this transition will affect their long-range prospects for greater power.

For most South Africans, the first five years of majority rule are a test of the ANC. Social life, the economy, crime, political violence, jobs, and the environment will all be laid at the door of the ANC-dominated government, though the party has little control over them. The government must work around an economy and social order systematically constructed by the Nationalists over 46 years of apartheid. Nor does the ANC have total control of the machinery of state. The state security apparatus—defense, police, and intelligence—is still dominated by agencies and figures identified with the apartheid regime, and much of the civil service is occupied by entrenched bureaucrats who were given five-year job guarantees in the pre-election negotiations. Even if the ANC were free to install replacements, it and the black community would be hard-pressed to find qualified personnel for all top positions. And how is the ANC going to finance its costly proposals without bankrupting government or scaring off businesses? Health care, housing, and job creation demand funds that, if raised in the white community, might not only jeopardize reconciliation but precipitate the flight of capital, managerial experience, and technical skills.

RECONSTRUCTING AND DEVELOPING

The government's social and economic agenda is embodied in the Reconstruction and Development Plan. The plan has undergone many changes since it was first drafted before the elections, and is still being debated. In some policy areas the resulting document still lacks specificity. A good deal of the wrangling in government has been between ministries competing for larger shares of the budget and for priority among plan projects. During his first three months in office, Mandela identified 22 projects to get the plan started and build momentum for change, pressing for land reform, redistribution, and restitution; electrification; improvements in rural water and sanitation; free health services for pregnant women and children under six; construction of housing and clinics; and promotion of agriculture and industry.

Progress has been slow, but the plan is now starting to move beyond the draft white paper and joint planning committee stages. But the desired transformation is enormous in magnitude, and cannot be brought about overnight, even in the best of circumstances.

Housing provides a good example. South Africa's housing backlog has been estimated at 1.35 million units. There are 9 million essentially homeless people in the country, most packed into the shack settlements that ring every sizable town and city. Squatters invade land set aside for low-income housing and delay construction. They occupy open land in affluent suburbs as well as near the townships, and have moved into empty buildings in city centers. Clashes between squatters and the authorities and local residents are commonplace. The government's plan promises 200,000 new homes every year for the next five years, but it is not clear what quality of housing it favors.

To add to the problems, millions of occupants of state housing refuse to pay rent and service fees; boycotts launched during the apartheid years have informally continued since the new government came to power. Moreover, in some townships law and order has collapsed. The culture of protest is entrenched, and to some still seems justified in dealing with local state agencies not yet fully transformed from their apartheid-era incarnations. Mandela insists that people start paying, but his pleas have not stirred compliance.

Mandela's first minister of housing, former Communist Party leader Joe Slovo, did his best to focus attention on the housing crisis, but just as his ministry was beginning to launch its program he succumbed to cancer in January. Slovo was the first cabinet minister to produce a credible plan for delivering on the ANC's campaign promises. In October and November he brought together government, financial institutions, construction companies, and civic organizations of residents and the homeless in a grand agreement for $500 million in new housing loans to township residents; in exchange, the government agreed to indemnify lenders against the payment boycotts and violence where they are building. The housing agreement is a distinctively new South African social contract: holistic, integrated, and involving leaders from across the social spectrum. It is a model understanding leading in the direction of the emergence of "civil society." And the ANC sees private ownership and private entrepreneurship (corporate as well as individual sweat equity) as the engines of change, spurred by an aggressive state leadership that virtually told the bankers, either you take the initiative and exercise social responsibility or the state will step in and force you to attend to the needs of the disadvantaged. The private financial institutions decided to cooperate.

POLITICS AS INVOLVEMENT

In each vital policy area—economic growth and job creation, land reform, health, education, infrastructure, crime—comprehensive negotiations are going forward that draw in almost anyone with a direct interest or who might make a difference. Difficult questions are wrestled with: What and how much is to be done? In what sequence? When? By whom? Who is in charge? Who is to pay? How much? The process has proved extremely time consuming, but when done carefully, it establishes a sound basis for cooperation and things are more likely to get done as planned.

Yet as South Africa stands ready to move beyond the strategizing stage, it is hampered by officials disagreeing with each other, jockeying for political or private gain, or dragging their feet because they oppose the development plan's outlines. Necessary government institutions have not yet been staffed, funded, or in some cases even established. Almost every existing government department must be reorganized, redirected, its resources rechanneled to meet the totally different tasks the government of national unity is setting it. In addition, too many local governments are ineffective, and chaos reigns in some provincial governments. Nevertheless, things are moving along, and where there are inspired leaders (Slovo was one, along with Kader Asmal at the Ministry of Water Affairs and Forestry, Derek Hanekom at Land Affairs, Trevor Manuel at Trade and Industry, Dullah Omar at Justice) progress has been visible.

But President Mandela and his lieutenants must still call for forbearance and austerity. In his address to the national conference of the ANC in December, Mandela admitted, "South Africa is not yet out of the woods." Be proud of our achievements, he said, but remember that "democratic forces in our country have captured only elements of political power." Social change is taking "longer than the situation demanded." By and large the people have been understanding, and realize that revolution is difficult. The predicted grassroots impatience has been muted. But though the national unity government and Mandela in particular receive high approval ratings in public opinion polls, no one knows how much time they have before frustrations boil over.

Considering South Africa's history of violence between groups and deep inequities in wealth, power, and opportunity, and considering the ANC's commitment to making major changes quickly in the lives of the masses, it is impressive how a consensus has been forged. Tangible results have come slowly, but positive changes in attitude are apparent. The poor have not risen up, and whites have not deserted the country. The police and the armed forces have remained largely obedient to the new government's dictates. Political violence has been reduced, though ordinary crime has continued at previous levels, if not increased.

Government has worked to keep the people informed of and relatively engaged in the policy process. Mandela has gone into the townships and conducted "people's forums" to learn firsthand about citizens'

goals and grievances. At base, the most remarkable aspect of the new order is the transformation of political discourse. In this highly stratified society, the leaders of most groups support the reconstruction and development plan. This does not mean that they agree on all its provisions, but that they accept that it is necessary to work together, that the country's resources should be redistributed, and that significant social transformation is required to see South Africa through this transitional period. They may argue about how and when this can best be accomplished, but not about whether it should be. Thus the language of politics has, by and large, ceased to be ideological, and become overwhelmingly pragmatic (as, for example, in the debate over privatization and nationalization).

This mood change is likely to last for as long as the ANC and its top leaders display reason, integrity, and goodwill. Mandela must ruthlessly root out corruption and Stalinist tendencies from government and his party where they occur. If the people sense that officials are using their positions for private gain, the still fragile consensus in the country will fall apart. Interest groups will scramble to bring short-term advantage to their constituents, and cynicism will replace cooperation.

In October Nobel Peace Prize winner Archbishop Desmond Tutu attacked the high salaries officials were awarding themselves, quipping that the new government had stopped the gravy train only long enough to clamber aboard. At first his views were criticized by some in the ANC, but eventually Mandela forced pay cuts. At the ANC's national conference, the president challenged his party: "We need to launch a campaign to set the country on a new moral footing." He cited recent problems—corruption, nonpayment for services, the blurred line between legal and illegal behavior in public office, and the "rampant pillaging of public funds" during the final days under de Klerk. But awkward and possibly corrosive cases have embarrassed the unity government. Allan Boesak, recently named ambassador to the United Nations in Geneva, was forced to withdraw after accusations that he had directed funds from European donors for his personal use. The immensely popular Winnie Mandela, the president's estranged wife, has allegedly been involved in dubious diamond deals in Angola. Joe Matthews, a deputy justice minister and Inkatha member, is wanted for fraud and theft from a trust fund in Botswana. Once regional governments get in gear, the opportunities for corruption ramify. How best should the central government oversee the regional governments without endangering federalism? Yet malfeasance at lower levels undermines the aims and achievements at the center, **bringing all government into disrepute.**

The ANC's style of governance requires a broad and deep pool of leadership relying on consultation, popular understanding, and mandates from below. For many ANC leaders, especially those tempered by the struggle within South Africa in the 1980s, process is as important as outcome. Mandela warned the December party conference of the "danger that the organization could turn into a conveyor belt of government decisions." But there is also a danger that the ANC, falling under the control of populist radicals, could become "a force steeped in [the] resistance mode." The country is engaged in a difficult balancing act in which the people must identify with the leaders and the leaders must reflect the wishes of the people. This interactive style is unlike anything South Africa has ever experienced, but "The People Shall Govern" is a slogan many take seriously.

Yet the ANC lacks the pool of talent it needs to accomplish this, and the financial resources to build one. A large proportion of ANC activists have been drawn into government, and experienced leaders have had little time to identify, energize, and train a younger cadre of leaders. "We managed to get into government," one ANC official put it, "but it almost cost us our organization."

This leads to a troubling question: What happens after Mandela? The prodigiously energetic 76-year-old president stands like a colossus astride the political scene. But the competition within the ANC in the selection of a deputy president after the election, and events at the December party conference, reveal party divisions and the personalities vying to replace the leader. The party's national executive, which is relatively close to Mandela, is largely a coterie that ran the ANC from exile, plus a number of leaders brought in by popular acclaim at national party meetings. Those identified with the United Democratic Front (an umbrella organization of more than 600 local and national civic organizations) or with the most militant sectors of the party generally did not fare well in gaining top national positions, though they did better at the regional level. The lion's share of senior cabinet posts went to the "pragmatic" or consensus-building wing of the ANC.

Yet at the 1994 national conference a "leftist" camp of populists, led by trade unionists and spokespeople for militant youth, asserted itself. In voting for the national executive, delegates rejected the idea of a slate of nominees handpicked by Mandela and cast ballots for their own favorites; thus Peter Mokaba, former head of the party's Youth League, and Winnie Mandela, leader of the Women's League, garnered the third- and fifth-highest number of votes. The left is still predomi-

nantly outside government; it feels the ANC's leaders have given too much away to the National Party in negotiations, are not forceful enough in dealing with Inkatha, and are preoccupied with reconciliation and with appealing to foreign investors and donors. Government is moving too slowly, leftists say, in bringing the benefits of political power to the masses.

The leadership struggle between Deputy President Mbeki and Cyril Ramaphosa, the secretary general of the ANC, is a personality contest, not an ideological or a policy one. Ramaphosa eschewed a cabinet position (after failing in his bid for the deputy presidency) and instead took up the reins of the party to ready it for mobilizing the people for the local elections expected in late 1995 and then the 1999 national elections. It looks increasingly likely that Mbeki will be Mandela's successor, but most South Africans hope that Mandela will continue as leader. Simply put, there are no obvious Mandelas on the horizon. And the ANC is in sufficient ferment that the factional lineup can shift before Mandela is ready to step down.

AFTER DEMOCRACY, THE HARD PART

While last April's elections were a marvelous beginning, elections alone do not a democracy make; they are a necessary but not a sufficient component of the democratic process. What seems vital at this point—and ANC leaders recognize this—is that the government continuously engage in keeping in touch with its base.

South Africa's accomplishments have so far surpassed most expectations, including those of the masses still waiting for tangible evidence that majority rule will deliver the benefits for which they struggled all those years. The poor have not revolted, though the culture of protest is still alive and many are hostile to reconciliation. The whites have not fled, though many dislike a "black" government. The security establishment has not undermined government. The unity government has avoided major mistakes. But all this is what did not happen.

On a more positive note, politics has been transformed and a climate of consensus has emerged, with some important exceptions. Overall, it has been a good opening for the ANC–government of national unity team.[1] South Africa still enjoys a season of goodwill, but success will ultimately depend on the government's ability to implement the reconstruction and development plan, thus expanding the economy, reducing crime and violence, creating jobs, and providing services for its constituents. Failing these achievements, no government, no matter how committed and popular, can last for long without relying on coercion.

---

[1]A more negative perspective is provided by R. W. Johnson, "Drift the Beloved Country," *World Press Review*, January 1995, pp. 8–11.

MEXICO

The Slippery Road to Stability

Nora Lustig

Nora Lustig is a senior fellow in the Brookings Foreign Policy Studies program. She is the author of Mexico: The Remaking of an Economy *(Brookings, 1993).*

Mexico, slowly emerging from its worst economic crisis in decades, is in the midst of a difficult political transition. America's neighbor to the south is struggling to break free of its authoritarian past to become a true democracy, complete with public accountability, clean and fair elections, and the rule of law. The path of political change, never expected to be smooth, became more unpredictable when, less than a month after President Ernesto Zedillo took office on December 1, 1994, a peso devaluation drove the economy into a sharp crisis.

Today political turbulence is one of the main threats to Mexico's financial stability and economic recovery. Likewise, a weak economy and volatile financial markets reduce the chances of a successful transition to democracy. A poor economic performance weakens Zedillo. And a weak government will be unlikely to be able to implement the changes necessary to produce genuine democracy and, especially, the rule of law. In addition, continued economic crisis might breed a political reaction that could jeopardize Mexico's fragile financial stability and the economic reforms under way to assure recovery.

Encouraging Signs

There are certainly reasons to be optimistic.

In early 1996 the economic picture brightened—a welcome relief after the bleak performance of 1995, when output contracted by an estimated 7 percent. After a surge in volatility last fall, the financial markets stabilized. The peso appreciated slightly, domestic interest rates and the open unemployment rate fell, and Mexico gained renewed access to private international capital markets. Most economic forecasts for 1996 chart a recovery, but not a brisk one. The official prediction is for output to grow 3 percent in 1996. Most predictions, though, are for 2 percent growth, practically stagnant in per capita terms.

On the political front, the government has shown its willingness to move forward with reform. President Zedillo has repeatedly stated, and taken initial steps on, his commitment to decentralizing power, fostering the separation between government and the long-ruling Institutional Revolutionary Party (PRI), completing ongoing electoral reforms, and strengthening the traditionally weak powers of Congress and the courts. Perhaps most important, Zedillo has indicated his intention to distance himself from the official party and, most significantly, to break with the practice, followed by all past presidents—of handpicking his successor. Zedillo's appointment of Antonio Lozano, a member of the opposition National Action Party (PAN), as attorney general is another sign of his apparent intent to govern Mexico by the rule of law. The arrest last year of Raul Salinas, brother of former president Carlos Salinas, in connection with the 1994 assassination of PRI Secretary-General Jose Francisco Ruiz Massieu was a powerful signal that the government was willing to break the unwritten rule of granting legal immunity to a former president and his family.

Political parties, civic organizations, and even the armed Zapatista rebels in Chiapas seem, judged by their actions, to favor a peaceful transition. Most local elections since early in 1995 have been free of violence or post-election rows, and their results, even when the PRI has been the loser, have been respected. The political crisis in Chiapas precipitated by a violent peasant uprising early in 1994 is being handled through peaceful negotiations. And the political parties and the government are in the process of negotiating the new terms that will rule the electoral processes, the relationship between the government and its party, and the allocation of power among the executive, the legislative, and the judicial powers and the federal and state and local governments.

But despite these bright spots, political reform is still vulnerable and financial stability fragile.

5. TRANSITIONS

Party Bosses Do Not Like Democracy

A primary threat to Mexico's democratic transition is the so-called old guard of the PRI, those who stand to lose if the political system becomes more open and competitive and if corruption is no longer tolerated. Members of the old guard, some now governors or leaders of blocs within the PRI, are well organized, have followers, and have access to financial resources.

They could create unmanageable conflicts within the party and exert considerable influence on its actions and programs. In exchange for their support, they could force even a well-intentioned Zedillo to look the other way while elections in some states continue to be fraudulent and while local governments continue their corrupt practices. The PRI governor of Tabasco, for example, though accused of spending outrageously far beyond Mexico's legal campaign limit, has successfully resisted pressure from the federal government to resign. The incident may be the first of more to come. In that case, Mexico's political picture would be mixed, with democratic practices being fully implemented in some areas, geographic and functional, and the old pattern of patronage and authoritarianism remaining in others. But what pattern will dominate cannot be answered yet.

Ironically, if Zedillo carries out his promise to give state and local governments more powers and financial resources, allowing them to raise more revenues locally, he could also increase the resources and autonomy of the local bosses and *caciques*. Any moves toward decentralization must therefore be accompanied by democratization. There is a danger that decentralization will not help political reform if local governments cannot be held accountable.

The PRI in Crisis

Together with the PRI's difficulty in coming to terms with political reform, revelations surrounding the investigations of two 1994 political assassinations and the economic crisis have touched off a crisis within the PRI itself. If the party's current crisis is not solved, the old guard is likely to be more successful in opposing reform.

One facet of the PRI crisis is financial. Long dependent on contributions from (or raised through) the government, the party is ill-prepared to find alternatives. It now faces the challenge of organizing to raise money. In this process, one particular danger is the temptation, on the part of some militants, to turn to "donations" from unsavory sources, such as narco-traffickers.

The party is also in the midst of an identity crisis. For many decades, the party, a product of the Mexican Revolution, endorsed a closed, largely state-led economy. The market-oriented reforms, particularly trade liberalization and privatization, introduced in the mid-1980s by President Miguel de la Madrid and his successor Carlos Salinas, were viewed with deep suspicion by most within the party. Although the prestige that Mexico won, particularly under Salinas, had attracted a number of PRI militants, the current economic crisis is raising renewed hostility. PRI candidates in next year's legislative elections know they will face an electorate ready to blame the crisis on the PRI government. Understandably, they will be strongly tempted to search for a platform both more congruent with the party's original ideology and more attractive to voters.

The party's morale is low. The assassination of PRI presidential candidate Luis Donaldo Colosio five months before the 1994 election was unnerving in itself, but the arrest of a presumed second gunman in March of last year gave support to the hypothesis that the assassination was the result of a plot. Though the second gunman has not been prosecuted and no one has been formally accused of orchestrating a plot, the public is convinced not only that there was a plot, but that the intellectual authors of the crime came from within the system itself.

Public rumors that former President Salinas or his foes were behind the plot inevitably create a tense atmosphere in the party since no one can be sure whom to trust or side with. The loss of prestige of former President Salinas following the peso devaluation of December 1994 and, in particular, the arrest of his brother Raul, first in connection with the assassination of Ruis Massieu and later for holding huge bank accounts outside Mexico under a false name, has only made matters worse.

Under these circumstances, the PRI could be ripe for a takeover by disaffected elements who promise to restore confidence, resources, and leadership. Such a takeover could pose severe problems for Zedillo, who would somehow have to govern and carry on the difficult political transition without being able to count on party support. And negotiating to win that support could cost Zedillo dearly.

In any case, discontent within the PRI has important implications for the consolidation of democracy. The "arm's length" relationship with the party exercised by Zedillo during his first year in office is likely to backfire later. In the upcoming months, the challenge for Zedillo is to work *with* his party in a number of crucial areas: in defining a platform that is congruent for both sides, organizing the party for fundraising, and making the party's internal rules of candidate selection more "bottom-up" and transparent. A reorganized, modernized, and energized PRI is all but essential to a successful transition.

> **TODAY POLITICAL TURBULENCE IS ONE OF THE MAIN THREATS TO MEXICO'S FINANCIAL STABILITY AND ECONOMIC RECOVERY. LIKEWISE, A WEAK ECONOMY AND VOLATILE FINANCIAL MARKETS REDUCE THE CHANCES OF A SUCCESSFUL TRANSITION TO DEMOCRACY.**

The Cleavage between Zedillo and Salinas

Once close allies in the struggle for economic liberalization, Zedillo and former president Salinas have been embroiled in an ugly fight. The tension between the two men reached its peak upon the arrest of Raul Salinas. Former president Salinas went on a hunger strike and demanded that Zedillo's government publicly acknowledge that he was responsible neither for the peso crisis nor for the assassination of Colosio, a rumor instigated by some of Mexico's leading columnists. Zedillo made no such public statement but sent a member of his cabinet, a former collaborator and friend of Salinas, as mediator. Following this episode the two men concluded some form of truce, whose terms for the moment remain unknown. At any rate, in March of last year Salinas left Mexico, and the issue seemed to have been put to rest.

Then last December, following the revelation of Raul Salinas's vast holdings in banks abroad, the former president wrote a long letter to the news media. In it he tried to disentangle himself from his brother's wrongdoings and accused Luis Echeverria, Mexico's president during the early 1970s, of orchestrating a plot against him. That Echeverria is actually engaged in such a plot is regarded by most observers as unlikely. Apparently the real purpose of the letter is to warn Echeverria, who publicly criticized Salinas last September, to keep quiet or risk the release of damaging information. The letter also implicitly contained a recurrent message from Salinas to Zedillo: "my enemies are your enemies." In other words, if Zedillo attacks Salinas or his family, he is strengthening a group within the system that opposes his own program of economic modernization. And Salinas is right in the sense that the more he is attacked, the more Zedillo's (and his) economic program and Zedillo himself are weakened and the old guard of the PRI strengthened.

Together with Mexico's poor economic performance and the crisis within the PRI, a rupture between Salinas and Zedillo would imperil Mexico's ongoing political transition and economic recovery. A cornered Salinas is in many respects a wildcard. As former president, Salinas probably has embarrassing, or worse, information about powerful members of the business community, the bureaucracy, and members of political parties. Last December 12, one day after NBC news reported that the U.S. government was investigating Salinas for his association with narcotics trafficking and money laundering (a report denied by Washington shortly afterwards), a rumor circulated that Salinas had written a letter naming former and current government officials and businessmen involved in shady activities. Although the next evening Salinas sent a short written statement denying writing the letter and called for public support for Zedillo, the possibility that he would implicate members of the business and political elite sent shivers down the backs of many.

In such a climate, powerful businessmen and politicians must be tempted to take their wealth out of the country, perhaps even prepare for some form of exile. If such people were to withdraw their capital in panic, the peso, financial stability, and the prospects for economic recovery could crumble.

Political Assassinations and the Rule of Law

The attorney general's arrest of a second suspect in connection with the assassination of Colosio was deeply troubling. The arrest, which reversed the finding of two former special prosecutors that Colosio had been killed by a lone assassin, raised fears of a plot.

Yet another disturbing possibility hinted at by the continuing investigation is that members of the military could be implicated in the murder.

How will the Zedillo government deal with that possibility? Getting at the truth, assuming that it is possible, poses extremely serious challenges and excruciating dilemmas for the government. If indeed the Colosio assassination was the result of a plot, what might the perpetrators be willing, and able, to do to prevent the truth from coming out? What might they do to confuse, obstruct, distort, and even impede the investigation? Not surprisingly, today Mexicans are prone to see conspiracies almost everywhere.

Are any of these scenarios ominous enough to frighten the government away from the case? Will Zedillo be forced to abandon the rule of law in perhaps the most important case in Mexico's recent history? If he does, will it damage irreparably his government's credibility? Will it also undermine the standing of the PAN, the party of the investigating attorney general? Clearly, the investigation can have very important implications for Mexico's economic and political stability.

Unfortunately, the rule of law is to a certain extent hostage to Mexico's financial vulnerability. The nation's leaders can probably not afford to uncover the questionable or illegal activities committed by prominent members of the political and business elites. The attempt to change the rules of the game too swiftly and prosecute people for past wrongdoings could trigger a wave of capital outflows large enough to threaten the fragile recovery.

Chiapas, Political Discontent, and the Military

At the moment the results of the negotiations in Chiapas are encouraging. But the equilibrium is fragile. Other tensions—those between landless peasants and the propertied, between Catholics and Protestants, between Indians and whites—could derail the peace process. Indeed, even the land redistribution measures envisioned by negotiators as part of the solution to the Chiapas conflict will not ultimately address the main cause of the uprising, which is deprivation without hope. A lasting peace will require a major effort to develop both a capable labor force and jobs.

The Mexican military have followed the instructions of the government and appear to be committed to a peaceful resolution of the Chiapas crisis. But while the increased militarization of the zone of Zapatista influence guarantees the peace by deterring the

Zapatistas from making a military move lest they be crushed, it also creates the conditions for bloodshed and violations of human rights. The military presence is also on the rise in other areas of the country where potentially similar movements, connected to the Zapatistas or not, exist. Again, the military presence can discourage other armed groups from violence. But under different circumstances, the military can be used to repress nonviolent protests, hurting innocent civilians in the process.

The possibility thus exists for Mexico to continue moving toward democracy in some areas, such as elections and the decentralization of power, but to remain repressive and authoritarian in others, particularly to be intolerant of civic, peasant, or labor organizations that reject government policies and pose a threat to financial stability.

Economic Performance and Popular Discontent

Despite the chaos produced by the financial crisis and despite important political faux pas, the government has been able to implement a tough adjustment program to counter the capital outflows that followed the peso devaluation and restore confidence in financial markets. Extensive lobbying, bargaining, and armtwisting also enabled Zedillo's government to win legislative approval of two highly controversial initiatives: increasing the value-added tax (last April) and reforming the social security system (in December).

Popular resistance to the adjustment program has been mild. There were fewer strikes in 1995 than in 1994, and neither labor nor peasant organizations have mobilized massive nationwide protests. Fear of joblessness probably saps workers' will to put up a fight. The debtors' movement known as *El Barzon* could turn into a powerful political force, but it seems to have been partially neutralized by a government program launched last summer to help debtors. For now, the most visible consequences of the economic crisis—the drastic fall in living standards, and the sharp increase in crime, suicides, and domestic violence—are more social than political.

But if economic recovery is slow, or, worse, if further financial instability postpones recovery, the political situation is likely to worsen. A poor economic performance will exacerbate popular discontent and weaken the government's ability to manage the country in this difficult period. The absence so far of a serious grassroots threat to the economic program or to social peace is no guarantee for the future. Urban riots don't happen until they happen. New and more militant organizations are likely to appear on Mexico's political landscape.

In the upcoming weeks, both major opposition parties, the center-right PAN and the left-wing Party of the Democratic Revolution (PRD), will be selecting their new leaders. The choices they make—whether pro-reform negotiators or proponents of greater confrontation with the government—may signal what is to come.

The good news is that discontent may be expressed primarily at the ballot box. But if the economy worsens or improves too slowly, the rise of more populist economic policies pushed by legislators from opposition parties or by the PRI itself becomes a real possibility. Desperation can foster unwise but popular economic policies.

Although the current forecast is for the economy to grow between 2 percent and 3 percent in 1996, the performance of real wages looks much bleaker. Estimated to have fallen about 12 percent in 1995, they could fall another 14 percent in 1996—a two-year plunge of 26 percent. Some optimistic scenarios see a fall of only 5 percent in 1996—still a cumulative drop close to 20 percent. Official predictions are that some 840,000 jobs will be added to the economy—about 400,000 short of the expected increase in the labor force.

Mexicans endured a worse fall in wages during the 1980s debt crisis. In 1983 alone, real wages plummeted about 25 percent. But the current crisis is exacerbated by large private-sector debt. High domestic interest rates combined with falling incomes for families and falling sales for businesses mean increasing defaults and bankruptcies. To the anguish of lower real wages and the fear, or the reality, of joblessness, families must add the threat of losing their homes, as many already have, because they cannot pay the mortgages. This is a new problem for Mexico, and the government's efforts to subsidize indebted families may not be enough, particularly if real interest rates stay high and real wages low throughout 1996.

In the medium term, maybe even as early as 1997, the Mexican economy, led by exports and foreign direct investment, should recover properly. But 1997 is ages away in political time, and even then there are no guarantees. The banking sector continues to be the Mexican economy's Achilles heel. Further bad economic news or more political turmoil could destabilize Mexico's peso and financial markets over and over again.

Clearly, the government's first priority should be economic recovery—but one that is sustainable. Unwise policy could lead to a run on the peso or to a balance of payments crisis. And, in fact, the degrees of freedom for an induced recovery are painfully slim. The government could perhaps relax fiscal and monetary policy, but only very little; it could privatize more state-owned industries and use the proceeds to reduce the debt burden. But the results would not be drastically different in terms of growth in the short run. Here is where the United States could be of great help.

What Can Washington Do?

Although the economic outlook is brighter and the quest for democracy has its own momentum, Mexico's financial vulnerability remains an important threat to political reform. It vastly complicates government efforts not only to prosecute prominent political leaders or the business and banking communities for past wrongdoing, but also to force local PRI officials to adhere to the new rules of electoral competition. Although the population at large would applaud such action, those under attack are likely to strike back. And although no one really knows how strong or effective these individuals or groups can be, the nation's financial volatility—easing now, but far from over—could make it extremely hard for the government to take the risk. Zedillo does not enjoy the full backing of the reform-minded. Many of his potential allies, while believing in his commitment to political reform, are concerned about his capacity to lead such a complex process. Economic improvements are likely to lessen the skepticism, strengthen Zedillo and make it easier for Mexico to undergo political reform.

The Clinton administration could help by clearing up questions about U.S. intentions to implement NAFTA. The president should offer reassurances, in both word and deed, that NAFTA is here to stay in full. The recent decision to postpone the licensing of Mexican trucks to operate in U.S. soil and the row over Mexican tomatoes are not good omens. Uncertainties about NAFTA could drive some direct foreign investment (how much is hard to tell) away from Mexico. If NAFTA is subject to recurrent onsets of U.S. protectionism, Mexican exports would suffer. Both exports and foreign direct investment are key to a sustained economic recovery in Mexico, and the United States is Mexico's largest market and source of investment flows. But more important than the potential economic loss, the equivocations over NAFTA make President Zedillo look weak and undermine his leadership when precisely the opposite is essential.

Obviously, it would also help if the U. S. government would make available the remaining funds—close to $10 billion—in the Mexican rescue package signed in February 1995. Releasing these funds in the form of guarantees, for example, could allow the Mexican government to borrow in the private capital markets on better terms. Giving the government such an option could enhance the stability of the peso and thereby reduce domestic interest rates further. Lower interest rates would offer relief to debtors, and hence the banking system, and allow lending to begin once again. With more credit available, economic growth

EVEN THE RULE OF LAW IS HOSTAGE TO MEXICO'S FINANCIAL VULNERABILITY. IF THE NATION'S LEADERS UNCOVER THE QUESTIONABLE PRACTICES OF POLITICAL AND BUSINESS ELITES, THEY RISK UNLEASHING A WAVE OF CAPITAL OUTFLOWS THAT COULD THREATEN THE FRAGILE RECOVERY.

could be higher than predicted even in the short run.

But in the current political climate and during a U.S. presidential election year, it is unlikely that the Clinton administration—under constant attack from critics in Congress who oppose lending to Mexico—will be ready to release more funds from the rescue package.

Washington should continue to support Zedillo, at least as long as he pushes Mexico to consolidate democracy. And the United States should treat Mexico as a partner—not as a defeated enemy—in managing the recurrent problems in the bilateral relationship—migration, narcotics trafficking, border pollution—as well as new ones arising from the implementation of NAFTA.

Unfortunately, electoral politics are pulling U.S. policy toward Mexico in the opposite direction. The results certainly do not help Mexico. But they do not help the United States either. A prosperous and stable Mexico is good for Mexicans first. But it is also good—in terms of higher exports, lower illegal immigration, fewer illicit activities, and an improved environment at the border—for the United States.

FORCE IS FOREVER

When pushed, Chile's army answers legal challenges with helicopters and menacing troops, raising a fundamental question: Does democracy ever fully recover from a coup?

TINA ROSENBERG

Tina Rosenberg is a senior fellow at the World Policy Institute and the author of "Children of Cain: Violence and the Violent in Latin America."

In a fourth-floor hospital room in a dismal city at the bottom of the world, an old man lies in bed. The city is Talcahuano, a fishing town in the south of Chile — its rowboats and wheeling gulls charming to the eye, its fish-meal factories spewing a noxious gas that blankets the city. The Naval Hospital, a sea-green building with bright green trim, surrounded by a barbed-wire fence, sits at the end of a road winding up the cliffs that overlook the ocean, high above the city. Even Talcahuano seems far away; here one has a sensation of infinite distance from the world. But the man in bed is the most notorious figure in Chile, and the question of how long he will remain there is one that may forever mark Chilean democracy.

The patient is retired Gen. Manuel Contreras, now 66 years old. After Gen. Augusto Pinochet's 1973 military coup against Chile's socialist President, Salvador Allende, Contreras ran the notorious National Intelligence Directorate, or DINA, and ranked a close second to Pinochet as the country's most powerful man.

It was Contreras who directed the first foreign terrorist assassination ever carried out in the United States. Orlando Letelier had held several Cabinet jobs in the Allende Government and in 1976 was in exile, lobbying foreign governments against the Pinochet regime from the Institute for Policy Studies, a left-wing think tank in Washington. On Sept. 21, 1976, a car bomb placed on the axle of Letelier's Chevy Malibu blew up as he rounded Washington's Sheridan Circle, cutting Letelier in two and piercing the carotid artery of Ronni Moffitt, his 25-year-old American fund-raising assistant. They were two of more than a thousand people killed or disappeared by the DINA. In 1978, the United States requested his extradition. Chile refused. It seemed Contreras would live out his life a free man.

But on Nov. 12, 1993, a judge of a now-democratic Chile convicted Contreras and Col. Pedro Espinoza, the DINA's No. 2, in the Letelier-Moffitt killings and sentenced them to prison terms of seven and six years, respectively. The conviction was affirmed this May. "They have violated my constitutional rights," raged Contreras on television from Viejo Roble, his 1,850-acre farm. "The judges were scared by Marxists. I am not going to any prison while there is no real justice." The army swooped in with planes and helicopters to snatch Contreras away to a military base and then to the Naval Hospital. And there he remains, claiming that his various illnesses — diabetes, high blood pressure, a hernia and now, according to his lawyers, anxiety and depression — would endanger him in prison.

Espinoza is now the sole inhabitant of Punta Peuco, a prison built this year 25 miles from Santiago as a concession to the military, which did not want its gentleman murderers sharing quarters with the scruffier variety. On the first Saturday of Espinoza's imprisonment, a thousand active-duty military officers — including Pinochet's chief aide — drove with their families to Punta Peuco to wave flags and sing the national anthem. "No prison is appropriate for a military man," one officer, Maj. Cristián Ilabaca, told a reporter.

According to Chilean news reports, on July 24 General Pinochet — no longer Chile's President but still its army commander — ended a meeting with the Defense Minister saying: "Minister, you know we don't want to stage another coup d'état. So don't force us to do so." Two months before elections in 1989 led to the end of his 17-year rule, Pinochet had warned, "The day they touch one of my men, the rule of law ends." At the time, the country was tipsy with the scent of democracy, and many dismissed it as an empty threat. Now, Chile is beginning to take him at his word.

This story is distressingly familiar in Latin America, where each new civilian government has struggled with how to bring to justice the human rights violators of the preceding military dictatorship. These efforts have produced little more than threats from the militaries and retreat on the part of civilians — and a continuation of the old cycle of militaries dominating civilian governments and blocking the rule of law.

It is not, however, the familiar story in Chile. Before 1973, Chile was thought to be the one country in Latin America where violent dictatorship couldn't happen: the nation with a history of democracy, human rights and civilian rule, the nation with a lawyer's soul. But Pinochet's coup showed that one long night was enough to turn the culture of ballots and habeas corpus into one of terror and silence. The question posed by General Contreras and Chile's response to him is this: What happens once a democratic culture is broken? Can full democracy be put together again, or does power never again truly relinquish its dominance over law?

MANUEL CONTRERAS CALLED THE DINA "THE shadow army." From its headquarters, a three-floor modern house on a dead-end street in downtown Santiago, its empire sprawled to some 10,000 agents, who murdered hundreds of student leaders, labor organizers, leftist politicians and human rights workers, tortured thousands more and took away hundreds of others who were never seen again. The DINA, with a little help from the air force, had a monopoly on violence.

And Contreras, although then just a colonel, had a monopoly on the DINA. A man described by one military school classmate as "a psychopath, with ingredients of sadism, delusions of grandeur and a superiority complex," he had few friends in the Government. Save one: Contreras reported not to the junta but to Pinochet alone.

In 1977, however, Pinochet cut him off. Civilian officials wanted closer ties with the United States, but Jimmy Carter, Mr. Human Rights, was now President. Contreras, the prime suspect in the Washington killings, was getting in the way. Pinochet replaced the DINA with a new secret police, retired Contreras from the army and held him in a military hospital for 14 months while the courts considered — and ultimately rejected — extradition. In 1978, the junta passed an amnesty law, exempting the armed forces from prosecution for all crimes. Only one crime was excluded from the amnesty: the murders of Orlando Letelier and Ronni Moffitt.

Before Pinochet's regime, crimes like those of Contreras were unknown in Chile. In 1965, a comprehensive comparison of democracies ranked Chile as more democratic than the United States, France, Italy or West Germany. Before the 1973 coup, constitutional succession was interrupted seriously only once in Chilean history, during a period of mild dictatorship from 1927 to 1932. In 1968, a prisoner's ears were boxed, creating such a scandal that the president of the Senate went to investigate. Political culture here reveres "institutionality," the authority of political and legal structures. Under Pinochet, Chileans joked that theirs was the only country where the tanks stopped at traffic lights during a military coup.

Several factors allowed Chile to escape Latin America's typical troubles. During the conquest, its lack of gold mines or large groups of Indians to press into labor saved it from the class divisions of the hacienda system and encouraged a more middle-class society. Chile's homogeneity also helped to prevent the rise of powerful regional leaders, or caudillos. It allowed the Santiago Government to impose its will nationwide and, fortunately, Santiago's leaders were democrats. Chile's liberator, Bernardo O'Higgins, was the only Latin American liberator who gave up power voluntarily — except for Simón Bolívar himself.

Democratic culture was strong, even under dictatorship. "The first thing you do if you form a soccer team is elect officers and write up pages of bylaws and rules," one Chilean told me in 1986. Politics is the national sport. Chileans do not just inhabit their country; they are its citizens.

In other Latin countries, the elite often stamped out the first signs of democracy, but not in Chile — in part because until Allende democracy usually produced governments the upper class liked. "Before 1973, the right was satisfied," says Raúl Sohr, a sociologist and documentary film producer who specializes in military issues. "The left had 15 to 20 percent in Parliament. The right here never felt the need to call out the armed forces."

And the military never became the landowners' personal army. From 1880 to World War I, the military was trained by Germans, who instilled hierarchy, discipline and loyalty to the nation. In 1973, Allende's most trusted general threatened to sue Tribuna, a conservative newspaper, for suggesting the military stage a coup. "Such things are not done here," said the general, Augusto Pinochet.

ON MAY 31, 1993, "RIDE OF THE VALKYries" blared through the loudspeakers of the San Bernardo military base. Pinochet and 20 generals, all wearing combat uniforms, watched as soldiers with painted faces descended on ropes from helicopters to simulate an assault on a radio station. Officially, it was a ceremony commemorating the 106th anniversary of the infantry school. But the aggressive dress and exercise were the continuation of an extraordinary week in which soldiers were called to barracks, elite black-bereted combat troops stood grimly in the street guarding the armed forces headquarters in downtown Santiago and helicopters circled the city. Patricio Aylwin, who had taken over the presidency from Pinochet in March 1990, was visiting Europe at the time, and Chileans whispered their fear that he might not be allowed to return.

The protest was the second warning to the Government to drop a case that had become known as "Pinocheques" — an investigation of army checks for $3 million paid to Pinochet's son for shares in his munitions company. The first protest, in December 1990, ended when a parliamentary commission looking into the payments promised that its report would make no explicit judgments about the involvement of General Pinochet. "But anyone who read it could come to no other conclusion," says Jorge Schaulsohn, the commission's head, who is now president of the center-left Party for Democracy.

In May 1993, the case proceeded to a judge, who called eight generals to testify. On May 28, the army's second protest began, the one scored by Wagner, and the court quickly dropped the investigation. At the urging of the military, politicians sought to soothe another source of discomfort, proposing bills — at the time, unsuccessful — either to stop or limit the few trials for human rights violations that were under way.

Talk about human rights violations had been a constant boiling irritant to the military. One of Aylwin's first acts as President was to establish a commission of eight citizens from across the political spectrum to investigate murder and forced disappearances under the dictatorship. The Rettig Commission and a subsequent investigation documented 2,000 murders and nearly 1,000 disappearances. The report was later endorsed by a unanimous Senate.

It was not, however, endorsed by many officers of the Chilean military, who routinely claim either that the murders and disappearances were necessary to win a civil war against the left or that they simply did not exist. "I don't know any disappeared people," says one colonel. "It doesn't mean that in some little town in the south some policeman didn't take Juan Pérez and shoot him because they were competing for the same woman. It could have happened. The Allende Government had left the climate so hate-filled and radical." I ask him who killed Letelier. "The C.I.A., working with the Cuban and Venezuelan intelligence services," he replies.

Espinoza is Chile's only military officer in prison for a human rights violation. One reason there are not more is, paradoxically, the post-Pinochet Government's respect for institutionality. Pinochet's successors continue to honor the constitution he wrote in 1980 that makes the armed forces "guarantors of institutionality" — in effect giving them the right to step in whenever they feel Chile's institutionality is threatened, as they did in 1973. It permits the chiefs of the three branches of the armed forces and the police to stay in office until 1998, regardless of the President's wishes. It also set rules that effectively allow Pinochet's supporters, although a minority, to control the Senate.

Those rules insured that the new Aylwin Government did not have the votes to overturn Pinochet's 1978 amnesty law, which covered the vast majority of the dictatorship's crimes. And Aylwin made no attempt to try to win public support for such a move, preferring to avoid conflict. In the study of his small one-story house (where he lived throughout his presidency), Aylwin protests that he had little choice. "The transition we chose left us tied up," he says. "The great challenge now is to fight for the majorities necessary to reform those enormous limits."

His successor, Eduardo Frei, has followed the Aylwin line. Like Aylwin, he is a cautious, colorless member of the centrist Christian Democrats. Frei's chief of staff, Genaro Arriagada, argues that Chile is doing all it can to deal with the military. "You can't compare this with a transition where the state disappeared, like the Soviet Union, or where the army was disgraced by a defeat by another power, as in Argentina," he says. "We have some justice, but not full justice. And we won't have it. We chose to keep the amnesty in exchange for social peace."

The need to buy off the military to win social peace is the Latin American disease to which, until 1973, Chile had thought itself immune. "The democratic and constitutional aspects of the military are gone," says Raúl Sohr, the sociologist. "They are now a political armed forces with a high grade of autonomy not compatible with a democratic system and, until this point, almost total impunity."

Pinochet, who cut Contreras loose in the late 70's, could easily have taken the position that Contreras is a bad apple who brought shame to the armed forces and deserves punishment. In fact, it seemed at first that he would. "The law is obeyed, that's all," he told a television interviewer in early June, a week after the Contreras and Espinoza convictions were upheld on appeal. But his position hardened, apparently because of pressure from his generals, who see themselves, the coup and the military government in the dock along with Contreras. "The armed forces were victorious militarily and politically," says Gen. Jorge Ballerino, who retired last year as Pinochet's principal adviser. "They feel current developments are trying to destroy the image of the armed forces and bury their successes."

Ever since, the military, in traditional Chilean fashion, has done everything possible short of breaking the law to keep Contreras out of prison. On June 11, as reporters freezing on stakeout were diverted by a farmhand who invited them to a lamb barbecue, an army convoy swept Contreras out of Viejo Roble and took him to the Sangra military base. Shocked Government officials ordered him back. The military took its time to comply. Two days later, a predawn convoy from Viejo Roble snuck Contreras into the army helicopter that brought him to the Talcahuano Naval Hospital.

Espinoza barricaded himself inside a Santiago army command, vowing he would never go to Punta Peuco. Perhaps conscious of his lesser symbolic weight, the army retired him and turned him over to the Government. Contreras, who underwent a successful operation for rectal cancer some years ago, argues that he is too sick to join Espinoza, but he seemed to suffer few limits on his activities until he faced arrest. In late August, naval doctors operated on a hernia and prescribed a month's convalescence. "No one is saying that his cancer is back," says Schaulsohn, the head of the Party for Democracy. "But where there's a will, there's a way."

PEDRO LIZANA, A MIDDLE-AGED MAN WITH A scruffy beard, flicks cigarette ash all over his desk while he talks and turns his chair to the side, allowing me a conversation-long view of his right profile. As head of the powerful industrialists'

association, Sofofa, Lizana leads the one community that has appeared to lend solidarity to Contreras. Sofofa had no comment on the case until it caused Frei to cancel a planned trip to a South American trade summit in Brazil. Then Lizana told the press: "People shouldn't be so nervous just because the general went for a walk around the block."

In an interview in Lizana's third-floor office in the posh, brand-new blue glass Sofofa skyscraper, I ask if he thinks the military's behavior could begin to scare off foreign investors. On the contrary, he responds, the problem is the Government's defiance of the military. "What will affect the economy is the sense that an arm of the state wants to pass over a sector as important as the armed forces."

The business community's traditional political allies do not agree. Although the two right-wing parties continue to emphasize their support for the 1973 coup and Pinochet's Government, especially its economic reforms, today they support a democratic system. The National Renovation and the Independent Democratic Union parties endorsed the Rettig report and called for Contreras to follow the law. Their firmness is a major reason that—Pinochet's rumblings aside—few believe a military coup is possible.

At least, that is, while the economy is booming. The upper class supports democracy in part because, once again, democracy supports the upper class. Since 1985, Chile's economy has grown an average of 7 percent a year. Unemployment stands at 6 percent and inflation is in single digits. The benefits have gone disproportionately to the rich, whose neighborhoods have been transformed, filled with new luxury shops and high-rise apartment buildings.

Indeed, the Contreras case has not yet had any visible impact on foreign investment. But politicians worry that his continued defiance could drive Chile's risk ratings downward or discourage the United States Congress — already spooked by Mexico's economic collapse and bizarre wave of political assassinations — as it considers admitting Chile to the North American Free Trade Agreement. "This crisis qualifies us as a political risk, " says Andrés Allamand, the 39-year-old president of National Renovation. "Pinochet is still strong. No one knows how stable we are."

More is at stake for Chile. If Contreras successfully defies the courts, Chile may fall permanently into the military-dominated democracy of most of its neighbors. "The case brings us back to basics," says Juan Pablo Letelier, the son of Orlando Letelier and a socialist parliamentarian. "Military subordination to civilian rule — does it exist or not? If Contreras doesn't go, then Chile's democracy stumbles."

Even if he does eventually enter Punta Peuco, Contreras's defiance has given the military the opportunity to press the Government for long-sought concessions. The first casualty will likely be human rights trials. Most of the dictatorship's crimes are covered by the 1978 amnesty law. While that precludes punishment, it has until now been interpreted to permit judges to investigate disappearances and reveal the identities of the killers. Such publicity galls military officers, who dread being confronted on the courtroom steps by a platoon of television cameras. Although polls show a huge majority of Chileans still favor bringing the killers to justice, President Frei recently proposed a deadline for ending trials and allowing soldiers to come forth in secret to reveal what happened to the disappeared.

Also last month, President Frei publicly asked the independent State Defense Council to drop its ongoing efforts to revive the prosecution of Pinochet's son for the Pinocheques case. The head of the council agreed, citing "the national interest." An-

other striking reminder of civilian intimidation is that in its extensive coverage of the Letelier murder case, the Chilean press has failed even to raise the obvious question of Pinochet's involvement. "It is hypocrisy to think that Pinochet didn't give the orders to kill Letelier," says Raúl Sohr.

The optimists in Chile believe that civilians will recover their traditional control after 1998. "I'm confident it will be possible to create a new relationship when those who were in the military government have left power, mainly Pinochet," Aylwin says. Others worry that the habits of power are not easily lost. "No one expected the army to be as hard-line as it has been," says Marcos Robledo, an editor at the pro-Government paper La Epoca who studies civil-military relations. "It has reminded us of what we wanted to forget — that the military are submissive here only when things are going their way."

OPEN FOR BUSINESS

Bereft of patrons, desperate to rescue his economy, Fidel turns to an unusual solution: capitalism

KEVIN FEDARKO

THE HEMISPHERE'S LAST COMMU-nist begins his evening with a martini. As he plucks the quintessentially American refreshment from the tray, Fidel Castro seems surprisingly muted. Or perhaps it is simply the mark of age: he is still a big man, trim and barrel-chested, but his 68 years are visible in the skin of his face, which is approaching the translucence of old parchment.

Taking his visitors on a slow walking tour of Havana's labyrinthine Palacio de la Revolución, Castro gestures toward an enormous mosaic of birds, animals and flowers that dominates the reception hall and quietly begins a story. The artist, he explains, cast the ceramic tiles at the same time the architect was completing the building's interior. Through some misunderstanding between the two men, the ceiling was built too low. When it came time to install the intricately etched tiles, the top two rows did not fit. The artist never forgave the architect whose miscalculations robbed his mosaic of its crown.

Someone asks what became of the architect. Was he fired for his mistake? Contemplating the missing top rows, Castro shrugs. "No," he deadpans, testing his listeners' sense of humor. "He was shot." Then Castro roars with laughter at his joke, a parody of his image as a bloodthirsty dictator. And with that, the evening and the aging commandant suddenly come alive.

In a dinner conversation two weeks ago with a group of TIME editors and correspondents, the Cuban leader talked of everything from the perfidy of his former Soviet allies to the numerous attempts on his life by the U.S., joking that he holds an "Olympic record" in surviving assassination plots. But in truth he faces now what may be his gravest challenge yet.

No matter how vehemently he may deny it—and he does—the Cuban leader cannot escape the fact that after 36 years of wily international gamesmanship, he is stranded on the wrong side of history. The Soviet patrons who financed his "socialist paradise" for three decades have collapsed. The communist bedrock upon which he built his edifice of power has proved itself bankrupt on virtually every continent of the globe. As his own people clamor for a better life, Cuba's socialist dream appears to be fading fast.

Castro remains firmly in power; despite an economic crisis that gives him no good options, he does not face the imminent collapse of his regime. His tactical skills, his powers of endurance and the affection of many Cubans are intact. There is no organized opposition to him inside the country. His army and security forces are large and efficient. Despite spasms of discontent, like the riot last August that helped unleash the rafter exodus, there is nothing like a Tiananmen brewing. And unlike many similar leaders, he has surrounded himself not with cronies and coat holders but with the best and the brightest his country has to offer. He may be constrained by a terrible economy and his enduring faith in the failed ideology that produced it, but Fidel is not finished yet. The trick he is trying to master, however, is a neat trick indeed: modifying Cuba's communist system enough to survive but not so much that he betrays the revolution.

SINCE THE FALL OF THE COMMUNIST BLOC in 1989 and the loss of Soviet subsidies in 1992, Cuba has suffered through a period of plummeting prosperity that is euphemistically known as the "special period." Imports have dried up. Industry has folded in on itself. Cuba's No. 1 money earner, the sugar crop, amounted to less than 4 million tons this year—a level not seen for decades. The island's factories are producing at only 30% capacity, giving rise to shortages in everything from clothes and cosmetics to pots and pans.

Castro has been loath to respond by renouncing his socialist credo in the fashion of former communists like Boris Yeltsin. But to salvage what remains of his economy, he has been forced to adapt, imposing some measures that are anathema to his beliefs. In 1990, for example, Castro began soliciting foreign investment. Though he continues to declare that Cuba will never sell off its state-run companies, he has opened up strategic areas such as telecommunications, oil exploration and mining to joint ventures. The latest shocker: condominiums for sale to foreigners, with titillating hints that even land ownership may soon be possible. Drawn by the promise of pent-up demand and the conviction that, in the words of a confidential British report to investors, the reform process is "cohesive, systematic and unstoppable," Canadian, Mexican and European businessmen are taking the gamble.

By the end of 1994, Cuba had signed deals for 185 foreign joint ventures. The Spaniards and Germans were among the first to invest in tourism, which grew at an annual rate of 17% between 1991 and 1993; now interest is rising in Canada and across Europe. Meanwhile, the Monterrey-based magnate Javier Garza-Calderón of Mexico's Grupo Domos bought up half the Cuban phone system in a $1.5 billion deal last year. June saw the arrival of Cuba's first foreign financial institution, the Dutch ING Bank. British companies are looking into oil exploration—even though France's giant Total has recently pulled out—and Unilever, the British-Dutch giant, produces toiletries and detergents for the domestic Cuban market. Italy's Benetton now boasts five retail stores on the island, and plans three more by the end of 1996, while Japanese automakers Mitsubishi and Nissan are now sold in Havana.

Even Israel, the only country to side with the U.S. in a recent United Nations vote condemning the American trade embargo, does business with Cuba: Israeli firms are second only to Mexican companies in textile investments. These days, the palm-lined patio at the elegant La Ferminia restaurant in suburban Flores is jammed with foreign businessmen power-lunching with government ministers and discreetly whispering into their cellular phones.

All of which has made for a singular irony: the only people left on the sidelines are the Americans. According to a White House source, the Clinton Administration doesn't feel the changes in Cuba have been substantial enough to justify a diplomatic rapprochement, while the conservative Republicans now in control of the U.S. Congress—pressured by Miami's community of Cuban Americans—are bent on keeping the door to Cuba firmly closed to U.S. companies. Just last week Senate Foreign Relations Committee chairman Jesse Helms introduced legislation that would tighten the 33-year-old economic embargo even more.

"Let me be clear," said Helms. "Whether Castro leaves Cuba in a vertical or horizontal position is up to him and the Cuban people. But he must and will leave Cuba."

NEVERTHELESS, CASTRO HAS ALSO TAKEN A number of other steps to ensure that this will not happen any time soon. In the doldrums of 1993 he legalized trade in dollars, widened opportunities for self-employment and turned over state farms to cooperatives or families. When food shortages became critical last fall, farmers were finally permitted to sell some of their produce on the open market.

Regardless of how disagreeable Fidel's apparatchiks may find these measures, they have produced real change. The trading ignited by newly legalized dollars has. been fueling the economy for the past 18 months. Despite Clinton's move last August to diminish the remittances sent by Cuban Americans to their families back on the island, millions manage to get through. Last year Cubans spent nearly a billion dollars buying imported consumer goods in 600 state-run stores across the island.

Moreover, since the opening of the farmer's markets last October, there has been a flurry of economic activity even within the moribund peso-driven sector of the economy. One such place is the Marianao farmer's market, in a drab workers' suburb of Havana, where customers seem to be complaining about high prices—but are still buying. A vendor named Jorge is doing a brisk trade in his homemade marinade of vinegar, garlic, onion, salt and cumin. "I used to teach language at the university," he explains. "But I was making only 325 pesos a month. Life is very expensive, so I have become a merchant."

His entrepreneurial efforts earn him 1,000 pesos a day.

IN GENERAL, CUBANS NOW SENSE THAT THE country has turned a crucial financial corner since the black days of 1993, when the worst effects of the economic collapse were being felt. "For a while, even among revolutionaries, there was a depressed mood," admits National Assembly President Ricardo Alarcón. "Now that's over. People realize there is a way out."

But as ordinary Cubans race to take advantage of the reforms, inequalities are swiftly giving rise to their inevitable by-products: class resentment, social unrest and crime. Prostitution once again flourishes in Havana. The influx of tourists (including some Americans, who slip onto the island illegally from Nassau) sets up a stark contrast between the fantasy playground being built for foreigners and the gritty reality that ordinary Cubans must contend with. As the inequalities increase, many poor but educated Cubans view the rush to the dollar with disgust.

For despite the recent flurry of economic activity, there are still few guarantees, many pitfalls and no safety net in Cuba's reformation. Castro's economic planner, Carlos Lage, told investors at the annual World Economic Forum in Davos, Switzerland, that the island's economy had ceased its free fall but warned that the recovery will be painful and slow. Cuba leaves much to be desired in basic infrastructure, such as communications and power supply. Moreover, the government has yet to face up to its most difficult challenge: paring down inefficient state-run industries and the loaded bureaucracies that serve as the backbone of the socialist state. Laid-off employees have nowhere to go for work, and the government has so far allowed only 160,000 people (out of a total population of 11 million) to seek self-employment.

Little wonder, then, that nowadays Castro's most frequent dinner guests are not fellow ideologues, but globe-trotting tycoons like Pierre Cardin, Ted Turner and Lee Iacocca, who can bring in the additional capital that Cuba desperately needs. In each meeting, Castro vows that he will never abandon socialism but also promises to continue holding open an economic window to the breezes of the free market. "We have to be ready to conduct the necessary reforms to adapt our country and our economy to the present world situation," he says. Rough translation: until Castro gets his country up and running again, he will use capitalist tools to survive. "But," he insists, "without renouncing our ideals!"

THE WAY OUT IS PROVING A DIFFICULT road for Castro's most loyal minions, since

it requires discarding—temporarily, they assure themselves—several pillars of Cuba's socialist dogma. The old Central Planning Board, which piloted the state-directed economy, has been abolished. Last year the government claims to have cut the budget deficit 72% by slashing its bloated work force, eliminating dozens of subsidies and imposing price increases on such things as cigars, alcohol and electricity. These measures do not sit well with party stalwarts. "We made these changes not because we like it, but because we had to," laments Communist Party official José Arbesú. "The point of no return would be to put all production in private hands. But we are not going to do it."

Cuban Americans and conservative politicians in Washington insist that keeping the trade embargo firmly in place will hasten Castro's demise. But this line of thinking ignores the bedrock of loyalty that many ordinary Cubans feel for Castro, whose revolution has provided every adult citizen with free health care, education and a social-welfare net. Castro has long profited by laying the blame for Cuba's economic troubles on the U.S. Resentment of the embargo—particularly when U.S. sanctions against Vietnam have been lifted—only reinforces a fierce pride. Cubans are nationalists even more than they are socialists or incipient capitalists, and pressuring them from the outside makes even more unlikely the full-scale rebellion that Cuban Americans would like to ignite.

The biggest impact of the U.S. economic restrictions is the damage they inflict on American businesses. For many foreign firms now attempting to establish a foothold in Cuba, the embargo represents a golden opportunity to do business without U.S. competition. One example is mining. By the end of last year, the Cubans had signed joint-venture exploration deals for nickel, gold, silver, copper, lead and zinc with a number of Canadian and Australian companies. "A company of our ilk would never have the opportunity if we had to compete with American capital," said Frank Smeenk, president of Canada's MacDonald Mines Exploration Ltd., as he celebrated the good news on drilling results with a Cuban minister.

While Smeenk and others make money, American businessmen can only sit back and salivate. American economists estimate that when the embargo is finally lifted, U.S. business could total as much as $1 billion in the first year alone. "The people in Miami have the best intentions, but the time has come to change," says Dwayne Andreas, head of Archer Daniels Midland. "The U.S. is missing hundreds of business opportunities, and we'll probably be locked out of Cuba for half a century."

It is a testament to the size of the prize that, despite the risks, an increasing number of Americans are sneaking into Havana with the hope of working out arrangements under the table. According to Cuba's Ministry of Foreign Investment and Economic Cooperation, representatives of more than 100 U.S. corporations have visited the island in the past year with hopes of doing business in a postembargo Cuba. At least 26 American firms signed nonbinding letters of intent in tourism, medicine and biotechnology. "We're upset that we're not getting a piece of the action," declares a frustrated investor from Arizona who was spotted in the Hotel Nacional investigating opportunities in marinas and real estate. "Why not us?"

Eager to help pave the way, a handful of savvy consultants from New York City, Washington and Miami jet in monthly to maintain relations with Cuban officials for American companies shy of openly violating U.S. law. Other firms simply take the risk themselves. Executives from such companies as Hyatt, Marriott, Merck and Eli Lilly have been seen around Havana. One Western diplomat in Cuba laughs at the increasingly flagrant violations, even by exiles in Miami who have spent 30 years condemning Castro. "The U.S. embargo is a sieve," he says. "Even Cuban Americans are coming here to look at business opportunities."

NO ONE, EXCEPT PERHAPS THOSE IN CAStro's inner circle, knows how far the old revolutionary is prepared to allow economic changes to go. Insiders say there is a lack of consensus in the government. The guiding philosophy seems to be to avoid any move that might threaten the social order and the political status quo. Castro appears resistant to any but the most modest concessions, and while a well-honed instinct for survival may drive him and his closest associates further into dalliance with free enterprise, they have not shown an intellectual acceptance of the superiority of market forces. Without an independent source of income, the Cuban regime will have to continue grudgingly to open up the economy, but the moves will be fitful and reverses inevitable.

Yet even as he flirts with capitalism, Castro continues to insist that communism is alive and well in Cuba. "I'm still a communist," he declared, when asked if he thought his experiment with Marx had been a failure. "I am proud to be one. Why do I have to renege on my principles? I have no choice but to continue being a communist." It is an intrepid defense of an idea whose time has passed.

—Reported by Cathy Booth/Havana, with other bureaus

Population, Development, and Environment

Population, development, and the environment are inextricably linked. The developing world's population continues to grow at an annual rate of between 2.5 and 3.5 percent, with some countries experiencing even higher growth rates. Although growth has slowed somewhat, world population is currently growing at the rate of approximately one billion people every 11 years. Most of this increase is taking place in the developing world, where poverty is widespread. The combination of higher population and poverty rates inevitably results in obstacles to development, increased exploitation of resources, and environmental degradation.

The United Nations estimates that if population growth rates continue, world population may double before it stabilizes sometime in the twenty-first century. Even if, by some miracle, population growth were immediately reduced to the level found in industrialized countries, the developing world's population would continue to grow well into the twenty-first century. Because such a large proportion of the population is young and will be starting new families, it will be some time before population growth slows substantially. There has been some progress in reducing fertility rates (that is, reducing the average number of children per family) through family planning programs, but much remains to be done. The 1994 International Conference on Population and Development in Cairo, Egypt, helped to focus worldwide attention on the crucial relationship between population and development.

There are differences of opinion about the best way to slow population growth. Some analysts regard development as the best contraceptive, while others view lower population growth as a prerequisite for development. These differences in perspective have politicized the population issue, dividing experts between those who favor family planning and wider availability of birth control and others who believe that development itself will slow population growth, as it did in the industrialized countries. Recent evidence, however, seems to confirm the view that family planning and birth control can have a favorable effect on birth rates. Debate over this issue is also related to the abortion controversy in the United States and elsewhere and resulted in static funding for family planning programs throughout the 1980s. The abortion question emerged as the most controversial issue during the Cairo conference on population and development, causing frustration among those who sought to deal with the broader dimensions of the population problem.

Estimates vary, but as many as one billion people may live in absolute poverty, as measured by a combination of economic and social indicators. As population increases, it becomes more difficult to meet the basic human needs of the developing world's citizens. Alleviating poverty is a daunting challenge and will require massive efforts on a number of fronts. Economic development, regarded by many as a panacea, has not only failed to eliminate poverty, it has exacerbated it in some ways. Ill-conceived economic development plans have diverted resources from more productive uses. Where economic growth has occurred, the benefits are often inequitably distributed and widen the gap between rich and poor. Rural-to-urban migration has caused an enormous influx of people to the cities, lured there by the illusion of opportunity and the attraction of urban life. In reality, opportunity is limited. Nevertheless, most opt for marginal lives in the cities rather than returning to the countryside. Additional resources are diverted to the urban areas in an attempt to meet demands for services. Meanwhile, food production may be affected, with those remaining in rural areas often choosing either to farm for subsistence because of artificially low prices, or to raise cash crops for export.

Population and poverty also contribute to environmental degradation. Larger populations of poor people place greater strains on scarce and fragile resources. Deforestation for agriculture and fuel has reduced forested areas and contributed to erosion, desertification, and global warming. Intensified agriculture, particularly for cash crops, has depleted soils. This necessitates increased fertilization, which is costly and also produces run-off that contributes to water pollution. Rapidly expanding urban populations overwhelm meager sanitation facilities, result-

ing in additional water pollution and increased incidence of water-borne diseases. In arid regions like the Middle East, added demand for scarce water resources has depleted aquifers, perhaps irreversibly.

The drive for economic development also contributes to pollution and generates toxic waste. The toxic waste problem is often compounded by the shifting of production facilities to developing countries to take advantage of cheaper labor and looser environmental regulations. In some cases, unscrupulous entrepreneurs have collaborated in the export of toxic waste from the industrialized countries to the developing world.

In her address to the opening session of the 1992 UN Conference on Environment and Development (UNCED), held in Rio de Janeiro, Brazil, Norway's prime minister Gro Harlem Brundtland noted that population, poverty, and the environment could not be separated. Nevertheless, the documents that came out of Rio did not explicitly address this connection, leaving substantive issues to follow-up conferences such as the 1994 Cairo conference. Moreover, the divisions between North and South on environmental issues became more pronounced at the Rio conference. The conference highlighted the fundamental differences between the industrialized world and developing countries over causes and solutions for global environmental problems. This politicization along North-South lines threatens to postpone constructive steps to preserve Earth's environment.

Looking Ahead: Challenge Questions

Why is population growing so rapidly? What are the consequences of continued population growth?

Identify the implications of the differing views on how to slow population growth.

Describe the demographic transition theory.

What could account for the dramatic growth in third world urban areas? What are the implications of this growth?

What steps should urban areas take to deal with this explosive growth?

Define sustainable development. How do views of sustainable development in the developing world differ from those of the West?

In what ways does economic growth threaten Earth's environment? How can these threats be handled?

Why have concerns about the environment sometimes been incompatible with human rights efforts?

The ICPD Programme of Action

Three years of what in the United Nations vernacular is called consensus-building—a painstaking and sometimes acrimonious process of debate, consultation, negotiation, and revision involving governments, non-governmental organizations, development agencies, scientists, and experts at national, regional, and international levels—culminated in the adoption on 13 September of the Programme of Action of the International Conference on Population and Development (ICPD).

Delegations from 179 states and seven observers took part in the official Conference. Their 16-chapter Programme of Action sets out a series of general pinciples as well as specific recommendations to guide future population policy-making and programmes.

As POPULI goes to print, the Programme of Action is being edited and printed for public distribution. What follows is a chapter-by-chapter description based on an unedited version of the document dated 19 September 1994, official ICPD press releases, and working summaries prepared by the United Nations.

Chapter 1: Preamble

The Preamble provides an overview of the main issues covered in the ICPD Programme of Action and sets the context for action in the field of population and development. It stresses that the ICPD is not an isolated event and that the Programme of Action builds on the considerable international consensus that had developed since the 1974 World Population Conference in Bucharest and the 1984 Mexico City International Conference on Population. The ICPD's broader mandate on development issues reflects the growing awareness that population, poverty, patterns of production and consumption, and other threats to the environment are so closely interconnected that none of them can be considered in isolation. The Conference follows and builds on other recent international activities, and the Programme of Action will make significant contributions to upcoming conferences, including the World Summit for Social Development and the Fourth World Conference on Women, both scheduled for 1995, and Habitat II, the Second UN Conference on Human Settlements, scheduled for 1996.

Chapter 2: Principles

This chapter lays out the document's guiding principles, and starts with a chapeau which states, in part, that the implementation of the Programme of Action is the sovereign right of each country, consistent with national laws and development priorities, with full respect for the various religious and ethical values and cultural backgrounds of its people, and in conformity with universally recognized human rights.

Principle 1 states that all human beings are born free and equal in dignity and rights, including all the rights and freedoms of the Universal Declaration of Human Rights, and have the right to life, liberty, and security of person.

Principle 2 calls on all nations to ensure that all individuals are given the opportunity to make the most of their potential.

Principle 3 states that the right to development is a universal and inalienable right and an integral part of fundamental human rights, and that the human person is the central subject of development.

Principle 4 calls for advanced gender equality and equity and the empowerment of women, and the elimination of all kinds of violence against women.

Principle 5 says that population-related goals and policies are integral parts of cultural, economic, and social development, the main aim of which is to improve the quality of life of all people.

Principle 6 indentifies sustainable development as a means to ensure human well-being and calls on states to

From *Populi* magazine, October 1994, pp. 6-11. Reprinted by permission of *Populi*, the magazine of the United Nations Population Fund.

pursue development which meets the needs of current generations without compromising the ability of future generations to meet their own needs.

Principle 7 calls on states to work together to eradicate poverty.

Principle 8 says that everyone has the right to enjoy the highest attainable standard of physcial and mental health and that states should ensure universal access to health-care services, including those dealing with reproductive and sexual health and family planning.

Principle 9 states that the family, which exists in various forms, is the basic unit of society and therefore should be strengthened.

Principle 10 says that all people—and particularly women—have the right to education, which should focus on the full development of human resources, dignity, and potential.

Principle 11 calls on states and families to give the highest priority to children, especially as regards their right to health and education.

Principle 12 calls on countries receiving documented migrants to provide adquate health and social welfare services and to ensure their physical safety.

Principle 13 states that everyone has the right to seek asylum, and that states have responsibilities toward refugees, as stated in the Geneva Convention on the Status of Refugees.

Principle 14 calls on states to consider the population and development needs of indigenous people, to recognize and support their identity, culture, and interests, and enable them to participate fully in the economic, political, and social life of the country.

Principle 15 requires that in the context of sustainable development and social progress, sustained economic growth be broadly based, offering equal opportunities to all people, within and between countries.

Chapter 3: Interrelationships between Population, Sustained Economic Growth, and Sustainable Development

This chapter reflects general agreement that persistent, widespread poverty and serious social and gender inequality have significant effect on, and are in turn affected by, demographic factors such as population growth, structure, and distribution. Governments must give priority to investment in human resource development in their population and development strategies and budgets. Programmes should seek to increase people's—especially women's—access to information, education, skill development, employment, and high-quality health services. Meeting the basic needs of growing populations is dependent on a healthy environment, however, hence the emphasis on sustainable development, which

includes environmentalism. The chapter includes a call for a supportive economic environment for developing countries and countries with economies in transition.

Chapter 4: Gender Equality, Equity, and Empowerment of Women

This chapter calls on countries to empower women and eliminate inequality between men and women; eliminate all forms of discrimination against the girl child and the root causes of son preference; increase public awareness of the value of girl children, beyond their potential for childbearing; and promote equal participation of women and men in all areas of family and household responsibilities.

Chapter 5: The Family, Its Roles, Rights, Composition, and Structure

This chapter describes the family as the basic unit of society. It calls for policies and laws that support the family, contribute to its stability, and take into account its various forms, particularly the growing number of single-parent families. It calls for equality of opportunity for family members, especially the rights of women and children in the family, with particular emphasis on protecting families, and individual family members, from the ravages of extreme poverty, chronic unemployment, and domestic and sexual violence.

Chapter 6: Population Growth and Structure

This chapter has five sections: fertility, mortality, and population growth rates; children and youth; elderly people; indigenous people; and persons with disabilities. It urges governments to: give greater attention to the importance of population trends for development; promote the health, well-being, and potential of all children, adolescents, and youth and enforce laws against their economic exploitation, physical and mental abuse, and neglect; develop social security systems that ensure greater equity and solidarity between and within generations and that provide support to elderly people; incorporate the perspectives and needs of indigenous communities at every step into population, development, and environmental programmes that affect them and address social and economic factors that serve to disadvantage them; and develop the infrastructure to address the needs of persons with disabilities, in particular with regard to their education, training, and rehabilitation, and eliminate discrimation against them.

Chapter 7: Reproductive Rights and Reproductive Health

This chapter covers some of the issues considered most controversial during the negotiating process; it begins by invoking the qualifying chapeau to Chapter 2. Chapter 7 contains five sections: reproductive rights and reproductive health; family planning; sexually transmitted diseases (STDs) and HIV (human immunodeficiency virus) prevention;

human sexuality and gender relations; and adolescents. It defines reproductive health as "a state of complete physical, mental, and social well-being and not merely the absence of disease or infirmity, in all matters relating to the reproductive system and to its functions and processes. Reproductive health therefore implies that people are able to have a satisfying and safe sex life and that they have the capability to reproduce and the freedome to decide if, when, and how to do so. Implicit in this last condition are the right of men and women to be informed and to have access to safe, effective, affordable, and acceptable methods of family planning of their choice, as well as other methods of their choice for regulation of fertitlity which are not against the law..."

And "reproductive rights embrace certain human rights that are already recognized in national laws, international human rights documents, and other relevant United Nations consensus documents. These rights rest on the recognition of the basic right of all couples and individuals to decide freely and responsibly the number, spacing, and timing of their children and to have information and means to do so, and the right to attain the highest standard of sexual and reproductive health. It also includes the right of all to make decisions concerning reproduction free of discrimination, coercion, and violence as expressed in human rights documents."

The chapter also states that "appropriate services" for adolescents "must safeguard [their] rights...to privacy, confidentiality, respect, and informed consent, respecting cultural values and religious beliefs. In this context countries should, where appropriate, remove legal, regulatory, and social barriers to reproductive health information and care for adolescents."

Chapter 8: Health, Morbidity, and Mortality

This chapter contains sections on: primary health care and the health-care sector; child survival and health; women's health and safe motherhood; and HIV/AIDS. It contains the paragraph that was subject to perhaps the most lengthy and heated debate, paragraph 8.25, which now states: "In no case should abortion be promoted as a method of family planning. All governments and relevant intergovernmental and non-governmental organizations are urged to strengthen their commitment to women's health, to deal with the health impact of unsafe abortion*** as a major public health concern and to reduce the recourse to abortion through expanded and improved family planning services. Prevention of unwanted pregnancies must always be given the highest priority and all attempts should be made to eliminate the need for abortion. Women who have unwanted pregnancies should have ready access to reliable information and compassionate counselling. Any measures or changes related to abortion within the health system can

only be determined at the national or local level according to the national legislative process. In circumstances in which abortion is not against the law, such abortion should be safe. In all cases women should have access to quality services for the management of complications arising from abortion. Post-abortion counselling, education, and family planning services should be offered promptly which will also help to avoid repeat abortions." The footnote, which cites the World Health Organization, reads: "***Unsafe abortion is defined as a procedure for terminating an unwanted pregnancy either by persons lacking necessary skills or in an environment lacking the minimal medical standards or both."

The chapter also urges countries to strive to achieve specific goals, such as:

- reducing infant and under-five mortality rates by one third, or to 50-70 per 1,000 live births, whichever is less, by the year 2000;
- reducing infant mortality to below 35 per 1,000 live births, and under-five mortality to below 45, by 2015; and
- reducing maternal mortality to half its 1990 level by 2000 and halving it again by 2015.

Chapter 9: Population Distribution, Urbanization, and Internal Migration

This chapter describes urbanization as "intrinsic" to economic and social development and calls on countries to adopt strategies that encourage the growth of small or medium-sized urban centres and to seek to develop rural areas while shoring up efforts to develop large municipalities' capacity to meet their own needs. It also states that "measures should be taken, at the national level with international cooperation, as appropriate, in accordance with the United Nations Charter, to find lasting solutions to questions related to internally displaced persons, including their right to voluntary and safe return to their home of origin."

Chapter 10: International Migration

This chapter states that poverty and environmental degradation, combined with the absence of peace and security, and human rights violations are all factors affecting international migration. It examines the specific circumstances of documented and undocumented migrants, refugees, asylum-seekers, and displaced persons. It urges governments to: address the root causes of migration, especially those related to poverty; encourage cooperation between sending and receiving countries; facilitate the integration of returning migrants; prevent the exploitation of undocumented migrants and ensure that their basic human rights are protected; protect migrants from racism and xenophobia; find durable solutions to the plight of refugees and displaced persons; and prevent the erosion of the right to asylum.

On the issue of family reunification, which was the subject of some debate at the Conference, the document states: "Consistent with Article 10 of the Convention on the Rights of the Child and all other relevant universally recognized human rights instruments, all governments, particularly those of receiving countries, must recognize the vital importance of family reunification and promote its integration into their national legislation in order to ensure the protection of the unity of families of documented migrants." And: "Governments are urged to promote, through family reunion, the normalization of the family life of legal migrants who have the right to long-term residence."

Chapter 11: Population, Development, and Education

This chapter describes education as a key factor in sustainable development and recommends providing universal access to quality education, especially primary and technical education and job training; eradicating illiteracy; eliminating gender inequality in educational opportunties and support; promoting non-formal education for young people; and introducing and improving the content of the curriculum so as to promote greater responsibility towards, and awareness of, the interrelationships between population and sustainable development, health issues, responsible parenthood, and gender equity.

Chapter 12: Technology, Research, and Development

This chapter stresses the importance of valid, reliable, timely, and internationally comparable data on all aspects of policies and programmes. It acknowledges that reproductive health research, especially biomedical research, has been instrumental in giving increasing numbers of people greater access to a wider range of safe and effective modern contraceptives. It adds that social and economic research is needed to enable programmes to take into account the views of their intended beneficiaries, especially women, the young, and other less empowered groups.

Chapter 13: National Action

This is the first of four chapters dedicated to implementation of the Programme of Action, and includes estimates of the funding levels required to meet the needs of developing countries and countries with economies in transition in the period 2000-2015 for basic reproductive health services including family planning and prevention of STDs and HIV/AIDS; population data collection, analysis, and dissemination; policy formulation; and research. The price tag: US$17.0 billion in 2000; US$18.5 billion in 2005; US$20.5 in 2010; and US$21.7 billion in 2015.

The chapter states that national legislators can have a major role to play in enacting domestic legislation to implement the Programme of Action, allocating appropriate financial resources, ensuring accountability of expenditure, and raising public awareness of population issues. It encourages governments to improve the skills and accountability of managers and others involved in national population and development strategies, policies, plans, and programmes.

Chapter 14: International Cooperation

This chapter urges the international community to fulfil the target, agreed upon for years, of committing 0.7 per cent of gross national product for overall official development assistance (ODA), and increasing the proportion of ODA dedicated to population to the levels necessary to implement the Programme of Action. Given the estimates laid out in Chapter 13, and assuming that developing countries and economies in transition will be able to generate sufficient increases in domestic resources, the need for complementary resources from "donor" countries would be roughly US$5.7 billion in 2000; US$6.1 billion in 2005; US$6.8 billion in 2010; and US$7.2 billion in 2015.

The chapter also takes note of an initiative to mobilize resources to give all people access to basic social services, known as the 20/20 Initiative, which will be studied further by the World Summit for Social Development.

Chapter 15: Partnership with the Non-Governmental Sector

This chapter acknowledges the vital roles of two sets of players in population and development: local, national, and international non-governmental organizations (NGOs); and the private sector. It calls on governments and development agencies to integrate NGOs into their decision-making and facilitate the contributions NGOs can make in implementing the Programme of Action. It also urges governments in the North and South to respect and help preserve NGOs' autonomy.

Chapter 16: Follow-up to the Conference

This chapter reiterates some of the points made in the preceding three chapters and adds that all interested individuals and organizations should be involved in the Conference follow-up; that they should publicize the Programme of Action as widely as possible and seek public support for it; that the international community, UN system, and anyone else in a position to provide financial and technical assistance should do so; and that South-South cooperation should play an important role in helping countries to implement the Programme of Action.

This article is a summary description of the ICPD Programme of Action, and is not an official version of the document. For more information, contact: ICPD Secretariat, 220 East 42nd Street, 22nd floor, New York, NY 10017, USA.

OPTIMISM AND OVERPOPULATION

Well, yes, the West must pay attention to the population problems of the Third World. But what sort of attention? The conventional wisdom holds that economic development —and thus economic aid from the West—is the key to curbing population growth in poor nations. Not true, says **VIRGINIA ABERNETHY**

Virginia Abernethy *is a professor of psychiatry and anthropology at Vanderbilt University and the editor of the journal* Population and Environment. *She is the author of* Population Pressure and Cultural Adjustment *(1979) and* Population Politics: The Choices That Shape Our Future *(1993).*

OVERPOPULATION afflicts most countries but remains primarily a local problem—an idea that this article will seek to explain. Reproductive restraint, the solution, is also primarily local; it grows out of a sense that resources are shrinking. Under these circumstances individuals and couples often see limitation of family size as the most likely path to success.

Many scholars, ancient and modern, have known that actual family size is very closely linked to the number of children people want. Paul Demeny, of The Population Council, is exceptionally clear on this, and the World Bank economist Lant Pritchett asserts that 85–95 percent of actual fertility rates are explained by parents' desires—not by mere availability of contraceptives. Pritchett writes that "the impressive declines in fertility observed in the contemporary world are due al-

most entirely to equally impressive declines in desired fertility." Of Paul Kennedy's contention, in his book *Preparing for the Twenty-first Century*, that "the only practical way to ensure a decrease in fertility rates, and thus in population growth, is to introduce cheap and reliable forms of birth control," Pritchett says, "We could not have invented a clearer and more articulate statement of the view we argue is wrong."

PROGRESS AND POPULATION

CROSS-CULTURAL and historical data suggest that people have usually limited their families to a size consistent with living comfortably in stable communities. If left undisturbed, traditional societies survive over long periods in balance with local resources. A society lasts in part because it maintains itself within the carrying capacity of its environment.

However, the perception of limits that derive from the local environment is easily neutralized by signals that promise prosperity. Quoting the late Georg Borgstrom, a renowned food scientist and a much-decorated specialist in Third World economies who died five years ago, a 1971 Population Reference Bureau publication explains,

> A number of civilizations, including India and Indonesia, "had a clear picture of the limitations of their villages or communities" before foreign intervention disrupted the traditional patterns. Technical aid programs . . . "made them believe that the adoption of certain technical advances [was] going to free them of this bondage and of dependence on such restrictions."

Economic expansion, especially if it is introduced from outside the society and is also broad-based, encourages the belief that formerly recognized limits can be discounted, that everyone can look forward to prosperity, and, as in recent instances, that the West can be counted upon to provide assistance, rescue, and an escape valve for excess population.

The perception of new opportunity, whether due to technological advance, expanded trade, political change, foreign aid, moving to a richer land, or the disappearance of competitors (who move away or die), encourages larger family size. Families eagerly fill any apparently larger niche, and the extra births and consequent population growth often overshoot actual opportunity.

Increase beyond a sustainable number is an ever-present threat, because human beings take their cue from the opportunity that is apparent *today*, and are easily fooled by change. Relying on what is near in space or time, we calculate with difficulty the long-term momentum of population growth, the limits to future technological advance, and the inexorable progression of resource depletion.

The appearance (and short-term reality) of expanding opportunity takes various guises. In the 1950s land redistribution in Turkey led formerly landless peasants to increase significantly the size of their families. Among African Sahel pastoralists, deep-water wells drilled by donor countries in the 1950s and 1960s prompted larger herds of cattle and goats, earlier marriage (because bride-prices are paid in animals and the required number became easier to accumulate), and higher fertility. Similarly, Ireland's widespread cultivation of the potato in the early eighteenth century increased agricultural productivity and encouraged peasants to subdivide portions of their farms into plots for their sons, which in turn promoted younger marriage and a baby boom. Still earlier, between the sixth and ninth centuries, the introduction in Europe of the stirrup, the rigid-collar harness, and nailed horseshoes greatly enhanced the agricultural output of Europe's northern plains. Better nutrition helped lead Europe out of the Dark Ages to economic recovery and thence, from about 1050 to 1350, to a tripling of population size in countries such as England and France.

India offers another example. Its population was nearly stable from 400 B.C. to about A.D. 1600. After the end of the Mogul invasions, and with the advent of new trade opportunities, the population began to grow (at about half the European rate). Later, European trade offered India further opportunity, and population growth accelerated. It took off for the skies shortly after the country shed its colonial status, in 1947; assistance from the USSR, the World Bank, and the International Monetary Fund bolstered perceptions of a prosperous future, and the rate of population growth accelerated up until about 1980.

Successful independence movements and populist coups are prominent among the kinds of changes that carry the message that times are good and getting better. China commenced its euphoric interlude with the expulsion of the Nationalists, in 1949. Communism triumphed, and its philosophy held that a greater nation required more people. The fertility rate and population size rocketed upward. A mainland-China population that was estimated to be 559 million in 1949 grew to 654 million in 1959, whereas in the preceding 100 years of political turmoil and war the average growth rate of the Chinese population had been just 0.3 per-

cent a year. Both lower mortality and higher fertility contributed to the increase. Judith Banister writes in *China's Changing Population*, "Fertility began rising in the late 1940s, and was near or above 6 births per woman during the years 1952-57, higher fertility than had been customary" in prior decades. Banister attributes China's baby boom to war's end and to government policy: "Land reform of 1950-51 redistributed land to landless peasants and tenant farmers."

Cuba experienced a baby boom when Fidel Castro displaced Fulgencio Batista, in 1959. Castro explicitly prom-

THE encounters with scarcity that are currently being forced upon billions of people by the natural limits of their environment are beginning to correct the consequences of decades of misperception. Now, as it has done many times in human history, the rediscovery of limits is awakening the motivation to limit family size.

ised a redistribution of wealth, and according to the demographers S. Díaz-Briquets and L. Pérez, fertility rose in response. Díaz-Briquets and Pérez write, "The main factor was the real income rise among the most disadvantaged groups brought about by the redistribution measures of the revolutionary government. The fertility rises in almost every age group suggest that couples viewed the future as more promising and felt they could now afford more children."

The populations of Algeria, Zimbabwe, and Rwanda grew rapidly around the time colonial powers left. Algeria, for example, achieved independence in 1962, and thirty years later 70 percent of its population was under thirty years of age. Zimbabwe gained independence in 1980, and soon achieved one of the highest population-growth rates in the world; the growth was encouraged by the Health Minister, who attacked family planning as a "white colonialist plot" to limit black power.

Because of their effect on family size, development programs entailing large transfers of technology and funds to the Third World have been especially pernicious. This kind of aid is inappropriate because it sends the signal that wealth and opportunity can grow without effort and without limit. That rapid population growth ensues should surprise no one. Africa, which in recent decades has received three times as much foreign aid per capita as any other continent, now also has the highest fertility rates. During the 1950s and 1960s the African fertility rate rose—to almost seven children per woman—at the same time that infant mortality was dramatically reduced, health-care availability grew, literacy for women and men became more widespread, and economic optimism pervaded more and more sectors of society. Extraordinarily high rates of population growth were new to Africa; during the 1950s the Latin American rate had been higher.

Even immigration can affect total world population. Studies of nineteenth-century England and Wales and modern Caribbean societies show that in communities already in the throes of rapid population growth, fertility stays high as long as the option to emigrate exists, whereas fertility falls rapidly in communities that lack such an escape valve. And while fertility rates are falling in most African countries, the rate remains high in Ghana (6.2 births per woman in 1993), perhaps because an established pattern of emigration (one per 1,000 in the population) provides a safety valve for excess numbers. This effect on fertility is consistent with independent reports that emigration raises incomes both among emigrants and among those they leave behind.

In sum, it is true, if awkward, that efforts to alleviate poverty often spur population growth, as does leaving open the door to immigration. Subsidies, windfalls, and the prospect of economic opportunity remove the immediacy of needing to conserve. The mantras of democracy, redistribution, and economic development raise expectations and fertility rates, fostering population growth and thereby steepening a downward environmental and economic spiral.

Despite this fact, certain experts and the public they inform nevertheless wish to believe that fertility rates have traditionally been high worldwide and have declined only in industrialized countries or in countries where modern contraception is available, and that the post–Second World War population explosion is explained mostly by better health and nutrition, which led to rapidly declining mortality rates and slight, involuntary increases in fertility. The possibility that larger family size resulted from wanting more children continues to be denied.

Experts in population studies were the first to be fooled. In the 1930s many demographers predicted a steady decline in population, because the low fertility of Western industrialized countries was attributed to development and modernization rather than to the endemic pessimism brought on by the Great Depression. Still missing the point, many failed to see that the high fertility after the Second World War was a response to the perception of expanding economic opportunity. The U.S. Baby Boom (1947–1961) and the slightly later booms in Western Europe took most demographers by surprise.

THE MESSAGE OF
SCARCITY

As it happens, the encounters with scarcity that are currently being forced upon literally billions of people by the natural limits of their environment are begin-

ning to correct the consequences of decades of misperception. The rhetoric of modernization, international development, and egalitarianism is losing its power to mislead. As Europe is revealed to be incapable of alleviating the suffering of the former Yugoslavia, as rich countries in general prove nearly powerless to help the countless distant multitudes, it becomes difficult to believe in rescue. Now, as it has done many times in human history, the rediscovery of limits is awakening the motivation to limit family size.

In Ireland land became scarce relative to the rapidly growing population in the early nineteenth century, whereupon fertility began a retreat to its low, pre-potato level. By 1830 only about two thirds of women married before age twenty-five. Ten percent married this young in 1851—a drastic postponement of marriage in response to the 1846–1851 potato famine. Following a brief recovery, as few as 12 percent married before age twenty-five. The pattern of late marriage persisted from about 1890 through the Second World War. In the United States the Baby Boom ended at about the time the jobs pipeline began to fill; the fertility rate dropped below replacement level after the 1973 oil shock occurred and many Americans' real income stopped rising. In post-revolutionary China population momentum built until famine, unrelieved by Western aid, forced a confrontation with limits. In 1979, mindful of severe food shortages, the government instituted a one-child-per-family policy, thus completing the evolution of incentives and controls that returned the country to the pre-Communist pattern of marital and reproductive restraint. In Cuba the Castro-inspired baby boom gave way to below-replacement-level fertility when communism's inability to deliver prosperity became manifest. In Eastern-bloc countries, including Russia, economic restructuring, the dissipation of government consumption subsidies, and the public perception of rising infant mortality have promoted lower fertility rates and created demand for the avoidance of pregnancy.

In Zimbabwe, prodded by the international economic retrenchment of the late 1980s, the government began to support family planning. According to *The Economist*, "The hefty cost of supporting a large family has helped persuade some men of the value of limiting its size." The fertility rate is falling among the Yoruba in Nigeria, owing to a combination of delayed marriage and increasing acceptance of modern contraception. Two thirds of the women who responded to a recent survey said that "the major force behind marriage postponement and the use of contraception to achieve it was the present hard economic conditions."

Elsewhere the demand for modern contraception is also rising, and again the reason seems to be that couples view early marriage and large families as unaffordable. In his new book, *Critical Masses*, the journalist George D. Moffett reports that a mother of two in Mexico defended her use of contraception before a village priest by explaining, "Things are difficult here. A majority of people are having hard times.

Jobs are hard to come by." Similarly, a day laborer in Thailand, in the words of Moffett, "would like to have one more child, but he understands that that is beyond his means."

Without the motivation to limit family size, access to modern contraception is nearly irrelevant. For six years in the 1950s a project directed by the British researcher John Wyon provided several villages in northern India with family-planning education, access to contraception, and medical care. The villagers had positive attitudes toward the health-care providers and toward family planning, and infant mortality had fallen way down. But the fertility rate stayed way up.

Wyon's group soon figured out why: the villagers liked large families. They were delighted that now, with lower infant mortality, they could have the six surviving children they had always wanted. The well-funded Wyon project may even have reinforced the preference for large families, by playing a part in making extra children affordable.

THINK LOCALLY

MISCALCULATION about the *cause* of the population explosion has led to irrelevant and even counterproductive strategies for helping the Third World to balance its population size and its resources. In the late 1940s and the heady decades that followed, trade, independence movements, populist revolutions, foreign aid, and new technology made people in all walks of life believe in abundance and an end to the natural limits imposed by the environments with which they were familiar.

Now it is a step forward for industrial nations, their wealth much diminished, to be retrenching and targeting aid more narrowly. Their remaining wealth must not be squandered on arming opposing factions, reckless foreign assistance, or support for international migrations that rob and ultimately enrage—to the point of violence and possibly civil war—resident populations. This retrenchment saddens many, but the former liberality did a disservice to every country targeted for development.

With a new, informed understanding of human responses, certain kinds of aid remain appropriate: microloans that foster grassroots enterprise, where success is substantially related to effort; and assistance with family-planning services, not because contraception is a solution in and of itself but because modern contraception is a humane way of achieving small family size when small family size is desired. This modest agenda remains within the means of industrialized countries even as they look to the needs of the growing ranks of their own poor. And it does not mislead and unintentionally harm intended beneficiaries.

The idea that economic development is the key to curbing world population growth rests on assumptions and assertions that have influenced international aid policy for some fifty years. These assumptions do not stand up to historical or anthropological scrutiny, however, and the policies they have spawned have contributed to runaway population growth.

The human capacity for adaptive response evolved in face-to-face interactions. Humanity's strong suit is quick response to environmental cues—a response more likely to be appropriate when the relevant environment is immediate and local. The mind's horizon is here and now. Our ancestors evolved and had to succeed in small groups that moved around relatively small territories. They had to succeed one day at a time—or not be anyone's ancestors. So, unsurprisingly, signals that come from the local environment are powerfully motivating.

Let the globalists step aside. One-world solutions do not work. Local solutions will. Everywhere people act in accord with their perception of their best interests. People are adept at interpreting *local* signs to find the *next* move needed. In many countries and communities today, where social, economic, and environmental conditions are indubitably worsening, the demand for modern contraception is rising, marriage and sexual initiation are delayed, and family size is contracting. Individuals responding with low fertility to signs of limits are the local solution. One prays that the hucksters of inappropriate development do not mess this up.

Poor Lands' Success In Cutting Birth Rate Upsets Old Theories

William K. Stevens

It used to be assumed that economic development was the best way for a poor country to reduce its population growth. But new studies suggest that a country like Bangladesh can cut its birth rate significantly if it aggressively promotes the adoption of modern contraceptive methods—without waiting for the reduction that traditionally comes with higher living standards.

In what some experts are calling a reproductive revolution, birth rates are falling in countries presumably too poor for economic development that would stabilize rapid population growth, as it did in Europe and North America early this century.

"Contraceptives are the best contraceptive," write three demographic researchers who are challenging the conventional theory of modern human population growth and decline.

The theory, predicated on the experience of the industrialized world before modern contraceptives, says that in a pre-industrial economy people tend to have many children but that high death rates hold the population down. As a country industrializes, living conditions improve, the practice of medicine advances and life spans increase, but the birth rate remains high and the population soars.

Birth rates drop only when education spreads and people find that too many children are an economic liability, according to the theory. Thus begins an era of low mortality, low fertility and stable but not runaway population growth—the condition of the industrialized world today.

This "demographic transition," as some social scientists call it, would also be the surest and most likely path to stable populations for developing countries.

Bangladesh is cited by the authors of the study as a "perfect example" of how the concept linking the fertility rate to developing economies has been disproved. The South Asian country, one of the world's poorest and most densely populated, has a traditional agrarian economy in which most families still depend on children for economic security. Yet fertility rates in Bangladesh declined by 21 percent between 1970 and 1991, to 5.5 children per woman from 7, according to Government figures. In the same period, the use of contraception among married women of reproductive age rose to 40 percent from 3 percent.

A LESSON IS DRAWN

To Bryant Robey of the Johns Hopkins School of Hygiene and Public Health and editor of American Demographics magazine, the lesson is clear: "If fertility rates are to fall, don't wait around for the forces of modernization to slowly work their way. Make family planning available, and you might be surprised by the number of couples that use them." Bangladesh, for one, "has a very effective family planning program," he said.

Population experts have considered Bangladesh's acceptance of family planning especially noteworthy and surprising because it is a predominantly Muslim country.

One reason for the spread of contraception in the third world is that demand is rising, Mr. Robey said. And a major factor behind increased demand, he believes, is the ease with which new ideas now spread into rural areas, changing people's attitudes about birth control.

"I think this was a big factor in Thailand," he said. "Even though the country is largely rural, communications are good and people are linked so that new ideas can travel fast."

The birth rate in Thailand dropped to 2.3 children per woman in 1987 from 4.6 in 1975. Condom use in Thailand has been vigorously promoted both as a contraceptive and an AIDS preventive.

A NOTION IS DISPUTED

"Fertility rates in developing countries have fallen much more rapidly than they did during the European demographic transition," Mr. Robey and two other population analysts wrote in Scientific American. These findings, they wrote, "dispute the notion that 'development is the best contraceptive;' " rather, "contraceptives are the best contraceptive."

Mr. Robey's co-authors are Dr. Shea O. Rutstein of Macro International, a private research organization, and Dr. Leo Morris of the Centers for Disease Control and Prevention.

The relative effectiveness of economic development and family-planning programs in bringing down the birth rate is much more than an academic concern. Even if the worldwide rate were to drop to the replacement level of 2.1 children per couple, United Nations demographers say, the current global population of 5.6 billion could double by the middle of the next century before eventually stabilizing at nearly 12 billion. Should fertility remain even 5 percent greater than replacement level, according to a United Nations analysis, the population would reach 21 billion in the year 2150.

The impact of humans on the global environment is already serious, in the view of most students of the subject. And there are widespread fears among ecologist and environmentalists that even if a human population growing out of control were somehow able to support itself, the result eventually could still be an environmental catastrophe.

U.S. POLICY REVERSED

The new findings have a bearing on United States policy. Under the Reagan and Bush Administrations, Washington refused to finance international population programs that provided women with counseling on abortion. The Clinton Administration, arguing that population control is crucial to the world's future, has reversed that policy.

The new study gives some cause for optimism about population control, Mr. Robey says, because birth rates in developing countries have declined by about one-third, to an average of four children, per woman, since the mid-1960's, when the average was six children per woman. This is about halfway to replacement level.

The plunge is still more evident in some cases, according to surveys of more than 300,000 women in 44 countries in sub-Saharan Africa, Latin America, the Caribbean, the Middle East, North Africa and Asia during the last eight years. The studies, part of an international effort that began 20 years ago, were largely financed by the United States Agency for International Development.

Not included in the surveys were the world's two most populous countries, China and India, but data from independent national surveys for those countries were included in the study. In China, where mandatory controls on family size are in effect, the birth rate dropped to

2.3 in 1988 from 5.99 in 1965; in India, where participation in family-planning programs is voluntary, it dropped to 4.2 in 1989 from 5.69 in 1965.

SHARP DROP IN COLOMBIA

Besides sharp drops in Thailand and Bangladesh, the study found that in Colombia the birth rate fell to 2.8 children in 1990 from 4.7 in 1975. In Indonesia, fertility declined by 46 percent between 1971 and 1991; in Morocco, by 31 percent between 1980 and 1991.

Family-planning programs have already reduced the world population by more than 400 million from what it would otherwise be, according to a 1990 study by Dr. John Bongaarts, W. Parker Mauldin and Dr. James F. Phillips of the Population Council, an independent international organization based in New York that conducts research on population and development.

Their study calculated that in the absence of family-planning programs, the population of the developing world would reach 14.6 billion by the year 2100 rather than the 10 billion now projected. But they also found a relationship between economic development and family-planning programs that enhances fertility reduction.

"You need economic development almost as a precondition," Dr. Bongaarts said, "but once you have some development, family-planning programs help accelerate the decline of fertility."

Two consequences of development stand out as influences on declining fertility, he said: falling death rates and better education, especially for women. When more children survive, it puts

pressure on the family's resources, encouraging people to have fewer offspring. And educated women tend to make better use of contraceptives, he said.

If a consensus is emerging that development and family-planning programs work synergistically, what is their potential for putting the brakes on world population growth?

The potential for development is difficult to gauge, governed as it is by complex factors of economics and politics, not to mention the chronically depressive effect of population growth itself. Similarly, it is difficult to assess how rapidly demand for contraceptives will grow. But Mr. Robey says it is clear that the potential for further decline in birth rates through expansion of family planning programs is substantial.

"The demand for family planning already far surpasses its supply," he and his colleagues wrote in Scientific American. "In the countries surveyed, between 20 and 30 percent of married women are not using contraception even though they want to avoid pregnancy."

If the demand were met, they calculated, the use of contraceptives in developing countries would rise to more than 60 percent from 51 percent. This, they wrote, would cause fertility to fall from the present average of four children per woman to about three, or one child more than replacement level.

Is that sufficient?

"We're certainly not saying that the population problem, so to speak, is solved," Mr. Robey said, "but certainly fertility has come down a lot faster than even experts thought a few decades ago. I guess we see reason for hope if money and effort can be found in the future to continue this process."

The Exploding Cities of the Developing World

Eugene Linden

Eugene Linden is a Contributor at Time *and author of* The Alms Race: The Impact of American Voluntary Aid Abroad.

VULNERABLE GIANTS

THE RHYTHM of history has been the rise, collapse, and occasional rebirth of cities. Until recently urban populations waxed and waned as disease, changes in trade and technology, and shifting political fortunes rewarded some cities and penalized others. In this century the rhythm has been interrupted in the developing world, where urban populations almost always rise. Lured by the bright lights, or driven from the countryside by political and economic turmoil, population pressures, and ecological breakdown, billions of people have been migrating to the cities.

This influx strains the resources, leadership, and infrastructure of already overburdened countries. Migrants from the desperately poor interior of sub-Saharan African continue to come to Kinshasa, Zaire, despite the collapse of its economy and services, which has led to rampant disease and malnutrition and brought the city to the edge of anarchy. Pakistanis pour into Karachi despite factional violence characterized by car bombings and gun battles in the streets. Question marks hang in the polluted air over megacities like Rio de Janeiro, São Paulo, Jakarta, Mexico City, Cairo, Delhi, and Beijing and tens of thousands of smaller cities in Asia, Africa, and Latin America. Many First World cities are also coping with waves of poor newcomers at a time when their tax base is eroding as companies and well-to-do citizens move out, driven away by high costs, crime, and a deteriorating quality of life.

More and more, the fate of cities determines the fate of nations and regions. Karachi, for instance, accounts for half of government revenues in Pakistan and 20 percent of GDP. It is the country's financial center and only port and has the highest concentration of literate people. Given the ties between Karachi's ethnic groups and powerful tribes elsewhere in the country, if the current factional violence in the city intensifies, unrest could engulf the rest of Pakistan's well-armed populace, perhaps leading to international conflicts and large crossborder movements of people.

With ever-increasing global integration, problems that arise in one city can quickly spread throughout its region and even worldwide. The health of cities in the developed world depends in some measure on developing nations' efforts to control new diseases and drug-resistant strains of old ones incubating in their slums. Moreover, as Earth becomes more and more crowded, how successfully developing world cities absorb continuing migration will have much to do with whether tides of humanity overwhelm nations and regions in years to come. The developed world ignores at its peril the problems of Third World cities.

MISMEASURE OF A METROPOLIS

AT THE turn of the century roughly five percent of the world's people lived in cities with populations over 100,000. Today an estimated 45 percent—slightly more than 2.5 billion people—live in urban centers. In recent years the most explosive growth has been in the developing world. Between 1950 and 1995 the number of cities in the developed world with populations greater than 1 million more than doubled, from 40 to 112; in the same period, million-plus cities in the developing world increased sixfold, from 34 to 213. The United Nations estimates that rural numbers will remain virtually steady while urban populations continue to soar: by 2025, it predicts, more than 5 billion people, or 61 percent of humanity, will be living in cities.

Determining what steps governments might take to lessen the shocks of this coming era of giant cities calls for information not available today. It is difficult, for example, to get a fix on something as elementary as the size of the larger cities. In 1992 some estimates put the population of Mexico City at 20 million. Now the United Nations set the number at 15.6 million—a difference bigger than Baghdad. Karachi may have 9.5 million residents, or it may have 12 million; São Paulo, at 16 million, has several million fewer than in earlier estimates. Part of the problem is the uncertainty of census data—where there has been a census at all—in nations that do not have the resources to conduct an efficient count and where squatters and legal residents may have sound reasons for evading the tally.

Migration to the cities is also difficult to analyze or predict. Often it is a product of both the pull of perceived opportunities and services in the metropolis and the push of rural unemployment caused by the mechanization of agriculture, oversubdivision of farmland, and environmental degradation. In China's rural Sichuan province, for example, where the land cannot come close to supporting the people on it, workers are squeezed out to join the country's "floating population" of some 100 million souls.

The conventional wisdom has been that megacities will continue to grow to horrific size. Experience, however, has sometimes proved otherwise, as in Mexico. As economic and political power was consolidated in Mexico City from the 1940s onward, peasants flocked to the capital, drawn by the prospect of jobs and lavishly subsidized transportation, health care, and education. Since the mid-1980s, however, when Mexico began opening its markets, many companies producing for domestic consumption have closed down; the job losses and cutbacks in government spending hit the capital disproportionately, and immigration has moderated in response. What might be called the rising costs of admission, as scarcity of land, water, and other resources drive up prices in the capital, is also having an effect. In recent years Mexicans have followed jobs to secondary cities like Monterrey. Thus U.N. projections for Mexico City's population at century's end have been halved since 1973, from 32 million to 16.4 million, and have been wildly off the mark for other cities, from Rio de Janeiro to Seoul.

The emphasis on megacities, argues David Satterthwaite of the International Institute of Environment and Development in London, is based on misapprehensions about what made them big and diverts attention from the real problems. There are probably 30,000 urban centers in the developing world, he says. "We concentrate on perhaps 100 of them." The fastest-growing cities on the planet, after all, are not the giant metropolises but anonymous secondary cities—agglomerations like El Alto, a sprawling collection of 500,000 people in Bolivia that has been expanding nine percent a year with virtually no planning and a haphazard infrastructure. The infant mortality rate in the million-plus Indian city of Kanpur is nearly four times that in Delhi. The second-rank cities must deal with all the problems facing a Karachi or Jakarta without the national attention and international assistance that go to the more visible megacities.

THE DISEASED CITY

THE GENERAL picture of the developing world in the latter half of the twentieth century painted by international institutions is one of tremendous progress in improving health and raising incomes: child mortality has been cut in half and income share more than doubled, according to the World Bank. These statistics, however, have been skewed by the tremendous health gains and economic growth of China and the newly industrializing Asian Tigers. Roughly one billion people—more than at any other time in history—live in households too poor to obtain enough food to provide nourishment for normal work, points out James Gustave Speth, the current head of the U.N. Development Programme. Another two billion live in conditions Speth describes as deplorable. About 1.5 billion poor people now live in cities, and many of them see their prospects dimming and family and community ties dissolving at the same time that assaults on their personal well-being have risen sharply.

Even the greatest and most enduring cities seem vulnerable when one considers the natural, political, and economic upheavals they must contend with. Poverty, unemployment disease, crime, and pollution have plagued urban centers for 10,000 years, since the earliest cities developed around granaries and armories in Mesopotamia and Anatolia. There is reason to believe, however, that while the individual problems facing cities are not new, an unholy synergy created in the developing world when explosive population growth, industrialization, and capital scarcity meet means dangers on an unprecedented scale.

After the decline of ancient Rome, nearly 1,800 years passed before a city again reached a population of one million, as London did in the nineteenth century. Until then, crowded slums without running water or sewers and inadequate public health procedures allowed microbes to flourish, and epidemics regularly decimated populations. Advances in sanitation and the discovery of antibiotics have given humanity a century's respite from the ravages of infectious disease. But many epidemiologists fear this period is drawing to a close as urban growth outruns the installation of sanitation in the developing world and resilient microbes discover opportunities in the stressed immune systems of the urban poor.

Disease transmitted by insects are staging a comeback from the ditches and trash heaps of squatter settlements. Mosquito hosts for the larvae of the parasite that causes filariasis can breed in polluted water. *Anopheles stephensi* mosquitoes need cleaner water but find it in open water tanks and the irrigated urban gardens of India and Africa. The malaria they carry is now the leading cause of hospital visits and deaths from infectious disease in Latin American and Africa, according to Carolyn Stephens, an epidemiologist at the London School of Hygiene and Tropical Medicine. The mosquito that transmits dengue has also benefited from urbanization, multiplying in old tires, flowerpots, and water drums.

While disease vary from city to city, one motif the megacities of the developing world share is pollution. To live in Mexico City or Delhi is to live in a place where the basic elements of life—air, water, and soil—have become inimical to health. Many of the cities in China have five to ten times the levels of particulates and sulfur dioxide found in the air of First World cities; a recent sampling in Guangzhou revealed concentrations of these pollutants among the highest ever measured anywhere. In Beijing and other Chinese metropolises ordinary people have been driven to riot by pollution ranging from incessant noise to choking clouds of coal dust. In some parts of Poland the land and water have been so poisoned by toxic waste that ten percent of babies are born with birth defects. Inadequate zoning regulations and enforcement, antiquated technologies, corruption, rising consumption, and burgeoning populations all play a part.

Pollution also has a role in the renewed spread of infectious disease. Untreated sewage flowing into the Bay of Bengal off Bangladesh made its way into the bilge tanks of a freighter headed for South America; a relatively new strain of cholera came along for the ride. According to Paul Epstein, an epidemiologist at the Harvard School of Public Health, when the tanker emptied its bilge off Peru, the microbe found a home in algal blooms in the coastal waters that had been nurtured by sewage from Lima. From there the cholera made its way into cities as people ate contaminated shellfish. Since arriving in Latin America in 1991, the disease has struck 320,000 people and killed 2,600.

Stephens' work has shown that poor people in cities die disproportionately from both infectious diseases and chronic illnesses, such as cancer and heart disease, associated with more developed societies. She and others argue that disease, along with pollution, is a symptom of a larger threat to urban dwellers: poverty. Many people endure these risks in the hope that work in the city will pay enough for them to move their families out of harm's way. But as cities continue to swell because of migration and births, workers face crowds of competitors like themselves. Beijing is now home to an estimated one million floating workers in search of jobs. Unemployment rates in scores of African cities top 20 percent and are unlikely to drop soon.

Disease, squalor, hopelessness, stress, and the decline of traditional cultural constraints in the atomized contemporary city conspire to aggravate yet another health hazard: violence. Homicides and other violence accounted for 86 percent of all deaths among teenage boys in São Paulo in a study Stephens conducted. Karachi, with roughly four million unemployed, many of them teens, has an endless supply of recruits for its ethnic militias and drive-by assassination teams. "You have a lot of people sitting around idly, and a lot of guns," says a World Bank official. "All you need is a little ideology and you can get your own army." The mixture helps fuel the Islamic uprising in Algerian cities and a crime wave in Rio that has driven the middle class into garrisons and encouraged vigilante justice.

Finally, there is war, which, as the stories that have emerged from Monrovia, Mogadishu, and Kigali show, inflicts unique horrors on those trapped in cities that at the best of times have trouble taking care of the injured, the hungry, and the displaced. Even without the stresses of war, the quality of life for the poor has declined to the point where observers who long believed city dwellers had the advantage now recognize that large numbers of impoverished urbanites are worse off than the rural poor.

Violence, disorder, pollution, and disease can ultimately become so severe that authorities abdicate, foreign investors retreat, and a city begins to slide into chaos. Karachi has flirted with this threshold in the past and after a few years of growth may be approaching it again. Kinshasa has long since crossed the line, and its slow contraction shows how a city dies from government corruption and incompetence.

KINSHASA DESCENDING

KINSHASA SHOULD be one of the more prosperous cities in sub-Saharan Africa. It is the capital of a country blessed with vast forests, rich agricultural lands, one of the world's great rivers, and huge reserves of copper, cobalt, manganese, and diamonds (now essentially privatized as a source of cash for the elite). During the Cold War, Zaire received billions in development aid, much of which disappeared, along with the nation's wealth, into the pockets of President Mobutu Sese Seko and his kleptocratic officials. Even so, the capital city of roughly four million people began the decade with an excellent water system, cheap and reliable electricity, and functioning public transportation.

In September 1991, however, ordinary citizens joined unpaid government troops in rioting and looting, reducing the city to a shambles; roughly $1 billion in goods changed hands. Foreign workers, many of whom provided critical services for the utilities, fled the city. Over the last three years Kinshasa has seen its formal economy shrink 40 percent. Thousands of government jobs have disappeared, the infrastructure has slowly crumbled, and businesspeople have replaced store windows with concrete facades and steel gates in anticipation of new rounds of civil disorder. Carjackers and gangs of bandits rove the streets. Those lucky enough to have work are paid in a shaky currency. Following rises of 8,500 percent in 1993 and 6,000 percent in 1994, inflation has been cut to three digits, but the economy is still extremely vulnerable. Many people eat only every other day, long-vanquished diseases such as plague are returning, and AIDS, tuberculosis, malaria, sleeping sickness, cholera, and river blindness spread.

What amazes visitors is that the city continues to function at all. Most Kinshasans live by what is facetiously called Article 25 of the constitution—debrouil-toi, or getting by on your own. A lively informal economy has sprung up and proved much more efficient than the bloated, corrupt state-owned organization. People grow crops and raise livestock on every available patch of ground. Families share good fortune and bad. Enterprising traders work the markets. Still, only food from outside donors has prevented outright starvation.

The situation is particularly frustrating because, as one U.S. State Department official put it, "Given the wealth of the nation, it would not take a lot to restore a semblance of order to the economy." The interim government of Prime Minister Kengo wa Dondo has wrested control of the central bank from Indiang Kabul, a Mobutu loyalist, and installed Patrice Djamboleka, a seasoned civil servant, who has imposed some discipline. But hopes for a savior are dim, as Mobutu has entangled most of the nation's best and brightest in his web of corruption. "There are no virgins in Zaire," it is said.

SWOLLEN CITIES, WEAKENED STATES

THE WORLD'S major cities already cast a long shadow, and as they absorb the great majority of those born in the coming decades, their economic and electoral significance will only grow—along with the danger of conflict as cities protect their interests.

How long, for instance, will China's central government be able to maintain control of booming coastal provinces dominated by industrial cities as the economy opens up and these local units gain clout? With the capitalist genie escaping from the bottle, the central government has less and less to offer in return for its claims on productivity. An attempt to reassert central control could cause provinces like Guangdong to break away and declare themselves free economic zones.

More and more, the fate of cities determines the fate of nations and entire regions.

Internal migration may also drive coastal cities to break with China. The 100 or 120 million surplus workers in the country gravitate toward cities in search of employment; Vaclav Smil of the University of Manitoba estimates that at any given time China's major urban centers each house between 500,000 and two million recent arrivals. Cities such as Guangzhou, which in 1990 averaged 5.7 people per room (the average in the United States is 0.5), are already too crowded to absorb migrants. Yet the great urban migration has only just begun in China, which is still more than 70 percent rural.

China may be fast approaching other limits. After a tenfold increase in agricultural productivity between 1978 and 1988, there may not be much room for improved yields. Recently the country went from being a net exporter to a net importer of grain. Factors including political turmoil following the death of paramount leader Deng Xiaoping, consolidation of land holdings, or protracted drought could trigger an enormous increase in the already heavy migration to the cities among China's rural population of 800 million. The government has allowed grain prices to jump more than 60 percent over the past year, possibly to boost rural incomes and encourage people to remain on the land. This, however, is a delicate game because higher food prices might inflame the urban poor. Should migration increase, the prosperous cities and provinces might try to close their gates, leaving rural China to cope with millions of desperate unemployed peasants. According to Jack Goldstone, a specialist on revolt and rebellion in China who teaches at the University of California at Davis, the tensions created by the contrast between coastal prosperity and rural poverty might even tear the country apart. This pattern of population pressures leading to collapse into warlorded states, Goldstone argues, has bedeviled the region since antiquity.

CITIES OF HOPE?

DESPITE THESE dangers, many economists view China's migrants in a positive light. Urbanization has long been seen as a necessary step in economic development (although studies of Brazil and Mexico have shown that urbanization does not necessarily lead to development). Urban living carries built-in incentives to have smaller families, take mass transportation, recycle garbage, use energy, water, and space carefully, and do other things deemed desirable in a crowded world with limited resources. In fact, the shift to the cities may be a major reason behind the present rapid drop in birthrates throughout the developing world. Concentration in urban areas may well be the only efficient way to house people and still preserve agricultural acreage and wilderness, given inexorable population growth.

But more than anything else, cities are a prism for the genius of civilizations. As Lewis Mumford put it, they are a "symbol of the possible," and this is true in the developing world no less than the developed. Cities are where entrepreneurs hatch their schemes and find the markets and financing to bring them to fruition, where the elites of technology, industry, and the arts meet to brainstorm, and where deep shifts in culture and politics might begin with an unexpected encounter.

Faced with budgetary restraints and capital scarcity, some developing world cities have adopted creative approaches to fundamental problems. Calcutta, Ho Chi Minh City, and Jakarta, for instance, have been experimenting with sewage treatment that uses wetland plants like water hyacinth and duckweed to purify waste naturally. Alternative energy sources such as wind and solar power are getting a much better reception in the developing world than they did in the developed, fossil fuel-based systems having been adjudged expensive, dirty, and a drain on foreign exchange.

Some urban cheerleaders foresee South-to-North technology transfers as cities in the developed world encounter dilemmas familiar to poorer countries, while confronting a similar scarcity of capital. One possibility is suggested by the Speedy Line, designed to meet mass transit needs in Curitiba, Brazil. Essentially a bus line with loading platforms and dedicated lanes, the Speedy Line achieves speeds and passenger capacity approaching that of a subway system at one-300th the cost. Moreover, it can be installed in six months, which means, notes Curitiba's former mayor, Jaime Lerner, "you don't have to waste a generation building a subway." Vancouver and Lyons are among the cities examining the idea's potential.

During the past few years Curitiba, a state capital in a predominantly agricultural region of southern Brazil, has become the poster child for the hopes of the developing world city. Its economy is now based on a healthy mix of manufacturing, services, and commerce. Although its 2.2 million citizens have an average annual income of only about $2,000, Curitiba offers amenities and services many First World cities fail to deliver. The city has managed to increase open space per capita by a factor of 100 since 1970 even as its population grew by 164 percent; today citizens enjoy nearly four times the open space available to New Yorkers. Curitiba has feeding centers for street children, immaculate public housing, and innovative programs like one in which the poor in neighborhoods beyond the reach of sanitation trucks trade garbage for fresh vegetables. Lerner argues that parks and good public transportation bolster ordinary people's dignity, and says, "If people feel respected, they will assume responsibility to help solve other problems."

What does Curitiba have that other cities don't? Most notably, quality leadership. Lerner and an idealistic team of technocrats with experience in urban planning have guided the city since 1970. When Lerner left office recently, he was the most popular mayor in Brazilian history. Now that he has been elected governor of Parana and a member of his mayoral administration, Rafael Greca, has succeeded him in Curitiba, the city and state may be able to mount a coordinated response to rural-urban migration, the one seemingly intractable problem for this successful city in a poor country.

THE PRECARIOUS FUTURE

CURITIBA, the Indian city of Bangalore, and a few other examples may indicate that the real problem facing poorer cities is not so much population growth or their resource base but a lack of competent leadership and sound regulations and policies that last beyond one administration. But the extreme rarity of success stories in the array of struggling municipalities suggests that this does not explain why so many cities are having trouble creating an environment in which citizens and businesses can prosper. Self-reliance among the indigent is also insufficient to pull a city up. There are those who say, get government out of the way of business, allow the poor to own their plots and homes, and watch human resourcefulness do the rest. This logic resonates with the libertarian mood of the times, but action tends to stop where the neighborhood stops, and a city is much more than a series of adjoining neighborhoods.

In fact, the fortunes of cities are increasingly hostage to factors beyond their control. Population pressures and the integration of the world economy have unleashed forces that can overwhelm a city, however well managed. To a degree, all poor cities today are at the mercy of a restless $4 trillion in institutional capital that roams the world like a giant ocean bird looking for profitable places to alight. When investment fund managers lose confidence in a nation's fiscal policies, as happened in Mexico in the fall of 1994, a country's or region's share of that capital can vanish, leaving cities to deal with the consequences of a ruined currency.

Developed world cities are now encountering dilemmas all too familiar to the developing world.

Even seemingly permanent foreign investments have become flighty. Competition among cities for what Adrian Atkinson of the Development Planning Unit of University College, London, calls "footloose foreign industry attracted to cheap labor" places constraints on the current panacea for improving the lot of the poor: jobs. Jabotatek, the name given to greater Jakarta, the Indonesian capital, has enjoyed formidable growth in manufacturing jobs since the 1970s as foreign investment took advantage of labor as cheap as $1.50 a day. Since the industries that have created those jobs import the bulk of their raw materials, they could move elsewhere if costs rise or a more attractive labor market beckons. This leaves workers little hope of better wages or working conditions, since their government is loath to impose costs that might scare away foreign money. Meanwhile unrelenting migration from overpopulated agricultural areas creates a situation in which ever more people could be chasing ever fewer jobs in an economic downturn.

Atkinson writes, "The city could, in this situation, become a mass graveyard."

As the global population climbs by nearly 100 million a year, starker limits appear on the horizon. Successful export-based economies can generate the money to buy food elsewhere, but somebody has to produce it. Even today China is simply too populous to count on exports to release its economy from inherent agricultural and resource limitations. Though the largest grain producer in the world, China has quickly become the second-largest importer of grain as well. Worldwide grain reserves, an estimated 48-day supply, are at their lowest level since the agricultural community began tabulating global statistics in 1963. Any disruption of the world market by either weather or grain exporters imposing export controls to protect their consumers could cause a staggering free-for-all over grain. Lester Brown of the Worldwatch Institute in Washington asks: what happens to countries that cannot compete with China and other hungry giants?

The usually optimistic International Food Policy Research Institute recently warned that the world cannot expect new breakthroughs to replicate the gains won during the now-sputtering Green Revolution. According to the World Bank, food production failed to keep pace with population growth in 75 countries during the 1980s, and 15 developing countries saw per capita food production decrease more than 20 percent during the decade. In per capita terms, fish production, fresh water, and arable land have all declined since 1980. As surpluses vanish, higher prices may temporarily spur production, but scores of developing countries may find themselves priced out of the market.

As limits begin to appear—or, equally important, are perceived to appear—the potential for strife and disorder rises, particularly if there are huge disparities in wealth within a city or society. The interplay between scarce land in the countryside, urban migration, and conflict in the cities is complicated, but the scramble for resources in a developing world city can create an environment ripe for exploitation by thugs and gangs. Thomas Homer-Dixon, director of the Peace and Conflict Studies Program at the University of Toronto, argues that crime and social instability resulting from environmental degradation and scarcity of land can prevent a society from establishing independent courts, open and honest markets, and other institutions necessary if it is to decouple its economy from resource limitations.

Other threats loom further off. Sometime in the next century, cities may have to deal with the serious consequences of climate change. Thirty of the world's 50 largest cities lie near coasts; a one-meter rise in the oceans caused by global warming would place an estimated 300 million people directly at risk. Many foreign investors already steer clear of Bangladesh because of its vulnerability to typhoons; a sea-level rise of one meter would put 16 percent of the densely populated country under water.

City dwellers have proved their resilience many times over. Kinshasa refuses to die, and Monrovia and Mogadishu still function despite hellish upheavals. But throughout history cities have expired, and there is no reason to believe the cycle has been permanently interrupted. One can envision a future in which the world's urban population swells from the 300 million of 1950 to perhaps 6 billion in 2050 without widespread collapse, but such a scenario is unlikely, if for no other reason than that it would run counter to the rhythm of history. In its own interest, the more developed world should help the developing cities with investments that promote family planning, foster education for girls as well as boys, improve sanitation and health care, and better the lot of those in rural areas. Broadcasting the rare success stories like Curitiba would also be useful. The world will have an opportunity to spotlight the problems of developing world cities at the U.N. conference on cities in Istanbul in June.

If the world's cities cannot absorb the unprecedented influx, masses of the desperate may overwhelm entire nations and regions. As populations grow and cities become more crowded, the margin for error narrows and the cost of mistakes rises. If peaceful, functioning cities are to exist in 2050, a law-abiding, harmonious, hardworking, ecology-conscious citizenry must be supported by enlightened leaders. Little in the cities of today suggests that this will come to pass.

Building a green economy

The global economy is going from bad to worse and the old solutions don't seem to work any more. Is there a better way?

Wayne Ellwood

MORE and more these days I get the feeling that something is wrong. It's an odd sense of unease, a dim registering that the world is 'out-of-joint' as Shakespeare might have put it. It happened most recently on a trip to my local corner store in Toronto, a family-owned greengrocer where the *signora* always gives me a welcome smile and her husband invariably drops cigarette ash onto the check-out counter as I pay for my milk or cold-cuts.

Today, when I ask him if the local strawberries have come in yet, he gives me a shrug and mumbles: 'Too expensive. California strawberries are cheaper and they last longer.' This seems odd to me but I let it pass and don't really start to put the pieces together until I'm fumbling around for a few cloves of garlic and notice the words 'Product of China' on the side of the box. China. This gives me pause: from where I'm standing China is approximately 15,000 miles away. These little, white bulbs have been harvested, transported overland, packed and shipped across the Pacific Ocean, then freighted three-quarters of the way across North America. It's at moments like these that the spectacular lunacy of the global economy comes crashing in on me.

California strawberries and Chinese garlic have muscled local produce out of the market for one reason only: they're cheaper. And in terms of actual cash out of my pocket here-and-now that's true. Economists argue that consumers like me are simply maximizing self-interest by buying from more efficient – ie cheaper – producers. That's the reason Chilean grapes fill supermarket shelves in Minneapolis and Dutch butter is half the price of local butter in Kenya.

But this word 'efficiency' is a double-edged sword. In fact, what's efficient in market terms is almost always damaging and costly in other ways – to employment, to social cohesion and to the environment. That's because the real costs of getting those mutant California berries onto breakfast tables in Montreal and Philadelphia are hidden. Or as economists would say, 'externalized'.

What's efficient in market terms is damaging and costly in other ways

Modern industrial agriculture is based on cheap, non-renewable fossil fuel: to run tractors and harvesters, to produce pesticides and fertilizers and to transport produce to market. That massive subsidy is not factored into final food costs any more than are the environmental costs of this high-tech approach to farming. Increased output per hectare over the last 50 years has come with a steep price: soil erosion, groundwater pollution, salinization of soils and diminished genetic diversity, to say nothing of the carbon dioxide and other greenhouse gases vented into the atmosphere. And this is a vicious circle. When soil fertility declines more fertilizer has to be dumped onto fields just to maintain yields. At the moment half the fertilizer used on US farmland is to replace nutrients lost to soil erosion.

So much for the hoopla about the 'efficiency' of the market. Ecologist and business consultant Paul Hawken argues that markets are good at setting prices but lousy at recognizing costs because they give us the wrong information. 'Whenever an organism gets wrong information, it is a form of toxicity,' writes Hawken. 'A herbicide kills because it is a hormone that tells the plant to grow faster than its capacity to absorb nutrients allows. It literally grows itself to death . . . Our daily doses of toxicity are the prices in the marketplace.'[1] Hawken's metaphor is apt: industrial society, too, is literally growing itself to death.

That's because there is a basic, potentially lethal, flaw at the heart of today's market-based economics. The varied and complex natural ecosystems, on which all life depends and on which the human economy is based, are treated as both limitless and, for the most part, free. The more oil we pump from the ground, the more forests we clear-cut, the more land we till, the more minerals we blast from the earth, the more the economy grows – and the richer we become. At least that's the theory. Except that as every economist knows, treating capital as current income is a recipe for disaster. Any business that operated along those lines would soon be bankrupt. For production to be sustainable, capital that is consumed (depreciated) must be replaced by investing some of the production. It's only what's left after this investment that can be counted as income.

A century ago this destruction of natural capital wasn't such a problem. The earth's bounty seemed infinite and its natural systems resilient enough to absorb whatever waste we could throw at them. That situation has changed dramatically over the last four decades. Since 1950 global economic output has jumped from $3.8 trillion to $18.9 trillion, a nearly five-fold increase.[2] We have consumed more of the world's natural wealth in this brief period than in the entire history of humankind.

And the great god growth continues to hold sway at the centre of economic policy. Every year at the World Economic Forum in Davos, Switzerland, the world's financial leaders, in a spasm of myopic optimism, close ranks in their quest for renewed economic growth. This year Renato Ruggiero,

Director-General of the new World Trade Organization, stressed the need for a 'universal system of free trade' which would be an 'unprecedented force for economic growth, for both rich industrial countries and the developing world'.

What's so depressing about this view is that it is widely shared by the power élite. There are few politicians, trade-union leaders or business bosses advocating anything other than growth as the key to prosperity and the solution to global poverty. Yet there is irrefutable evidence that growth is not the solution but the core of the problem. A central assumption of economists on both the Left and the Right has been that the 'carrying capacity' of the earth is infinitely expandable. A combination of human ingenuity and advanced technology will allow us all, eventually, to live like middle-class Americans – if only we can control our impatience and keep the economy growing.

Unfortunately, reality shows otherwise. It's clear there are limits to growth – and there is startling evidence that we've already breached them. According to University of British Columbia ecologist William Rees: 'Total consumption by the human economy already exceeds natural income; humankind is both liquidating natural capital and destroying our real wealth-creating potential. In this light, efforts to expand our way to sustainability through deregulation and trade can only accelerate global decline.'[3]

It is now estimated that 40 per cent of what ecologists call the 'net primary production' (NPP) of the earth's natural ecosystems is diverted to human activities. If global economic growth continues at the current rate

The production of goods and services cannot be detached easily from biophysical reality

and the earth's population doubles in the next 35 years (as would happen at the current pace) human beings, one species out of millions, would corral 80 per cent of NPP for their own use. Of course in some ways that's pure speculation. For the simple reason that a combination of environmental and social collapse will almost certainly kick in before we ever reach that point.

The iconoclastic American economist Herman Daly argues that we have moved from an 'empty world' to a 'full' one in what amounts to an historical eye-blink. But it is politically convenient, Daly says, not to admit to problems of carrying capacity because that would imply a limit to growth. And if growth is limited, Daly continues, 'then poverty must be dealt with, either by redistribution or by population control, both of which are taboo'.[4]

In his pioneering work on what he calls our 'ecological footprint', William Rees estimates that four-to-six hectares of land are needed to maintain the consumption of

the average person in the West. Yet in 1990 the total available productive land in the world was an estimated 1.7 hectares per person. The difference Rees calls 'appropriated carrying capacity'. The Netherlands, for example, consumes the output of a productive land mass 14 times its size. Most Northern countries and many urban regions in the South already consume more than their fair share, depending on trade or natural capital depletion for their survival. Such regions, Rees says, 'run an unaccounted ecological deficit – their populations either appropriating carrying capacity from elsewhere or from future generations'.[5] There are other more resonant names for this process, imperialism being the most obvious.

We don't have to search far for proof that growth-centred economics is pushing the regenerative capacities of the earth's ecosystems to the brink. The worry is not the one raised by the Club of Rome's *Limits to Growth* report of 20 years ago. There is no immediate shortage of basic non-renewable resources. Even at current rates of consumption there is enough copper, iron and fossil fuels to last centuries. More pressing is the concern that those basic life-support systems which we take for granted – the water cycle, the composition of the atmosphere, the changing seasons, the assimilation of waste and the recycling of nutrients, the pollination of crops, the delicate interplay of species – are everywhere on the verge of disintegration.

There is a now a large, unimpeachable body of research documenting this precipitous decline. Deserts are spreading, forests

being hacked down, fertile soils ruined by erosion and salinization, fisheries exhausted and ground-water reserves pumped dry. Carbon dioxide levels in the atmosphere due to our extravagant burning of fossil fuels continue to rise. On average we deposit 5.6 pounds of pure carbon into the atmosphere with every gallon of gasoline we burn— nearly six billion tons a year in total. And that doesn't include the estimated one to two tons released into the atmosphere every year from burning forests and grasslands. In September 1995 the Intergovernmental Panel on Climate Change, a select group of nearly 2,500 climate scientists, stated baldly that climate change is unstoppable and will lead to 'widespread economic, social and environmental dislocation over the next century'. Meanwhile oceanographers examining deep ocean sediments have confirmed that rapid, unpredictable shifts in climate can take place in as little as three or four decades.

So it seems the production of goods and services in the human economy cannot be

detached easily from biophysical reality. Yet the powerful myth that more production and greater consumption equals progress remains firmly entrenched. But 'progress' measured in this way is both relative and narrowly economistic. At the beginning of the industrial revolution in Britain the poet Oliver Goldsmith made an observation in verse that might just as easily apply today:

'Ill fares the land, to hast'ning ills
a prey,
Where wealth accumulates and
men decay.'

We have a growth that impoverishes rather than enriches. The dominance of the business perspective and an addiction to the 'bottom line' as the defining goal of human society have twisted the concept of community and perverted the notion of the public good. Thus in our modern economy the central purpose of life is shopping; the purpose of the family is to raise compliant future workers and consumers; the purpose of schools to teach marketable job skills; the purpose of government to boost business; and the purpose of Third World nations to provide cheap labour, raw materials and new markets.

Instead of an economy in service of community we have the reverse. In the original Greek, economics (*oikonomia*) means 'good housekeeping' and it is that broader humanitarian vision that has vanished. 'True economics,' writes Herman Daly, 'studies the community as a whole and locates market activity within it' in a quest for 'the long-term welfare of the whole community'.

Nor is our modern economy capable any longer of providing jobs and improving living standards for the majority. The evidence—and it's there for any who care to look—is unequivocal. The gap between rich and poor is widening in nation after nation. Real wages are declining as employment growth sputters. There are now more than 30 million unemployed in the West with no sign of the oft-promised outpouring of new jobs. Mainstream economists say this wrenching transformation to the new information age (what some have labelled the 'creative destruction' of the marketplace) will be worth it in the end. Don't count on it.

The truth is corporations are in the business of cutting jobs, not creating them. Witness the recent announcement by telecommunications giant AT&T that it would cut 40,000 jobs over the next three years. (The company's stock on the New York Exchange immediately rose $2.62 a share.) Or data that shows the top 500 companies in the US cut their workforces by 4.4 million between 1980 and 1993; this at a time when corporate assets more than doubled and the salaries of corporate executives increased more than six-fold. [6]

In the Third World, employment in the modern sector continues to grow in a few isolated enclaves. Chinese and Indonesian factories churn out an unending stream of Nike running shoes and Barbie dolls from non-unionized workers, often women, working 50-hour weeks for a few dollars a day. In Mexico – the lab test for economic globalization – it's been all downhill since the North American Free Trade Agreement (NAFTA) was signed three years ago. Over two million Mexicans lost their jobs after the 1994 peso devaluation and another two million peasants have been forced off their land since NAFTA.

Meanwhile, urban slums in the Third World proliferate, the total number of poor grows and overall living standards plummet. According to the World Health Organization a fifth of the world's nearly six billion people live in extreme poverty, almost a third of all children are undernourished and half the planet's population lacks access to basic essential drugs.

The global economy is not a total balls-up of course. It is working perfectly fine for some people. Like the world's 358 billionaires whose combined wealth now exceeds that of the world's poorest 2.5 billion people. And *Forbes* magazine tells us the number of non-Japanese, Asian multi-millionaires will double to 800,000 this year. The same article neglects to mention that 675 million Asians will continue to live in absolute poverty.

Orthodox economics and its seers have a lot to answer for in all this. As Canadian social critic John Ralston Saul notes: 'If economists were doctors, they would be mired in malpractice suits.' [7] He's right of course. The advice of economists has been treated as gospel when it should have been dismissed as self-serving cant.

And today's standard free-market prescription for economic health – deregulated markets, lower taxes for the wealthy, privatization and government cutbacks—is simply more of the same. It's a bit like re-arranging the deck chairs on the Titanic. Instead of this stale dogma we need a new vision of economics which puts people back at the centre of the human economy and subsumes economics to the interests of the public good.

I don't want to be naive about this; it's not going to be a stroll in the park. Those profiting from the current setup will not cede power voluntarily. Thankfully, there are hundreds of organizations and millions of people around the planet who share my deep sense of unease about the direction in which we're heading. And many of them are working hard to sow seeds of change, to develop a practical, realistic strategy for forging a new economy. . . .

There's even a new discipline called 'ecological economics' which is attempting to challenge mainstream growth-centered economics from within academia. Though you may not have got wind of it yet, there is a movement brewing—a movement which is attempting to turn conventional economics on its head by redirecting its focus from the narrow concerns of growth and efficiency to the broader concerns of community solidarity, democratic governance and environmental sustainability. The movement doesn't have a name or a leader or a headquarters. But it does have momentum. And more importantly it has a vision of a new green economy.

1 *The Ecology of Commerce*, Paul Hawken, HarperCollins, New York, NY, 1993. 2 *When Corporations Rule the World*, David C Korten, Kumarian Press, West Hartford, CT, 1995. 3 *Alternatives Magazine*, Vol 21, No 4, Oct/Nov 1995, University of Waterloo, Waterloo, ON. 4 *For the Common Good*, Herman E Daly and John B Cobb Jr, Beacon Press, Boston, MA, 1989. 5 'Ecological Footprints and Appropriated Carrying Capacity', William Rees and Mathis Wackernagel, from *Investing in Natural Capital*, Eds. Jansson, Hammer, Folke and Costanza, Island Press, Washington, DC, 1994. 6 From 'An agenda to tame corporations, reclaim citizen sovereignty and restore economic sanity', a speech by David Korten of the People Centred Development Forum, 3 Sept 1995. 7 *The Unconscious Civilization*, John Ralston Saul, Anansi Press, Concord, ON, 1995.

voices from the developing world

Progress Toward Sustainable Development

Tanvi Nagpal

Few would contest that we have an obligation to future generations: not to leave them an impoverished Earth and fragmented societies. In its simplest interpretation, sustainability is about this concern for intergenerational equity. Intellectuals and government decision makers are not alone in their concern about a long-term sustainable future. Small-scale farmers, community activists, leaders of women's groups and nongovernmental organizations (NGOs), and parents around the world are equally committed to leaving our children a world worth inheriting.

Much has been written about sustainability, what the term means, and what a sustainable future might entail. Global policy studies of the conditions required for sustainability abound, as do grassroots initiatives to improve the lives of common people by investing in their present and future. How do the recommendations of top-down analyses mesh with the bottom-up experience of leaders and activists? What have we in the West learned that must be shared with the East, and what can the proverbial "South" teach the "North"? Are the philosophical and methodological differences between the two irreconcilable? Most importantly, does a single definition of sustainability exist, and should we be searching for a globally acceptable plan for the future?

The 2050 Project was developed to explore the common elements—and the deep cleavages—in people's views of a sustainable future to design innovative, integrated strategies for achieving sustainability in the next century.[1] (See the box on page 206 for methodological details.) Eight-eight individuals in 47 countries were asked to submit essays on their visions of a sustainable world, and 19 interviews were conducted in 14 countries. The majority of those surveyed were from developing countries (the box on pages 208–209 lists the participants in the 2050 Project). This bias was intentional: The views of the industrialized world are already well known through a rich literature of Western visions. Sustainable development strategies cannot be based solely on these known views, both because they will be incomplete and because they will be rejected as "culture-bound" by the majority of the world's people. Those who were surveyed were asked to "imagine and describe a sustainable future, ideal yet plausible, that you desire for your grandchildren." The exercises yielded a varied set of responses: coherent visions of the future, immediate strategies to be implemented, and nostalgic commentaries on the link between the past and the future.

Envisioning sustainability is not about imagining utopias—perfect worlds without resource constraints and hard choices. Rather, it is about making decisions about the world we desire and, therefore, what should be sustained. Although the interviews and essays were as varied as the respondents themselves, many voiced common concerns. What was overwhelmingly evident was a desire to emphasize basic needs—ensuring food, shelter, clean water, health care, and education to all. An extension of this sentiment was a desire to protect basic values as well—to respect nature rather than dominate it and to use the wisdom of indigenous groups, elders, and tribal leaders to reexamine current structures of government and sources of knowledge.

The visions exercise of the 2050 Project did not bring us closer to a universally accepted definition of sustainability. Quite the opposite: The survey strengthens the belief that we should not be seeking a blueprint for a sustainable future because none exists. Instead, we should try to listen more carefully to one another, to learn from those whose knowledge we have long ignored. A sustainable future should be built on common aspirations and enriched with the diversity of cultures, languages, and belief systems. We face hard choices about our relationships with our communities and the Earth, but by working together, we can and must secure a sustainable future for our children.

Defining Sustainable Development

The term sustainable development was introduced in the 1987 report *Our Common Future*. There, the World Commission on Environment and Development (the Brundtland Commission) defined sustainable development as "development that meets the needs of the present generation without compromising the ability of future generations to meet their own needs."[2] Although this definition places needed focus on the importance of long-term planning, as a policy tool it is vague, providing no specifics about which needs and desires must be met and fulfilled and how.

Nonetheless, this definition has been adopted by several high-profile groups, including the Switzerland-based Business Council on Sustainable Development, a group of powerful business executives; the United Nations Commission on Sustainable Development, created to supervise and evaluate the achievement of the goals set by the Rio conference in 1992; and the President's Council on Sustainable Development, a U.S. group with representatives from environmental groups, industry, and local communities to formulate a strategy for sustainable development in the United States.[3] Indeed, the influential groups mentioned above are not alone in pondering sustainability. Sustainable development is a buzzword in even the smallest African countries, and commissions are being formed around the world to devise national and regional plans for the future. Thousands of small grassroots NGOs are grappling with these questions, and many indigenous leaders and grassroots activists are presenting their own priorities for the future. At times, the variety of agendas come together fortuitously, but more often than not there are major disconnects in the manner in which people define and understand sustainable development. However, in the years since it was first introduced, the Brundtland Commission's definition has been dissected and reconstructed dozens of times. Moreover, it has been criticized on grounds that it is

---

THE 2050 PROJECT

In August 1993, we invited colleagues to recommend essayists and solicited additional suggestions from the World Council of Indigenous Peoples, respected authors, and leaders of nongovernmental organizations. We contacted 88 people in 47 countries; of these, 52 individuals from 34 countries submitted essays in 5 languages. Although we sought as much diversity as possible given time and resource constraints, we cannot claim to have achieved a representative sample. Developing countries are over-represented because there is already a rich and readily accessible literature on the views of people from the "North." Our omission of contributions from Europe, Japan, and other highly industrialized regions is in no way intended to diminish the value of their people's visions; rather, our explicit aim is to supplement them. Finally, our method of selecting contributors brought us into contact with highly educated professionals, prominent in their fields or regions.

Besides the solicited manuscripts, 19 interviews were conducted between January and September 1994 with people from 14 countries to explore the visions of a group of people more diverse in terms of profession, educational background, and age.

Reprinted from T. Nagpal and C. Foltz, eds., *Choosing Our Future: Visions of a Sustainable World* (Washington, D.C.: World Resources Institute, 1995).

culturally bankrupt, dodges the issue of development without growth and redistribution, and pays little attention to human dignity, including the relationship that people have with the environment. Individuals and groups in less industrialized countries have led the protest, although they have many sympathizers in the West.

Those in developing countries argue that Western proponents of sustainable development "just don't get it." They point out that the debates on sustainability closely mirror those on development. By using terms of economic growth and efficiency, important issues are ignored: the urgency of nurturing human life and ecosystem health and the primacy of people, their communities, and the environment they depend on for their livelihood.[4]

In the project's survey, respondents echoed the same discontent. Some contributors gave scathing critiques of the Western influence on the definition of sustainability. For example, Saneh Charmarik (Thailand) asserted that "the whole issue of sustainability is fundamentally cultural and any effective solution to the current impasse requires nothing short of a shift in worldview."[5] Others argued that the predominant paradigms of our time are based on knowledge that has come exclusively from industrial societies, and they are angry that the West seems to have once again dominated the development of a new paradigm. To many, Western dominance implies that such issues as economic growth are paramount, and the environment is only superficially inserted into development plans. Those who challenge this domination are asking a fundamental question: Is the West ready to listen to those whose lives reflect a different set of values and priorities? As one contributor, Arshad Zaman (Pakistan), argues, perhaps our first task should be to explore whether a "global society can be created around a plural system of values, voluntarily." A consensus on that question may need to be reached before the hard work of sustainable development can truly begin.

Living in Harmony

What are the main features of a sustainable system, and how does it present itself? Both essays and interviews reflect a longing for peaceful coexistence within communities and nature. Contributors, whether from Africa, Asia, or the Americas voiced deep concern about the fragmantation of their communities and their growing detachment from the environment. Their concern stems in part from a somewhat idealized reconstruction of the past and in part from heatfelt anxiety about the lack of alternatives to the modern existence that has alienated them from the environment.

Communal Responsibility

Contributors from Africa offered many clear and compelling insights into how they see their communities changing. Families and communities remain the primary units of production in African society. For centuries, Africans have depended on extended families for economic and emotional support. Sometimes these ties have been blamed for holding back individuals. Now, with increasing urbanization and emphasis on nuclear families and individual achievements, many Africans are wondering what will replace old social structures and obligations. By highlighting the primacy of families and communities in their cultures, African contributors presented deep dilemmas about the battle between individual and communal achievement. Margaret Maringa (Kenya) outlined her ideas on the foundations of a sustainable future: empowerment of women, acknowledgment of the importance of religion, deep understanding of ethnicity, and management of natural resources through family holdings and communal responsibility. However, drawing on the customs, practices, and wisdom of her Agikuyu ancestors, she also idealized communities of the past:

Obligations rather than individual rights were advocated. Each age-set institution had an unwritten code of conduct. In this manner, the entire community was mobilized towards a common, positive standard with the least amount of supervision and waste. There were no policemen or prisons. The hoarding and misuse of resources was uncommon even in times of natural disaster.

Respondents often suggested that communal responsibility was essential for properly caring for natural resources. In a sustainable system, collective responsibility would ensure this care even if the structure and character of communities change. For example, Okyeame Ampadu-Agyei (Ghana) included communal management of resources in his definition of a sustainable system. He stated that in a desirable system, the inherited knowledge on resource management, which has been developed and refined over several generations, will not be disrupted but improved upon. Joseph Bedouma (Togo) echoes this sentiment, envisioning that traditional skills now forgotten by his children will be relearned by his grandchildren as they become protectors and builders of their environment and community. He feels humans have the power to destroy and protect the environment and hopes that his grandchildren will recognize this power.

Others surveyed pondered the contradictions of communities, their traditional hierarchies, and the knowledge systems they represent. We live in an era in which innovation, not experience, is revered; technological changes are accepted even when they do not improve the quality of human life or when they do more harm than good. This presents a significant dilemma for communities that are struggling to survive: Should they attempt to make progress using tried and tested methods and advice from the elders, or should they bypass traditional methods and follow the dictates of modern Western society? V. B. Mbaya (Kenya) admits that "there are pros and cons for either choice, as well as case studies that demonstrate the folly of naively choosing one over the other."

Education

Visions of sustainable communities varied, and family profiles, living arrangements, and social hierarchies differed substantially. However, a common element in many contributors' statements was a belief that communities need the ability to provide education and employment for their children, so that they do not have to leave for opportunities elsewhere. Schooling was seen by many as a basic human right, so they consider compulsory, universal primary education essential. Education is perceived as the single greatest equalizer of status and income, and a society that cannot assure it to all its members is neither desirable nor sustainable.

There was one universal caveat to this emphasis on education: It must contain the best the West has to offer while retaining elements of a location's unique culture. This is a challenge to those thinking about sustainability. Many acknowledge that wisdom comes not just from school books but also from traditional knowledge and customs, such as folk tales. It was widely felt that institutionalized schooling will become the norm. From Africa to Asia to South and Central America, participants voiced suggestions for

---

PARTICIPANTS IN THE 2050 PROJECT

Essayists

Fazle Hasan Abed
Executive Director
Bangladesh Rural Advancement
  Committee
Bangladesh

Abdiel Adames
Biologist
University of Panama
Panama

José Víctor Aguilar Guillén
Economist/Researcher
Fundación Nacional para el Desarrollo
El Salvador

Hussein Amach
Arab Fund for Economic and Social
  Development
Kuwait

Okyeame Ampadu-Agyei
Director
Environmental Protection Council
Ghana

German Ignacio Andrade
Executive Director
Fundación Natura
Colombia

Peggy Antrobus
Development Alternatives with Women
  for a New Era
Barbados

Elizabeth Ardayfio-Schandorf
Department of Geography
University of Ghana
Ghana

Christopher Ivo Atang
Executive Director
DETMAC Associates
Cameroon

Ruth Bamela Engo-Tjega
Advocates for African Food Security
Cameroon

Mariano Bauer
Director
Energy Program/UNAM
Mexico

Maristela Bernardo
Advisor
Brazilian Senate
Brazil

B. Bowonder
Dean of Research
Administrative Staff College
Hyderabad
India

Viviane Brachet-Marquez
Center for Sociological Studies
Colegio de Mexico
Mexico

Jacques Bugnicourt
Executive Secretary
ENDA-TM
Senegal

Urna Chahartogche
Inner Mongolia Dance and Music
  Company
China

Saneh Charmarik
Local Development Institute
Thailand

Pierre Dansereau
Professor Emeritus
University of Montreal
Canada

Graciela Diaz de Hasson
Instituto de Economica Energetica
Fundación Bariloche
Argentina

Souleymane Diop
Amicale Socio-Economique des
  Agriculteurs du Walo
Senegal

Marta Echavarria Uribe
Asocaña-Association of Cane Sugar
  Cultivators
Colombia

Abdelmohsen Farahat
College of Engineering
King Abdulaziz University
Saudi Arabia

Fabio Feldmann
Congressman
Brazil

Giap Van Dang
Assistant Research Professor
Asian Institute of Technology
Thailand

Mark Griffith
Environmental Systems, Inc.
Barbados

Chavannes Jean-Baptiste
Founder
Mouvement Paysen du Papaye
Haiti

Narpat S. Jodha
Head
Mountain Farming Systems Division
ICIMOD
Nepal

Mohammad Kassas
Department of Botany
Cairo University
Egypt

Emilio La Rovere
Federal University of Rio de Janeiro
Brazil

Demba Mansaré
Secretary-General
Committee for the Fight Against Hunger
Senegal

Margaret Maringa
Lawyer
Kenya

Uri Marinov
Environment and Development
  Management
Israel

Vernon Masayesva
Former leader
Hopi Nation
United States

V. B. Mbaya
Associate Professor of Biochemistry
University of Nairobi
Green Belt Movement
Kenya

reforming universities and combining culturally relevant material with technical education, as well as concern for the loss of civic learning. Several strategies were offered to retain cultural histories: schooling in native languages and graduate education in selected African tongues, combining the wisdom of traditional healers with the expertise of modern medicine, and establishing regional universities and centers of excel-lence that will stress integrated plans for development.

Welcoming Change

There is no prototypical African or Asian definition of a sustainable future. The visions heard were individual accounts of desires tempered by current reality, and the similarity that

Liberty Mhlanga
Agriculture Development Authority
Zimbabwe

Father Nzamujo
Executive Secretary
Centre Songhai
Benin

Joseph Palacio
Anthropologist
University of the West Indies
Belize

Qu Geping
Director
National Environmental Protection
Agency
China

Florence T. Robinson
Community activist
United States

Sixto Roxas
Foundation for Community Organization
and Management Technology
Philippines

Deborah Sandler
Wolfson College, Cambridge University
United Kingdom

S. Sathananthan
MANDRU
Sri Lanka

Francisco Serrano
Biologist
Salva-Natura
El Salvador

Youba Sokona
ENDA-Energie
Senegal

Alex Steffen
Freelance journalist
United States

Sri Supomo
Vice Secretary General
HKTI Indonesian Farmers Association
Indonesia

Pauline Tangiora
President
Women's League
Aotearoa/New Zealand

Jorge Terena
Director for Amazonian Regional
   Programs
IFAD
Ecuador

Anna Tibaijuka
Economic Research Bureau
University of Dar es Salaam
Tanzania

Eduardo Viola
Political scientist
Instituto Sociedade, Populaçao e Natureza
Brazil

Wen Dazhong
Head, Agroecology Department
Institute of Applied Ecology
China

Arshad Zaman
Arshad Zaman Associates, Ltd.
Pakistan

Interviewees

Alfred Ayeah-Tefuh
Water Technician
Cameroon

Virginia S. Bacay
Student
Philippines

Joseph Bedouma
Community leader
Togo

Alexander Buyentuev
Researcher
Institute of Geography
Russian Academy of Sciences
Russia

Maylene Dankers
Nurse
South Africa

Lamin Darboe
Chief
The Gambia

Alex Dawia
Criminologist
Australia

Andre Effa
Farmer
Cameroon

Priscilla Karumazondo
Secondary school teacher
Zimbabwe

Filimone Kau
Ministry of Information
Fiji

Li Wa Li
Former teacher
China

Albert Makina
Primary school teacher
Zimbabwe

Toum Mohammed
Secondary school teacher
Tanzania

Marla Muñoz
Centro de Estudios Europeanos
Cuba

Stella Mutasa
Secretary
Zimbabwe

Dennis Pantin
Economics Department
University of the West Indies
Trinidad and Tobago

Tobias Pavandiva
Ambulance driver
Zimbabwe

Sister Grace Yap
Order of Saint Francis
Jamaica

Erdeni N. Yelaev
Vice Executive Officer for Research
   and Development
Dershinsky National Park
Russia

emerged from respondents came from present shared experiences. In fact, both the similarities and differences among contributors merely highlighted how we are all to some extent shackled to the present: Our visions of distant futures hinge on solutions to current problems. Therefore, it was no surprise that Asian and South American contributors were more worried about changing patterns of energy use than were Africans; that South Americans spoke of simplifying consumption while African interviewees desired more consumer goods; and that concerns about population growth were clearly expressed by Asian authors, less so by Africans, and very little by South Americans. It is no revelation that Africans stressed agricultural practices and food security, or that South Americans spoke so eloquently about democracy, personal freedom, and safety.

Basic Necessities

African contributors spoke about the importance of fulfilling basic needs, especially food. The majority of Africans depend directly on the natural resource base for sustenance; more than 80 percent still grow their own food. Several contributors presented detailed strategies for improving food security. Many of these hinge on an appreciation of farmers' preexisting knowledge and increased freedom from centrally controlled pricing and marketing of crops. Pesticide-free production and the use of natural fertilizers were recommended, as well as improved farming techniques and investment in a "dry revolution" (nonirrigated agriculture). One can almost imagine a continent self-sufficient in food production, with a safe water supply, and a roof over everyone's head.

Among those interviewed, there was a strong desire for more equitable opportunities, especially for sustainable livelihoods and fair salaries. Toum Mohammed, a teacher from Tanzania, hoped that her grandchildren "will be paid enough money to buy the things they need and still have enough left over to save." Albert Makina, a Zimbabwean teacher, concurred:

My children will be educated and secure in their jobs. They will be doctors and engineers. They will not be teachers like me, because it does not pay well. . . . Farming is difficult and tiresome, and the financial rewards are poor. My parents are farmers and I think all of us should do better than our parents.

Sometimes this means bringing the city to the village. Chief Darboe of the Gambia is hopeful that the oil reserves off the Gambian coast will bring in wealth that will transform his villages into small cities. The trappings of a modern city—automobiles, televisions, VCRs—will all be available to villagers, and he hopes this will keep them in their ancestral homes. The disjuncture between this image and others of traditional idyllic pastoral villages is clear. Can communities survive the onslaught of modernization and retain the essence that has kept them alive for thousands of years? It appears as though this is strongly desired but difficult to achieve. Yet there are optimists such as Alfred Ayeah-Tefuh (Cameroon):

Customs and traditions will change. It is my vision that the cumbersome traditions will disappear, while only the strongest and best will remain. Do I worry about the loss of these traditions by the year 2050? No, I think that in order for a tree to grow up strong and tall it most lose some of its branches. This is the law of nature.

Participation in Governance

In some instances, the entire discussion of sustainability focused on the issue of human rights. People must have the rights and resources to make decisions about their environment and livelihood. Coming from a family of herders in Inner Mongolia, Urna Chahartogche's primary concern was the abrogation of the basic rights of herdsmen in her land. She remarks:

Sustainability must have its foundation. Culture, arts, economy, and freedom make up this foundation. The most important thing among them is freedom! Only after this foundation has been prepared can we talk about protecting the environment. It is senseless to talk about sustainability, not having created the most fundamental conditions for it.

Indeed, there was remarkable consensus that a sustainable society must be democratic, with multiple fora for negotiation. Democracy is not solely about the creation of a set of institutions but about much improved collective capacity to resolve common problems. In other words, sustainable societies should have the mechanisms to ensure that conflicts are resolved peacefully.

Describing a sustainable Cameroon, Christopher Atang envisions a democratically elected president and parliament that will work with people to not only speed up growth but also distribute its rewards more fairly. Graciela Diaz de Hasson (Argentina) refers to this as "economic democracy: greater participation of all social layers in the accumulation and distribution of the social product." Yet, this is by no means a universally accepted precondition of sustainability. Critics point out that several civilizations characterized by extreme inequities have been sustained for long periods. Giap Van Dang (Thailand) believes that the poor will always be among us. In a desirable future, he contends, they will not be abandoned by society, and their basic needs may be met.

A majority of contributors also emphasized the importance of responsible leadership and expressed a longing for increased authority at the local level. Respondents as diverse as a small farmer in Senegal and a fisherman on the Atlantic coast of Central America demanded that state and local governments stop imposing programs and dictating solutions to rural communities.

Both economies and the environment will gain from these sorts of changes. For example, Viviane Brachet-Marquez (Mexico) maintained that even our best efforts to protect human and biological resources will be wasted if ordinary people are not involved in the discussion of sustainability and governing elites continue to act as free, unchecked, and unaccountable agents, exercising their own will. Respondents pointed out that environmental conservation is not just a matter of technical, scientific, or sectoral debate. Therefore, stakeholders from both the private and public sectors should come together to make decisions about their collective well-being. Vernon Masayesva, speaking for the Hopi people of the Colorado Plateau, believes that sustainability at the local level depends on cooperation among federal, state, local, and tribal governments. Clearly, the ability of people to organize and express themselves at all levels is a fundamental precondition of sustainable systems.

No visions hinged on democracy in quite the same way as those of the Central and South American respondents. Again, this is evidence of how views of the future are unavoidably influenced by the present. From Haiti to Brazil, people called for popular participation and responsive leadership, equal participation of ethnic and linguistic minorities, access to information, and freedom of expression. The political and economic hegemony of the few was repeatedly challenged, not just because of the heartfelt desire for personal freedom and safety but also because contributors felt that pluralism would prevent future abuse of natural resources.

For example, Marta Echavarria Uribe (Columbia) wrote: *We have to relearn our capacity to disagree with respect, to give other people the treatment they deserve as fellow human beings—not based on social positions or income—and to live in some sort of harmony. For Columbian society to improve itself in the long term requires that all citizens adopt the principle of basic human and civil rights, which are essential for peace.*

What was most surprising (and perhaps inspiring) was the breadth of change that contributors imagined, much of which touched on long-standing laws and traditions. Joseph Palacio (Belize) suggested resource abuse in the small nations of the Atlantic coast can only be prevented by the creation of a United Nations-protected sanctuary. For peace and security to be achieved in South Asia, ethnic and linguistic groups must have autonomy, as S. Sathananthan (Sri Lanka) wrote; therefore, governments and electorates should review their inherited colonial borders and consider redefining sovereignty. Uri Marinov and Deborah Sandler (Israel) suggested that in view of the population pressures and resource scarcities in Israel, the famous Law of Return may have to be amended or revoked. Anna Tibaijuka (Tanzania) believes we need a Marshall Plan for Africa. This recommendation must be held up against Ruth Bamela Engo-Tjega's (Cameroon) image of an Africa rejuvenated by its inner strengths, not external assistance. And in the fiftieth year of the United Nations, maybe it is time to revolutionize international governance as Eduardo Viola (Brazil) suggested, and make representation proportional to population.

The Role of Indigenous Groups

Nowhere is the chasm between the developing and industrialized worlds more clear than in the discussion of the role of indigenous groups. Indigenous people and their spokespersons contend that Western societies place human beings in a position of dominance over nature, making the search for sustainability fruitless. In contrast, they feel that sustainability is not about prosperity but about living a life of dignity in harmony with nature. Although the lives of indigenous people have always been tied to the Earth, their knowledge and experience with sustainable practices have systematically been ignored by the West. Some argue that even attaching words as seemingly contradictory as "sustainable" and "development" reflects the industrialized world's inability to give priority to the environment.

Many of the survey respondents expressed deep concern for the survival of indigenous knowledge and culture. Those who have lived with and studied these groups are often convinced that modernization is forcing the extinction of indigenous languages and cultures and leading to the permanent loss of knowledge and practices that have allowed indigenous peoples to live in consonance with their environments for centuries. Respect for indigenous knowledge and the creation of mechanisms that will ensure its possessors equal participation in policymaking was a familiar refrain in the 2050 Project.

Many feel modern science has devalued traditional knowledge. Jorge Terena (Ecuador) faults both the insular world of modern scientists and technologists and the system that profits by appropriating communal knowledge and granting "intellectual property rights" to its usurpers. He believes that among the indigenous people, by contrast, collective wisdom is derived from group knowledge of natural laws that are pertinent for the group's sustenance and survival. This collective memory works for everyone's benefit, not solely for the interests of individual leaders and entrepreneurs.

Indigenous peoples see a natural link between their lives and environmental protection. Pauline E. Tangiora, a Maori woman from New Zealand, stated that "the instinct to preserve is present in all people but the indigenous live it. It is not a question of dedication because that would imply choice. For us, it is not a choice. It is a responsibility." Tangiora and others suggest that their relationship with the environment is a spiritual one, where nature provides more than physical sustenance. In a sustainable system, there is no place for a biotechnology firm that fells a tree for the extraction of a single medicine; instead, there must be appreciation for the complex life of the tree—that it is a giver of shade and decorative flowers and a home to birds and animals as well as a source of medicine. Coexistence with nature is the crux of a desirable future. The symbiosis she describes stands in contrast to the Western perception of the environment as an enabler of human activity; thus, humans have a responsibility to preserve it.

In sharp contrast to this indigenous view of the primacy of the environment is the argument that sustainability is about "a systematic shift in economic development patterns" and that there are no inherent inconsistencies between the object of the market system and the goals of sustainability as long as "markets internalize environmental costs."[6] While many essayists would agree that "getting prices right" is certainly a component of the transition to a sustainable future, they appear to be increasingly disenchanted with the exclusive focus on economic growth and market instruments. Moreover, many felt we are facing an important choice: economic growth or harmony with nature. In German I. Andrade's (Colombia) words:

6. POPULATION, DEVELOPMENT, AND ENVIRONMENT

From the perspective of minority groups it is clear that the concept of sustainability should include an ethical component. . . . In this region (the Amazon), it is clear that the only uses of nature that do not lead to losses in biodiversity are precisely those which can be interpreted as being antithetical to 'development.' Further, there are no known successful experiences of development which have not implied a loss of cultural diversity.

If economic growth must come at the expense of the Earth's ecosystem, as many contend it does, such growth is nonsustainable. Equating development with growth and growth with increases in wealth are at the heart of the struggle between development and sustainability. Indigenous leaders and grassroots activists, representing the priorities of people in the nonindustrialized world, argue for development with an emphasis not on growth but on a restructuring of economies and consumption patterns.[7]

Frugality in the consumption of nature is not antithetical to a system that ensures human survival and the satisfaction of basic needs instead of wealth and prosperity for all. Margaret Maringa (Kenya) asserted that in her desired future, "no person has more or less than he or she needs for basic survival." The suggestion that progress implies an increase in consumption was attacked not only by non-Western essayists but also squarely by two community activists from North America. Florence Robinson (United States) pointed to "classism" and the "excessive consumption of resources or materialism" as the two worst problems of America in the 20th century. She and Alex Steffen (United States) hoped for a future in which "luxury" will become a pejorative term.

Overemphasis on consumption was also addressed by Sixto Roxas (Philippines):

We must not only de-materialize consumption and production, we must, as in the far distant past, resacralize everything: nature, community, consumption, production, governance, science, and technology. Which also means that everything is repersonalized: the earth is our mother, the tree is our brother, as are the birds and all the fish and the deer. Every forest is a sacred grove, and every cow is a sacred cow, all lambs must be worthy of sacrifice, and all water is holy water. . . . In time, perhaps, the Asia which the West converted to a non-sustainable lifestyle will repay the West by teaching it the ways of sustainability.

The debate on the nonsustainability of growth and increased consumption illustrates the ideological divide between groups that appear to be equally concerned about the well-being of future generations. What is clear is that while the nonindustrialized world has learned a great deal about Western paradigms and priorities, the industrialized world has systematically ignored the unique and valuable knowledge of the developing world. Without such learning, a universal definition of sustainability, empty of ecological content and rife with cultural biases, can only lead to strategies, programs, and policies that project a false consensus.

Building Consensus

Global or even continent-wide formulas for sustainability may be an elusive goal for many reasons. First, as contributors have illustrated, there are many paths to a sustainable future, each determined by individualized priorities of what is desired and therefore worthy of sustaining. Second, the future is constrained by physical resources that are often finite or whose availability is difficult to determine. Third, the problems we face are multidimensional and interlinked, and no region can achieve sustainability in isolation. Hence, a desirable and sustainable future will be the result of many policy changes, some small and at the local level, others international and far-reaching. These will impact individuals, families, communities, businesses, and governments alike. We are only now taking the first steps toward understanding the complexity of the task that lies ahead.

Despite acceptance of the Brundtland definition of sustainable development, deep ideological divides must be overcome to progress toward sustainability. Desires for the future both unite and divide us. Accepting that our futures are inextricably linked could give us the humility to make compromises. Compromises around sustainability, however defined, should be based on open dialogues and partnerships among people in different nations and among diverse economic, linguistic, ethnic, and religious groups. If policymakers could share power with those whom their policies most readily impact, they may not only design better strategies but also see them succeed more often. Broader policy instruments—impressive conventions and treaties—will have little bearing if ordinary people have no authority to see them implemented.

There are millions of positive images of the future. Our responsibility is not to choose among them—that belongs to future generations. Our responsibility is to leave them social and natural resources that will allow them to make these images a reality.

NOTES

1. The 2050 Project, organized by the World Resources Institute, the Brookings Institution, and the Santa Fe Institute, seeks to combine empirical analyses about critical resources, trends, and transformations with a survey of what people actually desire for the future. Instead of forecasting, the project has adopted a backcasting approach. See also the full report of the study, T. Nagpal and C. Foltz, eds., *Choosing Our Future: Visions of a Sustainable World* (Washington, D.C.: World Resources Institute, 1995).

2. World Commission on Environment and Development, *Our Common Future* (New York: Oxford University Press, 1987), 8.

3. See J. Blumenfeld, "Institutions—The United Nations Commission on Sustainable Development," *Environment*, December 1994, 2; and J. Lash and D. Buzzelli, "Institutions—The President's Council on Sustainable Development," *Environment*, April 1995, 44.

4. See W. Harcourt, "Introduction," in W. Harcourt, ed., *Feminist Perspectives on Sustainable Development* (Atlantic Heights, N.J.: Zed Books, 1994), 1–5.

5. The ideas of contributors to the 2050 Project will be widely quoted throughout this article. Their home country will appear parenthetically. A complete list of those surveyed appears in the box on pages 32–33.

6. J. H. Faulkner, "Capital Formation and Sustainable Development," *Business and the Contemporary World* 6, no. 2 (1994): 69. A similar position was adopted by the United Nations Commission on Sustainable Development in its 1994 session. The commission agreed that sustainable consumption and production objectives would be best met by "encouraging greater efficiency in energy and resource use; minimizing waste; moving toward environmentally sound pricing; and making environmentally sound purchasing decisions." See N. Desai, "The Commission on Sustainable Development," *Ecodecision* 15 (Winter 1995): 52.

7. Noted economist Herman Daly has made a similar case for development without growth but with population control and wealth redistribution. See H. E. Daly, *Steady-State Economics* (Washington, D.C.: Island Press, 1991).

Upholding Human Rights and Environmental Justice

Aaron Sachs

The murder of Chico Mendes on December 22, 1988, in a remote section of the Brazilian Amazon, made international headlines largely because of Mendes' connection to the global environmental movement. "Brazilian Who Fought to Protect Amazon Is Killed," the *New York Times* reported. Yet Mendes, a lifelong rubber tapper and labor union activist, considered his struggle to be founded not on ecology but on social justice and human rights. He had not even been aware of environmentalism until about three years before his death.

Mendes' principal aim was to protect his fellow rubber tappers' right to earn a livelihood from the forest by extracting latex from rubber trees and gathering nuts in seasons when the rubber was not flowing. Once introduced to the environmental movement, though, he was quick to realize that the international struggle to save the rain forest and his local struggle to empower rain-forest inhabitants amounted to nearly the same thing—and in his felicitous blending of environmentalism and human-rights work lay the key to his legacy. Mendes pointed out that an intact forest ecosystem could sustain a substantial population of highly productive rubber tappers, who would have an obvious vested interest in keeping it intact. His advocacy eventually resulted in the creation of the Chico Mendes Extractive Reserve, a tract of nearly one million hectares of protected rain forest.

Tragically, by speaking out, by organizing protests, by fighting to ensure that the forests of his home region would be used sustainably and equitably rather than slashed and burned for the benefit of a few rich landowners, Mendes sealed his fate: an angry cattle baron was arrested for his murder. But Mendes' example—and those of hundreds of other environmental activists around the world whose human rights have been violated—serve as powerful reminders of the links between ecology and issues of human rights and social justice. In living, Mendes proved that the enjoyment of many basic rights depends on protection of the environment. In dying, the victim of frontier lawlessness, he proved that ongoing environmental protection depends on people's secure ability to exercise their basic rights.

Environmental degradation, even in areas that seem remote, usually carries a high human cost. That cost is behind struggles like the one Chico Mendes and his fellow forest dwellers waged—struggles for what has come to be known as environmental justice.

While ecologists have long warned of the damage caused by putting this planet's ecosystems under heavy stress, it took social activists like Mendes to point out that the immediate human toll of environmental destruction has usually been borne disproportionately by the people least able to cope with it—people already on the margins of society, who have perhaps been targeted as vulnerable and lacking resources to defend themselves.

In Chico Mendes' home state of Acre, in 1970, three-quarters of the land was publicly owned, unclaimed, and undeveloped. By 1980, almost all of it had been bought, and about half of Acre's land was held by only 10 people. By encouraging the fastest possible development of the frontier, the Brazilian government essentially forced the scattered inhabitants of the rain forest to pay the price of deforestation—ranging from air pollution to the spread of disease to flooding and soil erosion—while a few wealthy landowners reaped most of the rewards.

Environmental injustice—meaning the gap between our universally shared dependence on a healthy local environment and our inequitable access to such an environment—arises at all levels of society. Attacks against individual environmental activists often point to much broader injustices and human-rights violations, to attacks against entire communities—whether the destruction of the rubber tappers' resource base in the Amazon or the dumping of hazardous waste in an impoverished minority town in North Carolina or the forced relocation of thousands of people in India's Narmada Valley to make way for a gargantuan dam project or the pollution of black South Africans' drinking water by gold-mining operations. At the national level, environmental damage tends to be concentrated in poorer countries, which often overexploit their natural resources in order to feed overconsumption in richer countries. Working toward environmental justice will thus require wide-reaching policy changes in both the ecological and human-rights arenas.

Justice of any kind, however, is a fluid concept that depends on constant checks and balances. So one of the most important goals of the environmental justice movement may well be the protection of civil rights. The basic freedoms of civil society, after all—free speech, a free press providing access to information, fair elections, freedom to organize in groups—are the best ways of holding those who wield power accountable.

From *The Humanist*, March/April 1996, pp. 5-7. Adapted from "Eco-Justice: Linking Human Rights and the Environment" from *State of the World 1995*, Chapter 8, published by the Worldwatch Institute. © 1995 by Aaron Sachs. Reprinted by permission.

Much environmental destruction occurs in the first place simply because affected communities are powerless to prevent it. Although drastic, environmental policy reforms are essential; in other words, guaranteeing the implementation of such reforms will ultimately depend on the full protection of basic human rights—especially the rights of society's most vulnerable people.

Several badly planned ecological preservation projects have come at the expense of local peoples' basic human rights. And such mismanagement, in turn, often jeopardizes the integrity of the supposedly protected areas. This pattern has been especially devastating in the developing world. In many protected areas of India, for instance, local peoples have found themselves suddenly deprived of traditional land rights and

---

Some environmentalists have certainly deserved their reputation for neglecting the human element of conservation. Several badly planned ecological preservation projects have come at the expense of local peoples' basic human rights.

Since Chico Mendes' murder, environmentalists and human-rights workers all over the world have staked out common ground much more readily; they are finally beginning to blend their movements. In October 1995, the Sierra Club and Amnesty International issued their first joint letter, on the link between human-rights abuses and environmental degradation in Nigeria. The broader the coalition, both groups have realized, the more its policy agendas take on universal relevance and the more political power it attains. As Ashish Kothari, lecturer in environmental studies at the Indian Institute of Public Administration, has noted: "Most mass movements at the grassroots are not just human rights, nor just environmental, but inevitably both. They have to be, if they are conscious of the role of natural resources in their lives, and of the dominant forces exploiting those resources."

This collaboration is still tentative, however. Even though the agendas of the two movements have overlapped for quite a long time—on such issues as environmental health hazards and threats to indigenous peoples' resource bases—the two sets of activists still have a lot to learn from each other. Decades of fostering different approaches to advocacy have led to a certain amount of mutual distrust.

Members of Amnesty International, for instance, famous for their letter-writing campaigns on behalf of individual prisoners of conscience, have tended to feel little sympathy for eco-philosophers trying to make a case for "the rights of nature." They have a hard time understanding why ecologists seem willing to spend so much energy on abstractions—on efforts to prevent some possible future extinction of an obscure species of bird, supposedly for the eventual good of everyone—while human beings are being tortured right here in the present. Similarly, ecologists have tended to grow exasperated with the narrow human-rights focus on single cases of abuse, pointing out that far more people are threatened by such things as desertification and water pollution than by torture.

Some environmentalists have certainly deserved their reputation for neglecting the human element of conservation.

access to natural resources because of new conservation regulations. And they have responded, understandably, with increasing hostility. In one case, the creation of the Kutru Tiger and Buffalo Reserve in Madhya Pradesh displaced 52 villages of Maria tribals, many of whom have since joined an insurgent movement that occasionally conducts poaching missions and harasses park guards.

Because of such failures, and because so many developing-world preservation schemes originate with industrial-world environmental organizations, northern environmentalists have had to fend off constant accusations that they care more about the south's trees and birds than about its people. Over the last five to 10 years, though, as they learned to address the social and cultural context of their campaigns, they have been better able to demonstrate the immediate human value of intact ecosystems: the aloof tree-huggers became compassionate defenders of local peoples.

Similarly, human-rights activists have recently broadened their appeal by acknowledging the environmental factors behind many of the abuses they work on—but only after decades of dealing with the consequences of ignoring ecology. Sometimes an exclusively rights-based approach to protecting local peoples has opened the door to increased environmental degradation, which in turn tends to erode the peoples' basic rights and well-being.

Along the coasts of Ecuador's Galapagos Islands, for instance, local fishers are currently overharvesting sea cucumbers at a rate likely to wipe out supplies within about four years. By embracing the international economy and selling their bounty to wealthy gourmets in China and Japan, the cucumber fishers, known as *pepineros*, are able to make up to 20 times the profit they could earn from any other locally available species.

The original plan establishing the Galapagos National Park in 1974 pointedly protected indigenous peoples' right to continue their tradition of subsistence fishing. But Ecuadorean officials have failed to distinguish between indigenous peoples and new residents of the islands; many of the *pepineros* moved to the Galapagos region just a few years ago, specifically to collect sea cucumbers. Moreover, Ecuador's government has made no attempt to implement any monitoring mechanisms to ensure that the Galapaguenos are keeping their fishing within subsistence levels. As native Galapagueno ecologist Carlos A. Valle has noted, the *pepineros*, who have gone so far as to take hostages in their fight to keep the fishery open, seem intent on defending their "right to destroy their own future."

Conservationists have been accused of trying to deny the rights of the *pepineros*; yet they could make a strong case that better environmental regulation and monitoring would, in the long run, strengthen the rights of the fishing community. Indeed, if the *pepinero* community were composed more of indigenous peoples who had a longer-term investment in the local ecosystem, their harvesting strategies might be quite different. In general, when human rights and ecology are given equal weight and local people not only participate in the development decisions that are going to affect them but also have a strong ecological knowledge base, communities end up acting as stewards of the local environment and also flourish socially and culturally—as on the Chico Mendes Extractive Reserve.

An even broader overlap between the human-rights and environmental agendas is embedded within the history of the international human-rights movement. As early as 1948, just three years after the U.N. charter entered into force, the General Assembly adopted the Universal Declaration of Human Rights, representing the first international moral consensus about what people should be able to expect from civil society. Besides the personal civil liberties that form the basis of the human-rights movement, ranging from free speech to freedom from torture, the declaration also covered the broader, more communal rights to health, food, shelter, and work—the very rights at the core of the environmental movement. The Universal Declaration itself is not a binding legal document. But in later years, both sets of rights did enter into force as binding international laws in the Covenant on Civil and Political Rights and the broader Covenant on Economic, Social, and Cultural Rights.

Though the distinction between individual civil rights and more communal rights is sometimes perceived as a sticking point between human-rights and environmental workers, in the end it reveals the ultimate complementary of the two movements in working toward environmental justice. Human-rights activists, after all, have more and more frequently recognized that some of the worst abuses they deal with originate in environmental damage at the communal or regional level. And environmentalists have realized that upholding basic civil and political rights is one of the best ways of protecting the environment.

In the ecological context, the main difference between the relevant civil and political rights and the relevant economic, social, and cultural rights is that the first are largely procedural and the second are substantive: people exercise their individual rights (such as free speech) in order to protect their environment-related communal rights (for example, the right to an intact ozone layer). The human-rights movement and the environmental movement are fighting for both sets of rights. The substantive, communal rights combine moral and scientific perspectives to uphold the protection of life; they serve the crucial purpose of laying out the things all people should be able to expect from the environment—such as clean air and water. They explain just what would constitute an environmental injustice. But it is the procedural rights that perhaps provide the most common ground for the two movements, at the individual, communal, and even national level, because they are the rights that allow people to work toward the prevention of environmental injustice.

Aaron Sachs is a research associate at the Worldwatch Institute, studying issues in international development, human rights, and the social and environmental impacts of technology. He has authored numerous articles and is coauthor of the institute's latest annual report, State of the World 1995. *This article is adapted from chapter eight of that report, "Eco-Justice: Linking Human Rights and the Environment."*

Women and Development

Recognition is growing of the important role women play in the development process. Women are crucial to the success of family planning programs. Women bear much of the responsibility for food production, and they account for an increasing share of wage labor in developing countries. Despite their important contributions, however, women continue to face formidable social, economic, and political barriers.

Women's lives in the developing world are invariably difficult. Often female children are valued less than male offspring, resulting in higher infant and child mortality rates. In extreme cases, this undervaluing leads to female infanticide. Those females who do survive face lives characterized by poor nutrition and health, multiple pregnancies, hard physical labor, discrimination, and perhaps violence.

Clearly, women are central to any successful population policy. Evidence shows that educated women have fewer and healthier children. This connection between education and population indicates that greater emphasis should be placed on educating women. In reality, female school enrollments are lower than those of males for reasons having to do with state priorities, family resources that are insufficient to educate both boys and girls, female socialization, and cultural factors. Although education is probably the largest single contributor to enhancing the status of women and thereby promoting development, access to education is still limited for many women. Higher status for women also has benefits in terms of improved health, better wages, and greater influence in decision making.

Women make up a huge portion of the agricultural workforce. They are heavily involved in food production from planting to cultivation, harvesting, and marketing. Despite their agricultural contribution, women frequently do not have adequate access to advances in agricultural technology or the benefits of extension and training programs. They are also discriminated against in land ownership. As a result, important opportunities to improve food production are lost when women are not given access to technology, training, and land tenure commensurate with their agricultural role.

As industrialization takes place, larger numbers of women are entering the wage economy, primarily as production and clerical workers. Expanding opportunities for women in these positions contribute to family income and higher status. The informal sector, where jobs are smaller-scale, more traditional, and labor-intensive, has also attracted more women, because these jobs are often their only source of employment, due to family responsibilities or discrimination. Clearly, women play a critical role in economic expansion in developing countries.

Development does not always provide benefits to women, however. Advances in technology may further erode the status of women, relegating them to less valuable work or even eliminating their jobs. The industrialization that has accompanied the globalization of production has meant more employment opportunities, but often these are low-tech, low-wage jobs. The lower labor costs in the developing world that attract manufacturing facilities may come at the expense of women. Increasingly, women are recruited to fill these production jobs because wage differentials allow employers to pay women less.

The consequences of the structural adjustment programs that many developing world countries have had to adopt have fallen disproportionately on women. As employment opportunities have declined because of austerity measures, women have lost jobs in the formal sector and faced increased competition from males in the informal sector. Cuts in spending on health care and education also affect women, who already receive fewer of these benefits. Currency devaluations further erode the purchasing power of women.

Enhancing the status of women has been the primary focus of recent international conferences. The 1994 International Conference on Population and Development focused attention on women's health and reproductive rights and the crucial role these issues play in controlling population growth. The Fourth World Conference on Women held in Beijing, China, in 1995 proclaimed women's rights to be synonymous with human rights.

This represents a turning point in women's struggle for equal rights. These conferences not only focused attention on gender issues, but also provided additional opportunities for developing leadership and encouraging grassroots efforts to realize the goal of enhancing the status of women.

Looking Ahead: Challenge Questions

What types of cultural, political, and economic barriers do developing world women face?

How does female empowerment contribute to limiting population growth?

What myths contribute to gender bias? How does discrimination contribute to female poverty?

Why is gender a crucial part of development programs?

What types of concerns were addressed at the Beijing conference? What contentious issues emerged?

How have recent international conferences affected the status of women?

What were the achievements of the 1995 Fourth World Conference on Women in Beijing?

The Burden of Womanhood

Too often in the Third World, a female's life is hardly worth living

John Ward Anderson and Molly Moore

Washington Post Foreign Service

GANDHI NAGAR, India

When Rani returned home from the hospital cradling her newborn daughter, the men in the family slipped out of her mud hut while she and her mother-in-law mashed poisonous oleander seeds into a dollop of oil and forced it down the infant's throat. As soon as darkness fell, Rani crept into a nearby field and buried her baby girl in a shallow, unmarked grave next to a small stream.

"I never felt any sorrow," Rani, a farm laborer with a weather-beaten face, said through an interpreter. "There was a lot of bitterness in my heart toward the baby because the gods should have given me a son."

Each year hundreds and perhaps thousands of newborn girls in India are murdered by their mothers simply because they are female. Some women believe that sacrificing a daughter guarantees a son in the next pregnancy. In other cases, the family cannot afford the dowry that would eventually be demanded for a girl's marriage.

And for many mothers, sentencing a daughter to death is better than condemning her to life as a woman in the Third World, with cradle-to-grave discrimination, poverty, sickness and drudgery.

"In a culture that idolizes sons and dreads the birth of a daughter, to be born female comes perilously close to being born less than human," the Indian government conceded in a recent report by its Department of Women and Child Development.

While women in the United States and Europe—after decades of struggling for equal rights—often measure sex discrimination by pay scales and seats in corporate board rooms, women in the Third World gauge discrimination by mortality rates and poverty levels.

"Women are the most exploited among the oppressed," says Karuna Chanana Ahmed, a New Delhi anthropologist who has studied the role of women in developing countries. "I don't think it's even possible to eradicate discrimination, it's so deeply ingrained."

PHOTO BY JOHN WARD ANDERSON—THE WASHINGTON POST

Rani, 31, with Asha, 2, says she killed another daughter 3½ years ago. "I wanted to kill this child also . . . . Now I have killed, I still haven't had any sons."

This is the first in a series that will examine the lives of women in developing countries around the globe where culture, religion and the law often deprive women of basic human rights and sometimes relegate them to almost subhuman status. From South America to South Asia, women are often subjected to a lifetime of discrimination with little or no hope of relief.

As children, they are fed less, denied education and refused hospitalization. As teenagers, many are forced into marriage, sometimes bought and sold like animals for prostitution and slave labor. As wives and mothers, they are often treated little better than farmhands and baby machines. Should they outlive their husbands, they frequently are denied inheritance, banished from their homes and forced to live as beggars on the streets.

The scores of women interviewed for this series—from destitute villagers in Brazil and Bangladesh, to young professionals in Cairo, to factory workers in China—blamed centuries-old cultural and religious traditions for institutionalizing and giving legitimacy to gender discrimination.

Although, the forms of discrimination vary tremendously among regions, ethnic groups and age levels in the developing world, Shahla Zia, an attorney and women's activist in Islamabad, Pakistan, says there is a theme: "Overall, there is a social and cultural attitude where women are inferior—and discrimination tends to start at birth."

In many countries, a woman's greatest challenge is an elemental one: simply surviving through a normal life cycle. In South Asia and China, the perils begin at birth, with the threat of infanticide.

Like many rural Indian women, Rani, now 31, believed that killing her daughter 3 1/2 years ago would guarantee that her next baby would be a boy. Instead, she had another daughter.

"I wanted to kill this child also," she says, brushing strands of hair from the face of the 2-year-old girl she named Asha, or Hope. "But my husband got scared because all these social workers came and said, 'Give us the child.'" Ultimately, Rani was allowed to keep her. She pauses. "Now I have killed, and I still haven't had any sons."

Amravati, who lives in a village near Rani in the Indian state of Tamil Nadu, says she killed two of her own day-old daughters by pouring scalding chicken soup down their throats, one of the most widely practiced methods of infanticide in southern India. She showed where she buried their bodies—under piles of cow dung in the tiny courtyard of her home.

"My mother-in-law and father-in-law are bedridden," says Amravati, who has two living daughters. "I have no land and no salary, and my husband met with an accident and can't work. Of course it was the right decision. I need

a boy. Even though I have to buy clothes and food for a son, he will grow on his own and take care of himself. I don't have to buy him jewelry or give him a 10,000-rupee [$350] dowry."

Sociologists and government officials began documenting sporadic examples of female infanticide in India about 10 years ago. The practice of killing newborn girls is largely a rural phenomenon in India; although its extent has not been documented, one indication came in a recent survey by the Community Services Guild of Madras, a city in Tamil Nadu. Of the 1,250 women questioned, the survey concluded that more than half had killed baby daughters.

In urban areas, easier access to modern medical technology enables women to act before birth. Through amniocentesis, women can learn the sex of a fetus and undergo sex-selective abortions. At one clinic in Bombay, of 8,000 abortions performed after amniocentesis, 7,999 were of female fetuses, according to a recent report by the Indian government. To be sure, female infanticide and sex-selective abortion are not unique to India. Social workers in other South Asian states believe that some communities also condone the practice. In China, one province has had so many cases of female infanticide that a half-million bachelors cannot find wives because they outnumber women their age by 10 to 1, according to the official New China News Agency.

The root problems, according to village women, sociologists and other experts, are cultural and economic. In India, a young woman is regarded as a temporary member of her natural family and a drain on its wealth. Her parents are considered caretakers whose main responsibility is to deliver a chaste daughter, along with a sizable dowry, to her husband's family.

"They say bringing up a girl is like watering a neighbor's plant," says R. Venkatachalam, director of the Community Services Guild of Madras. "From birth to death, the expenditure is there." The dowry, he says, often wipes out a family's life savings but is necessary to arrange a proper marriage and maintain the honor of the bride's family.

After giving birth to a daughter, village women "immediately start thinking, 'Do we have the money to support her through life?' and if they don't, they kill her," according to Vasanthai, 20, the mother of an 18-month-old girl and a resident of the village where Rani lives. "You definitely do it after two or three daughters. Why would you want more?"

Few activists or government officials in India see female infanticide as a law-and-order issue, viewing it instead as a social problem that should be eradicated through better education, family planning and job programs. Police officials say few cases are reported and witnesses seldom cooperate.

"There are more pressing issues," says a top police official in Madras. "Very few cases come to our attention. Very few people care."

7. WOMEN AND DEVELOPMENT

Surviving childbirth is itself an achievement in South Asia for both mother and baby. One of every 18 women dies of a pregnancy-related cause, and more than one of every 10 babies dies during delivery.

For female children, the survival odds are even worse. Almost one in every five girls born in Nepal and Bangladesh dies before age 5. In India, about one-fourth of the 12 million girls born each year die by age 15.

The high death rates are not coincidental. Across the developing world, female children are fed less, pulled out of school earlier, forced into hard labor sooner and given less medical care than boys. According to numerous studies, girls are handicapped not only by the perception that they are temporary members of a family, but also by the belief that males are the chief breadwinners and therefore more deserving of scarce resources.

Boys are generally breast-fed longer. In many cultures, women and girls eat leftovers after the men and boys have finished their meals. According to a joint report by the United Nations Children's Fund and the government of Pakistan, some tribal groups do not feed high-protein foods such as eggs and meat to girls because of the fear it will lead to early puberty.

Women are often hospitalized only when they have reached a critical stage of illness, which is one reason so many mothers die in childbirth. Female children, on the other hand, often are not hospitalized at all. A 1990 study of patient records at Islamabad Children's Hospital in Pakistan found that 71 percent of the babies admitted under age 2 were boys. For all age groups, twice as many boys as girls were admitted to the hospital's surgery, pediatric intensive care and diarrhea units.

Mary Okumu, an official with the African Medical and Research Foundation in Nairobi, says that when a worker in drought-ravaged northern Kenya asked why only boys were lined up at a clinic, the worker was told that in times of drought, many families let their daughters die.

"Nobody will even take them to a clinic," Okumu says. "They prefer the boy to survive."

For most girls, however, the biggest barrier—and the one that locks generations of women into a cycle of discrimination—is lack of education.

Across the developing world, girls are withdrawn from school years before boys so they can remain at home and lug water, work the fields, raise younger siblings and help with other domestic chores. By the time girls are 10 or 12 years old, they may put in as much as an eight-hour work day, studies show. One survey found that a young girl in rural India spends 30 percent of her waking hours doing household work, 29 percent gathering fuel and 20 percent fetching water.

Statistics from Pakistan demonstrate the low priority given to female education: Only one-third of the country's schools—which are sexually segregated—are for women, and one-third of those have no building. Almost 90 percent of the women over age 25 are illiterate. In the predominantly rural state of Baluchistan, less than 2 percent of women can read and write.

In Islamic countries such as Pakistan and Bangladesh, religious concern about interaction with males adds further restrictions to females' mobility. Frequently, girls are taken out of school when they reach puberty to limit their contact with males—though there exists a strong impetus for early marriages. In Bangladesh, according to the United Nations, 73 percent of girls are married by age 15, and 21 percent have had at least one child.

Across South Asia, arranged marriages are the norm and can sometimes be the most demeaning rite of passage a woman endures. Two types are common—bride wealth, in which the bride's family essentially gives her to the highest bidder, and dowry, in which the bride's family pays exorbitant amounts to the husband's family.

In India, many men resort to killing their wives—often by setting them afire—if they are unhappy with the dowry. According to the country's Ministry of Human Resource Development, there were 5,157 dowry murders in 1991—one every hour and 42 minutes.

After being bartered off to a new family, with little education, limited access to health care and no knowledge of birth control, young brides soon become young mothers. A woman's adulthood is often spent in a near constant state of pregnancy, hoping for sons.

According to a 1988 report by India's Department of Women and Child Development: "The Indian woman on an average has eight to nine pregnancies, resulting in a little over six live births, of which four or five survive. She is estimated to spend 80 percent of her reproductive years in pregnancy and lactation." Because of poor nutrition and a hard workload, she puts on about nine pounds during pregnancy, compared with 22 pounds for a typical pregnant woman in a developed country.

A recent study of the small Himalayan village of Bemru by the New Delhi-based Center for Science and the Environment found that "birth in most cases takes place in the cattle shed," where villagers believe that holy cows protect the mother and newborn from evil spirits. Childbirth is considered unclean, and the mother and their newborn are treated as "untouchables" for about two weeks after delivery.

"It does not matter if the woman is young, old or pregnant, she has no rest, Sunday or otherwise," the study said, noting that women in the village did 59 percent of the work, often laboring 14 hours a day and lugging loads 1 1/2 times their body weight. "After two or three . . . pregnancies, their stamina gives up, they get weaker, and by the late thirties are spent out, old and tired, and soon die."

Studies show that in developing countries, women in remote areas can spend more than two hours a day carrying water for cooking, drinking, cleaning and bathing, and in some rural areas they spend the equivalent of more than 200 days a year gathering firewood. That presents an additional hazard: The International Labor Organization found that women using wood fuels in India inhaled carcinogenic pollutants that are the equivalent of smoking 20 packs of cigarettes a day.

Because of laws relegating them to a secondary status, women have few outlets for relaxation or recreation. In many Islamic countries, they are not allowed to drive cars, and their appearance in public is so restricted that they are banned from such recreational and athletic activities as swimming and gymnastics.

In Kenya and Tanzania, laws prohibit women from owning houses. In Pakistan, a daughter legally is entitled to half the inheritance a son gets when their parents die. In some criminal cases, testimony by women is legally given half the weight of a man's testimony, and compensation for the wrongful death of a woman is half that for the wrongful death of a man.

After a lifetime of brutal physical labor, multiple births, discrimination and sheer tedium, what should be a woman's golden years often hold the worst indignities. In India, a woman's identity is so intertwined and subservient to her husband's that if she outlives him, her years as a widow are spent as a virtual nonentity. In previous generations, many women were tied to their husband's funeral pyres and burned to death, a practice called *suttee* that now rarely occurs.

Today, some widows voluntarily shave their heads and withdraw from society, but more often a spartan lifestyle is forced upon them by families and a society that place no value on old, single women. Widowhood carries such a stigma that remarriage is extremely rare, even for women who are widowed as teenagers.

In some areas of the country, women are forced to marry their dead husband's brother to ensure that any property remains in the family. Often they cannot wear jewelry or a *bindi*—the beauty spot women put on their foreheads—or they must shave their heads and wear a white sari. Frequently, they cannot eat fish or meat, garlic or onions.

"The life of a widow is miserable," says Aparna Basu, general secretary of the All India Women's Conference, citing a recent study showing that more than half the women in India age 60 and older are widows, and their mortality rate is three times higher than that of married women of the same age.

In South Asia, women have few property or inheritance rights, and a husband's belongings usually go to sons and occasionally daughters. A widow must rely on the largess of her children, who often cast their mothers on the streets.

Thousands of destitute Indian widows make the pilgrimage to Vrindaban, a town on the outskirts of Agra where they hope to achieve salvation by praying to the god Krishna. About 1,500 widows show up each day at the Shri Bhagwan prayer house, where in exchange for singing "Hare Rama, Hare Krishna" for eight hours, they are given a handful of rice and beans and 1.5 rupees, or about 5 cents.

Some widows claim that when they stop singing, they are poked with sticks by monitors, and social workers allege that younger widows have been sexually assaulted by temple custodians and priests.

On a street there, an elderly woman with a *tilak* on her forehead—white chalk lines signifying that she is a devout Hindu widow—waves a begging cup at passing strangers.

"I have nobody," says Paddo Chowdhury, 65, who became a widow at 18 and has been in Vrindaban for 30 years. "I sit here, shed my tears and get enough food one way or another."

Female Empowerment Leads to Fewer Births

Cameron Barr

Staff writer to The Christian Science Monitor

DHAKA, BANGLADESH Batashi, a woman in her 30s wearing gold jewelry and a bright blue sari, stands in front of her tidy cement and packed-mud home in a village called Nabogram. She and millions of women like her in the developing world are helping to answer a question that is central to the effort to slow global population growth: Is it enough to hand a poor woman a contraceptive?

Batashi's village, about two hours outside Dhaka, Bangladesh, is perched on earthen ridges that divide rice paddies and keep people above the flood plain during the rainy season. Most people work tiny plots of land they don't own. But Batashi's economic situation is better than average because of small loans and other assistance she has received from a private development agency called BRAC, the Bangladesh Rural Advancement Committee.

She now owns three cows, tethered in a nearby shed, that produce 10 kilograms (22 pounds) of milk every day. She also owns three bicycle rickshaws, one pulled by her husband and the other two rented to men who earn their living by pulling them.

Do the cows and the rickshaws have any bearing on Batashi's decision to use family-planning services? "Yes, family planning is easier for me," she says. Economic opportunity "gives me freedom and . . . gives me power." Batashi has two sons and a daughter. "This is enough," she says, "because I want these three to be educated persons. I don't want my children to be rickshaw pullers."

Batashi's case illustrates why many population analysts now believe that "parallel efforts" and "holistic approaches" to overpopulation—that is, combining the delivery of family-planning services with programs that improve women's standing in society—are critical to slowing birthrates.

"What's clear," says Sharon Camp, senior vice president of the Population Crisis Committee in Washington, "is that if you can do good family planning and secure improvements in the status of women—legal, economic, social, and political—those things interact so powerfully that you can get declines in birthrates at breathtaking speeds. That's probably the solution to the world's population problem."

Even so, family-planning bureaucracies in many developing countries have been slow to expand beyond the traditional approach to family planning—providing contraceptives and advice on using them.

"From a program standpoint, the woman is a target to achieve demographic ends," says Saroj Pachauri, a program officer at the Ford Foundation in New Delhi. "It's not her concerns that are paramount."

Population experts have long understood the importance of "female empowerment"—a catchall term that covers women-centered health care, improvements in social and legal status, access to education and jobs, and a fairer distribution of responsibility for children between mothers and fathers.

But during the past 10 years, a growing body of evidence has verified the correlation between empowerment and reducing family size.

One of the best examples in the world is nearby in the southern Indian state of Kerala, where the fertility rate—on average, 2.3 children per woman—is one of the lowest in the developing world. One reason is a female literacy rate of 66 percent, several times the average in India's northern states, according to a United Nations report.

The other reason is the status of women. According to tradition, women inherit land in Kerala, and families pay a "bride price" to the parents of the bride, symbols, the UN Population Fund says, that women are considered an asset and not a liability.

Education changes outlook

There is plenty of evidence to show that eight or more years of education for women, because it encourages later marriages and broadens a woman's outlook, results in fewer births. "With education and economic opportunities, women begin to define themselves as citizens, not just family members," says Judith Bruce, a senior associate at the Population Council, a private research group in New York. "Interacting in a wider set of relationships means having access to more objective information [on the costs and benefits of having more children]. It means more equality in the marital relationship."

Research also links increased family planning with economic opportunity. One study looked at a group of 1,600 women members of the Grameen Bank, a Bangladeshi institution that provides small loans to promote small businesses. Fifty-nine percent of the bank members were using some sort of family planning, compared with 43 percent of women in a control group.

Economic insecurity, on the other hand, can have a reverse effect, driving up birthrates since children, especially sons, are considered essential to old-age security.

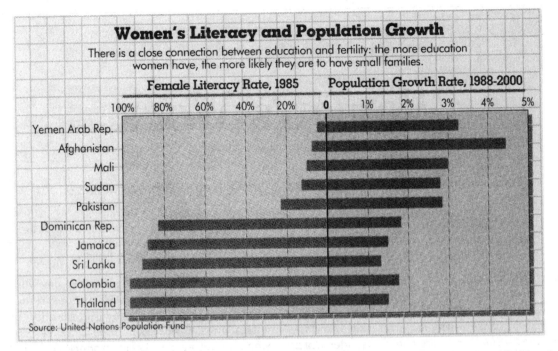

Women's Literacy and Population Growth

There is a close connection between education and fertility: the more education women have, the more likely they are to have small families.

Female Literacy Rate, 1985 | Population Growth Rate, 1988-2000

100% 80% 60% 40% 20% 0 1% 2% 3% 4% 5%

Yemen Arab Rep.
Afghanistan
Mali
Sudan
Pakistan
Dominican Rep.
Jamaica
Sri Lanka
Colombia
Thailand

Source: United Nations Population Fund

According to recent research, 60 percent of women in India over age 60 are widows. But some of India's many castes prohibit widows from returning to the village of their birth or joining the lineage of their married daughters.

"Unless she has adult or married sons, she is left virtually on her own," says Marty Chen of the Harvard Institute for International Development, in Cambridge, Mass., and author of the research.

In a village near Batashi's, a woman named Behula says she had three girls before she bore a boy.

"When my three daughters marry, my house will be completely empty," she says. "If I have a boy, he will be present in front of my eyes [and] in the end he will see me in my old age."

"To me it seems so obvious that we really don't have to explain it because women are [the] ones who make the choice," says Amina Islam, a program officer at the UN Population Fund in Khaka. "If you improve their status, they will be in a [better] position to make decisions about their fertility."

Sitting in the government family-planning office for Manikganj District, where Batashi's village is located and where BRAC has been active, two low-level male bureaucrats corroborate the point.

"It is very easy to talk about family planning with a working woman," says one, Motalib Hussain, the district family-planning supervisor. "It is very easy for us because she has already developed herself. [But] it is very difficult to talk about family planning with housewives."

At the higher levels of Bangladesh's family-planning bureaucracy, however, there is less regard for the impact that education and economic opportunity can have on fertility. "We are proud of our success," says A. K. M. Rafiquzzaman, director-general of Bangladesh's Family-Planning Directorate, sitting in an office air-conditioned against Dhaka's 100-degree heat.

"Bangladesh has disproved the theory," he asserts, that economic development and literacy are prerequisites to a contraceptive-prevalence rate of 40 percent.

'Can't wait for development'

"The main problem," writes Alia Ahmed in her 1991 book, "Women and Fertility in Bangladesh," "is that one cannot wait for socioeconomic development to solve the problem of overpopulation when development

itself is being stifled by the high rate of population growth."

But most experts insist that there are limits to relying exclusively on a "supply side" approach to family planning, providing contraceptive services to interested couples.

To produce deep cuts where they count most—in fertility rates—the "demand side" of the equation must be addressed as well by providing the education and economic opportunities that create a desire for smaller families and thus a wider demand for family-planning services.

"It's one thing to reduce fertility rates from five or six children per woman to three or four using traditional family-planning services," says Ronald Ridker, a senior economist at the World Bank in Washington. "But unless there is substantial social and economic progress, including improvements in the status of women, it will be impossible to get from three or four [per mother] to a replacement level of 2.1.

"We can't wait for social and economic progress to occur to accomplish these things," adds Dr. Ridker.

"We have to intervene selectively in the development process to ensure that the conditions that change attitudes toward family size are fostered."

Women's Work

Why "development" isn't always good news for the second sex

Jodi L. Jacobson

Jodi L. Jacobson is a senior researcher at the World-watch Institute in Washington. The research for this article was done for the Worldwatch study, Gender Bias: Roadblock to Sustainable Development.

The women of Sikandernagar, a village in the Indian state of Andhra Pradesh, work three shifts per day. Waking at 4 a.m., they light fires, milk buffaloes, sweep floors, fetch water, and feed their families. From 8 a.m. until 5 p.m. they weed crops for a meager wage. In the evening they forage for branches, twigs, and leaves to fuel their cooking fires, wild vegetables to nourish their children, and grass to feed the buffalo. Finally, they return home to cook dinner and do evening chores. These women spend twice as many hours per week working to support their families as do the men in their village. But they do not own the land on which they labor, and every year, for all their effort, they find themselves poorer and less able to provide what their families need to survive.

As the 20th century draws to a close, some 3 billion people—more than half the earth's population—live in the subsistence economies of the developing world. Most of these subsistence producers find themselves trapped in the same downward spiral as the women of Sikandernagar. Because they have cash incomes insufficient to meet their most basic needs, they must rely heavily on their own labor to secure whatever food, fuel, and water they can from the surrounding environment.

Women perform the lion's share of work in subsistence economies, toiling longer hours and often contributing more to real family income than their male relatives, but their work is not given monetary value and they are viewed as unproductive by many government statisticians, economists, development experts—even their husbands. A huge proportion of the world's real production, therefore, remains officially under-valued, and the essential contributions women make to the welfare of families and nations remain unrecognized. So, while the growing scarcity of resources within subsistence economies increases the burden on women and erodes their productivity, little is being done to reverse the cycle.

Ironically, by failing to address the pervasive gender bias that discounts the contributions of women, many development policies and programs intended to alleviate impoverishment actually are making the problem worse. There are development groups in both the private and public sector that focus on the role of women, but the flaws inherent in current development practices cannot be fixed by relatively minor allocations of funds to women. Fundamental changes are needed in mainstream policies and approaches.

18-HOUR DAYS

Gender bias is especially pernicious in less-developed nations, where most of women's activity takes place in the non-wage economy. Women's work is essential to survival, but because little or no money changes hands, it is not counted as economically productive. United Nations data indicate that on average, women work longer hours than men in every country except Australia, Canada, and the United States. Hours worked producing subsistence goods are rarely offset by a reduction of duties at home. Moreover, gender disparities in total hours worked are greatest among the poor: in developing countries, women work an average of 12 to 18 hours per day, producing food, managing and harvesting resources, and working at a variety of paid and unpaid activities, compared to 8 to 12 hours for men.

Since the cultivation or collection of food directly for the family is not considered a "business," the women who engage in such work usually are not granted access to land, credit, or other resources. While men are more likely both to have access to resources and to earn cash wages for their work, they are less likely than women to spend it on family maintenance—food, clothes, health care, and the like. Such patterns are disturbingly prevalent across countries and cultures.

Gender bias is thus a fundamental cause of poverty, because in its various forms it prevents hundreds of millions of women from obtaining the education, training, health services, child care, and legal status needed to escape from poverty. It is what prevents women from transforming their increasingly unstable subsistence economy into one that is not forced to cannibalize its own declining assets.

Gender bias is also the single most important cause of high birth rates. Where women have little access to productive resources, and little control over family income, they depend on children for social status and economic security. A necessary step in reducing births voluntarily, then, is to increase women's productivity and their control over resources.

REINFORCING GENDER BIAS

Conventional approaches to development not only fail to accomplish this goal, but by ignoring the obstacles faced by women they actually formalize and reinforce gender bias in several devastating ways.

First, many current development strategies do not benefit men and women equally. Although women are the main producers and procurers of household food supplies in subsistence economies, conventional agricultural development and strategies to promote cash crops have actually shifted resources *away* from female farmers. Environmental policies likewise discount the value of resources used in subsistence economies and thus work against environmental sustainability. Women, depending on croplands, forests, and other natural resources for food and fuel have a greater interest in guarding the long-term productivity of these resources, whereas men are more often concerned with converting these resources into immediate cash. Development programs that vest control over natural resources solely in the hands of men, or profit-making enterprises in general, are in effect explicitly supporting short-term consumption at the expense of long-term sustainability.

Second, women rarely are involved in designing or carrying out development programs. Consequently, these programs do not address women's needs or utilize their practical knowledge. For example, in rural Africa, 60 to 80 percent of all domestic fuel supplies are gathered from forests by women and girls. Yet, countless programs to reverse deforestation have failed because their planners did not consult village women who are the primary harvesters of forest products in their communities.

Third, conventional economic policies often contribute to increasing poverty within subsistence economies, which in turn increases the relative burden on women. In Sikandernagar, for example, the green revolution and other agricultural development schemes promised economic advancement but brought subsistence producers only greater impoverishment by further reducing their access to cropland and forest resources. With government and private interests controlling much of the once commonly owned land where subsistence families collected fuel and fodder, women were forced to go farther afield to meet their families' needs. At the same time, the replacement of human labor by tractors increased competition for, and lowered the wages of, the much smaller number of jobs available. So women who do work for wages now work longer for less money.

A FAMILY OF MYTHS

Implicit in the theory and practice of conventional economic development are three assumptions that are influenced by gender differences and that reinforce the biases. One assumption is that within a society, economic growth is gender-blind, and both men and women will benefit equally from it. The second is that the traditional Western model of a "household," in which a father, mother, and children share common interests and work toward common goals, is applicable to all societies. The third is that within households, the burdens and benefits of poverty and wealth will be distributed equally regardless of gender. Unfortunately, none of these assumptions holds true.

Economic growth is not gender blind. As economies develop, existing gender gaps in the distribution of wealth and in access to resources usually persist, and in many cases grow worse.

First, economic growth is not gender blind. As economies develop, existing gender gaps in the distribution of wealth and in access to resources usually persist, and in many cases grow worse. From the 1950s through the early 1980s, for example, worldwide standards of living as measured by widely used basic indicators, including life expectancy, per capita income, and primary school enrollment, rose dramatically. Yet women never achieved parity with men, even in the so-called developed countries. According to the Human Development Index, a measure created by the United Nations Development Program to gauge the degree to which people have available to them the resources needed to attain a decent standard of living, women lagged behind men in every country for which data were available. Gender differences were least pronounced in Finland, where measures of women's level of access as a share of men's reached 94 percent. They were most pronounced in South Korea and Kenya, where the index of women's access to resources did not even reach 70 percent of that for men.

Not only do women not automatically benefit from economic growth; they may even fall further behind. Unless specific steps are taken to redress inequity, gender gaps often increase over time, especially where access to resources is already highly skewed. This has happened with literacy. In 1985, 40 percent of the adult population worldwide was unable to read, compared to about 54 percent in 1970, clearly a significant improvement. The gender gap in literacy actually widened during these 15 years, however, as the number of women unable to read rose by 54 million (to 597 million), while that of men increased by only 4 million (to 352 million).

Second, individuals within poor families do not necessarily have common interests or work toward common goals. Development programs have been built on the premise that what is good for men is good for the family, but in many areas, this is patently not the case, because women effectively provide the largest share of the family's basic needs, and the incomes of men often are siphoned off by the purchase of alcohol, tobacco, or other consumer products. While a woman labors to produce food for her family, her husband may focus his energies on developing a business or pursuing cash interests that may not benefit his wife and children.

In much of sub-Saharan Africa, for example, both men and women plant crops, but they do so with different goals. Husbands and wives maintain separate managerial and financial control over the production, storage, and sale of their respective crops. Men grow cash crops, the income from the sale of which they retain, even though their wives still do the weeding and hoeing. Women, by contrast, use their land primarily for subsistence crops. They also are the ones expected to provide shelter, clothing, school fees, and medical care for themselves and their children. Given adequate acreage, high yields, or both, women do plant and market surplus crops to earn cash, but when land is scarce, or the soil poor, they put more time into other income-producing activities, or sell their labor for needed cash.

An increase in the income of a male within a household may not mean an increase in total consumption by family members. In Africa, according to a 1992 World Bank report, children's nutrition may actually deteriorate even while men in the household acquire wristwatches, radios, and bicycles. The connection between malnutrition and the diversion of income by males to personal consumption also has been found to be a problem in Belize, Guatemala, Mexico, and throughout

the Indian subcontinent. In Guatemala, for example, the children of women earning independent incomes had better diets than those of women who were not earning their own money and had little control over how their husbands' earnings were spent.

Finally, resources within poor households often are skewed toward the males. When household income rises, men and boys throughout the developing world fare far better than do women and girls. In parts of India, for example, male children consistently receive more and better food and health care than their sisters. Consequently, far more girls than boys die in the critical period between infancy and age five. And with the exception of girls aged 10 to 14, who are clearly economically productive, Indian females die from preventable causes at far higher rates than males through age 35. This pattern is contrary to that found wherever females have equal access to food and health care. Evidence of similar patterns of discrimination in the allocation of household resources has been found in Bangladesh, Nepal, Pakistan, throughout the Middle East and North Africa, and in parts of sub-Saharan Africa.

Globally, much of the discrimination against females in families and societies stems from another form of gender gap: the huge disparity that prevails between the actual economic and social benefits derived from women's work, and the social perception of women as unproductive.

Studies in every region of the Third World confirm that it is the mother's ability to grow or purchase food rather than the father's food production or cash income—and the degree of control she maintains over her production and income—that determines the relative nutrition of children. However, women's work that does not produce cash directly is heavily discounted. The low valuation of women's work is reinforced by women's lack of control over physical resources. In most subsistence economies, for example, females have few legal rights regarding land tenure, marital relations, income, or social security.

But ignoring the full value of women's economic contributions cripples efforts to achieve broad development goals. Lack of investment results in lower female productivity. Coupled with persistent occupational and wage discrimination, this prevents women from achieving parity with men in terms of jobs and income, and leads to further devaluation of their work. The omnipresence of this bias is a sign that virtually every country is operating below its economic potential.

CONSERVING THE LAND

In the not-so-distant past, subsistence farmers and forest dwellers were models of ecologically sustainable living, their numbers not threatening available resources. Today, however, as the subsistence producers' circumstances grow more and more tenuous, pressures on forests and croplands grow increasingly acute. Yet in an era when "sustainable development" has become a global rallying cry, most governments and international development agencies pay scant attention to this dilemma.

To provide for their families, women depend heavily on community-owned croplands, grasslands, and forests. Research shows women to be more effective at protecting and regenerating the environment than is either the state or private landowners. The reasons are obvious: community resources are as indispensable to land-poor women in subsistence economies as these women are to the maintenance of the resources.

Given access to appropriate land, traditional farmers employ "managed" fallowing, crop rotation, intercropping, mulching, and a variety of other soil conservation and enrichment techniques. Women farmers, who have a great deal of unacknowledged skill in these areas, also play a leading role in maintaining crop diversity.

Women in subsistence economies also are active managers of forest resources, and traditionally play the leading role in their conservation. Forests are a major source of fuel for home consumption as well as of plant fibers, medicinal plants and herbs, seeds, oils, resins, and a host of other materials used to produce goods or income for families.

Unfortunately, the widespread depletion and degradation of resources leads to equally widespread impoverishment of subsistence families. Women's access to farm lands and the goods they yield is fast diminishing. The results are already evident in the declining food security among subsistence households. Under strategies to promote cash crops in southern Ghana, for example, commonly owned village land traditionally available to women to grow food for their families is being "privatized" and shifted increasingly into the hands of male farmers who are not responsible for domestic food supplies. Left with smaller holdings, on poorer soil, Ghanaian women can no longer practice crop rotation and must farm the same plots year after year. As a result, soil becomes eroded and less fertile. Food production declines, and malnutrition deepens.

MISDIRECTED DEVELOPMENT

On balance, conventional agricultural development strategies have marginalized women farmers. Instead of increasing the productivity of food crops and domestic food production, which are controlled by women, governments and international agencies have promoted cash crops, which are generally controlled by men.

Four major—and interrelated—trends, all set in motion or perpetuated by the agricultural strategies of low-income countries since the 1950s, have been particularly damaging to the ability of rural women to produce or procure adequate supplies of food. All four are a product of the increasing emphasis on cash crops.

First, large amounts of land once jointly owned and controlled by villagers, and accessible to women, have shifted into the hands of government agencies and private landowners. Second, the distribution of resources on which cash crop agriculture is heavily dependent, including land, fertilizers, pesticides, irrigation, and hybrid seeds, has reflected persistent gender bias. Third, the mechanization of agriculture has reduced or replaced the labor traditionally done by men but increased that done by women without increasing their income. And, finally, the labor available to subsistence households in many countries has become increasingly scarce, largely as a result of the shift of male workers away from subsistence production into cash crops and urban-based industries.

The shifting of land out of the hands of those who are most responsible for producing food for domestic consumption has been hastened by development strategies that make false assumptions about who benefits from gross economic gains. Governments throughout the less-developed world since the end of the colonial era have privatized land in favor of male land-holders. As a result, the amount and quality of land available to women food producers in large parts of the developing world is declining. Legal and cultural obstacles prevent women from obtaining title to land and, therefore, from participating in cash crop schemes.

A woman's production is undercut when she spends more time working on her husband's land, and less tending the crops she needs to feed her family or sell in the market.... She is drawn into a cycle of more labor for lower gains.

Agricultural development schemes encourage expansion of cash crop operations by offering market incentives, improved agricultural technologies, credit, seeds, and the like, with access to these resources independent mainly on the use of land as collateral. But without ownership and control over land, women are further disadvantaged because they cannot compete in cash crop schemes and have fewer resources with which to produce food crops.

In Africa, men have responded to cash crop farming incentives by reserving the better land—and their own labor—for their crops. This has two damaging effects: it raises women's workloads, and it increases environmental degradation by forcing women to produce food crops on already exhausted fields. A woman's production is undercut when she spends more time working on her husband's land, and less tending the crops she needs to fee her family or sell in the market. Her personal income–an important source of community respect and economic independence–declines, and her labor is increasingly spent on activities for which she receives no remuneration. She is drawn into a cycle of more labor for lower gains, which only deepens her impoverishment and dependence.

Green revolution technologies also are skewed in favor of men. In India, investments in agriculture consistently bypass women even though most of the rural female population is engaged in agriculture. An International Labor Organization study of how rural women spend their time indicates that up to 90 percent of rural women in central India participate in agriculture. Nevertheless, the distribution of irrigation outlets favored large landholders at the expense of the small family farms on which women work and produce food for domestic consumption. And the credit needed to enhance productivity remains out of reach of women, again largely because they lack ownership of land as collateral.

Improving the status of women, and thereby the prospects for humanity, will require a complete reorientation of development efforts toward establishing an environment in which women and men can prosper together.

The focus of agricultural research and development, too, has often favored cash crops over food crops, to the detriment of women and of family nutrition. This has not only led to diminished production but increased the perception that cash crops are more "valuable."

THE LOSS OF JOBS

Mechanization has replaced millions of agricultural jobs, throwing large numbers of men out of their traditional occupations. Meanwhile, the privatization of commons lands has made large numbers of land-poor and landless female subsistence producers even more reliant on wage income. An increased number of both men and women were forced to compete for traditional jobs. For example, in many regions of India, the increased competition for agricultural work has further driven down wages and led to increasing pauperization among subsistence producers, and especially among women.

As wages fall and productivity declines, more and more men from the land-poor and landless households of the developing world migrate to towns and cities in search of work. Subsistence households may or may not benefit from male migration, however, depending on whether or not husbands or sons send back to their families the money they earn. Indeed, studies show that female-headed households are among the poorest in large part because the money sent back by male relatives tends to dwindle over time.

The growing number of female-headed households is one indication of how widespread these conditions are. Some estimates indicate that women are the sole breadwinners in one-fourth to one-third of the world's households. And at least one-fourth of all other households rely on female earnings for more than 50 percent of total income.

PROSPERING TOGETHER

Improving the status of women, and thereby the prospects for humanity, will require a complete reorientation of development efforts toward establishing an environment in which women and men can prosper together. This means creating mainstream development programs that increase women's control over income and household resources, improve their productivity, establish their legal and social rights, and increase the social and economic choices they are able to make.

The first step toward achieving these goals–a step that is consistently overlooked–is to ask women themselves what needs should be accorded top priority. Some answers were provided in a forum on international health held in June 1991. Among the key needs identified by participants from Africa, Asia, and Latin America were investments in the development and dissemination of appropriate technology to reduce women's work burden, and access for women to credit and training programs.

The second step is to act immediately to increase the productivity of subsistence producers, whether in rural or urban areas. Immediate gains can be realized by increasing women's access to land, credit, and the tools and appropriate technologies with which they can increase their own and their families' welfare. Enforcement of laws guaranteeing gender equity in the distribution of land resources, for example, needs to be assigned high priority. Given the intimate connections between women's lack of access to land, their increasing work burden, and their dependence on children as a force of labor, land distribution and allocation policies should be at the top of the agenda for groups concerned about the environment, human rights, hunger, and population issues.

The third step is to change the definitions and assumptions made by conventional development policies, in order to collect information that creates a realistic picture of subsistence economies. A redefinition of the concepts of "productivity," "value," and "work" is needed in many places to include activities that are indeed productive—such as those that yield family income in goods rather than in cash or that support people without degrading the environment—which would dramatically alter the base of relevant information sought by those who are truly interested in improving human prospects. This recognition, in essence, is a necessary precondition to environmentally sound economic systems.

The collection of this type of data on a small scale already has helped policymakers to recognize the different effects on men and women of conventional gender-blind development practices. But for many areas of the economy in which women play important but officially ignored roles, there are still too little data available to truly inform public policy. Such data need to be incorporated into all relevant areas of economics, health, and environment.

Research and development in the sciences and in appropriate technologies need to be far more gender sensitive, not only to benefit women but to benefit from them, especially in areas of crop production and biodiversity. Focusing research on the needs of women in subsistence economies could dramatically boost food crop and forest production within a decade.

But these objectives cannot be met unless women enjoy the same degree of independence and freedom of choice as men. Governments and international agencies also need to be pushed to recognize the effects of their policies on how such resources as money, food, and opportunities for learning are allocated within the household. Development should encourage more cooperation between the sexes with the goal of ending poverty, reducing fertility, and securing the environment.

These ends can most easily be achieved by directing resources into the education of young girls and the training of women, and by establishing policies that increase women's access to credit and opportunities to establish businesses, earn income, and create jobs.

Experience suggests that these reforms will not be easily accomplished. Gender bias dies hard. Much of the information regarding women's roles in agriculture and forestry, for example, has been available to governments and development planners for two decades and has yet to provoke real changes in policy. Yet it is in the interest of every person, from the poor farmers of Sikandernagar to the chiefs of industry, and from grassroots activists to heads of state, to combat gender bias. Nothing could be more important to human development than the reform of policies that suppress the productive potential of half the earth's people.

$$W = ♀ + ♂$$

Gender analysis has a crucial role in planning workable farming systems

Vicki L. Wilde

When project officers set out to implement a community forestry project in Nepal a few years ago, they wanted to do the right thing. They went directly to the villagers and asked what kind of trees they wanted to plant. "Hardwood trees," was the answer, so the project provided 3000 hardwood seedlings—and all 3000 seedlings subsequently died from lack of care.

Why? Because the project officers left gender issues out of their thinking. They consulted only the male villagers, who were only interested in wood for furniture-making and carving that would earn them cash. But, by tradition, it was the women who planted and watered tree seedlings. They saw no benefit for themselves in slow-growing hardwood trees, and so refused to take on the burden of caring for them. The women were spending some six hours a day collecting fuel and fodder, and—if they'd been asked—would have said they wanted fast-growing species to ease *their* burden.

The project officers learned a lesson from that false start, and things did improve. They called a second meeting and invited the women as well as the men to attend. This time it became clear that, to succeed, the project had to deliver both hardwood and fast-growing trees, so both sexes could get what they needed.

The Nepal project is a good example of why gender analysis is crucial to development, especially when new technologies or improvements on old ones are being introduced. In every culture and ethnic group, every environmental, economic and social setting, women and men have different roles, needs and priorities. In most development efforts, including those in the farm sector, the focus has been on men because they are considered community leaders and household decision-makers. This has warped the development process so that, in the long run, nobody benefits. Men may gain materially for a while, but when women end up worse off than they were

before, the whole family suffers to the detriment of entire communities and, eventually the nation as a whole.

As planners struggle to simultaneously boost crop production *and* achieve sustainability, experimenting with different combinations of low- and high-external-input farming techniques, the question of gender, and its inextricable links to the labor equations involved, should not be overlooked.

INCREASED MALNUTRITION

Another graphic example: in South India when irrigation technology was introduced for tea production, it was the men who were taught how to use it. For many years, women had earned their wages as agricultural laborers on these tea plantations, but with the introduction of irrigation, men took over the women's jobs. The result was that men's incomes were raised. That was fine until it was realized that, at the same time, their children had begun to suffer from increased malnutrition. This was because women had lost their source of income, and within households in this part of India, it was the women's responsibility to earn the income to buy food, while men spent their money in other ways. Women had lost their access to income, but they still had sole responsibility for feeding the family. And the whole family suffered.

Similar cases have been documented in other countries. An International Labour Organisation poverty study in the Gambia found that the small percentage of female-headed households were better fed than those with a male head because when women were in control their money went on food.

Development workers are only now beginning to recognize that introducing high-technology agriculture can cause a deterioration in the well-being of rural families. Most of these projects were designed for large landholdings and have required expensive inputs. Women have been left out on two counts—first, because women's

From *Ceres*, July/August 1994, pp. 28-31. © 1994 by the Food and Agriculture Organization of the United Nations. Reprinted by permission of *Ceres*, the FAO Review.

farms tend to be small and second, because even when projects do reach small farmers, only men have been invited to training sessions introducing new technologies and inputs.

FAO's 1989 *Global survey on agricultural extension* concluded that only about five per cent of all agricultural extension resources worldwide are directed to female farmers. The 1993 FAO publication *Agricultural Extension and Farm Women in the 1980s* said: "Whether by design or default, the result is a male-to-male system for transferring agricultural training, technologies and information. At best, the result is sub-optimal levels of agricultural production. At worst, female farmers are handicapped in both their subsistence and income-producing agricultural activities."

But the fact that women *don't* benefit from high-external-input systems doesn't necessarily mean that they *do* benefit from low-external-input systems. In fact, women emerge the losers in almost every kind of development effort because of three mistaken assumptions on the part of far too many planners:

• within a society, both women and men benefit equally from economic growth;
• if you raise men's income you improve the welfare of the whole family;
• within a household both burdens of poverty and the benefits of wealth are distributed equally.

None of these assumptions is true. Development planners go wrong when they view households as a single unit—a lump—and don't look at the interaction between females and males within them.

Gender analysis is a tool for understanding the relationship between gender issues and development. In its most basic form, gender analysis asks four questions:

1) **What is getting better, what is getting worse** in the lives of the people in economic, environmental, demographic, social and political terms?
2) **Who does what?** What is the division of labor and responsibilities between women and men?
3) **Who has what?** Who has access to and control of the key resources in the community?
4) **What should be done?** In other words, how do we close the gap between what people need and what development delivers?

In low-input systems, gender issues must be considered in the planning process and in the labor equation. During the planning process, gender analysis can help identify the needs and priorities of both women and men. On the basis of consultations with both in what are known as participatory rural appraisal exercises (PRA), decisions can be made about which development activities require support. Care must be taken to ensure that the types of crops, trees, animals and the placement of

wells, schools and other infrastructure are selected together with the women and men for whom they are intended. The planners need to be flexible enough to accommodate the sometimes overlapping, sometimes different priorities of women and men. The women may need help with their corn production while the men want to improve cotton processing.

In looking at the labor equation for low-input systems, the answers provided by the gender analysis questions enable planners to examine the existing division of labor and identify labor bottlenecks. Typically, women work more hours than do men. But if women are already overworked, leaving them out of the project is not the answer. Instead, planners must find ways to lessen their current work load and allow women to shift their labor over to new activities as they prefer. If women of a village are spending four hours a day looking for water, the project might provide for sinking a well close to the village to free that time for more lucrative activities.

Gender analysis also helps development specialists avoid working on the basis of stereotypes in making assumptions about labor patterns. It is often assumed that heavy labor tasks belong only to men, but as men migrate to the cities women are forced to take over traditionally male tasks, including heavy labor. On the other hand, it is accepted practice in Bhutan for men to take over the housekeeping for the first 30 days after a baby is born. Sometimes male and female labor overlaps, as often happens in Asia, sometimes it is distinct, as is usually the case in Africa. Not only do women and men have different labor roles; they also have different knowledge, concerns and priorities.

TWO PATTERNS

The division of responsibilities is very much a part of the culture of a country, but it can also vary greatly from village to village, depending on tradition, social customs, the economics, the environmental situation and the degree of development.

On a mountainside in the Khao Kho area of northeastern Thailand, two different patterns of gender roles are found within walking distance of each other.

Among the Hmong people in the highlands, women and men have distinct roles. Women are their husbands' property and handle household chores while men control the land, money, credit and their wives' labor. Midway down the same mountain, live the Thais. Here women and men work together in most of their tasks. Thai men help with the cooking and cleaning, and both men and women can sign for credit.

These ethnic-gender differences are important for afforestation of the area. Members of a forestry project staff now know that different extension strategies are needed for the two villages. They learned that meetings would only work well for the Hmong if they were held separately for women and men, whereas among the Thais, meetings should be held with women and men together.

Important as it is, there is still a lot of confusion about gender analysis. Unfortunately, "gender" has often been regarded as synonymous with "women." But gender analysis is about both women and men.

Twenty-five years of research has shown that if you leave out the women, millions of development dollars can go down the drain. The lack of women's participation in development has led not only to project failure, but also made life harder for rural families. But, leaving men out of the equation is not the answer either. In the Gambia, for example, projects that increased women's incomes through horticulture activities ultimately failed because the husbands felt so threatened by their wives' increased incomes that they drove their cattle through the women's gardens to let them fatten on the fruit and vegetables.

Clearly, for sustainability, both women and men must benefit from development. This is all the more important in low-input agriculture systems where labor is the primary input. Therefore, understanding the gender-based division of labor is crucial. It cannot be expected that anyone will put more labor into any particular activity unless the laborers—female, male or both—stand to gain. And this is where the planning comes in. Linking gender analysis to the planning of low-input agriculture efforts will clarify people's priorities.

When development efforts centre on people's priorities, motivations to participate are high, and everybody wins.

Breaking new ground ...

Women's Conference adopts 'Beijing Declaration and Platform for Action'

Acknowledging "the voices of all women everywhere" and declaring that "women's rights are human rights", the Fourth World Conference on Women—one of the largest world gatherings under UN auspices—concluded in China's capital city on 15 September with the adoption of the "Beijing Declaration and Platform for Action", a comprehensive, ground-breaking plan for the international community to promote the status of women.

"My dear sisters and brothers, we have made it", declared Conference Secretary-General Gertrude Mongella, as thousands of delegates cheered after almost two weeks of difficult deliberations and sometimes acrimonious debate at the Conference in Beijing (4-15 September).

"We have managed to transcend historical and cultural complexities; we have managed to transcend socio-economic disparities and diversities; we have kept aflame our common vision and goal of equality, development and peace", said Mrs. Mongella. "A revolution has begun and there is no going back."

Invited by the Platform for Action, which calls on States to respond with concrete commitments to improve the status of women, more than 100 countries and most UN organizations made formal commitments in their statements during the Conference plenary.

In addition to the Declaration and Platform for Action, these commitments constitute the major results of the Conference, most of them dealing with three areas: reform of national policies; numerical targets for the year 2000; and frameworks for international development cooperation.

Some 50,000 persons—more than two thirds of them women—came to Beijing for the Conference and related events. These included nearly 5,000 delegates from 181 Member States, 4,000 representatives of non-governmental organizations (NGOs) and 3,200 media representatives. A parallel NGO Forum on Women '95, held from 30 August to 8 September, attracted some 30,000 participants. As Mrs. Mongella noted, this was "an all-inclusive celebration of women's work" that helped "cement the bonds and networking among women from all corners of the globe".

Progress uneven

Among its 38 provisions, the Beijing Declaration recognizes that the status of women has advanced in some important respects in the past decade, but that progress has been uneven, inequalities between women and men

From *UN Chronicle,* December 1995, pp. 29-31. Reprinted by permission of *UN Chronicle,* a publication of the United Nations Department of Public Information.

have persisted and major obstacles remain, with serious consequences for the well-being of all people.

The 189 Governments taking part in the Conference pledged to dedicate themselves "unreservedly to addressing these constraints and obstacles and thus enhancing further the advancement and empowerment of women all over the world, and agree that this requires urgent action in the spirit of determination, hope, cooperation and solidarity, now and to carry us forward into the next century".

Platform for Action

The Platform for Action establishes a basic group of priority actions to be carried out over the next five years. It deals in depth with 12 critical areas of concern, considered as the main obstacles to women's advancement: poverty; education; health; violence against women; armed conflict; economic structures; power sharing and decision-making; mechanisms to promote the advancement of women; human rights; the media; the environment; and the girl child.

The Platform builds on progress made based on three previous UN conferences on women—in Mexico City in 1975, in Copenhagen in 1980, and in Nairobi in 1985—and reflects a review and appraisal of the Nairobi Forward-looking Strategies for the Advancement of Women.

The Beijing Conference is part of a cycle of world conferences convened by the UN in recent years, which have covered such global issues as environment and development, human rights, population and social development.

"From each of these global conferences emerged a more powerful recognition of the crucial role of women in sustainable development and protecting the environment, of the human rights of women as an inalienable, integral and indivisible part of universal human rights, of violence against women as intolerable violations of these rights, of health, maternal care and family-planning facilities, and of access to education and information, as essential to the exercise by women of their fundamental

rights", UN Secretary-General Boutros Boutros-Ghali said at the Conference's conclusion.

The Platform for Action also expands on the General Assembly's 1993 Declaration on the Elimination of Violence against Women, confronting issues once considered taboo, such as the problems of domestic and sexual abuse, forced pregnancy and sexual slavery. It explores the role of the media in "eliminating patterns of media presentation that generate violence" and calls for the establishment of professional guidelines and codes of conduct that address violent, degrading and pornographic media materials.

Some contentious issues

Several issues generated heated debates at the Beijing Conference, but eventually produced agreement on actions countries should take. Though the Platform was adopted by consensus, reservations were expressed, in writing and orally, by about 40 countries on specific provisions, mostly dealing with health.

Agreements that aim to broaden women's rights and propose qualitatively new measures include:

◆ **Women's rights as human rights:** Expanding on provisions already agreed upon in the ground-breaking 1979 Convention on the Elim-

ination of All Forms of Discrimination against Women, the Platform asserts women's right "to have control over and decide freely and responsibly on matters related to their sexuality, including sexual and reproductive health, free of coercion, discrimination and violence". A disputed text that called for elimination of discrimination due to "sexual orientation" was dropped after the Chairperson of the Conference's Main Committee ruled that there was not enough support for its inclusion.

◆ **Right to inherit:** Many African delegates, who felt that traditional legal structures often discriminate against women in land rights, supported the equal right of women and girls to inheritance. Delegates from some Islamic countries argued that their religious inheritance laws, which were based on the principle of equity, mandated a distribution of assets that gave a woman half the amount that her brother inherited. A compromise between the two positions in the Platform emphasizes the injustice and discrimination women and girls often face and calls for "enacting, as appropriate, and enforcing legislation that guarantees equal right to succession and ensures equal right to inherit, regardless of the sex of the child".

◆ **Parental responsibility:** The Platform recognizes the "rights and

UN Photo 191205

The Conference drew massive attendance: some 50,000, more than two thirds of them women.

duties of parents and legal guardians" to provide guidance in the exercise of the rights of young people, but it also upholds the rights of young people to information, privacy, confidentiality and informed consent on matters related to sexuality and reproduction.

◆ **Reviewing laws on illegal abortion:** The Platform commits nations to "consider reviewing laws containing punitive measures against women who have undergone illegal abortion". However, borrowing the formulation adopted at the International Conference on Population and Development, held in Cairo last year, it notes that "in no case should abortion be promoted as a method of family planning".

◆ **Role of the family:** The Platform recognizes the family as the basic

also acknowledges that any form of extremism may have a negative impact on women and can lead to violence and discrimination.

◆ **Rape is a war crime:** Rape in armed conflict, the Platform asserts, constitutes a war crime and, under certain circumstances, an act of genocide. It condemns "massive violations" of human rights, especially in the form of genocide. "Ethnic cleansing" as a strategy of war and rape as its consequence are also condemned. Such practices must be immediately stopped, the Platform states, and perpetrators of such crimes "must be punished".

◆ **Women's unremunerated work:** Although included in the UN System of National Accounts and in international standards for labour

ing but not limited to their experiences in balancing work and family responsibilities as mothers, professionals, managers and entrepreneurs. The Platform urges the media and the private sector to produce materials on women leaders that portray such diverse roles, and not to present women as inferior beings and exploit them as sexual objects and commodities.

Implementing the Platform

The Platform makes specific recommendations for its implementation and monitoring:

◆ Commitments by Governments to develop strategies to implement the Platform by the end of 1996.

◆ Review of policies by UN and

UN Photo 191206

unit of society, and acknowledges the "social significance of maternity, motherhood and the role of parents in the family and in the upbringing of children". It also asserts that maternity must not be a basis for discrimination or restrict the full participation of women in society.

◆ **Culture and religion:** Religion, thought, conscience and belief, the Platform asserts, can "contribute to fulfilling women's and men's moral, ethical and spiritual needs and to realizing their potential in society". However, it

statistics, women's household work and contribution to food production are largely undervalued and underreported. The Platform calls for developing methods for assessing the value of unremunerated work in quantitative terms for possible reflection in accounts that may be produced separately from, but consistent with, core national accounts.

◆ **Women leaders as mothers and professionals:** Women leaders bring to their positions of leadership many different life experiences, includ-

international financial institutions to ensure that their investments and programmes benefit women.

◆ Establishing a high-level post to act as adviser to the UN Secretary-General on gender issues and help ensure system-wide implementation of the Platform.

◆ Strengthening the UN Commission on the Status of Women, and a review of the work of the International Research and Training Institute for the Advancement of Women and of the UN Development Fund for Women.

WOMEN REDRAWING THE MAP: THE WORLD AFTER THE BEIJING AND CAIRO CONFERENCES

Joan Dunlop, Rachel Kyte, and Mia MacDonald

Joan Dunlop is President, Rachel Kyte, Senior Policy Analyst for Global Affairs, and Mia MacDonald, Special Assistant for Public Affairs of the International Women's Health Coalition. In Beijing, Ms. Dunlop helped lead efforts by NGO's to ensure inclusion of language supporting women's reproductive and sexual health and rights. Ms. Kyte acted as a key strategist for the push for sexual and reproductive health and rights, and Ms. MacDonald worked with the US and international media to ensure substantive coverage of the conference's key achievements.

In Beijing at the United Nations Fourth World Conference on Women, governments reaffirmed and moved beyond what they had agreed at recent global conferences on the environment (Rio 1992), human rights (Vienna 1993), population and development (Cairo 1994) and social development (Copenhagen 1995). Indeed, this series of conferences made the achievements in Beijing possible.

The Beijing Conference was a turning point in the world's understanding; an acknowledgment that women's issues are the world's issues, and vice versa. It provided a clear indication of global priorities for the next century, and of women's centrality to them. The Conference's final document, the Platform for Action, demonstrates that the agreements reached in Cairo at the International Conference on Population and Development (ICPD) is accepted global policy. And for the second time in 12 months, countries of the world reaffirmed the human rights of women and the critical importance of reproductive and sexual health and rights to women's empowerment and to development.

Beijing marked the first time a United Nations women's conference had as its central focus the human rights of women—economic, social, cultural, civil and political. Beijing also represents the coming of age of the international women's movement, with women playing key roles in the intergovernmental negotiations as delegates, advisors, and advocates.

Since the 1985 UN World Conference on Women in Nairobi, women around the world have mobilized in their communities, countries and internationally to gain access, successfully, to the arenas where policies are made and implemented.

Billed as a conference on equality, peace, and development, the Beijing meeting, at its core, was about eliminating coercion, discrimination, and violence in the public and private lives of women. Governments urged that: economic and employment policies recognize women's unpaid contributions to the economy; eliminate differentials in pay between men and women for equal work; and women be guaranteed equal access to public office, education, basic health care, and all other aspects of public and private life. In addition, they called for elimination of violence in the home and in public, where rape is not only a crime against the individual, but is still used as a weapon of war. Finally, the governments represented in Beijing reaffirmed what they had agreed in Vienna in 1993, that international human rights laws and standards must not be diluted by religious practices, or tradition when applied to women.

The conference opened with 35 percent of its Platform in "square brackets" because governments could not agree to terms. [Square brackets are placed around language that has not been accepted by consensus, pending further negotiation or, ultimately, reservation by a delegation at the end of the conference. All brackets must be removed by the conference's end; reservations are the means for countries to state on the record that they do not agree with particular sections or words of the final agreement.] Yet, by its final session, the conference had, as Norwegian Prime Minister Gro Harlem Brundtland said in her closing speech, "unbracket[ed] the lives of girls and women." When the negotiations ended, just before dawn on the morning of September 15, governments had agreed to the strongest international document ever detailing the reality of women's lives and which called for sustained and precise action.

From *SAIS Review*, Winter/Spring 1996, pp. 153-165. © 1996 by the Johns Hopkins Foreign Policy Institute, Paul H. Nitze School of Advanced International Studies. Reprinted by permission.

In this article, we will analyze how the Fourth World Conference on Women took the global community beyond the achievements of the recent series of global conferences in critical ways. In particular, we discuss the importance of the conference's strong reaffirmation of the new conceptualization of population-related health and development policies agreed on at the ICPD in 1994 which centered on women's reproductive health and rights. We also compare and contrast key dimensions of the process and outcomes of the ICPD and the Fourth World Conference on Women, including the genesis of leadership, political actors—not only government delegations but also non-governmental women's organizations—and the pattern and content of the diplomatic negotiations. We provide details of the most important points governments agreed in Beijing, many of which are unprecedented. A concluding section summarizes what the Beijing Platform for Action means for women's lives around the world, what it shows about the process of negotiating global agreements, and how real change can take place.

A Global Shift

The Fourth World Conference on Women was the culmination of a series of global conferences that caused a re-examination and reshaping of governments' understanding of the role of the international community, as well as the global understanding of development. The agreements reached at the Earth Summit in 1992 and the World Conference on Human Rights in 1993 created momentum for the breakthrough agreements reached at the International Conference on Population and Development (ICPD) in Cairo. There, 184 governments reached an unprecedented consensus on a twenty-year Programme of Action to balance the world's peoples with its resources. The Programme puts women's equality, empowerment, reproductive rights, and sexual health at the center of population and development policies.

Previous international agreements on population have set demographic targets for limiting population growth and have focused on contraceptive services as the method to achieve these goals. By contrast, in Cairo the international community recognized the interrelationships between consumption and production patterns, economic development, population growth and structure, and environmental degradation. Also in Cairo, the understanding of the term "population" was broadened significantly, in large part due to the influence of non-governmental organizations (NGOs), especially women's groups from all over the world.

Impact of the Women's Movement and Southern Leadership

The outcome of the ICPD provoked some conservative delegations to threaten to use the Beijing conference to turn back agreements women had achieved in Cairo. Most of the opposition came from delegations that had not fully accepted the Cairo accord, specifically its provisions on reproductive health and reproductive rights. Such groups included the Holy See, conservative Islamic countries, and several states in Latin America. Despite this challenge, governments of the world were able to achieve a consensus on a Platform for Action that included verbatim language from Cairo (including reproductive and sexual health and reproductive rights), as well as language that extends and operationalizes the Cairo Programme of Action in key areas.

As in Cairo, much of the progress achieved in Beijing was due to the capacity, skill, and tenacity of women's NGOs from all over the world, who worked at regional conferences, preparatory meetings and at the Beijing conference itself to move government delegations towards consensus. Rooted in the experience of domestic campaigns over the last 20 years, the series of international women's conferences (Mexico City, 1975; Copenhagen, 1980; Nairobi, 1985), and the force of women's organizations at the recent global conferences, women had refined an inside-outside lobbying strategy. They gave priority to ensuring that feminists were made members of government delegations, worked with delegations at preparatory meetings, and had crafted specific language for negotiation. Many of the over 7,000 women from NGOs who were accredited to the conference worked as a pressure group, and interpreted the complexity of issues and negotiations to the international media.

Contrary to assertions in the press and by opposition delegations, the bulk of the progress came not from Northern radical feminists, but from women of the South. It was clear, the political fulcrum had shifted from Northern to Southern countries, and from men to women. Consensus on sexual rights, abortion, adolescent access to services, the right to inheritance and succession, and most other issues covered by the Platform for Action were forged primarily by delegates who were neither white, nor liberal, nor necessarily feminist. What really happened is that governments of the world, represented by women delegates, stepped forward to acknowledge the realities of women's lives. Delegates wanted to leave Beijing with a document that reflected those realities and that committed the world's governments to take concrete and effective action to end coercion, discrimination, and violence against women of all forms.

Central to this process was the leadership of Africa which had been given focus and energy by the moral authority of South Africa; the courage of many Latin American countries in breaking free of the influence of the Vatican hierarchy; and the steadfastness of the Caribbean. These countries placed women in key positions in their delegations who were not swayed from progressive language on human rights, sexuality, and inheritance, among other contentious issues.

The Preparatory Process

The Conference in Beijing was prefaced by a preparatory process that gained momentum over a two year period. Part of the planning for Beijing took place in the context of the ongoing

7. WOMEN AND DEVELOPMENT

review of implementation of the recommendations of the last women's conference in Nairobi. Unlike other world conferences held in the 1990s, the focus of preparations for Beijing was at the regional level. Five regional conferences were held, in Indonesia, Argentina, Austria, Senegal, and Jordan, focusing on the specific priorities in each region. This process helped Africa, Latin America and the Caribbean, in particular, to work as strong regional groups in Beijing.

In March, 1995, at the annual session of the United Nations Commission on the Status of Women, the draft Platform for Action, compiled by the Conference Secretariat from the five regional conferences, was negotiated for the first time. With only this one chance to negotiate a document never seen in its entirety, the deliberations were tense. This mood was exacerbated by what were widely understood to be deliberate "blocking" tactics by delegations opposed to a constructive agreement on women's equality. Furthermore, many delegations were ill-prepared to negotiate and the Conference Secretariat was afraid of potential controversy. As a result, the draft Platform for Action emerged from the four week preparatory committee process with more than a third of its text unresolved. Among the concepts bracketed were "gender" and the "human rights of women."

Over the summer, a contact group convened to resolve the use of the word "gender" and informal negotiations were held in early August to remove some of the more redundant brackets. Apparently unsettled by the chaos of the preparatory process during the Commission on the Status of Women, diplomats in August tried to bring some order to negotiations, both in terms of process and tone. They were successful.

Indications of a Tide Turned

In the first few days of the official conference, which opened on September 4, events indicated that the negotiations would be painstakingly slow. But given the fact that most delegations were resolved not to reopen agreements reached in the recent past, it seemed likely that agreements made in Cairo would be fully reaffirmed. The first positive sign was the appointment of an experienced diplomat and skilled negotiator, Merwat Tallawy, Egypt's ambassador to Japan, as chair of the contact group on the health chapter. This task would not be easy. Achieving consensus on health, which included concepts of sexual and reproductive health and rights was expected to be a difficult and intricate process in itself. It was made even more difficult by the need to reconcile relevant language in the other sections of the document on poverty, the girl child, and human rights, as well as the preamble. Tallawy, who had led the Egyptian negotiating team at the ICPD, has years of experience regarding UN rules and procedures from her work on the Committee of the Convention on the Elimination of All Forms of Discrimination Against Women (CEDAW) and the Commission for the Status of Women. Tallaway steered the delegations through the most contentious issues, constantly reminding them that the conference was to achieve consensus by finding language acceptable to the majority of delegations.

After an effort by the Holy See and its few allies to unseat Tallaway had failed, and interventions by some delegations to slow the negotiations down were met with vocal derision by the other delegations, a consensus emerged by the end of the first week. As a result, the Holy See quietly announced that they would not challenge Cairo language. But the tide had not fully turned. Concepts outside, but related to, the specific language agreed in Cairo were challenged repeatedly not only by the Holy See but also by conservative delegations from Islamic states. Nonetheless, when language was agreed upon stating that "the right of all women to control all aspects of their health, in particular their own fertility, is basic to their empowerment," (Platform, Para. 94), it seemed clear that moving beyond Cairo was possible. That such a controversial statement, unattainable one year earlier, was possible in the first week suggested that the majority of delegates to Beijing were determined to secure agreements on women's empowerment. In essence, the mood in Beijing conference rooms was much different from the mood in the conference rooms in Cairo.

The Pattern of Diplomacy

Some threads of the pattern of diplomacy in Beijing were recognizable from Cairo, but they were overlaid with a more balanced global interplay with all regions of the world taking a significant role.

In Cairo, the negotiations were marked by the new assertiveness of the US under the Clinton Administration, a much hyped Holy axis of the Holy See and Iran, South Africa's first UN conference since its re-emergence onto the international scene, the decision by the Group of 77 to only operate as a block on economic issues—the group's original mandate—and the tentacles of the Holy See stretching from Malta to a rump of countries in Central and Latin America and West Africa.

In Beijing, the pattern of diplomacy included the emergence of Africa as a coordinated region and the strong voices of Senegal, Namibia, and Zambia, as well as South Africa. This was essential in reaching consensus on the sections on health, poverty, the girl child, and human rights. This coordinated African voice had been strengthened through the process of regional preparations which included a regional preparatory conference, regional ministerial meetings, sub-regional meetings, and a meeting sponsored by the Organization of African Unity. Also for the first time, representatives of African women's movements were represented on multiple delegations, and delegations spoke out with confidence on issues from which their diplomats had previously shied away.

Northern countries paid a price for approaching the conference as if it were only about the quality of women's lives in the South, and about the responsibility—or lack of responsibility—of the North for that quality of life. Most Northern delegations did not wish to discuss situations of inequality in their own countries, between women and men or between the wealthy and the poor.

The European Union (EU), now with a common position of 15 countries, did create political space for consensus by staking out strong positions in many areas, including sexual rights. However, other delegations and NGOs expressed frustration as the EU failed to develop a strategy to negotiate its positions, even as consensus was being built around language on women's rights to control their sexuality that was included in the Platform for Action. The fragile consensus on sexual rights that stretched from Iran to Norway nearly broke under the strain of the pressure within the EU for inclusion of the phrase "sexual rights." The same lack of negotiating skill held up other debates. But, Canada, New Zealand, Norway and Australia often found a way out, toward consensus, as the core of the JUSCANZ alliance.

In contrast to Cairo, at Beijing the US delegation played a low-key role in the negotiations. Silent at critical moments due to fear of domestic lobbies of the Christian right, the US delegation was uncomfortable being visibly in the lead on issues central to the Cairo consensus. However, echoing the First Lady's adoption of the women's rights community's phrase "women's rights are human rights," the US fought to defend the language of the 1993 Vienna conference in the human rights section.

Much has been said about the "unholy alliance" forged in both Cairo and Beijing between conservative forces of different fundamentalist religious standpoints. In Cairo, the alliance broke down as it became apparent that the motivations and concerns of each side of the alliance were different, and as the Holy See and Iran shrank from public association. In Beijing, a smaller core of countries associated themselves with each other much more visibly. Scripted and coordinated as a grouping that was fundamentalist in its approach, Sudan, Yemen, Malta and the Holy See were the only reliable members of such an alliance.

Opposition to the empowerment of women, expressed most vocally in negotiations on equal inheritance rights, sexual rights, and reproductive and sexual health, came from a diminished Catholic conservative bloc (much smaller and less united than in Cairo), and from conservative Islamic countries that were more vociferous than in Cairo. At times, these two blocs worked together, but were countered by the unfettered voices of many Latin American countries, including Brazil, Colombia and Mexico. For the first time in such a conference, the Organization of Islamic States acted as a country grouping to coordinate positions. This task proved difficult as secular Muslim countries, like Bangladesh and Indonesia, conservative fundamentalist states, including Sudan and Yemen, and dealmakers, such as Iran and Egypt, struggled to reach and maintain unified positions.

What Was Achieved

The key tenets established in the Beijing Platform for Action are:

- *The primacy of women's rights*: Human rights standards and international laws cannot be applied differently to women than to men, even if culture and tradition may

seem to sanction restrictions on women's rights. This is an unequivocal statement, like the stance taken at the Vienna World Conference on Human Rights. By comparison, the chapter on reproductive health and rights in the ICPD Programme of Action refers to culture specificity and national sovereignty in these matters. No such equivocation exists in the Beijing Platform.

- *Action to ensure reproductive and sexual rights*: The Platform reaffirms the human rights of women, including their reproductive rights and the right to control matters related to their sexuality, and directs governments to ensure that these rights are fully respected and protected. This paragraph (Platform for Action, Paragraph. 232f) operationalizes the agreements made in Cairo, where reproductive rights were defined. In Beijing, governments agreed to take action to ensure these rights and sexual rights were treated as human rights.

- *Abortion law review*: Included in the Platform for Action is a call for all countries to consider reviewing laws containing punitive measures against women who have undergone illegal abortions. (Platform, Para. 106k). In countries where abortion is legally restricted and women resort to clandestine or self-induced abortion, this agreement means that when a woman seeks treatment from a health clinic for an infection or hemorrhage caused by a botched abortion, she should be treated—not interrogated and arrested. This directive is a step toward decriminalizing abortion. It also keeps the focus, first recognized internationally in Cairo, on the number of women who die or are seriously injured from unsafe abortions worldwide.

- *Adolescent rights recognized*: An avalanche of conditional language asserting parental rights in sections of the Platform relating to reproductive and sexual health education, information and services for children and adolescents was streamlined. The final agreement recognized the primacy of adolescent rights, over the duties, rights and responsibilities of parents, thereby taking into account the evolving capacity of the child. This language is true to the basic premise that the needs of the child come first, as expressed by the international community in the 1990 Convention on the Rights of the Child.

- *Women's control over their sexuality*: Beijing established that the rights of women include the right to control their own sexuality, free from coercion, discrimination, or violence (Platform, Para. 96). This is much more than the right to say no to sex. It gives women the basis to be free from multiple abuses of their sexual rights, including trafficking, rape, battering, and female genital mutilation.

In the Conference's last negotiating session, an impassioned and unprecedented debate on sexual orientation took place. This debate ranged from outright denunciations of homosexuals and lesbians as deviant, to strong pleas to end discrimination in all its forms. A particularly eloquent and resonant statement was made by South African Health Minister Nkosazana Zuma when she assured the world that South Africa

7. WOMEN AND DEVELOPMENT

would not discriminate against anyone, no matter what his or her sexual orientation, and that the nation supported retaining the language on sexual orientation to show that South Africa has no short memory on how it feels to be discriminated against. However, despite the support of the majority of the delegations who took the floor to retain specific references to disallowing discrimination on the basis of "sexual orientation," it was ultimately stricken from the Platform for Action as part of an intricate bargain to achieve consensus on the document as a whole.

At the final plenary session of the Conference, more than 40 countries added interpretive statements or expressed reservations to specific passages of the Platform. Many other countries took the floor to express their "unqualified support" for the Platform, including Bolivia, El Salvador, Panama, India, and South Africa. In Cairo, 17 reservations and interpretive statements were made on multiple sections of the Programme of Action. By contrast, in Beijing, the majority of the 28 reservations and interpretive statements focused specifically on two of the 362 paragraphs comprising the Platform for Action: paragraph 96 (which establishes a woman's right to control her own sexuality) and paragraph 106k (which calls for countries to consider reviewing abortion laws that punish women who have had illegal abortions). The Holy See, as expected, expressed a reservation on the entire health chapter and additional paragraphs, but eventually joined the overall consensus. The reservations expressed were narrowly defined and, as such, do not undermine the value of the 125-page long Platform.

What It Means

To a great extent, the final consensus was due to the new dialogue witnessed in the negotiating rooms. More countries were represented than at previous conferences by women. As was not often the case in the past, these women were not tokens—there because of whom they married. In Beijing, women served as delegates because they were professionals, experts, elected officials, activists, and leaders of women's organizations. Many of them have backgrounds in women's movements, nurtured by the UN Decade for Women (1975–85), and the three previous women's conferences. Many of these women had participated, as government delegates or NGO observers in previous global conferences, and therefore were skilled in the process and substance of U.N. negotiations. Without question, their expertise and experience were critical to the outcomes of the conference.

The overall messages from this conference to the world are: First, equality is not for debate; it is desired, essential, and will come about. Second, coercion, discrimination, and violence must be eradicated from the lives of women, wherever they occur—in economics, politics, health care and within communities and families. Third, the vision of population and development adopted in Cairo is truly global policy. And fourth, women's rights are human rights. Governments and nongovernmental organizations must now deliver, and the women of the world, working in partnership with men, will hold them accountable.

What Beijing showed is that change can come about through intense collaboration, discipline, and a shared purpose. That change may not be immediately visible, especially heroic, or particularly sweeping. Still, it is hard to believe that the Beijing agreements will not have an impact. Such a diverse assembly *will* effect change, large and small, in public and private arenas. Positive energy pervaded the negotiations in Beijing—an intensely political conference about women's lives—and the first of the women's conferences not to be mired in other geo-political struggles. This energy will be kept alive by NGOs, as they press for realization of the commitments made not just in Rio, Vienna, Cairo, and Copenhagen, but those remade and extended in Beijing.

Index

Credits/Acknowledgments

Cover design by Charles Vitelli

1. Understanding the Developing World
Facing overview—United Nations photo by Jerry Frank.

2. Political Economy and the Developing World
Facing overview—United Nations photo by Ian Steele.

3. Conflict and Instability
Facing overview—United Nations photo by A. Hollmann. 124—UNICEF photo by Jacques Danois.

4. Weapons Proliferation and Arms Control
Facing overview—AP/Wide World photo by Allistair Sinclair.

5. Transitions
Facing overview—AP/Wide World photo.

6. Population, Development, and Environment
Facing overview—United Nations photo by John Isaac.

7. Women and Development
Facing overview—AP/Wide World photo by Anat Givon.

ANNUAL EDITIONS ARTICLE REVIEW FORM

■ NAME: _____ DATE: _____

■ TITLE AND NUMBER OF ARTICLE: _____

■ BRIEFLY STATE THE MAIN IDEA OF THIS ARTICLE: _____

_____

■ LIST THREE IMPORTANT FACTS THAT THE AUTHOR USES TO SUPPORT THE MAIN IDEA:

_____

_____

_____

_____

_____

■ WHAT INFORMATION OR IDEAS DISCUSSED IN THIS ARTICLE ARE ALSO DISCUSSED IN YOUR
TEXTBOOK OR OTHER READINGS THAT YOU HAVE DONE? LIST THE TEXTBOOK CHAPTERS AND
PAGE NUMBERS:

_____

_____

_____

_____

_____

■ LIST ANY EXAMPLES OF BIAS OR FAULTY REASONING THAT YOU FOUND IN THE ARTICLE:

_____

_____

_____

_____

■ LIST ANY NEW TERMS/CONCEPTS THAT WERE DISCUSSED IN THE ARTICLE, AND WRITE A SHORT
DEFINITION:

_____

_____

_____

_____

_____

We Want Your Advice

ANNUAL EDITIONS revisions depend on two major opinion sources: one is our Advisory Board, listed in the front of this volume, which works with us in scanning the thousands of articles published in the public press each year; the other is you—the person actually using the book. Please help us and the users of the next edition by completing the prepaid article rating form on this page and returning it to us. Thank you for your help!

ANNUAL EDITIONS: DEVELOPING WORLD 97/98
Article Rating Form

Here is an opportunity for you to have direct input into the next revision of this volume. We would like you to rate each of the 47 articles listed below, using the following scale:

1. **Excellent: should definitely be retained**
2. **Above average: should probably be retained**
3. **Below average: should probably be deleted**
4. **Poor: should definitely be deleted**

Rating	Article	Rating	Article
	1. The Third World and the New World Order in the 1990s		25. Arming Ethnic Conflict
	2. Don't Neglect the Impoverished South		26. The Pelindaba Treaty: Africa Joins the Nuclear-Free World
	3. Reverse Linkages: The Growing Importance of Developing Countries		27. Levers for Plowshares: Using Aid to Encourage Military Reform
	4. The 'New South'		28. Democracy's Trap
	5. Whither the North-South Gap?		29. On Course for . . . What?
	6. The Road to Third World Prosperity		30. Africa Tries Democracy, Finding Hope and Peril
	7. Immiserating Growth (2): The Third World		31. South Africa: Putting Democracy to Work
	8. Neoliberal Social Policy: Managing Poverty (Somehow)		32. Mexico: The Slippery Road to Stability
	9. Credit Where Discredit Is Due		33. Force Is Forever
	10. The Catch-22 of Debt		34. Open for Business
	11. Foreign Direct Investment in Developing Countries: Progress and Problems		35. The ICPD Programme of Action
	12. The Barefoot Bank with Cheek		36. Optimism and Overpopulation
	13. We Must Hear the Third World		37. Poor Lands' Success in Cutting Birth Rate Upsets Old Theories
	14. Political Islam: Beyond the Green Menace		38. The Exploding Cities of the Developing World
	15. The Middle East on the Brink: Prospects for Change in the 21st Century		39. Building a Green Economy
	16. The Gulf between the Rulers and the Ruled		40. Voices from the Developing World: Progress toward Sustainable Development
	17. Islam: Promise or Peril?		41. Upholding Human Rights and Environmental Justice
	18. Awaiting a New Spark		42. The Burden of Womanhood
	19. Nigeria: Inside the Dismal Tunnel		43. Female Empowerment Leads to Fewer Births
	20. No War, No Peace		44. Women's Work
	21. Culture Clash		45. W = Female + Male
	22. Refugees: The Rising Flood		46. Women's Conference Adopts 'Beijing Declaration and Platform for Action'
	23. Mixed Migration: Strategy for Refugees and Economic Migrants		47. Women Redrawing the Map: The World after the Beijing and Cairo Conferences
	24. Third World Militaries: New Suppliers, Deadlier Weapons		

(Continued on next page)

ABOUT YOU

Name _____ Date _____

Are you a teacher? ❏ Or a student? ❏

Your school name _____

Department _____

Address _____

City _____ State _____ Zip _____

School telephone # _____

YOUR COMMENTS ARE IMPORTANT TO US!

Please fill in the following information:

For which course did you use this book? _____

Did you use a text with this *ANNUAL EDITION*? ❏ yes ❏ no

What was the title of the text? _____

What are your general reactions to the *Annual Editions* concept?

Have you read any particular articles recently that you think should be included in the next edition?

Are there any articles you feel should be replaced in the next edition? Why?

Are there other areas that you feel would utilize an *ANNUAL EDITION?*

May we contact you for editorial input?

May we quote you from above?

ANNUAL EDITIONS: DEVELOPING WORLD 97/98

No Postage
Necessary
if Mailed
in the
United States

BUSINESS REPLY MAIL

| First Class | Permit No. 84 | Guilford, CT |

Postage will be paid by addressee

Dushkin Publishing Group/
Brown & Benchmark Publishers
Sluice Dock
Guilford, Connecticut 06437